THE OXFORD HAND

INTERNATIONAL RELATIONS

THE OXFORD HANDBOOKS OF POLITICAL SCIENCE

GENERAL EDITOR: ROBERT E. GOODIN

The *Oxford Handbooks of Political Science* is a ten-volume set of reference books offering authoritative and engaging critical overviews of all the main branches of political science.

The series as a whole is under the General Editorship of Robert E. Goodin, with each volume being edited by a distinguished international group of specialists in their respective fields:

POLITICAL THEORY
John S. Dryzek, Bonnie Honig & Anne Phillips

POLITICAL INSTITUTIONS
R. A. W. Rhodes, Sarah A. Binder & Bert A. Rockman

POLITICAL BEHAVIOR
Russell J. Dalton & Hans-Dieter Klingemann

COMPARATIVE POLITICS
Carles Boix & Susan C. Stokes

LAW & POLITICS
Keith E. Whittington, R. Daniel Kelemen & Gregory A. Caldeira

PUBLIC POLICY
Michael Moran, Martin Rein & Robert E. Goodin

POLITICAL ECONOMY
Barry R. Weingast & Donald A. Wittman

INTERNATIONAL RELATIONS
Christian Reus-Smit & Duncan Snidal

CONTEXTUAL POLITICAL ANALYSIS
Robert E. Goodin & Charles Tilly

POLITICAL METHODOLOGY
Janet M. Box-Steffensmeier, Henry E. Brady & David Collier

This series aspires to shape the discipline, not just to report on it. Like the Goodin–Klingemann *New Handbook of Political Science* upon which the series builds, each of these volumes will combine critical commentaries on where the field has been together with positive suggestions as to where it ought to be heading.

THE OXFORD HANDBOOK OF

INTERNATIONAL RELATIONS

Edited by

CHRISTIAN REUS-SMIT

and

DUNCAN SNIDAL

OXFORD

UNIVERSITY PRESS

OXFORD
UNIVERSITY PRESS

Great Clarendon Street, Oxford ox2 6dp

Oxford University Press is a department of the University of Oxford.
It furthers the University's objective of excellence in research, scholarship,
and education by publishing worldwide in

Oxford New York

Auckland Cape Town Dar es Salaam Hong Kong Karachi
Kuala Lumpur Madrid Melbourne Mexico City Nairobi
New Delhi Shanghai Taipei Toronto

With offices in

Argentina Austria Brazil Chile Czech Republic France Greece
Guatemala Hungary Italy Japan Poland Portugal Singapore
South Korea Switzerland Thailand Turkey Ukraine Vietnam

Oxford is a registered trade mark of Oxford University Press
in the UK and in certain other countries

Published in the United States
by Oxford University Press Inc., New York

British Library Cataloguing in Publication Data
Data available

Library of Congress Cataloging in Publication Data
The Oxford handbook of international relations / edited by
Christian Reus-Smit and Duncan Snidal.
p. cm. – (Oxford handbook of political science)
ISBN-13: 978–0–19–921932–2 (acid-free paper)
1. International relations. 2. World politics.
I. Reus-Smit, Christian, 1961– II. Snidal, Duncan.
JZ1242.O94 2008
327–dc22 2008006027

Typeset by SPI Publisher Services, Pondicherry, India
Printed in Great Britain
on acid-free paper by
Ashford Colour Press Ltd., Gosport, Hants.

ISBN 978–0–19–921932–2 (hbk.)
ISBN 978–0–19–958558–8 (pbk.)

7 9 10 8

ACKNOWLEDGEMENTS

Editing a project of this scale incurs many debts. The conversations with friends and colleagues that have shaped the *Handbook*'s contours are too many to acknowledge individually. However, several people stand out for their singularly important contributions. Robert Goodin is the mastermind behind the *Oxford Handbooks of Political Science*, and it is he whom we must thank for bringing us together as the editors of this volume. He has been a wonderful source of intellectual and editorial advice, and the path he started us upon has been immensely rewarding. A project such as this could not have been realized in its present form were it not for assistance provided by Lynn Savery and Mary-Louise Hickey. Lynn shouldered the early administrative burden, and her work was invaluable in getting the project off the ground. It was Mary-Louise, however, who shouldered the Herculean task of subsequent organization and editing. It is no exaggeration to say that without her efforts the *Handbook* would be a pale shadow of this final version. Finally, our contributors deserve special thanks. The brief we gave them was challenging, and in most cases we asked them for multiple iterations of their chapters. They rose to the task with good humor and energy, and the quality of their contributions is impressive and gratifying.

Chris Reus-Smit
Duncan Snidal

CONTENTS

PART IV THE QUESTION OF METHOD

PART V BRIDGING THE SUBFIELD BOUNDARIES

PART VI THE SCHOLAR AND THE POLICY-MAKER

PART VII THE QUESTION OF DIVERSITY

PART VIII OLD AND NEW

About the Contributors

Robert Ayson is Senior Fellow and Director of Studies at the Strategic and Defence Studies Centre, Australian National University.

Michael Barnett is the Harold Stassen Chair of International Affairs at the Humphrey Institute of Public Affairs and Professor of Political Science at the University of Minnesota.

Andrew Bennett is Professor of Government at Georgetown University.

Janice Bially Mattern is Associate Professor of International Relations at Lehigh University.

David L. Blaney is Professor of Political Science, Macalester College, St Paul.

Anthony Burke is Associate Professor of Politics and International Relations at the Australian Defence Force Academy, UNSW.

Michael Byers holds the Canada Research Chair in Global Politics and International Law, University of British Columbia.

Molly Cochran is Associate Professor in the Nunn School of International Affairs at the Georgia Institute of Technology.

Robert W. Cox is Professor Emeritus of Political Science at York University.

Phillip Darby is Director of the Institute of Postcolonial Studies, Melbourne, and a principal fellow of the School of Political Science, Criminology and Sociology, University of Melbourne.

Jack Donnelly is the Andrew Mellon Professor at the Graduate School of International Studies, University of Denver.

Tim Dunne is Professor of International Relations and Director of the Centre of Advanced International Studies at the University of Exeter.

Robyn Eckersley is Professor in the School of Political Science, Sociology and Criminology at the University of Melbourne.

Colin Elman is Associate Professor of Political Science at Arizona State University.

Toni Erskine is Lecturer in International Politics at Aberystwyth University.

James Goldgeier is Professor of Political Science and International Affairs at George Washington University and a senior fellow at the Council on Foreign Relations.

Ian Hurd is Assistant Professor of Political Science at Northwestern University.

Naeem Inayatullah is Associate Professor of Politics, Ithaca College.

Peter Katzenstein is the Walter S. Carpenter, Jr. Professor of International Studies at Cornell University.

Robert O. Keohane is Professor of International Affairs, Princeton University, a past president of the American Political Science Association, and a member of the National Academy of Sciences.

Friedrich Kratochwil is Professor of International Relations at the European University Institute.

Andrew H. Kydd is an Associate Professor of Political Science at the University of Wisconsin.

David A. Lake is Professor of Political Science at the University of California, San Diego.

Peter Lawler is Senior Lecturer in International Relations at the University of Manchester.

Richard Little is Professor of International Politics in the Department of Politics at the University of Bristol.

Edward D. Mansfield is the Hum Rosen Professor of Political Science and Director of the Christopher H. Browne Center for International Politics at the University of Pennsylvania.

Andrew Moravcsik is Professor of Politics and Public Affairs at Princeton University.

Terry Nardin is Professor of Political Science at the National University of Singapore.

Henry R. Nau is Professor of Political Science and International Affairs, Elliott School of International Affairs, George Washington University.

Joseph S. Nye, Jr., is Sultan of Oman Professor of International Relations and University Distinguished Service Professor at the John F. Kennedy School of Government, Harvard University.

Jon C. Pevehouse is Associate Professor at the Harris School of Public Policy, University of Chicago.

Richard Price is Associate Professor of Political Science at the University of British Columbia.

Joel Quirk is an RCUK Fellow, Department of Law and Wilberforce Institute for the Study of Slavery and Emancipation, University of Hull.

John Ravenhill is Professor of International Relations in the Department of International Relations, Research School of Pacific and Asian Studies, the Australian National University.

Nicholas Rengger is Professor of Political Theory and International Relations at St Andrews University.

Christian Reus-Smit is Professor and Head of the Department of International Relations, Research School of Pacific and Asian Studies, the Australian National University.

James L. Richardson is Emeritus Professor of the Australian National University.

Richard Rosecrance is Adjunct Professor at the Kennedy School of Government, Harvard University.

Richard Shapcott is Senior Lecturer in International Relations in the School of Political Science and International Studies, University of Queensland, Brisbane.

Kathryn Sikkink is a Regents Professor and McKnight Distinguished University Professor of Political Science at the University of Minnesota.

Rudra Sil is Associate Professor of Political Science at the University of Pennsylvania.

Gerry Simpson is Professor of International Law, London School of Economics.

Steve Smith is Vice-Chancellor and Professor of International Politics at the University of Exeter.

Duncan Snidal is Associate Professor in the Harris School, the Department of Political Science, and the College, at the University of Chicago.

Arthur A. Stein is Professor of Political Science at UCLA.

Douglas T. Stuart is the first holder of the J. William and Helen D. Stuart Chair in International Studies at Dickinson College, Carlisle, and Adjunct Professor at the US Army War College.

Benno Teschke is a Senior Lecturer in the Department of International Relations at the University of Sussex.

Philip Tetlock holds the Mitchell Endowed Chair at the University of California, Berkeley.

Jacqui True is Senior Lecturer in International Relations at the University of Auckland.

Sandra Whitworth is Professor of Political Science and Women's Studies at York University, Toronto.

William C. Wohlforth is Professor and Chair in the Department of Government, Dartmouth College.

PART I

INTRODUCTION

CHAPTER 1

BETWEEN UTOPIA AND REALITY: THE PRACTICAL DISCOURSES OF INTERNATIONAL RELATIONS

CHRISTIAN REUS-SMIT

DUNCAN SNIDAL

WHAT kind of work is this *Handbook*? Is it a reference book? Is it an introduction? Is it a commentary? Is it a contribution to research? Is it an account of international relations as a political practice, or of international relations as a field of study? If the latter, is it a statement of where the field has been or where it should be going?

It is, at once, all of these things and none of them. We hope that it will serve as a useful entry point to the study of international relations and global politics, a resource that junior and senior scholars alike can use to enhance their understandings of the multiple perspectives and approaches that constitute our field. It is thus, in

We thank Greg Fry, Robert Goodin, Richard Price, Heather Rae, and Alexander Wendt for their insightful comments on the penultimate draft of this chapter.

part, an introduction and a reference work. But it is envisaged as much more than this. We want it to be read as a critical, reflective intervention into debates about international relations as a field of inquiry. It is much more than a commentary, therefore, as our goal is to push debate forward, not merely to recount it. Because ideas about what we study, and why we study it, condition what we do as scholars, we see it as a contribution to research into international relations and global politics as political practice.

These ambitions have informed the *Handbook*'s gestation at two levels. To begin with, they have informed the choices we as editors have made about the volume's central themes and general structure. Because we see the *Handbook* as more than a survey—as an intervention—we have deliberately sought to read the field in a particular way. As explained below, two themes structure the content of the volume: the first being the relationship between empirical (and/or positive) theory and normative theory; the second being the dynamic interconnection between different theories, methods, and subfields. Our ambitions have also informed the *Handbook*'s development at a second level. In addition to asking our fellow contributors to respond to the above themes, we have asked them to reach beyond simple commentary or exegesis to advance new, and hopefully thought-provoking, arguments and interpretations.

This chapter explains the *Handbook*'s broad approach and advances a series of arguments about the nature of international relations as a field, arguments informed by our reading of the chapters that follow. We are concerned, in particular, with three interrelated questions. What is the nature of the theoretical endeavor in international relations? How have the empirical and the normative aspects of theories interacted to shape individual theories and the debates between them? And finally, has there been progress in the study of international relations, and if so in what sense?

Although there is no singular answer to these questions, our contributors have led us to a number of general conclusions. First, they have encouraged us to formulate a distinctive understanding of the theoretical enterprise, one broad enough to encompass the diverse forms of theorizing that populate the field. We argue that the art of theorizing about international relations has come to integrate three components: questions, assumptions, and logical arguments. Second, international relations theories are best conceived as contending practical discourses that, despite their significant differences, are all, implicitly or explicitly, animated by the question "how should we act?" This abiding feature of international relations theories explains the persistence of both empirical and normative aspects in all of them. Finally, our contributors' discussions of diverse theories, methods, and problems in international relations invite comment on the question of progress in the field. Across the board their chapters report increased sophistication in theory and method, greater communication and learning across theoretical boundaries, and more artful borrowing of ideas from other fields. However, progress within different areas remains heavily influenced by contestation among theoretical perspectives. Harnessed properly, such contestation is an engine of increased understanding even as it simultaneously explains the sometimes seeming lack of progress for the field as a whole.

1   OUR APPROACH

There is no shortage of overviews and introductions to international relations and global politics, either as a field or as a realm of political practice. New introductions—more or less advanced—appear each year, and this is not the first "handbook" on the subject. With few exceptions, however, these all adopt variations on a common approach. A choice is made by authors and editors about the topics worthy of discussion (a choice we too have made), and chapters are crafted to do these topics justice. Seldom, though, do these volumes have a "voice" of their own, above and beyond that of their individual, constituent chapters. The most recent handbook to appear, for example, has neither an introductory framing chapter nor a general conclusion (Carlsnaes, Risse, and Simmons 2002). Although an excellent volume, it has nothing to say or conclude about the field it has surveyed. Our goal is to step beyond this general approach to give the *Handbook* a voice of its own.

The first thing to note about the *Handbook* is our emphasis on theory, on conceptions of international relations as a discipline, on contending ideas of theoretical progress, on different theoretical perspectives, and on the methodological ideas that drive the study of world politics. We have adopted this emphasis not because we value theoretical over empirical inquiry or the pursuit of abstract ideas over more "practical" forms of scholarship. We have done so because we believe that theoretical assumptions (and debates surrounding them) determine the contours of the field and inform even the most empirical research. An inquiry into the field of international relations ought, first and foremost, to be an inquiry into the ideas that animate it—the ideas that distinguish international relations (or global politics) as a domain of social and political life, the ideas that determine what constitutes knowledge of this political realm, the ideas that dictate the questions that merit answers, and the ideas that shape the field's relations with other disciplines. Without these ideas, international relations would have neither identity, skeleton, nor pulse.

One consequence of this emphasis is our decision not to devote specific chapters to empirical issue areas, such as great power competition, weapons proliferation, environmental protection, human rights, nationalism, and international trade and finance. Again, this does not reflect a lack of interest in such issues; to the contrary. Rather, it reflects our belief that it is the ideas and debates canvassed in this volume that have informed and structured analyses of these issues. Theoretical and methodological ideas have determined which issues are legitimate foci of inquiry for international relations scholars, and they have provided the intellectual tools that scholars have taken up in the pursuit of understanding. The complexities of particular issue areas—especially new ones—do, of course, serve as catalysts for theoretical innovation, and grappling with them has often driven international relations scholars to conscript new ideas from other fields of inquiry. Our strategy, however, has been to concentrate on international relations as a milieu of ideas, and to ask our contributors to draw on their diverse empirical expertise to illustrate their arguments and propositions. This choice of strategy has been reinforced by our sense that the literature is now so saturated with survey chapters on new and old issue areas that yet another compendium is unwarranted.

The most distinctive feature of the *Handbook* is not its focus on theory but our reading of theory as *both* empirical *and* normative. Most surveys of international relations theory concentrate on empirical (and/or positive) theory; if normative theory receives any attention, it is left for a final chapter or two on "ethics and international affairs." Interestingly, this is as true of surveys originating outside the United States as from within (see Carlsnaes, Risse, and Simmons 2002; Baylis and Smith 2005; Burchill et al. 2005). The assumptions appear to be that empirical and normative inquiry can be segregated and that international relations theory is almost exclusively an empirical or positive project. Although it is acknowledged (in some limited fashion) that there is another body of theory—normative theory—that treats the international as its subject, this is the preserve of philosophers or political theorists. Thus the default position is that international relations is an explanatory endeavor, concerned with the "is" of world politics not the "ought."

We find this segregation both unsustainable and unhelpful. All theories of international relations and global politics have important empirical *and* normative dimensions, and their deep interconnection is unavoidable. When realists criticize national governments for acting in ways inconsistent with the national interest, or for acting in ways that destabilize international order, they base their criticisms on values of interest and order that can be defended only normatively. When postmodernists recommend a scholarly stance of relentless critique and deconstruction, they do so not for interpretative reasons (though this is in part their motive) but because this constitutes a practice of resistance against structures of power and domination. Indeed, as the *Handbook* authors demonstrate, every international relations theory is simultaneously about what the world *is* like and about what it *ought* to be like. One of the axes of diversity in our field is the different orientations scholars, and their attendant theoretical traditions, have had to the relationship between the normative and empirical aspects of theory. Some have embraced the intersection, many have sought to purge their theories of normative traits, and still others have gone in the opposite direction, privileging philosophical reflection over empirical. But the terrain between the empirical analysis and the normative is one trodden by all theorists, explicitly or implicitly.

The conventional explanation for why our theories all exhibit empirical and normative aspects is epistemological. Critical theorists have long argued that our values enter our enquiries from the moment we ask questions about the world, from the moment we make choices about what we will study to answer those questions, and from the moment we decide how we will study whatever it is we have chosen (for a classic statement, see Taylor 1979). Nothing we say here challenges this line of argument. Our explanation is different.

From the outset, international relations theory has been a practical discourse. We do not mean this in any deep Habermasian sense of the word, or say this to promote simplistic notions of the practical over the theoretical. Rather, we mean that all international relations theories, in one form or another, have at some level been concerned with the question "how should we act?" This is true for realists and liberals, Marxists and feminists. It is true of those who congregate under the umbrella of critical theory as well as those who pursue problem-solving theory. Different perspectives emphasize different issues that demand action, and arrive at different conclusions about types of action required. But whether they are concerned with the promotion of peace, order, institutional development, economic well-being, social empowerment, or ending global forms of discrimination, or whether they recommend the balancing of power, the promotion of free trade, the intensification of social contradictions, or resistance to all institutions and discourses of social power, they are nonetheless animated by the practical question of how we should act.[1]

This abiding nature of international relations theory as a practical discourse explains (above and beyond the epistemological reasons) the persistence of *both* the empirical *and* the normative in all our theories. We cannot answer the question of how we should act without some appreciation of the world in which we seek to act (the empirical) and some sense of what the goals are that we seek to achieve (the normative). This was E. H. Carr's central proposition in *The Twenty Years' Crisis*, that neither unadulterated realism nor idealism could sustain international relations if it were to be a practical discourse. Without idealism, realism is sterile, devoid of purpose; without realism, idealism is naive, devoid of understanding of the world in which one seeks to act. For Carr, international relations had to be a political science that brought the "is" and the "ought" together: "Utopia and reality are thus the two facets of political science. Sound political thought and sound political life will be found only where both have their place" (Carr 1946, 10).

Carr was appealing to the emergent field of international relations when he made this claim, appealing for it to take a particular form and direction. Our claim is not that his vision has guided the evolution of the field. For one thing, his message has been consistently lost in the misinterpretation of his work. Rather, our claim is that Carr identified a truth about all discourses with practical ambitions, that, once this

---

[1] The same is true for the field of public policy, of course. See Goodin, Rein, and Moran (2006).

ambition exists, however subterranean and unacknowledged it may be, theorists are forced onto the difficult terrain between the empirical and the normative. This is clearly the case for scholars who wish their work to have direct relevance to the question of action whether in the form of policy advice or in the form of political resistance. But even those whose concerns are mainly "scholarly" must tiptoe beyond the bounds of either empirical or normative theory to engage subject matter that is intrinsically intertwined with practical problems and so cannot be neatly partitioned. The field has never been able to reside comfortably in pure empirical or normative inquiry and this is destined to continue.

Instead of suppressing this duality of international relations theory, we have chosen to highlight it, to draw it out into full view. Our motive is not simply that this promises to be a particularly interesting and illuminating way to read the field, although we have certainly found this to be the case. We believe that it is important for international relations scholars to reflect on the status of international relations theory as a practical discourse and its consequences for what we do. As many of our contributors (from diverse quarters of the field) reinforce, we want international relations to be a field that ultimately speaks to the most pressing problems of political action in the contemporary world, even if we always speak with diverse voices, from diverse perspectives. But accepting this as an ambition means accepting that international relations scholars must navigate the difficult terrain between empirical and normative theory. Understanding how this terrain has been navigated to date—by realists and postmodernists, Marxists and constructivists—is an instructive first step. Furthermore, highlighting the empirical and normative aspects of all theories has the advantage of unsettling many of our established assumptions and conceits about the field. It challenges us to see different perspectives in different lights, and to reconsider the theoretical terrain of the field in different ways.

The second organizing theme of the *Handbook* is the dynamic interplay between different theoretical and methodological perspectives. Again, this is a departure from established practice. Most surveys, introductions, and compendia treat perspectives as isolated bodies of thought—this is realism, this is liberalism, this is constructivism, and so on. Individual chapters almost always cast their subject theory against theoretical "others," but the purpose is usually to highlight what is distinctive about a particular theory and only secondarily do they consider its evolution as part of a wider theoretical milieu. There have, of course, been many attempts to see the evolution of the field as the product of discussion, the most frequently invoked being the tale of recurrent great debates: realism versus idealism, classicism versus scientism, and reflectivism versus rationalism (Lapid 1989). But, whatever the merits of such accounts (and over the years they have helped acclimatize many students to the field), they work at a macro-level, obscuring much of the detailed interplay, conversation, and contestation between different perspectives. It is this level of interplay that interests us. How have the limitations of existing approaches prompted the development of new ones? How have established perspectives responded to new challengers? How have the ensuing debates and contestations shaped the nature of contending approaches? How have theories borrowed from each other to bolster their heuristic, interpretative, or critical power? Is the field, in the end, one marked by interchange and co-constitution or territoriality and mutual incomprehension?

These two organizing themes run through the *Handbook*, serving as both structuring devices and reference points for our contributors. The broad organization of the volume reflects our judgment about where the major debates over ideas are taking place. We open with a series of contending perspectives on what the central empirical focus of international relations ought to be: should its central concern be relations between sovereign states (Lake, Chapter 2, this volume), or should it address the wider constellation of political relationships operating at the global level (Barnett and Sikkink, Chapter 3, this volume)? More provocatively, are the very ideas of "international relations" or "global politics" misplaced, ontological frameworks that privilege certain standpoints over others (Cox, Chapter 4, this volume; Darby, Chapter 5, this volume)?

Having considered these questions, our attention shifts to the volume's largest part, that addressing the field's principal substantive theories and their ethics: realism, Marxism, neoliberal institutionalism, new liberalism, the English School, critical theory, postmodernism, and feminism.[2] It is here that our concern with the empirical and normative aspects of theory is most apparent. Instead of having one chapter on each of these theories, which is the established practice, the *Handbook* has two: the first providing a general overview of, and engagement with, the theory in question; the second drawing out its underlying ethical standpoint and propositions. We open this part with an essay on the merits on eclectic theorizing by Peter Katzenstein and Rudra Sil (Chapter 6, this volume). There appears to be a greater interest today in bridge-building across the theoretical traditions of the field, and it is appropriate to lead with a piece that explores systematically the merits of such dialogue.

The next part considers ideas about method. Our conception of method is broad and eclectic. For some, method is a positivist preserve, a preoccupation only of those who see international relations as a social science modeled on the natural sciences. But method, like theory, is unavoidable. Every table of contents betrays a method, a set of choices the author has made about how best to go about answering the question that animates his or her research. Sometimes this is the product of systematic reflection, at other times of intuition. But just as method is unavoidable, there is no "one size fits all" method—different questions demand different methods. Some questions are best answerable through quantitative methods, some through qualitative, some through historical, some through philosophical, deconstructive, and genealogical methods, and some through artful combinations of two or more of these approaches. Our contributors explore the principal

---

[2] These are complex and contested categories so we do not offer thumbnail sketches of them here but refer readers to the respective *Handbook* chapters. Table 1.1 below characterizes the different approaches in terms of three key dimensions of particular relevance to this chapter.

methodological approaches—rational choice (Kydd, Chapter 25, this volume), sociological and interpretative (Kratochwil, Chapter 26, this volume), psychological
(Goldgeier and Tetlock, Chapter 27, this volume), quantitative (Mansfield and Pevehouse, Chapter 28, this volume), qualitative (Bennett and Elman, Chapter 29, this
volume), and historical (Quirk, Chapter 30, this volume) methods—privileged by
the substantive schools of thought examined in the previous part, although we
readily acknowledge that our selection is not exhaustive.

The *Handbook* then turns to the borderlands of the field: the internal borders
between international relations' subfields, and the external borders between international relations and its near neighbors. As the "international" issues animating
scholarship have multiplied—from an initial focus on questions of war and peace
to a contemporary agenda that encompasses everything from global finance to population movements—two tendencies have been apparent. On the one hand, there
has been the proliferation of distinct communities under the broad umbrella of
"international relations." Some of these are so self-contained that their relationship
to the broad umbrella is an active topic of debate: are strategic studies, foreign-
policy studies, or international ethics subfields of international relations or distinctive fields of study? On the other hand, there has been a tendency for international
relations scholars to push out toward other disciplines, most notably economics,
law, and continental social theory. In some cases this has involved re-engagement
with realms of scholarship that were once seen as integral to the nascent field of
international relations, international law being the prime example. Part V of the
Handbook investigates the dynamics of these borderlands, paying particular attention to developments within international political economy (Ravenhill, Chapter
31, this volume), strategic studies (Ayson, Chapter 32, this volume), foreign-policy
analysis (Stuart, Chapter 33, this volume), international ethics (Nardin, Chapter 34,
this volume), and international law (Byers, Chapter 35, this volume).

Alongside debates over the substantive focus of the field, the nature of theoretical progress, the relative merits of various "isms," the appropriateness of particular methods, and the integrity of individual subfields, persistent anxiety has
surrounded the appropriate relationship between the scholar and the policy-maker.
For some, the scholar's role is "to speak truth to power," a stance reinforced by
Robert Keohane in one of the *Handbook*'s final chapters (Chapter 42, this volume).
For others, policy relevance and engagement with government are the true test
of scholarship. And for yet others, it is the very pretence of speaking truth that
makes international relations scholars so easily complicit in practices of power
and domination. At the heart of these debates are issues of scholarly identity,
the relationship between power and knowledge, the nature of social and political
engagement, and the relationship between "science" and objectivity. These issues
are taken up by a range of scholars across the various sections of the *Handbook*, but
in Part VI they are taken up directly by Henry Nau (Chapter 36, this volume) and
Joseph Nye (Chapter 37, this volume).

Part VII addresses the field's diversity, or lack thereof. Within the United States it is often assumed (often subconsciously) that the theoretical, methodological, and substantive concerns of American scholars define the nature and contours of international relations as a field of political inquiry—"American international relations is the field." Outside the United States, this chauvinism is frequently observed and linked to a widespread concern that the American academy exerts a hegemonic influence on the field, privileging those concerns, perspectives, and methods favored by American scholars and publishers—"international relations is an American social science." But, while the American academy exerts an undeniable centripetal pull on the field, a pull characterized by clear relations of power, the actual diversity of international relations scholarship globally deserves recognition. International relations scholarship in Britain, Canada, Australia, China, India, France, and Germany varies greatly, and none of it is identical to that conducted within the American academy. It is these issues of the field's homogeneity or heterogeneity—of the potential for diversity within hegemony—that our contributors address, focusing in particular on the "subaltern" view of international relations "from below" (Blaney and Inayatullah, Chapter 38, this volume), and on the perspective of international relations from within a former hegemon (Little, Chapter 39, this volume).

The *Handbook*'s final part consists of five short essays, each providing a different account of where the field has been and, more importantly, where it ought to be going. For much of its history, international relations has been a male-dominated field, and by some measures it remains so today. But in the past twenty years a significant demographic change has occurred, one that has seen the number of women undergraduates, graduate students, and faculty in international relations grow dramatically. Women's voices are central to multiple debates in the field, and often they are at the leading edge of conceptual, theoretical, and analytical innovation. We have sought to acknowledge and reflect this changing demographic by seeking the views not only of three eminent men—Robert Keohane (Chapter 42, this volume), Richard Rosecrance (Chapter 43, this volume), and Steve Smith (Chapter 44, this volume)—whose work has been influential in shaping the field, but also those of two women—Janice Bially Mattern (Chapter 40, this volume) from the United States, and Toni Erskine (Chapter 41, this volume) from the UK—who have established themselves as significant new voices.

2 THEORIZING IN INTERNATIONAL RELATIONS

Our understandings of international relations are organized by theory—and our multiplicity of understandings is reflected in the broad range of contending theoretical approaches canvassed in this *Handbook*. Some of these approaches are closely connected and largely complementary to one another (for example, rationalism and liberal institutionalism; feminism and critical theory), whereas other approaches are usually seen as competitive or even mutually hostile to one another (for example, realism and liberalism; rationalism and postmodernism). International relations further embraces a wide range of substantive topics and questions, some of which have an elective affinity with particular theoretical approaches. This cacophony of theoretical approaches reflects its subject matter and is key to understanding how the field has developed.

The tendency has been for international relations scholars to think divisively about theorizing, about the nature of theory in general and about particular theories. In a field centrally concerned with territoriality, fence-building is a prized craft. But our fellow contributors have encouraged us to think expansively about theorizing, to seek a conception of the theoretical endeavor that is broad enough to encompass a wide variety of theoretical projects without homogenizing them. Not only do many of our contributors advocate bridge-building, but we see in their work as many commonalities as differences.

The definition of theory is contested, and resolving that issue, even if it were possible, would be against the spirit of our enterprise of examining how the interactions of theories organize and drive the field. We have chosen, therefore, to focus on the art of theorizing in international relations rather than the nature of theory. We propose here that theorizing in international relations—in all its diverse manifestations—has come to exhibit three principal components and the dynamic interplay between them.

First, theorizing takes place in relation to the questions (empirical and normative) we ask about the "international" political universe. On the one hand, we construct theories to answer questions. These questions might be highly abstract—such as those animating formal theorizing—or very empirical. They might be broad in scope, or narrowly focused. But international relations theory always presupposes a referent question about the world we live in or could live in. On the other hand, theorizing often generates questions. For instance, theories that assume that anarchy generates like politics encourage questions about political variations across anarchic systems (Reus-Smit 1999). Secondly, theorizing rests on assumptions we make about what matters (empirically and normatively) in the "international" political universe, assumptions such as "states are the most important actors," "agents are rational utility maximizers," "norms constitute identities and interests," "discourses are politically constitutive," "truth statements condition power relations," "human rights are universal," "community is the source of all value." A distinction is often made between our ontological, normative, and epistemological assumptions (Price and Reus-Smit 1998). But in reality these are often inextricably linked. Postmodernists do not reject the ontological assumption that states are the most important actors, or the normative assumption that human rights are universal, because they are empirically false, but because they are epistemologically unsustainable (George 1994). Thirdly, theorizing necessarily involves logical argument. It is through argument that we mobilize our assumptions in relation to our questions to infer new conclusions. Arguments are the creative media through which we combine, enliven, hierarchize, and give meaning to our assumptions, and we do this in the process of answering our questions.

Logical coherence with heuristic or deductive power is the one criterion that all theoretical approaches accept and to which they give pride of place: Logical contradictions and non-sequiturs are no more tolerated by feminists than by neoliberal institutionalists. Good theory is distinguished by how well its internal logic leads us to new insights and conclusions. Like a good story, theory has an internal logic that drives the argument. Once certain elements are specified, conclusions begin to follow, new lines of argument develop, and other elements emerge as logical candidates for inclusion in the theory. This internal dynamic leads to new implications and arguments about the world. Indeed, when a theoretical logic is especially powerful, it not only drives the research but can even change and shape the very questions that are asked and create its own inward-looking theoretical "world." Good theory also opens up our assumptions and understandings about what is fixed and what can be changed—both in the theory and as a guide to action in the world.

This conception of the theoretical endeavor encompasses the wide spectrum of theoretical approaches in international relations. It is as applicable to ostensibly normative theories as it is to empirical ones. Charles Beitz's classic argument (1979) for a cosmopolitan ethic is concerned with the central question of what principles of justice ought to apply globally and rests on the primary assumption that practical interdependence (an empirical idea he draws from Keohane and Nye 1977) necessarily leads to moral interdependence. It is also as applicable to critical theories as problem-solving. Andrew Linklater (1998) has been centrally concerned with understanding patterns of inclusion and exclusion in world politics, and his argument about the expansion of moral community globally rests on assumptions about the logic of communicative action. Similarly, Keohane (1984) has focused on the question of explaining patterns of international institutional cooperation by building on assumptions about rational state action under conditions of interdependence. Finally, this conception is as applicable to theories addressing interpretative "how" questions as those concerned with explanatory "why" questions. The scholar who asks how chemical weapons have come to attract such high moral approbation (Price 1997) will build logically on the basis of assumptions about the international political universe as readily as the scholar who asks why states engage in balance of power politics (Kaplan 1957; Waltz 1979; Mearsheimer 2001).

Because international relations theory addresses questions about the world, it necessarily has empirical content. Even our normative questions have empirical referents—the nature of the use of force between states, patterns of global inequality, the subordination of women, the hierarchy of cultures. Although the boundaries of international relations are fluid and contested, the field is defined in large part by its evolving empirical domain and the questions we ask of this domain. Questions of security and order are enduring, but changing interrelations at the global level from transnationalism to interdependence have expanded the set of enduring issues to include prosperity and growth (Risse-Kappen 1995; Gilpin 2001) and, increasingly, rights and freedoms (Risse, Ropp, and Sikkink 1999). This evolution has been punctuated by important events including world wars, decolonization, the oil crisis, the end of the cold war, and the attacks of 11 September, events that have shaped and directed international relations scholarship. Of course, different theories and areas of international relations emphasize different aspects of the empirical domain, and even different aspects of the "same" empirics. Security and international political economy define themselves in terms of different though partially overlapping substantive problems, which lead them to contending understandings of world politics and possibilities. Differences reign even within areas. The meaning and origins of "security" are contested (Wæver 1995), as are the important questions and theoretical constructs—interdependence or dependency or globalization—of political economy (Ravenhill, Chapter 31, this volume). Even specific empirical "facts" are contested—is the world unipolar (Brooks and Wohlforth 2002)? Is globalization homogenizing or fragmenting (Scholte 2005)? Does free trade alleviate or accentuate global inequality (Rodrik 1997)? Often these disagreements provide the puzzles to be explained and the inspiration for introducing new elements into theory.

Most international relations theorizing relies on empirical evidence to distinguish good arguments from crazy ideas. While this position is most often identified with positivism, it undergirds most international relations scholarship. To take a seemingly hard example, postmodernists make the signature claim that texts are open to multiple interpretations, and that there is no Archimedean standpoint from which to determine the truth of one reading over another. But their increasingly sophisticated analyses of diverse political discourses nevertheless rest on the assumption that texts and events are amenable to better and worse interpretations (Price and Reus-Smit 1998; Hansen 2006). Pointing out that a broad spectrum of international relations theories rely on empirical evidence to support their arguments is not the same, however, as treating falsification as a paramount value. Insofar as positivism gives unreflective primacy to falsification, or treats theory only as a hook upon which to hang empirical results, it misses the fact that theory can be important even when it cannot be empirically validated or falsified. This is as true of positive theorizing, such as the Arrow (1951) theorem that establishes that every international voting or decision rule must fail to meet certain democratic aspirations,[3] as it is of normative theorizing, such as the claim that human rights

---

[3] The Arrow theorem is also an excellent example that positive theory can be deeply normative. Some of Arrow's conditions (e.g. nondictatorship, Pareto) are directly motivated on normative

are universal (Donnelly 2003). Neither can be validated or falsified empirically. Conceptual theorizing is also vitally important but not empirically verifiable. Thus, while theorizing is never independent of empirical questions, international relations theory has an autonomy from, and must take priority over, empirical analysis.

While many different stripes of international relations theory peacefully co-exist, disagreements are the most prominent feature of the landscape. Two axes of division stand out. The first is between critical and problem-solving theories. Robert Cox famously argued that the latter "takes the world as it finds it, with the prevailing social and political power relationships and the institutions into which they are organized, as the given framework of action," while the former "allows for a normative choice in favor of a social and political order different from the prevailing order; but it limits the range of choice to alternative orders which are feasible transformations of the existing order" (Cox 1986, 208, 210). This distinction remains an important one, pointing us to the crucial difference between theorizing that focuses on the emancipatory transformation of the "social and political complex as a whole" and that which concentrates on the technical management of particular aspects of that complex. The following chapters suggest, however, that it may no longer be a straightforward guide to differentiating particular international relations theories. As Richard Shapcott (Chapter 19, this volume) explains, one of critical theory's contributions to the field is that concern with the normatively oriented transformation of world politics is no longer the sole preserve of self-identified critical theorists: in different ways, constructivists, liberals, and English School scholars are all plowing this field. Equally important, it is now clear that theoretical approaches not traditionally associated with the critical project may fruitfully be conscripted to its aid. Notable here is the contribution methodological individualists have made to understanding the origins of the contemporary system of sovereign states (Spruyt 1994; 2007).

The second axis of division is between verbal and formal mathematical theory. Proponents see the formal approach as the highest form of theory whereas critics see it as the ultimate in abstract irrelevance. Neither position is correct. A theory that can be modeled mathematically engages a particularly powerful form of deductive reasoning. But even here the art is in the "modeling dialog" (Myerson 1992), which entails the pursuit of substantive as well as mathematical arguments. Moreover, many problems that cannot be modeled productively through mathematics are amenable to verbal theory as a means of advancing our theoretical understanding. Defining our questions by our techniques misses the point of developing theory about the world we care about. To reduce the field to what can be mathematically modeled would narrow it to a barren landscape; conversely, not to take advantage

grounds while others (e.g. independence of irrelevant alternatives, universal domain) raise implicit normative questions about what we desire in a "democratic" social choice process—the very desirability of which is itself a normative question.

of formal deduction when possible is to risk missing important theoretical insights and possibly allowing inconsistent arguments to stand.[4]

It is often contended that different international relations theories are fundamentally incompatible with one another. Approaches such as postmodernism and liberalism often seem irreconcilable, while others such as sociological (Kratochwil, Chapter 26, this volume) and psychological (Goldgeier and Tetlock, Chapter 27, this volume) may just have little to say to each other. Unfortunately, the field has a tendency to exaggerate and even glorify these differences: One purpose of theory is to clarify fundamental from nonfundamental differences and, where possible, to establish common ground. This has been occurring, for example, in the much discussed and somewhat overblown debate between rationalism and constructivism. There has already been some convergence with regard to the role of ideas—to which rationalists pay increasing attention (Goldstein and Keohane 1993; Snidal 2002)— and of strategic rationality (which constructivists are increasingly incorporating into their accounts; Keck and Sikkink 1998). Even the purported differences (Wendt 1999) between the causal theory of rationalism versus the constitutive theory of constructivism is exaggerated. After all, rational choice's central equilibrium concept is a constitutive statement that a set of elements are in harmony with each other; equilibrium analysis becomes causal only by asking what happens when one element is displaced and harmony disrupted. Conversely, constructivist theorizing about norms has been increasingly used as the theoretical underpinning for causal relations and empirical testing (Checkel 1999; Ruggie 2005). Even where common ground does not exist, lessons can migrate across perspectives, as, for example, has happened with the critical theory challenge to the positivist ideal of value-free research. This is not to argue that deep incompatibilities do not exist, only that international relations theorizing at its best serves to clarify which differences are fundamental and which can be bridged.

3 THE EMPIRICAL AND NORMATIVE FACES OF THEORY

Security studies have long been driven by the impetus to understand war so we can control and reduce it; human rights analysis is motivated by the desire to

---

[4] Relevant examples are myriad. Some involve fairly technical mathematical presentations (Downs and Rocke 1995; Powell 1999; Kydd, Chapter 25, this volume), but many other ideas founded in technical analysis have entered international relations through more accessible translations. Examples of the latter category include James Fearon's discussion (1995) of rational war, the widespread use of Mancur Olson's collective action analysis (1965, based on Paul Samuelson's quite technical analysis of public goods), or Thomas Schelling's discussion (1960) of credibility and deterrence.

stop atrocities ranging from genocide to slavery to torture; international political economy is ultimately about promoting mutually beneficial economic interactions among states, firms, and individuals; and we study institutions such as the World Health Organization and the Food and Agriculture Organization to understand how to improve global health and food, respectively. Although international relations theories often present themselves as scientific and even objective, the underlying choice of assumptions is never objective and neither are values that animate them. All theories contain significant normative elements through the questions they ask, the concepts they use, the factors they exclude or hold constant, and the values they seek to further. Nevertheless, much of contemporary international relations neglects and even denies its normative underpinnings out of concern that it will impede intellectual progress. In this section we argue the opposite position—so long as international relations remains a practical discourse, one ultimately (though often implicitly) concerned with the question of "how we should act," scholars will be compelled to occupy the difficult terrain between the empirical and the normative. Furthermore, closer attention to the variety of ethical underpinnings in the field can strengthen our understanding of what we do and, channeled properly, can motivate research progress as it enhances our ability, individually or collectively, to speak to the most pressing issue of political action in contemporary world politics.

The normative component has been falsely suppressed in international relations for a combination of substantive, methodological, and theoretical reasons. The traditional realist emphasis on national security as a seemingly uncontroversial goal, and the state as the uncontroversial actor, eliminated any need to problematize the goals of action. Early English School (Cochran, Chapter 16, this volume) and liberal American approaches (Richardson, Chapter 12, this volume) echoed this neglect of normative concerns in their emphasis on equally uncontroversial goals of order and efficiency, respectively. Of course, as Jack Donnelly (Chapter 8, this volume) shows, even the most hardcore security realism entails some ethical content; the English School has also invested heavily in normative theorizing, and liberals are increasingly aware of the shortcoming of efficiency as its singular normative concept. And questions of just war, treatment of foreigners, and fair exchange have long been with us. Currently, the changing and expanding range of questions of international politics—including new dimensions of security such as terrorism and ethnic conflict, new twists on long-standing North–South issues and new political economy issues such as regulation that penetrate into the domestic workplace and home, and deepened concern for issues such as human rights, the global environment, and effects beyond the great powers—all present issues where goals are contested and the myth of normative consensus is unsustainable.

Behavioralism, positivism, and the effort to create a "science" of international relations provided a second motivation for the neglect of ethical considerations. Although most positivists accept that normative considerations are relevant to what questions to ask and to the uses to which those answers are put, "science" is seen as the intermediate stage involving production of knowledge that is ostensibly value-free.[5] However, normative considerations are deeply, though often implicitly, embedded in this scientific stage itself. Thus quantitative international relations now pays close attention to selection bias within its analyses, but quantitative analysis itself is an important form of selection bias driven by measurability and data availability (Mansfield and Pevehouse, Chapter 28, this volume). Further value judgments are necessarily lodged in the definition of contested concepts such as power, liberty, and equality. These normative assumptions can be varied through alternative conceptualizations and measurements but they cannot be eliminated. Perversely, the choice to limit research to questions where it is (falsely) believed that value-free assessment is possible can have the unfortunate side effect of limiting the questions asked—itself an implicit value judgment. An outside example that has had profound effects on international relations is the "ordinalist revolution" of economics in the 1930s in which economists discovered that they could derive key market results without recourse to cardinal individual utility or interpersonal comparisons of utility—both of which raise thorny normative issues (Blaug 1985). This reorientation allowed economics to make important and fundamental progress—but at the cost of largely abandoning the social welfare questions that had been central to the discipline up to that time. The heritage of this methodological move is reflected within international relations in the emphasis on Pareto efficiency rather than distribution in liberal institutionalism, which in turn, implicitly gives the status quo normative pride of place. Liberals are well aware of this bias, but their analytic tools are not as powerful for addressing other values, which are therefore slighted. Of course, the procedures of science—especially its efforts at being systematic, comparable, and transparent—provide means to highlight these normative elements and perhaps evaluate their implications. But at best they can illuminate not eliminate the normative element.

The tendency to set aside ethical considerations has been reinforced by misleading efforts fully to substitute logic for values. This underlying impetus is well captured in the rational choice adoption of the distinction between "normative" theory as being about "ought" and "positive" theory as being about "is." Positive theory analyzes the consequences that logically follow from interactions among a set of actors, given their goals and their capacities without any evaluation or judgment of those goals. Of course, the assumptions regarding the actors, their goals, and their capacities are themselves partly normative assertions, while the normative content of the predictions is what motivates our interest in the analysis in the first place. More importantly, rational choice shortchanges itself by denying its normative heritage and possibilities. In addition to emanating from the distinctively normative utilitarian tradition, rational choice can be viewed as a normative theory about

---

[5] We thank Alex Wendt for suggesting this formulation.

what actors should do given their circumstance—what is rational action?—as much as an empirical prediction about what actors will do. This is especially important insofar as rationality is often impaired, so that actors cannot be assumed to be fully capable of achieving their goals (Levy 1997). Moreover, much of rational choice is directed toward understanding how to ameliorate the adverse consequences of individual rationality (as evidenced in problems such as the Prisoner's Dilemma, collective action, or principal–agent relations) and how to achieve better outcomes either through individual remedies such as precommitment (Martin 2000) or reputation (Tomz 2007), or through collective remedies such as arms control or institutional design (Koremenos, Lipson, and Snidal 2001). Such solutions are justified in terms of efficiency as the primary normative value in rational choice and one that is typically presented as a neutral or even "scientific" value. But efficiency claims can mask other values such as distribution or rights (Gruber 2000). Andrew Kydd (Chapter 25, this volume) argues more generally that rational choice is premised on liberal normative biases, including respect for the individual, and that it has an elective affinity for specific substantive outcomes such as free exchange and decentralized power. Thus, far from being a purely logical rather than a partially normative theory, rational choice is a logical theory based on normative premises that provides guidance regarding how to further our normative goals.

The problem of separating empirical from normative analysis has been reinforced by the tendency of scholars who do take normative considerations seriously to distance themselves from social scientific approaches. This is most pronounced among those whose central concern is philosophical, determining what constitutes right conduct in a variety of international situations, from global aid provision to humanitarian intervention. Very often the process of ethical reasoning is defined narrowly, to encompass only the logical determination of ethical principles. But ethical reasoning is in practice much broader than this, combining empirical propositions and assumptions with philosophical speculation (Reus-Smit 2008). Defining it narrowly, however, encourages a neglect of empirical inquiry and the theories and methods it necessarily entails. This tendency is also apparent, though to a lesser extent, among approaches that take normative concerns seriously but shun more "scientific" approaches to empirical inquiry. Until recently, this has been a weakness of the English School, whose critically important meditations on the relationship between order and justice have historically been limited by its unsystematic approach to the nature of social and institutional relations among states (Reus-Smit 2005). Instead of a proper engagement between normative and scientific positions, we typically see either mutual neglect or mutual critiques that fall on deaf ears. The result is a divide, with "science" on one side and "normative" on the other.

This separation severely impairs the ability of international relations to speak to practical concerns. On the one hand, the unwillingness of "scientists" to tackle ethical and seemingly unscientific problems means it often has little to say on the important problems of the day; on the other hand, insofar as normative international relations is insufficiently well grounded in empirical knowledge, it is not competent to say what we should do in specific cases. Advice on whether or not to intervene in the next Rwanda or Darfur, for example, rests both on an analysis of what is possible (do sanctions work? can military intervention be effective?), and on a judgment as to who has the right or obligation do so. In order to connect international relations theory back to the practical questions that motivate it, both normative and empirical legs of the analysis must be firmly in place. This is the long-standing position of critical theorists such as Cox and Linklater, who seek normatively compelling transformations of international order that are "realistic" and consistent with the empirical dynamics of the global system (Cox 1986, 208; Linklater 1998). It is also the position advocated more recently by Keohane (2001; see also Buchanan and Keohane 2004), who has called on international relations scholars to help bring about a new international institutional order, a project that demands the integration of empirical and normative theory.

Our purpose here, however, is not simply to encourage greater interaction and integration between empirical and normative theorizing; it is to show that all international relations theories already have empirical and normative dimensions. There are two reasons why this is necessarily so. The first, and most commonly observed, is that we as scholars can never escape our values; they permeate the questions we ask, the puzzles we seek to fathom, the assumptions we make, and the methods we adopt. There is, however, a second reason that we wish to highlight here. As explained in the first section, international relations has always been a practical discourse, in the sense that the question of "how we should act" has undergirded and informed scholarship across the field. This is no less true of postmodern scholarship—concerned as it is with how to respond to structures of domination— than realist scholarship with its concern for the effective prosecution of the national interest under conditions of anarchy. Because their practical questions exist as a motive force, however implicitly, scholars are drawn onto the difficult terrain between the empirical and the normative. Answering the question of "how we should act" in terms of the values we seek to realize demands an appreciation of "how we can act" in terms of the context of action we face.

This interconnection between empirical and normative theorizing exists not just at the stages of the questions we ask and the purposes for which we use theory but also at the intermediate stage of knowledge production. We made the point earlier that normative biases permeate this stage. But with practical discourses the empirical and the normative are even more deeply entwined in processes of knowledge production. Answering the question of how we should act requires empirical knowledge production that examines the causal, constitutive, and discursive structures and processes that frame political action. But it also requires normative knowledge production that examines who the "we" is that seeks to act, what principles we seek to realize, and what resources we are prepared to sacrifice to achieve our ends (such as the loss of compatriots to save strangers) (Reus-Smit 2008). With practical discourses, therefore, knowledge production cannot be confined to the "scientific" realm of empirical theory; it is necessarily more expansive, encompassing normative inquiry just as centrally.

One of our central goals in this *Handbook* has been to draw out these empirical and normative dimensions of international relations theories, and this has been done most systemically in our survey of the principal substantive theories. In the remainder of this section, we draw on our contributors' insights to map these theories' empirical and normative aspects, leading we hope to a markedly different characterization of the field than is common. We have found it illuminating to map them against three empirical and two normative axes, though others are no doubt possible.

With regard to their empirical–theoretic aspects, we have focused on their assumptions regarding agency and structure, ideas and materiality, and the nature of power. With the first of these, we have distinguished between theories that are agential (emphasizing individual choice in determining political outcomes), structural (emphasizing the opportunities and constraints that social structures place on individual choice), structurationist (emphasizing the mutually constitutive relationship between agents and structures), and poststructuralist (stressing the way in which systems of signification and meaning constitute subjectivities). With the second, we have differentiated between theories that are ideational (attributing constitutive power to intersubjective ideas and meanings), rational institutionalist (emphasizing the role of ideas in mediating the relationship between material or other interests and political outcomes), and materialist (highlighting the causal force of material factors). With the third set of assumptions, we distinguish between four different conceptions of "power" in different international relations theories. We have conscripted Michael Barnett and Raymond Duvall's typology (2005, 3, emphasis in original) where:

Compulsory power refers to relations of interaction that allow one actor to have direct control over another…*Institutional power* is in effect when actors exercise indirect control over others…*Structural power* concerns the constitution of social capacities and interests of actors in direct relation to one another…*Productive power* is the socially diffuse production of subjectivity in systems of meaning and signification.

When it comes to the normative–theoretic aspects of theories, we have concentrated on two axes of variation: value commitments and orientation toward change.[6] The first refers to the values or purposes that theories seek to realize, implicitly or explicitly. Drawing on our contributors, we have identified five distinct

---

[6] These are not the only axes of variation that could have been chosen here. For instance, we could have disaggregated value commitments into deontological and consequentialist subcategories, and we could have added an axis categorizing theories according to how they treat the relationship between means and ends.

value commitments: (1) the prudent pursuit of the national interest; (2) international cooperation (ranging from order through minimal norms of sovereignty to achievement of higher-order social values through international governance); (3) individual freedom (including negative freedom through the removal of constraints on individual liberty as well as positive freedom through the protection of individuals' basic rights); (4) inclusivity and self-reflexivity; and (5) responsibility to otherness. Our second axis—orientation toward change—refers to theorists' general inclinations to the question of moral and practical change: are they (implicitly or explicitly) optimistic or skeptical? The normative aspects of international relations theories are determined not only by the values scholars embrace, but by their willingness to entertain that moral change is possible. We have treated this as a separate axis on which to map theories, as the orientations toward change of different theories are reducible neither to their empirical understandings nor to their substantive value commitments—are realists generally skeptical about moral change because of the empirical assumptions they make, or do they favor these assumptions because they are moral pessimists?

Table 1.1 maps nine substantive theories of international relations against these empirical and normative dimensions. Our purpose here is not to reify these theories, reducing their complexities to singular, homogeneous, forms.[7] Nor is it to suggest that our chosen axes of comparison are the only relevant dimensions of similarity or difference. Our goal is to show (a) that indeed all theories of international relations entail empirical and normative dimensions, and (b) that a number of interesting patterns and overlaps emerge when theories are viewed in this way. Among other things, this reveals that a number of ritual characterizations that are used to divide the field are vastly overworked. The most notable is the much brandished distinction between realists and idealists, scientists and utopians—a distinction that rests on the purported ability to quarantine empirical theories from normative influence. A second is that the field is fundamentally riven by epistemological differences, by differences over what constitutes true knowledge. But while these differences are all too apparent, and their implications for how we conduct our scholarship important, they obscure multiple other significant points of convergence among theoretical approaches.

Our comparison reveals three patterns of note. The first is that of value resonance across seemingly opposed theories. This is perhaps most striking between critical theorists and new liberals. As Robyn Eckersley (Chapter 20, this volume) explains in her chapter on the ethics of critical theory, at the level of "normative ethics, critical

---

[7] Such categorizations are necessarily vulgar and disguise important internal variations within approaches. For example, some realists are optimists and some constructivists are pessimists. Elements of the English School are more structural than structurationist, while institutionalism might sometimes handle compulsory as well as institutional power. While our categorizations are necessarily imperfect, we believe they capture the general tendencies. The exceptions suggest other overlaps and intersections among perspectives.

Table 1.1. Empirical and normative faces of theory

THEORIES	EMPIRICAL ASPECTS			NORMATIVE ASPECTS	
	Agency–structure	Ideational–material	Conception of power	Value commitment	Orientation toward change
Realism	Structural (anarchy)	Material	Compulsory	National interest	Skeptical
Marxism	Structural (capitalism)	Material	Structural	Individual freedom (Negative—emancipation)	Skeptical
Neoliberal institutionalism	Agential (states)	Rational institutionalist	Institutional	International cooperation	Optimistic
New liberalism	Agential (individuals)	Rational institutionalist	Institutional	Individual freedom (Negative—liberty)	Optimistic
English School (ES pluralists)	Structural (anarchy)	Rational institutionalist	Institutional	International cooperation	Skeptical
(ES solidarists)	Structurationist	Ideational	Structural	Individual freedom (Positive—universal human rights)	Optimistic
Constructivism	Structurationist	Ideational	Structural	Individual positive freedom/ International cooperation	Optimistic
Critical theory	Structurationist	Ideational/material	Structural	Individual freedom (Negative—emancipation)	Optimistic
Postmodernism	Structurationist	Ideational	Productive	Responsibility to otherness	Skeptical
Feminism	Structurationist	Ideational	Productive	Inclusivity/Self-reflexivity	Skeptical

theory's overriding ethical goal is to promote emancipation, or remove constraints on human autonomy, by means of ever more inclusive and less distorted dialogue." The similarity between this normative standpoint and the priority given to individual liberty by new liberals is difficult to ignore. For both, the good of human individuals has ethical primacy and, for both, the removal of constraints on their freedom is prioritized. This is not to obscure important differences between these theories' ethical positions, but their similarities should not be surprising given their common Enlightenment origins. Value resonance is also apparent between English School solidarists and constructivists, both evincing a central concern for clarifying the conditions under which sovereignty can be compromised better to promote the positive freedom of individuals, particularly in the form of international human rights. Again, important differences should not be obscured, particularly over methodology and the priority given to philosophical inquiry, but convergence at the level of values is all too apparent.

Secondly, our comparison reveals a strong correlation between the orientations toward change of theories that adopt a compulsory conception of power and those that embrace a productive one. The prime example of this is the relation between realism and postmodernism. Both are skeptical of the possibility of moral change in international relations. For realists this is because the politics of morality is always eclipsed by the politics of power; for postmodernists it is because moral discourses are necessary for the production of power: all processes of moral signification produce relations of domination. Peter Lawler (Chapter 22, this volume) observes correctly that the postmodernists' critique of moral universalism does not lead them to the "moral despair" of realists, only to a preference "for localized, contingent responses to ethically troubling cases." However, theories that embrace compulsory or productive conceptions of power share a view of power as ubiquitous to international relations. For realists this is because it is the struggle for power that defines politics; for postmodernists it is that all processes of signification are constitutive of power. Both ultimately encourage a position of moral skepticism, even if this does not amount to despair.

The third pattern of note is the consistent correlation between structural theories and skepticism and between agential or structurationist theories and optimism. Realists, Marxists, and English School pluralists are all structural, in the sense that they see the structure either of anarchy or of capitalism providing the incentives and constraints for social actors. Not surprisingly their relative neglect of the role such actors can play in the constitution of social structures leaves little room for the possibility of moral change in international relations—with the partial exception of the Marxist view of the structure itself being unstable in the long term (Teschke, Chapter 9, this volume). Conversely, theories that are agential or structurationist—such as new liberalism, solidarism within the English School, or constructivism—leave greater space for the creative power of individual or collective human agency, providing the social theoretic foundations for more optimistic positions on the question of both moral and practical change. Of course, agency can work to bad ends as well—neoliberal institutionalists understand that cooperation can be aimed against third parties while constructivists recognize the possibility of bad norms leading to pathological consequences (Rae 2002). Finally, postmodernism and feminism are exceptions in being structurationist and skeptical, possibly because their emphasis on productive power overwhelms the impact of structurationism, encouraging skepticism not optimism.

4 The Question of Progress

While the above comparison reveals the diversity of contemporary theorizing in international relations, as well as diverse ways in which theories have traversed the difficult terrain between the empirical and the normative, has such diversity led to progress in the field? It is unfashionable to speak of progress in international relations, but it is also the case that some notion of progress informs all our scholarship. If we do not believe that our work makes some contribution to improving our understanding of world politics, and that our collective endeavors as a field yield some knowledge gains, what justifies our research? For this reason, we believe that progress in international relations can be evaluated in terms of the extent to which we have expanded our understanding of the subject matter—viewed broadly to include explanatory, interpretive, normative, and other approaches to understanding—and whether this has improved our ability to act effectively in international affairs. Simply put, can we do things better now than before in these two related spheres? An important distinction here is between progress within sub-areas of international relations—defined by substantive topic, methodology, or theoretical approach—versus progress of the field as a whole. We argue that the seeming lack of progress in the field as a whole is intimately related to the nature of progress within its subfields.

Evaluating progress is difficult for several reasons. We have no agreed criteria by which to measure what we know or how effectively it has been (or could be) applied to real world action. International relations' dynamic character makes it a moving target as both an object of inquiry and a field of study. Although some questions are enduring, others are changing with both world events and intellectual fashions. Most importantly, the field is inherently political and contested, so that any measure of progress is inherently value laden and depends significantly on beliefs regarding what is possible and what is desirable.

Nevertheless, the contributions to this volume clearly document multiple ways in which progress has been made. Conceptually, the field is much more rigorous;

even where it comes to no settled consensus, it is clearer about its differences. Fundamental concepts like power remain "essentially contested," but in differentiating types of power (Barnett and Duvall 2005) we have substantially advanced our understanding of its different facets. Similarly, the presumption of state-centrism has been increasingly challenged by analyses incorporating transnational and subnational actors (Moravcsik, Chapter 13, this volume), but the theoretical sophistication of both state-centric approaches and its competitors has advanced considerably. William Wohlforth (Chapter 7, this volume) shows how realism has flourished and multiplied in terms of more finely tuned arguments and debates, such as those between offensive and defensive realism; Ian Hurd (Chapter 17, this volume) and Friedrich Kratochwil (Chapter 26, this volume) show how constructivism has incorporated philosophical and sociological arguments to develop a novel ideational theory and norm-based explanations as a counterpoint to overly materialist traditional theory based solely on power and interests. Postmodernism, for all its skepticism about progress, has also developed ever more sophisticated methods of deconstruction, discourse analysis, and genealogical inquiry, yielding important insights into the discursive construction of post-cold war international relations (Burke, Chapter 21, this volume).

Other important aspects of the field's progress have been the incorporation of new approaches to long-standing questions, the opening of new areas of inquiry, and the asking of questions that either are new or have been neglected. These shifts have sometimes been prompted by emerging problems in the world, sometimes by the internal logic of theoretical approaches, sometimes by changing intellectual forces, and usually by a combination of all of these. For example, post-cold war and post-11 September security research has shifted to new concerns with ethnic conflict and terrorism, and its logics of assurance and deterrence have been adapted in light of the new challenges these problems present. The concept and boundaries of security (Buzan, Wæver, and de Wilde 1998) have been contested and seen to involve much deeper elements of personal security rather than simply military matters or state interests. International political economy has moved beyond its traditional concerns with trade and money, though those remain important, to look at emerging issues of standard-setting, transnational business regulation, and money-laundering (Abbott and Snidal 2001; Mattli and Büthe 2003; Drezner 2007). Institutions have been reconceptualized, with increasing attention paid to their different forms and specific properties (Koremenos, Lipson, and Snidal 2001). Similarly, the emergence of global warming as an issue and new regard for human rights around the globe have challenged traditional theories and sparked increased interest in new ones.

The field, or at least part of it, has become less complacent about the questions being asked. The proliferation of questions and approaches has been connected to a greater appreciation that questions asked are never neutral but always reflect underlying values and power relations. Critical approaches and feminism have challenged long-standing biases of "mainstream" realism and liberalism, while interpretivist and more historically oriented work have challenged the more universalistic ambitions of positivism. Ironically, some of these differences emerge because realism can also be criticized for being substantively less ambitious in assuming that the fundamental nature of international politics is unchanging, whereas liberals see possibilities for change within the system that need to be explained and more radical approaches problematize the existing international system to open up the need to explain large-scale system change.

The continuing relative neglect of Third World issues reminds us that the biases of our intellectual community, which remains a Northern and a Western one, continue to shape our discipline and limit its progress in at least some areas. Phillip Darby's critique (Chapter 5, this volume) of international relations as a discipline, Anthony Burke's discussion (Chapter 21, this volume) of postmodernism, and David Blaney and Naeem Inayatullah's "view from below" (Chapter 38, this volume), all argue that international relations theory excludes the questions and analyses most relevant to the Third World and continues to define progress in Western terms. Postcolonialism, postmodernism, and feminism all challenge the predominant focus on states and sovereignty, as well as the neglect of non-Western cultures and issues such as global injustice that receive little more than lip-service in the North. Blaney and Inayatullah (Chapter 38, this volume; see also Gilroy 2006) propose that such approaches need to engage "international relations from above" to expose their hidden assumptions and political purposes.

Progress in the use of increasingly sophisticated methodology is easy to document. Statistical and formal mathematical approaches have become both more widespread and more carefully tailored to substantive problems of international relations (Mansfield and Pevehouse, Chapter 28, this volume). There has been a continuing development of improved data-sets on an expanding set of questions, now including human rights (Hathaway 2002; Hafner-Burton 2005), the environment (Sprinz 2004), domestic institutions (Howell and Pevehouse 2007; Mansfield, Milner, and Rosendorff 2002), and democracy (Russett and Oneal 2001; Pevehouse and Russett 2006). Formal models (Snidal 2004) have become more common and more complicated and have driven theory in certain areas such as deterrence and cooperation. These approaches have also become better at recognizing and dealing with their limits—as reflected in increased attention to selection and identification problems in quantitative work (Drezner 2003; Vreeland 2003; von Stein 2005) or the use of agent models (Cederman 2003) to address problems not amenable to closed-form mathematical analysis.

Importantly, methodological progress has not been limited to these more technical approaches. Case study methods have advanced significantly not only in their use of historical and interpretative methods but also in the use of techniques such as process-tracing to combine careful causal analysis with close attention to underlying mechanisms (Bennett and Elman, Chapter 29, this volume). Postmodernism has advanced in its argumentation, as reflected in its genealogical analysis of discourses of security (Hansen 2006) and its practices and, more generally but perhaps also more controversially, in its closer attention to historical events and contemporary policy (Burke, Chapter 21, this volume). The different methods have also interacted to their mutual benefit. Statistical analysis of selection problems spurred considerable attention to selection problems in qualitative research, which in turn has led to a richer understanding of selection issues and research designs that go beyond the pure statistical models (Signorino 2002). The complementarity of different approaches has also been revealed by the widespread use of the combination of case studies and large-n analysis, which has almost become formulaic in some areas. In this vein, whereas early constructivist work was criticized by positivists as not being testable, constructivists have more than demonstrated their capacity to produce methodologically rigorous, empirical research (for a recent example see Acharya and Johnston 2007)—and positivists have been able to include some of the factors raised by constructivists in their own work (Tierney and Weaver 2007).

Methodologically driven progress has significant limits, however. While judicious use of methods improves empirical and theoretical analysis of international relations problems, methods are the means and not the goal. Overemphasis on methodological criteria can discourage research in areas that are not (yet?) amenable to the most advanced techniques. Just as it was valuable to study war before extensive data-sets had been developed for quantitative analysis, so it is useful to study problems such as human rights even if we cannot formally model normative action or if our statistical data are limited. Important research questions cannot always wait for method.

A related problem emerges when research is expected to meet the multiple standards of empirics and theory. Research can be first rate without doing everything. For example, inductive research that improves our knowledge of what the world looks like—and of important relationships that we care about—is useful even before the relationships are well theorized. Indeed, theoretical progress necessarily requires empirical facts even before they are deeply theorized. Conversely, theoretical analysis can improve the quality of international relations arguments even if they are not yet tested or, in some cases, cannot be tested: Good theory often takes us beyond our current empirical knowledge. In short, there is a virtue in a division of labor where not every article has to do everything—some papers should be largely theoretical with limited empirics, others largely inductive with thin theory, and others mainly normative, or even methodological. The corollary to this division of labor is that no piece of research is fully complete in and of itself. The meaning and value of individual projects depends vitally on their interconnections with international relations research in general.

How then does progress occur? It is useful to distinguish progress within individual research areas from progress in the field as a whole. *Handbook* authors who discuss a specific approach or issue all report on some type of progress within their area,[8] even if they sometimes express dissatisfaction with the rate or direction of progress. It might seem that, if all its areas have advanced, then presumably so has the field. However, there is no consensus that the field has advanced in the sense of moving toward a common and integrated understanding of international politics. International relations remains a diverse and contested field whose different areas are often claimed to be, and sometimes probably are, incompatible. To reconcile this coexistence of progress within areas with the seeming lack of overall progress, we need to consider the different ways that progress is made within and across areas.

Progress within areas often results from pursuing the internal logic of a theoretical argument and/or investigating the empirical realm that it identifies. In some cases, a key theoretical puzzle (for example, why is there cooperation?) or empirical fact (for example, democracies do not fight one another) has motivated enormous research effort and substantial advancement. Thus folk theorem results about the possibility of cooperation in anarchy have developed into a rich analysis of the institutions that surround cooperation; a few empirical facts about the relationship of democracy and war (Doyle 1986) has launched a thousand articles addressing the relation between domestic regimes and international outcomes (for a discussion see Mansfield and Pevehouse, Chapter 28, this volume). These more inward-looking logics of inquiry can be highly productive but, in isolation, promote relatively narrow specialization within areas, sometimes leading to some splintering of the areas itself. A prime example of this is Wohlforth's discussion (Chapter 7, this volume) of how the development of realist theory has increased the variety of different camps or types of realists.

The opposite extreme is when progress is based on the importation of external ideas. International relations always has been a deeply interdisciplinary enterprise, and one of its most important sources of progress has been borrowing from outside the field. The various chapters of this *Handbook* document extensive borrowing of theoretical ideas, substantive arguments, and methodological tools from the disciplines of sociology (Hurd, Chapter 17, this volume; Kratochwil, Chapter 26, this volume), history (Quirk, Chapter 30, this volume; Bennett and Elman, Chapter 29, this volume; Blaney and Inayatullah, Chapter 38, this volume), economics (Kydd, Chapter 25, this volume; Stein, Chapter 11, this volume), philosophy (Burke, Chapter 21, this volume), psychology (Goldgeier and Tetlock, Chapter 27, this volume), and political science (Donnelly, Chapter 8, this volume; Moravcsik, Chapter 13, this volume). We also see the incorporation of ideas from theoretical approaches such as feminism, critical theory, and postmodernism that cross over the social science disciplines as well as the humanities. Of particular note in this volume is the reinvigoration of international relations' borrowing from political theory. This is hardly

---

[8] Despite the obvious selection bias in terms of the criteria by which we solicited authors and that they accepted, the authors generally make compelling cases for progress within their areas—at least by that area's criteria.

new, since, as Donnelly notes, many of international relations' intellectual icons—including Thucydides, Thomas Hobbes, Hugo Grotius, and Immanuel Kant—are theorists of more than international relations. More recently, the field has begun to build on a wide range of more contemporary political theorists such as Jürgen Habermas, Carl Schmitt, Michel Foucault, John Rawls, Giorgio Agamben, Judith Butler, and Axel Honneth.

External borrowing is an important way to advance the field but poses problems of its own. One danger is that international relations problems will be adapted to fit to the theory rather than the other way round, as is appropriate. Theories developed in other contexts may not provide a good match: there is no reason to believe that states are socialized in the same way as individuals, that rational international actors are like marketplace consumers, or that individual psychology transfers to how leaders and bureaucracies act in international crises. Thus external borrowing needs to be carefully tailored to the circumstances of international relations in order to be valuable. Although there is no simple way to measure it, the quality of our intellectual "borrowing" and especially of our adapting it to the specific circumstances of international relations, has significantly improved. The probable reason is that international relations scholars are increasingly well versed in the particular external intellectual terrains from which they draw. However, this leads to a second danger that such borrowing fragments international relations as a field by connecting its sub-areas more to their respective external source than to each other. Even if we do not care whether international relations coheres as a "discipline," the commonality of our questions makes it desirable for different approaches to seek productive engagement with one another. Fortunately, there has also been extensive interaction across various international relations communities. Some of this has been in the form of borrowing ideas developed in one area better to understand another. In other cases, borrowing has been more competitive or even conflictual in nature. A prominent example is liberal institutionalism's adoption of realist premises to develop a nonidealist account of cooperation. This has led to competition and even conflict between the two areas on topics such as relative gains or the importance of institutions, since they have very different and even opposed explanations for the "same" phenomenon.

Contestation can be both productive and destructive. It is most productive when it is over what questions matter, and over the answers to those questions. This type of engagement can reveal shortcomings, challenge presuppositions, sharpen argument, and raise new questions. Debate also reinvigorates the contending theories and challenges the complacency toward which internal research programs sometimes gravitate. Contestation is least productive when it degenerates into defensive discussions that impede communication across areas. Arguments over ontology and epistemology, while sometimes important, are too often deployed in this fashion. Contestation also becomes destructive when vindication of the theory becomes more important than understanding the world—as illustrated by the so-called paradigm wars, where different international relations traditions engage in intellectual gladiatorial combat more focused on "victory" for their perspective than on explaining the world.[9] Whether contestation is productive or not depends on how we collectively channel our efforts. Trespassing across sub-areas of international relations is necessarily treacherous and difficult, but the goal is to make it easier not to raise barriers against it. Bially Mattern (Chapter 40, this volume) offers an interesting assessment of how contestation of the "power" concept has advanced international relations. On the one hand, it has helped broaden the discipline; on the other hand, it has separated international relations into niches. As she points out, this contestation can be productive only if it is channeled through enough common ground that diverse elements of the (un)discipline can truly challenge one another.

One of the key questions is whether different international relations approaches (or which ones) are sufficiently compatible that their competition can be productive. The realist–liberal interchange over relative gains suggests that the possibilities may be limited even among two traditions that share a rationalist underpinning. Perhaps surprisingly, the rationalist–constructivist interaction offers more grounds for optimism. Sometimes the debate has centered on questions of whether the two schools (which are themselves internally quite diverse) are sufficiently compatible in terms of either epistemology or ontology to allow a constructive exchange. Yet recent work has found substantial common ground, including successful efforts to accommodate key insights from the other. Table 1.1 above shows many points of intersection across ostensibly separate theoretical traditions at a very broad level. Such intersections can also be seen in the specific details of ongoing research. Constructivists have incorporated collective action and principal–agent relations into their analyses (Keck and Sikkink 1998; Nielson, Tierney, and Weaver 2006); rationalists have increased their attention to norms to deepen their analysis of institutions. The second generation of feminist work is much more empirically oriented, perhaps in part due to earlier criticisms, and more attuned to drawing connections to other factors that affect international politics. Sandra Whitworth (Chapter 23, this volume) illustrates this in terms of looking at the different ways in which various international institutions from the World Bank to the military use gender, while Jacqui True (Chapter 24, this volume) engages the compatibility of feminist theory with other international relations theories. Of course, the more radical postmodern and critical theorists suggest that mainstream international relations "doesn't get it" and holds out little hope that it will. Even here, however,

---

[9] Hasenclever, Mayer, and Rittberger (1997) provide a useful overview of the interaction among neorealists, neoinstitutionalists, and constructivists that highlight areas where the interaction has been positive (cooperation theory and institutions), where it has been more negative (relative gains), and where the ability of theories to improve each other is still unclear (ideas).

the criticism can still be valuable in raising awareness of hidden assumptions and presumptions and may cause some shift in the other work, although probably not to the satisfaction of the critics, who will be viewed as impossible to satisfy from the initial group. Finally, a striking challenge for more integration at an epistemological level is raised in Burke's endorsement (Chapter 21, this volume) of Lene Hansen's call (2006) "for poststructuralism to take methodology back [from rationalism]."

This then is the paradox of international relations theory—progress in individual areas does not aggregate into progress for the field as a whole—at least in the sense of developing a unified and synthetic understanding of the subject matter (Kitcher 1981). Instead of a grand synthesis based on a single logic of inquiry, we see the ongoing contestation among many diverse strands of theory using multiple logics. But, whereas this has generally been seen as a failure of international relations, it can also be seen as one reason for its success. Contestation provides vitality to the field that keeps it open to changing questions and provides access points for new ideas. This *Handbook* aims to further progress by bringing these different points of contention together in a constructive way. In particular, by emphasizing the importance of underlying normative arguments to all international relations theory, we locate common ground among seemingly uncommon approaches and elucidate these more fundamental reasons for our differences.

5 CONCLUSION

A central insight of postmodernism is that actors construct their identities through the construction of radical others—who we are is defined against an other who is everything we are not. Sadly, identity politics has been an all too prominent feature of international relations scholarship. Our theories have become our social identities, and in constructing these theoretical identities we have reified other theoretical positions to accentuate difference and suppress convergence. Our purpose in this chapter—and in how we have organized this *Handbook* more generally—has been to cut across these lines wrought by identity politics. We have not ignored genuine points of difference—in fact we have drawn attention to previously under-acknowledged differences. Nor have we downplayed the significance of such differences. Indeed, we have argued that they can be productive. We have, however, highlighted two similarities among all theories: the broad style of theorizing that approaches share, a style that integrates questions, assumptions, and logical argumentation; and the presence of empirical and normative aspects in all theorizing. While these similarities cut across existing theoretical differences, they do not homogenize international relations theory. Instead, they bring to the fore axes of difference and convergence previously obscured.

The existence of both empirical and normative aspects in all international relations theories is fundamental to their nature as practical discourses, concerned in their diverse ways with the question of how we should act. Only through practical discourses can international relations scholars speak to the complex problems of political action in the contemporary global system. And, if we embrace this as an objective for the field, then we must accept that the terrain between the empirical and the normative is one that we will need to tread, and to do so systematically. This interaction of empirical and normative considerations is what gives international relations its vitality. It is the source of the questions the field studies and the reason why it is never satisfied with the answers. The world is changing both because of shifts in international problems and because of shifts in what we care about. The scientific effort to wall off the normative issues is fundamentally misguided, as is normative theorizing that is innocent of empirical research.

This does not mean that the field has to be preoccupied by normative debates any more than it should be preoccupied by epistemological ones. Nor does it mean that every individual research effort need (or can) constantly engage the full panoply of empirical and normative issues. International relations is sufficiently developed and professionalized as a field that no individual scholar can cover everything and every project must "bracket" important considerations—which is not to say ignore or be unaware of them—for research to proceed. Thus scholarship closer to the empirical end may stipulate its research questions, assumptions about the actors, and the evaluation of the issue outcomes as relatively unproblematic, while focusing on developing explanations of how interactions occur. Conversely, a more normatively oriented project might stipulate certain "facts" about how the world works, and what is possible, as a prelude to evaluating prevailing circumstances and what we should do about them. This sort of basic research where scholars pursue the internal logic of their arguments, and competition among arguments is pursued for its own sake, is an important means of advancing the field. Such a division of labor is also inevitable and highly productive in a field where the questions are incredibly complex and always changing.

What is important, however, is that individuals recognize the partial nature of their research, acknowledge that their theorizing is infused with both empirical and normative elements, and accept that the parts must interact and communicate if divisions of labor are not to fragment into separate production lines. This latter task is something that can be implemented by the field as a community even if individual practitioners are not always attentive to the interconnections. Of course, it is important that individual researchers be kept aware of this intermittently— which is exactly what a diverse and interacting international relations community can achieve and which this *Handbook* highlights.

References

ABBOTT, K. W., and SNIDAL, D. 2001. International "standards" and international governance. *Journal of European Public Policy*, 8: 345–70.

ACHARYA, A., and JOHNSTON, A. I. (eds.) 2007. *Crafting Cooperation: Regional International Institutions in Comparative Perspective*. Cambridge: Cambridge University Press.

ARROW, K. J. 1951. *Social Choice and Individual Values*. New York: Wiley.

BARNETT, M., and DUVALL, R. 2005. Power in global governance. Pp. 1–32 in *Power in Global Governance*, ed. M. Barnett and R. Duvall. Cambridge: Cambridge University Press.

BAYLIS, J., and SMITH, S. 2005. *The Globalization of World Politics: An Introduction to International Relations*, 3rd edn. Oxford: Oxford University Press.

BEITZ, C. R. 1979. *Political Theory and International Relations*. Princeton, NJ: Princeton University Press.

BLAUG, M. 1985. *Economic Theory in Retrospect*, 4th edn. Cambridge: Cambridge University Press.

BROOKS, S. G., and WOHLFORTH, W. C. 2002. American primacy in perspective. *Foreign Affairs*, 81: 20–33.

BUCHANAN, A., and KEOHANE, R. O. 2004. The preventive use of force: a cosmopolitan institutional proposal. *Ethics and International Affairs*, 18: 1–22.

BURCHILL, S., LINKLATER, A., DEVETAK, R., PATERSON, M., DONNELLY, J., REUS-SMIT, C., and TRUE, J. 2005. *Theories of International Relations*, 3rd edn. New York: Palgrave Macmillan.

BUZAN, B., WÆVER, O., and DE WILDE, J. 1998. *Security: A New Framework for Analysis*. Boulder, Colo.: Lynne Rienner.

CARLSNAES, W., RISSE, T., and SIMMONS, B. A. (eds.) 2002. *Handbook of International Relations*. London: Sage.

CARR, E. H. 1946. *The Twenty Years' Crisis, 1919–1939: An Introduction to the Study of International Relations*, 2nd edn. London: Macmillan.

CEDERMAN, L.-E. 2003. Modeling the size of wars: from billiard balls to sandpiles. *American Political Science Review*, 97: 135–50.

CHECKEL, J. T. 1999. Social construction and integration. *Journal of European Public Policy*, 6: 545–60.

COX, R. 1986. Social forces, states and world orders: beyond international relations theory. Pp. 204–54 in *Neorealism and its Critics*, ed. R. O. Keohane. New York: Columbia University Press.

DONNELLY, J. 2003. *Universal Human Rights in Theory and Practice*, 2nd edn. Ithaca, NY: Cornell University Press.

DOWNS, G. W., and ROCKE, D. M. 1995. *Optimal Imperfection? Domestic Uncertainty and Institutions in International Relations*. Princeton, NJ: Princeton University Press.

DOYLE, M. W. 1986. Liberalism and world politics. *American Political Science Review*, 80: 1151–69.

DREZNER, D. W. 2003. Bargaining, enforcement, and multilateral sanctions: when is cooperation counterproductive? *International Organization*, 54: 73–102.

——— 2007. *All Politics is Global: Explaining International Regulatory Regimes*. Princeton, NJ: Princeton University Press.

FEARON, J. D. 1995. Rationalist explanations for war. *International Organization*, 49: 379–414.

GEORGE, J. 1994. *Discourses of Global Politics: A Critical (Re)Introduction to International Relations*. Boulder, Colo.: Lynne Rienner.

GILPIN, R. 2001. *Global Political Economy: Understanding the International Economic Order.* Princeton, NJ: Princeton University Press.

GILROY, P. 2006. Multiculturalism and post-colonial theory. Pp. 656–74 in *Oxford Handbook of Political Theory*, ed. J. S. Dryzek, B. Honig, and A. Phillips. Oxford: Oxford University Press.

GOLDSTEIN, J., and KEOHANE, R. O. 1993. Ideas and foreign policy: an analytical framework. Pp. 3–30 in *Ideas and Foreign Policy: Beliefs, Institutions, and Political Change*, ed. J. Goldstein and R. O. Keohane. Ithaca, NY: Cornell University Press.

GOODIN, R. E., REIN, M., and MORAN, M. 2006. The public and its policies. Pp. 3–35 in *Oxford Handbook of Public Policy*, ed. M. Moran, M. Rein, and R. E. Goodin. Oxford: Oxford University Press.

GRUBER, L. 2000. *Ruling the World: Power Politics and the Rise of Supranational Institutions.* Princeton, NJ: Princeton University Press.

HAFNER-BURTON, E. M. 2005. Trading human rights: how preferential trade agreements influence government repression. *International Organization*, 59: 593–629.

HANSEN, L. 2006. *Security as Practice: Discourse Analysis and the Bosnian War.* London: Routledge.

HASENCLEVER, A., MAYER, P., and RITTBERGER, V. 1997. *Theories of International Regimes.* Cambridge: Cambridge University Press.

HATHAWAY, O. A. 2002. Do human rights treaties make a difference? *Yale Law Journal*, 111: 1935–2042.

HOWELL, W. G., and PEVEHOUSE, J. C. 2007. *While Dangers Gather: Congressional Checks on Presidential War Powers.* Princeton, NJ: Princeton University Press.

KAPLAN, M. A. 1957. *System and Process in International Politics.* New York: John Wiley and Sons.

KECK, M., and SIKKINK, K. 1998. *Activists beyond Borders: Advocacy Networks in International Politics.* Ithaca, NY: Cornell University Press.

KEOHANE, R. O. 1984. *After Hegemony: Cooperation and Discord in the World Political Economy.* Princeton, NJ: Princeton University Press.

—— 2001. Governance in a partially governed world. *American Political Science Review*, 95: 1–13.

—— and NYE, J. S. 1977. *Power and Interdependence: World Politics in Transition.* Boston: Little, Brown.

KITCHER, P. 1981. Explanatory unification. *Philosophy of Science*, 48: 507–31.

KOREMENOS, B., LIPSON, C., and SNIDAL, D. 2001. The rational design of international institutions. *International Organization*, 55: 761–99.

LAPID, Y. 1989. The third debate: on the prospects of international theory in a post-positivist era. *International Studies Quarterly*, 33: 235–54.

LEVY, J. S. 1997. Prospect theory, rational choice, and international relations. *International Studies Quarterly*, 41: 87–112.

LINKLATER, A. 1998. *The Transformation of Political Community: Ethical Foundations of the Post-Westphalian Era.* Cambridge: Polity.

MANSFIELD, E. D., MILNER, H. V., and ROSENDORFF, B. P. 2002. Why democracies cooperate more: electoral control and international trade agreements. *International Organization*, 56: 477–513.

MARTIN, L. L. 2000. *Democratic Commitments: Legislatures and International Cooperation.* Princeton, NJ: Princeton University Press.

MATTLI, W., and BÜTHE, T. 2003. Setting international standards: technological rationality or primacy of power? *World Politics*, 56: 1–42.

MEARSHEIMER, J. J. 2001. *The Tragedy of Great Power Politics*. New York: W. W. Norton.

MYERSON, R. B. 1992. On the value of game theory in social science. *Rationality and Society*, 4: 62–73.

NIELSON, D. L., TIERNEY, M. J., and WEAVER, C. E. 2006. Bridging the rationalist–constructivist divide: re-engineering the culture of the World Bank. *Journal of International Relations and Development*, 9: 107–39.

OLSON, M. 1965. *The Logic of Collective Action: Public Goods and the Theory of Groups*. Cambridge, Mass.: Harvard University Press.

PEVEHOUSE, J., and RUSSETT, B. 2006. Democratic international governmental organizations promote peace. *International Organization*, 60: 969–1000.

POWELL, R. 1999. *In the Shadow of Power: States and Strategies in International Politics*. Princeton, NJ: Princeton University Press.

PRICE, R. 1997. *The Chemical Weapons Taboo*. Ithaca, NY: Cornell University Press.

—— and REUS-SMIT, C. 1998. Dangerous liaisons? Critical international theory and constructivism. *European Journal of International Relations*, 4: 259–94.

RAE, H. 2002. *State Identities and the Homogenisation of Peoples*. Cambridge: Cambridge University Press.

REUS-SMIT, C. 1999. *The Moral Purpose of the State: Culture, Social Identity, and Institutional Rationality in International Relations*. Princeton, NJ: Princeton University Press.

—— 2005. The constructivist challenge after September 11. Pp. 81–95 in *International Society and its Critics*, ed. A. J. Bellamy. Oxford: Oxford University Press.

—— 2008. Constructivism and the structure of ethical reasoning. In *Moral Limit and Possibility in World Politics*, ed. R. Price. Cambridge: Cambridge University Press.

RISSE, T., ROPP, S. C., and SIKKINK, K. (eds.) 1999. *The Power of Human Rights: International Norms and Domestic Change*. Cambridge: Cambridge University Press.

RISSE-KAPPEN, T. (ed.) 1995. *Bringing Transnational Relations Back In: Non-State Actors, Domestic Structures, and International Institutions*. Cambridge: Cambridge University Press.

RODRIK, D. 1997. *Has Globalization Gone Too Far?* Washington, DC: Institute for International Economics.

RUGGIE, J. G. 2005. What makes the world hang together? Neo-utilitarianism and the social constructivist challenge. Pp. 120–6 in *Foundations of International Law and Politics*, ed. O. A. Hathaway and H. H. Koh. New York: Foundation Press.

RUSSETT, B., and ONEAL, J. R. 2001. *Triangulating Peace: Democracy, Interdependence, and International Organizations*. New York: Norton.

SCHELLING, T. C. 1960. *The Strategy of Conflict*. Cambridge, Mass.: Harvard University Press.

SCHOLTE, J. A. 2005. *Globalization: A Critical Introduction*, 2nd edn. New York: Palgrave Macmillan.

SIGNORINO, C. 2002. Strategy and selection in international relations. *International Interactions*, 28: 93–115.

SNIDAL, D. 2002. Rational choice and international relations. Pp. 73–94 in Carlsnaes, Risse, and Simmons 2002.

—— 2004. Formal models of international politics. Pp. 227–64 in *Models, Numbers, and Cases: Methods for Studying International Relations*, ed. D. F. Sprinz and Y. Wolinsky-Nahmias. Ann Arbor: University of Michigan Press.

SPRINZ, D. F. 2004. Environment meets statistics: quantitative analysis of international environmental policy. Pp. 177–92 in *Models, Numbers, and Cases: Methods for Studying International Relations*, ed. D. F. Sprinz and Y. Wolinsky-Nahmias. Ann Arbor: University of Michigan Press.

SPRUYT, H. 1994. *The Sovereign State and its Competitors: An Analysis of Systems Change*. Princeton, NJ: Princeton University Press.

—— 2007. War, trade, and state formation. Pp. 211–35 in *Oxford Handbook of Comparative Politics*, ed. C. Boix and S. Stokes. Oxford: Oxford University Press.

TAYLOR, C. 1979. Interpretation and the sciences of man. Pp. 25–72 in *Interpretive Social Science: A Reader*, ed. P. Rabinow and W. M. Sullivan. Berkeley: University of California Press.

TIERNEY, M. J., and WEAVER, C. (eds.) 2007. The politics of international organizations: bridging the rationalist–constructivist divide. Unpublished typescript, University of Kansas.

TOMZ, M. 2007. *Reputation and International Cooperation: Sovereign Debt across Three Centuries*. Princeton, NJ: Princeton University Press.

VON STEIN, J. 2005. Do treaties constrain or screen? Selection bias and treaty compliance. *American Political Science Review*, 99: 611–22.

VREELAND, J. R. 2003. *The IMF and Economic Development*. Cambridge: Cambridge University Press.

WÆVER, O. 1995. Securitization and desecuritization. Pp. 46–86 in *On Security*, ed. R. D. Lipschutz. New York: Columbia University Press.

WALTZ, K. 1979. *Theory of International Politics*. New York: McGraw-Hill.

WENDT, A. 1999. *Social Theory of International Politics*. Cambridge: Cambridge University Press.

PART II

IMAGINING THE DISCIPLINE

CHAPTER 2

....

THE STATE AND INTERNATIONAL RELATIONS

....

DAVID A. LAKE

THE state is central to the study of international relations and will remain so into the foreseeable future. State policy is the most common object of analysis. States decide to go to war. They erect trade barriers. They choose whether and at what level to establish environmental standards. States enter international agreements, or not, and choose whether to abide by their provisions, or not. Even scholars who give prominence to domestic interests or nonstate actors are typically concerned with understanding or changing state practice. International relations as a discipline is chiefly concerned with what states do on the world stage and, in turn, how their actions affect other states.

Correspondingly, states are a common unit of analysis in theories of international relations. Many analysts focus on states and their interactions to explain observed patterns of world politics. The state is fundamental to neorealism (Waltz 1979) and neoliberal institutionalism (Keohane 1984). It is also key in many constructivist and English School theories (Bull 1977; Reus-Smit 1999; Wendt 1999). Even critical, postmodern, or feminist theories, which have arisen in opposition to existing forms of social power and are discussed elsewhere in this volume, often focus on deconstructing states and state practice.

Both as the object and as a unit of analysis, international relations is largely about states. The state is, thus, an indispensable component of theories of world politics. This chapter first reviews the rationales behind state-centric theories of international relations. The second section examines criticisms and probes the limits of state-centric theories. The third section identifies three promising areas of research within state-centric theory.

1 WHY STUDY THE STATE?

All theories are based on simplifying assumptions intended to render a complex reality explicable. Theories are typically grouped into families or paradigms by their shared assumptions.[1] In making simplifying assumptions, analysts place a method-ological "bet" on the most useful way to capture the essence of the phenomenon they wish to explain. These are bets because the assumptions must be made before the implications of the theory are fully explicated and tested.[2] Scholars can work for years or possibly generations building from a set of assumptions before they know whether their bet will pay off by providing a powerful explanation of the desired phenomenon.

State-centric theories of international relations assume that states are the primary actors in world politics. Theorists working in this tradition do not deny the existence of other political units. As Kenneth Waltz (1979, 93–4) writes, "states are not and never have been the only international actors . . . The importance of nonstate actors and the extent of transnational activities are obvious." Rather, the claim is that states, and especially great powers, are sufficiently important actors that any positive theory of international relations must place them at its core.

Scholars making this assumption are betting that a focus on states will yield parsimonious yet empirically powerful explanations of world politics. Central to this bet is a hunch that the parsimony or theoretical elegance derived from an emphasis on states will outweigh the loss in empirical richness that comes from including a broader range of actors. One's evaluation of state-centric theory rests, in part, on how one assesses the inevitable tradeoff between theoretical elegance and empirical power. This is a subjective choice over which reasonable scholars can disagree.

In addition to parsimony, there are at least three additional reasons why some scholars expect state-centric theory to be a good bet. First, states may possess, or be plausibly understood to possess, a national interest. A national interest can be reasonably assumed to exist when society has relatively homogeneous policy

---

[1] On assumptions and paradigms, see Kuhn (1970). On paradigms in international relations, see Elman and Elman (2003).

[2] On methodological bets, see Lake and Powell (1999, 16–20).

preferences or has internalized certain norms as appropriate. Alternatively, despite variation in preferences and norms between individuals or groups, a national interest may still plausibly exist when states have domestic institutions that aggregate individual or group attributes into a coherent collective ordering.[3] In both cases, analysts can safely abstract from the pushing and hauling of domestic politics and assume the state is a unitary entity with a collective preference or identity interacting with other similarly unitary entities.

In realist theories, the national interest is assumed to be state power (Morgenthau 1978), and in neorealist theories it is assumed to be state survival, at a minimum, or power, at a maximum (Waltz 1979). Survival is understood as a primordial goal that is necessary for the pursuit of all other political ends. The drive for power stems from human nature (Morgenthau 1978, 36–8) or the state of nature that characterizes the international system (Mearsheimer 2001, 32–6), but in either case it is instrumental for achieving other ends within the political arena. Since survival or power occurs at the level of the nation or society, these assumptions about the goals of politics lead to the further assumption that states are the appropriate unit of analysis in theories of world politics. Similarly, constructivists see norms as widely shared by domestic publics or embodied in a set of domestic institutions that then define a state's social purpose (Reus-Smit 1999; Ruggie 1996; 1998; Katzenstein 2005). Although constructivists largely treat them descriptively, it is the fact that norms are broadly held that allows such beliefs to be considered as historically contingent but nonetheless national interests. Other theories posit more context-specific national interests. Nuclear deterrence theory, not implausibly, presumes that everyone wants to avoid annihilation. Likewise, we can posit that nearly everyone benefits from freedom of the seas or stopping terrorism.[4] When it seems reasonable to assume that citizens possess relatively homogeneous interests or norms, it is then a convenient analytic short cut to treat states as unitary actors.

Secondly, even when they lack a plausibly construed national interest, states are authoritative actors whose duly enacted policies are binding on their citizens and thus regulate how individuals and the collective interact with other similarly bound societies. As sovereign entities, states possess ultimate or final authority over delimited territories and their inhabitants. Once a policy is enacted, the decision is binding on all citizens. If a state raises a tariff, all its citizens are affected by the higher price for imports, whether they support the tax or not. If a state declares war on another, all its citizens are belligerents, regardless of whether they personally

---

[3] Domestic institutions do not guarantee the aggregation of individual preferences into a stable collective preference. When individual preferences are socially intransitive, no nondictatorial institution can ensure a stable equilibrium (for an overview, see Schwartz 1987). Even if institutions induce an equilibrium (Shepsle 1979), these same institutions will be contested, with actors cycling through different institutions that privilege one or another outcome (Riker 1980). Despite these difficulties of collective choice, most states most of the time do not cycle through alternatives.

[4] As these examples suggest, public goods affect individuals in broadly similar ways (depending on individual preferences) and will often have a "national interest" character.

support the war or not. Just as states pass laws that bind their citizens at home, they also act authoritatively in ways that bind their own citizens in relations with other states. This is the analytic foundation of the adage that "politics stops at the water's edge." Given their internal hierarchy, it is again reasonable to treat states as unitary actors when interacting with other similarly hierarchical states.

A key assumption of Westphalian sovereignty is that authority is indivisible and culminates in a single apex (Hinsley 1986, 26; Krasner 1999, 11). Whether sovereignty is vested in a hereditary monarch or the people, there is an ultimate or final authority within each state. This is not to assert that states possess the ability to regulate all the possible behaviors of all citizens (see below), only that there is a single point where, in President Harry Truman's classic phrase, "the buck stops." States may, of course, differ in how they aggregate the interests and norms of their citizens. In autocratic regimes, a small group of elites may set policy for all. In more democratic states, representative institutions incorporate the interests and norms of voters into policy. But regardless of what type of regime exists, citizens are bound by the policies enacted by their governments.

It is this ability to bind their societies that make states virtually unique in international relations. However active a nongovernmental organization may be, it can claim to speak only for its members and, perhaps, for universal principles of justice or human rights; it cannot bind others through its actions, including its own members who join only in voluntary association. Because of their unique status as authoritative actors, and their ability to act on behalf of their citizens, it follows that states are central, more important actors than others, and thus oftentimes appropriate units of analysis in international politics.

Finally, theories of systems-level processes naturally assume states as units of analysis, especially when such processes affect states as states. Theories that include international evolutionary processes that select on certain unit attributes or reward behaviors by units differentially, logically and pragmatically assume those units are central actors (Kahler 1999). States that fail to balance against other states rising in power, Waltz (1979) hypothesizes, will be eliminated or "selected out" of the international system. Theories of systems-level processes are, at present, most highly developed by systemic constructivists, who posit that socialization or legitimation occurs at the level of the state within a society of states (Wendt 1994; 1999; Finnemore 1996; 2003). Going beyond states as relatively homogenous or authoritative actors, they theorize a systems-level process of diffusion and interaction that shapes the normative understanding of states about the nature of the society they comprise.[5] In this view, as Wendt (1992) famously observes, anarchy is what states—not individuals, groups, or transnational advocacy networks—make of it. The existence of states is not theorized explicitly, and thus systemic constructivists

---

[5] Holistic constructivists agree that socialization occurs at the systemic level but do not assume that it occurs strictly at that level (Price and Reus-Smit 1998, 268–9).

fall prey to Richard Ashley's critique of neorealism (1986) as being statist before it is structuralist.[6] But in focusing on and emphasizing these systems-level processes, states are understood to be shaped and reshaped *as states* by their material and ideational environment. As with any theory of systems process, it follows that states are useful units of analysis.

More importantly, to the extent that systems-level processes are significant, states and their behaviors cannot be reduced to the sum of their domestic attributes. A "bottom-up" or reductionist approach to theory that starts with individual or group preferences or norms and aggregates these desires into some national interest will not capture appropriately or fully the affect of the system on states. No individual or group necessarily has a direct interest in the systemically desirable actions that states are called upon to perform. As a result, the state as a whole has "interests" that cannot be reduced to its internal parts. This was the key insight of Waltz's argument (1959) about anarchy in the third image, but it holds more broadly for any truly systemic structure or process, including selection or socialization. For neorealists, anarchy demands attention to issues of security in ways likely to be different from the interests of either particular domestic groups or the collective interest aggregated through some set of domestic institutions (see Krasner 1978). Similarly, for all constructivists, the norms of the society of states within which individual states are socialized—even when reflecting a social purpose grounded in domestic politics—can be separate and distinct from the norms that exist within specific states.[7] Thus, not only does the assumption that states are central actors follow naturally from an emphasis on systems processes, but to the extent that such processes are important constraints on behaviour, a focus on states and their interactions is absolutely essential to a full understanding of international politics. If the states system really is more than the sum of its parts, then adding up the internal or domestic attributes of states will always fall short, and a systems approach focusing on states as states will always be necessary—even if systems effects are rarely if ever deterministic.

All three rationales share a pragmatic approach to theory. State-centrism is not a statement about the empirical world. No one working in this tradition is so naive as to mistake the billiard balls of state-centric theory as a description of states in the real world. Everyone recognizes that states have rich and sometimes highly consequential internal or domestic political lives. Likewise, everyone accepts that transnational forces can affect international politics in important ways. To point out that domestic or transnational politics exists and is not captured in state-centric theory is not an especially useful criticism; most state-centric theorists

[6] Wendt (1987) also makes this criticism, but then continues to treat states as primitives in his later writings.

[7] This is the problem of normative entrapment, in which powerful countries seed norms at the international level, often reflecting their domestic norms of governance, but then find themselves bound by those norms. See Ruggie (1993), Price (1998), and Reus-Smit (2004).

would certainly agree. Rather, the question is how much empirical power is lost relative to the parsimony that is gained, and whether we can identify any guidelines for when state-centric theory is likely to be more or less useful and necessary.

2 THE LIMITS OF STATE-CENTRIC THEORY

State-centric theories have been widely assailed. At root, most critics are simply making alternative methodological bets; although they may believe that the rationales that underlie their wagers are more reasonable, all such claims remain unproven. In this section, I probe two valid criticisms of state-centric theories, assessing the limits they identify but also the limits of the criticisms themselves. Both point to the need for more contextualized theories of international relations.

2.1 Domestic Politics

The first and perhaps most frequent criticism of state-centric theory is that there is no such thing as the "national interest." Over five decades ago, Arnold Wolfers (1952) famously recognized that its synonym, national security, was an ambiguous and possibly dangerous concept, more a rhetorical device used by those seeking support for particularistic policies than a real, concrete attribute of the nation as a whole. Rather than affecting everyone in similar ways, most policies are redistributive or have differential impacts on groups even in the same country. Even though global climate change, for instance, raises temperatures for everyone, and therefore might be thought of as the quintessential national interest, it will affect different groups in different countries in different ways. Likewise, policies aimed at mitigating global warming will hurt some interests but benefit others. Within each country there will be winners and losers from climate change and from every possible policy to slow or reverse it. In redistributive politics, the concept of a national interest shared equally by everyone evaporates.

This critique is undoubtedly correct. Even though Krasner (1978) persuasively argued that states do appear to pursue long-term interests that do not reflect the desires of particular groups or classes, even in the highly redistributive area of raw materials policy, many scholars today focus on domestic political interests and institutions to identify and explain more realistically what states want from international politics (for a review, see Gourevitch 2002). Different issues create and mobilize different political cleavages within societies. Countries are riven by internal cleavages—both material and normative—that mobilize individuals differently in different contexts (Moravcsik 1997). Varying political institutions serve to aggregate alternative sets of domestic interests with different degrees of bias (Rogowski 1999). To understand what states want, this new research holds, analysts must pay focused attention to how typically competing and disparate groups are mobilized into the political process and how institutions then transform interests into policy.

Yet, this critique is itself limited in three ways. First, as above, as long as states are authoritative, their decisions are binding on all citizens. Regardless of the divisiveness of the issue, the policy, once enacted, is equally authoritative for all individuals. To debunk the myth of national interests is not to undercut the importance of state authority in treating states as units of analysis.

Secondly, in many problems of international politics, domestic politics provides only an explanation of what states want, not what they do. That is, it might explain the preferences of a society on some international issue, but it cannot explain why that society adopts the policy or gets the outcome that it does. Most interesting puzzles of international politics arise from the strategic interaction not only of groups within countries but also from the interactions of states themselves (Morrow 1999). Domestic interests and institutions may produce in some countries an interest in reversing global warming, for instance, but for most states changing their own policies will have only a minimal effect on the global climate. Achieving consequential change requires the cooperation of other countries. Knowing this, each country has an incentive to free ride internationally on the efforts of others. The result is fewer efforts at mitigation and greater emissions of greenhouse gases than is collectively optimal or desired. The strategic interactions of states remains an important part of any explanation of world politics.

Increasingly, scholars of international relations accept a division of labor—what Jeffrey Legro (1996) calls the "cooperation two-step"—in which some focus on domestic politics with the ambition of explaining policy preferences and others, taking domestically generated interests as "given," focus on developing theories of strategic interaction between states.[8] In the latter, the state is assumed to be the unit of analysis, not because it is natural, as in the national interest rationale, but because theorists expect that they will gain some explanatory purchase on the problem they are studying. Perhaps because economic policies have more clearly redistributive effects, international political economists tend to emphasize domestic politics in the belief that more of the explanatory "action" will lay in understanding policy preferences, whereas international security scholars tend to devote more attention to the strategic interactions of states because issues of bargaining, information, and credible commitment appear more central to peace and war (Fearon 1995; Powell 1999). But, like all theories, these are just methodological bets about where we are most likely to find interesting and potentially important insights when we shine our spotlights on an otherwise dark landscape. Thus, even if we accept the validity of the

---

[8] For an effort to integrate this division of labor, see Milner (1997).

criticism that national interests seldom exist, state-centric theory may still be useful, especially when the strategic interaction of states is important to understanding how national preferences are translated into international political outcomes.

Thirdly, some state-centric theorists, in turn, question whether this "two-step" division of labor is likely to prove adequate. As explained above, reductionist and systemic theories are not just two different starting points that take the same set of attributes and arrive at the same sum, but rather identify two separate and incommensurate sets of processes that add up in very different ways. Systemic processes, to the extent that they are important, cannot be derived from within the two-step. More generally, theories that reverse the "second image" imply that the two-step will, for at least some portion of the time, yield inaccurate predictions (Gourevitch 1978). The discussion of systemic theory above focused on processes that affected states as states. But it is also clear that international factors also affect how individuals or groups define their interests, which they then seek to pursue in the domestic political arena. In an "open economy politics" approach, what groups want is determined, not by their position relative to other domestic groups, but, rather, by their relative abundance or competitive position within the international economy (Gourevitch 1977; Frieden 1988; Rogowski 1989). In turn, group strategy, including the coalitions the groups enter, may be conditioned not only by their position but also by the policy choices of other states (James and Lake 1989). Holistic constructivist theories identify similar limits. Not only do norms entrepreneurs, necessarily located within some territorial jurisdiction, organize and act transnationally in ways that change the normative environment in which states interact, but international norms themselves structure the political agenda, condition what these entrepreneurs can and cannot do, shape their political strategies, and determine when normative change succeeds and fails. Both the decolonization and anti-Apartheid campaigns, for instance, were fundamentally affected by the prior international norm of national self-determination and succeeded, in part, because the causes could be connected to this existing normative belief (Klotz 1995; Crawford 2002). Whenever the interests and capabilities of domestic actors are themselves affected by international structures, processes, and norms, the two-step that begins with domestically generated policy preferences and then adds in inter-state interactions will be insufficient to capture the reality of world politics.

2.2 Transnational Relations

The second, more substantive critique of state-centric theory is that states have lost control over private (nonstate) actors who can organize and move across national borders, be these cosmopolitan individuals, multinational corporations, or transnational advocacy networks.[9] Even if state-centric theory might once upon

---

[9] For a review of this literature, see Barnett and Sikkink, this volume.

a time have been a reasonable bet to explain international politics, the erosion of sovereignty and growth of transnational forces have now made this a less attractive wager (Keohane and Nye 1972; 1977).

Transnational actors entered the study of international relations in the early 1970s. Although some transnational actors, like the Catholic Church, have been present since the birth of the modern states system, the rise of multinational corporations that threatened to put "sovereignty at bay" (Vernon 1971) and the parallel rise of transnational advocacy networks (Keck and Sikkink 1998; Smith and Wiest 2005) led many to question the continued utility of state-centric theory. The international political landscape is certainly more crowded with a greater variety of actors than ever before.

In the face of this criticism, some scholars simply reaffirmed their bet that state-centric theory will retain its explanatory power (Waltz 1979, 93–7). Others argued that states remain sovereign and, rather than being challenged by non-state actors, actually permit such actors to exist and exert influence on world politics. For these analysts, the question is why states acquiesce in and perhaps even encourage the growth of transnational actors (Gilpin 1972; 1975; Krasner 1995). Neither the explanatory power of state-centric theories nor the ability of states to control transnational actors, however, is likely to be constant. Rather, sovereignty and effective control have to be theorized and, in turn, explained. Doing so helps us understand when state-centric theories are likely to remain useful and relevant, and when they must be augmented or perhaps radically transformed.

Sovereignty is variable. In international relations, scholars tend to focus on the external face of sovereignty or the status of being recognized as a state by the international community.[10] Recent research shows that the meaning of sovereignty and its practice has varied over time.[11] There is a second, "internal" face of sovereignty, however, that is more relevant to this discussion of transnational actors. Even within an external face, presumably similar for all states, the authority of states over their own citizens varies dramatically. "Liberal states" by law or custom have highly constrained ranges of authority. They have the right to regulate only certain practices by their constituents, mostly those that contribute to market failures. At the same time, they are restricted from regulating other practices—such as speech, assembly, or the press—except in extraordinary circumstances. The authority of such states is continually contested, at least at the margin, as suggested by the current debate over the rights of the government to monitor phone calls or financial transfers in conjunction with the global war on terror. "Strong states" may be no more or less autonomous than their liberal counterparts, but they possess greater authority over a greater range of behaviors, typically including some direct controls over

---

[10] This is "juridical" or "international legal" sovereignty. See Jackson (1990) and Krasner (1999).

[11] On the changing substantive content of sovereignty, see Biersteker and Weber (1996), Krasner (1999; 2001), Reus-Smit (1999), and Osiander (2001).

the commanding heights of the economy.[12] Even though states may be sovereign relative to one another, they possess clearly different authorities over their own societies.

It is perhaps not surprising, therefore, that transnational relations appear most fully developed and most consequential in liberal states (Keohane and Nye 1977; Risse-Kappen 1995). This is partly a function of interdependence, which creates additional "outside options" for actors, but it is equally a product of the larger private spheres of action in liberal democracies. In these countries, it may be less useful to think of private actors as escaping the authority of their states than it is to see them as enjoying a constitutionally protected sphere of autonomous action. Yet, this understanding severely qualifies the claim that states could if they wanted reassert control over private actors. Sovereignty abroad, which implies the authority to regulate transborder flows, is different from sovereignty at home, which as the dividing line between public authority and private freedoms is negotiated between the state and society. To claim new authority over, say, corporations requires renegotiating the constitutional compact that makes liberal states liberal. In determining the autonomy of transnational actors, external sovereignty is less important than the state's internal sovereignty.

Technology is also a variable with consequences for the scope of transnational relations. It is generally assumed that new communication and transportation technologies favor transnational groups and permit them to escape state control. Even though states might have the right to regulate their behavior, this suggests that transnational actors can exploit technology to gain even greater autonomy. Thus, new technologies permit multinational corporations to develop global networks that undermine the ability of states to regulate or tax production. Likewise, transnational advocacy networks use communications technologies to bring information to light on human rights and environmental practices that governments prefer to keep secret.

Yet, states are not without counter-strategies in the face of technological change. Given the design of the Internet, which requires traffic to move through particular "choke points," and the willingness of firms to cooperate with governments in order to preserve their market access (e.g. Google in China), states have been able to impose restrictions on the content available to their citizens (Cowhey and Mueller forthcoming). Similarly, the US government has greatly extended its authority and ability after 11 September to monitor phone calls, Internet traffic, and financial flows anywhere around the globe. Generating an ability to sift through the large number of communications they intercept each day, governments have been exploiting technology to reimpose control over transnational groups and activists. More generally, states exert extensive influence over which technologies

---

[12] This is a reformulation of earlier arguments about state strength; see Katzenstein (1978) and Lake (1999b, 42–8).

get developed, how they are used, and how they are regulated for what purpose. Technology cuts both ways. On balance, new technologies have most likely favored transnational actors, but the balance will ebb and flow over time.

The greater the autonomy of transnational actors, the more consequential they will be for international politics, and the less useful state-centric theories will be. This does not imply that state-centric theories are obsolete. Rather, theorists must now be more attuned to when nonstate actors are likely to be important for the outcomes they wish to explain and when it is reasonable to focus only on the actions and interactions of states. The answer is likely to vary by issue, time, and country. The old methodological bets of state-centric theory may not produce the same returns, but they are not yet without merit.

3 Frontiers of State-centric Theory in International Relations

States are important actors in world politics. State-centric theory remains useful both as a pragmatic tool and because it captures systemic effects that would escape strictly domestic or second image theories. If states and state-centric theory remain essential, what then are the most promising areas for further development? Where are the research frontiers? Since states are so important, such a survey might be synonymous with the field of international relations itself. In this final section, I highlight three research areas in which states are both the object and unit of analysis.

3.1 State Structure

As noted above, state structure conditions the possibilities and politics of transnational relations. Liberal states are more easily penetrated by the forces of global civil society; strong states are less hospitable. Globalization may be transforming state capabilities and how states and societies are integrated. State structure was a topic of vigorous analysis two decades ago. It is due for a revival.

State structure varies by how authority is distributed across political institutions (decentralized to centralized) and the degree of differentiation between state and society (low to high). Peter Katzenstein (1978; 1985) used this conception to identify "weak" and "strong" states in foreign economic policy, and then later liberal and social corporatist regimes. It was extended to nondemocratic regimes in Eastern Europe (Comisso and Tyson 1986) and less developed countries (Migdal 1988). This approach was superseded by a more narrow institutionalist research program that uses insights from American and comparative politics to study how the number of veto players, presidential versus parliamentary systems, single versus coalitional governments, unitary versus divided government, and other variations influence policy choice (Rogowski 1999). By specifying more precisely the ways in which political authority is distributed, this institutionalist literature is a significant advance, but it largely ignores the second dimension on how states and societies are differentiated. The more complete vision of state structure lives on in the varieties of capitalism literature (Hall and Soskice 2001), but the studies in this vein are mostly limited to developed countries.

Globalization is prompting new attention to questions of state structure, and especially how state and society are differentiated. One school sees globalization as forcing a convergence in state structures either in a race to the bottom or towards an Anglo-Saxon liberal state. In this view, global competition produces strong tendencies toward economic and political homogenization.[13] A second school, emerging from the varieties of capitalism literature, argues that dissimilar state structures are not necessarily better or worse, but that they simply work differently and co-evolve with particular forms of economic and social organization. Here, the dominant trait of globalization is not competition but specialization, which is compatible with and may even enhance differentiation (Gourevitch 2003; Gourevitch and Shinn 2005; Rogowski 2003). In both perspectives, however, state structure is, as above, a force for globalization and transnationalism and simultaneously a product of this same long-term historical process.

Globalization may be the most profound transformative process of the modern world, but we understand its processes, effects, and future only poorly. Although created by states that have intentionally liberalized their economies over the last half century, globalization works its effects primarily through individuals, firms, sectors, and other nonstate groups, including transnational advocacy networks that thrive on the new technologies and open borders that underlie market openness. These social forces, in turn, affect governments and policy differently depending on how they are mediated by state structure (Kahler and Lake 2003, 24–8). To unravel globalization's causes and effects it will be essential, in my view, to understand better variations in state structure.

Yet, we lack a full typology of state structures, and especially one that integrates the insights of the new institutionalism. In turn, analyses focus almost exclusively on developed democratic states, truncating the range of variation in state structure and attenuating or making more uncertain estimates of its effects (King, Keohane, and Verba 1994, 128–38). To understand fully the forces of transformation that are driving contemporary politics, and how states are likely to respond, analysts need to expand their horizons to include the full continuum of state structures. On

---

[13] This view predominates in the semi-popular writings on globalization. See Friedman (2000; 2005).

one end are "failed" or fragile states that retain their external sovereignty but lack authority within their own borders through the absence of a central government (for example, Somalia) or a government whose writ does not extend to all regions of its territory (for example, tribal areas of Pakistan). In terms of state structure, such states possess highly decentralized forms of political authority and near complete disintegration between state and society. One step along the continuum might be autocratic states that are relatively centralized but nonetheless have little ability to penetrate their societies, sharing the disintegration between state and society of their fragile cousins (Herbst 2000; Boone 2003). On the other end of the continuum are totalitarian states that aim to regulate all forms of social behavior, although this extreme is seldom realized in practice. In totalitarian states, authority is highly centralized and state and society are fused. Liberal and strong states, discussed above, take intermediate forms along this continuum. The effects of globalization may be most profound, and most easily observed, at the extremes of state structure, rather than in the middle, where scholars have so far concentrated their attention.

3.2 Unit Heterogeneity

Many state-centric theories assume that all units are sovereign territorial states, a unique form of political organization that survived a Darwinian struggle against city states, leagues, empires, and other "pre-modern" polities to dominate the world after Westphalia (Tilly 1990; Spruyt 1994).[14] Implicit in these theories are the further assumptions that sovereign territorial states are, first, composed of contiguous territories and, second, especially in more contemporary periods, formed as nation states in which all citizens possess relatively similar political rights and responsibilities and one titular group does not rule over other identity groups.

Yet, the assumption that all states are contiguous nation states is sustained only by an act of collective blindness by scholars of international relations. The modern states of Europe that form the basis for the model of sovereign territorial states were also empires, holding vast overseas territories for centuries. Imperialism is often cited as one of the possible causes of the great power rivalry that dominated late-nineteenth-century Europe and led to the First World War, one of the critical events of the first half of the twentieth century.[15] In turn, the most striking event of the second half of the twentieth century may not be the cold war, which appears to have come and gone without any fundamental change in the nature of international relations, but the breakup of the European empires, a rupture with history that nonetheless seldom warrants more than passing notice in international relations textbooks.

[14] On the problem of unit heterogeneity more broadly, see Kahler (2002, 66–74).
[15] The classic case is made in Hobson (1965). Two contemporary discussions include Doyle (1986) and Snyder (1991).

More recently, the post-cold war era has been shattered by the breakup of what are sometimes called multinational states in which one identity group dominates others—including the collapse of the Soviet Union, now recognized more appropriately in retrospect as a Russian (continental) empire and certainly never as a nation state in the full sense of that term (Dawisha and Parrott 1997; Esherick, Kayali, and van Young 2006). The problems of failed states and internal insurrections now facing the global community are similarly rooted in ethnic and religious competition between groups locked within sometimes arbitrarily drawn national borders, and often exacerbated by nations or identity groups that span those borders. The United States as of this writing, is sinking in the quicksands of a sectarian struggle spurred by generations of Sunni domination of Shi'ites and Kurds in Iraq.

The sovereign territorial state is, in many ways, a myth, or at best another convenient analytic fiction. Nonetheless, it has remarkable staying power within theories of international relations. The great trends of the twentieth century continue to involve the shaping and reshaping of political units. Yet, if states are not all alike, and do not conform to the model of a sovereign territorial state, we still lack a common set of dimensions along which to array different types of polities. Similarly, we lack theories that explain variation or, more importantly, that link heterogeneity in units to outcomes in clear, testable, and falsifiable ways. Taking seriously the history of world politics creates a lurking suspicion that different types of units have deep consequences for international relations—for instance, that the nineteenth-century world of imperial states was somehow different from the late-twentieth-century world of multinational states—but we lack the tools to examine and probe this intuition more deeply. This is an area that virtually demands greater attention if we are to explain the shifting forms of political organization that we confront in the world today.

3.3 International Hierarchy

State-centric theory also assumes that all states, as sovereign entities, are formally equal within the society of states. Waltz (1959) famously argued that international relationists made a fallacy of composition in reasoning about the whole (the system) from its parts (states), and thus put the concept of anarchy at the center of the field. But, in accepting this critique, scholars now make the opposite fallacy of division in reasoning about the parts from the whole. That the system is anarchic does not imply that all relationships between states in that system are likewise anarchic. Rather, as the existence of empires should have made clear, a variety of hierarchical relationships exists between states and other polities—including other apparently sovereign states.[16]

[16] For a key work that recognizes hierarchy within the system, see Bull and Watson (1984). Similarly, dependency theory was premised on a structural inequality of states. See Galtung (1971) and Cardoso and Faletto (1979), among others.

The great powers have always held a special place in world politics not just by their material capabilities but by the prestige they were accorded by other states (Gilpin 1981, 30–1), a status institutionalized in the Concert of Europe, the League of Nations, and especially the Security Council of the United Nations (Simpson 2004; Hurd 2007). Following in the footsteps of the cantons of Switzerland, the thirteen colonies that formed the original United States, the largely independent states that became Australia, and other federations, the European Union today is forming a new federal polity in which otherwise sovereign states cede authority over limited issue areas to a new, hierarchical center (Rector forthcoming). Less unique than sometimes supposed, the European Union is nonetheless a challenge to those who assume that states value their survival as states above all else (Grieco 1997, 184–6). At the level of the international community, moreover, new issues of international trusteeship are forcing themselves onto the international agenda (Bain 2003; Fearon and Laitin 2004; Krasner 2004; Lake 2007b).

Similarly, states exert authority over other states. In addition to formal empires, throughout modern history there has been a range of protectorates, dependencies, spheres-of-influence, economic zones, and informal empires in which one country has governed a greater or lesser range of actions of a second but stopped short of overthrowing the latter's formal sovereignty. The United States has ruled an informal empire in Central America since the turn of the twentieth century, a sphere-of-influence over Europe and northeast Asia since the Second World War, and economic dependencies around the globe (Lake forthcoming). Most dramatically, the United States today has asserted the right and actually overthrown the governments of two sovereign states, Afghanistan and Iraq, occupied their territories, installed new governments beholden to Washington, and retained a virtual veto over the institutions and policies of each even after their return to formal sovereignty. Russia continues to exert similar authority over several now sovereign states in its "near abroad" (Cooley 2005; Hancock 2006). Hierarchy did not disappear in international relations with the end of the overseas empires, but lives on in a variety of weaker and informal authority relationships even today (Dunne 2003).

These international hierarchies are only now beginning to be explored in a systematic way (see Lake 1999a). Yet, hierarchy appears to have important consequences for whether and how states balance against one another (Weber 2000), their levels of defense spending (Lake 2007a), the possibilities for economic and political reform (Cooley 2005), and even whether they choose to fight one another (Wimberley 2007). States governed more hierarchically by Germany during the Second World War were more vigorous in carrying out the "final solution" and killed larger fractions of their Jewish populations in the Holocaust (Hollander 2006). Hierarchy can have important constraints on dominant states as well, including the need to tie their hands or bind their power in order to demonstrate their limited ambition (Lake 1999a, 62–3; Ikenberry 2001). More consequences are likely to emerge as scholars dig deeper into theory and its empirical expectations. As the debate about the new American empire also suggests, hierarchy can have real implications for the conduct of contemporary foreign policy (Lake 2007c).

All three of these research frontiers maintain a focus on states as actors, but allow their internal attributes or external relationships to vary in ways that go beyond those now specified in state-centric theories. Even if we focus on states as states, there is more variation in the real world than we currently allow in our theories. States are more complicated entities and relations between states are more variegated than we commonly recognize. Capturing this richer and more complex world will greatly enhance and deepen even state-centric theories of international relations.

4 CONCLUSION

To develop or use state-centric theory is not to take an ethical position on the state as a form of political organization. State-centric theorists do not necessarily endorse the state as a social institution. Rather, state-centric theorists merely attempt to leverage the central role of states to explain the patterns and trends of world politics, including when violence is more or less likely, when economic interdependence will rise or fall, and whether societies will be able to address collectively threats to their common future. The question is not whether states are good or bad, but whether by focusing on states and their actions we can explain critical problems of international relations effectively and parsimoniously.

   States are likely to remain central actors in world politics. As such, they are necessary to any explanation of international relations. The critics of state-centric theory make important points. State-centric theories can be misleading when domestic interests are highly divided and their internal sovereignty is highly constrained. Scholars should be careful in specifying when states are likely to be important rather than assuming that their role in the real world and in our theories is constant. Yet, given the crucial role of states in international politics and the pragmatic need to build parsimonious yet powerful explanations, state-centric theory will continue to be a valuable—indeed, indispensable—tool for scholars seeking to understand the world in which we live. Scholars who ignore the state do so at their peril, since no analysis of international relations can do without it. Even so, the research agenda remains exciting and promises to improve our understanding of world politics in new and potentially important ways.

REFERENCES

ASHLEY, R. K. 1986. The poverty of neorealism. Pp. 255–300 in *Neorealism and its Critics*, ed. R. O. Keohane. New York: Columbia University Press.

BAIN, W. 2003. *Between Anarchy and Society: Trusteeship and the Obligations of Power*. New York: Oxford University Press.

BIERSTEKER, T. J., and WEBER, C. (eds.) 1996. *State Sovereignty as Social Construct*. New York: Cambridge University Press.

BOONE, C. 2003. *Political Topographies of the African State: Territorial Authority and Institutional Choice*. New York: Cambridge University Press.

BULL, H. 1977. *The Anarchical Society: A Study of Order in World Politics*. New York: Columbia University Press.

—— and WATSON, A. (eds.) 1984. *The Expansion of International Society*. New York: Oxford University Press.

CARDOSO, F. H., and FALETTO, E. 1979. *Dependency and Development in Latin America*. Berkeley: University of California Press.

COMISSO, E., and TYSON, L. D'A. (eds.) 1986. *Power, Purpose, and Collective Choice: Economic Strategy in Socialist States*. Ithaca, NY: Cornell University Press.

COOLEY, A. 2005. *Logics of Hierarchy: The Organization of Empires, States, and Military Occupations*. Ithaca, NY: Cornell University Press.

COWHEY, P., and MUELLER, M. forthcoming. Delegation, networks, and internet governance. In *Networked Politics: Agency, Power, and Governance*, ed. M. Kahler. Ithaca, NY: Cornell University Press.

CRAWFORD, N. C. 2002. *Argument and Change in World Politics: Ethics, Decolonization, and Humanitarian Intervention*. New York: Cambridge University Press.

DAWISHA, K., and PARROTT, B. (eds.) 1997. *The End of Empire? The Transformation of the USSR in Comparative Perspective*. Armonk, NY: M. E. Sharpe.

DOYLE, M. W. 1986. *Empires*. Ithaca, NY: Cornell University Press.

DUNNE, T. 2003. Society and hierarchy in international relations. *International Relations*, 17: 303–20.

ELMAN, C., and ELMAN, M. F. (eds.) 2003. *Progress in International Relations Theory: Appraising the Field*. Cambridge, Mass.: MIT Press.

ESHERICK, J., KAYALI, H., and VAN YOUNG, E. (eds.) 2006. *Empire to Nation: Historical Perspectives on the Making of the Modern World*. Lanham, Md.: Rowman and Littlefield.

FEARON, J. D. 1995. Rationalist explanations for war. *International Organization*, 49: 379–414.

—— and LAITIN, D. D. 2004. Neotrusteeship and the problem of weak states. *International Security*, 28: 5–43.

FINNEMORE, M. 1996. *National Interests in International Society*. Ithaca, NY: Cornell University Press.

—— 2003. *The Purpose of Intervention: Changing Beliefs about the Use of Force*. Ithaca, NY: Cornell University Press.

FRIEDEN, J. 1988. Sectoral conflict and foreign economic policy, 1914–1940. *International Organization*, 42: 59–90.

FRIEDMAN, T. L. 2000. *The Lexus and the Olive Tree: Understanding Globalization*, updated and exp. edn. New York: Anchor.

—— 2005. *The World Is Flat: A Brief History of the Twenty-First Century*. New York: Farrar, Straus and Giroux.

GALTUNG, J. 1971. A structural theory of imperialism. *Journal of Peace Research*, 8: 81–117.

GILPIN, R. 1972. The politics of transnational economic relations. Pp. 48–69 in Keohane and Nye 1972.

——1975. *US Power and the Multinational Corporation: The Political Economy of Foreign Direct Investment*. New York: Basic Books.

——1981. *War and Change in World Politics*. New York: Cambridge University Press.

GOUREVITCH, P. 1977. International trade, domestic coalitions, and liberty: comparative responses to the crisis of 1873–1896. *Journal of Interdisciplinary History*, 8: 281–313.

——1978. The second image reversed: the international sources of domestic politics. *International Organization*, 32: 881–912.

——2002. Domestic politics and international relations. Pp. 309–28 in *Handbook of International Relations*, ed. W. Carlsnaes, T. Risse, and B. A. Simmons. Thousand Oaks, Calif.: Sage.

——2003. Corporate governance: global markets, national politics. Pp. 305–31 in Kahler and Lake 2003.

——and SHINN, J. 2005. *Political Power and Corporate Control: The New Global Politics of Corporate Governance*. Princeton, NJ: Princeton University Press.

GRIECO, J. M. 1997. Realist international theory and the study of world politics. Pp. 163–201 in *New Thinking in International Relations Theory*, ed. M. W. Doyle and G. J. Ikenberry. Boulder, Colo.: Westview.

HALL, P. A., and SOSKICE, D. (eds.) 2001. *Varieties of Capitalism: The Institutional Foundations of Comparative Advantage*. New York: Oxford University Press.

HANCOCK, K. J. 2006. The semi-sovereign state: Belarus and the Russian neo-empire. *Foreign Policy Analysis*, 2: 117–36.

HERBST, J. 2000. *States and Power in Africa: Comparative Lessons in Authority and Control*. Princeton, NJ: Princeton University Press.

HINSLEY, F. H. 1986. *Sovereignty*, 2nd edn. New York: Cambridge University Press.

HOBSON, J. A. 1965. *Imperialism: A Study*. Ann Arbor: University of Michigan Press.

HOLLANDER, E. J. 2006. Swords or shields: implementing and subverting the final solution in Nazi-occupied Europe. Ph.D. dissertation, University of California, San Diego.

HURD, I. 2007. *After Anarchy: Legitimacy and Power in the United Nations Security Council*. Princeton, NJ: Princeton University Press.

IKENBERRY, G. J. 2001. *After Victory: Institutions, Strategic Restraint, and the Rebuilding of Order after Major Wars*. Princeton, NJ: Princeton University Press.

JACKSON, R. H. 1990. *Quasi-States: Sovereignty, International Relations, and the Third World*. New York: Cambridge University Press.

JAMES, S., and LAKE, D. A. 1989. The second face of hegemony: Britain's repeal of the Corn Laws and the American Walker Tariff of 1846. *International Organization*, 43: 1–29.

KAHLER, M. 1999. Evolution, choice, and international change. Pp. 165–96 in Lake and Powell 1999.

——2002. The state of the state in world politics. Pp. 56–83 in *Political Science: State of the Discipline*, ed. I. Katznelson and H. V. Milner. New York: W. W. Norton.

——and Lake, D. A. (eds.) 2003. *Governance in a Global Economy: Political Authority in Transition*. Princeton, NJ: Princeton University Press.

KATZENSTEIN, P. J. (ed.) 1978. *Between Power and Plenty: Foreign Economic Policies of Advanced Industrial States*. Madison: University of Wisconsin Press.

——1985. *Small States in World Markets: Industrial Policy in Europe*. Ithaca, NY: Cornell University Press.

——2005. *A World of Regions: Asia and Europe in the American Imperium*. Ithaca, NY: Cornell University Press.

KECK, M. E., and SIKKINK, K. 1998. *Activists beyond Borders: Advocacy Networks in International Politics*. Ithaca, NY: Cornell University Press.

KEOHANE, R. O. 1984. *After Hegemony: Cooperation and Discord in the World Political Economy*. Princeton, NJ: Princeton University Press.

——and NYE, J. S. (eds.) 1972. *Transnational Relations and World Politics*. Cambridge, Mass.: Harvard University Press.

————1977. *Power and Interdependence: World Politics in Transition*. Boston: Little, Brown.

KING, G., KEOHANE, R. O., and VERBA, S. 1994. *Designing Social Inquiry: Scientific Inference in Qualitative Research*. Princeton, NJ: Princeton University Press.

KLOTZ, A. 1995. *Norms in International Relations: The Struggle against Apartheid*. Ithaca, NY: Cornell University Press.

KRASNER, S. D. 1978. *Defending the National Interest: Raw Materials Investments and US Foreign Policy*. Princeton, NJ: Princeton University Press.

——1995. Power politics, institutions, and transnational relations. Pp. 257–79 in Risse-Kappen 1995.

——1999. *Sovereignty: Organized Hypocrisy*. Princeton, NJ: Princeton University Press.

——(ed.) 2001. *Problematic Sovereignty: Contested Rules and Political Possibilities*. New York: Columbia University Press.

——2004. Sharing sovereignty: new institutions for collapsed and failing states. *International Security*, 29: 85–120.

KUHN, T. S. 1970. *The Structure of Scientific Revolutions*, 2nd enl. edn. Chicago: University of Chicago Press.

LAKE, D. A. 1999*a*. *Entangling Relations: American Foreign Policy in its Century*. Princeton, NJ: Princeton University Press.

——1999*b*. Global governance: a relational contracting approach. Pp. 31–53 in *Globalization and Governance*, ed. A. Prakash and J. A. Hart. New York: Routledge.

——2007*a*. Escape from the state of nature: authority and hierarchy in world politics. *International Security*, 32: 47–79.

——2007*b*. International trusteeship: rebuilding authority after civil wars. Unpublished typescript, University of California, San Diego.

——2007*c*. The new American empire? Unpublished article, University of California, San Diego.

——Forthcoming. *Hierarchy in International Relations*. Ithaca, NY: Cornell University Press.

——and POWELL, R. 1999. *Strategic Choice and International Relations*. Princeton, NJ: Princeton University Press.

LEGRO, J. W. 1996. Culture and preferences in the international cooperation two-step. *American Political Science Review*, 90: 118–37.

MEARSHEIMER, J. J. 2001. *The Tragedy of Great Power Politics*. New York: W. W. Norton.

MIGDAL, J. S. 1988. *Strong Societies and Weak States: State–Society Relations and State Capabilities in the Third World*. Princeton, NJ: Princeton University Press.

MILNER, H. V. 1997. *Interests, Institutions, and Information: Domestic Politics and International Relations*. Princeton, NJ: Princeton University Press.

MORAVCSIK, A. 1997. Taking preferences seriously: a liberal theory of international politics. *International Organization*, 51: 513–53.

MORGENTHAU, H. J. 1978. *Politics among Nations: The Struggle for Power and Peace*, 5th rev. edn. New York: Alfred A. Knopf.

MORROW, J. D. 1999. The strategic setting of choices: signaling, commitment, and negotiations in international politics. Pp. 77–114 in Lake and Powell 1999.

OSIANDER, A. 2001. Sovereignty, international relations, and the Westphalian myth. *International Organization*, 55: 251–87.

POWELL, R. 1999. *In the Shadow of Power: States and Strategies in International Politics*. Princeton, NJ: Princeton University Press.

PRICE, R. 1998. Reversing the gun sights: transnational civil society targets land mines. *International Organization*, 52: 613–44.

——and REUS-SMIT, C. 1998. Dangerous liaisons? Critical international theory and constructivism. *European Journal of International Relations*, 4: 259–94.

RECTOR, C. forthcoming. *Federations*. Ithaca, NY: Cornell University Press.

REUS-SMIT, C. 1999. *The Moral Purpose of the State: Culture, Social Identity, and Institutional Rationality in International Relations*. Princeton, NJ: Princeton University Press.

——2004. *American Power and World Order*. Malden, Mass.: Polity.

RIKER, W. H. 1980. Implications from the disequilibrium of majority rule for the study of institutions. *American Political Science Review*, 74: 432–46.

RISSE-KAPPEN, T. (ed.) 1995. *Bringing Transnational Relations Back In: Non-State Actors, Domestic Structures, and International Institutions*. New York: Cambridge University Press.

ROGOWSKI, R. 1989. *Commerce and Coalitions: How Trade Affects Domestic Political Alignments*. Princeton, NJ: Princeton University Press.

——1999. Institutions as constraints on strategic choice. Pp. 115–36 in Lake and Powell 1999.

——2003. International capital mobility and national policy divergence. Pp. 255–74 in Kahler and Lake 2003.

RUGGIE, J. G. (ed.) 1993. *Multilateralism Matters: The Theory and Praxis of an Institutional Form*. New York: Columbia University Press.

——1996. *Winning the Peace: America and World Order in the New Era*. New York: Columbia University Press.

——1998. *Constructing the World Polity: Essays on International Institutionalization*. New York: Routledge.

SCHWARTZ, T. 1987. Votes, strategies, and institutions: an introduction to the theory of collective choice. Pp. 318–45 in *Congress: Structure and Policy*, ed. M. D. McCubbins and T. Sullivan. New York: Cambridge University Press.

SHEPSLE, K. A. 1979. Institutional arrangements and equilibrium in multidimensional voting models. *American Journal of Political Science*, 23: 27–59.

SIMPSON, G. 2004. *Great Powers and Outlaw States: Unequal Sovereigns in the International Legal Order*. New York: Cambridge University Press.

SMITH, J., and WIEST, D. 2005. The uneven geography of global civil society: national and global influences on transnational association. *Social Forces*, 83: 1279–85.

SNYDER, J. 1991. *Myths of Empire: Domestic Politics and International Ambition*. Ithaca, NY: Cornell University Press.

SPRUYT, H. 1994. *The Sovereign State and its Competitors: An Analysis of Systems Change.* Princeton, NJ: Princeton University Press.

TILLY, C. 1990. *Coercion, Capital, and European States, AD 990–1990.* Cambridge, Mass.: Blackwell.

VERNON, R. 1971. *Sovereignty at Bay: The Multinational Spread of US Enterprises.* New York: Basic Books.

WALTZ, K. N. 1959. *Man, the State, and War: A Theoretical Analysis.* New York: Columbia University Press.

——1979. *Theory of International Politics.* Reading, Mass.: Addison-Wesley.

WEBER, K. 2000. *Hierarchy amidst Anarchy: Transaction Costs and Institutional Choice.* Albany, NY: State University of New York Press.

WENDT, A. 1987. The agent–structure problem in international relations theory. *International Organization,* 41: 335–70.

——1992. Anarchy is what states make of it: the social construction of power politics. *International Organization,* 46: 391–425.

——1994. Collective identity formation and the international state. *American Political Science Review,* 88: 384–96.

——1999. *Social Theory of International Politics.* New York: Cambridge University Press.

WIMBERLEY, L. 2007. Pyrrhic peace: governance costs and the expected utility of war. Ph.D. dissertation, University of California, San Diego.

WOLFERS, A. 1952. "National security" as an ambiguous symbol. *Political Science Quarterly,* 67: 481–502.

CHAPTER 3

....

FROM INTERNATIONAL RELATIONS TO GLOBAL SOCIETY

....

MICHAEL BARNETT

KATHRYN SIKKINK

HISTORICALLY speaking, the study of international relations has largely concerned the study of states and the effects of anarchy on their foreign policies, the patterns of their interactions, and the organization of world politics. Over the last several decades worldly developments and theoretical innovations have slowly but surely eroded the gravitational pull of both anarchy and statism in the study of international relations. Although scholars of international relations continue to recognize that the world is organized as a formal anarchy and that states retain considerable power and privileges, they increasingly highlight an international realm where the international structure is defined by material and normative elements, where states share the stage with a multitude of other actors, and where trends in global politics are shaped not only by states but also by this variety of other actors and forces. Simply put, the discipline is moving away from the study of "international relations" and toward the study of the "global society." We use this shift in the name to symbolize a series of transformations in the last twenty years in the discipline regarding what and whom we study, and how and why we study them.

The cumulative effect of these transformations is that the overarching narrative of the field has changed from one of anarchy in a system of states to governance within a global society. Our notion of a global society parallels the arguments of the English School and its notion of world society, particularly the identification of an increasingly dense fabric of international law, norms, and rules that promote forms of association and solidarity, the growing role of an increasingly dense network of state and nonstate actors that are involved in the production and revision of multilayered governance structures, and the movement toward forms of dialogue that are designed to help identify shared values of "humankind" (Buzan 2004; Linklater and Suganami 2006). This shift from "international relations" to "global society" is reflective of several important developments that are the focus of this chapter.

We open with a discussion of the anarchy thematic and what John Agnew (1994) has called "the territorial trap" and survey some of the critical forces that compelled international relations scholars to free themselves from this trap. We then explore the shifts in the what, who, how, and why of the study of international relations. The assumption of anarchy and the territorial trap helped to define the discipline's agenda, fixating on how survival-seeking and self-interested states produce security and pursue wealth and how these states manage to produce cooperation under anarchy. Although these issues remain on the agenda, they increasingly share space with other topics, including "global" issues such as environmental politics and human rights, the sources of international change, the forces that define the identity, interests, and practices of states, and normative international relations and international ethics. A shift in what we study also has affected whom we study. The ecology of international politics is no longer dominated by states and increasingly includes nonstate actors such as nongovernmental organizations, transnational corporations, international organizations (IOs), and transnational networks of all kinds operating alongside states in a reconstituted "global public domain" (Ruggie 2004). Alterations in the ontology of the world polity have also shifted the epistemology of world politics— that is, *how* we study— encouraging scholars to move beyond a narrow conception of the "scientific" enterprise and adopt a diversity of epistemological positions. There has also been a reconsideration of *why* we study global—and not international—politics, a development driven by various factors, including a growing dissatisfaction with theory- and methods-driven research to the exclusion of puzzle-driven research and practical engagement.

This emerging field of global politics is increasingly focused on the study of global governance. Governance can be generically understood as "the maintenance of collective order, the achievement of collective goals, and the collective processes of rule through which order and goals are sought" (Rosenau 2000, 175). The discipline of international relations has always been concerned with issues of governance, venturing from the early twentieth-century study of IOs to the post-Second World War study of integration, transnationalism, international regimes, international institutions, and "governance without government" (Rosenau and Czempiel 1992). Traditionally the study of international governance has focused on how states have established norms, laws, and institutions to help them engage in collective action and create order. Over the last two decades, though, there has been a terminological shift from the study of *international* governance to the study of *global* governance, justified because the purposes of global governance no longer reflect solely the interests of states but now also include other actors, including IOs, transnational corporations, nongovernmental organizations, and new kinds of networks. Global governance is produced through networked relations among different kinds of actors with different kinds of authority and power that are embedded in both formal and informal arrangements. We need to think in more conceptually creative and intellectually diverse ways to understand the production, maintenance, and transformation of the global rules that define the global ends and the means to achieve them. We conclude by considering how governance, rather than anarchy, might be a candidate for narrating the study of international relations.

Our own work draws on and has contributed to constructivist theories of international relations in part because they gave us greater leverage over the changing and fundamentally social character of global relations. Constructivist theory, though, is not a disciplinary panacea, and we are aware of its limitations, the strengths of alternative theories, and the need for theoretical developments and synthesis to address the ongoing challenges of studying global society. Still, our position is deeply influenced by social constructivism, and we believe that it provides some critical intellectual tools that provide insight into both the central changes that have occurred in global relations over the decades and possible futures.

1 GOING GLOBAL

It is widely accepted that the discipline of international relations has undergone something of a sea change. As Brian Schmidt (2002) has forcefully argued, it was organized around the concept of anarchy, shaping the conceptualization of international relations, the boundaries of the field, and its research agenda.[1] International relations became the study of states. In state-centrism's extreme form, the territorial trap (Agnew 1994), international relations carves up the world into mutually exclusive territorial states and the study of international relations becomes the study of relations between these units. States are assumed to have authority over their

---

[1] However, William Wohlforth (this volume) argues that realism can live without the anarchy assumption.

political space, radiating power from the center to the territorial border, where it comes to a dead halt. This authority over a geographically defined and (mainly) contiguous space is reinforced and underscored by the principle of sovereignty, wherein states recognize each other's authority over that space and deny any authoritative claims made by those outside the state. Such matters inform the classic differentiation in international relations theory between anarchy, lawlessness, coercion, and particularism on the outside, and hierarchy, legitimate authority, dialogue, and community on the inside. State, territory, and authority became tightly coupled in international relations theory.

The discipline's anarchy narrative shaped a post-Second World War research agenda focused on how self-interested states pursue their security and welfare under a condition of anarchy that makes cooperation desirable but difficult. Under the shadow of the cold war, international relations scholars focused on patterns of war, how states manage their security relations, the impact of the nuclear age, and crisis management. When the once-neglected study of international political economy finally got the attention it deserved, the anarchy narrative shaped the framework employed and questions addressed by international relations scholars: a defining theme was the tension between the logic of capital and the logic of anarchy, how the state was constantly trying to intervene in markets in order to protect the *national* economy and the *national* security, and how the rise of global corporations could undermine the state's autonomy and sovereignty (Gilpin 2003). In the 1980s scholars began to address the question of "cooperation under anarchy" and the conditions under which states might produce sustained forms of coordination and collaboration in various issue areas (Keohane 1984; Oye 1986).

While the anarchy narrative illuminated some problems and issues, it dismissed and obscured many others. There was little attention paid to domestic politics. Ian Clark (1999) calls this "the great divide" in international relations—the presumption that the domestic and the international are distinct spheres that are defined by distinct organizing principles. There was little appreciation of the increasingly rule-bound nature of the decentralized global governance system and the interpenetration of rules in the domestic and international realm. There was little recognition of forms of authority outside the state—that is, disaggregated authority (Rosenau 2000). There was also little attention to important global trends, including the eye-opening development wherein certain regions were becoming more pacific in part because of developments in domestic politics and other regions were becoming undone from the ground up with horrific effects for civilian populations (however, see Buzan 1983).

Beginning in the 1980s, and picking up steam in the 1990s, various scholars from a range of disciplinary perspectives began to take aim at the territorial trap and those theories that were most closely associated with it, namely neorealism and neoliberal institutionalism. This is not the place to revisit the critiques of these theories or retell the rise of constructivism, but it is worth noting two critical dimensions of this development. One was the desire to find an exit option from the territorial trap, as scholars unpacked anarchy (Wendt 1992), sovereignty (Biersteker and Weber 1996), authority (Rosenau and Czempiel 1992), and the bundling of the state, territory, and authority (Ruggie 1992). The other was the failure of existing theories to explain much less predict important international change. Various global changes generated anomalies between existing theories and world developments—most famously and strikingly the remarkably peaceful end of the cold war and the dissolution of the Soviet Union. As Peter Katzenstein (1996) argued, the failure of existing international relations theories to predict let alone contemplate the end of the cold war was to international relations theory what the sinking of the Titanic was to the profession of naval engineering. The next decade of cascading globalization raised further challenges and agitation for new theoretical creativity.

The combination of new kinds of theorizing and rapid global change called into question the accuracy of the very label of international relations. As is well known, international relations was never inter*national* but instead was inter-*state*, but few challenged this sleight of hand. However, events of the 1990s, including globalization, ethno-national conflict, and identity politics, made scholars more aware that the term international politics obscured more than it illuminated. Scholars became more cognizant of transnational networks, relations, and associations that were both affecting inter-state relations and helping to define the very constitution of global society. For many, the label of international relations was no longer a convenient shorthand but was now a contrivance that hindered analysis. Accordingly, many went in search of labels that were more accurate representations of the subject, including international studies and global studies. Although the label of international relations has had clear staying power, scholars of international relations have gone global as they have become more comfortable with operating outside the territorial trap.

One last point. The territorial trap did not have the same hold on students of the international relations of the Third World as it did on students of the global North because the attending analytical assumptions were so glaringly distant from empirical reality. Hierarchy and not anarchy seemed to be the defining organizing principle. Colonialism's end did not transform North–South relations from hierarchy to anarchy (and equality) as economic, security, and political structures continued to place Third World states in a subordinate position, to challenge their authority in various domains, and to create a major chasm between their formal sovereignty and their effective sovereignty. Relatedly, the state in the global North was an accomplishment, while in the global South it was a project, needing to solidify its territorial base, to monopolize the means of coercion, and to eliminate all other rivals to its authority. In order to capture this reality, scholars began to modify their understandings of Third World states, calling them shadow, alien, weak, artificial, and quasi. Scholars of the global South developed a range of theories—including dependency, postcolonial, world-systems, and empire; for them, international relations was always global. Perhaps because Third World scholars saw international hierarchy instead of anarchy, they remained more committed to strengthening and defending sovereignty as a political project and were less likely to celebrate transnational processes that threatened it. Thus, for example, the benefits of global civil society have often been received with more skepticism in the global South than among critical international relations scholars in the North.

2 The What, Who, How, and Why of Global Society

2.1 What Do We Study?

Once scholars began to relax the assumption of anarchy and move beyond state-centrism, a whole new world became visible. There were two defining developments (a third—whom we study—will be discussed below). The first was the rise of topics other than classical security and international political economy. Scholars began to study a range of other issues, including human rights, the environment, gender, culture, religion, democracy, and law. And, even when scholars remained focused on political economy and security, they tracked very different features. The study of political economy underwent a rapid transformation in response to the growing observation that globalization was producing a qualitative shift in the global organization of capitalism, the character of the state and state–society relations, and international economic relations.

Historically, scholars of security focused on the state and inter-state relations—following the assumption that the object of security was the state (which represented the national community) and that the principal threat to the state's (and thus the "nation's") security was from another state. With the end of the cold war, however, there was a growing willingness by scholars to examine the meaning and practice of security (Katzenstein 1996). Whereas once security meant the security of the state, increasingly the object of security was the group or the individual, captured by the increasing circulation of the concept of human security. Shifting the object of security implied a re-examination of what constituted a threat. The state, once viewed as a unit of protection, was increasingly recognized as a principal source of insecurity in many parts of the world (Buzan 1983). In fact, in the twentieth century more individuals were killed by their own governments than in all international wars combined. The fact that states were failing in their responsibilities to protect their citizens implied that the study of human rights is related to security and not a marginal subfield that is irrelevant to the "real" issues of international relations.

Individuals, however, were not only passive victims of their governments; they were also increasingly active participants in the creation of new human rights rules and institutions, including some institutions that allowed these individuals to bring claims against their own government. Scholars and policy-makers called attention to "nontraditional" security threats such as famines, environmental degradation, and health epidemics, in some regions. In other regions, international relations scholars pointed out that states had established pacific relations and, importantly, no longer expected or prepared for war (Adler and Barnett 1998).

Another theoretical and empirical breakthrough was a growing recognition of the presence and impact of international normative structures. The individualism and materialism of the dominant theories presented international life as absent of any sort of sociality. In reaction to these axioms and various global developments, many scholars argued that power and interest did not exhaust explanations for global outcomes and change, and developed conceptions of normative structures that imagined how they might shape the state's identity, interests, and what counts as legitimate action. Now that international relations scholars were recognizing that global politics has a sociality, it was possible to resurrect once-banished concepts that are inextricably bound up with all political orders. Two concepts, in particular, are critical for the study of global society: legitimacy and authority.

Both legitimacy and authority are notoriously slippery concepts, difficult to define and measure, and inextricably related to theories of social control and thus bound up with questions of power. For these reasons international relations scholars have resisted them, only to be forced to wrestle, once again, with their causal importance, especially in the areas of compliance, cooperation, and governance. States and nonstate actors agree to be bound by rules, not only because the powerful impose them or because of self-interest, but also because they believe those rules to be legitimate—that is, they deserve to be obeyed (Kratochwil and Ruggie 1986; Hurd 1999; 2007; Bukovansky 2002; Clark 2005). To the extent that actors confer legitimacy on rules and institutions, they gain authority—thus the oft-heard phrase "legitimate authority." Scholars increasingly recognized that actors other than states have forms of legitimate authority in global society and that such authority derives from a variety of sources, including expertise. The existence of different kinds of authority conferred on different kinds of actors undermines the anarchy narrative and presumption that a distinguishing characteristic of the international sphere is that authority is monopolized by the sovereign state. IOs have become particularly important authorities in their own right, often working with states and nongovernmental actors in new hybridized forms of authority (Barnett and Finnemore 2004; Conca 2005).

A related and somewhat belated development is a growing interest in international normative theory and international ethics. The "scientific" study of international relations and normative international relations went their separate ways decades ago, lived parallel lives, and found little opportunity or incentive to cross-fertilize (Price 2008; Reus-Smit 2008). However, this segregation is beginning to break down for various reasons. Norms are defined as standards of appropriate behavior and thus, to study norms empirically, constructivists had to grapple with how and why actors come to believe certain behavior is appropriate or legitimate (Finnemore and Sikkink 1998). This led to a small and growing empirical investigation of international ethics, including studies of the changing ethical metrics that actors use to judge what counts as legitimate action and of the causes and consequences of the institutionalization of ethics in international arrangements. Constructivist investigations of state policies and of international society argue that they are shaped by deep beliefs, including ethical or moral beliefs about the purpose of the state, humanitarianism, and justice (Lumsdaine 1993; Reus-Smit 1997).

Although some of the constructivist research on norms demonstrated the importance of norms and the possibilities for moral change in world politics, most constructivists did not initially articulate their own normative or prescriptive position of those changes to be advocated (Price 2008). With the exception of a handful of scholars interested in questions of international political theory, including forms of global cosmopolitanism, communitarianism, and responsibility (Held 1995; Linklater 1998), scholars were often more committed to critiquing implicit notions of progress in many processes in global society than in articulating their own ethical or normative visions.

The study of global governance reflects these changes in the study of world politics. Whereas this was once limited to how states with pre-existing interests create norms, rules, laws, and institutions to regulate their relations, there have been a number of critical additions in the recent past. First, there is a greater interest in the social construction of what is to be governed—that is, how a problem becomes defined and gets placed on the agenda. Moreover, there is a growing consideration of how international and domestic structures, working through conceptions of self and logics of appropriateness, shape governance structures. The study of multilateralism, for instance, now includes a consideration of how national identity shapes the emergence of the multilateral form and then how the multilateral form came to be viewed as legitimate (Ruggie 1993). In addition to a rational design of institutions, there can also be a "sociological" design that incorporates logics of legitimation (Wendt 2001). There is also a growing desire to bring classical normative questions such as fairness, justice, accountability, and representation to bear on the study of governance and the sources of legitimacy (Kapstein 2005; 2006). Although political theorists have long worried about democracy in an age of internationalization (Held 1995), they are now joined by many international relations theorists who are focusing attention on questions of accountability, power, and legitimacy (Slaughter 2004; Grant and Keohane 2005; Hurd 2007).

2.2 Whom Do We Study?

What we study obviously relates to whom we study. International relations scholars justify the state-centric focus of the discipline on the grounds that nonstate actors either are captured by states or are causally irrelevant. This position, in our view, is now an embattled orthodoxy because states alone cannot account for important international outcomes or the very fabric of global politics.

Two developments deserve mention. The first is growing attention to domestic politics, and in particular to domestic regime type, as a significant factor for explaining global outcomes. Building on microeconomic analytics, one version of liberal theory examined how individuals form groups to shape the state's foreign policies (Slaughter 1995; Moravcsik 1997). Two-level game models demonstrated the importance of analyzing the interaction between domestic and international politics in order to understand inter-state negotiations, treaties, and policy collaboration. Having established the empirical regularity that democracies do not wage war with other democracies, scholars began to focus on the characteristics of democracies that might generate this unexpected outcome. Neoliberal institutionalists also increasingly turned their attention to domestic politics, both for models of how to study the global and for interactive models that helped incorporate domestic politics in efforts to understand global outcomes (Milner 1991). Constructivists, too, contributed to the growing interest in the relationship between domestic and international structures (Risse-Kappen 1995). We are now far beyond worrying about committing the sin of reductionism and are prepared to pick up the challenge of examining the relationship between these different "levels" (Gourevitch 2002). As scholars answer the challenge, though, they should be wary of falling back into the territorial trap—that is, treating the "domestic" and the "international" as necessarily ontologically distinct realms—and should consider their interrelationship and co-constitution.

Another important development is the growing awareness of the wider range of actors that are shaping global relations. Two kinds of actors are receiving increased attention precisely because of their causal importance and their perceived centrality to global governance—IOs and transnational actors. Although the study of IOs is almost as old as the discipline of international relations, it has fallen in and out of theoretical favor over the decades (this section draws heavily from Barnett and Finnemore 2007). The post-First World War emergence of the discipline of international relations included considerable attention to IOs; after the Second World War there was continuing interest in IOs because of the experiments in regional integration in Europe and postwar IO-building. Although international relations scholars lost interest in IOs during the 1970s and 1980s, a very powerful line of argument emerged concerning the conditions under which states will establish international institutions and the functions that they assign to them (Keohane 1984). Briefly, states create and delegate critical tasks to international institutions because they can provide essential functions such as providing public goods, collecting information, establishing credible commitments, monitoring agreements, and generally helping states overcome problems associated with collective action and enhancing collective welfare.

While this institutionalist perspective generates important insights into issues of international governance, its statism and functionalism obscure important features. First, the functionalist treatment of international institutions and IOs reduced them to technical accomplishments, slighting their political character and the political work they do. It also presumes that the only interesting or important functions that IOs might perform are those that facilitate cooperation and resolve problems of interdependent choice. Secondly, the statism of many contemporary treatments of IOs reduced them to mere tools of states, akin to how pluralists treated the state. IOs are mechanisms or arenas through which others (usually states) act. The regimes literature is particularly clear on this point. Regimes are not purposive actors. IOs are thus passive structures; states are the agents who exercise power in this view.

New studies of IOs argued that they have authority, autonomy, and agency, and are political creatures that have effects similar to the effects of other authority-bearing actors, including states. The impact of IOs is not limited to the functions assigned to them by states and the regulation of already existing state interests. IOs also construct the social world in which cooperation and choice take place. They help to define the issues that need to be governed and propose the means by which governance should occur (Barnett and Finnemore 2004). They help define the interests that states and other actors have, not only as a forum where persuasion takes place, but also as an actor that is engaged in processes of socialization (Checkel 2005). In fact, the growing recognition that IOs might have authority and power has encouraged scholars to worry that runaway IOs might become modern-day Frankensteins, where the inventors are no longer able to control their creation. Consequently, there is now a growing interest in what happens when decisional authority is scaled up to IOs that have more autonomy and more power than ever before; the issue is not only effectiveness but also legitimacy and accountability (Barnett and Finnemore 2004; Grant and Keohane 2005).

There has also been a burgeoning study of transnational relations. Similar to the study of IOs, the study of transnationalism had an earlier moment in the sun, faded in the shadow of state-centrism, and has now returned with a burst of energy. Robert Keohane and Joseph Nye (1972) introduced the study of transnational politics in the early 1970s, but that particular research agenda did not prosper in the short term, with the exception of some increased attention to transnational corporations in world politics. Ernst Haas and John Ruggie explored the role of various kinds of knowledge communities and transnational networks for understanding forms of international change and cooperation (Ruggie et al. 2005). These literatures proved to be ahead of their time.

By the early 1990s, though, international relations scholars began to rediscover transnationalism and transnational actors. One of the first important formulations was the work on epistemic communities, which focused on how transnationally connected experts with shared technical knowledge could influence state policy in situations of high complexity and uncertainty (Adler and Haas 1992; Haas 1992). A new literature on transnational advocacy networks, global civil society, and transnational social movements identified these actors as participants in global politics and documented their ability to create norms and contribute to regime formation and implementation (Sikkink 1993; Keck and Sikkink 1998; Price 1998; 2003; Thomas 2000; Tarrow 2005). In contrast to epistemic communities that were formed around scientific knowledge and expertise, these groups formed primarily around shared principled ideas. In either case, transnational communities could create new issue areas, project these issues into the international arena, prod states to "discover" their interests, identify new policy options, and help to constitute an independent global public sphere or public domain apart from the system of states (Wapner 1995; Ruggie 2004).

There was generally a "liberal" bias in much of the post-1990s research on transnationalism—that is, the assumption that these developments are desirable and help to pluralize power and advance basic human freedoms. A second wave of literatures looked at the "dark side" of transnationalism and pointed to the problematic nature of global civil society, its lack of autonomy from the world-views and funding sources of dominant states in the North, and its problems of accountability and representation. Another strand examines so-called dark networks including terrorist groups and criminal networks around drugs and trafficking (Kahler 2007). Regardless of whether one considers transnationalism, on balance, a good or a problematic development, there is general agreement that transnational actors can influence the course of global affairs.

A distinguishing characteristic of many of these transnational actors is that they are organized in network forms.[2] That is, while states and IOs are organized around hierarchies and have bureaucratic properties, networks are characterized by voluntary, reciprocal, and horizontal patterns of communication and exchange (Keck and Sikkink 1998). Organizational theorist Walter Powell calls them a third mode of organization, distinctly different from markets and hierarchy. "Networks are 'lighter on their feet' than hierarchy," and are "particularly apt for circumstances in which there is a need for efficient, reliable information" (Powell 1990, 303–4). International relations theorists are only now beginning to "see" network as an alternative form of organization, assess its presence, prominence, and causal importance in world affairs, and consider its normative implications. The dominant forms of communication in global politics (email and the World Wide Web) have

---

[2] Not all transnational actors are organized in networks (the Vatican is hierarchical, for example) and not all networks are made up of nonstate actors. As Ann-Marie Slaughter (2004) observes, intergovernmental relations also frequently use network forms of interaction.

networked forms that are increasingly beyond the complete control of states. Terrorist organizations are viewed as being organized around networks, making them more difficult for states to monitor, locate, and incarcerate. Global corporations are discovering and adopting network forms of organization.

Networks have various positive and negative attributes. They have flexibility, speed, informality, a greater chance for increasing multiple views, and perhaps even enhanced implementation capacities (Slaughter 2004; Weber 2004). Yet they lack "a legitimate organizational authority to arbitrate and resolve disputes" (Podolny and Page 1998); in short, they cannot provide the legitimate authority necessary for full-fledged global governance. Nevertheless, increasingly hybrid network forms of governance are emerging that may combine state and nonstate actors to carry out key governance tasks.

Finally, there is perhaps no more persuasive evidence of the rise of global society than the ability of nonstate actors and even individuals to participate directly in global politics without being mediated by the state. This ability finds formal recognition in human rights regimes, where increasingly individuals can bring claims against their own state to international human rights institutions, and where individuals can now be held accountable for acts (crimes against humanity or genocide) that previously were attributed to states. The rise of individual criminal accountability in the global system, as evidenced in the increase in human rights trials, can thus be seen as a broader metaphor for the emergence of individuals as direct participants in global society. Three decades ago Hedley Bull (1977, 152) recognized as much when he wrote that "if the rights of each man can be asserted on the world political stage over and against the claims of the state, and his duties proclaimed irrespective of his position as a servant or citizen of that state... The way is left open for a subversion of the society of sovereign states on behalf of the alternative organizing principle of cosmopolitan community." Contrary to some scholars of global civil society, we do not argue that a cosmopolitan community has emerged, but we would echo Bull's assertions that such changes imply that we have moved well beyond a global society composed only of sovereign states.

2.3 How Do We Study?

What and whom we study necessarily leads to a consideration of how we study. There is now greater epistemological eclecticism and methodological diversity than ever before. While there are various reasons for growing epistemological diversity, arguably most important was the recognition of the underlying social character of international relations. An important early contribution to this awareness was Friedrich Kratochwil and Ruggie's observation (1986) regarding the disconnect between epistemology and the study of international regimes. They argued that, while the very definition of regimes involves inherently intersubjective norms and principles, the prevailing positivist epistemology of international relations made it impossible to explain, assess, or capture the social aspect of life.

A genuinely *social* science cannot model itself only after the natural sciences; international relations scholars of a global society must embrace epistemologies that are appropriate to the task. There is no single path. Some have gravitated toward interpretative social science, frequently drawing from Max Weber and other classical sociological theorists, to understand how actors give significance and meaning to their actions and the intersubjective understandings that frequently constitute social action. Others have gravitated toward forms of scientific realism and theories of discourse, hoping to identify broad patterns of action and inaction. In this regard, there is an interest in "conditions of possibility," what makes possible certain action, what alternatives are seen as simply correct without any reflection or discussion, and which alternatives are seen as unthinkable (Wight 2006). In this important sense, post-positivist scholars operate with a much broader understanding of causality than do positivist scholars; underlying, unobservable structures that make some action possible, difficult, or unimaginable do important explanatory work.

Alongside an increasing diversity of epistemological positions is an increasing array of methodologies. The use of alternative methodologies to address the same questions has deepened our theoretical understanding and enhanced our empirical analysis. Consider two prominent areas in the study of global governance. The first is compliance. Behavioral approaches to the study of norms typically attempt to measure behavioral conformity with norms that are written in formal treaties and agreements (Simmons 2000; Raustalia and Slaughter 2002). Instances of compliance or noncompliance, in other words, are defined by the scholar as deviations from some measure developed by the analyst of what constitute behavior consistent with expectations codified in the agreement. Interpretative approaches go beyond behavior. They aspire to recover how actors interpret what counts as compliance and defection; whether there is an intersubjective understanding of what compliance demands in particular social situations; the kinds of justifications that are used for acts of noncompliance; and the motivations and reasons that actors give for compliance and noncompliance (Kratochwil and Ruggie 1986; Koh 1997; Kingsbury 1998).

Another area is the study of legitimacy. Certainly any international order that has a modicum of legitimacy will be reflected in behavior that is consistent with the international norms that define that order. Consequently, there should be behavioral effects, effects that can be observed and captured through comparative statics. In this regard, claims about the increasing or decreasing legitimacy of an IO, treaty, or agreement should be evident not only in rates of compliance but also with changes in the willingness of states to rally to its defense, to punish those who violate its norms, and to provide various kinds of resources (Clark 2005; Clark and Reus-Smit 2007). Yet we should also want to understand why legitimacy is conferred, what are the contests over what constitutes a legitimate international order, and what sorts of practices are considered to be appropriate as a consequence.

Not only are particular substantive areas benefiting from the application of diverse methodological approaches, but individual scholars are demonstrating greater agility as they are using multimethod approaches. Increasingly, some scholars who use quantitative methods are asked to supplement their large-n studies with well-selected cases, while qualitative scholars are also turning to some quantitative approaches or formal models. The reason for this development is the desire to balance the strengths and weaknesses of each approach: Large-n studies are very good at helping to determine broad patterns across space and time, but well-designed case studies can be essential for identifying and exploring the causal mechanisms that account for the relationship between independent and dependent variables.

2.4 Why Do We Study?

The what, who, and how raise fundamental issues regarding the why we study global politics. Or, more precisely, why *should* we study world politics? A vibrant discipline of international relations depends on the presence of a community of scholars who are collectively engaged in providing creative explanations and innovative insights into concerns of global importance that have potential relevance beyond that scholarly community. Theory development and methodological innovation is central to this task, but sometimes international relations theorists have become enamored with theory and method for their own sake, turning means into ends. This can lead to sterile paradigm wars and disengagement from the problems and practices of global relations. As Katzenstein and Rudra Sil (this volume) argue, we should judge progress in international relations by both the "quality and scope of dialogue among social scientists and the proximity of this dialogue to socially important normative and policy issues."

Most of us got into this business to explore and explain particular puzzles. We are motivated by the need to understand and explain developments and changes in global politics and to keep up with the world that often surprises and shocks us. In particular, we are motivated by the need to understand and explain change in global society. As early as 1983, Ruggie (1983) pointed to realism's inability to explain change as its greatest weakness. He argued that realism was unable to explain key changes in the international system because it was missing both a dimension of change and a determinant of change. Other authors have claimed that realism has likewise been unable to explain the most important changes in the late twentieth and early twenty-first centuries, in particular, the consolidation of the European Union, the end of the cold war, the emergence of the war of terror, and the explosion of IOs, international law, and networks. New theories have made some important contributions to understanding specific changes in global society, but have not yet provided a comprehensive theory of change. An increasingly common position is to reject the possibility of a grand theoretical synthesis. In this respect, we concur with Katzenstein and Sil (this volume) that a much more promising avenue is to develop eclectic theorizing that can be used to explain worldly problems with an eye toward how such eclecticism might or might not contribute to broader theoretical arguments.

Secondly, many of us decided on a career in international relations not only because we wanted to observe and explain from a cool distance but also because we hoped our knowledge might improve the conduct and character of global politics. The social sciences were founded with the expectation that they could solve societal problems and define the "public good." The field of international relations emerged from this tradition and with the desire to develop a scientific and rigorous study of war in order to help pacify a violent world. There is a long story about how, why, and when the social sciences largely abandoned the idea of practical engagement, a story that revolves around the quest for objectivity and the belief that practical engagement would pollute a pure science, the obsession with theory-building and methods, the desire to train graduate students for life in the academy and to forgo the idea of educating young professionals who might have a career in the public and nonprofit sectors (Anderson 2005). The consequence is that scholars are no longer actively engaged in practical politics. To be sure, there are moments when scholars attempt to comment on the controversies of the day in various forums, but the overall incentive structure is to orient scholars toward the community of scholars rather than toward policy-relevant research.

International relations scholars need to think through how to connect their theories and knowledge to practical action, and one possibility concerns a more substantial interest in marrying international ethics to empirical analysis. Because of its roots in critical theory and critical social science, critical international relations theory has always been attentive to the relationship between theory and praxis, particularly regarding how theory can lead to emancipation. For many, Robert Cox's (1981) distinction between a critical theory that unmasks relations of power with the hopes of changing them and problem-solving theory that takes the world as it is, has been a touchpoint. We are very sympathetic to the importance of attempting to uncover the structures that produce forms of oppression and hinder the ability of individuals to control their fates. However, this formulation has encouraged many who associate themselves with critical international relations theory to dismiss out-of-hand political interventions that are deemed insufficiently radical. But what, precisely, is ethically problematic with an engagement that aspires to make small but consequential changes in the lives of others? Is a practical politics that both makes small improvements and works toward more thoroughgoing change impossible? Where is the evidence that radical change has led to radical emancipation?[3]

---

[3] We recognize that there are potential links to pragmatism, especially pragmatism's interest in engagement with practical problems and in marrying forms of critical theory with social science methods, but we will leave it to others more conversant with pragmatism to draw the connections.

The empirical engagement with ethics underscores that moral judgment requires evaluation not just of principles but also of consequences. To answer the question "what to do," we need to ask not just "what is right" but also "what may work" to bring about outcomes consistent with our principles.[4] We study the world in part because we believe that our research does yield information about the consequences of human action that may be important for ethical judgment and for action in the world. Resolving empirical questions about consequences is important for making normative judgments about desirable policies. It is not only a question of determining which policies are good and bad, but rather specifying the conditions under which different policies can lead to better or worse outcomes.

Because the theorizing about consequences is an inherently comparative and empirical enterprise, empirically oriented scholars can make an important contribution (Nye 1986; Sikkink 2008). Thus ethical judgment requires the best empirical research we can do, using all the research tools at our disposal. The research will often involve difficult counterfactuals, complex research designs, and demanding evidence. Well-intentioned researchers will disagree about results. But we can improve our discussions by being more explicit about our processes of ethical reasoning and by relating our research findings more explicitly to their normative implications.

A paradigm-driven or methods-mad discipline is an intellectual and professional dead end because it allows scholars to feel satisfied with the resulting intellectual fragmentation and detachment from the world. There are many possible paths for reattaching these severed ties, and several of the chapters in this volume suggest different possibilities for greater dialogue among scholars and engagement with practical politics. Not every scholar needs to be equally engaged in dialogue or practical politics, and there are reasons to foster an intellectual division of labor. But such a division needs to be situated in the context of a general agreement that part of the responsibility that members of the community have to each other (and to the pursuit of greater understanding about the world) is to listen carefully and openly to alternative arguments and perspectives and then to consider how such perspectives might foster theoretical development, empirical analysis, and practical action.

3 CONCLUSION: FROM ANARCHY TO GLOBAL GOVERNANCE?

All disciplines, if they are to have any coherence whatsoever, must have an overarching narrative. The anarchy thematic has helped to generate coherence for the

---

[4] We are indebted to Richard Price for this particular formulation.

discipline of international relations. It provided a common narrative that focused on states as actors that were struggling to maintain their security and generate wealth in an inhospitable environment. It helped to define the boundaries of the field and distinguish the study of international relations from the study of comparative politics. It focused scholarly attention on a manageable set of issues that could be subjected to theoretical emendation and empirical analysis. It provided a coherent account of the discipline that could be passed down from one generation to the next. The anarchy thematic served various useful functions.

Yet this singular narrative also bred theoretical, intellectual, and empirical myopia. Theories that escaped the territorial trap were marginalized or ostracized on various grounds, including the view that they were not contributing to the core debates in the field. Students were advised against certain dissertation topics (for example, human rights, gender) because it would marginalize them in the field. At issue were not only diversity for diversity's sake but also the ability to construct alternative theories that had the capacity to provide new insights into the existing research agendas and identify new topics for research. The pluralization of the discipline did not occur because the mainstream digested the ethos of deliberative democracy, but rather because of theoretical shortcomings, empirical anomalies, and new items on the global agenda that demanded new approaches. Consequently, many scholars who once believed that they were on the outside of the discipline looking in rejoiced at the decline of the anarchy thematic and the demise of the territorial trap.

This growing diversity, however welcome, also risks generating disciplinary fragmentation, because there no longer exists a single, overarching story. We hesitate to propose an alternative narrative precisely because there is no magical formulation that can avoid prematurely foreclosing diverse perspectives and voices. However, the concept of governance has been emerging as a worthy alternative to anarchy because of its ability to interrogate enduring, heretofore neglected, and emerging issues in the theory and practice of international relations. Governance is about how actors work together to maintain order and achieve collective goals. Accordingly, the study of global governance is ultimately concerned with how rules are created, produced, sustained, and refined, how these rules help define the purpose of collective action, and how these rules control the activities of international, transnational, and increasingly domestic action.

A narrative of global governance, then, would have to consider both centralized and decentralized forms of governance. International relations scholars have tended to focus on centralized rules, particularly those that exist in inter-state agreements, treaties, and conventions. But we must become more aware of the different kinds of organizational forms and architectures through which global governance occurs. In particular, we must be attentive to the possibility of governance through decentralized rule, including governance through networks that link the public and private realms (Chimni 2004; Ruggie 2004). This suggests that we focus attention less on specific actors, such as specific IOs, and more on "rule systems" (Rosenau 2000) and often on multilayered structures where governance actually occurs (Conca 2005; Khagram 2005).

Global governance has evolved from a state-dominated affair to include a panoply of actors (even as states retain considerable privileges and prerogatives). Global rule-making is increasingly produced by private authorities such as global corporations and bond-rating agencies, transnational actors such as citizens' movements and indigenous groups, IOs such as the United Nations High Commissioner for Refugees, and nongovernmental organizations such as Doctors without Borders. In general, states do not exhaust the mechanisms of reproduction or transformation, and by stalking states we overlook other suspects that are the source and governor of international change.

Any consideration of global governance must necessarily be concerned not only with collective action and international cooperation but also with questions of power. But to see the power in global governance requires seeing power along its multiple dimensions, including compulsory power, the direct control of one actor over another; institutional power, the control actors exercise indirectly over others through diffuse institutional arrangements; structural power, the structural constitution of subject's capacities; and productive power, the discursive production of subjectivity. These different conceptualizations provide different answers to the fundamental question—when and in what respects are actors able to control their own fate?—and illuminate different forms of power in global governance (Barnett and Duvall 2005).

The narrative of global governance must also marry the theoretical and the normative. Indeed, much of the recent literature on global governance has moved from a consideration of the need for governance in order to enhance collective action and minimize market failures (all implicitly desirable outcomes) to a more thoroughgoing consideration of the relationship between the different forms of governance and their relationship to basic issues such as legitimacy, accountability, representation, and democracy. For instance, some forms of governance might be effective but illegitimate, and, if they are viewed by peoples as illegitimate, then they might be inherently unstable. Other forms may be legitimate but ineffective. This has led scholars to posit the possibility of alternative governance forms that can produce both effective and legitimate outcomes, a sterling instance in which theoretical and empirical analysis is married to practical politics.

In summary, we have argued that international relations is now a discipline focused on the governance of a global society. This has transformed whom, what, how, and why we study international politics. We now study a wider range of both public and private actors, recognizing that such actors both are engaged in governance tasks and, at times, embody legitimate authority. Rather than engaging in sterile struggles over paradigms and methods, we will need to use all the theoretical and methodological tools at our disposal to capture the complex and social nature of global society and global governance. These tools need to be capable of helping scholars understand processes and sources of global change, not only to explain the dynamics of global society, but also to permit scholars to engage more directly in helping shape the direction of that change.

REFERENCES

ADLER, E., and BARNETT, M. (eds.) 1998. *Security Communities*. Cambridge: Cambridge University Press.

——and HAAS, P. 1992. Conclusion: epistemic communities, world order, and the creation of a reflective research program. *International Organization*, 46: 367–90.

AGNEW, J. 1994. The territorial trap: the geographical assumptions of international relations theory. *Review of International Political Economy*, 1: 53–80.

ANDERSON, L. 2005. *Pursuing Truth, Exercising Power: Social Science and Public Policy in the Twenty-First Century*. New York: Columbia University Press.

BARNETT, M., and DUVALL, R. (eds.) 2005. *Power in Global Governance*. New York: Cambridge University Press.

——and FINNEMORE, M. 2004. *Rules for the World: International Organizations in Global Politics*. Ithaca, NY: Cornell University Press.

————2007. Political approaches. Pp. 41–57 in *The Oxford Handbook on the United Nations*, ed. T. G. Weiss and S. Daws. Oxford: Oxford University Press.

BIERSTEKER, T., and WEBER, C. (eds.) 1996. *State Sovereignty as Social Construct*. Cambridge: Cambridge University Press.

BUKOVANSKY, M. 2002. *Legitimacy and Power Politics: The American and French Revolutions in International Political Culture*. Princeton, NJ: Princeton University Press.

BULL, H. 1977. *The Anarchical Society: A Study of Order in World Politics*. London: Macmillan.

BUZAN, B. 1983. *People, States, and Fear: The National Security Problem in International Relations*. Columbia: University of South Carolina Press.

——2004. *From International to World Society? English School Theory and Social Structure of Globalisation*. Cambridge: Cambridge University Press.

CHECKEL, J. 2005. International institutions and socialization in Europe: introduction and framework. *International Organization*, 59: 801–26.

CHIMNI, B. S. 2004. International institutions today: an imperial global state in the making. *European Journal of International Law*, 15: 1–37.

CLARK, I. 1999. *Globalization and International Relations Theory*. Oxford: Oxford University Press.

——2005. *Legitimacy in International Society*. New York: Oxford University Press.

——and REUS-SMIT, C. (eds.) 2007. Resolving international crises of legitimacy, special issue. *International Politics*, 44: 153–339.

CONCA, K. 2005. Old states in new bottles? The hybridization of authority in global environmental governance. Pp. 181–206 in *The State and the Global Ecological Crisis*, ed. J. Barry and R. Eckersley. Boston: MIT Press.

COX, R. 1981. Social forces, states and world orders: beyond international relations theory. *Millennium: Journal of International Studies*, 10: 126–55.

FINNEMORE, M., and SIKKINK, K. 1998. International norm dynamics and political change. Pp. 247–78 in *Exploration and Contestation in the Study of World Politics*, ed. P. Katzenstein, R. Keohane, and S. Krasner. Cambridge, Mass.: MIT Press.

GILPIN, R. 2003. *Global Political Economy: Understanding the International Economic Order*. Princeton, NJ: Princeton University Press.

GOUREVITCH, P. 2002. Domestic politics and international relations. Pp. 309–28 in *Handbook of International Relations*, ed. W. Carlsnaes, T. Risse, and B. Simmons. Thousand Oaks, Calif.: Sage.

GRANT, R., and KEOHANE, R. O. 2005. Accountability and abuses of power in world politics. *American Political Science Review*, 99: 29–43.

HAAS, P. 1992. Introduction: epistemic communities and international policy coordination. *International Organization*, 46: 1–35.

HELD, D. 1995. *Democracy and the Global Order: From the Modern State to Cosmopolitan Governance*. Stanford, Calif.: Stanford University Press.

HURD, I. 1999. Legitimacy and authority in international politics. *International Organization*, 53: 379–408.

——2007. *After Anarchy: Legitimacy and Power in the United Nations Security Council*. Princeton, NJ: Princeton University Press.

KAHLER, M. 2007. Political networks: power, legitimacy and governance. Unpublished typescript.

KAPSTEIN, E. 2005. Power, fairness, and the global economy. Pp. 80–101 in Barnett and Duvall 2005.

——2006. *Economic Justice in an Unfair World: Toward a Level Playing Field*. Princeton, NJ: Princeton University Press.

KATZENSTEIN, P. (ed.) 1996. *The Culture of National Security: Norms and Identity in World Politics*. New York: Columbia University Press.

KECK, M., and SIKKINK, K. 1998. *Activists beyond Borders: Advocacy Networks in International Politics*. Ithaca, NY: Cornell University Press.

KEOHANE, R. O. 1984. *After Hegemony: Cooperation and Discord in the World Political Economy*. Princeton, NJ: Princeton University Press.

——and NYE, J. S. (eds.) 1972. *Transnational Relations and World Politics*. Cambridge, Mass.: Harvard University Press.

KHAGRAM, S. 2005. *Dams and Development: Transnational Struggles for Water and Power*. New York: Oxford University Press.

KOH, H. 1997. Why do nations obey international law? *Yale Law Journal*, 106: 2599–659.

KINGSBURY, B. 1998. The concept of compliance as a function of competing conceptions of international law. *Michigan Journal of International Law*, 19: 345–72.

KRATOCHWIL, F., and RUGGIE, J. 1986. International organization: a state of the art on an art of the state. *International Organization*, 40: 753–75.

LINKLATER, A. 1998. *The Transformation of Political Community: Ethical Foundations of the Post-Westphalian Era*. Cambridge: Polity.

——and SUGANAMI, H. 2006. *The English School of International Relations: A Contemporary Assessment*. New York: Cambridge University Press.

LUMSDAINE, D. H. 1993. *Moral Vision in International Politics: The Foreign Aid Regime, 1949–1999*. Princeton, NJ: Princeton University Press.

MILNER, H. 1991. The assumption of anarchy in international relations theory: a critique. *Review of International Studies*, 17: 67–85.

MORAVCSIK, A. 1997. Taking preferences seriously: a liberal theory of international politics. *International Organization*, 51: 513–53.

NYE, J. S. 1986. *Nuclear Ethics*. New York: Free Press.

OYE, K. (ed.) 1986. *Cooperation under Anarchy*. Princeton, NJ: Princeton University Press.

PODOLNY, J. M., and PAGE, K. L. 1998. Network forms of organization. *Annual Review of Sociology*, 24: 57–76.

POWELL, W. 1990. Neither market nor hierarchy: network forms of organization. *Research in Organizational Behavior*, 12: 295–336.

PRICE, R. 1998. Reversing the gun sights: transnational civil society targets land mines. *International Organization*, 52: 613–44.

—— 2003. Transnational civil society and advocacy in world politics. *World Politics*, 55: 579–606.

——(ed.) 2008. *Moral Limit and Possibility in World Politics*. Cambridge: Cambridge University Press.

RAUSTIALA, K., and SLAUGHTER, A.-M. 2002. International law, international relations and compliance. Pp. 538–58 in *Handbook of International Relations*, ed. W. Carlsnaes, T. Risse, and B. Simmons. Thousand Oaks, Calif.: Sage.

REUS-SMIT, C. 1997. The constitutional structure of international society and the nature of fundamental institutions. *International Organization*, 51: 555–89.

—— 2008. Constructivism and the structure of ethical reasoning. In Price 2008.

RISSE-KAPPEN, T. 1995. *Bringing Transnational Relations Back In: Non-State Actors, Domestic Structures, and International Institutions*. Cambridge: Cambridge University Press.

ROSENAU, J. 2000. Change, complexity, and governance in a globalizing space. Pp. 169–200 in *Debating Governance: Authority, Steering, and Democracy*, ed. J. Pierre. Oxford: Oxford University Press.

—— and CZEMPIEL, E.-O. (eds.) 1992. *Governance without Government: Order and Change in World Politics*. New York: Cambridge University Press.

RUGGIE, J. 1983. Continuity and transformation in the world polity: toward a neorealist synthesis. *World Politics*, 35: 261–85.

—— 1992. Territoriality and beyond: problematizing modernity in international relations. *International Organization*, 47: 139–74.

—— 1993. *Multilateralism Matters: The Theory and Praxis of an Institutional Form*. New York: Columbia University Press.

—— 2004. Reconstituting the global public domain: issues, actors, and practices. *European Journal of International Relations*, 10: 499–531.

—— KATZENSTEIN, P., KEOHANE, R., and SCHMITTER, P. 2005. Transformations in world politics: the intellectual contributions of Ernst B. Haas. *Annual Review of Political Science*, 8: 271–96.

SCHMIDT, B. 2002. On the history and historiography of international relations. Pp. 3–22 in *Handbook of International Relations*, ed. W. Carlnaes, T. Risse, and B. Simmons. Thousand Oaks, Calif.: Sage.

SIKKINK, K. 1993. Human rights, principled issue-networks, and sovereignty in Latin America. *International Organization*, 47: 411–41.

—— 2008. The role of consequences, comparison, and counterfactuals in constructivist ethical thought. In Price 2008.

SIMMONS, B. 2000. International law and state behavior: commitment and compliance in international monetary affairs. *American Political Science Review*, 94: 819–35.

SLAUGHTER, A.-M. 1995. International law in a world of liberal states. *European Journal of International Law*, 6: 503–58.

—— 2004. *A New World Order*. Princeton, NJ: Princeton University Press.

TARROW, S. 2005. *The New Transnational Activism*. Cambridge: Cambridge University Press.

THOMAS, D. 2000. *The Helsinki Effect: International Norms, Human Rights, and the Demise of Communism*. Princeton, NJ: Princeton University Press.

WAPNER, P. 1995. Politics beyond the state: environmental activism and world civic politics. *World Politics*, 47: 311–40.

WEBER, S. 2004. *The Success of Open Source*. Cambridge, Mass.: Harvard University Press.

WENDT, A. 1992. Anarchy is what states make of it: the social construction of power politics. *International Organization*, 46: 391–425.

—— 2001. Driving with the rearview mirror: on the rational science of institutional design. *International Organization*, 55: 1019–49.

WIGHT, C. 2006. *Agents, Structures and International Relations: Politics as Ontology*. New York: Cambridge University Press.

CHAPTER 4

THE POINT IS NOT JUST TO EXPLAIN THE WORLD BUT TO CHANGE IT

ROBERT W. COX

OVER three decades ago I participated in a panel at the annual conference of the American Political Science Association, the title of which was the question: "will the future be like the past?" It concerned the scholarly attempt to define a basic structure of world politics that would be valid everywhere and for all time as a framework for the analysis of world politics. Those who would answer "yes" to the question envisaged a way of explaining international relations in a world conceived as a bundle of data open to the observation of the analyst who stands apart from the action—an approach since called neorealism. This virtual world is invariably divided into a number of hard entities ("states") of different levels of material capabilities whose relationships (peace or war or something in-between) are governed by the "balance of power," which has its own inherent rules of practice. This basic approach is devised to explain what happens among the state entities as levels of military and economic capability among them change. Change in material capabilities takes place *within* the system, but the nature or basic structure *of* the system never changes.

Neorealism proved popular, particularly among American analysts, so long as it seemed to fit with the world into which it came. It proved to be adaptable to the bipolarity of the cold war. The question whether the structure of the system so conceived was indeed applicable to other times and places seemed at the time to be rather academic. In any case, history was not highly regarded by "neorealists." At best, history was a quarry for mining data to test the system. The point of "neorealism" was to explain shifting power relations in a world that did not change in its basic character.

1 CHANGE AS A LATENT FORCE IN HISTORY

"Neorealism" confronted another approach that did envisage basic change in the structure of world power. In its contemporary form this was Marxism, but Marxism had evolved out of a deeply rooted disposition of the human mind to posit a happy ending to the human story. It probably began with monotheism. If the world and all that has been and will be in it has been created by an all-powerful God, it was natural to assume that there was some ultimate purpose in it and that that purpose was ultimately good. The idea of an inherent purpose—a subjective notion—in the unfolding of human history is, of course, foreign to positive science and hence to neorealism. Historical actors, individual or collective (that is, states), can have purposes, but for the positivist observer, there can be no cosmic purpose inherent in the process of interaction itself.

Religious consciousness injects such a purpose. Its primitive form is what theologians call eschatology—the doctrine of final things, the individual's finality in heaven or hell, and history's end in the kingdom of God. The Jewish anticipation of the coming of the Messiah who would open the way toward the earthly paradise was taken over, adapted, and embellished by Christianity.

Civilizations untouched by monotheism saw history more naturally as a cyclical process by analogy to the spring, summer, autumn, and winter of the seasons and the biological cycle of birth, development, maturity, decline, and death. St Augustine, who had to debate with the assumptions of classical civilization in order to defend Christianity against the charge of undermining the imperial state, denounced Plato's teaching of the cyclical process. The moment in history when God had descended into the world in the Incarnation of Jesus Christ, Augustine argued, changed all that. Thenceforward history had a goal: the City of God. A twelfth-century monk from Calabria, Joachim of Floris, elaborated St Augustine's vision into a three-part historical process: the Age of the Father, in which God's law for humankind was laid down in the Old Testament; the Age of the Son, in which the revelation of Jesus Christ enabled men (note the patriarchal gender implication) to overcome the obstacle of sin through obedience to and guidance from the institutions of Church and state; and, ultimately, the Age of the Holy Spirit—heralded by some Franciscans reacting against the worldliness of the Church—in which men would live in mystical harmony without the need for coercive or directing institutions.

When Europe entered the Age of Enlightenment in the eighteenth century, the grip of religion loosened, but the three-stage vision of history remained entrenched in the European consciousness, taking on secularized forms. Georg Hegel spoke of history as a three-stage rational progress of freedom. Karl Marx's subsequent vision of history, inverting Hegel's idealism into materialism, appears as a mirror image of Joachim of Floris's vision. Class struggle, rather than religious revelation or Spirit and Reason, was his version of the dynamic of history. Social conflict, he explained, has transformed feudalism into capitalism and would proceed to transform capitalism into history's final form, the communist society, in which conflict is resolved into harmony as the coercive institution of the state "withers away."

Religious and secular visions of history are all about change, but change that is only indirectly the consequence of human endeavor. Change in these linear "progressive" theories comes from a latent nonhuman force: Providence for St Augustine and his followers; the "cunning of reason" for Hegel (to which we may associate Adam Smith's "hidden hand"); and the materialist logic of history in the Marxian version. The explanation of change lies within the process itself; human activity is guided by the dialectic of the process toward an ultimate happy ending.

It is well to recall that the modernist notion that history is governed by natural laws is the creation of three centuries of European history during which European ideas spread around the world. An older perspective sees the world as a realm of continuous and chaotic change with no ultimate final state—no "end of history." Contrary to modernism, which posits a separation between the subject as observer and the object as observed, the ancient perspective sees both observer and observed as reciprocally interacting in an unpredictable process of change. Purpose and fact cannot be separated.

2 CHANGE THROUGH CHAOS AND SELF-ORGANIZATION

In the Greece of the sixth century BCE, the pre-Socratic philosopher Heraclitus of Ephesus contemplated such a world of perpetual change, of eternal *becoming*. All change, he taught, comes from the dynamic and cyclical interplay of opposites. In China, about the same time, Lao Tzu, the legendary founder of Taoism, taught that transformation and change are the essential features of nature; and that change, resulting from the interplay of polar opposites, *yin* and *yang*, which are irrevocably bound together, is the ultimate reality—the Tao or the path.

Heraclitus and Lao Tzu, who, of course, knew nothing of each other's teaching, went further to say that the human intellect can never comprehend this ultimate reality, that concepts formed by the human mind to express the inner meaning of the world are illusions. Closer to our time, the French philosopher Henri Bergson, who had thought deeply about evolution, spoke about *homo faber*, the human being defined in its capacity to make and do things, rather than *homo sapiens*, who purports to understand the meaning of the universe (Bergson 1944, 153–4).

When we think now of "change" in world politics and society we think of what has to be done to ensure the survival of the human race and to moderate conflict among peoples. The primary task of the study of international relations along with the other departments of knowledge about human affairs is to help people to organize so as to achieve this.

To serve this purpose, social science should set aside the approaches of the past that sought to define persisting structures and laws and should adopt the less deterministic approach of the new physics and biology by being sensitive to emerging and declining historical structures and movements of self-organization in social and political relations. It should set aside illusions about "the end of history" and concentrate upon purposive change in a chaotic world.

3 PURPOSIVE CHANGE

The study of international relations should focus first on the key issues affecting the biological survival of the human race; and then on the pursuit of justice in the condition of peoples, which is essential to maintaining their support for a survivable world order.

A short list of the priorities would include:

- survival of the biosphere;
- avoidance of nuclear war;
- moderating the rich/poor gap;
- assuring protection for the most vulnerable people; and
- effective arrangements for negotiating conflict resolution.

The point for us now is to try to understand the world *as people are making it* so as to gain some control over where we are going; and to forgo speculation about an immanent logic of history that will turn out to be an illusion.

The modernist faith in universal laws began to fade in physics and biology during the past century, undermining the model that had been emulated in the social sciences. The basic theoretical challenges came in physics from relativity theory and quantum theory. These concerned the infinitely large (astrophysics) and the infinitely small (particle physics) and they showed that the apparent certainties of classical mechanics did not apply in these areas (Prigogine 1996).

Further challenges came in physics from the second principle of thermodynamics, or tendency toward entropy, in which loss of energy leads toward disorganization; and in biology when it showed how a movement toward disorganization in the neurons of the brain could be countered by autonomous movements of "self-organization." The French biologist Jacques Monod (1970) popularized the discovery of indeterminism, disorder, and chance in his book, *Le Hasard et la nécessité*.

These discoveries opened a new approach in the physical and biological sciences called "complexity" (Waldrop 1993). It departs from a mechanical conception of causality by envisaging vast interacting networks—an approach facilitated by advances in cybernetics. The French philosopher Edgar Morin (1973) has speculated about what he calls *hyper-complexity*: a system that reduces constraints while increasing its capacity for self-organization, in other words its capacity for autonomous change.

These developments in scientific thinking have implications for thinking about change in human affairs. Implications for the social sciences are:

- a shift from being to becoming, from emphasis on innate structures to emphasis on processes, and from causality (in a billiard-ball sense) to complexity (in the sense of interactive networks);
- to renounce searching for basic causes; change takes place through interactions in a complex network in which no single force is determining;
- that processes are irreversible, that is, tendencies toward entropy and disorganization may be countered by self-organization, which means that the future will not predictably reproduce the past;
- that the search for absolute certainty of scientific propositions is abandoned in favor of determining their "domain of validity," which converts such propositions into exploratory hypotheses rather than universal laws;
- that observer and observed are equally involved in change, which means discarding the subject/object dichotomy of so-called objective science in favor of an "epistemic" science that pursues findings within a particular and transitory paradigm.

The terms chaos, complexity, and uncertainty are characteristic of the new scientific approach, whereas order, simplicity, and certainty characterized modernist science. The natural sciences are moving away from the notion that their purpose is to facilitate humans' domination and control over nature, toward understanding humanity as a part of nature through an emerging theory of living, self-organizing systems. The impact of these changes on social science—which has heretofore been constructed on the model of Enlightenment physics—is bound to be resisted and delayed by professional conservatism; but new paradigms are emerging here too in more holistic, more relativistic, and more historically oriented approaches.

This means looking for the recurrent "self-organizing" of the human species so as to discern the patterns of reorganization that have been created collectively in response to the sequence of challenges to human society. The structures that emerge in this process are human creations, neither something innate within a supposed invariant "human nature" and "natural order," nor something inherent within a cosmic historical process. What we have here are *historical* structures, the forms of collective organization, and the mentalities that fit them, both reacting from and adapted to the material conditions of existence of human groups.[1]

The distinction between data and facts is important here. It is clearer in the Latin languages than in English. The word "data" derives from the verb "to give" (*dare*, *datum*); and the word "fact" derives from the verb "to make" (*facere*, *factum*): a given is just there; a fact presupposes a maker and the maker's purpose. Positivist science deals with givens. History deals with facts; or, as R. G. Collingwood (1946) said, with the inside as well as the outside of an event, not just that which can be observed but also the intentions and purposes of the action that went into making the fact. With facts and history the ethical and the observable are one.

4 CHANGE IN HISTORICAL STRUCTURES

Action begins with an assessment of prevailing conditions. If the purpose of action is to remedy some anomaly or dysfunction, then the prevailing conditions are taken as given; but if the goal is change in some fundamental way—that is, in the structure of society, whether local or global—then action must also aim at changing the prevailing conditions. These conditions can no longer be taken as givens. They have to be viewed critically as products of history. Only thus can we understand how they came to be and how we may work to change them. Fundamental change means change in the historical structures that create the framework for everyday activities.

Hegel (1967, 13) wrote: "The owl of Minerva spreads its wings only with the falling of dusk." The world is not shaped by theory. Theory comes from reflection on what happens in the world; and there has been much to reflect upon recently as a spur to thinking about emerging and persisting historical structures:

[1] The French *Annales* school of history has developed this approach. See Braudel (1980).

- the collapse of the Soviet Union, and with it of the bipolar world, and the emergence of what French diplomacy calls the *hyper-power* of the USA;
- growing concern about ecological instability and its impact on the biosphere;
- the persistent tendency of capitalism to widen the gap between the rich and the poor;
- a resurgent affirmation of identities of an ethnic, national, religious, or cultural kind;
- a new salience of irregular or extralegal activities like "terrorism" and organized crime;
- increasing skepticism of people toward all forms of established authority.

I would suggest that in the context of these changes at the beginning of the twenty-first century there are three configurations of power, three interacting historical structures that circumscribe the problems of international politics and world order.

5 Existing Historical Structures

The first is what has been called the "American empire," or now often simply "Empire." "Empire" penetrates across borders of formally sovereign states to control their actions from within through compliant elites in both public and private spheres. It penetrates first into the principal allies of the United States but also into many other countries where US interests wield influence. Transnational corporations influence domestic policy in countries where they operate; and economic ties influence local business elites. Military cooperation among allies facilitates integration of military forces under leadership of the core of "Empire." Cooperation among intelligence services gives primacy to the security concerns of the imperial leadership. The media generalize an ideology that propagates imperial values and justify the expansion of "Empire" as beneficial to the world. Economic systems of the component territories of "Empire" are restructured into one vast market for capital, goods, and services. In the imagined future of "Empire," the "hard power" of military dominance and economic coercion is both maintained and transcended by the "soft power" of attraction and emulation.[2] "Empire" constitutes a movement tending to absorb the whole world into *one civilization*. Its governing principle is unity and homogeneity.

The second configuration of power is the Westphalian inter-state system that was inaugurated in Europe in the seventeenth century and spread throughout the world during the era of European dominance. The sovereign state, though weakened by

---

[2] The concept of "soft power" comes from Nye (1990, 32).

"Empire," remains a hardy structure. Sovereignty has a dual aspect. One aspect is the autonomy of each sovereign state in the society of nations. The other is the authority of each state within its own territory and population. Both aspects are protected by respect for the principle of nonintervention in the internal affairs of other states. Both external and internal sovereignty remain a defense against absorption into "Empire."

The two fronts on which the residue of the Westphalian world structure confronts the impact of "Empire" are, first, the defense of the inter-state system and its creations, international law and the United Nations; and, second, the strengthening of the bonds linking citizens to political authorities. These protect national autonomy in economic and social organization, and thereby sustain a plural world of coexisting cultures and civilizations. Multilateralism within the inter-state system is the realpolitik of middle powers. The governing principles of the Westphalian world are pluralist diversity and a continuing search for consensus.

The third configuration is what is often called "civil society." This exists within states and within "Empire" and it also takes a transnational form. This configuration of forces has defended the environment and women's rights. It has mobilized for peace and to combat poverty. It has been especially active in recent decades initially as a movement for an alternative to the economic globalization of transnational corporate power and then as a direct confrontation of "Empire" in the popular mobilization against the Anglo-American invasion of Iraq.

It has also, in the form of so-called people power, provoked "regime change" in some countries, most recently in Serbia, Georgia, and Ukraine. In these cases, external ideological influence and finance from "Empire" merged with internal discontent to create a formula for nonviolent revolution. Civil society was, in a measure, co-opted to become an instrument for the penetration of "Empire" into Eastern Europe and Central Asia.

"Civil society" differs from both "Empire" and the state system in that it functions as a decentred network rather than as a disciplined hierarchical structure. Modern information technology in the form of the Internet and the cell phone has helped it to develop and to mobilize for action. This loose flexible character is an asset in being able to bring together a diversity of groups around some central issue. It is also a weakness by making it difficult to articulate a clear program of action because of this very diversity; and also by leaving the movement open to disruption by *agents provocateurs* or to being co-opted by well-financed and well-organized state or ideological interests either domestic or foreign. Civil society is inherently opposed to the centralizing and homogenizing force of "Empire" but is always vulnerable to being subverted or manipulated.

Behind and below these three rival configurations of power lies a covert world including organized crime, so-called terrorist networks, illegal financial circuits, intelligence operatives, arms dealers, the drug trade and the sex trade, and sundry religious cults, all of which are transnational in reach. This covert world functions in the interstices of the three overt configurations of power. Some of its component elements, like "terrorist" networks, conspire to subvert and destroy established powers. Other components, like organized crime, are parasitical upon established power and live in symbiosis with it. The covert world is always present in some measure. Its expansion signals trouble for the established order—a loosening of confidence in the security that order is supposed to ensure for people in general.

The three configurations of power in the world today overlap geographically. They are not confined by territorial boundaries. They have points of geographical concentration but are in contest everywhere asserting rival claims to legitimacy, while the expansion of the covert world, in both its subversive and parasitical aspects, undermines legitimacy everywhere.

6 Legitimacy and Change

When we think of the world in dynamic terms as being open to change, the legitimacy of authority becomes the condition for effective action. Legitimacy enables authority to act with sustained support and public acquiescence. A revolutionary act or an imperial incursion may precipitate change, but the change becomes durable only to the extent that legitimacy comes to prevail. Government is legitimate when people accept the institutions and procedures of authority and the decisions that emerge, even if they do not like them. When that general acceptance becomes eroded, when there is no general acceptance that decisions have been properly arrived at, the relationship becomes illegitimate.

Fear is a critical factor—fear on the part of the rulers as well as among those subject to authority. The tyrant is in constant fear of being overthrown; and those over whom the tyrant rules are kept in obedience through fear. Legitimacy calms fear on both sides—for the governors and for the governed. When the public is gripped by a fear that authority seems impotent to calm, the scene is set for arbitrary power—for the "man of destiny." When governments provoke fears among the public, as is now a common aspect of the "war on terror," they are preparing for oppressive measures. The inverse relationship between fear and legitimacy is the key to the problem of public and social order today as always. This is perhaps the one durable transhistorical truth. The establishment of legitimacy is the primary condition for the ethical pursuit of change.

Legitimacy in global governance thus becomes the central problem of world order. "Empire" aspires to global legitimacy by claiming to know the one best way of organizing society—what the agents of "Empire" call "democracy" and "capitalism." The overwhelming military power of "Empire," its capacity for economic coercion, and its communications and ideological resources have not, however, been able to gain support or acquiescence from a broad sector of humanity. The claims of "Empire" remain illegitimate on a global scale. Indeed, the overwhelming "hard power" of "Empire" has generated "terror" as the response of those who utterly reject "Empire."

The alternative concept of global governance—a continuing process of negotiation among states under recurrent pressure from the manifold manifestations of civil society—has been faltering in its ability to establish confidence in its efficacy. Civil society is the ultimate anchor of legitimacy. This is the major dilemma of international relations today.

One civilization versus a *plural world* of coexisting civilizations: How this basic issue of global governance is decided will affect the way in which the major issues confronting the future of humanity can be dealt with. These issues are all global in scope: protecting the biosphere; moderating the extreme inequalities between rich and poor; protecting the vulnerable; and minimizing violence within and among peoples. To deal effectively with these issues requires broad consensus with legitimate power behind it. The challenge to world politics and to the study of international relations is to build that consensus. The conditions in which this can be done are shaped by the ongoing contest for legitimacy among the rival configurations of power: "Empire," state system, and civil society. The outcome is uncertain—the historically transitory product of ethical conviction, will, skill, and chance. Such is life in a Heraclitan world.

REFERENCES

BERGSON, H. 1944. *Creative Evolution*, trans. A. Mitchell. New York: Modern Library.

BRAUDEL, F. 1980. History and the social sciences: the *longue durée*. Pp. 25–54 in *On History*, F. Braudel, trans. S. Matthews. Chicago: University of Chicago Press; originally published (in French) 1958.

COLLINGWOOD, R. G. 1946. *The Idea of History*. Oxford: Clarendon Press.

HEGEL, G. W. F. 1967. *Hegel's Philosophy of Right*, trans. T. M. Knox. Oxford: Oxford University Press; originally published (in German) 1821.

MONOD, J. 1970. *Le Hasard et la nécessité: Essai sur la philosophie naturelle de la biologie moderne*. Paris: Seuil.

MORIN, E. 1973. *Le Paradigme perdu: La Nature humaine*. Paris: Seuil.

NYE, J. S. 1990. *Bound to Lead: The Changing Nature of American Power*. New York: Basic Books.

PRIGOGINE, I. 1996. *The End of Certainty: Time, Chaos, and the New Laws of Nature*. New York: Free Press.

WALDROP, M. 1993. *Complexity: The Emerging Science at the Edge of Order and Chaos*. New York: Touchstone.

CHAPTER 5

A DISABLING
DISCIPLINE?

PHILLIP DARBY

THIS chapter's title may seem perverse when from some perspectives international relations appears to be riding high. The discipline now straddles the globe and provides a common language with which to analyze world politics. In recent years, it has expanded its purview, bringing in new fields of study ranging from culture to ecology. As this volume shows, there has also been a movement within the discipline to embrace a politics of change and to free up methodologies to this end. Especially since 11 September, student interest has swelled undergraduate enrolments and led to a proliferation of postgraduate courses. A succession of international crises has ensured a constant demand for disciplinary scholars to produce opinion pieces for the press and to give commentaries on radio and television. On the basis of such criteria, the discipline appears to be thriving.

Yet there is another side. For some years, there has been anxiety about the discipline's explanatory capacity, which came into question with the loss of meaning that accompanied the end of the cold war and the failure to predict the collapse of Communism in the Soviet Union. Of late, attention has been directed to the disorder and the violence that has erupted within and between the successor states of empire. It is the contention of a growing number of scholars at the margins of international relations that processes on the ground in these societies challenge Western imagery of a world being set right by the workings of the market, the promotion of

I would like to thank Chris Reus-Smit for his incisive comments on the first draft and Devika Goonewardene for her help throughout.

democratization, and the commitment to development. One indication of how far removed established scholarly thinking is from daily life in large parts of the world is the construct of "emergencies," which presents recurrent breakdowns as somehow exceptional rather than the norm (Calhoun 2004). The realization appears to be growing that existing disciplinary knowledge—not only in international relations but also in adjacent discourses such as development and security studies—is ill equipped to address the problem, all the more so since it cuts across the boundaries of different knowledge formations. Criticisms of this nature intersect with a more long-standing indictment that international relations remains wedded to a colonial world-view that both distorts its understanding of what is happening in the South and skews its normative horizons.

This chapter will focus on the discipline's failure over most of its history to engage with the non-European world except as an appendage to the body of thought developed in relation to the First World. It will go on to ask how far this situation is changing and whether international relations is now set to engage in a process of decolonizing its thinking. I will conclude with some more general remarks about the discipline's knowledge procedures, which inhibit the development of alternative political agendas.

In large part, the story of international relations has been told as the internationalization of a system of thought and practice that arose within Europe, the foundational event being Westphalia. It is a narrative of progress: a reading (or more accurately several different readings) of the reordering of relations between polities in one part of the globe that were then transposed to cover the world. Such theorizing has been damaged by the claim that the settlement of 1648 was not the signal point in the emergence of the modern state system—as has become almost scriptural. Rather, the Westphalian system was characterized by distinctly non-modern geopolitical relations, rooted in absolutist pre-capitalist property relations (Teschke 2003, ch. 7). More importantly, and in some ways prefigured by Samir Amin's exposure (1989, 89) of the myth of an "eternal Europe," unique since the moment of its origin, the narrative has been challenged by the growing recognition of the crucial part played by Europe's relationship with its colonial other in the making of modern sovereignty (Hardt and Negri 2000, 70, 103; Barkawi and Laffey 2002) and the modern economy (Mitchell 2002, 80–119). That for so long this has remained unacknowledged in international relations must largely be attributed to the deep reluctance to engage with the international politics of European imperialism. Recent research on the historiography of international relations suggests that imperialism was a pervasive theme in the discipline in the early decades of the twentieth century (Long and Schmidt 2005). A good deal more research needs to be done to clarify the perceived linkages between the imperial and the international on the part of pioneering scholars and how widely such views were held. What is abundantly clear, however, is that after the Second World War Europe's subjugation of the tropical world was forgotten or repressed in the memory of the discipline.

As a result, the processes that helped shape the futures of two-thirds of the world's peoples and indelibly marked the domestic politics of the metropoles were left to other knowledge formations—most notably imperial history—to take up in their own ways (Darby 1997, 3). It is indicative that a generation and more of international relations scholars seemed content to accept Hedley Bull and Adam Watson's summation (1984, 1–9) of European colonialism as the "expansion of international society"—a formulation that repressed or at best glossed over the violence, racism, and economic expropriation involved.

It is worth touching on some of the ways in which an engagement with the colonial archive might have enabled the discipline to get a better purchase on the international relations of North and South, not only then but also now. Modern colonialism was responsible for instituting the flows of people, ideas, values, and commodities that we understand to be intrinsic to globalization today. It can thus be seen to have contributed in substantial measure to the contemporary instabilities in the Third World. The violence, for instance, that is commonly presented as having endogenous causes cannot adequately be explained by reference to local cultural formations or to the phenomenon of failed states. Its roots can be traced back to colonial conquest and rule, which created new divisions within traditional societies and exacerbated old ones. Of particular significance here were the accentuation of religious and ethnic identifications and the processes of uneven development, which advantaged some local people and disadvantaged others. All this focuses, as it should, on the damaging consequences of colonialism for its victims overseas. But colonialism also had damaging consequences for the victors. Ashis Nandy is one who has given this side of the story much thought. Writing of gender and sexuality (at a time when neither was a subject of inquiry in international relations), Nandy (1983) shows how the colonizing experience in India elevated hyper-masculine values and downgraded those aspects of British political culture that were tender, humane, and associated with the feminine. Some of his arguments are controversial, but he works out from his analysis of gender to suggest that the experience of co-suffering has the potential to bring major civilizations closer together—in marked contrast to monocultural "one-world" approaches that still underline so much Western thinking today. These and other fragments serve to remind us that, although colonialism flew the flag of modernity, it also had a darker side rooted in absolutism and the valorization of power. Thus informed, we may see resonances of this darker side in recent international doctrines of intervention and the way their universalist pretensions shield from view their complicity with Western dominance. But there is also the hope that through an imaginative engagement with the colonial period—such as Nandy's work on suffering—ways out of the present impasse may be found.

The marginalization of the non-European world survived the end of empire. The Western powers must be held to be primarily responsible for the perpetuation of a profoundly unequal world order, but international relations and its ancillary discourses offered little by way of sustained critique and were mostly resistant to alternative thinking. The problem was that, confronted by Third World challenges, policy-makers and disciplinary scholars worked from much the same traditional assumptions. Whereas for the nationalist leaders decolonization offered the hope of a new politics, from the perspective of the West the primacy of the cold war ensured that any rethinking about the formerly colonized world was subordinated to calculations of power and strategy directed to the maintenance of the central balance. In this way, the globalization of violence introduced by the cold war served to conceal a continuing imperial interest in resources and trade and in an international hierarchy based on power and race.

The nationalist leaders attempted to advance their claims by drawing on such resources as were at their disposal. This meant pursuing unconventional strategies for gaining influence in world councils, in some ways akin to guerrilla war, in others anticipating Joseph Nye's ideas (2004, 1–32) about soft power. In the main, they were not part of the stock-in-trade of established international relations. These strategies included the promotion of nonalignment and associated schemes about zones of peace as a means of communication; bringing the Third World's weight of numbers to bear through collective action, as at the Bandung Conference of 1955, and through bodies such as the nonaligned movement, the Group of 77, and the Organization of African Unity; challenging some of the major strands of international law that derived from its colonial past and served the interests of the major Western powers; using dependency theory as a political weapon; and embarking on agitational diplomacy within the United Nations system, focusing especially on economic issues in the General Assembly. Ali Mazrui has in fact argued that the Western powers, which were largely responsible for the charter of the United Nations, wrote it in such a way that peace and security were treated as the primary objectives and the promotion of human rights was secondary. It was his view that the Afro-Asian states were concerned to reverse the order of priority (Mazrui 1967, 135).

The Third World challenge, of course, failed. The power of the discursive as it was deployed was no match for the economic clout of the West—and anyway the West had the means to get across its own story more effectively, at least at home. Outside the Third World, nonalignment was never taken to have much credibility and, after the border war between India and China in 1963, it lost much of its appeal even there. Collective action proved more rhetorical than substantive as Third World states pursued what they took to be their distinctive interests. The attempt to rewrite international law was largely thwarted by entrenching neoimperial economic relations in the private sphere, thus compromising the sovereignty of Third World states (Anghie 2005, 226–44). Dependency was pronounced dead after being dismissed by economists in the West and receiving only belated and limited recognition in international relations. One after another of the radical thinkers of the 1960s and 1970s—people of the stature of Michael Manley and Andre

Gunder Frank—came around to accepting the orthodoxies of development along Western lines. Notwithstanding United Nations declarations, the new international economic order failed to materialize.

Having stymied the tricontinental diplomatic assault, the Western states found new allies and settled to pursue an agenda of their own. This most recent chapter, which covers the period of structural adjustment programs in the 1980s, the globalization of neoliberalism in the 1990s, and the aftermath of September 11, can be understood in very different ways. Nonetheless, as the main issues are familiar, our account can be abbreviated and rather starkly themed. With the strong state more or less neutered, the West began to intervene more extensively in the internal affairs of Third World societies. Very often acting in conjunction with international agencies such as the World Bank and international nongovernmental organizations, the objective became the restructuring of Third World states in ways that could advance the further integration of their societies into the international system. The initial concern—and on most accounts the primary consideration throughout—was the "reform" of domestic economic structures involving privatization, cutbacks in welfare, and the freer entry of foreign capital (for an incisive analysis of how this threatens the politics of the world economy, see Ruggie 1994). Other elements then came to be grafted onto this stock. First was good governance, which was understood in essentially Western terms. Democracy, civil society, and social capital were not only seen as important in their own terms; increasingly they were presented as prerequisites for development. Then, after September 11, some states—mostly Muslim—were pressured to overhaul their approaches to security so that they conformed with the United States' new strategic paradigms. It can also be said that the very phraseology of the war against terrorism—"pre-emptive self-defence," "rogue states"—and the animalization of the other threatened the sovereignty of Third World states. As can be seen from the literature on complex political emergencies, the tendency for humanitarian relief to serve as a basis for state reconstruction and, above all, the attempt to rebuild Iraq along democratic and market-oriented lines, we are witnessing the re-emergence of an imperial politics. What is insufficiently recognized, however, is that the policies now being put in place in the former colonial world are far more interventionist than those pursued in the period of formal empire.

For most of the period, the reconstitution and extension of the power of the center was not seen in international relations for what it was. The discipline was perhaps too preoccupied with making sense of its own corpus in the face of the growing reach of the international, the rise of interdependence, and the impact of globalization. It was also the time when realism was under challenge from constructivism, critical theory, and feminism. Still, there were powerful invitations to rethink the politics of the world system as they affected the South. Alongside the work of John Ruggie and the insights of the complex emergency theorists, there was the discovery of poverty by the editors of *Millennium: Journal of International*

Studies (1996). These suggestive lines of thought, however, were overshadowed by democratic peace theory—not to mention Francis Fukuyama's "end of history" thesis—which pointed in quite the wrong direction. Equally important, knowledges that could have provided critical leads were neglected: Third World critiques of the major tenets of international law were not given the attention they deserved; development, which was usually assigned a chapter in the international relations readers, was seldom seen to reflect back on the theorizing of the discipline. One of the few texts that took the discipline to task, Stephanie Neuman's *International Relations Theory and the Third World* (1998), made some promising moves, then rather lost its way.

Two crucial points emerge from this interpretative survey. Both are fundamental to postcolonial studies and are now gaining some recognition at the margins of international relations. First, for a very long period, the non-European world has been constituted by its lack (Doty 1996, 162). Whereas earlier it was the lack of clothes, the lack of cultivation, and the lack of civilization, it is now the lack of a modern market economy and the lack of good governance. The guiding principle appears to have remained that of the mandate system of the League of Nations: the tutelage of peoples "not yet able to stand by themselves under the strenuous conditions of the modern world" must be entrusted to "advanced nations." Yet, taking our cue from feminist thought, lack may be reconfigured as enabling, as generating alternative precepts and policies. The second is the need to recognize and to work with difference. On one count, this involves "not so much the rejection of the 'West', but its reimagination" (Inayatullah and Blaney 2004, ix; see also Salter 2002; Yew 2003).

The challenge that confronts international relations is to tackle these related issues. Taken together, they constitute a project that involves both decolonizing the discipline and engaging with different ways of knowing the world. There will be divergent views as to whether international relations is now so positioned as to carry through the project. Unarguably difference is now on the agenda and the need for decolonization is more widely acknowledged (see Jones 2006). The chapters in this volume attest to the fact that the discipline is no longer cast in the statist-realist mould. There is a growing concern with "domestic politics," on the one hand, and "global society," on the other. There is also a new interest in experimentation and political activism. Yet there are also signs that the process of rethinking may be cut short—as the nationalist leaders believed was the case with decolonization after the Second World War. Realism may be flagging but liberalism is not. I do not wish to quibble unduly about words, but some of the phraseology suggests continuities or parallels. Given its earlier usage in the discipline, "domestic politics" has its implied exclusions and misses the not-yet political. "Global society" raises the specter of "one-worldism" and certainly is in need of speed bumps. At this point, we might take a lead from Partha Chatterjee's *The Politics of the Governed* (2004), which although not about international relations as such, is a book all international relations students should read. As Chatterjee tells it, in most of the world the business of government has been emptied of politics. Civil society is the closed association of modern elite groups. The real political struggle is now conducted by subaltern groups very largely outside Western imposed or inspired political systems—for which he coined the phrase "political society." What is really at stake, Chatterjee is suggesting, is the nature of non-European societies and how they relate to the international system.

It might be thought that one way forward is for international relations in the North to take its bearings from the practice of international relations in the South. The situation, however, is not so straightforward. The position is now changing, but mostly the hold of tradition has been as strong in the South as in the North (regarding security, see Darby 2006, 457–8). While Third World scholars have been at the forefront in denouncing the continuing hold of Eurocentric thought—one thinks immediately of Amin, Edward Said, Mazrui, Achille Mbembe, Mahmood Mamdani, Nandy, Dipesh Chakrabarty—the role played by international relations has not excited much interest. As a consequence, the discipline's writ has remained very largely undisturbed. Its authority has been invoked not merely in Singapore (which one might expect), but also in Delhi and Beijing (which one might not); Hans Morgenthau on the national interest continues to stud Ph.D. theses throughout much of Africa. Frequently, powerful alternative lines of approach such as dependency or subalternality feature on syllabi and invariably inform oral exchange, but somehow they fail to dislocate the larger structure of disciplinary thought. This may be taken as a sign of the discipline's universality, but it is my contention that it constitutes an as yet largely unexamined case of what Chatterjee (1985) has called "derivative discourse." Hence it might be said that the dominant thrust of the discipline is doubly disabling because it has so colonized the minds of international relations scholars in the South that it renders their priorities and understanding of the key issues irrelevant.

To this point, we have focused on the politics of international relations' marginalization of the non-European world. I now want to reflect on the established knowledge conventions of the discipline in the light of the task of engaging with different ways of knowing the world. Granted perspectives are changing, but the weight of disciplinary lineage must be borne in mind. Two swallows do not make a summer, as the saying goes. There is a strong case to be argued that the discipline's internal scholarly procedures work to screen out knowledges that appear regressive, messy, or fragmented, and knowledges embedded in ways of life that are seldom recognized as knowledge at all (for exceptions, see Keck and Sikkink 1998; Sylvester 2000; Shaw 2002; Magnusson and Shaw 2003). The major debates in international relations have been mainly in-house affairs, and they have had the effect of insulating international relations from other ways of seeing the international. The process of organizing and contesting knowledge between various schools of thought all too often works against novelty and imaginative reach. So also the need to relate to familiar reference points, the often deadening vocabulary, even the style of writing, inhibit departures from established disciplinary moorings (Bleiker 1997). In this regard, it is not that there is no space for difference, but that difference tends to solidify into set positions, which represents a form of closure. It is as if the adherence to emplaced scholarly conventions serves as a bulwark against vulnerability.

There are two footnotes that might be made here. The first relates to research and it applies not only to international relations but across the disciplinary board. With the globalization of the academy and the increasing competition between universities for funding, brownie points go to those who publish internationally, but internationally is widely understood to mean written in English and published in journals in the First World. Secondly, it needs to be remembered that teaching is part of the practice of international relations and it is especially important in terms of whose knowledge goes out into the world. There is a good deal of evidence to suggest that, when it comes to non-European knowledges, the record is not very encouraging (Nossal 2001; Hovey 2004).

All this is the more serious because, for most of its history, the politics of international relations have been spatially circumscribed. Traditionally the discipline's concern was with "high politics." It surveyed the world from the "top down." Even now there is a resistance to addressing the impact of international processes on the lives of ordinary people. That politics takes different forms at the grass roots from at the summit is unsettling to the order of things. Sankaran Krishna is insightful about how international relations discourse has negotiated its way out of this dilemma. Examining the case of race, he argues that the "discourse's valorisation, indeed fetishization, of abstraction is premised on a desire to escape history" (Krishna 2001, 401). One might add, not only to escape history but to escape a politics of the here and now. Hence the appeal, not only of abstractions such as the state of nature or periods of peace, but with model-building and game theory, the calculus of rational choice, and the power of the systemic. By working along these lines we may be better placed to answer questions that should be asked but seldom are. Why is there so little interest in international relations scholars having knowledge of societies other than their own? Why is there so little teaching about the international and the everyday?

These questions direct attention to the politics of the divide between here and there and between the self and the other. The publication of Tzvetan Todorov's remarkable volume, *The Conquest of America*, was a major landmark in theorizing responses to alterity and what is at stake. He approaches the encounter between the Spaniards and the Indians in the fifteenth and sixteenth centuries—"the most astonishing encounter of our history" (Todorov 1984, 4)—with the perspective of a moralist, and with an eye to the future. On his telling, it is not enough to understand or to identify with the other. Knowledge of the other must be put to the task of better knowing the self, thereby revealing the relativity of self-knowledge (Todorov 1984; see also Todorov 1995). Other scholars, at times building on Todorov, more often drawing on different traditions of thought, have contributed distinctive insights, as, for example, showing the continuities between the victors and the victims, identifying commonalities such as suffering and vulnerability, emphasizing the diversity of traditions within all cultures and the need to reclaim recessive voices, and exploring the psychological processes at work (in particular, see Nandy 1987; Kristeva 1991; Das 2002). What is so significant about these narratives is that sifting the historical material and analogous contemporary experience pertaining to encounters between different cultures makes it possible to think about the future in a way that is not simply spun from the self-image of the powerful. Recognizing the other in the self, plus all the self-reflectivity that goes with it, is a necessary first step in moving toward a dialogue between cultures. Yet, as Todorov (1984, 247) suggests, for most of the period of European ascendancy the West has assimilated the other.

It is not, I think, straining the category of self/other to suggest that it applies to discourses as well as to people and cultures. If this is so, we are brought face to face with another facet of the discipline's failure to engage with the other: its reluctance to enter into sustained dialogue with other knowledge formations concerned with the international. Now it is of the very nature of disciplinary thought to privilege its own knowledge specializations, its language of analysis, and its ways of proceeding. And there are good reasons for questioning whether interdisciplinarity, in any of its various forms, can further the process of integrating different knowledges without a general "dumbing-down," let alone negotiate an agreed ethics of knowledge production (Klein 1990; Coles and Defert 1998). Still there is a range of possibilities between disciplinary closure to the outside and inter-disciplinarity: selective border crossing, drawing on alternative source materials and methodologies, Said's eclecticism, anti-disciplinary moves such as Gayatri Spivak's "rule-breaking," embarking on short-term collaborative projects that might loosen disciplinary attachment (Readings 1996). If in some instances such initiatives falter, they can still challenge mindsets, and it is worth remembering that getting things wrong can be productive—as arguably was true of dependency theory.

Except for a scattering of dissidents at the margins, however, such moves have been uncommon in international relations. The discipline's assurance that the main issues of international politics can be tackled from within its own corpus has been too strong for this. Leaving aside the mostly selective trafficking with globalization, international relations has not found it necessary to have dialogue with other discourses about the international. Yet the enabling potentialities of border-crossing can hardly be doubted—most of all perhaps regarding other knowledges. One pertinent study, for instance, examines how the poor see and engage with the state on an everyday basis (Corbridge et al. 2005); another addresses the politics of performance in Asia and Africa (Strauss and Cruise O'Brien 2007). The costs of nonengagement are strikingly demonstrated by returning to the mutual "stand-off" that prevails between international relations and development studies. Largely as a result, I would argue, development has not been seen as a crucial constituent of the international order. Yet, were it not for the promise of redemption held out by development, neoliberalism could never have become international ideology.

We are left with the question of where the critic of disciplinary international relations might position him or herself. There are weighty arguments that working for change involves targeting the mainstream international relations constituency because this is where power resides. On one account, potentially the most effective strategy is to identify and probe the cracks within the discourse that reveal self-doubt and uncertainty in the discipline (Marcus 1999, xi). Once inside the house of international relations, however, it is difficult to withstand the discipline's encaptive capacities. The risk is that new perspectives may be incorporated within the established knowledge order, thus blunting their radical edge (see, e.g., Weber 1999). There is also the possibility of establishing yet another school within international relations, but whether this is what is needed is problematic, to say the least. It is instructive given the arguments rehearsed in this chapter to consider Krishna's view (2001, 407) that a "postcolonial IR is an oxymoron—a contradiction in terms. To decolonize IR is to deschool oneself from the discipline in its current dominant manifestations."

Alternatively, the critic might position him- or herself at the margins of the discipline or outside it, making occasional forays into its heartland. The problem with critiques so situated is not only that they are unlikely to have much purchase on orthodox thinking, but that the chances of getting the discipline right will be much reduced because their in-house knowledge base will be poorer. Of course it is unlikely that critics will make decisions about their positionality in such a rational manner. Rather they will gravitate each way, depending on what excites their curiosity, how they write, and the company they keep. This is probably for the best, as the discipline needs critics both inside and outside. Moreover, as the international comes increasingly to reside within societies—as it surely will—knowledge debates about its politics will less and less be confined within a single discipline, whatever the claims made in its name.

REFERENCES

AMIN, S. 1989. *Eurocentrism*, trans. R. Moore. London: Zed Books.

ANGHIE, A. 2005. *Imperialism, Sovereignty and the Making of International Law*. Cambridge: Cambridge University Press.

BARKAWI, T., and LAFFEY, M. 2002. Retrieving the imperial: empire and international relations. *Millennium: Journal of International Relations*, 31: 109–27.

BLEIKER, R. 1997. Forget IR theory. *Alternatives*, 22: 57–85.

BULL, H., and WATSON, A. (eds.) 1984. *The Expansion of International Society*. Oxford: Clarendon Press.

CALHOUN, C. 2004. A world of emergencies: fear, intervention, and the limits of cosmopolitan order. *Canadian Review of Sociology and Anthropology*, 41: 373–95.

CHATTERJEE, P. 1985. *Nationalist Thought and the Colonial World: A Derivative Discourse?* New Delhi: Zed Books.

—— 2004. *The Politics of the Governed: Reflections on Popular Politics in Most of the World.* New York: Columbia University Press.

COLES, A., and DEFERT, A. (eds.) 1998. *The Anxiety of Interdisciplinarity.* London: BACKless Books in association with Black Dog.

CORBRIDGE, S., WILLIAMS, G., SRIVASTAVA, M., and VÉRON, R. 2005. *Seeing the State: Governance and Governmentality in India.* Cambridge: Cambridge University Press.

DARBY, P. (ed.) 1997. *At the Edge of International Relations: Postcolonialism, Gender, and Dependency.* London: Pinter.

—— 2006. Security, spatiality, and suffering. *Alternatives*, 31: 453–73.

DAS, V. 2002. Violence and translation. Pp. 205–9 in *Sarai Reader 02: The Cities of Everyday Life*, ed. R. Vesudevan, R. Sundaram, J. Bagchi, M. Narula, G. Lovink, and S. Sengupta. Delhi: Centre for the Study of Developing Societies.

DOTY, R. L. 1996. *Imperial Encounters: The Politics of Representation in North–South Relations.* Minneapolis: University of Minnesota Press.

HARDT, M., and NEGRI, A. 2000. *Empire.* Cambridge, Mass.: Harvard University Press.

HOVEY, R. 2004. Critical pedagogy and international studies: reconstructing knowledge through dialogue with the subaltern. *International Relations*, 18: 241–54.

INAYATULLAH, N., and BLANEY, D. L. 2004. *International Relations and the Problem of Difference.* New York: Routledge.

JONES, B. G. (ed.) 2006. *Decolonizing International Relations.* Lanham, Md.: Rowman and Littlefield.

KECK, M. E., and SIKKINK, K. 1998. *Activists beyond Borders: Advocacy Networks in International Politics.* Ithaca, NY: Cornell University Press.

KLEIN, J. T. 1990. *Interdisciplinarity: History, Theory, and Practice.* Detroit: Wayne State University Press.

KRISHNA, S. 2001. Race, amnesia, and the education of international relations. *Alternatives*, 26: 401–24.

KRISTEVA, J. 1991. *Strangers to Ourselves*, trans. L. Roudiez. New York: Columbia University Press.

LONG, D., and SCHMIDT, B. C. (eds.) 2005. *Imperialism and Internationalism in the Discipline of International Relations.* Albany, NY: State University of New York Press.

MAGNUSSON, W., and SHAW, K. (eds.) 2003. *A Political Space: Reading the Global through Clayoquot Sound.* Minneapolis: University of Minnesota Press.

MARCUS, G. 1999. Foreword. Pp. vii–xv in *Cultures of Insecurity: States, Communities, and the Production of Danger*, ed. J. Weldes, M. Laffey, H. Gusterson, and R. Duvall. Minneapolis: University of Minnesota Press.

MAZRUI, A. A. 1967. *Towards a Pax Africana: A Study of Ideology and Ambition.* Chicago: University of Chicago Press.

Millennium: Journal of International Studies. 1996. Special issue on poverty. 25: 521–779.

MITCHELL, T. 2002. *Rule of Experts: Egypt, Techno-Politics, Modernity.* Berkeley: University of California Press.

NANDY, A. 1983. *The Intimate Enemy: Loss and Recovery of Self under Colonialism.* Delhi: Oxford University Press.

——1987. *Traditions, Tyranny, and Utopias: Essays in the Politics of Awareness*. New Delhi: Oxford University Press.

NEUMAN, S. G. 1998. *International Relations Theory and the Third World*. London: Macmillan.

NOSSAL K. R. 2001. Tales that textbooks tell: ethnocentricity and diversity in American introductions to international relations. Pp. 167–86 in *International Relations—Still an American Social Science? Toward Diversity in International Thought*, ed. R. M. A. Crawford and D. S. L. Jarvis. Albany, NY: State University of New York Press.

NYE, J. S. 2004. *Soft Power: The Means to Success in World Politics*. New York: Public Affairs.

READINGS, B. 1996. *The University in Ruins*. Cambridge, Mass.: Harvard University Press.

RUGGIE, J. G. 1994. At home abroad, abroad at home: international liberalisation and domestic stability in the new world economy. *Millennium: Journal of International Studies*, 24: 507–26.

SALTER, B. 2002. *Barbarians and Civilization in International Relations*. Sterling, Va.: Pluto Press.

SHAW, K. S. 2002. Indigeneity and the international. *Millennium: Journal of International Studies*, 31: 55–81.

STRAUSS, J. C., and CRUISE O'BRIEN, D. B. (eds.) 2007. *Staging Politics: Power and Performance in Asia and Africa*. London: I. B. Tauris.

SYLVESTER, C. 2000. *Producing Women and Progress in Zimbabwe: Narratives of Identity and Work from the 1980s*. Portsmouth, NH: Heinemann.

TESCHKE, B. 2003. *The Myth of 1648: Class, Geopolitics, and the Making of Modern International Relations*. New York: Verso.

TODOROV, T. 1984. *The Conquest of America: The Question of the Other*, trans. R. Howard. New York: Harper and Row.

——1995. *The Morals of History*, trans. A. Waters. Minneapolis: University of Minnesota Press.

WEBER, C. 1999. IR: the resurrection or new frontiers of incorporation. *European Journal of International Relations*, 5: 435–50.

YEW, L. 2003. *The Disjunctive Empire of International Relations*. Aldershot: Ashgate.

PART III

MAJOR THEORETICAL PERSPECTIVES

CHAPTER 6

ECLECTIC THEORIZING IN THE STUDY AND PRACTICE OF INTERNATIONAL RELATIONS

PETER KATZENSTEIN

RUDRA SIL

The prescriptions directly derived from a single image [of international relations] are incomplete because they are based upon partial analyses. The partial quality of each image sets up a tension that drives one toward inclusion of the others...One is led to search for the inclusive nexus of causes.

(Waltz 1959, 229–30)

FOR most of the past three decades, international relations scholarship has typically been embedded in discrete research traditions, each proclaimed by its adherents to be either inherently superior or flexible enough to be able to subsume the others. Competition among discrete research traditions is certainly one motor for intellectual vitality within a given tradition of international relations. However, vitality within particular traditions does not necessarily constitute a basis for progress for the field of international relations as a whole (Elman and Elman 2003). As Gunther Hellmann (2002, 3) notes: "although the sort of professionalization which Waltzian 'realists' and Wendtian 'constructivists' have helped to bring about in international relations has rightly and widely been hailed as a blessing, it must not be mistaken for intellectual progress."

The editor of *Perspectives in Politics*, one of the two leading journals of the American Political Science Association, writes about the field from a highly informed perspective:

the standard IR article consists of pushing a huge rock of theory up a steep hill, in order to roll it down to smash a few pebbles of fact at the bottom. That is, the modal manuscript starts by outlining the three standard theories: realism, liberalism, constructivism (sometimes subdivided into neo-realism, neo-liberalism, and so on). Articles then diverge slightly—some seek to show that these apparently different theories can really be combined to show X; others seek to show that one of the theories is right and the other two are wrong, as evidenced by an explanation of X; a few argue that none of the three quite suffices to explain X, so we need a new theory (or more frequently, a variant of one of the old ones).

(Hochschild 2005, 11)

The sound editorial advice proffered was to eliminate paradigms, to focus attention on a central question, and to engage that question fruitfully—that is, to follow the road of problem-driven rather than paradigm-driven research. Indeed, a growing number of scholars, albeit still a minority, have been self-consciously forgoing metatheoretical and methodological battles in favor of approaches that explicitly seek to explore the interfaces between, and build bridges across, problematics and analyses originally constructed within seemingly incommensurable research traditions (Bernstein et al. 2000; Makinda 2000; Sil and Doherty 2000; Dow 2004; Suh, Katzenstein, and Carlson 2004; Zürn and Checkel 2005).

Because research traditions are typically founded on metatheoretical principles that are distinct from those informing competing traditions, each intrinsically favors some types of scholarly endeavors over others, as evident in the selection and framing of research puzzles, the representation and interpretation of relevant empirical observations, the specification of evidentiary standards, and the attention to certain causal mechanisms at the expense of others. Given the lack of a definitive consensus on such fundamental issues, this chapter calls for the accommodation of eclectic modes of scholarship that trespass deliberately and liberally across competing research traditions with the intention of defining and exploring substantive problems in original, creative ways, selectively drawing upon a variety of existing and emerging research traditions, eclectic scholarship is in a position to contribute to both a deeper understanding of a critical problem and theoretical progress for international relations as a whole. What we refer to as analytic eclecticism is distinguished by the fact that *features of analyses in theories initially embedded in*

*separate research traditions can be separated from their respective foundations, trans-
lated meaningfully, and recombined as part of an original permutation of concepts,
methods, analytics, and empirics.*

Our conception of analytic eclecticism is premised on a pragmatist foundation
that eschews metatheoretical debates and encourages scholarly practices aimed at
generating creative forms of knowledge that engage adherents of different traditions in meaningful conversations about substantive problems in international
life. Analytic eclecticism also suggests a reflexive process aimed at generating fresh
theoretical perspectives that have practical value beyond the academe, speaking to
both the normative and policy debates in which actors in international relations
are enmeshed. This does not suggest that anything goes or that established research
traditions need to be dismantled. Rather, following Albert Hirschman (1981), we
note that self-conscious "trespassing" across research traditions can enable us to
make better use of the innovative and creative analyses produced within these
traditions in the process of recognizing socially important problems and building
interpretations and hypotheses. Even if not especially parsimonious, such scholarship can be analytically coherent, intellectually interesting, and responsive to
normative concerns and policy debates surrounding these problems.

Below, we first outline a pragmatist view of social knowledge in which intellectual
progress is understood as expanding the possibilities for dialogue and creative
experimentation. In the following section, we elaborate on the definition of analytic
eclecticism, identifying its distinctive characteristics and payoffs vis-à-vis those
of preexisting research traditions. We then consider a small sample of scholarship in international relations that illustrates the meaning and value of analytical
eclecticism with specific reference to issues of international security and political
economy. We conclude that alongside, and in dialogue with, scholarship produced
in specific research traditions, analytic eclecticism is a necessary and valuable asset
in enabling the discipline of international relations to evolve beyond recurrent
metatheoretical debates and to hold forth some promise for having meaningful
practical significance beyond the academe.

1 A PRAGMATIST VIEW OF PROGRESS

Much research in international relations has been founded on a positivist conception of social knowledge. Positivists generally gravitate toward a view of social
inquiry in which patterns of human behavior are presumed to reflect *objective* principles, laws, or regularities that exist above and beyond the subjective orientations
of actors and scholars, and that can be deduced, inferred, or falsified through the

rigorous application of replicable methods and logics across a specified universe of cases. A positivist image of scientific progress generally suggests some common notion of an objective reality that can be approximated with increasingly greater accuracy through the application of increasingly more sophisticated techniques in conjunction with theories that explain a larger slice of reality than their predecessors did (Laudan 1996, 21). The implication is that the accumulation of knowledge is desirable, possible, and indeed, inevitable.

However, positivism has many variants, and the variations are significant enough to preclude consensus on the indicators of intellectual progress. Empiricists, for example, assign priority to observation and measurement and proceed to generate inferences, with the expectation that the standardized application of replicable methods will generate progressively better descriptions and explanations of specific phenomena. Although quantitative and qualitative scholars generally constitute separate communities with distinct practices (Mahoney and Goertz 2006), empiricists in both camps encourage standardized research techniques and gauge progress in terms of the discipline and consistency with which these techniques are applied to interpret empirical observations and replicate empirical findings (King, Keohane, and Verba 1994; Brady and Collier 2004; Bennett and Elman 2006; Klotz and Lynch 2007). By contrast, what Ian Shapiro and Alexander Wendt (2005, 24–8) refer to as "logicism" derives from Carl Hempel's formulation (1966) of the deductive-nomological model, with the emphasis placed on the deduction of testable causal propositions from axiomatic covering laws. In a logicist view of social science, temporal and intellectual priority is assigned to the construction of concepts and the articulation of assumptions that inform internally consistent theoretical axioms from which predictive and explanatory claims are logically derived (Bueno de Mesquita 1985). Thus, even among positivists, there is no agreement on what matters most for generating and measuring intellectual progress in a given field of research.

In contrast to positivist research traditions, other traditions proceed from a subjectivist conception of social reality as fluid, viewed through the particular lenses actors rely upon to make sense of their experiences and social relations. Such a stance precludes general explanatory theory altogether. Instead, it favors context-bound interpretative approaches by focusing on the meanings actors attach to ordinary practices within their immediate social environments, as evident in Clifford Geertz's conception (1973) of "thick description" or Hans Gadamer's articulation (1976) of hermeneutics. To the extent that the term "theory" is in evidence at all, it is usually critical theory, which privileges critique and praxis over the search for explanation or understanding, as evident in the writings of Frankfurt School philosophers such as Herbert Marcuse and Jürgen Habermas (cf. Held 1980). In international relations, varying degrees of subjectivism are evident in critical perspectives that seek to reconnect empirical inquiry and normative reflection

(Reus-Smit 2008; see also Luke 2003; Haacke 2005) and in variants of constructivism that emphasize discourse analysis (Hopf 1998; Neumann 2002; Wæver 2004; see also Checkel 2007). Here, too, the differences between alternative nonpositivist positions is not as important for our argument as the common a priori rejection of a clear-cut distinction between interpretation and explanation (Shapiro 2005, 2) along with a deep skepticism about the very possibility of cumulative progress in social scientific analysis.

In between these different strands of positivism and subjectivism, pragmatism may be considered an ideal-typical center (Sil 2000b; see also Hellmann 2002). Far from representing a residual category, a pragmatist perspective is predicated on co-herent philosophical principles about what kinds of knowledge are worth pursuing, in what manner, and with what aims. Pragmatism has its roots in the late nineteenth and early twentieth centuries in the philosophical positions articulated by Charles Pierce, William James, and John Dewey as well as in the symbolic–interactionist view of social action as formulated by George Herbert Mead. Following a period of marginalization precipitated by the behavioral revolution and the quest for grand theory, pragmatism has been revived and carried forward by Richard Rorty (1982; 1999) and other contemporary philosophers who have offered nuanced critiques of positivism without surrendering to relativism or subjectivism (e.g. Bernstein 1983; 1992; Putnam 1981; 2002). Although multiple strands of pragmatism have emerged from quite different intellectual milieus and philosophical perspectives (Joas 1993), they collectively embrace some common understandings about the nature, limits, and uses of social inquiry. These understandings suggest a different conception of progress from what is assumed in positivist research traditions, one that stresses the quality and scope of dialogue among social scientists and the proximity of this dialogue to socially important normative and policy issues.

One common theme has to do with an aversion to excessively abstract ontolo-gies and rigid analytic principles in favor of useful interpretations that can be deployed to cope with concrete problems. Following James (1997, 94), pragmatists seek to bypass "metaphysical disputes that otherwise might be interminable," and instead "try and interpret each notion by tracing its respective consequences" in concrete situations. Given the complexity of social life and the heterogeneity of social contexts, covering laws or general theories are viewed by pragmatists such as Dewey as merely fleeting efforts to exert "control" over the real world (Cochran 2002, 527). At the same time, in contrast to subjectivists, pragmatists are concerned with the *consequences* of various truth claims for resolving pressing social problems (Bohman 2002). The making of practically relevant knowledge cannot wait for the emergence of a definitive consensus on methodological procedures or axiomatic principles that may reveal "final" truths. As Hellmann (2002, 8) puts it: "Due to the necessity to act today we cannot afford to wait until we 'know' The Truth." Thus, knowledge needs to be formulated and evaluated within fixed timeframes in terms of its immediate practical consequences for addressing specific empirical and conceptual problems in discrete contexts (Johnson 2006, 227).[1]

Related to this is a second theme in which the production of knowledge is seen as a process of integrating different aspects of "knowing" and "doing" through creative experimentation. For Dewey (1920, 121), experimental science "means a certain kind of intelligently conducted doing; it ceases to be contemplative and becomes in a true sense practical." The kind of experimentation pragmatists encourage is not the controlled experiment scientists rely on to validate or falsify cause–effect relationships but rather the creative exploration of how varied stocks of knowledge can be adapted and integrated with new knowledge in different permutations over time to resolve certain types of problems. "We take a piece of acquired knowledge into a concrete situation, and the results we get constitute a new piece of knowledge, which we carry over into our next encounter with our environment" (Dewey 1926; cf. Menand 1997, xxiii). The aim, according to Hellmann (2003b, 149), is to develop a "holistic" approach to problems "by combining experience and intelligence in creative ways to come up with solutions to the puzzles at hand." This does not preclude theoretical knowledge. It does, however, require that theoretical knowledge be sufficiently close to the experience of real-world actors who are themselves trying to match the vocabularies and interpretations at their disposal with their normative commitments and their successive encounters with real-world problems.

A third theme has to do with the centrality of dialogue among a more inclusive and democratically structured community of scholars. Pragmatists view the production of knowledge as a social project and put a high premium on a fluid and open process of communication and deliberation among all who are interested in a given problem (Joas 1993; Menand 1997). This perspective is captured by Rorty (1982, 165), who views pragmatism as "the doctrine that there are no constraints on inquiry save conversational ones—no wholesale constraints derived from the nature of the objects, or of the mind, or of language, but only those retail constraints provided by the remarks of our fellow-inquirers." Pragmatists understand that knowledge claims are offered and explored within the context of scholarly communities, but they have a distinct preference for more inclusive and egalitarian communities in which open dialogue is seen as facilitating and legitimizing whatever consensus emerges in relation to specific problems.[2] Moreover, the emphasis on open deliberation does not constitute only a procedural commitment aimed at

---

[1] Thus, for scholars adopting historical approaches to the study of international relations but encountering contending historical narratives, a pragmatist perspective suggests continuous engagement with different strands of historiography in the process of identifying what historical "facts" can be tentatively agreed upon so that these may be employed in constructing solutions to contemporary problems (Isacoff 2006).

[2] In this context, a pragmatist view of knowledge has much in common with modes of "deliberative democracy" that emphasize participation and engagement among informed actors for the purpose of generating consensus on collective decisions or shared standards of governance (Elster 1998, 5; see also Bohman 1999; Knight and Johnson 1999; Buchanan and Keohane 2006).

improving the quality of knowledge available to policy-makers; it is intended to reduce moral disagreement and facilitate the negotiation of consensual norms that can support the legitimation of institutions governing human behaviors (Buchanan and Keohane 2006).

A fourth unifying theme relates to the relationship between individuals and the different social milieus in which they are situated. Mead's symbolic interactionism—where the self is constructed and reconstructed in continuous dialogue with society—provides a foundation for a dialectical understanding of the multifaceted relationships between agency and structure, between individuals and the patterned social relations in which they are embedded. This flexibility is one reason why pragmatism, especially Mead's work, has been invoked in support of quite different intellectual perspectives. For some, the role of rational, intelligent agents in the deliberative process not only makes rational-choice theory consistent with the spirit of pragmatist inquiry, but also compensates for the weaknesses of formulations preoccupied with the analysis of institutions as entities in their own right (Knight and Johnson 1999). Josh Whitford (2002) rejects the linkage between pragmatism and rational-choice theory, noting that the stark dualism of means and ends in the latter is not consistent with a pragmatist emphasis on the integration of thought and action, of knowledge and experience. Indeed, for Peter Haas and Ernst Haas (2002, 586), the significance of pragmatism lies precisely in the rationale it provides for the role of institutions in generating shared concepts and meanings that can aid in the production of a new consensual discourse. And, for Wendt (1999), Mead's symbolic interactionism draws attention to processes of collective identity formation in relation to actors' identities, actions, and social environments. To us, the linkages between pragmatism and these varied perspectives suggest an open-ended approach to processes and mechanisms that cuts across levels of analysis and connects actors' individual self-conceptions and common world-views to evolving social institutions.[3]

These tenets suggest that, while pragmatists and positivists share a broad commitment to uncovering "truth" that can be of use to policy-makers (Chernoff 2005), pragmatists reject the application of standardized methods and techniques for the purpose of definitively verifying or falsifying truth claims. For they regard all such claims as tentative, providing at best "a temporary resting place for inquiry" (Cochran 2002, 527). Similarly, the rejection of a clear separation between judgments of facts and judgments of values (Putnam 2002) is something that pragmatists can, in principle, share with critical theorists who reject the notion of a value-free science protected by rigid structures of institutionalized knowledge (Bohman 2002; White 2004). But critical theory proceeds to the conclusion that

---

[3] This aspect of pragmatism has much in common with "structurationism" insofar as the latter's flexible ontology allows for an entire range of processes through which individual actions and choices can shape, transform, and conform to material and ideal structures (Giddens 1984; Sewell 1992; Sil 2000a).

all knowledge claims need to be treated skeptically because of their political implications. In contrast, pragmatists call for dialogue across communities of scholars for the purpose of incrementally reducing moral disagreement and uncertainty and generating consensual norms and standards for social and international life, as evident in Allen Buchanan and Robert Keohane's calls (2006) for a "complex standard" for legitimizing global governance institutions.

In sum, a pragmatist perspective points to a modest, nonlinear view of progress that depends on the practical utility of various knowledge claims in the collective problem-solving efforts of open communities connected through encompassing dialogues. For pragmatists, the markers of intellectual progress are not the extent of theory cumulation, the level of technical sophistication, or the success of replication efforts in the eyes of a given research community. What counts are the consequences of scholarship for the quality of communication among all who express concern with a given problem and for the possibilities for creatively reconfiguring particular stocks of knowledge to generate new ways of framing real-world problems and devising potential solutions for those problems. A pragmatist conception of intellectual progress thus paves the way for a deeper appreciation of the contributions of analytic eclecticism to the study—and practice—of international relations.

2 WHAT ANALYTIC ECLECTICISM IS—AND IS NOT

We concur with Robert Dahl (2004) that, because politics encompasses an extraordinarily complex set of phenomena involving multiple types of units connected through a wide range of relations, understanding this complexity initially requires a more specialized examination of particular elements, institutions, and actors. The analytic accentuation and empirical focus facilitated by the boundaries of research traditions can be intellectually fruitful, enabling scholars with similar assumptions, vocabularies, standards, and skill sets to examine more thoroughly selected aspects of a problem. Moreover, debates among adherents of multiple research traditions can generate progress within each tradition as scholars respond to critiques and alternative knowledge claims generated in competing traditions.

However, viewing social inquiry solely through the lens of competing research traditions risks excessive compartmentalization of knowledge unless some effort is made to illuminate connections and complementarities between the various problems, interpretations, and mechanisms posited by different research traditions. As Shapiro (2005, 184) notes, because scholarship embedded in a single approach reflects the theoretical priors privileged by that approach, social inquiry is inherently restricted to those aspects of the social world that can be readily problematized employing the preferred conceptual apparatus and methodological tool kit of that approach. Thus, while the debates among research traditions may generate refinements within each tradition, they also serve to block off the sort of communication and intellectual versatility needed to recognize potentially relevant conceptual and empirical connections across analyses developed in separate traditions. In security studies, for example, articles in each of two leading journals—*Journal of Conflict Resolution* and *International Security*—rarely acknowledge scholarship produced in the other, even when considering the same topic (Bennett, Barth, and Rutherford 2003). Moreover, there are very large intellectual, financial, professional, and psychological investments that go into producing and sustaining a research tradition, and these investments militate against addressing important aspects of problems that are not easily represented in the conceptual apparatus and analytic frameworks privileged in that tradition. As Friedrich Kratochwil (2003, 125) puts it: "The desire to win, to stand one's ground, perhaps not surprisingly, is most of the time stronger than the genuine search for an acceptable solution to a problem."

To overcome these barriers to intellectual engagement, to gain depth in insight and improve the accuracy of observations and, especially, to make research more relevant to the practical and normative concerns of real-world actors, it is intellectually productive to reconsider a problem from the vantage point of a "multiperspectival mode of social inquiry" (Bohman 2002, 502). This is where the very advantages that enable adherents of a research tradition to proclaim progress become *disadvantages* in terms of exploring real-world puzzles that force scholars to confront the question of the empirical accuracy and the practical and normative relevance of their work rather than justify their work primarily on methodological or epistemological grounds (Grofman 2001). The benefits of embedding scholarship within research traditions—the cultivation of a recognizable professional identity, efficient communication based on shared stocks of knowledge and skills, a common set of evaluative standards linked to explicit methodological assumptions, and the psychological and institutional support provided by fellow members— need to be sacrificed for the purpose of recognizing and framing problems in ways that more closely approximate the complexity of the social world and that can be explored through different permutations of concepts, data, methods, and interpretative logics taken from separate research traditions. As distinct scholarly communities seek to make their intellectual products relevant to policy-makers and other actors, eclectic scholarship enables these communities to recognize related aspects of a problem and to move toward richer interpretative frameworks that selectively integrate artificially segmented schemes and logics initially devised in separate research traditions. The emergent theoretical framework, whatever its limitations with regard to such scientific ideals as parsimony and replicability, comes to constitute "a tool for problem-solving rather than an instrument for truth-production" (Hellmann 2002, 7).

It is true that moving between research traditions founded on competing on-tological and epistemological principles runs some risk of introducing concep-tual fuzziness (Johnson 2002). However, as Ted Hopf (2007) notes, the analytic foundations of given traditions may not be as far apart as is often assumed, and these foundations can be adjusted or bracketed so as to enable the translation, comparison, and integration of substantive theories and narratives developed in different research traditions. So long as there is clarity with regard to concepts and definitions, differences in metatheoretical postulates do not inherently pre-clude recognition of complementarities and linkages in *substantive* processes in international life, even if these are normally represented in distinct theoretical vocabularies and cast at different levels of analysis (Sil 2000a; 2004; Katzenstein and Sil 2004; Parsons 2007). Eclectic approaches cannot ignore or substitute for the intellectual products generated within separate traditions. However, by expanding the repertoire of assumptions, analytic tools, theoretical concepts, methodological devices, and empirical data, analytic eclecticism allows for the development of complex explanations that reveal how different kinds of causal mechanisms and processes might relate to each other.

Analytic eclecticism should not be confused with theoretical synthesis or the building of a unified theory. Although some have used the term "synthesis" to capture the kind of "pragmatic fusion" (Hellmann 2003a, 149) among diverse ap-proaches that we associate with analytic eclecticism, a genuinely synthetic theoreti-cal framework would require the dismantling of existing research traditions and the construction of a new unified system of concepts, assumptions, and analytic prin-ciples that can be deployed over a broader range of problems. Analytic eclecticism, by contrast, is focused on a given problem and assumes the continued existence of, and growing engagement between, competing research traditions. At the same time, analytic eclecticism is more than the kind of augmentation of claims implied in Andrew Moravcsik's understanding (2003) of theoretical synthesis (contested by Hellmann 2003b) in which the rigorous use of standardized data-sets and replicable methods allows for the testing of different components of a complex theory. The kind of synthetic theory that can be broken down into discrete components, each to be tested separately, is not without value, but this is not the same thing as eclectic theorizing intended to illuminate the complex interactions among processes and mechanisms that bear on a given problem.

The value-added of eclectic scholarship thus lies not in neglecting existing re-search traditions but in self-consciously engaging them in pursuit of empirical and conceptual connections that recognize the complexity of international life in ways that no single research tradition can. Indeed, eclecticism that is inattentive to the benefits and pitfalls of approaching problems in line with the specifications of existing research traditions can lead to uncompelling, ad hoc arguments that are often unintelligible to other scholars and add little to the work being done in a more systematic fashion within distinct research communities. Eclectic scholarship that *does* engage existing research traditions can help generate a wider range of alternative combinations of analytic and empirical components; and these components can then be brought to bear in redefining and solving problems of practical and normative import, even if these components are initially formulated in separate research traditions. For intellectual progress to be made in the social sciences, it is as important to be aware of the menu of possibilities as it is to engage in deterministic or probabilistic analyses. Analytic eclecticism is oriented toward recognizing those empirical and moral possibilities that elude the grasp of the theoretical frameworks constructed in existing research traditions while still continuing to recognize and engage those traditions in the hope of expanding the scope and quality of dialogue concerning practical problems in international life.[4]

3 ECLECTICISM IN INTERNATIONAL RELATIONS SCHOLARSHIP

The notion that different approaches are necessary to make sense of problems in international relations is not entirely new, even among scholars traditionally identified with one or another research tradition. We have already quoted from Kenneth Waltz's *Man, the State, and War* (1959); writing in a realist perspective, Hans Morgenthau also noted, long ago, the limitations of scholarship aimed at defining the boundaries of particular intellectual perspectives. Most theories of international relations, he argued,

provide a respectable protective shield behind which members of the academic community may engage in noncontroversial theoretical pursuits. International relations in our period of history are by their very nature controversial. They require decisions concerning the purposes of the nation and affecting its chances for physical survival. By dealing with the subject matter but not with the issues underlying these decisions, a theory can appear to contribute to the rationality of the decision without actually doing so.

(Morgenthau 1970, 247)[5]

---

[4] This intellectual move is also mirrored in economic theory in recent calls for "structured pluralism" (Dow 2004), with the existence of separate schools of thought providing a provisional structure and language for the development of communication *within* research communities while also creating new lines of communication *across* these communities. Moving beyond the academe, a similar logic is also apparent in the world of business, where the success of the most dynamic firms depends on improving "dialogue within and across groups of individuals with proximate knowledge of a particular problem" (Helper, MacDuffie, and Sabel 2000, 484), and in the observation that firms that pursue "combinative capabilities" (Kogut and Zander 1992, 391) are better suited to experiment and recombine different types of knowledge to cope with changing market opportunities than firms relying on existing stocks of knowledge that have produced their current capabilities.

[5] We thank Ido Oren for alerting us to this reference.

Morgenthau would not have been surprised that, at the very time at which the cold war ended, international relations scholars were consumed by the latest iteration of an old controversy. The debate between neorealism (or structural realism) and neoliberalism (or institutional liberalism) absorbed most of the attention of scholars, even though neither approach had anticipated this revolutionary transformation in world politics or was able to offer consistent advice on how to think coherently about a world transformed. Paradigmatic debate was drowning out problem-focused research at a pivotal moment in history.

In the remainder of this section we review a small sample of recent international relations scholarship on questions of security and political economy that we see as eschewing such paradigmatic debate and putting forward a more eclectic perspective. We do not view these examples as a comprehensive review of eclectic scholarship in international relations; nor do we assume that the substantive narratives or claims contained in any of these studies are necessarily "correct." We do, however, view these as exemplars of eclectic scholarship that prevents us from getting stuck in recurrent debates over metatheoretical issues that defy resolution. Such eclectic scholarship holds forth the promise of making scholarly conversations more productive and perhaps leading to purposeful actions that help address concrete dilemmas in international life.

3.1 Eclectic Perspectives on National Security

Recent changes within realist theorizing (Rose 1998; Walt 2003) have created space for eclectic approaches to the problem of national security, a subject once thought to lie entirely within the domain of realism. Henry Nau's (2002) combination of balance of power and balance of identity theorizing offers insights into the nature of US foreign policy and, by implication, into how to conceptualize the direction of balancing over time. The United States' self-image as an exceptional and unique part of the "New World" sharply divides it from the rest of the world, which, for reasons of power, wealth, and myriad other factors, seeks ever closer engagement. The history of US foreign policy records a continuous battle between internationalists and isolationists, within both realist and liberal orientations. The result is seen in recurring swings between competing coalitions that reflect the temporary victory of one camp or the other, or unstable coalitions between the two. As a result, the relations between the United States and the world rarely prove unproblematic for long. Thus, Nau's eclectic integration of traditional balancing logics and balancing in national identity points to a host of new questions that would normally elude sparse formulations of neorealist or neoliberal theory.

David Kang's (2007, 11–12) analysis of China's rise is also designed to search for "interconnections between causal factors, rather than isolating one factor at the expense of others." Kang asks why East Asia, with the possible exception of Japan, is not so much balancing against as bandwagoning with China. This question clearly speaks to the core concerns of realists, but an adequate response requires consideration of ideas, broadly conceived to include preferences, intentions, beliefs, norms, identities, and assessments of the world. Kang's interpretation, while taking account of both absolute and relative capabilities as well as domestic politics, places great emphasis on shared ideas about China's relationship to the East Asian region in the past and future. Given that a weak and fragmented China has historically created problems for its neighbors, whereas a prosperous China has usually benefited its neighbors, a shared East Asian understanding has emerged over the centuries, that China holds a special position in the region and that Chinese policies are geared toward getting richer *with* its neighbors, rather than at their expense. The practical implication of this analysis is that China needs to be understood as a status quo and not as a revisionist state in international affairs. Right or wrong, Kang's complex interpretation challenges existing theories—whether realist, liberal, or constructivist—that focus on certain factors at the expense of others in characterizing China's rise as problematic for stability in East Asia.

This treatment resonates strongly with Jason Lyall's (2005) analysis of post-Communist Russia. Lyall's approach engages, and seeks to refine, the work of Randall Schweller (1998; 2006), who, following a long tradition of realist scholarship, has emphasized the significance of revisionist states. Lyall argues convincingly that the hard-and-fast distinction between status quo and revisionist power actually refers to fixed identities that generate powerful predictions. Put differently, very heavy lifting in this version of realist theory is actually done by a concealed identity variable. This is not to deny the importance of absolute and relative capabilities in Schweller's work as much as to reveal its unacknowledged, eclectic character. For the categories of "revisionist" and "status quo" ultimately denote understandings of the role that states are seen as filling in the society of states. That is, they suggest important social dynamics in the relations among states, dynamics that cannot be conceptualized in a realist conception of the international system. In both Kang's and Lyall's analyses, the explanations offered would not be possible without the prior conceptualization of revisionist states and their significance for conflict or stability in international affairs. At the same time, the originality of their arguments depends on the willingness to sacrifice parsimony in order to consider a number of concepts and facts that are central to a more comprehensive grasp of the issues at hand.

Robert Jervis (2005) inquires into what he regards as perhaps the most striking change in conceptions of security in contemporary world politics, the fact that war has become unthinkable among the most developed great powers in the world. While he acknowledges their respective weaknesses, Jervis's list of explanatory factors draws on each of the three main research traditions (Jervis 2005, 16–26): the norm of nonviolence and the shared identity among capitalist democracies, stressed by constructivist theories; the pacifying effects of democratic politics, economic interdependence, and joint membership in international organizations, emphasized by liberal theories; and the presence of external threat, American hegemony, and the pacifying effects of nuclear weapons, underscored by realist theories. He then offers (Jervis 2005, 26–9) what he calls a "synthetic interactive explanation . . . [that] reformulates and combines several factors," specifically three: the belief that conquest is difficult; the fact that war is very costly; and, rooted in the spread of democracy, shifts in identity that reflect a sharp decline in militarism, territorial disputes, and nationalism along with a far-reaching growth in value compatibility among the most advanced major powers. Jervis does not argue that these changes explain all world politics; far from it. Still his analysis of what he regards as the most astonishing change in world politics, the growth of a security community among its most developed great powers, is self-consciously eclectic in its recognition of the interactions among mechanisms typically conceptualized and deployed in separate research traditions.

3.2 Eclectic Perspectives on International Political Economy

Eclectic work has also contributed to progress in the field of international political economy (IPE). Following Robert Gilpin's seminal writing (1975), a generation of scholarship thought of IPE as being divided into three distinct traditions of scholarship: realist-mercantilist, liberal, and Marxist. This conceptualization has now become outdated thanks to recent work that not only cuts across the three camps but also incorporates new concepts and variables that were generally ignored in all three. This is powerfully evident in treatments of political economy that explicitly seek to add ideational factors to the traditional focus on state power in realist thought and on economic incentives in liberal thought.

One example is Rawi Abdelal's analysis (2001; see also Helleiner and Pickel 2005) of the radically different economic strategies of successor states of the former Soviet Union in the face of pervasive economic dependence on Russia. For Abdelal (2001, 13–18), realist and liberal explanations, although contributing to a comprehensive account of these states' choices, come up short in their efforts to make sense of post-Soviet economic strategies because their theoretical frameworks treat actor identity as exogenous. Abdelal sets out to rectify this situation by relying on the concept of economic nationalism to understand the divergent political choices evident in the economic strategies of the successor states. Nationalism gives policy a fundamental social purpose that relates to protecting and cultivating the nation. It engenders the sacrifices necessary to achieve societal goals. And it lengthens the time horizon of state and society (Abdelal 2001, 2). Taking these effects into account allows Abdelal not only to understand specific state choices but also to explain the variation across the paths traveled by post-Soviet successor states in engaging the international economy.

Leonard Seabrooke's (2006) inquiry into the social foundations of state financial power is eclectic in a different way, going beyond interactions between state and big business to incorporate the understandings and practices evident among marginal economic actors, specifically lower-income groups typically excluded from the "big end of town." Theories emphasizing factor endowments and institutional constraints and opportunities are too static to capture the complexity of this dynamic, for they do not recognize the significance of the social consensus that gives meaning to credit and money. Theories focusing on state capacity or the varieties of capitalism have also overlooked political and social dynamics that, Seabrooke argues, are central to a state's international power and the stability of national and international financial systems. Seabrooke thus focuses on the importance of *legitimacy* in economic life, referring to the political and economic practices, including those of lower-income groups, which endow a political order with a sense of rightness and fairness. Thus, positive government policies toward lower-income groups—such as lowering their tax burdens and enhancing their access to credit and property—are significant because they provide an important social foundation for a state's financial power. Such policies broaden and deepen the domestic pool of capital and encourage financial practices that return capital to the state in the form of added revenues and greater international clout. Case studies of early twentieth-century England and Germany and the late-twentieth-century United States and Japan offer compelling plausibility probes of this novel and eclectic approach.

In stressing the social nature of global finance, Timothy Sinclair's analysis (2005) of the politics of rating agencies complements existing rationalist theories of international political economy. Rationalists argue that in an era of financial globalization rating agencies more than banks are now deciding on creditworthiness, and states and corporations are both submitting to the judgments of these self-regulating agencies. In an environment of high uncertainty and risk, rating agencies thus give economic agents the transparent and impartial assessments of conditions that they need for a rational assessment of conditions and efficient allocation of scarce resources. Sinclair does not reject this rationalist account but seeks to enrich it with a deeper and more political understanding of the processes through which this knowledge is created and monitored. Rating agencies are not narrowly technical in the sense of providing to their clients and the general public only the condensation of massive amounts of data about natural market developments. They also offer interpretative frameworks that specify what constitutes proper economic conduct that should be rewarded by the flow of additional private investments. Rating agencies provide a store of expert knowledge that is authoritative but that may or may not be correct in the conventional understanding of the term. The fact that the major international rating agencies are all located in the United States is one important aspect of the character of the embedded knowledge networks they incorporate.

Finally, an eclectic perspective that integrates questions of security and political economy is evident in an emerging literature on the significance of *regions* in international affairs. Regions have been defined and analyzed within at least three separate research traditions (Katzenstein 2005, 6–13). Classical theories of geopolitics stress the material base of regions: For example, one argument posits that the nature of the terrain or the imperatives of land or sea power determine the overall shape of world politics. Ideational theories of geography insist that regions are not given but politically and culturally made: Not only are regions shaped by processes that separate economic cores from peripheries, but regional symbols act as instruments or labels designating the domination of specific places in the world by particular groups of people. Space, in ideational theories, is a social invention and practice. Finally, regions have also been analyzed from the perspective of behavioral theories of geography, with the variable of spatial distance treated as having a direct and statistically robust effect on actors' behaviors. Material, ideational, and behavioral theories of regions each offer important partial insights, but none independently provides a satisfactory account of how actors in international affairs define and understand regions or their place in them. Here is where eclectic analysis, supported by the inherent interdisciplinarity of geographical science, can open the door to more comprehensive frameworks that reveal the connections between variables or processes privileged by each of the three separate traditions. This is precisely what Katzenstein (2005) has sought to do in understanding and theorizing the differences between Europe and Asia in the context of the American "imperium."

4 CONCLUSION

The contribution of analytic eclecticism to intellectual progress does not depend on any specific criteria of rigor. Rather, it depends on expanding the scope and quality of communication among all concerned with a given problem, and in encouraging creative efforts to recognize, define, connect, and solve substantive problems in international life that are usually parsed in different ways in different research traditions and that have normative aspects that are often bracketed out in the name of a more "pure" science of international politics (Reus-Smit 2008). We are not arguing for the proliferation of research in which "anything goes" or in which there is little attention paid to relevant arguments developed within existing research traditions. Nor do we see eclectic approaches as indicative of caution through the hedging of one's bets (Therborn 2005, 325–6). To us eclecticism is both focused, in seeking out the best available answer for a given problem at any given time, and courageous, in pursuing intellectual engagements with diverse styles of thought and putting its wager unconditionally on the dialogical model of science. Moreover, because analytic eclecticism is also self-conscious in engaging separate research traditions, it is in a position to enhance the scope and quality of communication between research communities, revealing connections and complementarities across clusters of empirical puzzles, normative concerns, and theoretical interpretations. For the field of international relations writ large, "the achievement of most progress depends on continuing the conversation among all of us" (Haas and Haas 2002, 587).

A commitment to eclectic approaches does entail costs and risks. First, eclectic approaches lack the "protective belt" (Lakatos 1970) that can shield substantive analyses from questions about core epistemological and methodological assumptions; they also lack the standards and norms that enable research communities to reward individual contributions and proclaim some degree of internal progress. Secondly, eclectic approaches are likely to leave themselves open to a wider range of criticism motivated by standards and practices developed within the various research communities whose products are being disaggregated and selectively redeployed in a different type of analysis. Thirdly, eclectic analyses also share with attempts at theoretical synthesis the dangers of conceptual muddiness as they work with multiple analytic languages in conjunction with a wider range of empirics cast at different levels of generality (Johnson 2002). Fourthly, trafficking in more than one research tradition typically takes considerable time and effort, requiring scholars not only to read widely but also to engage in shifting "multilingual" conversations with diverse scholarly communities, each confidently speaking a single theoretical language that its members have been wedded to for their entire careers. These costs and risks do beg the question of whether the limited resources available for social scientific research should be expended on eclectic projects in the absence of prior indications of their utility and of the standards to which they may be held. As Stephen Sanderson (1987, 321) puts it in his critique of eclecticism: "Because the vast majority of these leads will not produce anything of value, to follow this strategy is to waste enormous amounts of time and energy. A better alternative...is to adopt the theoretical tradition that seems at the time most useful and to follow it as intensively as possible."

For better or worse, these concerns do not justify the marginalization of eclectic scholarship, especially considering the track record of the major research traditions in international relations. If anything, the benefits that accompany the production of scholarship within research traditions often lead also to an increasing gap between scholarly endeavors and the problems requiring attention in the real world. As Shapiro (2005, 2) has argued: "In discipline after discipline, the flight from reality has been so complete that the academics have all but lost sight of what they claim is their object of study." The fundamental problem of devising standardized indicators of "progress" for the social sciences as a whole remains as elusive as before, and devoting resources only to scholarship that is disciplined by the postulates and practices of separate research traditions serves only to perpetuate this problem. While analytic eclecticism does not resolve the issue, it does bypass it, enabling eclectic scholarship to recognize and evaluate what is going on in different research traditions concerned with different aspects of problems that may be, in empirical terms, very much intertwined. Moreover, by recognizing the complexity of real-world problems and the practical consequences of different strategies for addressing these problems, analytic eclecticism openly and directly embraces the often unacknowledged normative concerns animating scholarship (Reus-Smit 2008).[6] For this reason alone it is desirable to gamble at least *some* of our resources on the intuition that eclectic modes of analysis can advance our collective ability to communicate across the boundaries of research communities and, in the process, create greater space for experimenting with different permutations of concepts, theories, and empirics in relation to complex problems encountered in international life. Compared to the flaws of clashing dogmatisms, the flaws of analytical eclecticism are small indeed and well worth the costs (Hoffmann 2006, 11).

References

ABDELAL, R. 2001. *National Purpose in the World Economy: Post-Soviet States in Comparative Perspective*. Ithaca, NY: Cornell University Press.

BENNETT, A., BARTH, A., and RUTHERFORD, K. R. 2003. Do we preach what we practice? A survey of methods in political science journals and curricula. *PS: Political Science and Politics*, 36: 373–8.

—— and ELMAN, C. 2006. Complex causal relations and case study methods: the example of path dependence. *Political Analysis*, 14: 250–67.

BERNSTEIN, R. 1983. *Beyond Objectivism and Relativism: Science, Hermeneutics, and Praxis*. Philadelphia: University of Pennsylvania Press.

—— 1992. The resurgence of pragmatism. *Social Research*, 59: 813–40.

BERNSTEIN, S., LEBOW, R. N., STEIN, J. G., and WEBER, S. 2000. God gave physics the easy problems: adapting social science to an unpredictable world. *European Journal of International Relations*, 6: 43–76.

BOHMAN, J. 1999. Democracy as inquiry, inquiry as democratic: pragmatism, social science, and the cognitive division of labor. *American Journal of Political Science*, 43: 590–607.

—— 2002. How to make a social science practical: pragmatism, critical social science and multiperspectival theory. *Millennium: Journal of International Studies*, 31: 499–524.

---

[6] As Reus-Smit (2008) notes, even classical realists such as Carr and Morgenthau, while committed to a "science" of international relations and critical of the utopianism of liberals, incorporated normative reflection and moral reasoning into their conceptions of realism.

BRADY, H., and COLLIER, D. (eds.) 2004. *Rethinking Social Inquiry: Diverse Tools, Shared Standards*. Lanham, Md.: Rowman and Littlefield.

BUCHANAN, A., and KEOHANE, R. O. 2006. The legitimacy of global governance institutions. *Ethics and International Affairs*, 20: 405–37.

BUENO DE MESQUITA, B. 1985. Toward a scientific understanding of international conflict: a personal view. *International Studies Quarterly*, 29: 121–36.

CHECKEL, J. 2007. Constructivism and EU politics. Pp. 57–76 in *Handbook of European Union Politics*, ed. K. E. Joergensen, M. Pollack, and B. Rosamond. London: Sage.

CHERNOFF, F. 2005. *The Power of International Theory: Reforging the Link to Foreign Policy-making through Scientific Enquiry*. London: Routledge.

COCHRAN, M. 2002. Deweyan pragmatism and post-positivist social science in IR. *Millennium: Journal of International Studies*, 31: 525–48.

DAHL, R. 2004. Comments on the confluence of American and comparative politics. *APSA-CP Newsletter: Organized Section in Comparative Politics of the American Political Science Association*, 15: 4–6.

DEWEY, J. 1920. *Reconstruction in Philosophy*. New York: Henry Holt and Company.

——1926. *Democracy and Education: An Introduction to the Philosophy of Education*. New York: Macmillan.

DOW, S. C. 2004. Structured pluralism. *Journal of Economic Methodology*, 11: 275–90.

ELMAN, C., and ELMAN, M. F. 2003. Introduction: appraising progress in international relations theory. Pp. 1–20 in *Progress in International Relations Theory: Appraising the Field*, ed. C. Elman and M. F. Elman. Cambridge, Mass.: MIT Press.

ELSTER, J. 1998. Introduction. Pp. 1–18 in *Deliberative Democracy*, ed. J. Elster. New York: Cambridge University Press.

GADAMER, H. 1976. *Philosophical Hermeneutics*. Berkeley: University of California Press.

GEERTZ, C. 1973. *The Interpretation of Cultures: Selected Essays*. New York: Basic Books.

GIDDENS, A. 1984. *The Constitution of Society: Outline of the Theory of Structuration*. Cambridge: Polity.

GILPIN, R. 1975. *US Power and the Multinational Corporation: The Political Economy of Foreign Direct Investment*. New York: Basic Books.

GROFMAN, B. 2001. Introduction: the joy of puzzle solving. Pp. 1–11 in *Political Science as Puzzle Solving*, ed. B. Grofman. Ann Arbor: University of Michigan Press.

HAAS, P. M., and HAAS, E. B. 2002. Pragmatic constructivism and the study of international institutions. *Millennium: Journal of International Studies*, 31: 573–601.

HAACKE, J. 2005. The Frankfurt School and international relations: on the centrality of recognition. *Review of International Studies*, 31: 181–94.

HELD, D. 1980. *Introduction to Critical Theory: Horkheimer to Habermas*. Berkeley: University of California Press.

HELLEINER, E., and PICKEL, A. (eds.) 2005. *Economic Nationalism in a Globalizing World*. Ithaca, NY: Cornell University Press.

HELLMANN, G. 2002. Creative intelligence: pragmatism as a theory of thought and action. Presented at the *Millennium* Special Issue Conference on Pragmatism in International Relations Theory, London, Oct 12.

——2003a. In conclusion: dialogue and synthesis in individual scholarship and collective inquiry. Pp. 147–50 in Hellmann 2003b.

——(ed.) 2003b. The forum: are dialogue and synthesis possible in international relations? *International Studies Review*, 5: 123–53.

HELPER, S., MacDUFFIE, J. P., and SABEL, C. 2000. Pragmatic collaborations: advancing knowledge while controlling opportunism. *Industrial and Corporate Change*, 9: 443–88.

HEMPEL, C. G. 1966. *Philosophy of Natural Science*. Englewood Cliffs, NJ: Prentice Hall.

HIRSCHMAN, A. O. 1981. *Essays in Trespassing: Economics to Politics and Beyond*. New York: Cambridge University Press.

HOCHSCHILD, J. 2005. Symposium I: Ian Shapiro's *The Flight from Reality in the Human Sciences* (Princeton University Press, 2005). *Qualitative Methods: Newsletter of the American Political Science Association Organized Section on Qualitative Methods*, 3: 11–13.

HOFFMANN, S. 2006. *Chaos and Violence: What Globalization, Failed States, and Terrorism Mean for US Foreign Policy*. Lanham, Md.: Rowman and Littlefield.

HOPF, T. 1998. The promise of constructivism in international relations theory. *International Security*, 23: 171–200.

—— 2007. The limits of interpreting evidence. In *Theory and Evidence in Comparative Politics and International Relations*, ed. R. N. Lebow and M. I. Lichbach. New York: Palgrave Macmillan.

ISACOFF, J. 2006. *Writing the Arab–Israeli Conflict: Pragmatism and Historical Inquiry*. Lanham, Md.: Lexington.

JAMES, W. 1997. What pragmatism means. Pp. 93–111 in *Pragmatism: A Reader*, ed. L. Menand. New York: Vintage.

JERVIS, R. 2005. *American Foreign Policy in a New Era*. New York: Routledge.

JOAS, H. 1993. *Pragmatism and Social Theory*. Chicago: University of Chicago Press.

JOHNSON, J. 2002. How conceptual problems migrate: rational choice, interpretation, and the hazards of pluralism. *Annual Review of Political Science*, 5: 223–48.

—— 2006. Consequences of positivism: a pragmatist assessment. *Comparative Political Studies*, 39: 224–52.

KANG, D. 2007. *China Rising: Peace, Power, and Order in East Asia*. New York: Columbia University Press.

KATZENSTEIN, P. J. 2005. *A World of Regions: Asia and Europe in the American Imperium*. Ithaca, NY: Cornell University Press.

—— and SIL, R. 2004. Rethinking Asian security: a case for analytic eclecticism. Pp. 1–33 in Suh, Katzenstein, and Carlson 2004.

KING, G., KEOHANE, R. O., and VERBA, S. 1994. *Designing Social Inquiry: Scientific Inference in Qualitative Research*. Princeton, NJ: Princeton University Press.

KLOTZ, A., and LYNCH, C. 2007. *Strategies for Research in Constructing International Relations*. Armonk, NY: M. E. Sharpe.

KNIGHT, J., and JOHNSON, J. 1999. Inquiry into democracy: what might a pragmatist make of rational choice theories? *American Journal of Political Science*, 43: 566–89.

KOGUT, B., and ZANDER, U. 1992. Knowledge of the firm, combinative capabilities, and the replication of technology. *Organization Science*, 3: 383–97.

KRATOCHWIL, F. 2003. The monologue of "science." Pp. 124–8 in Hellmann 2003*b*.

LAKATOS, I. 1970. Falsification and the methodology of scientific research programmes. Pp. 91–196 in *Criticism and the Growth of Knowledge*, ed. I. Lakatos and A. Musgrave. New York: Cambridge University Press.

LAUDAN, L. 1996. *Beyond Positivism and Relativism: Theory, Method, and Evidence*. Boulder, Colo.: Westview.

LUKE, T. 2003. Real interdependence: discursivity and concursivity in global politics. Pp. 101–20 in *Language, Agency, and Politics in a Constructed World*, ed. F. Debrix. Armonk, NY: M. E. Sharpe.

LYALL, J. 2005. Paths of ruin: why revisionist states arise and die in world politics. Ph.D. dissertation, Cornell University.

MAHONEY, J., and GOERTZ, G. 2006. A tale of two cultures: contrasting quantitative and qualitative research. *Political Analysis*, 14: 227–49.

MAKINDA, S. M. 2000. International society and eclecticism in international relations theory. *Cooperation and Conflict*, 35: 205–16.

MENAND, L. 1997. An introduction to pragmatism. Pp. xi–xxxiv in *Pragmatism: A Reader*, ed. L. Menand. New York: Vintage.

MORAVCSIK, A. 2003. Theory synthesis in international relations: real not metaphysical. Pp. 131–6 in Hellmann 2003*b*.

MORGENTHAU, H. J. 1970. Common sense and theories. Pp. 241–8 in *Truth and Power: Essays of a Decade, 1960–70*, H. J. Morgenthau. New York: Praeger.

NAU, H. R. 2002. *At Home Abroad: Identity and Power in American Foreign Policy*. Ithaca, NY: Cornell University Press.

NEUMANN, I. 2002. Returning practice to the linguistic turn: the case of diplomacy. *Millennium: Journal of International Studies*, 31: 627–51.

PARSONS, C. 2007. *How to Map Arguments in Political Science*. New York: Oxford University Press.

PUTNAM, H. 1981. *Reason, Truth and History*. New York: Cambridge University Press.

——— 2002. *The Collapse of the Fact/Value Dichotomy and Other Essays*. Cambridge, Mass.: Harvard University Press.

REUS-SMIT, C. 2008. Constructivism and the structure of ethical reasoning. In *Moral Limit and Possibility in World Politics*, ed. R. Price. Cambridge: Cambridge University Press.

RORTY, R. 1982. *Consequences of Pragmatism: Essays, 1972–1980*. Minneapolis: University of Minnesota Press.

——— 1999. *Philosophy and Social Hope*. Harmondsworth: Penguin.

ROSE, G. 1998. Neoclassical realism and theories of foreign policy. *World Politics*, 51: 144–72.

SANDERSON, S. K. 1987. Eclecticism and its alternatives. Pp. 313–45 in *Current Perspectives in Social Theory: A Research Annual*, vol. viii, ed. J. Wilson. Greenwich, Conn.: JAI Press.

SCHWELLER, R. L. 1998. *Deadly Imbalances: Tripolarity and Hitler's Strategy of World Conquest*. New York: Columbia University Press.

——— 2006. *Unanswered Threats: Political Constraints on the Balance of Power*. Princeton, NJ: Princeton University Press.

SEABROOKE, L. 2006. *The Social Sources of Financial Power: Domestic Legitimacy and International Financial Orders*. Ithaca, NY: Cornell University Press.

SEWELL, W. 1992. A theory of structure: duality, agency, and transformation. *American Journal of Sociology*, 98: 1–29.

SHAPIRO, I. 2005. *The Flight from Reality in the Human Sciences*. Princeton, NJ: Princeton University Press.

——— and WENDT, A. 2005. The difference that realism makes: social science and the politics of consent. Pp. 19–50 in Shapiro 2005.

SIL, R. 2000*a*. The foundations of eclecticism: the epistemological status of agency, culture, and structure in social theory. *Journal of Theoretical Politics*, 12: 353–87.

—— 2000*b*. Against epistemological absolutism: toward a "pragmatic" center? Pp. 145–75 in Sil and Doherty 2000.

—— 2004. Problems chasing methods or methods chasing problems? Research communities, constrained pluralism, and the role of eclecticism. Pp. 307–31 in *Problems and Methods in the Study of Politics*, ed. I. Shapiro, R. Smith, and T. Masoud. New York: Cambridge University Press.

—— and DOHERTY, E. (eds.) 2000. *Beyond Boundaries? Disciplines, Paradigms, and Theoretical Integration in International Studies*. Albany: State University of New York Press.

SINCLAIR, T. J. 2005. *The New Masters of Capital: American Bond Rating Agencies and the Politics of Creditworthiness*. Ithaca, NY: Cornell University Press.

SUH, J. J., KATZENSTEIN, P. J., and CARLSON, A. (eds.) 2004. *Rethinking Security in East Asia: Identity, Power, and Efficiency*. Stanford, Calif.: Stanford University Press.

THERBORN, G. 2005. In lieu of conclusion: more questions. Pp. 321–32 in *Welfare Politics Cross-Examined: Eclecticist Analytical Perspectives on Sweden and the Developed World from the 1980s to the 2000s*, ed. E. Carroll and L. Erickson. Amsterdam: Aksant.

WÆVER, O. 2004. Discursive approaches. Pp. 197–216 in *European Integration Theory*, ed. A. Wiener and T. Diez. Oxford: Oxford University Press.

WALT, S. M. 2003. The progressive power of realism. Pp. 58–67 in *Realism and the Balancing of Power: A New Debate*, ed. J. A. Vasquez and C. Elman. Upper Saddle River, NJ: Prentice Hall.

WALTZ, K. N. 1959. *Man, the State, and War: A Theoretical Analysis*. New York: Columbia University Press.

WENDT, A. 1999. *Social Theory of International Politics*. New York: Cambridge University Press.

WHITE, S. 2004. The very idea of a critical social science: a pragmatist turn. Pp. 310–35 in *The Cambridge Companion to Critical Theory*, ed. F. Rush. New York: Cambridge University Press.

WHITFORD, J. 2002. Pragmatism and the untenable dualism of means and ends: why rational choice theory does not deserve paradigmatic privilege. *Theory and Society*, 31: 325–63.

ZÜRN, M., and CHECKEL, J. T. 2005. Getting socialized to build bridges: constructivism and rationalism, Europe and the nation-state. *International Organization*, 59: 1045–79.

CHAPTER 7

....

REALISM

....

WILLIAM C. WOHLFORTH

Iᴛ is only a slight exaggeration to say that the academic study of international relations is a debate about realism. Realism provides a foil against which many other schools of thought define themselves and their contributions. Take realism out of the picture and the identities of these other schools as well as the significance of their arguments become much less clear. The study of international politics thus is in an important sense inexplicable without a grounding in realism.

Gaining such a grounding, however, is harder than it seems. Precisely because realism is so influential, it is also systematically misunderstood. Whether favorably or unfavorably disposed toward realist ideas and theories, scholars face powerful incentives to make realism into something it is not. As a result, many of the most popular criticisms of realism miss the mark. My purpose in this chapter is to set the record straight (portions of the chapter overlap with Wohlforth 2007).

The most important point is that realism is not now and never has been a single theory—if that term is defined properly. Unfortunately, scholars use the word "theory" to refer to three distinct things: realism (a large and complex tradition of statecraft and scholarship); subschools within realism such as neorealism (complex schools of thought fitting within the realist tradition); and specific realist theories like the balance of power, the security dilemma, or the offense–defense balance (propositions about patterns of relations among states or pressures facing a particular state). In this chapter, I keep these things clear, reserving the term "theory" for specific propositions or arguments. These distinctions are not academic quibbles. The notion that realism—this centuries-old foundational school of thought—can be and has to be reduced to a single, internally consistent, and logically coherent theory is the taproot of the greatest misunderstanding.

1 WHAT IS REALISM?

Political realists typically claim to be part of a tradition that stretches back, through Thomas Hobbes and Niccolò Machiavelli, to Thucydides.[1] In the academic study of international relations, which is not much more than a century old, four principal generations can be identified: an interwar and wartime generation, the best-known figures of which were Reinhold Niebuhr and E. H. Carr; a postwar or early cold war generation, symbolized by Hans Morgenthau's *Politics among Nations* (1954),[2] and including most prominently George Kennan and Raymond Aron; a détente generation, best represented by Kenneth Waltz's *Theory of International Politics* (1979), and including among its leading exponents Stephen Krasner and Robert Gilpin; and a post-cold war generation, led by John Mearsheimer (2001) (whose book *The Tragedy of Great Power Politics* seems to be emerging as emblematic) and prominently represented in the work of Steven Walt, Randall Schweller, and Charles Glaser.[3]

Realism is best seen as "a spectrum of ideas...rather than as a fixed point of focus with sharp definition" (Haslam 2002, 249); an "attitude of mind" with "a quite distinctive and recognizable flavour" (Garnett 1984, 110); "a philosophical disposition" (Gilpin 1986, 304); "a 'big tent,' with room for a number of different theories" (Elman 1996, 26). C. A. J. Coady (2005, 122) draws a penetrating analogy to a religion, understood as involving "a combination of an often loosely related set of beliefs, a way of thinking and responding, a sometimes desperate desire to preach to the uncomprehending heathen, and a pantheon of canonical exemplars or saints whose very diverse intellectual and practical lives are seen to embody the virtues of the religion."

Definitions of realism[4] vary considerably in their details but reveal a striking family resemblance. Realists tend to converge around four central propositions, which in this and the following chapter we will take as providing a working definition of the tradition of realism.

---

[1] This section was written jointly with Jack Donnelly and was jointly designed as a common introduction for this and the following chapter.

[2] Although the first edition appeared in 1948, *Politics among Nations* acquired its famous first chapter, which lays out Morgenthau's six principles of political realism, only in the 1954 second edition.

[3] These generations are divided by major internal disagreements. For example, Mearsheimer, Glaser, and Schweller are representatives, respectively, of what today are usually called offensive, defensive, and neoclassical realism. This list is quite incomplete: leading figures who could readily be added include Robert Schuman, Nicholas Spykman, Herbert Butterfield, Henry Kissinger, Robert Tucker, Kenneth Thompson, John Herz, and Glenn Snyder.

[4] In addition to the canonical definitions of Morgenthau (1954, 4–13), Waltz (1979, 117), and Mearsheimer (2001, 30–1), see, e.g., Carr (1946, 63–4), Keohane (1986, 164–5), Frankel (1996, xiv–xvii), Gilpin (1996, 7–8), Grieco (1997, 164–8), Crane (1998, 64–71), Nicholson (1998, 67), Haslam (2002, 12, 17, 250), and Schweller (2003, 322–9).

1. *Groupism.* Politics takes place within and between groups. Group solidarity is essential to domestic politics and conflict and cooperation between polities is the essence of international politics. To survive at anything above a subsistence level, people need the cohesion provided by group solidarity, yet that very same in-group cohesion generates the potential for conflict with other groups. Today the most important human groups are nation states and the most important source of in-group cohesion is nationalism. For convenience, I shall use the term "states" henceforth. But it is important to stress that realism makes no assumption about the nature of the polity. It may apply to any social setting where groups interact.[5]

2. *Egoism.* When individuals and groups act politically, they are driven principally by narrow self-interest. This egoism is rooted in human nature. Its expression, though, may be exacerbated, moderated, or even temporarily overcome by national and international political structures, institutions, and values.

3. *Anarchy.* The absence of government dramatically shapes the nature of international politics. Anarchic political systems of self-help both impose distinctive constraints on the ability of international actors to achieve their purposes and exacerbate group egoism.

4. *Power politics.* The intersection of groupism and egoism in an environment of anarchy makes international relations, regrettably, largely a politics of power and security.[6] Once past the hunter-gatherer stage, human affairs are always marked by great inequalities of power in both senses of that term: social influence or *control* (some groups and individuals always have an outsized influence on politics) and *resources* (some groups and individuals are always disproportionately endowed with the material wherewithal to get what they want). Key to politics in any area is the interaction between social and material power, an interaction that unfolds in the shadow of the potential use of material power to coerce. As Waltz (1979, 186) put it, "The web of social and political life is spun out of inclinations and incentives, deterrent threats and punishments. Eliminate the latter two, and the ordering of society depends entirely on the former—a utopian thought impractical this side of Eden." One corollary, to which the following chapter is devoted, is the characteristic realist skepticism toward pursuing moral objectives in international relations.

---

[5] This point is often misformulated in the claim that states are the central actors of international politics. If by "state" we mean a particular kind of polity (defined, for example, by territorial sovereignty), then this is clearly not essential to realism. Quite the contrary, no realist believes that the theory is restricted to a particular form of polity. But if by "state" we mean polity or group, we should simply say that in order to avoid confusion.

[6] Rationality is the other premise most frequently identified (e.g. Keohane 1986, 164; Frankel 1996, xviii; Mearsheimer 2001, 31). The rationality assumption, however, is either in a thin sense shared by almost all theories of international politics (except certain psychological theories) or in a thick sense not actually essential to realism (cf. Schweller 2003, 324–5).

Note that groupism and egoism apply to both domestic and international politics. In fact, canonical realists such as Thucydides and Machiavelli made no categorical distinction between the two, and in the twentieth century Niebuhr and Carr advanced realism as a general approach to the study of politics. Over the past century, however, most have treated realism as pertaining mainly to international politics. In this understanding, anarchy—or, more precisely, government or its absence—qualitatively transforms politics,[7] making power politics characteristic principally of international relations. Given the focus of this volume, in both this and the following chapter, without denying the possibility of applying realist analysis to domestic politics, we focus on realism as an intellectual tradition for understanding international politics.

2 Realism's Unity: The Signature Argument

If you believe the world generally works by these four rules, then many important consequences follow for how you think about international politics: that the main groups with which people identify—be they tribes, city states, empires, or nation states—will exert a major influence on human affairs and thus that it pays analytically to focus on the most powerful (that is, most resource-rich and influential) groups at any given time; that the group's collective interest, however defined, will be central to its politics, and thus that it pays analytically to be skeptical toward professed aims of foreign policy other than the state interest; and that necessity as the group interest defines it will trump any putatively universal morality, and thus that it pays to look beyond rhetoric to the power realities that realists expect nearly always underlie policy. In analyzing international relations, realists thus look for where the power is, for what the group interests are, and to the role power relationships play in reconciling clashing interests.

Certain types of thinkers tend to share similar bets about how the world works. Critics like to say that the kind of person most likely to accept the core realist propositions is a congenital pessimist and cynic. Realists counter that these propositions are simply realistic—based on the dispassionate observation of human affairs the way they are as opposed to the way we might wish them to be. There is a degree of truth to both views, and they add up to produce a unity of realist thought that links the writings of the highly diverse thinkers realists claim as their canon.

[7] Herbert Butterfield (1950, 31) put the point in a particularly striking form: "the difference between civilization and barbarism is a revelation of what is essentially the same human nature when it works under different conditions."

For international relations theory, the most important intellectual thread that provides coherence to the realist tradition is what might be called realism's signature argument: If human affairs are indeed characterized by groupism, egoism, and power-centrism, then politics is likely to be conflictual unless there is some central authority to enforce order. When no authority exists that can enforce agreements— "anarchy"—then any state can resort to force to get what it wants. Even if a state can be fairly sure that no other state will take up arms today, there is no guarantee against the possibility that one might do so tomorrow. Because no state can rule out this prospect, states tend to arm themselves against this contingency. With all states thus armed, politics takes on a different cast. Disputes that would be easy to settle if states could rely on some higher authority to enforce an agreement can escalate to war in the absence of such authority. The signature realist argument is therefore that anarchy renders states' security problematic and potentially conflictual, and is a key underlying cause of war.

The four general propositions and the arguments they yield provide coherence to the realist tradition, while debates about the relative importance or priority of each proposition, their overall implications, and the conditions under which they apply generate diversity. In explaining the recurrence of war, for example, some realist writings stress egoism, arguing that human nature is the prior and main cause, while others insist that the condition of anarchy takes explanatory priority (Spirtas 1996). Some writings derive from the four propositions the implication that all states will always seek more power, while others hold that power-seeking is far more variable. Some stress the potential of very powerful states to impose a rudimentary political order that may constrain power politics, while others stress the severe limits of that potential. Some stress agency, contending that enlightened or particularly skilled statesmen can ameliorate the destructive potential of power politics. Others stress structure, highlighting the constraints generated by the inter-action of egoism and groupism in anarchy.

In short, scholars who agree with each other on the centrality of the core realist premises have nonetheless built out of these premises a bewildering array of arguments, theories, and debates. To organize this diversity, it helps to consider it along two dimensions: theoretical schools within realism, and specific realist theories.

3 REALISM'S DIVERSITY: THEORETICAL SCHOOLS

Scholars routinely describe the recent development of realist thought as a linear succession of attempts to fashion comprehensive theories of international politics, sometimes called "grand theories" or "research programs." In this portrayal, by the 1960s Morgenthau's initial attempt to pull together classical realist thought into such a theory was widely seen as a failure. In the late 1970s, Waltz tried again, with a new, revivified realist theory that came to be called "neorealism." For a time during the 1980s, neorealism "ruled the theoretical seas," but it soon began to wither in the face of theoretical critiques and empirical setbacks. By the 1990s, it was widely seen as a "degenerating" research program, and a key indicator of that degeneration was the emergence of a proliferation of new realist schools: offensive realism, defensive realism, and eventually neoclassical realism.

This story is mainly mythical. It has been sustained for so long in part because realists themselves have often bought into it, agreeing that the evolution of their scholarly tradition ought to be viewed as a succession of single integrated and internally consistent theories.[8] In reality, realist research has always been highly diverse, even in neorealism's heyday. There is nothing new about the existence of multiple schools within realism. What is new—and helpful to scholars seeking to survey the literature and chart developments in research—is that these schools now have names.

3.1 From Classical to Neorealism

After the development of neorealism in the 1980s, scholars began referring to all the realist works of the interwar and early cold war years as classical realism (Ashley 1986). In recent years, scholars have even widened the term to include all realist works from Thucydides to Morgenthau (e.g. Lebow 2003). Classical realism is thus not a subschool; it simply *is* the realist tradition in all its diversity as it unfolded prior to the publication of Waltz's *Theory of International Politics* in 1979. For the subsequent development of international relations theory, however, one classical realist text stands far above all others: Morgenthau's *Politics among Nations*. This book inaugurated the practice of seeking to translate the realist tradition of scholarship and statecraft into what Morgenthau, in the famous first chapter of his text, called "a realist theory of international politics."[9]

In one sense, Morgenthau came closer to the Holy Grail of a realist theory of international politics than any of his successors. His major text brings realist arguments to bear on a very large number of phenomena: war, peace, cooperation, international law, diplomacy, ethics, international organization, world public opinion, and more. Even though Morgenthau left out some important aspects of international politics—notably what we would today call international

---

[8] Or, as Waltz (1991) himself rather grandly pictured it, the replacement of classical realist "thought" with neorealist "theory."

[9] Carr's *Twenty Years' Crisis* (1946) does seek to advance international relations as a science, but does not explicitly articulate an overarching theory.

political economy—none of his subsequent imitators came close to matching his comprehensiveness. Where Morgenthau more obviously fell short was in convincing the scholarly community of the plausibility and internal logical coherence of his theory. Even fellow realists found Morgenthau's theory beset by "open contradictions, ambiguity and vagueness" (Tucker 1952, 214). Key concepts such as the "national interest" or "the balance of power" were either undefined or defined in multiple and mutually contradictory ways. And, not surprisingly, arguments deployed in different issue areas did not always cohere.

As scholarly criticisms of realism mounted and the interest in the scientific approach to the study of politics grew (especially in the United States), Waltz sought to revivify realist thinking by translating some core realist ideas into a deductive, top-down theoretical framework that eventually came to be called neorealism. Waltz (1959) held that classical realists' powerful insights into the workings of international politics were weakened by their failure to distinguish clearly among arguments about human nature, the internal attributes of states, and the overall system of states. His *Theory of International Politics* brought together and clarified many earlier realist ideas about how the features of the overall system of states affect the ways states interact.

Waltz's text had a profound influence on the development of international relations scholarship in general and realist thought in particular. But it is not really a theory of international politics. It does not address in any explicit way most of the phenomena that are encompassed by that term. Rather, by restating in the clearest form yet realism's signature argument about how the mere existence of groups in anarchy can lead to powerful competitive pressure and war—regardless of what the internal politics of those groups might be like—Waltz presented a theory that purported to answer a few important but highly general questions about international politics: why the modern states system has persisted in the face of attempts by certain states at dominance; why war among great powers recurred over centuries; and why states often find cooperation hard. In addition, the book forwarded one more specific theory: that great-power war would tend to be more frequent in multipolarity (an international system shaped by the power of three or more major states) than bipolarity (an international system shaped by the power of two major states, or superpowers).

Waltz left to others the task of exploring his book's implications for all other questions of international politics, both general (for example, theories of alliances, arms races, rivalries, international institutions, and so on) and specific (for example, why the cold war began and why the superpower rivalry waxed and waned). The overwhelming majority of scholars seeking to address those questions not surprisingly found Waltz's theory—constructed to address different and usually much more general questions—insufficient. Most responded by using Waltz's work as a foil for developing self-consciously nonrealist explanations of specific puzzles or, more ambitiously, for developing alternative theoretical schools, most notably institutionalism (Keohane 1984) and constructivism (Wendt 1999). But some responded by developing their own realist theories even as they endeavored to make use of Waltz's. For example, in seeking to explain alliance behavior, Walt (1987) integrated insights from Waltz into a new, related but clearly distinct "balance of threat" theory (discussed below), while Glen Snyder (1997) combined Waltz's theories with other complementary theories. In explaining cooperation, Joseph Grieco (1988) supplemented Waltz's theory with propositions from game theory. And a great many scholars used Waltz's theory as part of more complex explanations for more specific puzzles or events.

Thus, even though Waltz, like Morgenthau, presented his work as a single stand-alone realist "theory of international politics," the natural development of scholarly inquiry led to the development of neorealism as a complex subschool within realism encompassing many Waltz-inspired theories. What linked the research of these scholars was a common bet that Waltz's reformulation of realism was the best place to start inquiry, even if it was never the place to end it. To be sure, these links were often unclear, and the boundaries of the school debatable. But the term neorealism captures the profound influence Waltz had on the thinking and research of many other realist scholars.

Even in its heyday of the 1980s, neorealism never subsumed all realist research. Waltz and his followers focused on a few core realist ideas, especially those that helped explain basic continuities in international politics. They downplayed or ignored theories of change that were also part of the classical realist canon. Two years after Waltz's *Theory of International Politics*, Gilpin (1981) published *War and Change in World Politics*, which sought systematically to bring together realist ideas about hegemonic war and change in international politics. Conceived and written independently of Waltz's *Theory*, this book could not possibly be seen as somehow derivative of it. It could hardly have been clearer that neorealism was but a part of a larger, ongoing, and vibrant realist scholarly tradition. Yet, wedded as they were to the idea of single dominant theories or research programs, both realists and their critics tried either to shoehorn Gilpin's work into the neorealist scheme or to downplay it.

3.2 Offensive and Defensive Realism

The advent of neorealism caused scholars to think much harder and more clearly about the underlying forces that drive international relations. Realists working with Waltz's theory discovered that, depending on how they thought about the core assumptions, and what they saw as the most reasonable expectations about real-world conditions, neorealism could lead to very different predictions. Written in a highly abstract manner, Waltz's neorealism ignored important variations in international relations, including geography and technology. Depending on how one conceptualized those factors, the very same neorealist ideas could generate widely disparate implications about the dynamics of inter-state politics. Out of this realization were borne two new theoretical subschools, each of which built on the basic insights of neorealism.

Defensive realists reasoned that under very common conditions the war-causing potential of anarchy is attenuated (Taliaferro 2000–1). Proceeding from the core realist assumption about groupism, these theorists argued that the stronger group identity is—as in the modern era of nationalism—the harder it is to conquer and subjugate other groups (Van Evera 1999). And the harder conquest is, the more secure all states can be. Similarly, technology may make conquest hard—for example, it is hard to contemplate the conquest of states that have the capacity to strike back with nuclear weapons. Thus, even accepting all Waltz's arguments about how difficult it is to be secure in an anarchic world, under these kinds of conditions states could still be expected to find ways of defending themselves without threatening others, or could otherwise signal their peaceful intentions, resulting in an international system with more built-in potential for peace than many realists previously thought (Glaser 1997). The result was to push analysts to look inside states for the domestic/ideational causes of war and peace.

Offensive realists, by contrast, were more persuaded by the conflict-generating, structural potential of anarchy itself. They reasoned that, with no authority to enforce agreements, states could never be certain that any peace-causing condition today would remain operative in the future. Even if conquest may seem hard today owing to geography, technology, or group identity, there is no guarantee against the prospect that another state will develop some fiendish device for overcoming these barriers. Given this uncertainty, states can rarely be confident of their security and must always view other states' increases in power with suspicion. As a result, states are often tempted to expand or otherwise strengthen themselves—and/or to weaken others—in order to survive over the long haul. The result is to reinforce the classic realist argument about the competitive nature of life under anarchy, regardless of the internal properties of states.

Defensive and offensive realism emerged in the 1990s as outgrowths of Waltz's neorealism. In keeping with the tradition established by Waltz and Morgenthau, many of the scholars who developed these theories saw them as articulating *the* realist theory. Thus, scholars framed much defensive realist theorizing as developments of Waltz's neorealism. And, in *The Tragedy of Great Power Politics*, Mearsheimer portrays offensive realism as *the* successor to Waltz's neorealism, which he equates with defensive realism. But it is impossible to put the genie of realism's diversity back into the bottle. It is clear that defensive and offensive realism coexist as distinct subschools. And those two subschools hardly exhaust realism's diversity, for many other realist theories fall outside both of them.

3.3 Neoclassical Realism

Neoclassical realism is a problem-focused subschool within realism that embraces rather than denies realism's diversity. Works in this subschool share two features: a focus on the explanation of specific puzzles or events; and the effort to recapture important realist insights lost in neorealists' obsessive search for the one overarching realist theory of international politics. As clear and elegant as neorealism and its immediate outgrowths were, it remained unclear just how relevant they were to any given foreign-policy problem. So focused were realists on defining the single best and most universal formulation of their theory that it began to seem as if the development of realism had taken a completely different path from the analysis of foreign policy. Waltz (1996) himself argued famously that "international politics is not foreign policy," implying that theory development and foreign-policy analysis had become two distinct endeavors with little connection to each other.

Neoclassical realism seeks to rectify this imbalance between the general and the particular. It accepts from neorealism and its descendants the basic utility of thinking theoretically about the international system as distinct from the internal properties of states (Rose 1998). Having carefully specified their assessment of the international conditions particular states face, however, neoclassical realists go on to factor in specific features of a given situation to generate more complete explanations. They seek to recapture the grounding in the gritty details of foreign policy that marked classical realism while also benefiting from the rigorous theorizing that typified neorealism.

Neoclassical realists are not driven by the dream of creating the one universal theory of international politics. For them, the question is: Which realist school or theory (if any) is most useful for explaining a given puzzle or analyzing issues of foreign policy at a given place and time? To some extent, the choice of theory is a contextual issue. For example, offensive realism provides a powerful shorthand portrayal of the incentives and constraints states faced in parts of Europe for long stretches of the eighteenth to twentieth centuries. In other periods, and for some groups of states in Europe, defensive realism arguably provides a more accurate model of the international setting. For some problems and issues, the theory presented in Gilpin's *War and Change* may be far more relevant.

The degree to which a theoretical picture of the international system really applies is a matter of judgment, based on the analyst's reading of the context. Neoclassical realists remain agnostic over which theoretical proposition may apply; they bring to bear those theories that are arguably relevant. While they are agnostic over which theory or theoretical school may apply, they agree that theory helps strengthen analysis. From the perspective of realism, a basic set of questions constantly recurs in foreign-policy analysis. To what degree is state X's policy a response to external pressures and incentives as opposed to internally generated? If a new party were to come to power, how much would the policy change? Would state X respond more favorably to incentives or threats? To answer these questions, one has to imagine what any state would do in X's position. The key contribution of neorealism and its offshoot subschools of offensive and defensive realism is rigorous thinking about exactly these questions. For neoclassical realists, theoretical structures like offensive and defensive realism are not always and everywhere true or false. Rather, they make it easier to perform the key mental experiments that lie at the core of foreign-policy analysis by helping analysts frame their assessments of the external constraints and incentives states face.

4 REALISM'S DIVERSITY: THEORIES

Theoretical subschools do not capture realism's full diversity. Equally important are specific theories about the fundamental constraints and incentives that shape behavior and outcomes in international politics. Subschools help you figure out the intellectual connections among scholars, how various arguments are related, and how scholarship progresses. But when the issue at hand is a real explanatory problem—such as the effort to explain some puzzling foreign-policy behavior—reach for the specific theories that appear to be relevant.

Arguably the best-known theoretical proposition about international relations is *balance-of-power theory*. Given the basic problem that under anarchy any state can resort to force to get what it wants, it follows that states are likely to guard against the possibility that one state might amass the wherewithal to compel all the others to do its will and even possibly eliminate them. The theory posits that states will check dangerous concentrations of power by building up their own capabilities ("internal balancing") or aggregating their capabilities with other states in alliances ("external balancing"). Because states are always looking to the future to anticipate possible problems, balancing may occur even before any one state or alliance has gained an obvious power edge. Thus, Britain and France fought the Russian Empire in Crimea in the middle of the nineteenth century less because they saw an immediate challenge to their position than because they reasoned that, if unchecked, Russian power might someday be a threat to them. However wise or unwise it may have been, the thinking in London and Paris at that time strikes many historians as being entirely consistent with the expectations of balance-of-power theory.

Balance-of-threat theory adds complexity to this picture. As its name implies, this theory predicts that states will balance against threats. Threat, in turn, is driven by a combination of three key variables: aggregate capabilities (that is, its overall military and economic potential), geography, and perceptions of aggressive intentions. If one state becomes especially powerful and if its location and behavior feed threat perceptions on the part of other states, then balancing strategies will come to dominate their foreign policies. Thus, the United States began both external and internal balancing after the end of the Second World War, even though the Soviet Union remained decidedly inferior in most categories of power. Ultimately, the Western alliance overwhelmed the Soviet-led alliance on nearly every dimension. Balance-of-threat theory holds that it was the location of Soviet power in the heart of Europe, as well as the threat inherent in its secretive government and perceived aggressiveness, that produced this outcome (Walt 1985).

Security-dilemma theory. The "security dilemma" is a term coined by John Herz (1950) for the argument that in arming for self-defense a state might *decrease* its security via the unintended effect of making others insecure, sparking them to arm in response. In a hugely influential article, Robert Jervis (1986) showed how this consequence of anarchy could lead security-seeking states into costly spirals of mistrust and rivalry. He argued that the severity of the security dilemma depends on two variables: the balance between offense and defense, and the ability to distinguish offense from defense. Thus, although anarchy is theoretically a constant, "there can be significant variation in the attractiveness of cooperative or competitive means, the prospects for achieving a high level of security, and the probability of war" (Glaser 1997, 172). The article prompted a major debate among realists that eventually ended up in the two subschools of offensive and defensive realism.

Offense–defense theory is an offshoot of Jervis's development of security dilemma theory. As developed by Glaser, Stephen Van Evera, and others, this is a set of theoretical propositions about how technology, geography, and other factors affect the ease of conquest as opposed to defense, as well as the ease of distinguishing between offensive and defensive postures.

Hegemonic stability theory builds on the observation that powerful states tend to seek dominance over all or parts of any international system, thus fostering some degree of hierarchy within the overall systemic anarchy. It seeks to explain how cooperation can emerge among major powers, and how international orders, comprising rules, norms, and institutions, emerge and are sustained. The theory's core prediction is that any international order is stable only to the degree that the relations of authority within it are sustained by the underlying distribution of power. According to this theory, the current "globalization" order is sustained by US power and is likely to come undone as challengers like China gain strength.

Power transition theory is a subset of hegemonic stability that seeks to explain how orders break down into war. Building from the premises of hegemonic stability theory, it deduces that dominant states will prefer to retain leadership, that lesser states' preference for contesting that leadership will tend to strengthen as they become stronger relative to the dominant state, and that this clash is likely to come to the fore as the capabilities of the two sides approach parity. Applied to the current context, the theory posits that the stronger China gets the more likely it is to become dissatisfied with the US-led global order. It predicts that a war or at least a cold war-style rivalry between the United States and China will become likely unless China's growth slows down or Washington finds a way to accommodate Beijing's preferences.

There are numerous other realist or realist-related theories, but even this list makes my main point: Realist theories, which do the real work of explanation, are far more diverse than any one theoretical subschool. Neither the security dilemma nor hegemonic stability nor power transition figured in Waltz's neorealist theory. The development of defensive realism owes as much if not more to Jervis as it does to Waltz. Equating any one subschool with realism as a whole lets important and potentially useful theories fall through the cracks.

5 MYTH-INDUCED MISCONCEPTIONS

The foregoing discussion suggests that many of the most common criticisms of realism miss the mark in part because of myths of a monolithic and universally valid realism—myths propagated with the willing connivance of many self-proclaimed realists.

The monolithic myth leads to a tendency to equate diversity with degeneration. Many scholars want to think of international relations scholarship as a neatly defined competition between grand theories or paradigms, where each such paradigm is internally consistent, focused on contrasting core principles, and highlighting mutually exclusive sets of explanatory variables (see, e.g., Vasquez 1998; Legro and Moravcsik 1999). Diversity within realism undercuts this vision and makes the world of scholarship messier and harder to organize, and so is portrayed as degeneration, a sign of decline. The problem with this vision is that it is normative, not positive. It is how some scholars think their profession *ought* to work, not how it actually does. Hence, it is profoundly misleading.

The universalistic myth leads to a failure to see the contingent nature of realist theories (see, especially, Brooks 1997). No single subschool or theory is always right or always the source of the master explanation to which others are subservient. Different strands of realism are more or less relevant to different problems and cases. The question for contemporary researchers is which subschools or specific theories apply to a given problem or case? The answer lies in being clear about how the various parts of any theory fit together.

Recall the signature realist argument I spelled out above: groupism, egoism, and power-centrism conspire to make politics under anarchy conflictual. Many realists and critics of realism make the mistake of universalizing one or all components of this argument. For example, many assert that conflict is an assumption that defines realism. This is wrong, and leads to major analytical mistakes on the part of scholars both favorably and unfavorably disposed toward realism. Realists do not assume conflict. Rather, realism contains theories that identify the conditions under which inter-state interactions are likely to be conflictual. Two simple but commonplace misconceptions follow.

First is to deny variation in the salience of any part of the argument. To clarify their theories, scholars seek pure and clean conceptual building blocks. In other words, they strive to put the basic ideas out of which their theories are built in the clearest possible way so that the basic logic at work is clear for all to see. The notion of "anarchy" is an example. Theorists require a clear understanding of anarchy in order to construct a coherent theory of what international politics in an anarchical setting looks like. Scholars mainly interested in building theory are thus very resistant to understanding anarchy as a matter of degree. Hence, realist scholars squabble over whether the logic of anarchy spelled out in defensive or offensive realism is universally valid. And critics of realism cite this squabbling as irrefutable evidence of realism's degeneration.

If you think anarchy is really a constant, then you are likely to think realist theories that highlight anarchy apply equally strongly to all states everywhere. But in practice anarchy varies. States' ability to rely on some authority to enforce agreements is a matter of degree. For example, great powers sometimes seek to enforce order among nearby small states. For those smaller states, anarchy is attenuated. On some set of issues, those states might reasonably expect the local great power to enforce agreements. Realist theories that highlight anarchy, therefore, would not apply particularly strongly to those states on that set of issues. Thus, for example, the United States in Central America, the European Union in the Balkans, and perhaps Russia in Central Asia may all perform this anarchy-attenuating role (albeit in very different ways). The only way to know where and to what degree anarchy is attenuated is to acquire in-depth knowledge about specific states. Only then can the analyst know which realist theories apply.

The second kind of error is to confuse assumptions with predictions. If you mistakenly think that conflict is a core assumption of realism, you might well conclude that whenever states are nice to each other, realist theories must not apply. But this is not necessarily so. Because realist theories explain war, they also explain peace. For realists, peace results when the key causes of war are absent. Thus the amity you might observe among some group of states may be a result of the attenuation of anarchy among them caused by a local order-providing great power. Or amity among one group of states may arise from their shared need to oppose another state or group. In either case, realist theories predict that the absence of conflict is contingent on a particular configuration of power and that conflict might return when that configuration changes.

6 Realism Today

I have argued that realism is not now and never has been a monolithic and universal "theory of international politics." It has always been diverse, even its grandest theories contingent in scope if not name. The chief development of the last fifteen years is a greater recognition of this fact, as well as a possibly associated decline in realism's centrality to the discipline. In the United States, hopes and fears for a new universal approach have largely turned to formal theory, which has ascended to a dominance of the country's top journals that realists never experienced. With the advent of neoclassical realism, meanwhile, realist research has become more problem focused, and its interactions with research from other traditions more complex and arguably more productive. To be sure, the publication of Mearsheimer's *Tragedy of Great Power Politics* has led to further elaboration of offensive realism as a new candidate "theory of international politics." But given changes in the discipline and within the realist tradition, it is unlikely that this approach will attract the aspirations and illusions occasioned by Waltz's *Theory of International Politics*.

As a result, three key trends are evident. First is a *reduced salience of interparadigmatic competition*. Like all scholars, realists are often motivated by dissatisfaction with existing (often nonrealist) explanations, but the impulse to prove the overall explanatory priority of realism over other theoretical approaches has receded. Instead the focus is increasingly on what realist theories might add to knowledge about more specific problems or issues. Most recent realist research represents attempts either to answer general empirical puzzles or to explain particular events or behavioral patterns whose causes and implications remain matters of debate.

The declining salience of paradigm wars has facilitated a second trend: *more productive interactions with other theoretical schools*. Scholars always operate in a competitive scholarly world, where theories and schools of thought are often seen to be competing against others. Adjustments to a theory, recognition of its contingent nature, may be seized upon by intellectual rivals as admissions of the theory's weakness or irrelevance. Realism is often the fulcrum of these academic debates. Most other schools of thought and theories are written in one way or any other as a response to realism. Perhaps responding in turn, realist scholars sometimes have been very reluctant to acknowledge the contingent nature of their theories or the degree to which the explanation of key phenomena requires theories from many different traditions. At the same time, inter-paradigm rivalries fed the pernicious notion that certain explanatory variables are the special province of particular theoretical approaches. Domestic politics is for liberals, ideas are for constructivists, power is for realists, and so on. Scholars sometimes wrote as if any explanation that incorporates variables from the other side of the paradigmatic fence was somehow suspect.

Competition is inevitable and necessary in scholarship, but there is a difference between competing over the best universal theory and competing over the explanation of specific phenomena. As scholars move increasingly toward the latter approach, the incentives and opportunities for productive interchange increase. In practice, both realists and their counterparts adhering to other research traditions show sensitivity to the complexity of the social world they seek to explain, the contingent nature of all theories, and the consequent premium on integrating arguments and variables long associated with different theoretical traditions. This has been particularly evident in the cross-fertilization of ideas and conjectures between neoclassical realists and constructivists (e.g. Sterling-Folker 2002; 2004; Jackson and Nexon 2004). In addition, works by self-identified realists increasingly incorporate theory and findings from other disciplines, notably psychology (e.g. Wohlforth 1993; Taliaferro 2004).

Third and most important is the *cumulation of new and important research by scholars working within the realist tradition.* This includes work that seeks to account for general phenomena, such as the origins of war (Copeland 2000); suboptimal provision of security by states (Schweller 2006); great-power military interventions (Taliaferro 2004); threat assessment (Lobell 2003); the origins of revisionist state preferences (Davidson 2006); the constraints on peace settlements after major wars (Ripsman 2002); and the dynamics of unipolarity (Wohlforth 1999; Pape 2005), to mention only a few. It also includes research explaining more discrete events or behaviors, such as US foreign policy in the cold war (McAllister 2002; Dueck 2006); the end of the cold war (Schweller and Wohlforth 2000); US, South Korean, and Japanese strategies vis-à-vis the North Korean nuclear crisis (Cha 2000); the evolution of US monetary policy after the demise of the Bretton Woods monetary system (Sterling-Folker 2002); the origins of the George W. Bush administration's approach to foreign policy and the invasion of Iraq (Dueck 2006; Layne 2006), and many others.

These works are eclectic. Most avoid chest-thumping advocacy on behalf of realism. Yet, if they had to be classified as being in one theoretical school, all would end up in the realist column. All have in common sensitivity to realist core insights, a central role for the four key propositions that define realism, and an appreciation of how neorealism and its successor subschools can aid in the mental experiments that lies at the core of causal explanation of international phenomena. At the same time, most are open to the insights of classical realism and lack dogmatic attachment to one theory or the other. While they hardly represent the last word on their respective subjects, in aggregate they stand as testimony to the ongoing contributions realism makes to the discipline.

7 CONCLUSION: THE ADVENT OF MODEST REALISM

The decline of the aspiration for a monolithic and universal realist theory of international relations may well be associated with the relative decline of realism's centrality in the discipline. In the years ahead, the contention with which I began this chapter—that international relations is in many ways a sustained debate about realism—may well read as an anachronism. Diehard realist partisans may regret that development and pine for the days when neorealism seemed to some to have a claim as the field's "master theory." And diehard antirealists may miss the days when an overreaching realism made it easy to tout the most banal observation as a major contribution. But if the interest is in productive scholarship, such regret would be misplaced. Realism's diversity is increasingly transparent, realist scholarship is more problem focused, more empirical, more historically and methodologically sophisticated, and more open to other traditions and disciplines than it ever was in the heyday of classical or neorealism. As a result, scholars working within the realist tradition are arguably adding more to knowledge about their subject today than ever before.

REFERENCES

ASHLEY, R. K. 1986. The poverty of neorealism. Pp. 255–300 in *Neorealism and its Critics*, ed. R. O. Keohane. New York: Columbia University Press.

BROOKS, S. G. 1997. Dueling realisms. *International Organization*, 51: 445–77.

BUTTERFIELD, H. 1950. *Christianity and History*. New York: Charles Scriber's Sons.

CARR, E. H. 1946. *The Twenty Years' Crisis, 1919–1939: An Introduction to the Study of International Relations*, 2nd edn. New York: St Martin's Press.

CHA, V. 2000. Abandonment, entrapment, and neoclassical realism in Asia: the United States, Japan, and Korea. *International Studies Quarterly*, 44: 261–91.

COADY, C. A. J. 2005. The moral reality in realism. *Journal of Applied Philosophy*, 22: 121–36.

COPELAND, D. 2000. *The Origins of Major War*. Ithaca, NY: Cornell University Press.

CRANE, G. 1998. *Thucydides and the Ancient Simplicity: The Limits of Political Realism*. Berkeley: University of California Press.

DAVIDSON, J. W. 2006. *The Origins of Revisionist and Status-Quo States*. New York: Palgrave Macmillan.

DUECK, C. 2006. *Reluctant Crusaders: Power, Culture, and Change in American Grand Strategy*. Princeton, NJ: Princeton University Press.

ELMAN, C. 1996. Horses for courses: why *not* neorealist theories of foreign policy? *Security Studies*, 6: 7–53.

FRANKEL, B. 1996. Restating the realist case: an introduction. *Security Studies*, 5: ix–xx.

GARNETT, J. C. 1984. *Commonsense and the Theory of International Politics*. London: Macmillan.

GILPIN, R. G. 1981. *War and Change in World Politics*. Cambridge: Cambridge University Press.

—— 1986. The richness of the tradition of political realism. Pp. 301–21 in *Neorealism and its Critics*, ed. R. O. Keohane. New York: Columbia University Press.

—— 1996. No one loves a political realist. *Security Studies*, 5: 3–26.

GLASER, C. L. 1997. The security dilemma revisited. *World Politics*, 50: 171–201.

GRIECO, J. 1988. Realist theory and the problem of international cooperation: analysis with an amended prisoner's dilemma model. *Journal of Politics*, 50: 600–24.

—— 1997. Realist international theory and the study of world politics. Pp. 163–201 in *New Thinking in International Relations Theory*, ed. M. W. Doyle and G. J. Ikenberry. Boulder, Colo.: Westview.

HASLAM, J. 2002. *No Virtue Like Necessity: Realist Thought in International Relations since Machiavelli*. New Haven, Conn.: Yale University Press.

HERZ, J. H. 1950. Idealist internationalism and the security dilemma. *World Politics*, 2: 157–80.

JACKSON, P., and NEXON, D. 2004. Constructivist realism or realist-constructivism? *International Studies Review*, 6: 337–41.

JERVIS, R. 1986. Cooperation under the security dilemma. *World Politics*, 30: 167–214.

KEOHANE, R. O. 1984. *After Hegemony: Cooperation and Discord in the World Political Economy*. Princeton, NJ: Princeton University Press.

—— 1986. Theory of world politics: structural realism and beyond. Pp. 158–201 in *Neorealism and its Critics*, ed. R. O. Keohane. New York: Columbia University Press.

LAYNE, C. 2006. *The Peace of Illusions: American Grand Strategy from 1940 to the Present*. Ithaca, NY: Cornell University Press.

LEBOW, R. N. 2003. *The Tragic Vision of Politics: Ethics, Interests, and Orders*. Cambridge: Cambridge University Press.

LEGRO, J. W., and MORAVCSIK, A. 1999. Is anybody still a realist? *International Security*, 24: 5–55.

LOBELL, S. E. 2003. *The Challenge of Hegemony: Grand Strategy, Trade, and Domestic Politics*. Ann Arbor: University of Michigan Press.

MCALLISTER, J. 2002. *No Exit: America and the German Problem, 1943–1954*. Ithaca, NY: Cornell University Press.

MEARSHEIMER, J. J. 2001. *The Tragedy of Great Power Politics*. New York: Norton.

MORGENTHAU, H. J. 1954. *Politics among Nations: The Struggle for Power and Peace*, 2nd edn. New York: Alfred A. Knopf.

NICHOLSON, M. 1998. Realism and utopianism revisited. Pp. 65–82 in *The Eighty Years' Crisis: International Relations 1919–1999*, ed. T. Dunne, M. Cox, and K. Booth. Cambridge: Cambridge University Press.

PAPE, R. 2005. Soft balancing against the United States. *International Security*, 30: 7–45.

RIPSMAN, N. M. 2002. *Peacemaking by Democracies: The Effect of State Autonomy on the Post-World War Settlements*. University Park: Pennsylvania State University Press.

ROSE, G. 1998. Neoclassical realism and theories of foreign policy. *World Politics*, 51: 144–72.

SCHWELLER, R. L. 2003. The progressiveness of neoclassical realism. Pp. 311–47 in *Progress in International Relations Theory: Appraising the Field*, ed. C. Elman and M. F. Elman. Cambridge, Mass.: MIT Press.

—— 2006. *Unanswered Threats: Political Constraints on the Balance of Power*. Princeton, NJ: Princeton University Press.

—— and WOHLFORTH, W. C. 2000. Power test: evaluating realism in response to the end of the Cold War. *Security Studies*, 9: 60–107.

SNYDER, G. H. 1997. *Alliance Politics*. Ithaca, NY: Cornell University Press.

SPIRTAS, M. 1996. A house divided: tragedy and evil in realist theory. Pp. 385–423 in *Realism, Restatements and Renewal*, ed. B. Frankel. London: Frank Cass.

STERLING-FOLKER, J. 2002. Realism and the constructivist challenge: rejecting, reconstructing, or rereading. *International Studies Review*, 4: 73–97.

—— 2004. Realist-constructivism and morality. *International Studies Review*, 6: 341–3.

TALIAFERRO, J. W. 2000–1. Security seeking under anarchy: defensive realism revisited. *International Security*, 25: 128–61.

—— 2004. *Balancing Risks: Great Power Intervention in the Periphery*. Ithaca, NY: Cornell University Press.

TUCKER, R. W. 1952. Professor Morgenthau's theory of political "realism." *American Political Science Review*, 46: 214–24.

VAN EVERA, S. 1999. *Causes of War: Power and the Roots of Conflict*. Ithaca, NY: Cornell University Press.

VASQUEZ, J. A. 1998. *The Power of Power Politics: From Classical Realism to Neotraditionalism*. Cambridge: Cambridge University Press.

WALT, S. M. 1985. Alliance formation and the balance of world power. *International Security*, 9: 3–43.

—— 1987. *The Origins of Alliances*. Ithaca, NY: Cornell University Press.

WALTZ, K. N. 1959. *Man, the State, and War: A Theoretical Analysis*. New York: Columbia University Press.

—— 1979. *Theory of International Politics*. New York: Random House.

—— 1991. Realist thought and neorealist theory. Pp. 21–37 in *The Evolution of Theory in International Relations: Essays in Honor of William T. R. Fox*, ed. R. L. Rothstein. Columbia: University of South Carolina Press.

—— 1996. International politics is not foreign policy. *Security Studies*, 6: 54–7.

WENDT, A. 1999. *Social Theory of International Politics*. Cambridge: Cambridge University Press.

WOHLFORTH, W. C. 1993. *The Elusive Balance: Power and Perceptions during the Cold War*. Ithaca, NY: Cornell University Press.

—— 1999. The stability of a unipolar world. *International Security*, 24: 5–41.

—— 2007. Realism and foreign policy. Pp. 31–48 in *Foreign Policy: Theories, Actors, Cases*, ed. S. Smith, A. Hadfield, and T. Dunne. Oxford: Oxford University Press.

CHAPTER 8

....

THE ETHICS
OF REALISM

....

JACK DONNELLY

THIS and the preceding chapter treat political realism[1] as a loose but distinctive tradition of international theory centered on four propositions.

1. *Anarchy*. The absence of government makes international relations a qualitatively distinct domain of political action.
2. *Egoism*. Individuals and groups tend to pursue self-interest narrowly defined.
3. *Groupism*. Politics takes place within and between groups.
4. *Power politics*. Egoistic groups interacting in anarchy generate a politics of power and security. "International politics are always power politics" (Carr 1946, 145).

The priority of the pursuit of power marginalizes *all* other objectives. This chapter focuses on the standard realist argument that international politics "is a practical exercise and not a moral one" (Kennan 1954, 48), that "no ethical standards are applicable to relations between states" (Carr 1946, 153). "Universal moral principles cannot be applied to the actions of states" (Morgenthau 1954, 9). The "reality" of international politics "justifies and necessitates political policies which a purely individualistic ethic must always find embarrassing" (Niebuhr 1932, xi).

---

[1] Political realism has no obvious connection with either moral realism, the view that moral judgments refer to or are based on natural or objective features of the world, or scientific realism, the view that theory-independent knowledge of unobservable entities is possible, making it in principle possible to obtain accurate scientific knowledge of the "true" nature of reality.

I show that such categorical denials of the ethical dimension of international relations, although rooted in important insights, are both descriptively inaccurate and prescriptively perverse. Sophisticated realists, however, acknowledge that the "realities" of power politics are but one dimension of an adequate theory or practice of international politics. Initial appearances to the contrary, most leading realists grant ethics a necessary if subordinate place in international relations—although they generally fail to grapple with the contradictions between this account and their more familiar calls for an amoral foreign policy.

Realism fits the structure of this part of this *Handbook* quite well. It has typically been understood by its leading proponents and critics alike as both an explanatory account of the way the world is (the subject of the preceding chapter) and a set of prescriptions, based on this reading of political "reality," for how societies and their leaders ought to practice international relations (my subject here). The difference in substantive focus, however, leads this chapter to deal with a rather different part of the realist literature. Where the preceding chapter focused on relatively recent work by (primarily American) social scientists, this chapter draws primarily on the work of earlier generations. Part of the reason is that social scientists today are much less inclined than their predecessors to address moral issues in their professional work. No less important, though, is the unrivaled power and vitality of the arguments of these "classical" realist authors.

1 Moral Relativism

Some realists claim that morality is relative to a particular community rather than widely shared across states, societies, or cultures. For example, E. H. Carr (1946, 2, 87) claims that "morality can only be relative, not universal." "Supposedly absolute and universal principles [are] not principles at all, but the unconscious reflexions of national policy based on a particular interpretation of national interest at a particular time." George Kennan (1954, 103, 47, 36) similarly contends that "our own national interest is all that we are really capable of knowing and understanding" and counsels against assuming that "our moral values ... necessarily have validity for people everywhere." Kennan even claims that "in most international differences elements of right and wrong, comparable to those that prevail in personal relations, are—if they exist at all, which is a question—simply not discernable to the outsider."

In fact, however, we can and do have considerable knowledge of the values and interests of others. Numerous international issues do involve genuine questions of right and wrong. And in contemporary international relations there is widespread agreement, for example, that aggressive war is impermissible and that genocide is a legitimate subject of international concern and action.

The breadth, depth, and policy implications of such shared values certainly are matters of intense controversy. The claim that political values are merely national, however, is descriptively false. An admirable caution against an inappropriate belief in the universality of one's own values has been overgeneralized into a deeply mistaken denial of shared values.

Kennan (1985–6, 206) also confuses the discussion when he claims that the national interest is a matter of "unavoidable necessit[y]" and therefore "subject to classification neither as 'good' or 'bad'." This is clearly false. Any "necessity" is neither natural nor inescapable. And unless the national interest is in some sense good, there is no obvious reason to follow it.

Not surprisingly, then, most realists reject moral relativism, particularly in its stronger forms. Reinhold Niebuhr (e.g. 1932; 1941; 1953) and Herbert Butterfield (e.g. 1960; 1953) are the most prominent of many Christian realists. Among secular realists, Hans Morgenthau (1979, 10) argues that "there is one moral code ... [which] is something objective that is to be discovered" (cf. Morgenthau 1946, 178–80, 195–6; 1962b, 43, 237). This view is also shared by no less radical a realist than Niccolò Machiavelli (1970; 1985).

Consider Machiavelli's conception of "cruelties well used." "Those can be called well used (if it is permissible to speak well of evil) that are done at a stroke, out of the necessity to secure oneself, and then are not persisted in but are turned to as much utility for the subjects as one can" (The Prince, ch. 8, para. 4; cf. ch. 17, para. 1). Although morality cannot be applied directly to politics, Machiavelli insists that one must "not depart from good, when possible, but know how to enter into evil, when forced by necessity" (The Prince, ch. 18, para. 5). Note his very conventional understandings of good and evil. Might does not make right. Immoral means are intrinsically bad and thus should be kept to a minimum—and even when necessary must be judged by the standard of "utility for the subjects," the common public good.

Rather than reject conventional notions of morality and justice, most realists claim instead that these standards either do not apply to (international) politics or are appropriately overridden by other considerations. Human nature, international anarchy, and the special character of the state and statesmanship are the principal grounds on which realists argue that "other criteria, sadder, more limited, more practical, must be allowed to prevail" (Kennan 1954, 49).

2 NATURAL IMPULSION

The Athenian envoys in Thucydides' "Melian Dialogue" (1982, bk. V, chs. 85–111) present the most radical, and probably best-known, realist rejection of ethics in international affairs. "Right, as the world goes, is only in question between equals in power, while the strong do what they can and the weak suffer what they must" (bk. V, ch. 89). "Of the gods we believe, and of men we know, that by a necessary law of their nature they rule wherever they can" (bk. V, ch. 105). As another group of anonymous Athenians claimed just before the outbreak of the war, they acquired and held their empire under "the pressure of three of the strongest motives, fear, honor, and interest. And it was not we who set the example, for it has always been the law that the weaker should be subject to the stronger" (bk. I, ch. 76; cf. bk. I, ch. 72).

Even setting aside the difficulties of establishing such "facts" and "laws" and of deriving "ought" from "is," these arguments are deeply problematic. If the impulse to rule were indeed an overwhelming force of nature, then, following the moral maxim "ought implies can," conquerors and tyrants might be excused from the requirements of justice. Thucydides' Athenians, however, do not act out of irresistible natural compulsion. Immediately after appealing to the law of the rule of the stronger, they claim that they have treated their allies with greater respect for justice than their position compelled them to do (bk. I, ch. 76). And at Melos they *could* have taken justice into consideration. They chose, rather than were compelled, to act unjustly—in the end, killing all the men and enslaving the women and children, because the Melians refused to abandon their neutrality.

Even if "all men lust for power" (Morgenthau 1962*a*, 42), most realists appreciate that such impulses are not inevitably overwhelming. For example, Thomas Hobbes (1986) in Chapter 13 of *Leviathan* stresses the roots of violent conflict lying in the passions of competition, diffidence, and glory, and the associated desires for gain, safety, and reputation. He concludes the chapter, however, by noting that human nature also includes passions that incline us to peace, as well as reason, which allows us to devise alternatives to war. Likewise, Niebuhr, although he emphasizes "the universality of... egoistic corruption" (1953, 13), also insists that we are, and always remain, under a moral obligation to struggle against our fallen nature. "The Christian doctrine of original sin with its seemingly contradictory assertions about the inevitability of sin and man's responsibility for sin is a dialectical truth which does justice to the fact that man's self-love and self-centeredness is inevitable, but not in such a way as to fit into the category of natural necessity" (1941, 263).

This vacillation between one-sided and bifurcated accounts of human nature reflects a tension that, as we shall see, runs through realist arguments. Realists regularly, sometimes spectacularly, overstate the nature and significance of the "facts" that constrain the pursuit of moral objectives in (international) politics. Yet some realists—often the same individuals in more reflective moods—recognize that these "facts" do not justify, let alone require, amoral power politics.

3 ANARCHY

International anarchy, the absence of government above the level of the state, regularly leads realists to argue that "the cleavage between individual morality and international morality corresponds to the difference between social relations in a community and those in a society bordering on anarchy" (Schwarzenberger 1951, 231). But international relations simply is not a domain where "the law of the jungle still prevails" (Schuman 1941, 9). And it is obviously false to claim that "states in anarchy cannot afford to be moral. The possibility of moral behavior rests upon the existence of an effective government that can deter and punish illegal actions" (Art and Waltz 1971, 6). Just as individuals may behave morally in the absence of government enforcement of moral rules, so moral behavior is possible in international relations.

Once more, the archetypical realist argument stretches an important insight well beyond the breaking point. The absence of centralized enforcement of norms and agreements will increase the incidence of immoral or illegal behavior. But *all* national interests and objectives run up against anarchy. No one would argue that we should abandon pursuing economic interests or stop trying to avoid war with our adversaries because anarchy complicates realizing such objectives. Similarly, anarchy does not require abandoning ethical goals of foreign policy. The difficulty of achieving particular ethical, economic, military, or political objectives in anarchic orders is no reason never to try.

4 REASON(S) OF STATE

Perhaps the strongest realist arguments appeal to the nature of states and statesman-ship. The doctrine of *raison d'état* (reason(s) of state) holds that, "where interna-tional relations are concerned, the interests of the state predominate over all other interests and values" (Haslam 2002, 12). In international relations, it is claimed, the interests of one's own political group appropriately take priority over the interests of other groups and other normative considerations. Because the "primary oblig-ation" of any government "is to the *interests* of the national society it represents," "the same moral concepts are no longer relevant to it" (Kennan 1985–6, 206; 1954, 48).

Such arguments, however, are ethical arguments. They concern *which* values are appropriate in international relations, not whether foreign policy is appropriately subject to normative evaluation. "Power politics may be defined as a system of international relations in which groups consider themselves to be ultimate ends"

(Schwarzenberger 1951, 13). Thus Morgenthau (1951, 33) talks of "the moral dignity of the national interest," and Heinrich von Treitschke (1916, 54) considers the state "a high moral good in itself."

Unfortunately, though, realists rarely present an explicit defense for choosing *these* values over others when they conflict. *Raison d'état* arguments usually simply draw our attention to the values associated with states and other political communities. Other rationalities and normative standards typically are set aside rather than argued against. And the limits that other values place on the pursuit of national interests and values are generally ignored.

5 SURVIVAL

A more limited, and more powerful, realist argument appeals to the preemptory value of (national) survival. For example, Henry Kissinger (1977, 46) argues that "the statesman manipulates reality; his first goal is survival." Robert Tucker likewise claims that "the statesman has as his highest moral imperative the preservation of the state entrusted to his care" (Osgood and Tucker 1967, 304 n. 71). When survival truly is at stake, all else may indeed appropriately give way, much as domestic law and most moral theories permit private individuals to use deadly force in self-defense.

Survival, however, rarely is at stake. It simply is not true that "the struggle for power is identical with the struggle for survival" (Spykman 1942, 18). Only rarely is it the case that "the system forces states to behave according to the dictates of realism, or risk destruction" (Mearsheimer 1995, 91).

Other national interests, though, no matter how "vital," lack the preemptive force of survival. They must be balanced against competing political, legal, moral, and other imperatives. The resulting dilemmas are real and important. But realists typically ignore these problems. And at their worst they advance the monstrously misguided claim that national interests ought always to take precedence over all other values in the decisions of statesmen.

6 THE OFFICE OF THE STATESMAN

Turning from states to statesmen, realists regularly argue that different standards apply to the public actions of national leaders and the actions of private individuals (e.g. Carr 1946, 151; Kennan 1954, 48; Thompson 1985, 8). Like other professionals, statesmen have a professional obligation to give priority to the interests of their "clients." Much as a defense lawyer is ethically bound to (within certain limits) give an aggressive defense to a guilty client, and a doctor (within certain limits) is required to do what is best for her patient rather than society as a whole, so a statesman is, by the nature of her office, required to do what is best for her state and its interests. "Unlike the solitary individual who may claim the right to judge political action by universal ethical guidelines, the statesman will always make his decision on the basis of the state's interest" (Russell 1990, 51).

This regularly leads to policies that treat the lives and interests of nationals and foreigners differently. For example, Western embassies evacuated their own nationals but few locals when the genocide began in Rwanda in April 1994. Morally problematic as this may be, we not only expect and regularly accept but often even demand such behavior. National leaders are agents charged with a special *ethical* responsibility to protect the rights and further the interests of their citizens, the principals for whom they work.

The resulting foreign policy may be "amoral" in the sense that it is not shaped or directly judged by the principles of ordinary morality. It is, however, neither "value free" nor beyond ethical or other normative limits. Much as an attorney is obliged to divulge knowledge of a future crime planned by her client or a doctor is prohibited from purchasing an organ for her patient, there are limits on how statesmen may legitimately pursue the interests of their citizens.

Some limits arise from international law and the ethical (and other) norms of the society of states.[2] For example, today states may legitimately use force only in self-defense and only within the restrictions imposed by the laws of war and humanitarian law.

National interests and values, however, may also constrain a state's foreign policy. Consider, for example, the commitment of many states to famine and disaster relief, democracy promotion, development assistance, or human rights. "The national interest" is what the term manifestly indicates—namely, those interests/values that are held by the nation. The insistence of some realists (e.g. Morgenthau 1954, 5, 10) that states define their interest in terms of power reflects a deeply contentious, and descriptively inaccurate, prescriptive theory of foreign policy.

There is no compelling theoretical reason why a state should not place a high value on, for example, fighting communism, or Islamo-fascism, or world poverty. Appeals to *raison d'état* and statesmanship cannot determine what interests the state has or ought to have. These questions of values exceed the reach of the insights of realism.

---

[2] If an international society has few if any shared norms and values, that is an empirical fact about that particular international society rather than a general theoretical feature of international relations.

7 PRUDENCE

An even more explicitly ethical argument for an "amoral" foreign policy appeals to "prudence," which Machiavelli defines as "knowing how to recognize the qualities of inconveniences, and … picking the less bad as good" (*The Prince*, ch. 21, para. 6). Because "one always finds that, bound up with what is good, there is some evil," Machiavelli counsels emulating the Romans, who "always took the lesser evil to be the better alternative" (*Discourses*, bk. III, ch. 37, para. 1; bk. I, ch. 38, para. 2).

Morgenthau similarly argues that "prudence—the weighing of the consequences of alternative political actions—[is] the supreme virtue in politics. Ethics in the abstract judges action by its conformity with the moral law; political ethics judges action by its political consequences" (1954, 9). "Political ethics is indeed the ethics of doing evil … choose, since evil there must be, among several possible actions the one that is least evil" (1946, 202; cf. Thompson 1985, 13). This is a variant on Max Weber's famous distinction between an ethic of ultimate ends and an ethic of responsibility.[3]

The public good of one's own state, however, is not the only appropriate standard for judging the actions of statesmen. Prudence does regularly conflict with morality, religion, and other values. There is no reason to believe, though, that it *always* appropriately takes priority over all other values and concerns. And strikingly absent from most realist discussions is any account of how to balance these competing normative demands.

I suspect that much of the realist tendency to exaggerate arises from failing to explore the complex but unavoidable interactions of the demands of power, morality, and statesmanship. Dazzled by the power of their insights into the (undeniably important) limits on pursuing moral, legal, and humanitarian objectives, realists typically fail to reflect systematically on the limits of power politics. And it is particularly tragic for a tradition that emphasizes responsible statesmanship that realists not only fail to grapple seriously with the problems of balancing competing values but that their characteristic exaggerations short-circuit serious engagement with this central issue of statesmanship.

8 REALISM AND MORALISM

A defensible realist ethic is perhaps best seen as a warning against the inappropriate application of moral standards to international political action. "The realist target

---

[3] See Weber's 1919 essay, "Politics as a vocation," widely reprinted—e.g. in Weber (1958; 2004); cf. also Williams (2005, ch. 5). For an excellent brief account of Weber as a realist, see Smith (1986, ch. 2).

is, or should be, not morality but certain distortions of morality, distortions that deserve the name of moralism" (Acheson 1958; cf. Thompson 1985, 5; Lefever 1998, ch. 9; Coady 2005, 123). Thus leading figures such as Carr, Niebuhr, and Kennan explicitly cast their work as a critique of "idealism," understood as a combination of rationalism, moralism, and legalism.

Here too, though, a valuable caution regularly is unreasonably exaggerated. For example, Carr (1946, 153) claims that "theories of international morality tend to fall into two categories. Realists...hold that relations between states are governed solely by power and that morality plays no part in them. The opposite theory, propounded by most utopian writers, is that the same code of morality is applicable to individuals and to states." In fact, though, not only are there many other positions but few people actually hold either of these views. Most people, both lay and professional, understand that statesmen are subject to the demands of competing systems of values. And, on careful examination, we find that most leading realists acknowledge that moral and ethical principles are, as Kenneth Thompson (1985, 22) puts it, "operative but not controlling."

Carr (1946, 235) himself, in a more restrained moment, argues that "it is an unreal kind of realism which ignores the element of morality in any world order." Morgenthau talks of "the curious dialectic of ethics and politics, which prevents the latter, in spite of itself, from escaping the former's judgment and normative direction" (1946, 177) and allows that "nations recognize a moral obligation to refrain from the infliction of death and suffering under certain conditions despite the possibility of justifying such conduct in the light of...the national interest" (1948, 177). Niebuhr (1932, 233, xxiv) not only insists that "an adequate political morality must do justice to the insights of both moralists and political realists" but argues that the "ultimate purpose" of realist analysis "is to find political methods which will offer the most promise of achieving an ethical social goal for society."

Realists rightly remind us of the dangers of ignoring "realities" rooted in groupism, egoism, and anarchy. A narrow vision of "the national interest defined in terms of power" (Morgenthau 1954, 5, 10) certainly deserves consideration in debates over a state's international objectives. But arguments that "no ethical standards are applicable to relations between states" (Carr 1946, 153) and that "universal moral principles cannot be applied to the actions of states" (Morgenthau 1954, 9) not only cannot bear critical scrutiny but prove not even to reflect the considered views of most leading self-identified realists—despite their unfortunate tendency to repeat and emphasize such indefensibly exaggerated claims.[4] As John Herz (1976,

----

[4] Joel Rosenthal's social history (1991) of the postwar generation of American realists, *Righteous Realists*, nicely captures the crusading spirit of these critics of moralism, who in their deeply held belief in their own insight and righteousness were unusually prone to exaggerating both the power of realism and the shortcomings of other approaches. Consider, for example, the inaccurate and unfair labels "idealists" and "utopians" with which they regularly tarred analysts who took seriously the demands of morality, law, or reason in international relations.

11) notes, "the mitigation, channeling, balancing, or control of power has prevailed perhaps more often than the inevitability of power politics would lead one to believe."

9 THE CONTRIBUTIONS AND LIMITS OF REALISM

The implication of the preceding assessment is that realism is best read as a cautionary ethic of political prudence rooted in a narrow yet insightful vision of international politics.[5] But realism can avoid encouraging a monstrously distorted foreign policy only if we take to heart Carr's insistence (1946, 89) that "we cannot ultimately find a resting place in pure realism." "Political action must be based on a co-ordination of morality and power." "Sound political thought and sound political life will be found only where both [reality and utopia, power and morality] have their place" (Carr 1946, 97; cf. Schwarzenberger 1951, xv).[6]

We must also guard against a very different sort of exaggeration. Not every appeal to anarchy, egoism, or groupism is realist, in either inspiration or application. Analysts of virtually all traditions and theoretical perspectives take anarchy as a defining feature of international relations. Only radical cosmopolitans, libertarians, and anarchists challenge the assumption of groupism. Most ethical traditions and moral theories see the struggle with egoism as central to the problems of moral action. Realism does not have a monopoly or copyright on these explanatory variables, let alone on conflict.

Nonetheless, the combination of anarchy, egoism, and groupism, leading to strong pressures to conflict-generating power politics, does give realist analyses a recognizable style and character—and value. So long as realism does not claim too much for itself, its central place in the discipline is deserved. Realism, however, is not, and cannot be, the general theory of international politics or international ethics that many of its proponents present it to be.

I thus share William Wohlforth's stress, at the end of the preceding chapter, on the importance of modesty among realists. I am, however, less sanguine about

---

[5] Elsewhere (Donnelly 2005, 52–4; 2000, ch. 9) I make a parallel argument about realism as a social scientific theory. For other summary assessments of realism, in addition to the preceding chapter, see Gilpin (1986), Keohane (1986), Doyle (1997), Grieco (1997), Guzzini (1998), Jervis (1998), Vasquez (1998), and Walt (2002).

[6] Niebuhr (1944, 14–15) similarly stresses combining the insights of "the children of darkness" and "the children of light;" that is, "moral cynics, who know no law beyond their will and interest," and thus are characteristically evil but wise, and "those who believe that self-interest should be brought under the discipline of a higher law," who Niebuhr paints as characteristically virtuous but foolish.

the systematic change that he discerns. For example, John Mearsheimer seems to me hardly modest in his theoretical aspirations or claims and Stephen Walt's arguments (2002; 1997) for "the enduring relevance of the realist tradition" and "the progressive power of realism" are not much more modest than those of his teacher, Kenneth Waltz. Conversely, the more consistent modesty of recent realists such as Charles Glaser or Randall Schweller is no greater than that of, say, Niebuhr, Herz, Tucker, or Glenn Snyder. I see more continuity and recurrence than change. In particular, I expect the peculiar mixture of modesty and exaggeration, and a striking tendency to forget or suppress the limits that one "knows" apply, to remain characteristic of the realist tradition in the coming years.

References

ACHESON, D. 1958. Morality, moralism, and diplomacy. *Yale Review*, 47: 481–93.

ART, R. J., and WALTZ, K. N. 1971. Technology, strategy, and the uses of force. Pp. 1–25 in *The Use of Force: International Politics and Foreign Policy*, ed. R. J. Art and K. N. Waltz. Boston: Little, Brown.

BUTTERFIELD, H. 1953. *Christianity, Diplomacy and War*. London: Epworth Press.

——1960. *International Conflict in the Twentieth Century: A Christian View*. New York: Harper.

CARR, E. H. 1946. *The Twenty Years' Crisis, 1919–1939: An Introduction to the Study of International Relations*, 2nd edn. New York: St Martin's Press.

COADY, C. A. J. 2005. The moral reality in realism. *Journal of Applied Philosophy*, 22: 121–36.

DONNELLY, J. 2000. *Realism and International Relations*. Cambridge: Cambridge University Press.

——2005. Realism. Pp. 29–54 in *Theories of International Relations*, 3rd edn., S. Burchill, A. Linklater, R. Devetak, J. Donnelly, M. Paterson, C. Reus-Smit, and J. True. London: Palgrave.

DOYLE, M. W. 1997. *Ways of War and Peace: Realism, Liberalism, and Socialism*. New York: Norton.

GILPIN, R. G. 1986. The richness of the tradition of political realism. Pp. 301–21 in *Neorealism and its Critics*, ed. R. O. Keohane. New York: Columbia University Press.

GRIECO, J. M. 1997. Realist international theory and the study of world politics. Pp. 163–201 in *New Thinking in International Relations Theory*, ed. M. W. Doyle and G. J. Ikenberry. Boulder, Colo.: Westview.

GUZZINI, S. 1998. *Realism in International Relations and International Political Economy: The Continuing Story of a Death Foretold*. London: Routledge.

HASLAM, J. 2002. *No Virtue Like Necessity: Realist Thought in International Relations since Machiavelli*. New Haven, Conn.: Yale University Press.

HERZ, J. H. 1976. *The Nation-State and the Crisis of World Politics: Essays on International Politics in the Twentieth Century*. New York: D. McKay.

HOBBES, T. 1986. *Leviathan*. Harmondsworth: Penguin.

JERVIS, R. 1998. Realism in the study of world politics. *International Organization*, 52: 971–91.

KENNAN, G. F. 1954. *Realities of American Foreign Policy*. Princeton, NJ: Princeton University Press.

—— 1985–6. Morality and foreign policy. *Foreign Affairs*, 64: 205–18.

KEOHANE, R. O. 1986. Theory of world politics: structural realism and beyond. Pp. 158–201 in *Neorealism and its Critics*, ed. R. O. Keohane. New York: Columbia University Press.

KISSINGER, H. A. 1977. *American Foreign Policy*, 3rd edn. New York: Norton.

LEFEVER, E. W. 1998. *The Irony of Virtue: Ethics and American Power*. Boulder, Colo.: Westview.

MACHIAVELLI, N. 1970. *The Discourses*, trans. L. J. Walker. Harmondsworth: Penguin.

—— 1985. *The Prince*, trans. H. C. Mansfield. Chicago: University of Chicago Press.

MEARSHEIMER, J. J. 1995. A realist reply. *International Security*, 20: 82–93.

MORGENTHAU, H. J. 1946. *Scientific Man versus Power Politics*. Chicago: University of Chicago Press.

—— 1948. *Politics among Nations: The Struggle for Power and Peace*. New York: Alfred A. Knopf.

—— 1951. *In Defense of the National Interest: A Critical Examination of American Foreign Policy*. New York: Alfred A. Knopf.

—— 1954. *Politics among Nations: The Struggle for Power and Peace*, 2nd edn. New York: Alfred A. Knopf.

—— 1962*a*. *Politics in the Twentieth Century*, vol. i. *The Decline of Democratic Politics*. Chicago: University of Chicago Press.

—— 1962*b*. *Politics in the Twentieth Century*, vol. iii. *The Restoration of American Politics*. Chicago: University of Chicago Press.

—— 1979. *Human Rights and Foreign Policy*. New York: Council on Religion and International Affairs.

NIEBUHR, R. 1932. *Moral Man and Immoral Society: A Study in Ethics and Politics*. New York: Charles Scribner's Sons.

—— 1941. *The Nature and Destiny of Man: A Christian Interpretation*, vol. i. *Human Nature*. New York: Charles Scribner's Sons.

—— 1944. *The Children of Light and the Children of Darkness: A Vindication of Democracy and a Critique of its Traditional Defence*. New York: Charles Scribner's Sons.

—— 1953. *Christian Realism and Political Problems*. New York: Charles Scribner's Sons.

OSGOOD, R. E., and TUCKER, R. W. 1967. *Force, Order, and Justice*. Baltimore: Johns Hopkins University Press.

ROSENTHAL, J. H. 1991. *Righteous Realists: Political Realism, Responsible Power, and American Culture in the Nuclear Age*. Baton Rouge: Louisiana State University Press.

RUSSELL, G. 1990. *Hans J. Morgenthau and the Ethics of American Statecraft*. Baton Rouge: Louisiana State University Press.

SCHUMAN, F. L. 1941. *International Politics: The Western State System in Transition*, 3rd edn. New York: McGraw-Hill.

SCHWARZENBERGER, G. 1951. *Power Politics: A Study of International Society*, 2nd edn. London: Stevens.

SMITH, M. J. 1986. *Realist Thought from Weber to Kissinger*. Baton Rouge: Louisiana State University Press.

SPYKMAN, N. J. 1942. *America's Strategy in World Politics: The United States and the Balance of Power*. New York: Harcourt, Brace.

THOMPSON, K. W. 1985. *Moralism and Morality in Politics and Diplomacy*. Lanham, Md.: University Press of America.

THUCYDIDES 1982. *The Peloponnesian War*, trans. R. Crawley, rev. edn. New York: Modern Library.

VASQUEZ, J. A. 1998. *The Power of Power Politics: From Classical Realism to Neotraditionalism*. Cambridge: Cambridge University Press.

VON TREITSCHKE, H. 1916. *Politics*, 2 vols. London: Constable.

WALT, S. M. 1997. The progressive power of realism. *American Political Science Review*, 91: 931–5.

——2002. The enduring relevance of the realist tradition. Pp. 197–230 in *Political Science: The State of the Discipline*, ed. I. Katznelson and H. V. Milner. New York: W. W. Norton.

WEBER, M. 1958. *From Max Weber: Essays in Sociology*. New York: Oxford University Press.

——2004. *The Vocation Lectures: Science as a Vocation, Politics as a Vocation*. Indianapolis: Hackett.

WILLIAMS, M. C. 2005. *The Realist Tradition and the Limits of International Relations*. Cambridge: Cambridge University Press.

....

CHAPTER 9

MARXISM

....

BENNO TESCHKE

MARXIST thought on international relations pre-dates its formal establishment as an institutionalized field of study. Its integration into the Western canon of international relations approaches is belated, partial and problematic, and symptomatic of the politics of social science governed by the great twentieth-century contest between communism and capitalism. While Marxist international relations during the interwar years and the "first cold war" was marginal to the discipline, its resurgence after the end of the "long boom," unchallenged US hegemony, and deepening North–South conflicts led in conjunction with the post-positivist and critical turn during the 1980s to its increasing internal differentiation and overall consolidation as a recognizable tradition within the field. Today, after the removal of the intellectual strictures imposed by the geopolitics of bipolarity and released from doctrinal party lines, Marxist international relations presents a vibrant and rich subfield that produces some of the most trenchant challenges to mainstream international relations theory and general social science.

1 MARX AND ENGELS ON INTERNATIONAL RELATIONS

....

This renaissance presents as much a Marxist challenge to international relations as a challenge of the problematique of international relations to Marxism that reaches back into the very core premises of its founders. For Karl Marx and Friedrich Engels never systematically addressed, much less successfully resolved, the question of the spatial and interspatial dimensions of social processes over time on a universal scale (Berki 1971; Soell 1972; Kandal 1989; Harvey 2001). This absence of an explicit theorization of relations between spatiotemporally differentially developing political communities exposes a fundamental deficiency that pervades their conceptions of world history in general and their theory of capitalism in particular. This deficiency underwent several permutations in the intellectual trajectories of Marx and Engels without ever receiving a definitive resolution.

Marx and Engels's initial position was influenced by liberal cosmopolitanism and premised on the transnationalizing power of capitalism and the pacifying consequences of "universal interdependence" based on international commerce—assumptions that ultimately implied a world-historical convergence toward a "world after capitalism's own image." This perspective, first sketched in the 1846 *German Ideology*, received its canonical definition in the 1848 *Communist Manifesto*:

> The need of a constantly expanding market for its products chases the bourgeoisie over the whole surface of the globe. It must nestle everywhere, settle everywhere, establish connections everywhere. The bourgeoisie has through its exploitation of the world-market given a cosmopolitan character to production and consumption in every country ... In place of the old local and national seclusion and self-sufficiency, we have intercourse in every direction, universal interdependence of nations ... The bourgeoisie, by the rapid improvement of all instruments of production, by the immensely facilitated means of communication, draws all, even the most barbarian nations into civilisation (Marx and Engels 1998, 39).

The core dynamic behind this process was driven by the progressive universalization of capitalism, understood as the contradictory relation between waged workers and capitalists whose market-mediated reproduction imposed the need for expanded reproduction through competitive accumulation. This would lead to a series of social transformations in noncapitalist societies whose cumulative result was the creation of the capitalist world market. While this perspective retained the role of states as guarantors of exploitative and antagonistic class-divided societies, militarized inter-state conflicts would be gradually replaced by the consolidation and polarization of classes, leading to the intensification of class struggle on a global scale, culminating eventually in a synchronized proletarian world revolution. Here, the notion of a "simultaneous development on a world scale" prevails (Soell 1972, 112). This original conception provides a singular analytic revolving around the vertical deepening and horizontal widening of capitalism progressively unifying the world geographically, homogenizing national differences sociopolitically, while polarizing class relations universally. This narrative would eventuate in the abolition of national histories and prepare the terrain for world history proper (even though the term *Geschichte* as a consciously planned collective enterprise was reserved for the post-capitalist age). Yet, Marx and Engels never clarified how exactly the trade-mediated expansion of capitalism would transform prevailing regional class relations and state forms in a capitalist direction. They rather imputed an automaticity to a transnationalizing process that discounted domestic class conflict (resistance) and geopolitics (war). This pristine conception extrapolated directly from the national to the universal, eliding the international as the mediating instance that frames the national and fractures and disables the universal to this day.

Such supra-historical abstractions, based on logical deductions untempered by historical experience, received several qualifications after the failed 1848 revolutions that transformed Marx and Engels's perspective on the nexus between capitalist development, revolutions, and war. Prior to 1848, Marx and Engels expected progress through the internationalization of revolutions by means of inter-state wars, pitching a democratic and united Germany against late-absolutist states (Denmark, Russia, and Austria). A successful German bourgeois revolution would end the "Holy Alliance" and shift the European balance of power toward the progressive Western countries. This would lead to a division of Europe into a revolutionary and counter-revolutionary camp. The new constellation was depicted as a struggle between freedom and despotism carried out by "world war." After the failed 1848 revolution, the formula "domestic revolution plus war equals international progress" was now reversed to "war plus revolution equals domestic progress." The world-historical march toward communism came now to be derived less from the unfolding of domestic class dynamics, spilling over into the international, as from defeat in inter-state wars. The consequent delegitimation of the European Old Regimes would facilitate revolutionary change in specific countries. But a third complication came into view: In contrast to earlier confident assumptions of international working-class formation, Marx and especially Engels started to envisage the prospect of the national incorporation of working classes into their respective nation states, most directly through "social imperialism" and the replacement of international class solidarity with national loyalty through warfare.

Overall, the general insight into the variability of country-specific resolutions of particular social and geopolitical conflicts led to a shift from the notion of "simultaneous development on a world scale" to the empirical recognition of socio-temporally differentiated national trajectories, encapsulated in the notion of "unevenness" (Soell 1972, 113–15). Still, the growing recognition of "unevenness" and of force as an integral component of an expanding capitalist world market (India, China, American Civil War, Ottoman Empire, etc.) generated only a series of tergiversations that never resulted in an encompassing praxis-guiding theory that properly accounted for the relation between world-market formation, revolution, and geopolitics. More fundamentally, the move toward "unevenness" relied on a taken-for-granted prior determination: the existence of a system of states that was the precondition for regionally multiple differential developments; hence, the precondition for unevenness. However, as this spatial fragmentation of the total historical process was captured only in its results—differences between separately existing entities—"unevenness" as a central category of analysis discounted both, an explanation of this geopolitical pluriverse and the causative dimension of cross-regional geopolitical dynamics. In this respect, the statement that "bourgeois society comprises...the total commercial and industrial life of a particular stage and transcends in this respect each state and nation, although it is required to represent itself externally as a nation and internally as a state" (Marx and Engels 1976, 50) raises precisely the question in what exactly this requirement consists, insofar as the territorial fragmentation of the states system cannot be derived from the formation of a transnationalizing capitalist bourgeoisie.

While this "geopolitical deficiency" received intermittent attention in Marx and Engels's journalistic and historical writings (however unsatisfactorily), its full challenge surfaces most dramatically where Marxism turns most theoretical: the three volumes of *Das Kapital*. Here, the central object of investigation is "capital" in the abstract, unfolding according to its inner contradictions (the "laws of accumulation"), conceived as a dialectical self-movement that relegates agency and history to the margins as mere illustrations of the "capital-logic." Although "Capital" is adorned with illustrative references to Victorian Britain, it was essentially conceptualized in ideal-typical fashion in a political and geopolitical vacuum—beyond history. While the working plan for the 1857 *Introduction* envisages a theory of the state and international relations (that would remain eventually unfinished), the problem as to *why* political power constitutes itself territorially in the shape of a world system of multiple sovereign states and *how* the dynamics between these political jurisdictions relate to the national and transnational reproduction of capitalism is not even formulated as a research desideratum. Marx and Engels's interest in geopolitics remained primarily tied to the tactical consequences of alterations in world politics for communist strategy and, hence, limited to very perceptive but primarily ad hoc interventions, rather than governed by a sustained reflection on geopolitical and transsocietal relations for the general course of history.

2 CLASSICAL THEORIES OF IMPERIALISM

Classical Marxist theories of imperialism constitute a more systematic and sustained attempt to ground the changing geopolitical dynamics and the crisis and breakdown of world order in the changing dynamics of capitalism. The second generation of Marxists located the "new imperialism," "the scramble for Africa," the arms race, and the final descent into world war in a profound transformation in the nature of capitalism, following a significant slump in the rates of return across the capitalist economies during the world economic crisis of 1873–98. Socialist tactics and strategy were redefined in the light of these developments (Mommsen 1980; Brewer 1990; Chilcote 2000).

This transformation was conceptualized, with various emphases, by Rudolf Hilferding (1981), Nicolai Bukharin (1972), and Vladimir Lenin (1973) in a transition from the era of free competition to the centralization and concentration of capital, leading eventually to national monopolies (trusts and cartels)—the era of monopoly capitalism (Luxemburg 1951) understands imperialism somewhat differently as a permanent component of capitalism in general). The notion of "finance capital" expressed the fusion between industrial and banking capital, uniting previously fractured capitalist interests nationally with a view to instrumentalize the state for expanded reproduction through the political promotion of monopoly profits. Both the concentration of capital and the reliance on the state were rooted in tendencies of overproduction and overaccumulation (underconsumption), thought to be generic to capitalism's long-term dynamics, especially in the age of industry. Domestically, protectionism (high tariffs and quotas) restricted foreign competition, allowing price-setting above world-market levels in home markets and controlled overseas areas. Internationally, the quest for raw materials, the search for new export markets, and the export of capital demanded the territorialization and politico-military control of colonies, leading to empire formation, the regionalization of the world market, and the formation of rival national blocs. According to Bukharin and Lenin, "super-profits" reaped from colonial exploitation were central for the integration of working classes into their "fatherlands" through the prospect of higher wages and social welfare (social imperialism). These "bribes" nurtured a metropolitan "labor aristocracy" rooted in national contexts that betrayed the causes of internationalism. The direct role of the state in the national and international promotion of "finance capital" implied the transformation of private economic competition between firms into public politico-military competition between states, encapsulated in the notion of "inter-imperial rivalry." Intensifying inter-imperial strategic competition over the territorial redivision of the world was bound to lead to world war, increasing the chances that bourgeois power could be broken in defeated states that formed "the weakest link" in the chain of capitalist states. Thus reformulated, the classical expectation that socialist revolution would occur first in the most advanced capitalist countries received a geographical dislocation toward the least developed—Russia, in particular. Through this reversal of the original Marx-Engels position, the transnationalizing tendency of capitalism was renationalized, the relation between the world market and interstate conflict rearticulated, the relative impotence of working classes in the capitalist heartland rendered plausible, while socialist revolution in Russia received a theoretical justification.

Classical Marxist theories of imperialism can be criticized on empirical grounds, specific to the assumptions made relating to a circumscribed period, and on wider theoretical grounds, regarding their relevance as general Marxist theories of international relations. Empirically, few price-setting and market-distorting monopolies actually existed, while cartels were loose inter-firm agreements subject to collapse.

Underconsumptionism was, on the one hand, posited as a phenomenon intrinsic to the capital-logic, yet also deemed to be reversible through "social imperialism." Real wages were rising in the last quarter of the nineteenth century. The account of "finance capital" relied primarily on the example of the German and Austrian banking sectors, which contrasted strongly with more fragmented and competitive banking sectors in Britain and France. Capital exports to the colonial periphery, although rising sharply before the First World War, were significantly lower than capital exports (both portfolio and direct investments) between imperialist powers. Inter-imperial volumes of trade were significantly higher than imperial–colonial commerce. Colonial capital exports were small in absolute terms relative to domestic investments. Rates of return from colonial capital exports were not higher relative to the rates from domestic investment, yet subject to higher risks. "All the evidence suggests that the long-run effects of empire on the development of the imperialist centers was small" (Brewer 2000, 83). Although aggregate results cannot be interpreted as nullifying the economic case for empire since profit expectations may have provided the initial motives for economic and political imperialism (although they raise the question of its sustained character), a simple cost–benefit analysis alone sheds insufficient light on the complexities involved. Special interest groups may have gained privileged leverage on the state, privatizing benefits and socializing costs in terms of significant public expenditures for the military and political maintenance of empire. Still, the historical record is ambiguous.

In a wider theoretical perspective, classical Marxist theories of imperialism are self-limiting by their attempt to explain a particular juncture (c.1873–1917) of capitalist international relations. They cannot be expanded to provide a general theory of *capitalist* international relations. Even the partial character of theories of imperialism is open to a range of powerful theoretical criticisms. The attempt to present a particular phenomenon—with huge variations within specific advanced capitalist countries, in their respective imperial–colonial relations, in the rates of intra-colonial development, and in inter-imperial relations—as a necessary byproduct inscribed in the dynamics of a particular phase of capitalism objectifies its rise, reproduction, and fall. Especially Lenin's interpretation of imperialism as "the highest stage of capitalism" reifies this juncture as a definite and necessary stage (the monopoly stage) intrinsic to the overall development of capitalism, rather than understanding it as a particular (and reversible) outcome of the conflicts between nationally differentially developed societies.

Karl Kautsky (1970, 45–6) raised a similar objection, arguing that "imperialism...represents only one among various modes of expansion of capitalism." His notion of "ultra-imperialism" envisaged the likelihood of cooperation among national capitals—a "holy alliance of imperialists" that was not reduced to an economically necessary logic of capitalism, but that emphasized the variable class (geo)politics of capitalism. In this respect, the theorization of the role of the state in Hilferding, Bukharin, and Lenin was not only reductionist, but also mechanistic and functionalist, both domestically and internationally. Diplomacy, international alliance patterns, and geopolitical crises were deduced from, but not historically analyzed in relation to, nationally variable sociopolitical interests (as a close reading of the 1885 "Berlin Conference" or the 1914 "July Crisis" demands). The tendency to objectify country-specific developments and to generalize them as holding for the capitalist states system as a whole discounted the differential development of political constellations of social forces in the imperialist core countries in their implications for inter-imperialist as well as core–periphery relations. Moreover, social forces in the colonies are generally portrayed as passive recipients, rather than as active participants in specific geopolitical encounters with diverse results, raising the charge of Eurocentrism. These criticisms are ultimately grounded in the failure to address social and political agency more generally.

Although Marx's original direct move from "the national" to "the global" defined as the world market (silencing "the inter-national") was not repeated, the collapsing of multiple and unevenly developing national trajectories into one systemic logic reified the "inter-imperial" as an abstract extrapolation, restrictively defined as a sphere of strategic competition and war. And behind this failure to uncover the variable and interactive dimension of the politics and geopolitics (rather than logic) of the "inter-imperial" lies the absence of an inquiry into the precondition for military conflict—the inter-state system. Classical theories of imperialism took the nation state as a social relation in its plural manifestations—the states system—as given, failing to problematize, much less theorize, the fact that nation states were "relevant units" (Brewer 1990, 123) in the world economy.

3 WORLD-SYSTEMS THEORY

World-systems theory, most prominently represented by Immanuel Wallerstein, draws on classical Marxist theories of imperialism, dependency theory as developed by Andre Gunther Frank, and the work of the *Annales* historian Fernand Braudel (Wallerstein 1974*a*; 1974*b*; 1983; Chase-Dunn 1991). Its objective is to provide a theoretical framework for the interpretation of the entire history of the capitalist world system. Its central unit of analysis is the world economy, understood as an integrated totality defined by a single international division of labor based on different "regimes of labor control" (wage labor, sharecropping, serfdom/slavery) between multiple states. Their strength and geopolitical location within the world economy (core, semi-periphery, periphery) correspond in descending order to their labor regimes. States are hierarchically tied into a system of unequal exchange maintained by their differential power capacities that govern politically set monopolistic terms of trade. Unequal exchange leads to the transfer of surplus from the periphery to the core, consolidating, in turn, the political hierarchies and developmental differentials within it. World economies are generically contrasted to world empires as single territorial units in which tribute is extracted by a central authority. The modern world system originated in the "long sixteenth century" (1450–1640) (in the thirteenth century according to Braudel (1982, 433)) in Europe due to an original regional specialization and division of labor, theorized by a weak technological determinism (high-skilled manufacture in "Western Europe" versus low-skilled agriculture in "Eastern Europe" and raw material production overseas). This enabled European core states to incorporate the semi-periphery/periphery into the world system on their terms, entailing the reproduction of their economic underdevelopment and political dependency. The modern world system, spanning regionally different labor regimes, is invariably described as capitalist, since economic activity beyond the core countries is generically conceived as profit-oriented production for the world market.

This organization of international capitalism on a world scale exhibits a strong tendency toward a self-reinforcing system maintenance. Specifically, it is immune to a reversal to world empires since only a world economy allows for global capital accumulation without the prohibitive politico-military costs of empire-building. In fact, the states system is a precondition for the rise and continuing reproduction of capitalism, since plural sovereignties are needed for the transfer of surplus from peripheries to cores through state-organized competition, preventing the direct absorption of surplus by a centralized imperial formation. A recurring cycle of successive hegemonic states (Genoa/Venice, Holland, Britain, and the United States) periodically alters intra-core hierarchies, rearranging and realigning geocommercial core–(semi-)periphery relations (Arrighi 1994). In contrast to realist hegemonic stability theory that anchors hegemony in military–political capacity alone, hegemony is here grounded in innovations in capital-intensive production systems (which spill over into commercial and then financial superiority), allowing hegemonic states to position themselves at the summit of the international division of labor. Hegemonic transitions are decided by hegemonic intra-core wars between rising challengers and declining status quo powers.

World-systems theory is an evolving theoretical tradition that has undergone several permutations and partial revisions. However, at the center of this approach stands a problematic conception of capitalism as a worldwide commercial network that transfers surplus from the periphery to the core. Implicit in this conception is a failure to consider the origins of capitalist class relations and the specific dynamics of capitalist economic development (Marx's "primitive accumulation" arguably first achieved in seventeenth-century England), leading to a problematic timing of the origins of the modern world system—the Italian–Iberian "age of discovery" during the "long sixteenth century" and a distinct overall narrative of modern world history defined in terms of successive commercial hegemonies (Brenner 1977; Brewer 1990, 161–78; Teschke 2003, 129–39). The tendency to generalize the monopolistic and inter-regional character of capitalism—derived from Marxist theories of imperialism—leads to the equation of all four historical hegemonies as invariably capitalist, downplaying their differences in the types of social relations and state forms that constitute their economies (merchant capitalism, mercantilism, free-trade capitalism, regime-regulated capitalism) and especially the crucial difference between a structurally monopolistic system of merchant capital that defined the Italian, Spanish, and Dutch experiences and the competitive capitalism, rooted in capitalist class relations as defined by Marx, of their British and US successors. This underspecifies the profound variations in the sociopolitical dynamics of different hegemonic powers, their diverse strategies of managing intra-core (competition or cooperation) and core–periphery relations, and the different projects of territorialization over which they presided (Gowan 2006). The flattening of their qualitative differences leads to a highly static depiction of the modern world system revolving around the geographical redistribution of surplus, supervised by changing hegemonic powers.

Wallerstein's definition of capitalism merely interconnects in the sphere of circulation regionally diverse labor regimes that technically adapt to and specialize according to the requirements of international commerce. Since classes and class conflict play a derivative role in the regionally specific construction of "labor regimes" during the moment of their encounter with and integration into the trade-based worldwide division of labor (since labor regimes and class relations are reduced to the kind of product specialization demanded by their export orientation for the world market), world-systems theory is unable to explain the regionally variegated outcomes of these encounters that engendered different class conflicts with different outcomes; that is, the reinforcement of preexisting labor regimes (for example, east-Elbian "second serfdom"), the imposition of completely new pre-capitalist labor regimes (slave-based plantation systems or *encomiendas* in the Americas), or their transformation in a capitalist direction. Labor regimes did not simply emerge as a passive and functional adaptation to the requirements of the world market and the technical exigencies of product specialization, but as class-contested, highly politicized, and active responses to external pressures. Since these regionally diverse resolutions, mediated by prevailing balance of class forces, are short-circuited, the differential paths of economic development and nondevelopment and the chances of states that underwent a successful capitalist transformation to rise to the rank of core state remain obscure to world-systems theory.

Relatedly, Wallerstein's state theory remains spurious. State interests are directly reduced to trade-dependent ruling classes, rather than reflecting diverse class-contested strategies of reproduction within an international force field that also allows the construction of alternative geostrategic projects. A state's strength and position in the world system are directly inferred from its dominant labor regime. The "strength" of core states is premised on a high-skill/high-capitalization regime that simultaneously generates the resources to state-organized surplus transfer from the periphery, thus reinforcing inter-regional hierarchies. The "weakness" of peripheral states expresses their low-skill/low-capitalization regime. This purely quantitative conceptualization of power differentials fails to understand the specific qualitative character of state forms in their relation to class politics across all zones (Brenner 1977; Skocpol 1977).

The states system itself, in turn, is deemed to be a structural feature of the capitalist world economy. "Capitalism and a world-economy (that is, a single division of labour, but multiple polities and cultures) are obverse sides of the same coin" (Wallerstein 1974b, 391; Chase-Dunn 1991, 107). In this perspective, the states system not only performs a functional complementarity to capitalism, but constitutes the very condition of possibility for capitalist expansion and surplus transfer. However, world-systems theory neither addresses nor answers the question whether the states system is itself causally created by—and not simply encountered by—capitalism. The statement that "the interstate system is the political superstructure of the capitalist world-economy and was a deliberate invention of the modern world" (Wallerstein 1995, 141) remains assertoric and without proof. An explanation of the world economy's "obverse side" is missing. Since capitalism—whether defined as commercial exchange or a specific relation of production—originated in a geopolitical context that was already prestructured as a system of plural sovereignties, this geopolitical pluriverse and its attendant strategic pressures demand a theoretical and historical account and not merely a statement on its functionality to capitalism (Teschke 2003; Lacher 2006). This genetic disjuncture between states system and capitalism allows for the explanation of profound historical variations in the configurations between the spaces of capitalist accumulation and political jurisdiction. For the geopolitics of world history since the "long sixteenth century" was marked not only by successful, though not universal, empire formations by capitalist and noncapitalist polities, but by an immense diversity of spatial orders (Teschke 2006, 136). In contrast, even the most dynamic part of world-systems theory—hegemonic successions—repeatedly relapses into a circular account of the essential sameness of successive hegemonies, erecting hegemonic orders on an ever-expanding geographical scale, while maintaining the qualitatively identical mechanisms of international order/hierarchy among multiple states plus surplus transfer. Similarly, the account of hegemonic transitions in terms of hegemonic wars fails to square with the historical record. Venice/Genoa did not clash with Holland; Holland only partially with England (France was the greater challenger); Britain was not militarily defeated by the United States. The overemphasis on hegemonic agency fails fully to incorporate geopolitical contexts into the equation.

Overall, world-systems theory is premised on a deep structural functionalism in which the function, strength, and location of specific states on the world system's core–semi-periphery–periphery spectrum is determined by their trade-mediated integration into the economic structure of the international division of labor. This tends to reinforce existing economic (the "development of underdevelopment") and political hierarchies ("dependency"). The subsumption of very different historical cases under one law-like generalization of rise, expansion, challenge, war, and demise levels their respective specificities. It also tends to reify a cyclical pattern of capitalist world history that leads to theoretical rigidities that jar with actual historical developments while prescribing determinate theoretical expectations for the future course of history. These prescriptions are repeatedly revised in light of the long delay in the "decline of US hegemony" (Arrighi 2005a; 2005b; Wallerstein 2006).

4 Neo-Gramscian International Political Economy

Neo-Gramscian international political economy (IPE, or "transnational historical materialism") presents the most influential Marxist theory in the contemporary international relations discourse. Based on the noneconomistic writings of the Italian communist Antonio Gramsci, the concept of hegemony constitutes the central analytical category to understand historical world orders with a view to devise counter-hegemonic prescriptions against them.

Neo-Gramscian thought entered international relations primarily through the work of Robert Cox (1987, 1–15; 1996, 124, 135), who "derived" categories of analysis from Gramsci's writings and "applied" them to international relations (see also van der Pijl 1984; Gill and Law 1988; Gill 1990, 33–56; 1993; Arrighi 1994; Rupert 1995, 14–38). Hegemonic power is conceptualized as a mutually irreducible configuration between dominant ideas, institutions, and material capacities that are widely accepted as legitimate. Social forces, states, and world orders are interrelated as dialectical wholes, bound together in world hegemonies. A dominant "structure of accumulation," defined as a spatiotemporally specific combination of different "modes of social relations of production," lies at the core of these hegemonies. Cox distinguishes twelve modes (subsistence, peasant lord, primitive labor market, household, self-employment, enterprise labor market, bipartism, enterprise corporatism, tripartism, state corporatism, communal, central planning). Different "monad-modes"—presented simultaneously as Leibnizian self-enclosed entities and as interrelated practices—coexist in different societies, yet are orchestrated and hierarchized by the state, constituting a "structure of accumulation" in which one "monad-mode" is hegemonic. This "structure of accumulation" is then projected abroad, through both the transnationalizing agency of the hegemonic class and the international agency of its hegemonic state. The mechanisms of exercising hegemony consist internationally in specific international organizations (World Bank, International Monetary Fund, G8, UN) that co-opt talent from nonhegemonic foreign elites and allow for a degree of co-determination by and concessions to subaltern states. Transnationally, a hegemonic class universalizes itself through private international fora (Trilateral Commission, Rotary Club, Bilderberg Group, think tanks), fostering the formation of a global civil society—a transnational historic bloc (van der Pijl 1984; Gill 1990). The transnationalization of a hegemonic project, in turn, exercises pressures on subaltern states to align their respective composites of "structures of accumulation" with those of the hegemonic state, often through processes of "passive revolution" and *trasformismo* (state-led reformist processes). These states become internationalized and act as "transmission belts" (Cox 1992, 30) between the hegemon and their respective domestic arrangements and are, ultimately, incorporated into the world hegemonic bloc.

In contrast to realism, which introduced the notion of international hegemony based on the concentration of material power in one dominant state, neo-Gramscians claim that liberal international hegemonies are based on the universalization of particular state–society complexes, maintained primarily by consensus formation (although coercion remains latent) between hegemonic and hegemonized states, rather than on crude power politics alone. The specification of distinct state–society complexes at the heart of successive world hegemonies allows us to distinguish between different inter-state systems with different forms of conflict and cooperation, rather than to collapse their variety into a circular and cyclical realist (or world system's) narrative of the transhistorical rise and fall of world hegemonies. Modern world history is periodized in terms of two successive hegemonies, the *Pax Britannica* and the *Pax Americana*, interrupted by a nonhegemonic period of inter-state rivalry. Other neo-Gramscians, like Giovanni Arrighi (1994), list four world hegemonies—Genoese, Dutch, British, and American. Whereas Cox originally envisaged that the construction of counter-hegemony was possible neither within international organizations, nor within the sphere of a transnational civil society, but in national contexts first, he later renounced this position by arguing for "inter-civilizational dialogue."

Centrally, the replacement of Marx's term "mode of production" with the concept of "structures of accumulation" entails fundamental problems for the neo-Gramscian tradition. For most of Cox's "structures of accumulation" present only historical variations within the capitalist mode of production, whereas the latter is taken as given and never historically theorized. In this perspective, the social conflicts associated with capitalist transformations and the novelty and specific dynamics of capitalist modernity disappear from view (Lacher 2002, 150). The attendant emphasis on inter-ruling class relations—a fixation on inter-elite agency and ideology formation (Scherrer 1998) rather than on class conflict and "primitive accumulation" (Shilliam 2004)—is radicalized by a failure to trace the geographical expansion of capitalism across a territorially preconstituted inter-state system, which is itself taken for granted, but described as being in place by the time of the Treaty of Westphalia (Cox 1987, 111). For Cox, the states system becomes progressively transnationalized/internationalized; for Arrighi, it is, following Wallerstein, a persistent condition for the flowering of capitalism, defined as "a fusion between capital and state," that reproduces inter-state competition over surplus. Yet, it was this protracted but progressive inter-national expansion of the capital relation in its encounter with specific territorially contained correlations of social forces that gave rise to regionally specific resolutions of state–society relations. In this respect, the specific combination of "monad-modes" in diverse national contexts cannot be accepted as pre-given, since these "developed and (in some cases) regressed not as monads, but in 'geo-political' and temporal relation to each other through the exigencies of the expansion and intensification of capitalist sociality" (Shilliam 2004, 83).

The missing political geography of uneven capitalist expansion is addressed by Kees van der Pijl (1998; 2006), who conceives of this process as a three-century cycle in which an expanding "Lockean heartland," composed of ever-larger coalitions of liberal-capitalist states, is repeatedly challenged by successive waves of "Hobbesian contender states." These confrontations are decided not by the balance of military capacities alone, but by the differential ability of these competing state/society complexes to mobilize human productivity, tending to lead to the absorption of defeated contenders into the Lockean heartland. The origin of the heartland lies in the British export of the Lockean state/society complex to its settler colonies, generating a transnational society among its integrated regions. Since the conditions for political autonomy and development outside the heartland are heavily circumscribed by the expanding world economy, state classes outside the heartland tend to generate state-led late-industrialization "catching-up strategies" to resist peripheralization, often leading to the introduction of capitalism by "passive revolutions." This mobilization of society by authoritarian means, necessitated by "relative backwardness," produces very different state/society complexes (in which civil society remains confiscated by and subordinated to the "Hobbesian contender state") that, in some cases, ultimately resolve their tensions with the liberal heartland in a series of contests over world hegemony; that is, world wars. While there remains competition for the leadership of the heartland, each new hegemon coordinates the "international socialization of state functions," incorporating defeated contender states into the heartland and sustaining the interests of capital in general on an expanding geographical scale, leading eventually to an "immanent world state," characterized by governance without government. While realpolitik within the heartland is suspended, transnational policy planning groups, staffed by a transnational managerial class of cadres, set the agendas for the successful integration, reproduction, and continuing expansion of the heartland's transnational society, including the formulation of "comprehensive concepts of control." This reading holds the considerable advantage of setting out a substantive and generative account of the lateral dynamics of capitalist expansion that goes beyond Cox's abstract typologies of state forms and monad-modes (and does not homogenize capitalist space under the heading of hegemony "from above") by tying their emergence and transformations in temporal and geopolitical relation to each other into an overall framework of uneven expansion. It thus opens up a theoretically integrated perspective on the geographical trajectory of the social and geopolitical processes and crises in the transformative conflicts that characterize the long-term dynamics of hegemonies in their internal and external relations.

In a wider perspective, however, the concept of world hegemony as a general category for world history is of very limited applicability. Equivocations over the definition and historical origins of capitalism have contributed to exaggerated claims over the capitalist character and transnationalizing success of specific historic blocs and the attendant restructuring of particular international orders by and for a hegemonic state. Arrighi's "Dutch hegemony," for example, fails to understand the limits posed to Dutch commercial supremacy by an absolutist-mercantilist European states system that imposed its specific competitive patterns of international relations on the Dutch Republic, rather than being hegemonized along the lines of the Dutch social model (Teschke 2003, 133–6). Even the historical record for the first capitalist world hegemony, the *Pax Britannica*, is equivocal. While Britain's nineteenth-century role overseas was of crucial importance, it failed to become hegemonic in continental Europe, where its central objective was negatively defined as preventing the ascendancy of a dominant European challenger through power-balancing (Congress of Vienna and Concert of Europe), rather than the positive pursuit of internationalizing its state–society relations through consensual means (Lacher 2006, 123).

Neo-Gramscian IPE is best equipped to provide a conceptual framework for understanding one particular world order—the *Pax Americana*. While the politics of class is central to Mark Rupert's important work (1995), even here the charge of reducing the analysis of US hegemony to inter-elite relations applies (see Bieler et al. 2006); the depiction of states within the hegemonic order as "transmission belts" between the global and the national discounts their relative autonomy and characterizes them as passive mediators of global forces (Panitch 1996); the privileging of consensus over and against coercion remains dubious, both in intra-core relations and in those between hegemons and nonhegemonized states; and the concentration on hegemonic order de-emphasizes the contradictions and fault lines within transnational historical blocs, including a marginalization of analyses regarding counter-hegemonic movements (Drainville 1994). Finally, neo-Gramscian IPE slides towards a "pluralistic empiricism," far removed from the rigours of Marx's original critique of political economy (Burnham 1991).

While neo-Gramscian IPE has opened up powerful avenues of research, its central category of hegemony is, in the end, unable to provide a more encompassing perspective on the dynamics of capitalist international relations. In line with Gramsci's original twin omissions—lack of an inter-national perspective and discounting

of class politics and social relations in favor of consensual ideology formation—
the passage from the national/hegemonic to the transnational/hegemonic has once
again eliminated the inter-national (with the partial exception of van der Pijl's
work) as a terrain of sociopolitical and geopolitical conflicts and transformations.

5 THE (RE)TURN TO CLASSICAL MARXISM AND POLITICAL MARXISM IN INTERNATIONAL RELATIONS

The return to classical Marxism followed Fred Halliday's programmatic call (1994)
for a "necessary encounter" between historical materialism and international relations. It provoked a refoundation of Marxist international relations theory, reformulated as an international historical sociology, through a sustained reflection
on the relation between capitalism, the state, and the states system in historical
perspective. Justin Rosenberg (1994; for a similar, though less structuralist perspective see Bromley 1994; 1999) demonstrates in his early work the structural correspondence between different geopolitical systems—the classical Greek polis system,
the Italian renaissance city-states system, early modern empires, and the modern
system of sovereign states—and different modes of production/social structures.
Although most geopolitical systems are characterized by anarchy, a "structural
discontinuity" separates all pre-capitalist systems from the modern capitalist international order, premised on the distinction between personalized domination
under pre-capitalist relations of production and impersonal modern sovereignty,
anchored in the separation between the economic and the political in capitalism
(Wood 1995). This structural discontinuity explains the co-constitution and compatibility of a system of bordered (but porous) sovereign states and a transnational
international economy—the "empire of civil society." In this perspective, the capitalist anarchy of the market, regulated by a desubjectified price mechanism, is not
simply analogous to international anarchy, regulated by a desubjectified balance
of power, but its condition of possibility. Modern power politics and its realist
discourse are thus premised on an abstract notion of the state, grounded in a generalized differentiation between the economic and the political under capitalism.

Rosenberg's study is marked by a tension between a structuralist understanding
of Marxism and its attention to historical development (Lacher 2002; Teschke
2003, 39–41). European history is essentially reconstructed as a series of successive, discrete, and self-contained geopolitical orders, leading to the elision of the
transitions between them. The crises—social conflicts, revolutions, and wars—
inherent in these transformations disappear from view. Agency and especially class

conflict are underrepresented. Relatedly, the suggested structural interrelation and functional compatibility between a territorially divided states system and a private, transnational, world market obscures the complex historical dynamics of the co-development of capitalism, the modern state, and the modern states system. The latter two are analytically derived from the first, while all three are regarded as causally and temporally coeval aspects of capitalist modernity. This thesis overplays the explanatory power of capitalism, leaving the historical co-development (but not co-genesis) of capitalism, state, and states system underexplored.

These criticisms are central to Benno Teschke's historical-dialectical reinterpretation of the long-term development of the changing political geographies and geopolitical dynamics of "Europe" from the end of the Carolingian Empire to the emergence and expansion of a capitalist state-society complex in seventeenth- and eighteenth-century Britain, tied into a cumulative narrative of regionally differential class and state formation (Teschke 2003). Theoretically, the account is premised on transformations in politically constituted and class-contested social property relations grounded in different balances of class forces, which generate variable geopolitical strategies of reproduction that define different modes of territoriality and geopolitical relations. Developing the tradition of "political Marxism" (Brenner 1985), the project examines the *sui generis* character of feudal geopolitics (Teschke 1998), reconstructs the emergence of a medieval geopolitical pluriverse, and retraces the diverging, yet interconnected, trajectories of class and state formation in late medieval and early modern France and England. Since French and continental "absolutisms" remained mired in pre-capitalist social property and authority relations, dynastic sovereignty and the persistence of "geopolitical accumulation" among European powers imparted specific premodern practices of international relations (inter-dynastic marriages, personal unions, wars of succession, mercantilist trade wars, predatory equilibrium, and empire formation) on the "Westphalian System" (Teschke 2002). Although these practices constituted a system of multiple territories, it remained composed predominantly by the social relations of dynastic-absolutist sovereignty. The Westphalian Settlement as international relations' foundational moment of the modern states system is thus fundamentally revised. In contrast, the sixteenth century rise of agrarian capitalism in England and a de-personalized form of capitalist sovereignty in post-revolutionary Britain led to the emergence of a uniquely dynamic state/society complex. Regulating continental inter-dynastic relations through the active management of the balance of power, Britain exerted economic and geopolitical pressures that forced continental polities to design diverse counter-strategies of class and state formation through "revolutions from above" in a process of spatiotemporally differentiated and geopolitically combined development (Teschke 2005). Since the states system was not "the obverse side" of capitalism, but the cumulative consequence of century-long medieval and early modern class conflicts over rights of domination and exploitation over land and people, which finally crystallized in a plurality of militarily competing dynastic territories, the interrelation between capitalism and the states system is not the-orized in terms of an invariant capitalist structural functionalism. It is rather conceived in a processual perspective that is attentive to the protracted expan-sion, transformation, and sometimes negation of capitalism within a territorially prefigured geopolitical pluriverse that itself underwent manifold alterations in the process. Capitalist expansion was not a transnational and even process, generating a world "after its own image," but refracted through a series of geopolitically con-tested encounters between polities with diverse results in different regions of the world. This opens up a nondeterministic perspective on the historically changing geopolitical strategies of reproduction and the construction of variable capitalist territorial orders by and between capitalist states.

Hannes Lacher draws out the theoretical implications of the historical disjunc-ture between multiple territory formation and capitalism by tracing the changing articulations between the national and international/global, premised on the notion of strategies of spatialization (Lacher 2006). In contrast to the widespread Marxist and non-Marxist assumption of a twin birth of and co-constitution between cap-italism and the states system, their interrelation cannot be conceived in terms of an invariant "logic of capital," which either eternally reproduces the territorially segmented form of capitalist rule (as in world-systems theory) or progressively deterritorializes and homogenizes states through the transnational expansion of capitalism (as originally envisaged by Marx and Engels and many contemporary globalization theorists). Given the inherited quality of the inter-state system, the spaces of global capital accumulation and territorial forms of rule are incongruent. Competition in the world market is not directly between individual firms, but is mediated by state boundaries, enabling states to organize the external projection of national class interests through diverse strategies of spatialization. The persistent centrality of the state militates against any functional long-term trend line in the correlation between forms of governance and global capital accumulation, calling for close attentiveness to the historically changing dialectic of state projects of de- and re-territorialization (cooperation and competition) that characterize the course of capitalist modernity. Instead of identifying unchanging structural im-peratives underlying "capitalist geopolitics" or a linear-evolutionary developmental trajectory—such as the alleged contemporary shift from the "international" to the "global"—there is neither a realm of "the international" spanning the period from 1648 to today based on inter-territorial competition, nor a space of "capitalist international relations" following a single identifiable logic.

Rosenberg's later work (1996; 2006) problematizes "the international" based on a paradigm shift from Marx's central category "mode of production" to Leon Trotsky's notion of "uneven and combined development," developed as a "general abstraction." In contrast to Marx's vision of the progressive creation of a world after capitalism's own image, Trotsky drew attention to the generic unevenness of coexisting multiple patterns of historical development. Even in their encounter with the spread of capitalism, these differentiated regional trajectories would re-inforce themselves, rather than even out, through "combined development"—an amalgamation of the old and the new. This insight is generalized to yield a sociological—and not merely a geopolitical—theory of the international, since it arises from the unevenness of development itself, mediating the multilinear and in-teractive dimension of social development over time without being subsumed by it.

This raises the narrower question whether socioeconomic unevenness itself pro-vides a criterion powerful enough to explain or sustain geopolitical multiplicity and the wider epistemological question of whether a theory of "the international" can be constructed at the level of a "general abstraction." For unevenness has never stopped—in fact, it was usually the precondition for—the incorporation of the less developed into the more developed entity, whether by conquest, contract, marriage, cession, or migration. Inversely, empires disintegrated and fractured along a wide range of diverse fault lines (ethnic, strategic, political, linguistic), among which the lines of domestically differentially developing regions are but one. Uneven development is only contingently linked to territorial multiplicity and reveals per se little about the territorial scales and social modalities of concrete political geogra-phies. More fundamentally, the generic terms that Rosenberg deploys—"society," "state," "the international," and "development"—are themselves, as any historical semantics suggests, historical categories that refer to specific spatiotemporally cir-cumscribed phenomena with strictly limited historical life cycles. Consequently, the method of abstraction entails a tendency toward the reification of "the in-ternational" that is simultaneously posited as the expression of and condition of possibility for uneven development, but is itself beyond history. The ontologization of "the international" as a "spatial category" (Rosenberg 2006, 318) obstructs its understanding as a "socio-historical practice" that underwent infinite alterations, as any analysis of 1,000 years of "feudal" territoriality exemplifies. More con-cretely, the theory provides no pointers for explaining the inter-stateness of capi-talist modernity—arguably the central *explanandum* of any Marxist theory of "the international"—even though "uneven and combined development" is only opera-tional on the basis of its prior existence. Furthermore, the theory of combined and uneven development does not specify—at the level of theory—a distinct explana-tory principle that accounts for the dynamics of unevenness and combinedness and appears thus socially evacuated. Ultimately, the method of general abstraction jars with Marx's dialectical historicization of phenomena that emerge from concrete human praxes and incurs his injunction that "the only immutable thing is the abstraction of movement—*mors immortalis*" (Marx 1976, 166). While "uneven and combined development" provides a powerful heuristic that immunizes against a facile collapsing of difference into (capitalist) identity, its elevation to "a general law" and formulation in an overly abstract and contentless register opens up a gap between the universal and the particular that requires substantiation—at the level of theory and not simply history—to recover the distance between abstraction and concretion.

6 GLOBALIZATION, EMPIRE, AND NEOIMPERIALISM

Widespread agreement among Marxists and non-Marxists on the intensifying reality of "globalization" since the late 1970s, compounded by the post-11 September US–American "unilateralist turn," have thrown into sharp relief the inadequacy of notions of classical sovereignty and the "Westphalian system" to capture the contemporary reconfiguration between the national and the international/global. The relative decline, if not the very end, of the politically autonomous nation state has generated a proliferation of alternative but competing concepts on a scale from the internationalization of the state, via the global state, to empire and neoimperialism (for a Marxist critique of mainstream globalization theory, see Rosenberg 2000; 2005).

A dominant tendency assumes a transition from the national–international to the global, first conceptualized as "the internationalisation of the state" (Palloix 1977). The shift from international trade to integrated transnational production patterns and "finance capital" has led to a convergence of interests among transnationally oriented capitals, creating a "transnational business class" that transcends national boundaries. It simultaneously renders national states responsive to transnational class interests as "transmission belts" (Cox 1992; van der Pijl 1998), coordinating and integrating inter-state policies. This line of argument is reinforced and developed by William Robinson's concept (2002; 2004) of "global state formation." Locating the internationalization of the state in the postwar period, post-Bretton Woods economic globalization has brought about the subordination of the nation state to international institutions, as national bourgeoisies are metamorphosing into local (national) contingents of an emergent transnational bourgeoisie, eclipsing national rivalries. "Economic globalisation has its counterpart in transnational class formation and in the emergence of a transnational state . . . which has been brought into existence to function as the collective authority for a global ruling class" (Robinson 2002, 210). This argument is further radicalized by Michael Hardt and Antonio Negri's notion of "empire." "Along with the global market and global circuits of production has emerged a global order, a new logic and structure of rule—in short, a new form of sovereignty." Drawing on Michel Foucault's desubjectified notion of power, empire is conceived as a *"decentered* and *deterritorializing* apparatus of rule"* that "realize[s] ... a properly capitalist order" in which even *"the United States does not . . . form the center of an imperialist project"* (Hardt and Negri 2000 xi, xii, 9, xiii–xiv, emphasis in original; for critiques, see Balakrishnan 2003; Bromley 2003).

Underlying these strong globalization theses is a profound economic functionalism and instrumentalism, couched into a teleological narrative, which imputes that global structures of political rule, while previously territorially segmented, have now been restructured, aligned, and rescaled—irresistibly and irreversibly, it is often argued—to complement the universalistic potentials inherent in the unfolding of capital. Yet, the instrumentalist reduction of state orientations to transnational elites or transnationally oriented class fractions (rather than to diverse balances of class forces) glosses over regional specificities in state/class articulations and their often competing foreign-policy projects. These disparities continue to reproduce contradictions and countervailing forces in capitalist inter-state relations that any totalizing notion of "empire" or "global state" obliterates. A coherent aggregation of class interests and political authority at the global level, comparable to the institutional capacities of the nation state, is hard to detect.

More specifically, the directive role—in fact, the overwhelming organizing agency—of the United States has been underspecified in these accounts. Leo Panitch and Sam Gindin argue that, instead of a multilateral system of global governance or a global state, the current geopolitical moment is marked by a specifically American informal empire that, while formally maintaining plural sovereignties, has suspended the balance of power and moved beyond inter-imperialist rivalries to organize capitalism on a global scale (Panitch and Gindin 2003). Similarly, Peter Gowan (1999; 2006) and Perry Anderson (2002, 20–1) reject the argument that post-cold war US national interests can be straightforwardly equated with or extended to encompass the interests of transnational capital—a merger of capitalists of all countries that would herald a universal capitalist empire or, alternatively, a benign US hegemony. According to Gowan (2006, 216), the United States is a "*sui generis* hegemon*," incomparably more powerful than its predecessors and possessing economic and politico-military strengths (unipolar core, unchallenged US predominance in intra-core relations, overwhelming regime-making capacities, and feedback mechanisms for cycle-breaking) that transcend the vocabulary of hegemony and "universal capitalist empire," calling for its appellation as an "American world empire." Gowan and Anderson emphasize the neomercantilist dimension of US-led global restructuring that combines consensual claims to universality with the promotion of specific coercion-backed national economic and strategic interests. In this sense, while the United States is less than a global state, it has effectively resolved the coordination problem of inter-state anarchy among multiple capitalist centers of power—not by fabricating consent, but by sheer geopolitical weight. American "exceptionalism" transcends the original dichotomous conceptions of either Lenin's inter-imperialist rivalry or Kautsky's ultra-imperialism.

In contrast to strong "globalists," the counter-claim regarding the persistence of the states system runs the opposite danger of overinvesting the national form with a durability that leaves the real changes in the restructuring of political territoriality unaccounted for. Ellen Wood suggests that globalization and the states system have entered into a mutually reinforcing relationship, since global capital accumulation requires a reliable system of states as the adequate form for protecting and policing capitalist social property relations. "The political form of globalization is not a global state but a global system of multiple states" (Wood 2003, 6). US imperial hegemony is therefore primarily defined as economic imperialism, working through a reliable system of plural capitalist states. The American inter-state empire is, paradoxically, "the empire of capital." Since coercion is necessary only at the point of implanting capitalist property relations and state structures in pre-capitalist locales and for the policing of market-sustaining institutions once capitalist markets and sovereignty are established, inter-imperial rivalry is eclipsed. In this sense, the US imperial turn, is objectless—"surplus imperialism." This position is premised on her understanding of capitalism as a social relation in which all economic actors are market dependent, so that economic power is detached from political power, allowing for capitalist expansion across borders without the political subjugation of the penetrated state—economic imperialism. This conception defines, similar to world-systems theory, the multi-state system in terms functional to the global reproduction of capitalism, attributes to unevenness a politico-territorial blocking character, which implies a fixed multi-territorial landscape as the adequate geopolitical carapace of capitalism, and fails to offer either a theoretical derivation or a historical specification of the conditions under which capitalist class relations took shape, politically, in the form of multiple and competing sovereign states. Because of this depoliticized reading of the nature of "economic imperialism," the current US military–political imperial turn is not theorized as a positive manifestation of specific sociopolitical dynamics within the United States, but, given the "systemic imperatives" of economic capitalist accumulation, is somehow surplus to requirement.

David Harvey, finally, suggests a reading of the neoliberal "new imperialism" grounded in the fall of profitability due to overaccumulation and the ensuing problems of capital accumulation since the 1960s. Before the onset of the long downturn, the United States followed a hegemonic project that through the international framework established at Bretton Woods was designed "to coordinate growth between the advanced capitalist powers" and "to bring capitalist-style economic development to the rest of the non-communist world" (Harvey 2003, 54–5). Consent prevailed over coercion. Post-1973, American hegemony was restructured around a much more aggressive neoliberalization project that had run its course by the turn of the millennium, leaving coercion as the only viable exit option to maintain US primacy, especially through direct territorial control of the oil spigot. Inter-imperial rivalries are optional again. Theoretically, this account draws on two distinct, competing, and separate logics—a "territorial logic of power," pursued by state managers, and a transnational "capitalist logic of power," pursued by firms, that are irreducible to each other but intersect in variable ways (Harvey 2003, 26–30). There are, however, two conflicting readings of the "two logics" in Harvey. One, drawing on Hannah Arendt's definition of imperialism, suggests that unlimited capital accumulation functionally requires a geographically coextensive sphere of direct politico-territorial control, assuming compatibility if not identity of interests between state and capital; the other suggests two separate and conflicting logics between state managers and capitalists that might contradict each other. The implication is that, if the first reading holds, much of US postwar foreign policy cannot be accounted for; if the second reading holds, then the current Afghanistan–Iraq fiasco—the "territorial logic"—is beyond an explanation in terms of capitalist interests. In any case, the theoretical ascription of *one* generic rationality of permanent politico-territorial (imperial) accumulation to state managers is as historically unwarranted and fraught with dangers of reification (constituting also an unnecessary relapse into realist verities), as the ascription of *one* generic rationality of transnational capital accumulation to capitalists. The dualistic conception of power stands in stark tension with the dialectical approach that Harvey also champions.

7 CONCLUSION

Marx and Engels left a problematic legacy for theorizing international relations because of their neglect of inter-spatial relations and alterations in political geographies for processes of social reproduction. This "geopolitical deficiency" still haunts the collective Marxist imagination. If significant progress has been made to rectify this defect, the tradition still stands in need of devising a theoretical framework wide and open-ended enough to conceptualize the nexus between social reproduction, power, and inter-spatial relations across the entire spectrum of human history. Because of the ever-growing recognition of the variable rates of regional development, the efficacy of geopolitical and transnational relations on domestic dynamics, and the complexities involved in articulating the relation between the domestic and the foreign, there has been a strong tendency to move away from teleological conceptions of history, economic reductionism, and structural determinism—legacies that have been dislodged by greater attentiveness to historical specificity and the agency of historically situated actors. The challenge remains to develop an understanding of different types and patterns of geopolitical competition and co-operation that is not held hostage to the structural functionalisms of a desocialized "logic of anarchy" or a depoliticized and de-geopoliticized "logic of capital." In line with its critical vocation, Marxism needs to reconceptualize how balances of social forces affected the historical evolution of political communities in their internal and external aspects, to reconstruct the changing dynamics of their interactions and interpenetrations, and to specify the full range of spatial orders (within the capitalist epoch as before) devised by them in order to reproblematize the variable relations between domination and exploitation—and chances of resistance to them. It is a sign of the ambition and ongoing vitality of Marxism as a living tradition that this monumental research agenda has finally moved right into the center of critical reflection on the human condition.

REFERENCES

ANDERSON, P. 2002. Force and consent. *New Left Review*, 17: 5–30.

ARRIGHI, G. 1994. *The Long Twentieth Century: Money, Power, and the Origins of our Times*. London: Verso.

—— 2005a. Hegemony unravelling—1. *New Left Review*, 32: 23–80.

—— 2005b. Hegemony unravelling—2. *New Left Review*, 33: 83–116.

BALAKRISHNAN, G. (ed.) 2003. *Debating Empire*. London: Verso.

BERKI, R. N. 1971. On Marxian thought and the problem of international relations. *World Politics*, 24: 80–105.

BIELER, A., BURNHAM, P., BONEFELD, W., and MORTON, A. 2006. *Global Restructuring, State, Capital and Labour: Contesting Neo-Gramscian Perspectives*. London: Palgrave Macmillan.

BRAUDEL, F. 1982. *The Wheels of Commerce*. New York: Harper and Row.

BRENNER, R. 1977. The origins of capitalist development: a critique of neo-Smithian Marxism. *New Left Review*, 104: 25–92.

—— 1985. The agrarian roots of European capitalism. Pp. 213–327 in *The Brenner Debate: Agrarian Class Structure and Economic Development in Pre-Industrial Europe*, ed. T. H. Aston and C. H. E. Philpin. Cambridge: Cambridge University Press.

BREWER, A. 1990. *Marxist Theories of Imperialism: A Critical Survey*, 2nd edn. London: Routledge.

—— 2000. Imperialism in retrospect. Pp. 65–83 in Chilcote 2000.

BROMLEY, S. 1994. *Rethinking Middle East Politics: State Formation and Development*. Cambridge: Polity Press.

—— 1999. Marxism and globalisation. Pp. 280–301 in *Marxism and Social Science*, ed. A. Gamble, D. Marsh, and T. Tant. London: Macmillan.

—— 2003. Reflections on *Empire*, Imperialism and US Hegemony. *Historical Materialism*, 11: 17–68.

BUKHARIN, N. 1972. *Imperialism and World Economy*. New York: Monthly Review Press; originally published 1915.

BURNHAM, P. 1991. Neo-Gramscian hegemony and the international order. *Capital and Class*, 45: 73–93.

CHASE-DUNN, C. 1991. *Global Formation: Structures of the World-Economy*. Oxford: Blackwell.

CHILCOTE, R. H. (ed.) 2000. *The Political Economy of Imperialism: Critical Appraisals*. Lanham, Md.: Rowman and Littlefield.

COX, R. 1987. *Production, Power, and World Order: Social Forces in the Making of History*. New York: Columbia University Press.

—— 1992. Global perestroika. Pp. 26–43 in *Socialist Register 1992*, ed. R. Miliband and L. Panitch. London: Merlin Press.

—— 1996. Gramsci, hegemony, and international relations: an essay in method (1983). Pp. 124–43 in *Approaches to World Order*, R. Cox with T. J. Sinclair. Cambridge: Cambridge University Press.

DRAINVILLE, A. 1994. International political economy in the age of open Marxism. *Review of International Political Economy*, 1: 105–32.

GILL, S. 1990. *American Hegemony and the Trilateral Commission*. Cambridge: Cambridge University Press.

——(ed.) 1993. *Gramsci, Historical Materialism and International Relations*. Cambridge: Cambridge University Press.

——and LAW, D. 1988. *The Global Political Economy: Perspectives, Problems, and Policies*. New York: Harvester.

GOWAN, P. 1999. *The Global Gamble: Washington's Faustian Bid for World Dominance*. London: Verso.

——2006. Contemporary intracore relations and world-systems theory. Pp. 213–38 in *Global Social Change: Historical and Comparative Perspectives*, ed. C. Chase-Dunn and S. J. Babones. Baltimore: Johns Hopkins University Press.

HALLIDAY, F. 1994. A necessary encounter: historical materialism and international relations. Pp. 47–73 in *Rethinking International Relations*, F. Halliday. London: Macmillan.

HARDT, M., and NEGRI, A. 2000. *Empire*. Cambridge, Mass.: Harvard University Press.

HARVEY, D. 2001. The geopolitics of capitalism. Pp. 312–44 in *Spaces of Capital: Towards a Critical Geography*, D. Harvey. New York: Routledge.

——2003. *The New Imperialism*. Oxford: Oxford University Press.

HILFERDING, R. 1981. *Finance Capital: A Study of the Latest Phase of Capitalist Development*. London: Routledge and Kegan Paul; originally published 1910.

KANDAL, T. R. 1989. Marx and Engels on international relations, revolution and counterrev-oluton. Pp. 25–76 in *Studies of Development and Change in the Modern World*, ed. M. T. Martin and T. R. Kandal. New York: Oxford University Press.

KAUTSKY, K. 1970. Ultra-imperialism. *New Left Review*, 59: 4–6; originally published 1914.

LACHER, H. 2002. Making sense of the international system: the promises and pitfalls of contemporary Marxist theories of international relations. Pp. 147–64 in *Historical Materialism and Globalization*, ed. M. Rupert and H. Smith. London: Routledge.

——2006. *Beyond Globalization: Capitalism, Territoriality and the International Relations of Modernity*. London: Routledge.

LENIN, V. I. 1973. *Imperialism: The Highest Stage of Capitalism: A Popular Outline*. Peking: Foreign Languages Press; originally published 1917.

LUXEMBURG, R. 1951. *The Accumulation of Capital*. London: Routledge and Kegan Paul; originally published 1913.

MARX, K. 1976. The poverty of philosophy. In *Collected Works*, vol. vi, K. Marx and F. Engels. London: Lawrence and Wishart; originally published 1847.

——and ENGELS, F. 1976. *Collected Works*, vol. v. London: Lawrence and Wishart.

————1998. *The Communist Manifesto: A Modern Edition*. London: Verso; originally published 1848.

MOMMSEN, W. J. 1980. *Theories of Imperialism*. London: Weidenfeld and Nicolson.

PALLOIX, C. 1977. The self-expansion of capital on a world scale. *Review of Radical Political Economics*, 9: 3–17.

PANITCH, L. 1996. Rethinking the role of the state. Pp. 83–13 in *Globalization: Critical Reflections*, ed. J. H. Mittelman. Boulder, Colo.: Lynne Rienner.

——and GINDIN, S. 2003. Global capitalism and American empire. Pp. 1–42 in *Socialist Register 2004*, ed. L. Panitch and C. Leys. London: Merlin Press.

ROBINSON, W. I. 2002. Capitalist globalization and the transnationalization of the state. Pp. 210–29 in *Historical Materialism and Globalization*, ed. M. Rupert and H. Smith. London: Routledge.

—— 2004. *A Theory of Global Capitalism: Production, Class, and State in a Transnational World*. Baltimore: Johns Hopkins University Press.

ROSENBERG, J. 1994. *The Empire of Civil Society: A Critique of the Realist Theory of International Relations*. London: Verso.

—— 1996. Isaac Deutscher and the lost history of international relations. *New Left Review*, 215: 3–15.

—— 2000. *The Follies of Globalisation Theory: Polemical Essays*. London: Verso.

—— 2005. Globalization theory: a post mortem. *International Politics*, 42: 2–74.

—— 2006. Why is there no international historical sociology? *European Journal of International Relations*, 12: 307–40.

RUPERT, M. 1995. *Producing Hegemony: The Politics of Mass Production and American Global Power*. Cambridge: Cambridge University Press.

SCHERRER, C. 1998. Neo-gramscianische Interpretationen internationaler Beziehungen. Pp. 160–74 in *Gramsci-Perspektiven*, ed. U. Hirschfeld. Hamburg: Argument-Verlag.

SHILLIAM, R. 2004. Hegemony and the unfashionable problematic of "primitive accumulation." *Millennium: Journal of International Studies*, 33: 59–88.

SKOCPOL, T. 1977. Wallerstein's world capitalist system: a theoretical and historical critique. *American Journal of Sociology*, 82: 1075–90.

SOELL, H. 1972. Weltmarkt–revolution–staatenwelt: zum problem einer theorie internationaler beziehungen bei Marx und Engels. *Archiv für Sozialgeschichte*, 12: 109–84.

TESCHKE, B. 1998. Geopolitical relations in the European Middle Ages: history and theory. *International Organization*, 52: 325–58.

—— 2002. Theorizing the Westphalian system of states: international relations from absolutism to capitalism. *European Journal of International Relations*, 8: 5–48.

—— 2003. *The Myth of 1648: Class, Geopolitics, and the Making of Modern International Relations*. London: Verso.

—— 2005. Bourgeois revolution, state formation and the absence of the international. *Historical Materialism*, 13: 3–26.

—— 2006. Imperial doxa from the Berlin republic. *New Left Review*, 40: 128–40.

VAN DER PIJL, K. 1984. *The Making of an Atlantic Ruling Class*. London: Verso.

—— 1998. *Transnational Classes and International Relations*. London: Routledge.

—— 2006. *Global Rivalries from the Cold War to Iraq*. London: Pluto Press.

WALLERSTEIN, I. 1974a. *The Modern World-System: Capitalist Agriculture and the Origins of the European World-Economy in the Sixteenth Century*. New York: Academic Press.

—— 1974b. The rise and future demise of the world capitalist system: concepts for comparative analysis. *Comparative Studies in Society and History*, 16: 387–415.

—— 1983. The three instances of hegemony in the history of the capitalist world-economy. *International Journal of Comparative Sociology*, 24: 100–8.

—— 1995. *Historical Capitalism with Capitalist Civilization*. London: Verso.

—— 2006. The curve of US power. *New Left Review*, 40: 77–94.

WOOD, E. M. 1995. The separation of the "economic" and the "political" in capitalism. Pp. 19–48 in *Democracy against Capitalism: Renewing Historical Materialism*, E. M. Wood. Cambridge: Cambridge University Press.

—— 2003. *Empire of Capital*. London: Verso.

CHAPTER 10

....

THE ETHICS OF MARXISM

....

NICHOLAS RENGGER

ONE of the many happy ironies of the study of the political theory of international relations is the recognition of odd couples in the history of ideas. Realism and Marxism, for example, are generally supposed to occupy different conceptual worlds and to be, in broad terms at least, completely opposed to one another. And so, at some levels at least, they are. The former pessimistic, where the latter is utopian; the latter determinist, where the former is persuaded of the power of contingency in human affairs. Yet astute students of both have always seen degrees of commonality lurking just beneath the surface, and among the most commonly noted similarities is a similar suspicion, not to say downright opposition, to the notion of ethics. Realism, it is said, has no place for ethics in political life at all and Marxists seem equally skeptical of moral arguments; Karl Marx, allegedly, "burst out laughing whenever anyone used the word morality" (Brown 1992, 228).

Given that this chapter is concerned with the ethics of Marxism in international relations, such skepticism might seem problematic. The ethics of realism, of course, occupies an earlier chapter in this book and so I will not comment on that here. However, as with realism, Marxism's relationship to ethics is much more complex than it appears on the surface and I will therefore take as my chief task in what follows to lay out the character of that relationship, to emphasize certain key features of Marxist thinking in relation to the ethics of international relations—not

I am grateful to Chris Reus-Smit and Duncan Snidal and, for comments on an earlier draft, to Chris Brown, Patrick Hayden, Tony Lang, Andrew Linklater, Oliver Richmond, Justin Rosenberg, and Ian Taylor.

all of which are necessarily congruent with one another—and then, finally, to point to what I take to be the fundamental problem with the Marxist tradition in thinking about the ethics of international relations in particular and indeed, the social world in general. To tip my hand in advance, I want to explore whether it is likely that Marxism, as an independent tradition of thought, has, can, or will offer serious points of departure for ethical reflection on international relations, and I will suggest, toward the end of this chapter, that it cannot. Along the way, however, I hope to show that, as a *contributor* to ethical reflection on international relations, Marxism indeed offers some important and arresting insights.

1 MARXISM AND ETHICS

To begin with, however, I must outline how I will understand "Marxism" in what follows and from the outset I should make it plain that Marxism has to be understood as a highly variegated tradition of thinking about the social world, culled from a wide range of sources and stretching, now, over 150 years. Leszek Kolakowski (1978), in his classic history of Marxist thought, suggests that the history of Marxist thought can be divided into three stages, which he names the "founders"—the period dominated by Marx himself and his collaborator Friedrich Engels from the mid-nineteenth century; the "golden age"—roughly the period of the so-called Second International, the thirty or so years leading up to the outbreak of the First World War in 1914, when a wide variety of movements took inspiration from Marx's ideas; and then, finally, the so-called breakdown, the period after the Bolshevik revolution in Russia when the unity of Marxism was sundered and a wide range of separate "Marxisms" became rivals. I suppose we might perhaps add to Kolakowski's triptych a fourth period, which we might call "eclipse," following the collapse of "really existing socialism" in the Soviet Union and its satellites after 1989, though Marxism as an intellectual doctrine has proved much tougher than its political manifestations.

To complicate matters still further, there are profound questions of interpretation at every level, in all periods. To give just one example, despite Marx's own skepticism toward morality, many have suggested that at least in his earlier work, most especially in the so-called 1844 manuscripts but also in the *Grundrisse*, he displays a much more obvious commitment to an ethic that derives from thinkers like Jean-Jacques Rousseau, an image of human beings as "naturally" free and self-governing but as currently enslaved by modes of production that "alienate" them from their true selves. The problem is whether this represents an "ethical" Marx versus a "scientific" Marx or whether this is simply an ambiguity that runs throughout Marx's theory. Indeed, this dilemma seems to be writ large in many of Marx's best-known claims; for Marx, as we know, the point about philosophy was that hitherto it had sought to understand the world, but the point was to change it; but to change the world (always assuming you can, of course) invites the question, are you changing it for the better or the worse?

And it is perhaps from that point that we can start to orient this discussion of Marxism and ethics. While there are indeed many different trajectories visible within Marxism, all of them work within two broad intellectual assumptions, naturalism and materialism, and it is these two assumptions, taken together, that generate the broad horizon of Marxism's engagement with ethics. It is because the material forces operative within any society structure the moral claims made about it that Marx is so dismissive of the language of morality. As Steven Lukes (1991, 181) points out, quoting *The German Ideology*, "(Morality) like religion, metaphysics . . . all the rest of ideology and their corresponding forms of consciousness" had "no history, no development, but men, altering their material production and their material intercourse alter—along with these—the real existence and their thinking and the products of their thinking."

Underpinning such materialism, however, is a naturalism that identifies a "good" for human beings as such—a "good" that is expressed not in terms of the language of morality but rather in the language of interest (again the parallelism with realism is pointed). This "good," however, is perhaps best understood as a "eudaimonistic" concept derived originally from Marx's immersion in Greek thought, especially Aristotelian thought. Marx's aim throughout his life was to understand how it would be possible for people to acquire "true happiness" and so make "morality" redundant; and how this would occur would be through the abolition of the "conditions of morality." As Lukes (1991, 187) puts it, "Marx's view of morality . . . is exactly parallel to his view of religion, concerning which he wrote, 'the abolition of religion as the illusory happiness of the people is a demand for their true happiness. The call to abandon illusions about their condition is the call to abandon a condition which requires Illusions.' "

What this suggests, as Chris Brown (1992, 234) has pointed out, echoing Lukes, is that much mainstream Marxism has an attitude to ethics that is essentially an extreme consequentialist one. Moral claims may often be made, but they will be made as tactical moves in a game of interests and will be justified if they advance the interests of the working class and not justified if they do not. But they are not justifiable in "moral terms," since all such terms are essentially ideological, in the special sense that Marxism gives to that term. Nonetheless, they are concerned with "ethics" at least in the sense that in the world as it (materially) is, such claims are part of the fabric of political action. Given this, however, and given further that after the "breakdown" there are many different versions of "Marxism" out there, it is hardly surprising that the "purity" of what we might term the orthodox Marxist position on ethics has become somewhat diffuse over time. This has become particularly obvious with the split between orthodox (that is, Soviet-style Marxist Leninist) versions of Marxism and so-called Western Marxism in the 1920s and after, and with the emergence of various different forms of "Western Marxism" as well. However, more of this in a moment.

Of course, for much of the twentieth century, one aspect of Marxism that was of considerable relevance for thinking about the way it discussed ethical questions was the practice of governments and other actors that claimed adherence to Marxism as a doctrine (that is, the Soviet Union, the People's Republic of China, and so on). In his earlier article discussing Marxist ethics, Brown (1992, 240–4) offers a superb *tour d'horizon* detailing the broad outlines of how the practice of "really existing socialism" mapped onto ethical debates in world politics, but points out that in effect such ethical discourse as there was could be seen simply either as an extreme version of the consequentialism that was such a strong hallmark of Marxism from the beginning, or as a result of the inevitable messiness of international politics in an age of geopolitical confrontation. In neither case, however, does it alter the general shape of the dilemma that we have already seen confronts Marxism in its dealing with the ethical from its inception.

There has been, of course, some work that dissents from this. Lawrence Wilde's *Marxism's Ethical Thinkers* (2001), for example, traces the lineaments of a Marxist ethical sensibility from the revisionist debates to the present, and suggests that there certainly is an ethical imperative to be found within Marxism. Perhaps the most sophisticated attempt to discuss precisely what this might entail and the dilemmas underpinning it can be found in Lukes's pioneering work (1985; 1991, chs. 8–10). It is perhaps useful to say something about his argument, since I shall use it to structure my reflections on the way in which Marxism has been applied to international ethics in the next section. Lukes makes a distinction between two kinds of morality, which he calls the morality of *Recht* and the morality of *emancipation*. The morality of *Recht* "comprises ... an area of morality (the morality of law) which has special characteristics ... occupied by the characteristics of justice, fairness, rights and obligation" (Lukes 1985, 198, quoting Hart 1955). The morality of emancipation, by contrast, "denotes a setting free from the prehistory of human bondage, which culminated in wage slavery and exploitation, and thus it refers to that ideal of transparent social unity and individual self realization in which 'the contradiction between the interest of the separate individual ... and the common interest of all individuals who have intercourse with one another has been abolished' " (Lukes 1985, 198, quoting Marx and Engels 1975, 46). Lukes's argument is that it is the morality of *Recht* that Marx—and the Marxist tradition in its pure form—dismisses, but the morality of emancipation that it seeks to make its own, and that it is *because* of this that the form of morality that Marxism most often subscribes to is effectively a version of consequentialism.

Lukes's own view is that this amounts to a serious weakness within Marxism, since it does not allow Marxism any real response to the crimes and injustices committed in the name of emancipation; indeed, it suggests that they cannot be seen as "crimes or injustices," since these are terms of *Recht* that are ideologically constructed, which is simply, hopelessly, counter-intuitive. A second weakness, connected to the first, is what Richard Norman (1986, 272) in his review of *Marxism and Morality* referred to as "Marxism's failure to spell out in a substantial and detailed way the form of political community which might embody the ideal of emancipation." Nonetheless, for Lukes, Marxism does contain important ethical resources. "It offers a conception...of freedom and of the constraints upon or the obstacles to it that is far deeper and richer than negative and classical liberal views...[and it] raises some deep and unanswered questions about the morality of *Recht*, which non-Marxists have yet to answer" (Lukes 1985, 198).

To sum up where we have reached so far, then. The Marxist tradition in all its variety has a fairly clear mainstream position on ethics—broadly consquentialist, interest based, and naturalistic—but some positions more sympathetic to at least some versions of the morality of *Recht* on its fairly extensive—and sometimes quite influential—fringes. The next question, then, is how all this relates to international relations.

2 MARXIST "ETHICS" AND INTERNATIONAL RELATIONS

The way in which Marxist thought engages with international relations in general is every bit as complex as its engagement with ethics. In the way in which international relations is traditionally understood, Marx did not have a "theory" of international relations at all, of course; rather he had a theory about social formation that had implications for the international dimensions of social organization. This is a point that has been emphasised by a number of scholars of international relations, perhaps most prominently Martin Wight (1966), as well as by scholars of Marxism more generally, for example R. N. Berki (1971). Some of Marx's successors in the "golden age" did, of course, offer more fully formed thoughts on international relations—or at least on aspects of it, such as imperialism—but again these hardly amounted to a fully thought through theoretical approach to the topic. More recently some Marxist-influenced scholars have remedied this defect in Marxist theorizing, with, to my mind, more or less successful results (Rosenberg 1994; Halliday 1999; Teschke 2003). However, since these attempts are the subject of the companion piece to this chapter, I will not dwell on them here.

Marxism was hardly alone in not treating the "ethical" in international relations seriously. Many of the most influential currents in political science and international relations scholarship in general throughout the twentieth century also avoided explicit ethical reflection, at least until relatively recently. There are, of course, many reasons for this that space does not allow (see Rengger 2000 for a more elaborate discussion). Instead, let me say something about the gradual re-entangling of international relations and what I will call "large-scale ethical reflection," before turning to what, in general terms, Marxism—and the dilemmas within it touched on above—might have to say about it.

It is a commonplace, of course, that the revival of normative theorizing in international relations has been fed by a number of tributaries. To begin, it was given a powerful fillip with the general revival of what we might term strong normative theory in general that followed both political events—such as the Vietnam War—and academic ones—such as the publication of John Rawls's *A Theory of Justice* (1971). The former was, of course, not insignificantly connected to a topic that had long been a central question in international relations—the legitimacy of the use of force. The latter, coupled with the gradual realization that issues such as globalization raised as many normative questions as it did explanatory ones, and allied as well to the first wave of responses to Rawls, kick-started what we might term the global justice industry, which has become hugely important as a site of ethical reflection about world politics over the last thirty years. Then again, the importation into international relations scholarship of assumptions, methods, and questions from other areas of the human sciences (signaled by the rise of "critical theory," poststructuralist, and feminist approaches, to name but three) all had normative significance, even if of a very different kind from more analytic approaches to ethical reflection, as did the development of challenges to the conventional explanatory assumptions in political science and international relations, such as the varied diet of "constructivist" approaches that developed exponentially during the 1990s.

International relations today, then, has a wide range of normative questions that are being increasingly widely debated, a debate fueled by both academic and political developments and focused around the twin poles of the use and role of force and how we evaluate it (an aspect that has gone into overdrive after the 11 September attacks and all that they have brought in their train) and the perhaps more recessed but equally central question of the justice of contemporary international relations *tout court* (that is to say, both procedurally and in terms of the distribution of goods, resources, wealth, and well-being). However, Marxism in the sense discussed above has, by and large, been a ghost at the feast in these debates. While Marxist, or quasi-Marxist, sensibilities have been very visible in world politics—they have been influential on various different strands of the antiglobalization movement, for example—what might they offer to ethical reflection upon the contemporary conditions of world politics?

I want to suggest that there are two broad trajectories of Marxist thought in the context of these debates and that each represents a serious and important set of reflections on the ethical aspects of international relations, in part because such aspects are simply not detachable from "international relations proper" in the way that many (including many Marxists) thought they were. The first trajectory takes what I referred to above as the "purist" form of Marxist engagement with ethics—essentially it adopts a consequentialist ethic predicated on a morality of emancipation. The second follows Lukes's argument—though not necessarily the manner in which he articulates it—and suggests that some form of bridge needs to be built between the morality of *Recht* and the morality of emancipation, and that, in doing so, Marxism can provide an important perspective on the normative debates just mentioned.

Let me take this latter perspective first. I do so simply because this is probably the most influential articulation of Marxist thought and international ethics at present, partly because it overlaps with the manner of thinking adopted by a number of influential theories of international relations strongly influenced by Marxism but that would now generally be seen as lying outside Marxism itself. Frankfurt School-influenced critical theory, for example, has certainly been an important voice in the growing debates in international political theory and ethics, with the work of Andrew Linklater being particularly significant. One might see in Linklater's work a profound attempt to do what Lukes was suggesting needed to be done; that is to say, put *together* in important ways the morality of *Recht* and the morality of emancipation, though to be sure not in the way Lukes himself would (Linklater 1982; 1997).

But such attempts are not unique to self-confessed "critical theorists," who while certainly drawing on the Marxist tradition, are also amending it in more or less profound ways. Many other scholars of politics and international relations, with roots—sometimes very deep roots—in various versions of Marxism, have clearly been developing ideas along similar lines. Fred Halliday, for example, in both *Rethinking International Relations* and *Revolution and World Politics*, is clearly engaged in a not dissimilar enterprise, arguing that however important explanations of the phenomena of world politics are, "the ought will not go away" (Halliday 1994, 236).

Perhaps the most important area where such work has tended to focus is precisely on the question of the "justice" or otherwise of capitalism, a question that goes hand in hand, of course, both with explanatory accounts of what capitalism is and how it develops and evolves (and thus now with questions over globalization and the like) and with discussions of what might replace it (or even whether it is replaceable). Jeffery Reiman (1991), in an important overview of the relationship between Marx and morality in general, pointed to this as one of the two outstanding contributions of Marxism to moral philosophy (the other was to force a confrontation with the notion of ideology), and by definition, this is a central aspect of contemporary international relations, where the structure, trajectory, and impactions of a globalizing world economy are a major area of debate. G. A. Cohen (1978), one of the leading contemporary Marxist philosophers and one of the founders of so-called analytical Marxism, is perhaps the person who has done most to claim that Marxism does have (or rather can have) a theory of justice, in that he claims that Marx himself was mistaken when he assumed Marxism did not have an account of justice because he was simply confused about justice. Similar arguments can be found in writers such as Phillipe van Parijs and Kai Nielson. These arguments obviously overlap with more general arguments about distributive justice put forward by liberals and cosmopolitans such as Henry Shue, Onora O'Neill, Charles Beitz, and Thomas Pogge, but they retain the Marxist emphasis on exploitation and the elimination of capitalism as a social form, which cosmopolitan liberal arguments lack, and they develop (in many cases at least) much more radical claims about the need for, and scope of, global redistribution.

This overlaps with another way in which Marxism has been influential on such debates—the influence it has had on Latin American liberation theology. Theologians such as Gustavo Gutiérrez, Enrique Dussel, and the brothers Colodovis and Leonardo Boff have developed a theological activism focused on the poor and exploited and deriving much from classical Marxian analysis (C. Boff 1976; L. Boff 1978; Dussel 1978; Gutiérrez 1978). Gutiérrez, perhaps the most influential of all the liberation theologians, is also the one closest to classical Marxism. His portrayal of liberation theology is dependent on a philosophy of history that mirrors that of classical Marxism, and he makes much use of terms from Marxism, such as praxis, which underpins the centrality of the "liberating" of the poor. Here, too, there is an attempt to weld traditional moral notions (though not the rights or obligations one might usually discuss in the context of *Recht*) to a morality of emancipation; though, of course, the emancipatory potential in liberation theology is still a distinctly Christian one. Nonetheless, it has had marked impact on questions of exploitation and injustice and has also fed into many contemporary antiglobalization movements.

Yet, however much such ideas might appeal and however much they might chime with other contemporary international theories that draw on Marxian ideas, there is still, it must be said, something slightly problematic about them. In his defense of his heavily altered Marxist program, van Parijs (1993, 1) argued that "the right attitude towards such bulky artefacts as the Marxist tradition is not one of dutiful conservation, but of ruthless recycling...only the unashamed adoption of this attitude can keep the Marxist tradition alive as an essential component of the political culture of the left." But one might add that, if things are recycled, very often they turn out to be something completely different from what they originally were. For many in Marxist circles, such "ruthless recycling" simply takes such Marxists out of the ambit of Marxism altogether, as has happened (they would say) with the critical theory of Jürgen Habermas and those influenced by him.

So, if one adopts a more "purist" Marxist stance, does that mean that there is nothing that can be said about the ethics of international relations? Perhaps somewhat surprisingly, I want to suggest that the answer to this question is no. In the first place, a more traditional Marxist view of ethics provides a very powerful base for a *critique* of the rather elevated conceptions of ethics that are often at least the *rhetoric* of contemporary world politics, if not very often its reality. Here again the parallel with realism is very acute. A traditional Marxist reading of ethics puts Marx, as Allen Wood (1991) has pointed out in an important essay, alongside Freidrich Nietzsche, Sigmund Freud, and (perhaps more radically still) later thinkers who explicitly drew on him such as Theodor Adorno, as a "master of suspicion;" someone who brings profound questions to bear on the moral/ethical reflections of traditional European thought and who asks difficult questions of the internal coherence of the ethical traditions we have inherited. This aspect of Marxist thinking about ethics has some powerful contemporary advocates and can involve far more than just reflections upon exploitation or economic justice, but can involve sweeping critiques of the geopolitical and military aspects of world politics and in these respects can often draw on the pronounced interest classical Marxist writers—most especially Engels—had in military affairs (Neumann 1943). This can also be seen in less obviously Marxist writers; for example, Raymond Geuss's recent book *Outside Ethics* (2002) displays something of this sensibility (though Geuss is hardly a traditional Marxist), and it is already becoming influential on some younger scholars of international ethics and political theory who are dissatisfied with the broadly Habermasian and dialogic thrust of a good deal of contemporary critical theory in international relations.[1]

Beyond this, however, more traditional modes of Marxist analysis certainly have things to offer normative analysis of international relations, even if it is still primarily negative rather than positive. The now huge literature around dependency or world-system analyses of the global economic system certainly has normative implications, even if those making the analysis do not always draw it out themselves, though scholars such as Frank and Immanuel Wallerstein have certainly not been shy of drawing certain sorts of normative conclusions from their analyses, albeit ones that could be seen largely in consequentialist terms and dependent on an appeal to the morality of emancipation (Kubálková and Cruickshank 1985).

Perhaps the most influential version of Marxist analysis in contemporary international relations, the "neo-Gramscian" version developed by Robert Cox, and then further developed by a whole range of scholars, especially in international political economy and international organization, can also have real normative power and can be seen from a variety of perspectives. In a recent article, one of the most influential neo-Gramscians, Craig Murphy (2007), has emphasized the normative, reformist aspect of neo-Gramscian research, and while he accepts that many would see his version as *too* reformist (and, by implication, not Gramscian, or Marxist, enough), he also points out that, in the context of contemporary international relations, it is precisely such a multiple, reformist, inclusive version of radical

---

[1] See, e.g., the currently unpublished paper cited at <www.st-andrews.ac.uk/intrel/pgcourses/students/ks.html>.

politics that is most likely to have an impact and make a difference—the aim, after all, of all Marxist thought is not just to understand the world, but to change it. Other versions of neo-Gramscian thought—for example, the extremely influential version developed by Ernesto Laclau and Chantal Mouffe (1985) in general political theory, and that developed by Stephen Gill (1990) in international political economy—have been criticized for lacking precisely the normative component that Murphy emphasizes. So, within neo-Gramscian approaches in general there appears to be a debate that mirrors the wider debate within Marxism as a whole.

Perhaps we might close this section by briefly offering a comment on the most generally influential contemporary neo-Marxist meditation on world politics as a whole, Michael Hardt and Antonio Negri's *Empire* (2000; see also the (to my mind) less successful Hardt and Negri 2004). Hardt and Negri offer an account of globalization and the emergence of the eponymous "empire" that draws on many sources other than Marx, but they make it clear that they see their book as recasting Marx for our time (and indeed others saw them in these terms, as well; one of the comments on the book's dust jacket referred to them as the "Marx and Engels of the internet age"). For Hardt and Negri, the emergence of empire, for all its baleful consequences, is a hopeful time that will lead to a new "militancy" (a rather baroque description of which closes the volume) in the "multitude." In Hardt and Negri's vision, then, we see another version of an attempt to broaden and strengthen Marxism's ethical reach, though not along the lines suggested by Lukes but rather by taking on board ideas about social movements, civic action, and empowerment (Hardt and Negri are strong supporters of the antiglobalization movement, for example) that unite many on the left. But it is significant that, among the many criticisms of their argument, many of the most severe come from other Marxists. Laclau (2001), for example, took them sternly to task for having (effectively) abandoned politics for the assertion of a universal immanentist ethic. Thus the permanent dilemma of Marxist thinking about ethics reasserts itself.

3 A FUTURE FOR THE ETHICS OF MARXISM IN INTERNATIONAL RELATIONS?

I hope that the above suggests that Marxism retains a power to illuminate at least some of the growing range of ethical debates that are becoming increasingly central to international relations. In this respect, as I remarked at the outset, the demise of "really existing socialism" may have helped Marxism to develop an awareness of both its strengths and its weaknesses as a theoretical and normative approach to politics in general and international politics in particular.

But it is equally obvious that the debates about Marxism's normative capacity *within Marxism* are hardly likely to go away. They have, after all, been present from the beginning. And the danger, for many Marxists, is that any attempt to do what Lukes suggests they should do and somehow bridge the morality of *Recht* with the morality of emancipation will effectively mean co-opting Marxism into simply one more, perhaps slightly more radical, version of left-liberalism. Look at Habermas, they might say, and the current trajectory of critical theory; that would be the future, and just how Marxist is it (Callinicos 1986)? Yet many Marxists also see the point of Lukes's claim; as Wood (1991) suggests, it is an uncomfortable and difficult thing for moderns to reject "morality" *tout court*, as he suggests Marx does, because it seems uncomfortably close to allowing the morality of "anything goes." What stops Marx asserting that is, of course, his belief that Marxism has found the hidden key to human history and human development; that it is, in truth, scientific. Indeed, one might say that it is *only* that claim that warrants traditional Marxism's dismissal of traditional ethics and morality while at the same time asserting the language of emancipation. For, if it is the case, not that human beings and human history *will* develop in a certain way, but only that they *could* (and perhaps should) do so, then you need a *reason* to persuade people to do so, and you are plunged back into a morality of *Recht* with a vengeance, albeit not necessarily of a deontological kind.

And this, it seems to me, is the fundamental wager that Marxism, in anything resembling its traditional form, must make. So we are obliged to ask, how plausible is it to claim that, at least in general terms, Marxism has understood both the past, the present, and the future of human history and, crucially, *their necessary relations*? One might hold, as indeed I would, that there is much to learn from Marx, and from other Marxists, about discreet aspects of human social relations, and one could certainly admit that the way in which Marxism was interpreted and practiced by some of its twentieth-century advocates no more condemns it out of hand than Christianity is condemned by the Inquisition or the rampant anti-Semitism that has disfigured its history. But for Marxism to be able to stand as a coherent explanation of the social world and especially (in the current context) for it to be able to offer any moral guidance of whatever sort as an independent system, we must believe that Marxism offers not just a, but *the*, appropriate way to conceptualize the relations between the past, the present, and the future. Though I cannot elaborate here, such a claim strikes this writer, at least, as deeply implausible—for reasons that are both epistemological and ontological. But if so, then the only way that the legacy of Marx will be able to live on in the context of the ethics of international relations—and in terms of explaining it as well—lies in it existing as a tributary that can feed other traditions not so generally problematic. In that sense, perhaps, the future of Marxism in international relations indeed lies in its contribution to developments such as critical theory, but in that context it will no longer be "Marxism" that offers a contribution to the ethics of international relations. The point, perhaps, might be not just to understand Marxism; the point might be to change it.

REFERENCES

BERKI, R. 1971. On Marxian thought and the problem of international relations. *World Politics*, 24: 80–105.

BOFF, C. 1976. *Theology and Praxis: Epistemological Foundations*. New York: Maryknoll Press.

BOFF, L. 1978. *Jesus Christ Liberator: A Critical Christology for our Time*. New York: Maryknoll Press.

BROWN, C. 1992. Marxism and international ethics. Pp. 225–49 in *Traditions of International Ethics*, ed. T. Nardin and D. R. Mapel. Cambridge: Cambridge University Press.

CALLINICOS, A. 1986. *Marxism and Philosophy*. Oxford: Oxford University Press.

COHEN, G. A. 1978. *Karl Marx's Theory of History: A Defence*. Princeton, NJ: Princeton University Press.

DUSSEL, E. 1978. *Ethics and the Theology of Liberation*, trans. B. F. McWilliams. New York: Maryknoll Press.

GEUSS, R. 2002. *Outside Ethics*. Princeton, NJ: Princeton University Press.

GILL, S. 1990. *American Hegemony and the Trilateral Commission*. Cambridge: Cambridge University Press.

GUTIÉRREZ, G. 1978. *A Theology of Liberation: History, Politics, and Salvation*. New York: Maryknoll Press.

HALLIDAY, F. 1994. *Rethinking International Relations*. London: Macmillan.

——1999. *Revolution and World Politics: The Rise and Fall of the Sixth Great Power*. London: Palgrave.

HARDT, M., and NEGRI, A. 2000. *Empire*. Cambridge, Mass.: Harvard University Press.

————2004. *Multitude: War and Democracy in the Age of Empire*. Cambridge, Mass.: Harvard University Press.

HART, H. L. A. 1955. Are there any natural rights? *Philosophical Review*, 64: 175–91.

KOLAKOWSKI, L. 1978. *Main Currents of Marxism: Its Rise, Growth, and Dissolutions*, 3 vols., trans. P. S. Falla. Oxford: Clarendon Press.

KUBÁLKOVÁ, V., and CRUICKSHANK, A. A. 1985. *Marxism and International Relations*. Oxford: Oxford University Press.

LACLAU, E. 2001. Can immanence explain social struggles? *Diacritics*, 31: 2–10.

——and MOUFFE, C. 1985. *Hegemony and Socialist Strategy: Towards a Radical Democratic Politics*, trans. W. Moore and P. Cammack. London: Verso.

LINKLATER, A. 1982. *Men and Citizens in the Theory of International Relations*. London: Macmillan.

——1997. *The Transformation of Political Community: Ethical Foundations of the Post-Westphalian Era*. Cambridge: Polity.

LUKES, S. 1985. *Marxism and Morality*. Oxford: Oxford University Press.

——1991. *Moral Conflict and Politics*. Oxford: Clarendon Press.

MARX, K., and ENGELS, F. 1975. *Marx and Engels Collected Works*, vol. v. *April 1845–April 1847*. London: Lawrence and Wishart.

MURPHY, C. N. 2007. The promise of critical IR, partially kept. *Review of International Studies*, 33: 117–33.

NEUMANN, S. 1943. Engels and Marx: military concepts of the social revolutionaries. Pp. 155–71 in *Makers of Modern Strategy: Military Thought from Machiavelli to Hitler*, ed. E. M. Earle. Princeton, NJ: Princeton University Press.

NORMAN, R. 1986. Review of *Marxism and Morality*. *Philosophy*, 61: 272–4.

RAWLS, J. 1971. *A Theory of Justice*. Cambridge, Mass.: Belknap Press.

REIMAN, J. 1991. Moral philosophy: the critique of capitalism and the problem of ideology. Pp. 143–67 in *The Cambridge Companion to Marx*, ed. T. Carver. Cambridge: Cambridge University Press.

RENGGER, N. 2000. Political theory and international relations: promised land or exit from Eden? *International Affairs*, 76: 755–70.

ROSENBERG, J. 1994. *The Empire of Civil Society: A Critique of the Realist Theory of International Relations*. London: Verso.

TESCHKE, B. 2003. *The Myth of 1648: Class, Geopolitics, and the Making of Modern International Relations*. London: Verso.

VAN PARIJS, P. 1993. *Marxism Recycled*. Cambridge: Cambridge University Press.

WIGHT, M. 1966. Why is there no international theory? Pp. 17–34 in *Diplomatic Investigations: Essays in the Theory of International Politics*, ed. H. Butterfield and M. Wight. London: George Allen and Unwin.

WILDE, L. (ed.) 2001. *Marxism's Ethical Thinkers*. New York: Palgrave.

WOOD, A. 1991. Marx against morality. Pp. 511–24 in *A Companion to Ethics*, ed. P. Singer. Oxford: Blackwell.

C H A P T E R 11

NEOLIBERAL INSTITUTIONALISM

ARTHUR A. STEIN

INTERNATIONAL politics today is as much institutional as intergovernmental. International institutions can be found in every functional domain and in every region in the world. Modern reality consists of an alphabet soup of institutions, that includes the United Nations (UN), World Trade Organization (WTO), International Monetary Fund (IMF), Nuclear Non-Proliferation Treaty (NPT), International Atomic Energy Agency (IAEA), Trade-Related Aspects of Intellectual Property Rights (TRIPS), Missile Technology Control Regime (MTCR), European Union (EU), Shanghai Cooperation Organization (SCO), Association of Southeast Asian Nations (ASEAN), Organization of the Petroleum Exporting Countries (OPEC), Asia-Pacific Economic Cooperation (APEC), North Atlantic Treaty Organization (NATO), North American Free Trade Agreement (NAFTA), Gulf Cooperation Council (GCC), and so on.

Even when people discuss the seeming irrelevance of institutions, the argument presumes institutions. The complaint of US unilateralism only makes sense in a world where the presumption is that states do not act unilaterally as a matter of course. If the world truly approximated the realist vision of autonomous independent states acting in their self-interest in an anarchic setting, then unilateralism would be the norm and would elicit little comment or even the characterization of unilateral.

The study of international institutions has grown alongside their growing number. It draws upon diverse analytic traditions and impacts the broad range of international relations scholarship.

1 A LEXICAL AND HISTORICAL INTRODUCTION

1.1 Institutionalism

The moniker of neoliberal institutionalism is a product of scholarly branding and product differentiation and is one I would prefer to do without. Just as everyone uses a computer but typically not for computing, and even as we talk about game theory though it is not a theory of games, so this chapter will talk of neoliberal institutionalism. Ironically, those who use the label never address whether the "liberal" qualification means that there is an "illiberal institutionalism," or whether it is possible to talk of institutions and not be a liberal. Unfortunately, scholarly literature in the field revolves around labels and "isms," and so this chapter will use the common parlance of international relations even though it is essentially about institutions in international politics.

1.2 A Reactive Field Discovers International Organizations

The field of international relations responds to real-world events and historically has shifted the substantive focus of investigation to reflect changing reality. Following the First World War, and with the creation of the League of Nations and the emergence of international law, the field necessarily focused on international organizations. The literature was largely descriptive and normative. When the League failed to deal with aggression in the 1930s and the Second World War broke out, the reaction was to castigate the emphasis on international organizations and international law. The critics dubbed those who promoted international organizations as idealists who believed in the possibility of international cooperation and contrasted them with realism and its emphasis on power and conflict (Carr 1940).

Yet, following the Second World War, there was even more of a broad-scale effort to construct international organizations (Ikenberry 2001). The UN was created, as were the World Bank (initially called the International Bank for Reconstruction and Development) and the IMF, among others. Moreover, the steps taken toward European integration, especially the creation of the European Economic Community, also constituted important institutional developments. Scholars necessarily took note, and international organizations and regional integration became established subfields of international politics.[1]

---

[1] Ironically, the key victim of the realist shellacking of idealism was not the study of international organizations, but rather the study of international law. What had been part of the core curriculum in

The emergence of European integration was especially momentous. On the Continent, where the state system had developed and which had been witness to centuries of great-power rivalry and war, states were combining aspects of governance in some new creation. The project of European unification has undergone fits and starts over the past half-century, but the very project itself implies some transcendence of the anarchic state of nature in which realists presume states find themselves.

1.3 From Organizations to Regimes to Institutions

During the more than half-century since the end of the Second World War, the field of international organizations has undergone significant changes, captured by the changing terms used to characterize it. In general, and consistent with broader changes in political science, the subfield became less normative and increasingly theoretical. What began as the study of international organizations and regional integration took a dramatic turn in the early 1980s in what came to be called regime theory, and was subsequently rechristened neoliberal institutionalism. The turn consisted of both a broadening of the focus and a specific formulation of the causal logic.

The original post-1945 focus was on international organizations, concrete entities with a physical presence—names, addresses, and so on. A typical definition was that of "a formal arrangement transcending national boundaries that provides for the establishment of institutional machinery to facilitate cooperation among members in the security, economic, social, or related fields" (Plano and Olton 1979, 288). This rather narrow conceptualization was broadened with a focus on regimes, defined as "principles, norms, rules and decision-making procedures around which actor expectations converge in a given issue-area" (Krasner 1982, 185).

The second critical feature of this intellectual turn was that it rooted the existence of international institutions in the core elements of realist theory: states, power, and interests. Rather than argue that regimes were somehow a different feature of international life, that they constituted an alternative way of thinking about international politics, regime theorists accepted the realist view of states as the central actors of international politics, and they accepted the central realist premise that state behavior is rooted in power and interest.[2] In addition, they used

international relations before the Second World War, the study of international law, was relegated to law schools and was systematically ignored by political scientists for more than half a century.

[2] Emblematic of the convergence implied in this formulation is the fact that the critical contributions to regime theory are in a special 1982 issue of *International Organization*, which was edited by a prominent realist, Stephen Krasner. For more on regimes see Young (1986); Rittberger with Mayer (1993); Hasenclever, Mayer, and Rittberger (1997).

the intellectual tools of conflict analysis such as game theory and derived a self-interested basis for the existence of international institutions.

Before long, the term regime was replaced with that of institution. The key reason is that it allowed those in international relations to connect intellectually with the re-emergence of the study of institutions in economics, political science, and sociology. In all these fields and in various subfields, an "old institutionalism" which had focused on formal institutions was being replaced by a "new institutionalism" which embodied a broader conceptualization. Across fields and subfields, scholars could accept the definition of "institutions," as "the rules of the game in a society, or more formally, [the] humanly devised constraints that shape human interaction" (North 1990).

The expansion in focus made it possible to recognize a broader array of international politics as being comparable and similar. Take, for example, the efforts by states to stop the proliferation of nuclear weapons and their delivery systems. In the 1960s, the vast majority of states signed the NPT and constructed an IAEA to monitor compliance. Years later, to deal with the ancillary issue of delivery systems, states capable of exporting missiles came together and created the MTCR. Although dealing with similar concerns, preventing the spread of particular weapons systems, the two arrangements were constructed quite differently (Rasmussen and Stein 2001). The IAEA was an international organization, but there was none created by the MTCR. Yet both the NPT and the MTCR could be considered international regimes or international institutions. One implication of this broader focus is that scholars could assess the role of international institutions prior to the arrival of actual international organizations.

1.4 Liberalism

Those who studied the post-Second World War international organizations were called liberals. In part, this was because they focused on the cooperation that underlay the new post-Second World War international arrangements. Realists after all focus on conflict and minimize the prospect for, and the nature of, international cooperation. In addition, in focusing on international cooperation and new institutional arrangements, scholars were accepting the possibility of change and improvement (both classically liberal notions) in contrast to the realist emphasis on the continuous and unchanging nature of the reality of international anarchy and the omnipresent prospect of war.

This intellectual turn to a focus on regimes, although it was intended by some to bridge the gap between realists and institutionalists, was nevertheless considered liberal for two reasons. Even though realists had by this point rooted their arguments in microeconomic arguments about competition among the few, the core argument that international institutions constituted mutually beneficial

arrangements reflected the classically liberal argument of economists about individuals and firms engaging in mutually beneficial exchanges. In addition, this
new institutional turn also drew on arguments made by economists to explain
the integration of firms. Economics was built on the logic of large numbers of
producers and consumers exchanging in an efficient market. In classical economic theory, the size of firms could be explained only by economics of scale—
that is, efficiency improvements from becoming larger. But firms had clearly
grown beyond simply scale efficiencies. Economists thus had to explain why
firms replaced market transactions and internalized them in a corporate structure that included production facilities in multiple locations. Economists developed an argument about market transaction costs, and that in some cases
firms found hierarchy more efficient than the market. This argument was appropriated by international relations scholars to explain international institutions
(Keohane 1984; Lake 1996; Weber 2000). Thus, this new institutional literature,
despite emphasizing self-interest as realists do, despite drawing on microeconomics
as realists do, and despite using game theory as realists do, was dubbed neoliberalism and neoliberal institutionalism because of its emphasis on cooperation and
institutions.

1.5 Rationalism: The Grand Union

The use of game theory and the demonstration that institutionalized cooperation
could be explained from a starting point of the power and interest of independent
actors made possible not only a rapprochement between realists and neoliberal
institutionalists but even an intellectual union in a perspective some dubbed as
rationalism. Game theory made possible integrating conflict and cooperation in
a unifying framework in contrast to having the field divided between those who
studied conflict, especially crises and war, and those who studied cooperation and
institutions. It also held the prospect for an integration of those who focus on
security and typically emphasize the conflictual nature of international politics and
those who study international political economy with its substantial domain of cooperation between states. It made possible a recognition that there were cooperative
elements even in the midst of conflict and conflictual elements even in the midst of
cooperation.

By the late 1990s, one could detect two distinct views. On the one hand, some
accept a view of limited difference between neorealism and neoliberal institutionalism and talk of a single perspective of rationalism (Katzenstein, Keohane, and
Krasner 1998). On the other hand, one continues to come across studies setting realism and liberalism against one another as competing explanations (Baldwin 1993;
Kegley 1995) and assessing their subtle differences (Schweller and Priess 1997; Jervis
1999).

2 COMPETING FORMULATIONS
AND PERSPECTIVES

2.1 Institutions as Marginal and Epiphenomenal

Those who do recognize the seemingly obvious reality that international politics is riddled with institutions must perforce confront the implications of this development. Those who believe they have a set of concepts and theories that have explained international politics all along are quite reasonably chary of discarding them because of the emergence and growth of international institutions. Realists trace their intellectual roots to Thucydides and see states as the primary actors and emphasize the role of power in determining outcomes in the anarchic setting of international politics. And realists see international institutions as a relatively small and irrelevant component of international relations and in any case reducible to the twin realist verities of power and interest (Stein 2001b).

Realists have downplayed the role of institutions in international politics for two general reasons. While not denying the obvious reality of a vast array of institutions, they have argued that institutions exist typically in "low politics" domains of lesser importance such as transportation, communication, health, and the like, and not in the "high politics" domains of national security and defense. In these areas, institutions constitute a "false promise" (Mearsheimer 1994–5).

The second main criticism is that institutions are epiphenomenal, that they merely reflect power and interest. Institutions have no independent standing, they have no independent causal role, they constitute the same world of power politics familiar to realists. Institutions may exist, but they do not mitigate in any way the anarchy of the international system. Institutions are created by the powerful to serve their interests, and they are dissolved when power and interest shift. Realists beg the question of why institutions would be needed in the first place to achieve the interests of the powerful.

The post-cold war period thus makes possible a test of the resilience and continuity of institutions. The collapse of the Soviet Union clearly transformed the international distribution of power. The bipolar world of US–Soviet rivalry was replaced by one of US predominance, and this led realists to argue that an institution such as NATO, whose sole purpose was to contain Soviet power, was doomed. The departure of the enemy removed any reason for the continued existence of the institution (Mearsheimer 1990). Yet NATO has not only continued to function; it has expanded its membership and its tasks. For realists, only a concern by former Soviet satellites and newly independent former Soviet republics about the return of Russian imperialism can explain NATO's expanded membership. More difficult for them to explain is the expansion of NATO missions to "out-of-area operations" such as those in the former Yugoslavia and in Afghanistan.

2.2 How Wide to Cast the Net?

The expansion of the focus of inquiry raises the problem of how widely to cast the net. If institutions are simply rules of the game, and if all recurrent behavior is guided by some rule, then the entire study of international politics can simply be redefined as the study of international institutions. Even the definition's requirement that the rules be "humanly devised constraints" does not do much to delimit a domain of inquiry. In a sense, all social reality is humanly devised, and since what actually happens can always be contrasted against a range of possibility, what actually occurs can be seen as the product of constraints. States interacting in an anarchic international system follow some rule (even one such as "all's fair in war"), and thus anarchy can simply be redubbed an institution. Nothing is then delimited by a focus on institutions, because all international politics is institutional.

The field continues to be in some disarray from an inability to agree on a definition that circumscribes some well-defined domain for the study of international institutions. What I said once about regimes could as easily be applied to today's use of institution: "scholars have fallen into using the term … so disparately … that it ranges from an umbrella for all international relations to little more than a synonym for international organizations" (Stein 1982, 299). One study assessing historical change in a set of international institutions deals with the following: statehood, territoriality, sovereignty, international law, diplomacy, international trade, colonialism, and war (Holsti 2004). To that list, some add borders as institutions (Simmons 2005). The key question is whether all these can be profitably conceptualized and studied as institutions.

Two literatures, often described separately, are similar in casting a wide net that in effect redefines all international politics along institutional lines. One school is that of social constructivism, in which all social reality is constructed intersubjectively through interaction. The very units of international politics, states, are social constructions, as is the sovereign state system in which they interact. Combining a broad view of institutions with a view of social and political reality as socially constructed leads to the argument that the sovereign state system is itself an institution of international political life. In this view all international politics is subject to a set of rules that are human constructions and in which actors are subsequently socialized.

A second literature is in many ways similar; it is known as the English School and it emphasizes the existence of international society. Although the School recognizes an international system that involves the mere interactions of states and that is subject to power politics, it argues that typically an international society, rather than system, constitutes international reality. The definition of international society provided by the School seems delimiting: An international society exists "when a group of states, conscious of certain common interests and common values, form a society in the sense that they conceive themselves to be bound by a common set of rules in their relations with one another, and share in the working of common institutions" (Bull 1977, 13). But this definition appears in a book titled *The Anarchical Society*, whose point is that states do not really interact in an anarchic international system but rather in an anarchical society guided by rules and norms of behavior. Relations both create and reflect some rules of a game, and these are socially constructed and constitute the basis of an international society.

Both social constructivism and the English School characterize (if not define) the study of international institutions so broadly as to make all international relations institutional. In doing this, they in effect argue that recent developments do not constitute anything new but merely a continuation or a development on what has always been there (a feature they share with realists). Although they both provide essential insights for an understanding of international relations, they do not help circumscribe the role of institutions in international relations.

3 INSTITUTIONS AS SOLUTIONS TO DILEMMAS OF SELF-INTEREST

As already alluded to, the heart of neoliberal institutionalism is a view of international institutions as the self-interested creations of states. States find that autonomous self-interested behavior can be problematic and they prefer to construct international institutions to deal with a host of concerns.

States experience many coordination problems, situations in which their interests generate multiple equilibria and for which they need some mechanism for what has come to be called equilibrium selection. In some cases, there is little conflict of interest, and international institutions are easily constructed. In other cases, there are conflicts of interest between equilibria, yet here too institutional solutions may be preferable to the risk of coordination failure (Stein 1982; 1990; Snidal 1985a; Martin 1992).

States also experience collaboration problems, in which their autonomous self-interested behavior results in deficient outcomes. The Prisoner's Dilemma game is the quintessential example of a situation in which autonomy results in poorer outcomes. In such cases, institutions can resolve the collective action problems and allow states to reach mutually preferred outcomes. Many situations, from trade to arms races, have been characterized as Prisoner's Dilemma games, and these are precisely ones in which states have either created, or tried to create, international institutions.

This institutional solution is akin to the social contract arguments of political theorists for the creation of states. These theorists explain the state as an institutional solution to the problem of autonomous choice in the state of nature. Individuals, they argue, out of their self-interest, voluntarily cede some of their freedom of action in order to achieve better outcomes than those arrived at in the state of nature. The argument of these political theorists came to be analyzed using modern game theory, and they were seen as offering a statist solution to Prisoner's Dilemma problems.[3]

Finally, states may also create institutions in order to reduce the governance costs associated with autonomous decision-making. The costs of organizing coalitions of the willing for every specific problem and circumstance are quite high. Just as firms find it more efficient to take external arm's length transactions and internalize them within a corporate governance structure, so too states find that transaction costs can be reduced by creating international institutions.

4 THE DARK SIDE OF THE FORCE

Realists responded to these arguments about cooperation and collective action.[4] Their response focused on what they saw as too rosy a picture about the prospects for, and the nature of, international institutions. International cooperation and international institutions were harder to construct than the picture provided by institutionalists. In addition, not only did international institutions themselves reflect the power of the states that created them, but their construction itself entailed the exercise of power even as it was the product of voluntaristic and autonomous choice.

4.1 Relative Gains and the Problem of Institutions

One realist retort was to emphasize that institutional cooperation in international relations was more difficult than imagined because states had distributional concerns and not simply welfare-maximizing ones. That is, they argued that, even

---

[3] It should be noted that anarchic solutions to Prisoner's Dilemma problems could still arise if there were repeated interactions and sufficient weight attached to future payoffs. Ironically, within civil society, the statist solution is omnipresent. In international politics, the statist and anarchy solutions are both present.

[4] The title of this section pays homage to Jack Hirshleifer (2001), who continually emphasized that the voluntaristic domain of economics has a coercive component to it.

if states found themselves in situations in which they would be better off cooperating with one another, it remained the case that states were concerned about the relative gains that would accrue from cooperation. In short, cooperation was more difficult to achieve and sustain because states would give up potential gains if the cooperation that brought them these gains meant that others gained even more (Grieco 1988). States were concerned about their relative standing and the relative gains from cooperative arrangements and did not just focus on their own returns.

The issue of relative gains led to a mini-literature, the net result of which remains open to competing interpretations (Stein 1990, ch. 5; Powell 1991; Snidal 1991a; 1991b; Busch and Reinhardt 1993). What is clear, however, is that relative gains concerns do not do away with the possibility of cooperation and especially so as the number of powers in the system increases.

The point to be made, however, is that relative gains notwithstanding, there is a great deal of institutionalized cooperation and much of it having quite differential payoffs. The international hierarchy of power and wealth has changed over the last half-century, and those shifts have occurred in part because of, and certainly in the context of, the workings of international institutions.

4.2 Coercive Cooperation: The Power of Clubs and First Movers

A second line of criticism argues that international institutions are less benign than they are pictured and reflect the actions of the powerful. States differ in power and they use that power in the creation of international institutions. They use their bargaining power as well as their power to structure the choices for others in the construction of institutions. Realists argue that this vitiates their view of the world.

Stephen Krasner (1991) argues that when there is a set of acceptable outcomes (a Pareto frontier), great powers use their bargaining power to obtain outcomes they most prefer. I described this as "coordination for the powerful" (Stein 1982, 311), and it arises whenever there are multiple equilibria, and states have conflicting preferences over which they want to see emerge. But the existence of such cases in no way reduces the importance of institutions and voluntaristic agreement. It simply reminds us that there is a coercive aspect to mutually beneficial exchanges. Actors have different endowments and different possibilities and different bargaining strengths, and these determine outcomes. But this was the point of neoliberal institutionalism, that one could begin with the power and interests of states and deduce a role for international institutions. That such outcomes were described as cooperative does not imply the complete absence of power and even coercive threats.

There are also cases in which especially powerful states can get together in a less than universal grouping and leave other countries with the difficult choice of joining or staying out of the arrangement. The creation of the inter-state club changes the status quo and means that what may have been a preferable alternative is no longer available. States outside the club are left with a choice: they may join the club but there is a substantial component of coercion along with the voluntarism in the choice. The states creating the club have exercised a form of power (Gruber 2000).

This latter point is also a long-recognized one. The emergence of a liberal trading order began with the inclusion of most-favored-nation clauses in bilateral trade agreements (Stein 1984; 1990). States bound by such agreements created a "club good." Those in the club shared a collective benefit, that of the lowest negotiated tariff rates between them. Those not in the club were excluded and paid the standard and often substantially higher tariff rate. Such clubs provide benefits to members and exclude nonmembers, and their existence changes the incentives for future prospective entrants. They are *clubs of agglomeration* and constitute "regime creation by accretion" (Rosecrance and Stein 2001, 225–6). Such a sequential admission of members based on their preference for cooperation results in an institution exhibiting more cooperation than could have been achieved by an initial strategy of complete inclusion (Downs, Rocke, and Barsoom 1998). Those on the outside might prefer not to have to choose between joining and staying out. They might even have preferred to join initially when they could have had a larger role in writing the rules. But this exercise of power is hardly the coercive vision of classical realism (Rosecrance 2001).

4.3 Institutional Failure

International organizations were also faulted as failures on their own terms. The fact that they were created to improve outcomes for states provides no assurance that they actually accomplish their objective. The argument is much like that made regarding states and domestic policy. State intervention is a desirable outcome when there is market failure. But the fact of market failure and the possibility of better outcomes is no guarantee that states deliver. Instead, government failure is itself a possibility. So citizens in democratic societies debate when markets fail and whether government intervention would provide improvement.

A similar debate exists about international organizations. There may indeed be failures of autonomous independent behavior, and the possibility for improved coordinated and collaborative behavior. But creating international institutions may not provide the hoped-for improved outcomes, because they may themselves exhibit a form of international organizational failure (Gallarotti 1991; Barnett and Finnemore 1999).

5 Intellectual Agendas of Neoliberal Institutionalism

5.1 Do Institutions Matter?

Central to an interest in institutions is the notion that they matter, that they make a difference in the behavior of states and in the nature of international politics. Otherwise they are the irrelevancies that realists claim.

In one area after another, then, there are literatures devoted to assessing the impact, or effectiveness, of international institutions. There are many studies, mostly by economists, assessing the impact of regional and global trade arrangements (Goldstein, Rivers, and Tomz 2007). There are many studies on the effectiveness of international environmental regimes.

Similarly, scholars have focused on the question of state compliance with international institutions, and have found that states by and large comply with the agreements they make. They have demonstrated that compliance is not easy to ascertain (Chayes and Chayes 1993) and is related to the design of the institution (Mitchell 1994). Much of the force of the original wave of work on compliance was that compliance occurred even without enforcement mechanisms, and a mini-literature developed on the possibility of a managerial alternative to enforcement as the basis for compliance.

Yet the empirical assessment of compliance is bedeviled by the problem of selection bias. As George Downs, David Rocke, and Peter Barsoom (1996, 380) put it in discussing the first wave of work on compliance, the problem is that compliance with minimal enforcement results "from the fact that most treaties require states to make only modest departures from what they would have done in the absence of an agreement." More recent extensive statistical work on compliance has been subject to the same charge (Simmons 2000; von Stein 2005). While it may be difficult analytically to assess the impact of institutions, it remains striking that states use institutions to arrive at the outcomes they want.

5.2 How they Come into Being

That international institutions serve state purposes provides an explanation but no process for how they come into being. One answer, and one that oddly links institutionalist and realist thought, is that hegemonic powers create institutions. Yet imposition is only one mechanism (Young 1982), and hegemonic powers often provide inducements to create institutions (Stein 1984; Snidal 1985b). They provide a variety of forms of leadership central to the process of regime formation (Young 1991).

5.3 Institutional Design

International institutions vary along many dimensions. They vary in their membership and size. Some are universal and encompass almost all states in the international system. Others are purely regional in character and encompass only a small set of countries. Some focus on very narrow issues, whereas others are broader and multipurpose in character. As discussed above, some are embodied in formal organizations, whereas others have no building, no address, no secretariat, and so on. They vary in the degree of attention paid to issues of monitoring and enforcement, in their mechanisms for dispute resolution, and in how they deal with possible noncompliance by states. They vary in their rules of procedure—in how collective decisions are selected.

These issues are the same ones that underlie domestic institutional construction and are at the heart of constitutional arrangements (Rogowski 1999). Domestically we speak of the franchise rather than membership, but the issue is the same: who is part of the enterprise and who is not. In international organizations, as within countries, representation mechanisms and decision rules determine how preferences are aggregated into a collective choice.

All these issues are negotiated by states in the course of dealing with the problems that underlie the search for institutional responses. Why particular institutional designs are chosen and with what consequence are the focus of a growing literature.

The original formulation of international organizations as solutions to collective action problems contained the broad implication that the design of international institutions was related to the nature of the problem they were intended to solve. Institutions that provided coordination, for example, were self-enforcing and did not require extensive mechanisms for monitoring and enforcement. Thus they were unlikely to be highly institutionalized and formalized. In contrast, collaborative solutions to Prisoner's Dilemma problems were subject to defection and cheating and exhibited extensive concern with monitoring and enforcement (Stein 1982; 1990).

There has been a heightened interest in institutional design, as evidenced by a special issue of *International Organization* on the topic that appeared in 2001 (reprinted as Koremenos, Lipson, and Snidal 2004). The special issue lays out five dimensions of design: membership, scope of issues covered, centralization of tasks, rules for control of the institution, and the flexibility of arrangements in dealing with new and unanticipated circumstances. In addition, the special issue argues that design choices along the above dimensions are a function of distribution problems, enforcement problems, the number of actors as well as asymmetries between them, and uncertainty.

These design features do not exhaust the possibilities. Thinking of international institutions as forms of governance and thinking of governments as analogues, one can characterize the structure of international institutions as including legislative, executive, and judicial features. The above items capture aspects of the first two, but some international institutions even embody a judicial function. These institutions are designed with mechanisms that provide disaffected states an alternative to exit. States, for example, can depart from their institutional obligations, and quasi-judicial procedures exist for distinguishing acceptable departures from opportunistic behavior. In addition, institutions also have mechanisms for dispute resolution that embody different design features (Smith 2000).

Another design feature of international institutions has to do with how they treat property and provide the good in question. It is a misconception that international institutions deal only with public goods. Indeed, they deal with both private and public goods.

Some international institutions are constructed to change the nature of the good being provided. Environmental problems such as clean air are quintessential examples of public goods. Yet the international institution created to clean the air did not approach the problem by instituting a global regulatory regime for air quality; rather it created a market in emissions trading. On the other hand, international trade is an inherently private good, and it is only the design feature of including most-favored-nation clauses in bilateral agreements that provide it with a collective character (Stein 1984; 1990; Rosecrance and Stein 2001). In some cases, international institutions make collective what is inherently a private good.

There is much work to be done characterizing the design features of international institutions, the trade-offs associated with different design features, their bases, and their consequences.

5.4 Domestic Politics and International Institutions

One of the major developments in the study of international relations has been the breaking down of the intellectual wall separating domestic and international politics. It is increasingly recognized that international relations has domestic roots and domestic consequences.

The link between domestic and international politics applies as well to the study of institutions. On the one hand, domestic political institutions must typically be supportive of membership, and thus we can talk of the domestic political requisites of joining international institutions. Further, there must be domestic support for subsequent compliance as well (Dai 2005).

But international institutions also affect domestic ones. First, because there are often domestic requisites to joining international institutions, membership conditionality has an important effect on internal political arrangements (Skålnes 1998; Kelley 2004). Secondly, since membership in an institution subjects a state to continuing restraints, joining one has the affect both of locking in domestic changes and of making credible a domestic commitment to a particular policy path (Pevehouse 2002; Grigorescu 2003). Thirdly, international institutions may provide a degree of legitimacy (Franck 1988; Hurd 1999) and make difficult domestic changes more palatable by providing political cover (Vreeland 2003; Allee and Huth 2006). In these cases, domestic actors come to frame their arguments in terms of international institutions (Cortell and Davis 1996).

The relationship between domestic politics and international institutions is an important one that requires further exploration. And it is an evolving one, as shown by the next section, which describes the growth of international intrusiveness into domestic life and how such increasing constraints on sovereignty interact with domestic politics.

5.5 Toward a Historical Institutionalism

Alongside the development of the new institutionalism in the social sciences has been the emergence of a historical institutionalism, emphasizing the ways in which institutions change. Some institutions arise and decay and disappear. Others arise and grow and develop (Shanks, Jacobson, and Kaplan 1996), and become more complex (Holsti 2004). They take on new members and even new tasks.

Even more broadly, institutions can themselves substantially change the circumstances under which they were created. Although the original regime literature emphasized that institutions reflected power and interest, it left open as a question what would happen to institutions as the distribution of power changed and as the constellation of interest shifted. The possibility was raised that the creation of institutions would itself change the nature of interests and subsequent calculations (Stein 1982; 1990).

The discussion above about how institutions can begin with a small set of countries and then grow signals the role of accretion and agglomeration in institutional development. Most international institutions have grown in size. Even narrowly crafted security ones, such as NATO, took on new members.

Institutions also develop and become formalized and organized. The Group of Seven (G7) economic summits began as informal exercises but became routinized over time. The institutional structure that is NATO was not at all foreseen in the founding arrangements (Wallander 2000).

Institutions also change and take on new tasks with changing conditions. The IMF, for example, proved inadequate for its originally intended role and thus did little in its early years. It then functioned as intended during the 1950s and 1960s, but found a new role as the major states left the system of fixed exchange rates. The IMF today functions in a way never intended or imagined by its founders (Pauly 1999).

Perhaps the most important development is that institutions have become more intrusive and constraining over time. To deal with the challenges that have led them to construct international institutions in the first place, states have demanded and accepted unprecedented levels of intrusiveness in their domestic affairs (Stein 2001*a*). In both security and economic arrangements, states expect and tolerate more involvement in their internal affairs by international institutions. On-site monitoring by foreigners, an item that was once an immense stumbling block in obtaining security arrangements, is now much more readily accepted. International economic institutions now lecture and grade member states on a host of political variables that were once deemed as off-limits and not related to economic management. It has even become accepted practice to have external monitors for internal elections (Santa-Cruz 2005; Hyde 2006). Nowhere is the decline of sovereignty more apparent than in Europe, where states still exist and matter but where significant governance operates at levels above the state (Mattli 1999; Wallace 1999).

5.6 Multilevel Governance

The number of international institutions has become sufficiently large for scholars to have begun to focus on the implications of competing and overlapping institutions and the choices that states have regarding institutions. Faced with new problems, states can extend the scope of extant institutions or create new ones. And as institutions proliferate, states have a choice in which institutional setting to deal with their problems and concerns.

In a rich institutional environment, states have a choice between creating new institutions or reforming existing ones in order to deal with new problems. As mentioned above, rather than extend the scope of the institutions already dealing with proliferation of nuclear weapons, a new institution, quite different in character, was created to deal with the proliferation of missile technology (MTCR). On the other hand, as also mentioned above, states have changed the character of extant institutions, such as NATO and the IMF, when facing new challenges.

In a number of areas there are multiple institutions that are either nested or overlap (Aggarwal 1998; Rosecrance and Stein 2001). In the area of trade, for example, bilateral trade agreements and regional trade agreements coexist with the global WTO. In such cases, states have the opportunity to engage in forum shopping, deciding in which venue to pursue their interests and concerns (Alter and Meunier 2006; Busch 2007).

A wide array of international institutions exist, some regional and some global, some narrowly focused and others quite broad. The result is a more complex world of multilevel governance which states navigate (Stein 2008).

5.7 Ideas

Ideas are central to many of the above agendas. As social constructions, institutions inherently reflect ideas about governance, and many of the illustrations above implicitly demonstrate this (Goldstein and Keohane 1993). For example, as discussed above, the transformation of trade from a private to a club good depended on the idea of an unconditional most-favored-nation clause. The idea of a market in pollution rights is the key underpinning of the institutional design that transforms that public good into a private one. Similar cases can be made about other elements of institutional design. In addition, institutional change is also related to ideational change.

6 CONCLUSION

The world is full of international institutions. Disagreement about definitions, about how old or new the phenomenon, and about its exact impact cannot mask the reality of a growing number and role of international institutions. How much and how adequately these institutions of international governance tame anarchy is open to question, but the world is witnessing an increase in supranational governance, created by states and in which states increasingly live. Understanding and explaining international politics (and indeed even many areas of national politics) increasingly requires incorporating the role of international institutions. Scholarship on international institutions is growing and developing commensurately.

REFERENCES

AGGARWAL, V. K. (ed.) 1998. *Institutional Designs for a Complex World: Bargaining, Linkages, and Nesting*. Ithaca, NY: Cornell University Press.

ALLEE, T. L., and HUTH, P. K. 2006. Legitimizing dispute settlement: international legal rulings as domestic political cover. *American Political Science Review*, 100: 219–34.

ALTER, K. J., and MEUNIER, S. 2006. Nested and overlapping regimes in the transatlantic banana trade dispute. *Journal of European Public Policy*, 13: 362–82.

BALDWIN, D. A. (ed.) 1993. *Neorealism and Neoliberalism: The Contemporary Debate*. New York: Columbia University Press.

BARNETT, M. N., and FINNEMORE, M. 1999. The politics, power, and pathologies of international organizations. *International Organization*, 53: 699–732.

BULL, H. 1977. *The Anarchical Society: A Study of Order in World Politics.* New York: Columbia University Press.

BUSCH, M. L. 2007. Overlapping institutions, forum shopping, and dispute settlement in international trade. *International Organization*, 61: 735–6.

—— and REINHARDT, E. R. 1993. Nice strategies in a world of relative gains: the problem of cooperation under anarchy. *Journal of Conflict Resolution*, 37: 427–45.

CARR, E. H. 1940. *The Twenty Years' Crisis, 1919–1939: An Introduction to the Study of International Relations.* London: Macmillan.

CHAYES, A., and CHAYES, A. H. 1993. On compliance. *International Organization*, 47: 175–205.

CORTELL, A. P., and DAVIS, J. W. 1996. How do international institutions matter? The domestic impact of international rules and norms. *International Studies Quarterly*, 40: 451–78.

DAI, X. 2005. Why comply? The domestic constituency mechanism. *International Organization*, 59: 363–98.

DOWNS, G. W., ROCKE, D. M., and BARSOOM, P. N. 1996. Is the good news about compliance good news about cooperation? *International Organization*, 50: 379–406.

—— —— —— 1998. Managing the evolution of multilateralism. *International Organization*, 52: 397–419.

FRANCK, T. M. 1988. Legitimacy in the international system. *American Journal of International Law*, 82: 705–59.

GALLAROTTI, G. M. 1991. The limits of international organization: systematic failure in the management of international relations. *International Organization*, 45: 183–220.

GOLDSTEIN, J., and KEOHANE, R. O. (eds.) 1993. *Ideas and Foreign Policy: Beliefs, Institutions, and Political Change.* Ithaca, NY: Cornell University Press.

—— RIVERS, D., and TOMZ, M. 2007. Institutions in international relations: understanding the effects of the GATT and the WTO on world trade. *International Organization*, 61: 37–67.

GRIECO, J. M. 1988. Anarchy and the limits of cooperation: a realist critique of the newest liberal institutionalism. *International Organization*, 42: 485–507.

GRIGORESCU, A. 2003. International organizations and government transparency: linking the international and domestic realms. *International Studies Quarterly*, 47: 643–67.

GRUBER, L. 2000. *Ruling the World: Power Politics and the Rise of Supranational Institutions.* Princeton, NJ: Princeton University Press.

HASENCLEVER, A., MAYER, P., and RITTBERGER, V. 1997. *Theories of International Regimes.* New York: Cambridge University Press.

HIRSHLEIFER, J. 2001. *The Dark Side of the Force: Economic Foundations of Conflict Theory.* New York: Cambridge University Press.

HOLSTI, K. J. 2004. *Taming the Sovereigns: Institutional Change in International Politics.* New York: Cambridge University Press.

HURD, I. 1999. Legitimacy and authority in international politics. *International Organization*, 53: 379–408.

HYDE, S. 2006. Observing norms: explaining the causes and consequences of internationally monitored elections. Ph.D. dissertation, University of California, San Diego.

IKENBERRY, G. J. 2001. *After Victory: Institutions, Strategic Restraint, and the Rebuilding of Order after Major Wars.* Princeton, NJ: Princeton University Press.

JERVIS, R. 1999. Realism, neoliberalism, and cooperation: understanding the debate. *International Security*, 24: 42–63.

Katzenstein, P. J., Keohane, R. O., and Krasner, S. D. (eds.) 1998. *International Organization* at fifty: exploration and contestation in the study of world politics, special issue. *International Organization*, 52: 645–1061.

Kegley, C. W. (ed.) 1995. *Controversies in International Relations Theory: Realism and the Neoliberal Challenge*. New York: St Martin's Press.

Kelley, J. 2004. International actors on the domestic scene: membership conditionality and socialization by international institutions. *International Organization*, 58: 425–57.

Keohane, R. O. 1984. *After Hegemony: Cooperation and Discord in the World Political Economy*. Princeton, NJ: Princeton University Press.

Koremenos, B., Lipson, C., and Snidal, D. (eds.) 2004. *The Rational Design of International Institutions*. New York: Cambridge University Press.

Krasner, S. D. 1982. Structural causes and regime consequences: regimes as intervening variables. *International Organization*, 36: 185–205.

—— 1991. Global communications and national power: life on the Pareto frontier. *World Politics*, 43: 336–66.

Lake, D. A. 1996. Anarchy, hierarchy, and the variety of international relations. *International Organization*, 50: 1–33.

Martin, L. L. 1992. Interests, power, and multilateralism. *International Organization*, 46: 765–92.

Mattli, W. 1999. *The Logic of Regional Integration: Europe and Beyond*. New York: Cambridge University Press.

Mearsheimer, J. J. 1990. Back to the future: instability in Europe after the Cold War. *International Security*, 15: 5–56.

—— 1994–5. The false promise of international institutions. *International Security*, 19: 5–49.

Mitchell, R. B. 1994. Regime design matters: intentional oil pollution and treaty compliance. *International Organization*, 48: 425–58.

North, D. C. 1990. *Institutions, Institutional Change, and Economic Performance*. New York: Cambridge University Press.

Pauly, L. W. 1999. Good governance and bad policy: the perils of international organizational overextension. *Review of International Political Economy*, 6: 401–24.

Pevehouse, J. C. 2002. With a little help from my friends? Regional organizations and the consolidation of democracy. *American Journal of Political Science*, 46: 611–26.

Plano, J. C., and Olton, R. 1979. *The International Relations Dictionary*, 2nd edn. Kalamazoo, Mich.: New Issues.

Powell, R. 1991. Absolute and relative gains in international relations theory. *American Political Science Review*, 85: 1303–20.

Rasmussen, G., and Stein, A. A. 2001. Non-proliferation regimes. Pp. 181–202 in *The New Great Power Coalition: Toward a World Concert of Nations*, ed. R. Rosecrance. Lanham, Md.: Rowman and Littlefield.

Rittberger, V., with Mayer, P. (eds.) 1993. *Regime Theory and International Relations*. Oxford: Clarendon Press.

Rogowski, R. 1999. Institutions as constraints on strategic choice. Pp. 115–36 in *Strategic Choice and International Relations*, ed. D. A. Lake and R. Powell. Princeton, NJ: Princeton University Press.

Rosecrance, R. 2001. Has realism become cost–benefit analysis? A review essay. *International Security*, 26: 132–54.

ROSECRANCE, R., and STEIN, A. A. 2001. The theory of overlapping clubs. Pp. 221–34 in *The New Great Power Coalition: Toward a World Concert of Nations*, ed. R. Rosecrance. Lanham, Md.: Rowman and Littlefield.

SANTA-CRUZ, A. 2005. Constitutional structures, sovereignty, and the emergence of norms: the case of international election monitoring. *International Organization*, 59: 663–93.

SCHWELLER, R. L., and PRIESS, D. 1997. A tale of two realisms: expanding the institutions debate. *Mershon International Studies Review*, 41: 1–32.

SHANKS, C., JACOBSON, H. K., and KAPLAN, J. H. 1996. Inertia and change in the constellation of international governmental organizations, 1981–1992. *International Organization*, 50: 593–627.

SIMMONS, B. A. 2000. International law and state behavior: commitment and compliance in international monetary affairs. *American Political Science Review*, 94: 819–35.

——2005. Rules over real estate: trade, territorial conflict, and international borders as institution. *Journal of Conflict Resolution*, 49: 823–48.

SKÅLNES, L. S. 1998. From the outside in, from the inside out: NATO expansion and international relations theory. *Security Studies*, 7: 44–87.

SMITH, J. McC. 2000. The politics of dispute settlement design: explaining legalism in regional trade pacts. *International Organization*, 54: 137–80.

SNIDAL, D. 1985a. Coordination versus prisoners' dilemma: implications for international cooperation and regimes. *American Political Science Review*, 79: 923–42.

——1985b. The limits of hegemonic stability theory. *International Organization*, 39: 579–614.

——1991a. International cooperation among relative gains maximizers. *International Studies Quarterly*, 35: 387–402.

——1991b. Relative gains and the pattern of international cooperation. *American Political Science Review*, 85: 701–26.

STEIN, A. A. 1982. Coordination and collaboration: regimes in an anarchic world. *International Organization*, 36: 299–324.

——1984. The hegemon's dilemma: Great Britain, the United States, and the international economic order. *International Organization*, 38: 355–86.

——1990. *Why Nations Cooperate: Circumstance and Choice in International Relations.* Ithaca, NY: Cornell University Press.

——2001a. Constrained sovereignty: the growth of international intrusiveness. Pp. 261–81 in *The New Great Power Coalition: Toward a World Concert of Nations*, ed. R. Rosecrance. Lanham, Md.: Rowman and Littlefield.

——2001b. Realism/neorealism. Pp. 12812–15 in *International Encyclopedia of the Social and Behavioral Sciences*, ed. N. J. Smelser and P. B. Baltes. New York: Pergamon Press.

——2008. Incentive compatibility and global governance: existential multilateralism, a weakly confederal world, and hegemony. Pp. 1–68 in *Can the World be Governed?*, ed. A. Alexandroff. Waterloo: Wilfrid Laurier University Press for the Centre for International Governance Innovation.

VON STEIN, J. 2005. Do treaties constrain or screen? Selection bias and treaty compliance. *American Political Science Review*, 99: 611–22.

VREELAND, J. R. 2003. Why do governments and the IMF enter into agreements? Statistically selected cases. *International Political Science Review*, 24: 321–43.

WALLACE, W. 1999. The sharing of sovereignty: the European paradox. *Political Studies*, 47: 503–21.

WALLANDER, C. A. 2000. Institutional assets and adaptability: NATO after the Cold War. *International Organization*, 54: 705–35.

WEBER, K. 2000. *Hierarchy amidst Anarchy: Transaction Costs and Institutional Choice*. Albany, NY: State University of New York Press.

YOUNG, O. R. 1982. Regime dynamics: the rise and fall of international regimes. *International Organization*, 36: 277–97.

——1986. International regimes: toward a new theory of institutions. *World Politics*, 39: 104–22.

——1991. Political leadership and regime formation: on the development of institutions in international society. *International Organization*, 45: 281–308.

CHAPTER 12

THE ETHICS OF NEOLIBERAL INSTITUTIONALISM

JAMES L. RICHARDSON

CONTEMPORARY liberal institutional theory, originating in an enhanced awareness of interdependence in the 1970s, broke with earlier liberal thought in accepting some of the central assumptions of realist theory and defining itself solely in empirical terms. To the extent that normative presuppositions or implications may nonetheless be discerned, they remain implicit. This chapter focuses on the most prominent theoretical school, usually termed "neoliberal institutionalism," which, it is argued, narrowed down liberalism's traditional normative commitments no less than its empirical assumptions. The chapter also takes note of certain alternative formulations of institutionalist theory and of the broadening scope of institutional theorizing in the present decade, and its re-emphasis on the normative. The norma- tive writings of Robert Keohane, the central figure in the neoliberal school, demand special attention: while in some respects quite distinctive, they may reasonably be taken as representative of a widely shared American liberal outlook. It is argued that the values endorsed by these variants of liberal institutionalism are limited by their shared perspective: that of the predominant power of the day with its distinctive political culture.[1]

I should like to thank Ursula Vollerthun and the editors for their comments and searching questions, from which this chapter has greatly benefited.

[1] Institutionalist theory outside the United States, notably in Germany, has been strongly influenced by American theorists; for reasons of space it is not discussed here.

1 Historical Context

In response to the devastation occasioned by the First World War, liberal institutionalists pursued one overriding goal: the establishment of peace. Initially it
was sought directly, through creating an institution, the League of Nations, which
would embody a new liberal order in place of the discredited realist "power politics."
The League's failure to fulfil this expectation prompted a radical reformulation: a
new approach, functionalism, sought to achieve the goal indirectly. A network of
specialized institutions regulating specific areas of international relations would, it
was maintained, foster habits of cooperation that would gradually moderate the
conflicts that would otherwise lead to war. The early moves toward integration in
Western Europe offered some encouragement, but in the intellectual climate of the
cold war functionalism never won credibility as a general theory.

By the 1970s the increasing salience of economic interdependence prompted
a further radical reformulation of institutionalism, culminating in Keohane and
Joseph Nye's *Power and Interdependence* (1977), which foreshadowed core ideas of
neoliberal institutionalist theory. They did not seek to replace realist theory, but to
limit its scope: They saw it as valid when security concerns were uppermost, but
introduced the term "complex interdependence" to identify areas of international
relations governed by a different logic—namely, regulation through cooperative
regimes. In a further departure from traditional institutionalist thinking, there was
no explicit reference to the normative purpose, the promotion of peace. While this
might remain the ultimate aim, it was no longer claimed that institutions have the
system-transforming potential formerly ascribed to them.

Thus far, changes in institutionalist theory had been prompted mainly by perceived changes in "the world." The shift to neoliberal institutionalism, it may be
suggested, was mainly theory driven. The replacement of the comparative-socio-
logical style of *Power and Interdependence* by the economics-based "rationalist"
style of neoliberal institutionalism was occasioned by acceptance on the part of
a group of liberal scholars of the metatheoretical assumptions of rational choice
theory and of the core realist assumptions that states remain the central actors
in international politics, and that they pursue self-interested goals, in particular
security and material interests. The main difference with neorealism was the claim
that, nonetheless, there was far greater scope for international cooperation than
neorealist theory would have it, and that institutions played an important role in
facilitating this cooperation (see, e.g., Keohane 1989, 1–20, 101–31).

The critique of hegemonic stability theory offered persuasive support for this
institutionalist claim. Contrary to the realist thesis that the maintenance of cooperative economic regimes requires the presence of a hegemon to enforce the
system's norms, it was argued on both theoretical and empirical grounds that this
is not the case: Egoistic state actors can find ways to cooperate to advance their

shared interests (Keohane 1984; Snidal 1985). The argument was soon broadened: The same game-theoretical logic can provide a common framework of analysis for the whole of international relations—for conflict and cooperation, international security and political economy. These are not separate realms, and conflict is not always paramount (Oye 1986; Stein 1990). However, this left open the question of the scope for cooperation, and of how much institutions "matter," relative to power capabilities—for realists the basic determinant. The debate over relative gains versus absolute gains clarified these issues up to a point, but they remain the crux of the divergence between the two theories (Keohane and Martin 2003).

During the 1990s institutionalists sought to remedy certain omissions identified by critics—notably the role of ideas and the linkage to internal politics—through rationalist analyses complementing their systemic theory (Goldstein and Keohane 1993; Keohane and Milner 1996). But, with the possible exception of the legalization project (Goldstein et al. 2000), there were no further theoretical landmarks. Moreover, the counterpart to the close engagement with neorealism was a failure to engage with other theoretical traditions, and the debate with realism appeared to have run its course. By the late 1990s Keohane was looking back to it as "yesterday's controversy," and embarking on an agenda shaped more by perceived changes in the world than by theoretical puzzles (Keohane 2002, 27–38, 193–287).

Keohane's subsequent institutional studies are so wide-ranging as to raise the question whether there is continuity with neoliberal institutionalism or an entirely new departure. Again in collaboration with Nye, he returns to a sociological style of analysis, seeking to define the nature and extent of changes in the international system: state actors remain important, but theory also needs to take account of new actors and the significance of networks. Normative issues relating to democratic accountability now figure prominently (Keohane 2002, 193–244). In addressing a major new issue, "governance in a partially globalized world," Keohane (2002, 245–71) retains rational choice theory, but now combined with other approaches—sociological, historical, and normative. He retains major elements of neoliberal institutionalism, but has moved beyond its confines.

Certain other theorists offer a wholly different conception of liberal institutionalism—as a theory not of cooperation or of institutions in general, but rather of the character of the contemporary institutional order. Two are especially notable: John Ruggie, moving toward constructivism; and John Ikenberry, drawing on rational choice theory along with other approaches.

Ruggie's contribution is mainly conceptual. His starting point is not a world of egoistic state actors but a historically grounded conception of state–society relations. An international order and its major institutions are not simply a function of the power of the leading actor, but result from "a fusion of power with legitimate social purpose" (Ruggie 1982, 382). Since 1945 the United States, the leading actor (but not the hegemon as usually understood), has promoted an institutional order consistent with its normative identity. This has a certain "architectural form," multilateralism, defined in terms of principles of nondiscrimination, indivisibility, and diffuse reciprocity (Ruggie 1993, 8–16). Similarly the US-inspired post-1945 economic order had a distinctive normative character, "embedded liberalism" (economic liberalism qualified by certain overarching political goals), whose subsequent disembedding raised major concerns (Ruggie 1982; 1996, 135–56).

Ikenberry (2001) identifies a historical trend, the creation of increasingly institutionalized international orders by the victors in hegemonic wars, but his main concern is to examine and explain the order constructed by the United States after the Second World War, and still providing the framework for international politics. He sees this order as part-hegemonic, but in view of the nature of this particular hegemon, it is a liberal, constitutional order: Power is exercised through rules and institutions, the hegemon accepts binding institutional restraints, its decision-making is relatively open, thus its junior partners enjoy access and "voice" opportunities. These liberal characteristics explain the persistence and relative stability of the order after the cold war, and indeed the further institutionalization in this period: the extension of the North Atlantic Treaty Organization and the establishment of the World Trade Organization, the North American Free Trade Agreement, and Asia-Pacific Economic Cooperation.

2 THE ETHICAL DIMENSION

Neoliberal institutional theorists did not question the prevailing assumption that value judgments have no place in the social sciences—even though they might provide the motive for a scholar's choice of subject matter. This assumption, never uncontested, is now widely questioned, but there is no new consensus on the role of value judgments. This section inquires to what extent implicit normative commitments—judgments about what is good, desirable, legitimate, obligatory, and so forth—are entailed in contemporary institutionalism, and what are these commitments? Are they indeed liberal, and in what sense of that term? While the focus is on the neoliberal school, inclusion of the alternative theories permits a more differentiated response.

There is no canonical method for teasing out implicit value commitments, but several aspects of the theories will be examined: the use of evaluative language; values implicit in the conceptual framework, or excluded by it; the research agenda; silences; and finally, the question whether a pattern can be discerned, and to what extent it is liberal. No more than a provisional sketch can be completed within the space available, hopefully in a way that invites further inquiry.

Some empirical concepts have evident normative connotations: Negative terms such as genocide, terrorism, or totalitarianism provide clear examples, but the positive connotations of peace, security, or order equally convey taken-for-granted value judgments (see, e.g., Putnam 2002). Cooperation is one such concept. Even though Keohane (1984) insists that it is not necessarily benign, but can be exploitative, it is often used with positive connotations, as when Arthur Stein (1990, ix) writes of "an era of hope, of the promise of international cooperation" or Keohane (1989, 160) himself contrasts "fragile cooperation" with "persistent zero-sum conflict and warfare." And the regimes studied by the neoliberal school are normally assumed to be welfare promoting, not exploitative.

Even the realist theory of hegemonic stability is not value free, but claims that the hegemon provides highly valued public goods, essential for maintaining a liberal international economic order. The attraction of *After Hegemony* is its persuasive argument that these public goods can be achieved through nonhegemonic regimes. Such evaluative concepts, like "reciprocity" with its connotation of equal exchanges, are very general expressions of commendation. More specific values are signaled in the language on the functioning of regimes: providing reliable information, deterring cheating, providing focal points for coordination, or reducing transaction costs (more generally, "efficiency"). These suggest a managerial orientation, an economist's view of administration.

The foregoing might be termed "cool" evaluations, compared with the relative warmth of the language with which Ruggie and Ikenberry characterize their favored ideal-types, evoking a richer mix of liberal values. This is heightened by the contrast with negative ideal-types: for Ruggie, the kind of world order envisaged by Nazi Germany or the Soviet Union; for Ikenberry, the balance of power or hegemony.

While evaluative language can suggest no more than a general orientation, a theory's conceptual framework can have stronger implications for values promoted or excluded. As Charles Taylor expresses it, a framework "secretes a certain value position:" it charts the geography of the phenomena in question, the range of possible variation. "A given map will have ... its own built-in value-slope." Certain outcomes being ruled out, the framework "will usually determine for itself" what is the best possible state of affairs (Taylor 1973, 153–4).[2]

Utilitarianism, as employed in neoliberal institutional theory, may be construed in this light. It is not the utilitarian framework as such that predetermines the valued outcome—for actors determine their own utilities—but rather its use together with the assumption that states, the relevant actors, are necessarily egoistic and define their individual self-interest in material terms.[3] If this is how the world is, the most that is achievable is that states cooperate to pursue their interests in an enlightened manner—to maximize gains and minimize losses. No other ethical framework seems relevant. Within this general framework, the economists' concept

---

[2] Taylor refers to well-known studies by Seymour Martin Lipset, Harold Lasswell, and Gabriel Almond.

[3] While Keohane (1984, 125) allows for explanation other than in terms of "narrowly defined self-interest," he sees this as limited to "relatively small spheres of activity."

of Pareto optimality—referring to situations in which no actor's welfare can be increased except at the expense of that of other actors—offers a sharper illustration. If institutions are seen as enabling actors to reach the "Pareto frontier" or to choose among "Pareto-optimal equilibria," a high level of welfare is being presupposed. More importantly, this particular concept of welfare excludes by definition the question of redistribution, since this would leave some individual actors worse off.[4] Elsewhere, Keohane allows that liberalism can make for a tendency to accommodate dominant interests and to adopt the perspective of governments, not of the disadvantaged (1990, 192–3) and, in a telling aside, dubs the present institutions "of the privileged, by the privileged and for the privileged" (2002, 256).

The neoliberal institutionalists' treatment of distributive issues offers a striking illustration of the way in which the framework narrowed down the normative agenda. In the initial phase of regime theorizing in the 1970s, "distribution" could refer to the larger, societal consequences of regimes: for example, in Raymond Hopkins and Donald J. Puchala's study of the international food regime, its effects on "wealth, power, autonomy, community, nutritional well-being...and sometimes physical survival," leading to the conclusion that in this regime there were "broad and endemic inadequacies" (cited in Martin and Simmons 1998, 737). In neoliberal institutional theory, regimes came to be evaluated, rather, as "efficient or efficiency-improving:" distributional issues were understood as conflicts over the allocation of gains and costs through bargaining among the state actors (Martin and Simmons 1998, 744–6).

The game-theoretic framework opened up an agenda for explaining significant aspects of institutions previously neglected or passed over lightly—questions relating to information, incentives, commitment, and compliance. But what was excluded from the research agenda was no less striking. A framework premised on bargaining on (more or less) equal terms is not conducive to the study of relations characterized by extreme inequalities such as those encountered in "North–South" relations, nor of hierarchical institutions such as those in the international financial domain, controlled by the major Western governments. Not surprisingly, the typical examples chosen by the neoliberal institutionalists are of bargaining among relative equals: the European Union and the international trade regime, the latter viewed from the perspective of its leading members. Keohane's suggestion (1984, 7) that the analysis might be extended to include North–South relations was not followed up; and indeed this must have created difficulties for applying the framework, or have led to questioning its generality.

The framework makes for a further silence, whose normative consequences are more difficult to discern. Can the United States really be regarded as just one actor like the others? Is the basic model of egoistic state actors, fundamentally alike, a

---

[4] For the Pareto formula see, e.g., Martin and Simmons (1998, 744–5), referring *inter alia* to Krasner (1991).

valid starting point for theory in the present international system? The United States may not be hegemonic, but it is preponderant, its influence not just greater than that of others, but different in kind; the theory has no place for such an actor. The question of the normative consequences of the invisibility of the United States is taken up below.

Keohane's normative discussion of regimes adds a further dimension to the foregoing. It stands apart from his empirical theory—a commentary interrogating the theory from a different perspective (Keohane 1984, 10–11, 247–57). He by no means offers a robust defence of cooperative regimes. Rather, with reference to utilitarian and Rawlsian theory, he finds existing regimes seriously deficient, insufficiently responsive to the needs of the least well off. Nonetheless, he argues that they are superior to the politically feasible alternatives: Those disadvantaged under the present regimes would be even worse off if the powerful were not constrained by their rules. The analysis is searching, the conclusion unsatisfying: He does not acknowledge the problematic character of the politically feasible, nor allow for potential alternatives between the ideal world and the actual regimes. Indeed, his conclusion is at odds with the conception of liberalism that he outlines a few years later, as a gradualist striving for improvement (Keohane 1990, 194).

This discussion redresses the silence on North–South relations but is not incorporated into subsequent institutionalist theorizing. And, although there is no reference to the role of the United States, there is a clue as to what this omission may signify. Why is the politically feasible so circumscribed? Arguably, it was the Reagan administration's total rejection of the various North–South initiatives under discussion in the 1970s, and its subsequent imposition of the "Washington consensus," that rendered reformist alternatives irrelevant—not any systemic constraint. Through excluding the concept of a leading actor, the theory foreclosed inquiry into the potential negative consequences of its role.

That role, as we have seen, is central in Ruggie's and Ikenberry's institutionalist theorizing. Both evaluate it positively. Ikenberry, while highly critical of the turn to unilateralism, remains close to the mainstream American foreign-policy discourse; Ruggie's focus on key concepts invites more searching questioning of the way in which the United States exercises its role. Neither engages in normative theorizing, but their explicit evaluations could serve to prompt normative debate on the American role and on the kind of institutionalization that the United States has promoted.

Do the normative commitments that have been identified in neoliberal institutionalism form a pattern, and is it a liberal one? They can be seen as relating to welfare, a very general value in liberal theory, but not exclusively liberal, and also to efficiency, highly valued in contemporary liberal economics; a certain conservatism, an orientation to the status quo, is also evident. There is no reference to the central liberal values—the freedoms and rights of the individual—but given the basic "levels of analysis" framework, this should perhaps not be expected of a theory at the level of the international system.[5] Neoliberal institutionalism can be seen as an updating and synthesis of two of the main traditions in international liberal theory, commercial and regulatory liberalism, both essentially systemic (Keohane 1990), and its values are characteristic of those traditions.

International relations theory has not been much concerned with differences within liberalism—the contrasting philosophical rationales and contending political orientations uneasily constituting the liberal "tradition."[6] Tension between conservative and radical strands has been ever present. Neoliberal institutionalism, its perspective essentially that of the leading governments of the day, is readily located near the conservative end of the spectrum, and its restrictive concepts of welfare and distribution bear the hallmarks of the American political culture. The radical strand, now prominent in normative political theory, is under-represented in the international relations discipline.[7]

Ruggie's and Ikenberry's normative commitments fall within the same general pattern: a system ("order")-oriented, relatively conservative, and more explicitly American liberalism. Ikenberry's constitutionalism offers some further classical liberal values such as the virtues of institutional limits on the exercise of power; and among the institutionalists he is the most explicitly supportive of the existing order. Ruggie's societal orientation extends the framework beyond the governmental, and indeed suggests an affinity with the social liberal, not the utilitarian liberal tradition. His concern for the viability of embedded liberalism holds the potential for a more radical analysis of the political–economic order, but neither he nor other liberal institutionalists have followed this up.[8]

3 KEOHANE'S NORMATIVE TURN

As indicated earlier, since the late 1990s Keohane has developed a broader version of liberal institutionalist theory in order to address the kinds of questions that are raised by current changes in world politics. Issues chosen for research are related to explicit, theoretically grounded normative premises derived from a distinctive view of liberalism (Keohane 1990), one that falls within what might be termed the liberal pessimist tradition of thinkers such as James Madison, Adam Smith, and Judith Shklar (Keohane 2002, 246–7).

[5] For a comprehensive normative critique of neoliberal institutionalism that does not make this concession, see Long (1995).

[6] On differences within liberalism, see, e.g., Gray (2000); Richardson (2001).

[7] There are important exceptions, such as Richard Falk (1999).

[8] Steffek (2006) brings out embedded liberalism's underlying conservatism, oriented to the needs and interests of relatively well-off Western societies, not to those of the disadvantaged.

This is a cautious, wary liberalism that sees human progress as possible but by no means inevitable, and achievable only if human and social limitations are taken into account. He sees liberalism as first and foremost a theory that highlights the scope for human action and choice, but he insists that the constraints that are emphasized—indeed overemphasized—in theories such as realism and Marxism be taken very seriously. Thus, while rejecting the pursuit of impracticable ideals regardless of consequences, he endorses a gradualist reformism that, over time, can extend the limits of political choice. In terms of standard liberal assumptions his theorizing is uncomfortable: In particular, he is skeptical of the association of liberalism with peace, allowing that radical critics may be correct in claiming that the needs of the open capitalist economy make for intervention and war (Keohane 1990, 186–90). This is a sober, seemingly dispassionate liberalism, offering little orientation to those deeply concerned over human rights violations or the intolerable living conditions of those at the margins of subsistence.

Keohane's discussion of global governance brings out some of the practical implications of this general conception of liberalism. In collaboration with Nye, he presents a critique of the existing "club model" of decision-making in the major international institutions—that is, their informal control by a few key members—showing why this has become unacceptable and outlining the practical and normative issues raised by the demand for greater democratic accountability (Keohane 2002, 219–44). They seek to scale down unrealistic expectations, looking to incremental improvements, not radical institutional restructuring.

His presidential address to the American Political Science Association proposes a general framework for such inquiries into the problems of "governance in a partially globalized world." The goals are defined normatively and he draws on several kinds of empirical theory—rational choice theory perhaps *primus inter pares*—to guide research into how they might be realized in institutional practice (Keohane 2002, 245–71). He refers to Amartya Sen's concept of enhancing human capabilities and to John Rawls's concept of justice, but his immediate discussion limits itself to issues raised by democratic legitimacy: accountability, participation, and persuasion. Even so, the project outlined here involves a major expansion of the institutional research agenda, and the inclusion of the issues raised by Sen and the Rawlsian debates would require an even more radical expansion. From a perspective outside the United States, however, the discussion reads as quintessentially Western: a response to the concerns of Western publics and nongovernmental organizations. There is no reference to non-Western perspectives on governance: for example, to the issue of greater representativeness, whether of states or of peoples.

The Western—and sometimes distinctively American—perspective is even more evident in certain of Keohane's other recent papers, such as his argument for "unbundling sovereignty" in the context of reconstructing political institutions after humanitarian interventions (Keohane 2003). However cogently reasoned in its own terms, the argument does not engage with the reasons why sovereignty is so highly valued outside the West. And the volume of which it is part, like virtually all the literature on humanitarian intervention, remains a conversation among Western scholars.

The American world view comes through most strongly in his proposal, in collaboration with Allen Buchanan, for a new institutional process to authorize the preventive use of force if the United Nations Security Council is unable to act to forestall dire threats to security or to check massive violations of human rights. Subject to carefully defined conditions, a coalition of democracies, not exclusively Western, could then authorize preventive action (Buchanan and Keohane 2004). Has the cautious reformer turned radical in his readiness to set aside long-established norms and procedures? Radical or not, the argument—and in particular the apotheosis of democracy—may be seen as representative of the liberal interventionist outlook that has become characteristic of the American foreign-policy community since the ending of the cold war. It is to be hoped that Keohane's provocative formulation of this orientation will prompt a genuinely international debate within the discipline—and one not confined to the Western scholarly community.[9]

4 Conclusion

Contemporary institutionalist theories may be located in different liberal traditions—utilitarian, social liberal, and constitutional—and Keohane has developed a version of liberalism that stands apart as something of a pessimist–realist hybrid. However, for all their diversity, the theories share a common perspective, that of America as a "leading" power with a distinctive political culture.

For all its liberal virtues, this perspective does not make for sensitivity toward the concerns of those less well placed in the international hierarchy or those with different cultures or values. In the case of "North–South" relations this raises major issues for policy but presents no new challenge for theory, where the issues date back to the late-nineteenth-century debates over social liberalism (Richardson 2001). Far more intractable issues are raised by relations between Western and non-Western (more precisely, nonliberal) societies: the tension between liberal norms of universalism versus respect for diversity and self-determination (e.g. Gray 2000) may prove unresolvable. These issues are subject to lively debate among political theorists but remain at the margins of international relations theory.

The trend towards normative explicitness, here exemplified by Keohane, holds much promise for the discipline. Normative reasoning is surely preferable to assumption in guiding research. And, if it tends initially to bring out national

---

[9] Such a debate may be foreshadowed in Reus-Smit (2005).

perspectives underlying contemporary international relations scholarship, it may subsequently lead to a certain distancing from the assumptions of one's own political culture, and serve as a catalyst for debate that could overcome the invisible barriers that separate national scholarly communities.

REFERENCES

BUCHANAN, A., and KEOHANE, R. O. 2004. The preventive use of force: a cosmopolitan institutional proposal. *Ethics and International Affairs*, 18: 1–22.

FALK, R. 1999. *Predatory Globalization: A Critique*. Cambridge: Polity.

GOLDSTEIN, J., KAHLER, M., KEOHANE, R. O., and SLAUGHTER, A.-M. (eds.) 2000. Legalization and world politics, special issue. *International Organization*, 54: 385–703.

——and KEOHANE, R. O. (eds.) 1993. *Ideas and Foreign Policy: Beliefs, Institutions, and Political Change*. Ithaca, NY: Cornell University Press.

GRAY, J. 2000. *Two Faces of Liberalism*. Cambridge: Polity.

IKENBERRY, G. J. 2001. *After Victory: Institutions, Strategic Restraint, and the Rebuilding of Order after Major Wars*. Princeton, NJ: Princeton University Press.

KEOHANE, R. O. 1984. *After Hegemony: Cooperation and Discord in the World Political Economy*. Princeton, NJ: Princeton University Press.

——1989. *International Institutions and State Power: Essays in International Relations Theory*. Boulder, Colo.: Westview.

——1990. International liberalism reconsidered. Pp. 165–94 in *The Economic Limits to Modern Politics*, ed. J. Dunn. Cambridge: Cambridge University Press.

——2002. *Power and Governance in a Partially Globalized World*. London: Routledge.

——2003. Political authority after intervention: gradations in sovereignty. Pp. 275–98 in *Humanitarian Intervention: Ethical, Legal and Political Dilemmas*, ed. J. L. Holzgrefe and R. O. Keohane. Cambridge: Cambridge University Press.

——and MARTIN, L. L. 2003. Institutional theory as a research program. Pp. 71–107 in *Progress in International Relations Theory: Appraising the Field*, ed. C. Elman and M. F. Elman. Cambridge, Mass.: MIT Press.

——and MILNER, H. (eds.) 1996. *Internationalization and Domestic Politics*. Cambridge: Cambridge University Press.

——and NYE, J. S. 1977. *Power and Interdependence: World Politics in Transition*. Boston: Little, Brown.

KRASNER, S. D. 1991. Global communications and national power: life on the Pareto frontier. *World Politics*, 43: 336–66.

LONG, D. 1995. The Harvard school of liberal international theory: a case for closure. *Millennium: Journal of International Studies*, 24: 489–505.

MARTIN, L. L., and SIMMONS, B. 1998. Theories and empirical studies of international institutions. *International Organization*, 52: 729–57.

OYE, K. A. (ed.) 1986. *Cooperation under Anarchy*. Princeton, NJ: Princeton University Press.

PUTNAM, H. 2002. *The Collapse of the Fact/Value Dichotomy, and Other Essays*. Cambridge, Mass.: Harvard University Press.

REUS-SMIT, C. 2005. Liberal hierarchy and the licence to use force. *Review of International Studies*, 31: 71–92.

RICHARDSON, J. L. 2001. *Contending Liberalisms in World Politics: Ideology and Power*. Boulder, Colo.: Lynne Rienner.

RUGGIE, J. G. 1982. International regimes, transactions, and change: embedded liberalism in the postwar economic order. *International Organization*, 36: 379–415.

——1993. *Multilateralism Matters: The Theory and Practice of an Institutional Form*. New York: Columbia University Press.

——1996. *Winning the Peace: America and World Order in the New Era*. New York: Columbia University Press.

SNIDAL, D. 1985. The limits of hegemonic stability theory. *International Organization*, 39: 579–614.

STEFFEK, J. 2006. *Embedded Liberalism and its Critics: Justifying Global Governance in the American Century*. New York: Palgrave Macmillan.

STEIN, A. A. 1990. *Why Nations Cooperate: Circumstance and Choice in International Relations*. Ithaca, NY: Cornell University Press.

TAYLOR, C. 1973. Neutrality in political science. Pp. 139–70 in *The Philosophy of Social Explanation*, ed. A. Ryan. Oxford: Oxford University Press.

CHAPTER 13

....

THE NEW
LIBERALISM

....

ANDREW MORAVCSIK

THE universal condition of world politics is *globalization*. States are, and always have been, embedded in a domestic and transnational society that creates incentives for its members to engage in economic, social, and cultural interactions that transcend borders. Demands from individuals and groups in this society, as transmitted through domestic representative institutions, define "state preferences"—that is, fundamental substantive social purposes that give states an underlying stake in the international issues they face. To motivate conflict, cooperation, or any other costly political foreign policy action, states must possess sufficiently intense state preferences. Without such social concerns that transcend borders, states would have no rational incentive to engage in world politics at all, but would simply devote their resources to an autarkic and isolated existence. This domestic and transnational social context in which states are embedded varies greatly over space and time. The resulting globalization-induced variation in social demands and state preferences is a fundamental cause of state behavior in world politics. This is the central insight of liberal international relations theory.

Three specific variants of liberal theory focus are defined by particular types of state preferences, their variation, and their impact on state behavior. *Ideational* liberal theories link state behavior to varied conceptions of desirable forms of cultural, political, socioeconomic order. *Commercial* liberal theories stress

For more detailed analysis and a literature review, see Moravcsik (1997; 2003), on which this chapter draws.

economic interdependence, including many variants of "endogenous policy theory." *Republican* liberal theories stress the role of domestic representative institutions, elites and leadership dynamics, and executive–legislative relations. Such theories were first conceived by prescient liberals such as Immanuel Kant, Adam Smith, John Stuart Mill, John Hobson, Woodrow Wilson, and John Maynard Keynes—writing well before the independent variables they stressed (democratization, industrialization, nationalism, and welfare provision) were widespread.[1]

The liberal focus on variation in socially determined state preferences distinguishes liberal theory from other theoretical traditions: realism (focusing on coercive power resources), institutionalism (focusing on information), and most nonrational approaches (focusing on patterns of beliefs about appropriate means–ends relationships).[2] In explaining patterns of war, for example, liberals do not stress inter-state imbalances of power, bargaining failure under incomplete information, or particular nonrational beliefs, but conflicting state preferences derived from hostile nationalist or political ideologies, disputes over appropriable economic resources, or exploitation of unrepresented political constituencies. For liberals, a necessary condition for war is that these factors lead one or more "aggressor" states to possess "revisionist" preferences so extreme that other states are unwilling to submit. Similarly, in explaining trade protectionism, liberals look not to shifts of hegemonic power, suboptimal international institutions, or misguided beliefs about economic theory, but to economic incentives, interest groups, and distributional coalitions opposed to market liberalization.

Liberal theory is a paradigmatic alternative theoretically distinct from, empirically at least coequal with, and in certain respects analytically more fundamental than, existing paradigms such as realism, institutionalism, or constructivism. This chapter presents three core theoretical assumptions underlying liberal theories, elaborates the three variants of liberal theory, and draws some broader implications. Perhaps the most important advantage of liberal theory lies in its capacity to serve as the theoretical foundation for a shared multicausal model of instrumental state behavior—thereby moving the discipline beyond paradigmatic warfare among unicausal claims (Lake and Powell 1999 outline a similar vision).

---

[1] In a Lakatosian sense, this should increase our confidence in liberal predictions (Moravcsik 2003).

[2] Some who engage in the pre-scientific practice of classifying theories according to "optimism" and "pessimism," or political pedigree, classify theories of international organizations as liberal (though in fact, in the nineteenth and early twentieth centuries, international institutions were more often espoused by monied conservatives). For modern international relations theorists, however, what matters are core assumptions, and modern regime theory rests on a distinctively different set of assumptions from the liberal theories discussed here. Regime theory concerns the distribution of information, with state preferences treated as exogenous. The liberal theories discussed here seek to endogenize state preferences. For more discussion, see Moravcsik (1997, 536–8); cf. Keohane (1990).

1 CORE ASSUMPTIONS OF LIBERAL THEORY

Liberal international relations theory's fundamental premise—state preferences derived from the domestic and transnational social pressures critically influence state behavior—can be restated in terms of three core assumptions.

Assumption 1: The Nature of Societal Actors.
Globalization generates differentiated demands from societal individuals and groups with regard to international affairs.

Liberal international relations theory rests on a "bottom-up" or pluralist view of politics. Functionally differentiated individuals and groups define material and ideational goals independently of politics, then seek to advance those ends through political means.[3] Social actors favor some economic, social, cultural, and domestic political arrangements rather than others—that is, particular structures of economic production and exchange, social relations, cultural practice, or domestic political rule. For the purpose of studying world politics, the critical source of social interests is *globalization*—that is, the changing opportunities and incentives to engage in transnational economic, social, and cultural activity—which changes the prospects for realizing domestic objectives. Without globalization, societal actors, like states, would have no rational incentive to attend to world politics. Such incentives vary from individual opportunities for glory or plunder (say, in the epoch of Alexander the Great) to the maintenance of complex networks of transnational production, immigration, and cultural discourse (more often found in our own). The most fundamental theoretical task of liberal international relations theory is to define the impact of the shifting terms of economic, social, and cultural globalization on social actors and the competing demands they will thus place upon states.

A simple analysis starts by assuming that, the stronger the aggregate benefit from social interactions across borders, the greater the demand to engage in such interactions. In pursuing such goals, individuals can be assumed to be, on the average, risk averse—that is, they defend existing private opportunities for investment while remaining more cautious about assuming cost and risk in pursuit of new gains. All this can generate strong incentives for peaceful coexistence and *status quo*-oriented policies. This starting point often leads critics, not least realists, to caricature liberals as espousing a utopian belief in an automatic harmony of interest among social actors.

In fact liberal theory—as reflected in liberal philosophers and social scientists alike—rests on the contrary premise. Societal demands are a variable, shifting

---

[3] The critical distinction here is *not* the "level of analysis"—that is, that liberal theory offers a "domestic" explanation ("level of analysis" is an outmoded and misleading concept; see Fearon 1998; Lake and Powell 1999, ch. 1). Essential is rather that liberals take seriously, rather than arbitrarily suppress, Kenneth Waltz's notion of "functional differentiation," grounding it in domestic and transnational society (Ruggie 1983).

with factors such as technology, geography, and culture. A harmonious pattern of interest associated with liberal "utopianism" is no more than one ideal endpoint. In nearly all social situations, shifts in control over material resources, authoritative values, and opportunities for social control have domestic and transnational distributional implications, which almost invariably create winners and losers. Moreover, while the average individual may be risk averse, particular individuals may be willing to risk costly conflict for improbable gain. Any liberal theory must therefore specify more concrete conditions under which the interests of social actors converge toward particular patterns vis-à-vis other societies.

Broadly speaking, conflictual societal demands about the management of globalization tend to be associated with three factors. First, contradictory or irreconcilable differences in core beliefs about national, political, and social identity promote conflict, whereas complementary beliefs promote harmony and cooperation. Secondly, resources that can be easily appropriated or monopolized tend to exacerbate conflict by increasing the willingness of social actors to assume cost or risk to enrich themselves. Thirdly, large inequalities in domestic social or political influence may permit certain groups to evade the costs of costly conflict or rent-seeking behavior, even if the result is inefficient for society as a whole. These general tendencies are developed in more detail in the next section, where we will link them to the three major strands of liberal theory.

Assumption 2: The Nature of the State.
States represent the demands of a subset of domestic individuals and social groups, on the basis of whose interests they define "state preferences" and act instrumentally to manage globalization.

For the purpose of analyzing international politics, an essential characteristic of the state is its set of underlying *preferences*: the rank ordering among potential substantive outcomes or "states of the world" that might result from international political interaction. States act instrumentally in world politics to achieve particular goals on behalf of individuals, whose private behavior is unable to achieve such ends as efficiently. Internationally, the liberal state is a purposive actor, but domestically it is a representative institution constantly subject to capture and recapture, construction and reconstruction, by coalitions of social interests. It constitutes the critical "transmission belt" by which the preferences and social power of individuals and groups are translated into foreign policy. In the liberal conception of domestic politics, state preferences concerning the management of globalization reflect shifting social demands, which in turn reflect the shifting structure of domestic and transnational society. Deriving state preferences from social preferences is thus a central theoretical task of liberal theory.

State preferences, the ultimate ends of foreign policy behavior, are distinct from "strategies"—the specific policy goals, bargaining demands, institutional arrangements, tactical stances, military or diplomatic doctrines that states adopt, advocate, or accept in everyday international politics. From rational choice theorists to constructivists, analysts now recognize such a distinction as a necessary precondi-tion for rigorous analysis of world politics. When a government increases military spending and declares an interest in confronting an adversary, for example, it is essential to distinguish a shift resulting from changing preferences over states of the world (as when confrontation is initiated by a new ruling elite intrinsically committed to territorial aggrandizement) from a shift resulting from changing strategies with preferences fixed (as when two states respond to each other's arms build-ups in a "security dilemma"). Even support for apparently "fundamental" political strategies—say, sovereignty, national defense, open markets—vary consid-erably depending on underlying patterns of state preferences concerning "states of the world." Few modern states are Sparta: Most compromise security or sovereignty in order to achieve other ends, or, indeed, just to save money. Nor do modern states seek ideal free markets, but rather strike complex and varied trade-offs among economic goals. To see how consequential the results can be, one need look no further than the implications for international relations of Germany's evolution from Adolf Hitler's preference for militant nationalism, fascist rule, and ruthless exploitation of German *Lebensraum* to the social compromise underlying the post-war *Bundesrepubik* for national reunification, capitalist democracy, and expanding German exports (Katzenstein 1987).

This last example highlights the importance, in the liberal conception, of the selective nature of domestic representative institutions. Representation is a key determinant (alongside the basic nature of social demands themselves) of what states want, and therefore what they do. No government rests on universal or un-biased political representation. At one ideal extreme, representation might equally empower everyone equally. At the other, it might empower only an ideal-typical Pol Pot or Josef Stalin. Myriad representative practices exist in between, each priv-ileging different sets of demands. Powerful individuals and groups may be entirely "outside" the state, bureaucratic clients and officials "within" it, or some com-bination thereof (for example, a "military-industrial complex"). Representation may be centralized and coordinated or disaggregated, subject to strong or weak rationality conditions, socialized to various attitudes toward risk and responsibility, and flanked by various substitutes for direct representation (Achen 1995; Grant and Keohane 2005).

It is important to note one qualification to the assumption that states have pre-strategic preferences. Over the longer term there is, of course, feedback, which makes it more difficult to treat preferences as pre-strategic. The fundamental pref-erences of states may adapt to strategic circumstances. When, to take a simple example, a conqueror exterminates a linguistic group, imposes a new political order, or reshapes a domestic economy, the preferences of the target state will be different in succeeding iterations. Similarly, the outcomes of economic cooperation agreements often alter economic structure for good—often in a self-reinforcing way that encourages further movement in a similar direction. Indeed, it is often precisely to induce such feedback that individuals engage in international politics.

Still, any meaningful analysis of international politics as instrumental behavior requires, at the very least, that we distinguish *within any given iteration* between "pre-strategic" preferences, akin to "tastes" in economics, and strategic calculations. Even in explaining dynamic change over a long period, analysts often neglect at their peril to distinguish change caused by constantly evolving exogenous factors from change that is triggered by policy feedback.[4]

Assumption 3: The Nature of the International System.
The pattern of interdependence among state preferences shapes state behavior.

The critical theoretical link between state preferences, on the one hand, and state behavior, on the other, is the concept of *policy interdependence.* Policy interdependence refers to the distribution and interaction of preferences—that is, the extent to which the pursuit of state preferences necessarily imposes costs and benefits upon other states, independent of the "transaction costs" imposed by the specific strategic means chosen to obtain them.

Liberals argue that patterns of interdependent preferences belong among the most fundamental structures influencing state behavior. In areas of modern life where policy externalities remain low and unilateral policies remain optimal for most states, there is an incentive for sovereignty to remain the norm and states to coexist with low conflict and politicization. Where policy alignment can generate mutual gains with low distributive consequences, there is an incentive for international policy coordination or convergence. The lower the net gains, and the greater the distributional conflict whereby the realization of interests by a dominant social group in one country *necessarily* imposes costs on dominant social groups in other countries, the greater the potential for inter-state tension and conflict. Where motives are mixed such that coordination of policies generates high benefits but also high benefits from unilateral defection, then strong incentives will exist for precommitment to social cooperation to limit cheating. Games such as coordination, assurance, Prisoner's Dilemma, and suasion have distinctive dynamics, as well as precise costs, benefits, and risks for the parties (Oye 1986). While such strategic incentives can, of course, be influenced by power, information, beliefs, and other nonliberal variables, they are often very fundamentally influenced by the structure of transnational interdependence itself—that is, by the extent to which basic national goals are compatible.

By drawing on the relative intensity or "asymmetrical interdependence" among state preferences, liberalism highlights a distinctive conception of inter-state power (Keohane and Nye 1977). In this view, the willingness of states to expend resources or make concessions in bargaining is a function of preferences, not (as in realism) linkage to an independent set of "political" power resources (Baldwin 1979). Nations are in fact rarely prepared to mortgage their entire economy or military

---

[4] A major weakness of neofunctionalist integration theory, for example, was its lack of any strong liberal theory of preferences, which led Ernst Haas consistently to attribute policies to "feedbacks" or "spillovers" that were in fact the result of shifts in exogenous factors (Moravcsik 2005).

capabilities in pursuit of any single foreign-policy goal. Few wars are total, few peaces Carthaginian. On the margin, the binding constraint is more often "resolve" or "preference intensity"—a view set forth by Albert Hirschman and others, and more fundamentally consistent with conventional Nash bargaining theory than is realist theory (Hirschman 1945; Raiffa 1982). Even in "least-likely" cases, where military means are used to contest political independence and territorial integrity, "preferences for the issues at stake...can compensate for a disadvantage in capabilities." In the Boer War, Hitler's remilitarization of the Rhineland, Vietnam, and Afghanistan, for example, the relative intensity of state preferences arguably reshaped the outcome to the advantage of a "weaker" party (Mack 1975; Morrow 1988, 83–4). Such examples suggest that the liberal view of power politics, properly understood, generates plausible explanations not just of international cooperation and coexistence, but of the full range of systemic phenomena central to the study of world politics, including war.

2 THEORETICAL VARIANTS OF LIBERALISM

The three core liberal assumptions outlined above, like those of institutionalism, realism, or any other broad paradigm, are relatively "thin" or content free. The focus on variation in preferences, rather than autonomous capabilities, beliefs, or information, does exclude most realist, institutionalist, and nonrational theories. But alone it is insufficient to specify a single sharply defined set of theories or hypotheses. This is as it should be.[5] A paradigm should instead clearly define a theoretical field, and the question is whether a coherent, rich, and focused research program emerges. While the analysis of state preferences over managing globalization might appear in theory to be impossibly unparsimonious, as many have argued, the range of viable liberal theories has proven in practice to be focused and empirically fruitful. Three variants have emerged in recent theorizing, stressing respectively identity, interest, and institutions.

2.1 Identity and Legitimate Social Orders

One source of state preferences is the set of core domestic social identities. In the liberal understanding, social identity stipulates who belongs to the society and what is owed to them. Liberals take no distinct position on the ultimate origins of such

---

[5] The Lakatosian understanding of a "paradigm" leads us to expect that core assumptions and concepts define a paradigm, but auxiliary propositions are required to specify it (Moravcsik 2003).

identities, which may stem from historical accretion or be constructed through conscious collective or state action, nor on the question of whether they "ultimately"
reflect ideational or material factors—just as long as they are not conceived as endogenous to short-term inter-state interaction. (The ultimate origin of preferences
"all the way down" is an issue on which international relations theorists, the speculations of constructivists notwithstanding, have little comparative advantage.) But
liberals have long argued that identity is essential to state preferences—a tradition
reaching back through William Gladstone, Mill, Giuseppe Mazzini, Wilson, and
Keynes. More research is required to isolate precise causal mechanisms at work.
Liberals focus in particular on legitimate domestic order across three dimensions:
national identity, political ideology, and socioeconomic order.[6]

The first type of social identity concerns beliefs about the proper scope of the
political "nation" and the allocation of citizenship rights within it. Where inconsis-
tencies arise between underlying patterns of political identity and existing borders,
liberals argue, the potential for inter-state conflict increases. Where they coincide,
peaceful coexistence is more likely. Where identities are more fluid, more complex
arrangements may be possible. Empirical evidence supports such claims. From
mid-nineteenth-century nationalist uprisings to late-twentieth century national
liberation struggles, claims and counterclaims involving national autonomy constitute the most common issue over which wars and interventions have been waged:
antinationalist intervention under the Concert of Europe and the Holy Alliance,
Balkan conflicts preceding the First World War and following the cold war, and
ethnic conflicts today (Van Evera 1990; Holsti 1991).[7] Not by chance is scenario planning for China/United States conflict focused almost exclusively on Taiwan—the
one jurisdiction where borders and national identity (as well as political ideology)
are subject to competing claims (Christensen 2001). Recent literature on civil wars
increasingly focuses on contention over the social identity, political institutions,
and the political economy of the state (Walter 1997; Fortna 2004; Kaufman 2006).
Ironically, the current era of fixed borders may lead civil wars to proliferate then
spill over, rather than being resolved by succession or adjustment (Atzili 2006–7).

A second relevant social identity concerns fundamental political ideology. Where
claims of political legitimacy or ideology conflict directly, and the realization of

---

[6] Here is a point of intersection between traditional liberal arguments and more recent constructivist works, which tend to stress the social rather than inter-state origins of socialization to particular
preferences (Risse-Kappen 1996). Yet the concept of preferences across public goods is deliberately
more focused than Ruggie's "legitimate social purpose" (1982) or Katzenstein's "collective identity"
(1996).

[7] Even those who stress the absence of domestic credible commitment mechanisms or the interaction between ideational and socioeconomic variables in explaining patterns of nationalist conflicts
concede the importance of underlying identities (Fearon and Laitin 2000). Dissidents include realist
John Mearsheimer (1990, 21), who bravely asserts that nationalism is a "second-order force in world
politics," with a "largely...international" cause—namely, multipolarity. Greater problems since 1989
in Eastern Europe and the former Soviet Union, where there are more overlapping national claims
than in democratic, capitalist Western Europe, belie Mearsheimer's prediction.

legitimate domestic political order in one jurisdiction is perceived as threatening its realization in others, conflict becomes more likely. Whether during the wars of the French Revolution, the nineteenth-century Concert of Europe, the Second World War, the cold war—or now the post-cold war era—the degree of ideological distance among the domestic systems of the great powers appears to have been a critical determinant of international conflict (Gaddis 1997; Haas 2005; 2007). Some argue a similar dynamic of mutual ideological recognition underlies the "democratic peace" (Doyle 1986; Owen 1994).

More recently, some within modern societies have adopted a more cosmopolitan attitude toward political rights, extending political identity beyond the nation state. To be sure, the most intense concerns remain focused on co-religionists and co-nationals abroad, but altruistic campaigns are increasingly organized to defend human rights on behalf of others. Where such goals clash with the goals of foreign governments, they can spark international conflict (Keck and Sikkink 1998). Recent literature on the sources of such concern, the conditions under which states take them up, and the ways in which issue networks can increase their salience, reflect core liberal theoretical concerns.[8]

A third important type of social identity concerns the nature of legitimate domestic socioeconomic regulation and redistribution. In a Polanyian and Keynesian vein, John Ruggie reminds us that legitimate social compromises concerning the provision of regulatory public goods impose limits on markets. Such social compromises, domestic and transnational, underlie variation in state preferences and behavior regarding immigration, social welfare, taxation, religious freedom, families, health and safety, environmental and consumer protection, cultural promotion, and many other issues (Ruggie 1982). Recent research on environmental policy and many other areas reveals the emergence of "Baptist-bootlegger" coalitions around regulatory issues, combining economically self-interested producer groups with those interested in regulatory outputs (Ruggie 1995; Vogel 1995).

2.2 Commercial Liberalism: Economic Assets and Cross-border Transactions

A second source of social demands relevant to foreign policy is the pattern of transnational market incentives—a liberal tradition dating back to Smith, Richard Cobden, and John Bright. This argument is broadly functionalist: Changes in the structure of the domestic and global economy alter the costs and benefits of

---

[8] This has spawned an enormous literature on social movements designed to promote the interests of such individuals and groups. Some of this literature involves the construction of international institutions and use of coercive sanctions. But the material on the mobilization of social movements to pressure governments to act is a quintessentially liberal argument—e.g. Carpenter (2007).

transnational economic activity, creating pressure on domestic governments to facilitate or block it.[9]

Commercial liberal theory does not predict that economic incentives automatically generate universal free trade and peace, but focuses instead on the interplay between aggregate incentives and distributional consequences. Contemporary trade liberalization generates domestic distributional shifts totaling many times aggregate welfare benefits (Rodrik 1992). Losers generally tend to be better identified and organized than beneficiaries. A major source of protection, liberals predict, lies in uncompetitive, undiversified, and monopolistic sectors or factors of production. Their pressure induces a systematic divergence from laissez-faire policies—a tendency recognized by Smith, who famously complained of mercantilism that "the contrivers of this whole mercantile system [are] the producers, whose interest has been so carefully attended to".[10]

This commercial liberal approach to analyzing conflict over foreign economic policy is distinct from those of realism (emphasizing security externalities and relative power), institutionalism (informational and institutional constraints on optimal inter-state collective action), and constructivism (beliefs about "free trade"). Extensive research supports the view that free trade is most likely where strong competitiveness, extensive intra-industry trade or trade in intermediate goods, large foreign investments, and low asset specificity internalize the net benefits of free trade to powerful actors, reducing the influence of net losers from liberalization (Milner 1988; Alt and Gilligan 1994; Keohane and Milner 1996). Similar arguments can be used to analyze issues such as sovereign debt (Stasavage 2007), exchange-rate policy (Frieden 1991), agricultural trade policy (Gawande and Hoekman 2006), European integration (Moravcsik 1998), foreign direct investment (Elkins, Guzman, and Simmons 2006), tax policy (Swank 2006), and migration policy.

The effect of economic interdependence on security affairs varies with market incentives. A simple starting point is that the collateral damage of war disrupts economic activity: the more vulnerable and extensive such activity, the greater the cost. A more sophisticated cost–benefit calculation would take into account the potential economic costs and benefits of war. Where monopolies, sanctions, slavery, plunder of natural resources, and other forms of coercive extraction backed by state power are cost-effective means of elite wealth accumulation—as was true for most of human history—we should expect to see a positive relationship, between transnational economic activity and war. Where, conversely, private trade and investment within complex and well-established transnational markets provide a less costly means of accumulating wealth and one that cannot be cost-effectively appropriated—as is most strikingly the case within modern multinational

---

[9] Keohane and Milner (1996) provide a review and discussion of the relationship between commercial and republican liberal theories, properly conceptualizing interdependence as a structure of incentives, or potential costs and benefits, not as a pattern of behavior.

[10] *An Inquiry into the Nature and Causes of the Wealth of Nations* (Oxford Edition, 1993), p. 378.

investment and production networks—the expansion of economic opportunities will have a pacific effect. Along with the spread of democracy and relative absence of nationalist conflict, this distinguishes the current era from the period before the First World War, when high levels of interdependence famously failed to deter war (Van Evera 1990; Brooks 2007; Kirshner 2007). We see in current Western relations with China a very deliberate strategy to encourage the slow evolution of social preferences in a pacific direction by encouraging trade. Eric Gartzke (2000) has recently argued that the "democratic peace" phenomenon can largely be explained in terms of a lack of economic and other motives for war. Even among developed economies, however, circumstances may arise where governments employ coercive means to protect international markets. This may take varied forms, as occurred under nineteenth-century empires or with pressure from business for the United States to enter the First World War to defend trade with the allies (Fordham 2007).

2.3 Republican Liberalism: Representation and Rent-seeking

A final source of fundamental social preferences relevant to international politics is the institutional structure of domestic political representation. While ideational and commercial theories stress, respectively, particular patterns of underlying societal identities and interests related to globalization, republican liberal theory emphasizes the ways in which domestic institutions and practices aggregate such pressures, transforming them into state policy. The key variable in republican liberalism, which dates back to the theories of Kant, Wilson, and others, is the nature of domestic political representation, which helps determine *whose* social preferences dominate state policy (Russett 1993).

A simple consequence is that policy tends to be biased in favor of the governing coalitions or powerful domestic groups favored by representative institutions—whether those groups are administrators (rulers, armies, or bureaucracies) or societal groups that "capture" the state. Costs and risks are passed on to others. When particular groups with outlier preferences are able to formulate policy without providing gains for society as a whole, the result is likely to be inefficient and suboptimal policy. Given that (as we assumed earlier) most individuals and groups in society tend generally to be risk averse, the broader the range of represented groups, the less likely it is that they will support indiscriminate use of policy instruments, like war or autarky, that impose large net costs or risks on society as a whole. Republican liberal theory thereby helps to explain phenomena as diverse as the "democratic peace," modern imperialism, and international trade and monetary cooperation. Given the plausibility of the assumption that major war imposes net costs on society as a whole, it is hardly surprising that the most prominent republican liberal argument concerns the "democratic peace," which one scholar has termed "as close as anything we have to an empirical law in international relations"—one that applies to tribal societies as well as modern states (Levy 1988, 668). From a liberal perspective, the theoretical interest in the "democratic peace" lies not in the greater transparency of democracies (a claim about information), the greater political power of democracies (a realist claim), or norms of appropriate behavior (a constructivist claim), but the distinctive preferences of democracies across states of the world.

This is not, of course, to imply that broad domestic representation *necessarily* generates international cooperation. In specific cases, elite preferences in multiple states may be more convergent than popular ones. Moreover, the extent of bias in representation, not democracy per se, is the theoretically critical point. There exist conditions under which specific governing elites may have an incentive to represent long-term social preferences in a way that is less biased—for example, when they dampen nationalist sentiment, as may be the case in some democratizing regimes, or exclude powerful outlier special interests, as is commonly the case in trade policy.

The theoretical obverse of "democratic peace" theory is a republican liberal theory of war, which stresses risk-acceptant leaders and rent-seeking coalitions (Van Evera 1999; Goemans 2000). There is substantial historical evidence that the aggressors who have provoked modern great-power wars tend either to be extremely risk-acceptant individuals, or individuals well able to insulate themselves from the costs of war, or both. Jack Snyder, for example, has refurbished Hobson's classic left-liberal analysis of imperialism—in which the military, uncompetitive foreign investors and traders, jingoistic political elites, and others who benefit from imperialism are particularly well placed to influence policy—by linking unrepresentative and extreme outcomes to log-rolling coalitions (Snyder 1991).[11] Consistent with this analysis, the highly unrepresentative consequences of partial democratization, combined with the disruption of rapid industrialization and incomplete political socialization, suggest that democratizing states, if subject to these influences, may be particularly war prone (Mansfield and Snyder 1995; Snyder 2000). This offers one answer to the paradox posed by James Fearon—namely, why rational states would ever enter into war rather than negotiate their way out. For war or other costly conflict to break out among rational actors, not only must opposed preferences be intense enough to motivate the acceptance of extremely high cost, but the actors must be risk acceptant in pursuit of those goals.

Parallels to the "democratic peace" exist in political economy. We have seen that illiberal commercial policies—trade protection, monetary instability, and sectoral subsidization that may manifestly undermine the general welfare of the population—reflect pressure from powerful domestic groups. In part this power results from biases within representative institutions, such as the power of money in electoral systems, the absence or presence of insulated institutions (for example,

---

[11] It is indicative of the muddled metatheoretical mislabeling that besets the field that arguments by Stephen Van Evera, Stephen Walt, Randall Schweller, and Snyder have been termed "neoclassical realism"—despite their clear liberal intellectual pedigree and theoretical structure. See Legro and Moravcsik (1999).

"fast-track" provisions in the United States), and the nature of electoral institutions (for example, proportional representation or majoritarianism) (Haggard 1988;
Ehrlich 2007).

3 Broader Implications of Liberal International Relations Theory

Having considered the core assumptions underlying liberal theory, and three concrete variants of it, we turn now to three broader implications: its unique empirical predictions, its status as systemic theory, and its openness to multitheoretical
synthesis.

3.1 Distinctive Predictions of Liberal Theory

Liberal international relations theory, we have seen, generates predictions concerning war and peace, trade liberalization and protection, and other important
phenomena in world politics—predictions that challenge conventional accounts. It
also generates some predictions about broad political phenomena for which other
international relations paradigms generate few, if any, plausible explanations.

One such phenomenon is *variation in the substantive content of foreign policy
across issues, regions, or hegemonic orders*. Why do we observe such different preferences, levels, and styles of cooperation and conflict across different sorts of issues,
such as trade and finance, human rights, and environmental policy? Or within issue
areas? Or across different countries and regions? Why, for example, do regions vary
from highly war prone to de-facto "security communities?" Why do hegemons and
great powers seem to have such different schemes for global order?

From a liberal perspective, with its focus on the issue-specific and country-
specific social preferences, there are straightforward explanations for such substantive differences. One can easily see why regimes with ideologies, economies,
and governmental systems as different as the United States, UK, Nazi Germany,
and Soviet Union should generate such disparate plans for the post-Second World
War world. One can see why the United States should care so much more about
modest, perhaps nonexistent, North Korean or Iraqi nuclear arsenals, but remain
unconcerned about far greater British, Israeli, and French forces. One can explain
why the compromise of "embedded liberalism" underlying Bretton Woods was
struck on entirely different terms from arrangements under the Gold Standard, or
why the European Union and the Council for Mutual Economic Assistance differed,
though their hegemonic structure was similar, or why the protectionist agricultural
trade policy and the open industrial trade policy of OECD countries today differ so

strikingly. Such differences continue to have a decisive effect on world politics today. Theories that treat preferences as exogenous, like realism and institutionalism, like constructivist-inspired theories of ideas and beliefs, have difficulty explaining the extreme substantive and geographical variation we observe in the goals and purposes over which states conflict and cooperate. Abstract political forces—relative power, issue density, transaction costs, or strategic culture—provide similarly little insight.

Another related phenomenon is *long-term historical change in the nature of world politics*. Classic realists like Kenneth Waltz, Robert Gilpin, John Mearsheimer, and Paul Kennedy predict unchanging cycles of rise and decline among the great powers, with little impact on the substantive content or form of international order. Liberal theory, by contrast, forges a direct causal link between long-term economic, political, and social transformations, such as economic and political modernization, and state behavior (Ikenberry 2000). Global economic development over the past 500 years has been closely related to greater per capita wealth, democratization, education systems that reinforce new collective identities, and greater incentives for transborder economic transactions (Huntington 1991). Over the modern period the principles of international order have decoupled from dynastic legitimacy and are increasingly tied to national self-determination and social citizenship, economic prosperity, and democratic legitimacy—factors uniquely highlighted by liberal theory.

One result has been that, among advanced industrial democracies, inter-state politics is increasingly grounded in reliable expectations of peaceful change, domestic rule of law, stable international institutions, and intensive societal interaction. Liberal theory argues that the emergence of a large and expanding bloc of pacific, interdependent, normatively satisfied states has been a precondition for such politics. This is the condition Karl Deutsch terms a "pluralistic security community," Robert Keohane and Joseph Nye call "complex interdependence," and John Ikenberry labels "self-binding" (Keohane and Nye 1977; Ikenberry 2000). Consider, for example, the current state of Europe, in particular the absence of serious conflict among Western powers over a case like Yugoslavia—in contrast to the events that led up to the First World War a century before. For liberals, the spread of democracy, commerce, and national self-determination explain why the geopolitical stakes among democratic governments are low and competitive alliance formation absent from modern Europe—an outcome that baffles realists (Van Evera 1990). Overall, these trends have contributed to historically low levels of warfare across the globe in recent decades.

3.2 Liberalism as Systemic Theory

Another fundamental implication of liberal theory concerns its status as a "systemic" theory. To some, the central liberal claim—in essence, "what states want determines what they do"—may seem commonsensical, even tautological. Yet for the past half-century, mainstream international relations theories, notably realism and institutionalism but also nonrational theories, have defined themselves in opposition to precisely this claim. In his classic postwar redefinition of realism, Hans Morgenthau (1960, 5–7) explicitly points to its assertion of "the autonomy of the political," which he says gives realism its "distinctive intellectual and moral attitude" and which he contrasts with "two popular fallacies: the concern with motives and the concern with ideological preferences." Waltz follows Morgenthau almost *verbatim*: "Neo-realism establishes the autonomy of international politics and thus makes a theory about it possible" (Waltz 1979, 29, also 65–6, 79, 90, 108–12, 196–8, 271).

One basic reason why theorists are often skeptical of variation in state preferences as a fundamental cause is because such a claim appears utopian. It seems to imply states do as they please, unconstrained by others. Realists pride themselves, by contrast, on being hard-headed, which they associate with demonstrations that states are forced to pursue objectives strikingly at variance with their underlying desires. Foreign policy, they insist, has *ironic* consequences: The best is the enemy of the good (Waltz 1979, 60–7, 93–9). Waltz, echoing not just Morgenthau but Max Weber, concludes from this that the preferences of states must be unimportant: "Results achieved seldom correspond to the intentions of actors," he argues, therefore "no valid generalizations can logically be drawn" from an examination of intentions— thus runs Waltz's oft-cited argument for structural and systemic theory (Waltz 1979, 29). Hegemonic stability theory and institutionalist regime theory—a combination that Keohane, a scholar otherwise clearly more open to preference-based theory, initially termed "modified structural realism"—rests on a similar distinction: "even where common interests exist, cooperation often fails ... cooperation is evidently not a simple function of interests" (Keohane 1984, 6, 12). As Robert Powell (1994, 318) observes, such approaches "lack a theory of preferences over outcomes."

These realist criticisms simply misunderstand liberal preference-based theory, which is in fact nonutopian precisely because it is "systemic" in the Waltzian sense. Liberal theory implies neither that states get what they want, nor that they ignore the actions of others. The distribution of state *preferences*, just like the distribution of capabilities, information, or beliefs, is itself an attribute of the state system (that is, in Waltzian terms, of the *distribution* of state characteristics) outside the control of any single state. Every state would *prefer* to act as it pleases, yet each is compelled to realize its ends under a constraint imposed by the *preferences* of others. Liberal theory thereby conforms to Waltz's own understanding of systemic theory, explaining state behavior with reference to how states stand in relation to one another.

Liberal theory is systemic and nonutopian in a second, less Waltzian sense as well. National preferences emerge not from a solely domestic context but from a society that is transnational—at once domestic and international. Foreign policy, liberals argue, is about the management of globalization—that is, it is about managing the results of interaction between societies. This interactive or systemic quality goes all the way down. Commercial liberal analyses, for example, explain the interests of domestic groups by situating their domestic economic assets in the context of international markets. Ideational liberal analyses explain the concerns of domestic groups by situating their values in the context of a transnational cultural field. Liberalism does not draw a strict line between domestic and transnational levels of analysis. Critiques that equate theories of state preferences with "domestic" or "second-image" theorizing are not simply misguided in their criticism, but are conceptually confused in their understanding of international relations theory. Liberals side with those who view the "level of analysis" as a misleading concept best set aside.[12]

3.3 Liberalism and Multicausal Synthesis

We have seen that liberal assumptions generate powerful unicausal explanations based on variation in state preferences alone. Yet complex inter-state behavior is rarely shaped by a single factor. Coercive capabilities, information, beliefs about appropriate means, and other facts often play a role as well. To analyze such situations, theoretical synthesis between different types of theory is required. Perhaps the most attractive characteristic of liberal theory is that it suggests a simple and conceptually coherent way of combining theories—in contrast to biased and incoherent means of theory synthesis often proposed.

The explanation of state preferences must receive analytical priority in any such synthesis. That is, variation in state preferences must be explained using liberal theory *before* attempting to apply and assess the role of strategic factors like coercive power resources, information, or strategic culture. This is not a distinctively "liberal" claim; it is the only procedure consistent with the assumption of instrumental (soft rational) behavior shared by realism, institutionalism, liberalism, and even many variants of constructivism.[13] This is because preferences shape the nature and intensity of the game that states are playing; thus they help determine which systemic theory is appropriate and how it should be specified.

The necessary analytical priority of preferences over strategic action is hardly surprising to political scientists. It is the fundamental lesson of Robert Dahl's classic work on political influence: We cannot ascertain whether "A influenced B to do something" (that is, power) unless we first know "what B would otherwise do"

---

[12] In rejecting "levels of analysis," I side with Fearon (1998) and Lake and Powell (1999), as well as Gourevitch (1978); Putnam (1988).

[13] Many recent constructivist analyses argue that states act instrumentally on the basis of particular cultural beliefs about ends or appropriate means–ends relationships. These can be synthesized with rationalist accounts, as many constructivists have productively pointed out.

(that is, preferences) (Dahl 1969; Baldwin 1989, 4; Coleman 1990, 132–5). It would be inappropriate, for example, to employ realist theory to explain state behavior unless state preferences are arrayed so that substantial inter-state conflict of interest exists and the deployment of capabilities to achieve a marginal gain is cost effective. Similarly, institutionalist explanations of suboptimal cooperation are inappropriate unless states have sufficient interest in resolving particular inter-state collective action problems. Without controlling for preference-based explanations, it is easy to mistake one for the other. As Kenneth Oye (1986, 6) notes: "When you observe conflict, think Deadlock—the absence of mutual interest—before puzzling over why a mutual interest was not realized."

State behavior should thus be modeled multicausally—that is, as a *multi-stage process* of constrained social choice in which variation in state preferences comes first. In modeling the process, however, states nonetheless first define preferences, as liberal theories of state–society relations explain, and *only then* debate, bargain, or fight to particular agreements, and thereafter commit in subsequent stages to institutional solutions, explained by realist and institutionalist (as well as liberal) theories of strategic interaction. *This is not to say, of course, that liberal theory is more powerful or that it explains more.* That is an empirical judgment that will vary across cases (indeed, adopting a standardized procedure for synthesis would help us reach and aggregate such empirical results; for more, see Moravcsik 1997). Hence we increasingly see realists and institutionalists retreating to what Keohane terms a "fall-back position," whereby exogenous variation in the configuration of state interests defines the range of possible outcomes within which capabilities and institutions are used to explain specific state behavior—so-called "neoclassical realism" being a prime example (Keohane 1986, 183).[14] Methodologically, however, we must generally theorize and explain preferences, not just assume them, as a basis for strategic analysis.[15] Practice speaks louder than theory: We need less doctrinaire and more pragmatic theory syntheses, with analytical priority going to theories that endogenize varying state preferences.

This claim about the priority of preference-based theories of state behavior in a multistage explanation reverses the near-universal presumption among contemporary international relations theorists that "liberalism makes sense as an explanatory theory within the constraints" imposed by other theories (see Waltz 1979; Keohane 1990, 192; Matthew and Zacher 1995).[16] The methodological procedure that follows from this conventional misconception, whereby the analyst tests a realist theory first, then turns to theories of preferences (often wrongly termed

---

[14] There is an implicit subdisciplinary consensus on this view—e.g. Legro (1996); Schweller (1996); Moravcsik (1997); Lake and Powell (1999).

[15] For a very persuasive argument along these lines, as a basis for a programmatic statement of rational choice theorizing, see Frieden (1999) and more generally Lake and Powell (1999).

[16] There is "something particularly satisfying about systemic explanations and about the structural forms of . . . explanations" (Keohane 1986, 193). This claim may or may not be true, but is often wrongly conflated with setting preferences aside—since, as we have seen, liberalism is a systemic theory.

"domestic" or "second-image") to explain anomalies, is both conceptually incoherent (because it is inconsistent with rationality) and empirically biased (because it arbitrarily ignores results that might confirm liberal theories; for a more detailed argument, see Moravcsik 1997). Yet this intellectual residue of misguided realist criticism of liberalism remains visible in the subdiscipline to this day.

Much of the most vibrant mid-range theorizing in international relations, we have seen, is distinctively liberal. Yet the paradigmatic language of international relations does not reflect it. Much of the work in this chapter is termed "realist" (even though it violates the core premises of any reasonable definition of that paradigm), "domestic" (even though that term describes no theory at all and little empirical work), or "constructivist" (even though that label describes an ontology not a theory).[17] Indeed, the broad categories of "grand" international relations debates remain almost entirely unchanged since the 1950s, when realists squared off against legalists (today: neoliberal institutionalists) and idealists (today: constructivists) (Legro and Moravcsik 1999). No wonder so many scholars today eschew such labels altogether. Yet this is no solution either. Without a recognized paradigm of its own, theories that stress variation in the preferences of socially embedded states are still too often dismissed in theoretical discussions, ignored in comparative theory testing, and, most importantly, disregarded in multicausal syntheses.

REFERENCES

ACHEN, C. 1995. How could we tell a unitary rational actor when we saw one? Presented at the Midwest Political Science Association annual meeting, Chicago, 16–18 April.

ALT, J., and GILLIGAN, M. 1994. The political economy of trading states: factor specificity, collective action problems, and domestic political institutions. *Journal of Political Philosophy*, 2: 165–92.

ATZILI, B. 2006–7. When good fences make bad neighbors: fixed borders, state weakness, and international conflict. *International Security*, 31: 139–73.

BALDWIN, D. A. 1979. Power analysis and world politics: new trends versus old tendencies. *World Politics*, 31: 161–94.

——1989. *Paradoxes of Power*. Oxford: Basil Blackwell.

BROOKS, S. G. 2007. *Producing Security: Multinational Corporations, Globalization, and the Changing Calculus of Conflict*. Princeton, NJ: Princeton University Press.

CARPENTER, R. C. 2007. Studying issue (non)-adoption in transnational advocacy networks. *International Organization*, 61: 643–67.

CHRISTENSEN, T. J. 2001. Posing problems without catching up: China's rise and challenges for US security policy. *International Security*, 25: 5–40.

COLEMAN, J. S. 1990. *Foundations of Social Theory*. Cambridge, Mass.: Harvard University Press.

DAHL, R. A. 1969. The concept of power. Pp. 79–93 in *Political Power: A Reader in Theory and Research*, ed. R. Bell, D. V. Edwards, and R. Harrison Wagner. New York: Free Press.

[17] For a lucid and exceptionally fair-minded effort to distinguish constructivism from ideational liberalism, see Johnston (2005, ch. 1).

DOYLE, M. W. 1986. Liberalism and world politics. *American Political Science Review*, 80: 1151–69.

EHRLICH, S. D. 2007. Access to protection: domestic institutions and trade policy in democracies. *International Organization*, 61: 571–605.

ELKINS, Z., GUZMAN, A. T., and SIMMONS, B. A. 2006. Competing for capital: the diffusion of bilateral investment treaties, 1960–2000. *International Organization*, 60: 811–46.

FEARON, J. 1998. Domestic politics, foreign policy, and theories of international relations. *Annual Review of Political Science*, 1: 289–313.

—— and LAITIN, D. 2000. Violence and the social construction of ethnic identity. *International Organization*, 54: 845–77.

FORDHAM, B. 2007. Revisionism reconsidered: exports and American intervention in World War I. *International Organization*, 61: 277–310.

FORTNA, V. P. 2004. *Peace Time: Cease-Fire Agreements and the Durability of Peace*. Princeton, NJ: Princeton University Press.

FRIEDEN, J. 1991. Invested interests: the politics of national economic policies in a world of global finance. *International Organization*, 45: 425–51.

—— 1999. Actors and preferences in international relations. Pp. 39–76 in Lake and Powell 1999.

GADDIS, J. L. 1997. *We Know Now: Rethinking Cold War History*. Oxford: Oxford University Press.

GARTZKE, E. 2000. Preferences and the democratic peace. *International Studies Quarterly*, 44: 191–212.

GAWANDE, K., and HOEKMAN, B. 2006. Lobbying and agricultural trade policy in the United States. *International Organization*, 60: 527–61.

GOEMANS, H. E. 2000. *War and Punishment: The Causes of War Termination and the First World War*. Princeton, NJ: Princeton University Press.

GOUREVITCH, P. 1978. The second image reversed: the international sources of domestic politics. *International Organization*, 32: 881–912.

GRANT, R. W., and KEOHANE, R. O. 2005. Accountability and abuses of power in world politics. *American Political Science Review*, 99: 29–43.

HAAS, M. L. 2005. *The Ideological Origins of Great Power Politics, 1789–1989*. Ithaca, NY: Cornell University Press.

—— 2007. The United States and the end of the Cold War: reactions to shifts in Soviet power, policies, or domestic politics? *International Organization*, 61: 145–79.

HAGGARD, S. 1988. The institutional foundations of hegemony: explaining the Reciprocal Trade Agreements Act of 1934. *International Organization*, 42: 91–119.

HIRSCHMAN, A. O. 1945. *National Power and the Structure of Foreign Trade*. Berkeley: University of California Press.

HOLSTI, K. J. 1991. *Peace and War: Armed Conflicts and International Order 1648–1989*. Cambridge: Cambridge University Press.

HUNTINGTON, S. P. 1991. *The Third Wave: Democratization in the Late Twentieth Century*. Norman: University of Oklahoma Press.

IKENBERRY, G. J. 2000. *After Victory: Institutions, Strategic Restraint, and the Rebuilding of Order after Major Wars*. Princeton, NJ: Princeton University Press.

JOHNSTON, I. 2005. Social states: China in international institutions, 1980–2000. Unpublished typescript, Harvard University.

KATZENSTEIN, P. J. 1987. *Policy and Politics in West Germany: The Growth of a Semisovereign State*. Ithaca, NY: Cornell University Press.

——(ed.) 1996. *The Culture of National Security: Norms and Identity in World Politics*. New York: Columbia University Press.

KAUFMAN, S. J. 2006. Symbolic politics or rational choice? Testing theories of extreme ethnic violence. *International Security*, 30: 45–86.

KECK, M., and SIKKINK, K. 1998. *Activists beyond Borders: Advocacy Networks in International Politics*. Ithaca, NY: Cornell University Press.

KEOHANE, R. O. 1984. *After Hegemony: Cooperation and Discord in the World Political Economy*. Princeton, NJ: Princeton University Press.

——(ed.) 1986. *Neorealism and its Critics*. New York: Columbia University Press.

——1990. International liberalism reconsidered. Pp. 165–94 in *The Economic Limits to Modern Politics*, ed. J. Dunn. Cambridge: Cambridge University Press.

——and MILNER, H. V. (eds.) 1996. *Internationalization and Domestic Politics*. Cambridge: Cambridge University Press.

——and NYE, J. S. 1977. *Power and Interdependence: World Politics in Transition*. Boston: Little, Brown.

KIRSHNER, J. 2007. *Appeasing Bankers: Financial Caution on the Road to War*. Princeton, NJ: Princeton University Press.

LAKE, D., and POWELL, R. (eds.) 1999. *Strategic Choice and International Relations*. Princeton, NJ: Princeton University Press.

LEGRO, J. W. 1996. Culture and preferences in the international cooperation two-step. *American Political Science Review*, 90: 118–37.

——and MORAVCSIK, A. 1999. Is anybody still a realist? *International Security*, 24: 5–55.

LEVY, J. S. 1988. Domestic politics and war. *Journal of Interdisciplinary History*, 18: 653–73.

MACK, A. 1975. Why big nations lose small wars: the politics of asymmetric conflict. *World Politics*, 27: 175–200.

MANSFIELD, E. D., and SNYDER, J. 1995. Democratization and the danger of war. *International Security*, 20: 5–38.

MATTHEW, R. A., and ZACHER, M. W. 1995. Liberal international theory: common threads, divergent strands. Pp. 107–50 in *Controversies in International Relations Theory: Realism and the Neoliberal Challenge*, ed. C. Kegley. New York: St Martin's Press.

MEARSHEIMER, J. J. 1990. Back to the future: instability in Europe after the Cold War. *International Security*, 15: 5–56.

MILNER, H. 1988. Trading places: industries for free trade. *World Politics*, 40: 350–76.

MORAVCSIK, A. 1997. Taking preferences seriously: a liberal theory of international politics. *International Organization*, 51: 512–53.

——1998. *The Choice for Europe: Social Purpose and State Power from Messina to Maastricht*. Ithaca, NY: Cornell University Press.

——2003. Liberal international relations theory: a scientific assessment. Pp. 159–204 in *Progress in International Relations Theory: Appraising the Field*, ed. C. Elman and M. F. Elman. Cambridge, Mass.: MIT Press.

——2005. The European constitutional compromise and the neofunctionalist legacy. *Journal of European Public Policy*, 12: 349–86.

MORGENTHAU, H. J. 1960. *Politics among Nations: The Struggle for Power and Peace*, 3rd edn. New York: Alfred Knopf.

Morrow, J. D. 1988. Social choice and system structure in world politics. *World Politics*, 41: 75–97.

Owen, J. 1994. How liberalism produces democratic peace. *International Security*, 19: 87–125.

Oye, K. (ed.) 1986. *Cooperation under Anarchy*. Princeton, NJ: Princeton University Press.

Powell, R. 1994. Anarchy in international relations theory: the neorealist–neoliberal debate. *International Organization*, 48: 313–44.

Putnam, R. D. 1988. Diplomacy and domestic politics: the logic of two-level games. *International Organization*, 42: 427–60.

Raiffa, H. 1982. *The Art and Science of Negotiation*. Cambridge, Mass.: Harvard University Press.

Risse-Kappen, T. 1996. Collective identity in a democratic community: the case of NATO. Pp. 357–99 in Katzenstein 1996.

Rodrik, D. 1992. The rush to free trade in the developing world: why so late? why now? will it last? NBER Working Paper No. 3947, National Bureau of Economic Research.

Ruggie, J. G. 1982. International regimes, transactions, and change: embedded liberalism in the postwar economic order. *International Organization*, 36: 379–415.

—— 1983. Continuity and transformation in the world polity: toward a neorealist synthesis. *World Politics*, 35: 261–85.

—— 1995. At home abroad, abroad at home: international liberalization and domestic stability in the new world economy. Jean Monnet Chair Paper, Robert Schuman Centre, European University Institute.

Russett, B. 1993. *Grasping the Democratic Peace: Principles for a Post-Cold War World*. Princeton, NJ: Princeton University Press.

Schweller, R. L. 1996. Neorealism's status-quo bias: what security dilemma? *Security Studies*, 5: 90–121.

Snyder, J. 1991. *Myths of Empire: Domestic Politics and International Ambition*. Ithaca, NY: Cornell University Press.

—— 2000. *From Voting to Violence: Democratization and Nationalist Conflict*. New York: Norton.

Stasavage, D. 2007. Cities, constitutions, and sovereign borrowing in Europe, 1274–1785. *International Organization*, 61: 489–525.

Swank, D. 2006. Tax policy in an era of internationalization: explaining the spread of neoliberalism. *International Organization*, 60: 847–82.

Van Evera, S. 1990. Primed for peace: Europe after the Cold War. *International Security*, 15: 7–57.

—— 1999. *Causes of War: Power and the Roots of Conflict*. Ithaca, NY: Cornell University Press.

Vogel, D. 1995. *Trading Up: Consumer and Environmental Regulation in a Global Economy*. Cambridge, Mass.: Harvard University Press.

Walter, B. F. 1997. The critical barrier to civil war settlement. *International Organization*, 51: 335–64.

Waltz, K. N. 1979. *Theory of International Politics*. Reading, Mass.: Addison-Wesley.

CHAPTER 14

THE ETHICS
OF THE NEW
LIBERALISM

GERRY SIMPSON

1 NEW LIBERALS AND INTERNATIONAL RELATIONS

A great deal of international relations theory defines itself in relation to the three traditions (Wight 1991). In the past two decades, this act of self-definition has taken two broad forms. In one case, scholars have sought to transcend these traditions and their various affiliates. For them, Thomas Hobbes, Immanuel Kant, and John Locke establish modernity. Writing that configures these individuals as central, therefore, is itself keyed into a particular moment in time and a particular way of thinking through the world. The work of poststructuralists or critical theorists, then, is an expression of distance from, and dissatisfaction with, these categories of enlightenment thought reproduced in much international relations theorizing (Der Derian 1992; Walker 1993). This is work that positions itself as *after* the three great projects of modernity (Der Derian and Shapiro 1989).

A less iconoclastic (perhaps less baleful) form of critique works within these traditions and has sought to deepen and extend the insights found in the classical categories. The neo-neo debates are an obvious example of this refinement project. More recently, though, the two most appealing intellectual refurbishments have occurred in the work of constructivists and new liberals. Constructivists have sought to understand the way in which ideas are socially constitutive. Put bluntly, while actors have ideas, it is true also that ideas have actors. One aspect of this, important for the purposes of this chapter, is that international legal norms are thought to perform a dynamic role in constituting the global political order.

New liberalism, the subject of this chapter, makes two important contributions. First, it wants to place liberal theory on a scientific footing and offer it (at least) parity with the other major paradigms of international relations thought (by giving it empirical bite, by grounding it in testable propositions, by bringing some coherence to its textual formulations) (this is Andrew Moravcsik's project). Secondly, it takes the vague entreaties of Wilsonian liberalism and the outmoded sovereigntisms (statisms) of public international law, and converts them into a legal theory about how norms are created and how they operate in a world defined not by the interaction of opaque nation states but by transgovernmentalism: a multileveled international law, policy, and politics operating across highly permeable national boundaries (this is Anne-Marie Slaughter's project). These projects have been, deservedly, celebrated. They are imaginative and supple responses to a changed global environment.

In order to untangle some of the key propositions of new liberalism, I propose to consider three key new liberal texts. These are Moravcsik's "Taking Preferences Seriously" (1997), Slaughter's *A New World Order* (2004), and the recent Princeton Project's *Forging a World of Liberty under Law* (Ikenberry and Slaughter 2006). The first text is new liberalism's methodological blueprint; it is a persuasive, widely read, and considered piece of theorizing that sought to position new liberalism alongside the great "isms" of international relations theory. The second text, Slaughter's *A New World Order*, seeks to describe a world already transformed by the norms and institutions produced by liberal law and politics. This represents a move from the sometimes dry theorizing of Moravcsik (1997) to a more popular normativism. The third text marks the first explicit effort to present new liberal theory as government policy. *Forging a World of Liberty* self-consciously mimics the style and intentions of the George W. Bush administration's two National Security Strategies (e.g. White House 2006). This prospectus for US foreign policy combines the feel-good normativity of new world order with a hard-headed pragmatism about violence and war; it as an approximation of what new liberal foreign relations might look like.

2 TAKING PREFERENCES TOO SERIOUSLY

Moravcsik (1997) faces a familiar liberal paradox—how to be liberal and scientific, or how to combine the crusading spirit of liberal policy with heavyweight international relations theory. His response is to do away largely with liberalism's ethical (or political) tendencies altogether. The "non-ideological, non-utopian" project of Moravcsik involves liberating liberalism from its normative biases (its celebration of progress, its concerns about poverty and redistribution, its benevolent paternalism) by predicating liberal theory on the strategic calculations and interactions of rational persons, groups of whom at the domestic level determine state interests and preferences at the international level.

How, then, might we characterize the "ethics of new liberalism?" This denuded liberalism of Moravcsik's is illuminating as a description of strategic interaction, but it leaves some questions unanswered. These can be divided into a set of questions around the identity of the "political," and a tranche of problems surrounding Moravcsik's assumptions about the state.

First, to the problem of politics; there is little discussion of how rational actors come to possess preferences in the first place (Moravcsik 1997, 517). In particular, the possibility that there exists some sort of feedback loop in which political and strategic interaction might play a role in defining preferences and demands is not acknowledged. According to Moravcsik (1997, 517), people have tastes, commitments, and endowments, but these are regarded as somehow prior to politics. Individuals bring these attributes *to* politics; political life, then, involves competition and cooperation between and among these preconstituted actors. Their tastes and commitments are "pre-political" (Reus-Smit 2001), though their "deep, irreconcilable differences in beliefs about the provisions of public goods..." (Moravcsik 1997, 517) presumably are political. This distinction between the pre-political (the social?) and the political is surely questionable. Is it plausible, for example, to think of a person brought up, say, as a Labour Party supporter in England possessing a set of "social commitments" (held independently of politics) and a repertoire of "beliefs" (forged, engaged, and modified in political action)?

A second problem with new liberalism is the way in which it conceives of the state. State preferences are shaped and constituted at the domestic level by the political interplay of individuals and groups seeking to maximize leverage at the international level. Once these interests have been constituted, they remain largely unmodified by the operation of other actors in the international system. These fundamental preferences may shift but only in response to political reconfigurations at the domestic level (Moravcsik 1997, 519). This theoretical construct has the merit of dislodging some realist assumptions about the universalizability and homogeneity of state behavior (for example, that states will always maximize security or defend sovereignty), but what it replaces them with is a set of unsustainable demarcations between national and international space. This is problematic in two respects. First, it resurrects the very distinction between international and domestic politics that much liberal theory was supposed to eliminate and, secondly, it suggests that "fundamental preferences," in thrall to political reorientations internally, are nonetheless independent of convulsions or changes in the international environment. This version of new liberalism, then, has too little to say about the way in which states establish self-understandings as a consequence of their international position and regardless of the caprices of internally constituted elites (Australia's self-image as a "good international citizen" is an example of this).

The deeper question about Moravcsik's strategy is whether liberal states *do* behave differently, as new liberalism predicts that they will. This question links Moravcsik's work to Slaughter's more transparently normative agenda. If states' behavior is conditioned by their internal preferences, then this has very great implications for international order generally. It means, for example, that the realist focus on material power, the institutionalist faith in international machinery, and the legalist obsession with creating and identifying autonomous norms are each in their own way misplaced, and likely to generate inconclusive or disappointing research agendas and errant policy. For new liberals, norms and institutions will work better, and power will be rendered relatively peripheral, among states where domestic preferences are mutually reinforcing. Moravcsik argues that both war and intensified cooperation can be explained by the configuration of domestic preferences. So, war in the twentieth century is marked by global conflict between rival ideologies (communism, liberalism, and fascism), while supranational cooperation (involving the pooling of sovereignty) is a feature of regions in which there is uniform commitment to "democratic norms" (Moravcsik 1997, 527). The most salient and certainly most disseminated insight derived from all this is the democratic peace: "as close as anything we have to an empirical law in international relations" (Russett 1993, 139, quoting Jack Levy). As Moravcsik (1997, 531) puts it: "Liberal democratic institutions tend not to provoke such [major] wars because influence is placed in the hands of those who must expend blood and treasure and the leaders they choose."

Liberal states, though, have been far from pacific in their relations with other states (including embryonic democracies). The two most recent large-scale aggressions (in Kosovo and Iraq) have been committed by liberal coalitions.[1] Indeed, there may be three reasons why liberal societies have a greater propensity to go to war than other states. First, late-modern liberal polities have become hugely adept at shaping and cajoling public opinion. Secondly, it is not at all clear, contra Moravcsik, that liberal states must expend (much) blood in pursuing contemporary war (and are accordingly more likely to be restrained by citizens bearing the costs of those wars). Thirdly, the north Atlantic states now regard themselves as representatives of humanity (fighting humanitarian wars or wars against terror). No longer engaged in war at all but rather in what Carl Schmitt (2003) called "pest control," they are free to engage in armed action without the stigma of "war." What we are left with is not the democratic peace but the abolition of war as a juridical

---

[1] I have used a neutral definition of aggression derived from the *United Nations 1974 Definition on Aggression*.

or political category and its displacement by forms of violence in the name of humanity (Simpson 2004*a*).

Ultimately, preferences—changeable, protean, contingent not on values but on success, and subject to linguistic reformulations—may turn out to be poor predictors of behavior in the sphere of war. But what of liberalism in other domains? Is it the case that liberal states are more likely to adopt and support international legal rules (based largely, after all, on liberal principles)? Here I turn to the work of Slaughter.

3 The Ethics of *A New World Order*

Slaughter's work has two related strands. The first is a magnification and clarification of the new liberal commitment to distinguishing between liberal and illiberal states. This distinction is at the heart of some of this work, and generates a particular and heterodox view of international law. Public international law, traditionally a body of law that treated sovereigns as equals, is reinterpreted as a system whose subjects are to be differentiated for methodological and normative reasons. The problem of compliance, international law's *bête noire*, is solved by reference to the domestic preferences of relevant actors; liberal states comply, illiberal states defect. The task of international law is to promote liberal democracy in order to secure an internally generated culture of compliance.

The second strand involves de-emphasizing the state altogether in favor of "transgovernmentalism." The thankless, professional task of imposing liberal norms on illiberal agents (traditional international law) is abandoned or, at least, downgraded in favor of encouraging transnational judicial cooperation among liberal judicial organs (Slaughter 1995; 2004); developing informal networks of like-minded government instrumentalities (Slaughter 1997; 2004); prompting recalcitrant legislators to collaborate across borders (Slaughter 2004), and build formal institutions and informal machineries composed of liberal states (Slaughter 1994).

Before considering transgovernmentalism as a theory of governance, I want to return to the first precept of Slaughter's work and consider the behavioral suppositions that undergird it. Are liberal states better behaved? Or, to ask the question differently, do liberal states tend to comply with international law more regularly than nonliberal states, as we would anticipate from a reading of Moravcsik (1997)?

The answers are equivocal. Frequently, liberal states have pursued war in defiance of existing legal frameworks. In the area of violence and force (always a realist stronghold), it is not the case that liberal states have been more compliant with the international legal norms drafted in 1945 making the unilateral use of force illegal.

Breaches of the nonintervention norm have been widespread (often to depose democratically elected governments, for example in Chile and Guatemala). Neither liberal institutions nor liberal law has greatly constrained the appetite of liberal states for military intervention (Franck 1970).

In the case of participation in international judicial institutions, the evidence is again ambiguous. The International Court of Justice (a Wilsonian institution through and through) has failed to attract the support of the major liberal powers. It seems that factors other than domestic configurations or interest group dynamics seem to be critical in determining commitment to the international rule of law in this sphere at least.

The human rights and humanitarian law fields, each imbued with liberal ideals, have not always garnered the support of liberal states either. Australia, a state with compulsory voting and therefore very high rates of participation in the democratic process, has adopted an increasingly hostile attitude toward human rights norms in recent years. The United States, meanwhile, is now notorious for its rejection of several important multilateral initiatives (for example, the Ottawa Convention banning landmines, and the International Criminal Court Statute), and its commitment to human rights institutions and norms has been patchy to say the least. Meanwhile, Jose Alvarez has documented many other ways in which liberal states do not behave better (with respect to participation in environmental regimes (2001, 205), in the adoption of common trade commitments (2001, 207), or in their enthusiasm for regional human rights machinery (2001, 222)).

Indeed, it may be that the ethics of liberalism obstructs the sort of convergences that new liberalism describes and prescribes. If liberals are right about the normative and analytic priority to be accorded representative interests within states, then this might lead to an expectation that liberal states and domestic institutions will scrutinize and reject many international legal norms. It might also suggest that this *ought* to occur given the sentiments of the internally constituted elites.

But perhaps little of this matters when states themselves are being superseded, and here I turn to the transgovernmental aspect of Slaughter's work. Her most recent book, *A New World Order*, is imbued with a sort of Wilsonian American optimism (she admits as much at one point (2004, 257)) but one that departs from both Woodrow Wilson's reliance on states as the engines of change, and the romantic claims of cosmopolitans.[2] The dream of powerful public institutions or world government has been superseded by an embryonic reality of world governance. This is manifesto and diagnosis at the same time. What makes Slaughter's work so attractive is that she takes an existing set of relationships, encompassing everything from international conferences of judges to ad hoc mechanisms for economic management to regulatory cooperation across borders, and translates them into a theory of global governance or world law. Then she calls for the deepening of these

---

[2] Parts of the discussion in this section are drawn from Simpson (2004*b*).

relationships and offers some prescriptions for making this incipient system both just and effective.

Her recent work is a corrective to the dominant view that diplomacy is about executive-level inter-state exchange. It is not that law and politics do not continue to be managed and developed at these executive levels; rather, Slaughter's argument goes, it gets done in many other places as well. While the global media remain fixated on the elected leaders of the United States, the United Kingdom, and France, the stuff of global law is being molded and transformed in other places, by other people—by the Bank for International Settlements, by the International Association of Insurance Supervisors, by the Committee on International Judicial Relations, or by the Global Parliamentarians.

This is apiece with Slaughter's career-long commitment to demolishing the image of states as monolithic unitary actors (as in "the United States is opposed to the International Criminal Court") or organized around the inclinations of great men (as in "Blair and Bush have plans for the international order"). Billiard balls are displaced by "regulatory, judicial and legislative channels" (Slaughter 2004, 5) through which parts of states engage with each other transnationally. In this way, Slaughter purports to solve a paradox of global relations: We need more government but we want less. The answer is found in the transition from government (hierarchical, sometimes sclerotic, inflexible, and inattentive) to governance (multiple, lateral, adaptable, permeable), and from the unitary state ("Blair," the "United Kingdom") to the disaggregated state (Britain's regulators, legislators, and judges, among others). At the same time, Slaughter seeks to dislodge a clichéd view of the world in which the hegemony of the great powers or rapacity of global capital is tempered only by civil, nongovernmental society. This view merely opposes the "passion" (of nongovernmental organizations) to the "interests" (of governments) and "profit-motive" (of corporate actors). What is required to keep all these elements in check is the neutral expertise of transnational actors; a technocratic turn, in other words, toward networks of regulators, judges, and legislators engaging in three types of behavior: information or cooperation, enforcement or compliance, and harmonization or convergence.

In the networked world order, regulatory, judicial, and legislative networks will spread. Networks of networks, such as the Commonwealth or the Asia-Pacific Economic Cooperation, will facilitate the business of global interaction, while vertical networks make transgovernmentalism more effective and international organizations continue to foster and encourage networks.

Slaughter's work, then, is a retort to two highly fashionable images of international society: the hegemony of the great powers and the power of civil society. At this level, it succeeds. It alerts us to the rise of an international technocracy capable of wielding power or converting soft power into hard power. In the remainder of this section, I want to pursue two possible lines of critique. The first involves challenging the picture of the world on offer here. The second demands of new liberals like Slaughter a better account of what these governmental networks are *for*. What is the ethical content of transgovernmetalism? In particular, is it open to the same criticism as Moravcsik (1997)—that is, that it does not take politics seriously enough?

The world of war, death, poverty, and resistance does not feature large in Slaughter (2004). (When Slaughter (2004, 26) talks about Iraq she uses it as a concrete example of how government networks could rebuild a society. Networks of foreign judges could offer technical training to Iraqi judges, regulators could rebuild banking systems, and legislators could teach democracy.) There is little reference to the way in which the new world order is so congenial to what is often a highly exploitative capitalist class or the way in which extreme poverty is viewed as largely acceptable by the political classes by whom Slaughter sets so much store. Politics, repeatedly, is sidelined.[3] What, though, of the content of new liberal norms? What is it that new liberalism seeks to achieve? There is a revealing sentence toward the end of Slaughter's book (2004, 260): "the content of these specific principles is less important in many ways than the simple fact that there be principles." *A New World Order* promises novelty, change, and prescription. And, as well as this, it tells us where, and by whom, this new order is being created. The revolutionary class is the technocratic class.

But if it is, what is it that these networks are trying, or ought to be trying, to create? What is the content of the new world order? No doubt, it is "a deeply human creation motivated by human aspiration" (Slaughter 2004, 133), but what is it being created *for*? When the underlying assumptions are that people want to work together to build a decent world order, then the underlying normative commitments surely have to be quite thin, since the deep-seated conflicts about the specifics are, inevitably, elided. The UN Secretary-General's Global Compact is a case in point. This is commended as "collective learning in action" (Slaughter 2004, 192). The image is of corporate actors working with civil society, labor, and the UN to offer the global market "a human face."[4] The emphasis is on solutions and learning. But solutions to what? Judged by the conduct of corporations in the early twenty-first century, it is legitimate to argue that often what corporations want and what the market demands are buying and selling in the absence of a human face. If corporations are psychopathic then the Global Compact is likely to be hugely

---

[3] For example, the sharp politics of Guantanamo Bay and the anxieties it has provoked do not feature. Yet, the detention without trial of those incarcerated there is not without relevance to Slaughter's thesis. In particular, the four aspects of judicial comity described by Slaughter (deference, localism, rights, and engagement) (2004, 87) each seem relevant to the way judges have approached the detention of nationals in Cuba. In the English Appeal Court decision of *Abbasi*, for example, the Court was critical of the United States for breaching fundamental norms of human rights law, engaged with US courts over the appropriate norms to be applied, and deferred to these better-situated courts in the hope that they would provide resolution (see *Abbasi* v. *Secretary of State* 2002).

[4] UN Secretary-General Kofi Annan's address to the World Economic Forum, Davos, 28 Jan. 1999, quoted in Slaughter (2004, 192).

helpful to them in presenting a human face to the world (human faces after all are marketable), while continuing with business as usual (Achbar, Abbott, and Bakan 2004).

But Slaughter is at the vanguard of a liberal internationalism that views itself as progressive and humanitarian: for better "stewardship" of the earth, in favor of human dignity (and human rights), hostile to the death penalty, worried about the "excesses" of capitalism, and multilateralist (in the broadest sense). Her just world order is as "inclusive, tolerant, respectful and decentralised as possible" (Slaughter 2004, 217), but is this new liberal vision of technocratic networks thick enough to sustain its own normative preferences? Much of Slaughter's work is about procedure—more transparency, deliberative equality, legitimate difference—but there is not enough by way of substantive commitments. To be sure, inclusiveness as a procedural norm has certain substantive implications. It may be that the Montreal Consensus, with its emphasis on permitting "developing countries and poor countries [to] share in the benefits of the global economy" (Slaughter 2004, 246), is something to support, but if this is so we want to know more about which networks will encourage this sort of policy, what the opposition is, and what sort of sacrifices need to be made to achieve a just global political economy.

Ultimately, the "global transgovernmental constitution" (self-consciously mimicking the principles of James Madison and others), unless it grapples with the origins of politics and the hard choices of global redistribution, may well allow the reproduction of many of those hierarchies, oppressions, and substantive inequalities that many new liberals sincerely wish to resist.

4 FORGING A WORLD OF LIBERTY UNDER LAW

If Moravcsik provides the theoretical muscle and Slaughter the descriptive power, then *Forging a World of Liberty under Law* (Ikenberry and Slaughter 2006—a restatement and development of themes found in earlier work but this time conjoined, sometimes awkwardly, to a project to re-envisage US national security) is a full-blown set of policy prescriptions—an application to join the "rulership cadre of states, promoting wise and effective statecraft" (Kennedy 1999, 103).

The title enunciates some of the main conceits of new liberalism. This is an order that, if it is to emerge, will do so not through an incremental flourishing of local projects or an accretion of good deeds or the facilitation of ideas and practices on a small scale. This is a world to be "forged," sometimes through military intervention, sometimes through economic integration. It is a world of liberty (not justice or equality or opportunity) in which states that practice the virtues of freedom and democracy will flourish. Finally, it is a world in which law is the handmaiden to liberty, promoting it at every turn.

Some classic new liberal themes are prominent in this document. There is a call for the creation of a world of "mature liberal democracies" (Ikenberry and Slaughter 2006, 19). There is a Kantian tolerance for (imperfect) existing institutions combined with the promise that much of this will be swept away by new, more authentically liberal institutions. Thus, there are suggestions for a tinkering with Security Council membership and an endorsement of the High Level Panel's proposal for a "Responsibility to Protect"—the latter a reaffirmation of the Rawlsian principle that liberal states ought to have the right to intervene in illiberal states (Rawls 1999; United Nations 2004).

The Princeton Project contains a great deal of good sense (the need to update conceptions of deterrence), liberal ethics (concern for issues of global health, a genuine reaching out to the citizens of foreign states), and some political daring (a national gasoline tax in the United States). I am more interested, for these purposes, in concentrating on three proclivities that hover over this document (and cast into relief some of the preoccupations of new liberalism as an ideological program, whatever the nature of its scientific ambitions).

First, there is a curious lack of faith in the domestic processes that are supposed to energize the new liberal project. Hugo Chavez, for example, a man elected three times, is a "populist" guilty of "fomenting a continent-wide anti-US coalition" (Ikenberry and Slaughter 2006, 11). This cold war rhetoric sits uneasily with the ardor for democratic processes on display elsewhere. A deeper contradiction lies at the heart of the democratic governance project in international law. It may be that the purpose of international law is to restrain sovereigns (liberty under law), but, if those sovereigns exercise authority as an expression of popular will, then international law must have to be, at times, antidemocratic and antilibertarian (Rabkin 2004; Anderson 2005, 1308–9). In *Forging a World of Liberty*, members of the Concert of Democracies are required to "pledge not to use force against one another" (Ikenberry and Slaughter 2006, 7). If such pledges are necessary in a world of democratic states, it may be because the popular will can become bellicose or because liberal states might have good reason to attack one another (for example, over remaining oil stocks, in response to mass refugee flows, because of chauvinistic media campaigns). It is not clear, in such cases, why international law is to be taken more seriously than these (sometimes warmongering) domestic preferences.

Secondly, there is a classic split between the political and the pre-political. Thus, just as "preferences" have a pre-political origin, so, too, do "threats." Some threats, according to the authors, are political (extremists inflicting catastrophic damage), while others are naturally occurring and "not politically motivated" (such as nuclear meltdown, climate change, and infectious disease). Only an emaciated conception of the political could permit these sorts of distinctions, and they are buttressed by analogous divisions between culture (them) and strategy (us). Extremists, usually Islamic fascists who would "willingly martyr themselves," are to be distinguished from rational actors like the Soviet Union or the United States (both of which participated in a deterrence regime that assumed a capacity and willingness to martyr whole nations).

There is, thirdly, an unstable dual commitment to both global justice and American well-being. The centrality of US exceptionalism (mostly unstated in early new liberal work) becomes a non-negotiable norm in the *Forging a World of Liberty* proposals. The basic objective of US strategy must be "to protect . . . *the American way of life*" (Ikenberry and Slaughter 2006, 14, emphasis added). What is not fully explained is how the American way of life can be protected in a way that is compatible with a liberal global order. It may be, instead, that the levels of consumption, the degree of ecological destruction, and the militarism that is required to sustain the American (and, indeed, Western) project are fundamentally at odds with building a stable and decent political order. This centrally important question is confronted in neither the Princeton Project document nor Slaughter's *New World Order*. Indeed, sometimes the ethics of new liberalism is best demonstrated by its aporia; some matters (fear, retribution, poverty, the skewing effects of private wealth) are screened out.

In the end, new liberalism is an important and rigorous approach to world politics and international relations. Its virtues are manifold (a refusal readily to accept the primacy of raw power, an attention to domestic spaces as engines of international change, a genuinely parsimonious and compelling initial theorization, an ambitious and intellectually confident grand theory of global order). As a theory of politics and ethics, however, it remains insensitive to the enormity of private power, the subtlety of political motivation, and the intermingling of the social and the political.

REFERENCES

Abbasi v. Secretary of State for Commonwealth and Foreign Affairs 2002. www.courtservice. gov.uk/judgmentsfiles/j1354/abassi_judgment.htm.

ACHBAR, M., ABBOTT, J., and BAKAN, J. 2004. *The Corporation: A Documentary*. London: Constable and Robinson.

ALVAREZ, J. 2001. Do liberal states behave better? A critique of Slaughter's liberal theory. *European Journal of International Law*, 12: 183–246.

ANDERSON, K. 2005. Squaring the circle? Reconciling sovereignty and global governance through global government networks. *Harvard Law Review*, 118: 1255–311.

DER DERIAN, J. 1992. *Antidiplomacy: Spies, Terror, Speed, and War*. Cambridge, Mass.: Blackwell.

——and SHAPIRO, M. J. (eds.) 1989. *International/Intertextual Relations: Postmodern Readings of World Politics*. Lexington, Mass.: Lexington Books.

FRANCK, T. M. 1970. Who killed article 2(4)? Or: changing norms governing the use of force by states. *American Journal of International Law*, 64: 809–37.

IKENBERRY, J., and SLAUGHTER, A.-M. 2006. *Forging a World of Liberty under Law: US National Security in the 21st Century, Final Report of the Princeton Project on National Security*. Princeton, NJ: Woodrow Wilson School of Public and International Affairs, Princeton University.

KENNEDY, D. 1999. The disciplines of international law and policy. *Leiden Journal of International Law*, 12: 9–133.

MORAVCSIK, A. 1997. Taking preferences seriously: a liberal theory of international politics. *International Organization*, 51: 513–53.

RABKIN, J. 2004. *The Case for Sovereignty: Why the World Should Welcome American Independence*. Washington, DC: American Enterprise Institute Press.

RAWLS, J. 1999. *The Law of Peoples: With, The Idea of Public Reason Revisited*. Cambridge, Mass.: Harvard University Press.

REUS-SMIT, C. 2001. The strange death of liberal international theory. *European Journal of International Law*, 12: 573–94.

RUSSETT, B. 1993. *Grasping the Democratic Peace: Principles for a Post-Cold War World*. Princeton, NJ: Princeton University Press.

SCHMITT, C. 2003. *The Nomos of the Earth in the International Law of the Jus Publicum Europaeum*. New York: Telos.

SIMPSON, G. 2004a. *Great Powers and Outlaw States: Unequal Sovereigns in the International Legal Order*. Cambridge: Cambridge University Press.

—— 2004b. What is to be done? Who is to do it? *Finnish Yearbook of International Law*, 15: 395–403.

SLAUGHTER, A.-M., 1994. The liberal agenda for peace: international relations theory and the future of the United Nations. *Transnational Law and Contemporary Problems*, 4: 377–419.

—— 1995. A typology of transjudicial communication. *University of Richmond Law Review*, 29: 99–137.

—— 1997. The real new world order. *Foreign Affairs*, 76: 183–97.

—— 2004. *A New World Order*. Princeton, NJ: Princeton University Press.

UNITED NATIONS 2004. *A More Secure World: Our Shared Responsibility, Report of the High-Level Panel on Threats, Challenges and Change*. New York: United Nations.

WALKER, R. B. J. 1993. *Inside/Outside: International Relations as Political Theory*. Cambridge: Cambridge University Press.

WHITE HOUSE 2006. *National Security Strategy of the United States of America*. Washington, DC: White House. www.whitehouse.gov/nsc/nss/2006/

WIGHT, M. 1991. *International Theory: The Three Traditions*. Leicester: Leicester University Press.

CHAPTER 15

···

THE ENGLISH
SCHOOL

···

TIM DUNNE

INTERNATIONAL relations is no longer an American social science, as Stanley Hoffmann (1977) proclaimed. This is true in a literal sense: The subject is taught in universities in dozens of countries and is becoming a global discipline. It is also true insofar as the study of international relations outside the United States is often committed to theoretical orientations that are hostile to the dominant approach encapsulated by the phrase "an American social science." The English School of international relations is the oldest and arguably the most significant rival to the American mainstream. By English School, I mean a group of scholars located mainly in the UK who have a common ontological disposition and are critical of the kind of scientific method advanced by positivists. During the classical period in its evolution (1950s–1980s), the leading figures in the School were Charles Manning, Herbert Butterfield, Hedley Bull, Adam Watson, and R. J. Vincent. In the post-classical phase (1990s onwards), the most prominent writers are Barry Buzan, Andrew Hurrell, Robert Jackson, Edward Keene, Andrew Linklater, Richard Little, James Mayall, Hidemi Suganami, and Nicholas J. Wheeler.

The claim that the English School constitutes a distinctive and systematic approach to international relations is one that is relatively uncontroversial today but would not have been accepted in the 1980s, when the landscape of international relations was carved up into the paradigms of realism, pluralism, and structuralism.

I would like to thank Chris Reus-Smit for extremely helpful feedback on an early draft of this chapter.

Today the English School is not only more confident of its own contribution; it is increasingly being taken seriously by other theoretical approaches. What evidence can be cited in support of this claim? To begin with, key textbooks surveying international relations theory today include the English School (Burchill et al. 2001; Dunne, Kurki, and Smith 2007). Additionally, the influential Cambridge University Press/British International Studies Association series is consistently publishing books on the School, including Buzan (2004) and Linklater and Suganami (2006). A final indicator is the extent to which international relations researchers—primarily in the United States, Canada, Australia, and Scandinavia—are engaging with the work even though many do not identify themselves as being part of an English School project per se (Finnemore 1996; Epp 1998; Reus-Smit 1999; Wendt 1999; Jackson 2000; Shapcott 2004; Adler 2005).

This geopolitical diversity points to an anomaly with the label "English School" in that even in its heyday some of its leading contributors were not English (though all built their academic reputations at British universities). The empirical deficiencies with the label has generated a great deal of debate and to some extent resentment on the part of those who symphathize with the ideas but not the act of union to a particular place. While recognizing this deficiency, it is probably time to admit that the label has taken hold and is understood by just about every undergraduate studying international relations.

Those who identify with the English School today see it as occupying the middle ground in international relations alongside constructivism: This location is preferable to the dominant mainstream theories of neorealism and neoliberalism and the more radical alternatives (such as critical theory and poststructuralism). They are drawn to an English School perspective because it offers a synthesis of different theories and concepts. In so doing, it avoids the "either/or" framing of realism versus idealism, as set out in the writings of many great figures during the 1930s and 1940s. It also avoids the explanatory versus interpretative dichotomy that generated so much heat during the "fourth debate" in the 1990s. In place of these dichotomies, the English School purports to offer an account of international relations that combines theory *and* history, morality *and* power, agency *and* structure.

One obvious consequence of this level of theoretical ambition is that the boundaries of the English School often appear to be unclear, which in part explains the ongoing debate about who belongs in the School and how it differs from other theoretical accounts of world politics. To shed light on these questions, Section 1 of this chapter will consider in more depth the contextual emergence of the English School, and in particular its determination to develop an original account of inter-state order. Section 2 takes its central claim—that the practice of states is shaped by international norms, regulated by international institutions, and guided by moral purposes—and explores this in relation to the countervailing forces of the states system and world society. In the course of this exploration, the argument opens up a number of "axes of difference" within the School (Reus-Smit 2002, 496–9) such as the extent to which ontological primacy is accorded to international society, and, at a deeper level, whether that society is understood in procedural or substantive terms.

In Section 3, the focus shifts away from debates inside the English School and toward a wider reflection on its place within international relations as a whole. What do leading US theorists regard as the contribution of the School, or, putting it more negatively, what do they see as being wrong with the English School? Perhaps the most significant conversation of them all is the one with constructivism. The broadly sociological assumptions shared by both schools generated excitement on the part of adherents to the English School: Suddenly works that had seemed outdated and idiosyncratic were opened up for new critically informed readings. Over a decade later, the initial excitement has waned as the English School has come under "friendly fire" from constructivists. As I argue in this chapter, while the English School has a great deal to learn from constructivism, it should maintain its distinctive voice primarily because it has greater synthetic potential and is more openly committed to certain ethical standpoints.

1 CONTEXT AND EMERGENCE

The English School can claim to be a distinctive theory of international relations because of a shared history and a sense that its approach to the subject was a living tradition. What is apparent from existing accounts of the development of the School is the extent to which the main protagonists believed themselves to be part of a collective enterprise, and consciously sought to carry its debates forward.

The emergence of a self-conscious research program, with an open yet distinct agenda, can be seen in the writings of early post-1945 writers working in leading UK universities. Manning developed a curriculum in which the idea of international society played a prominent role. In the 1950s, his colleague Martin Wight developed an approach to the subject that viewed international society as a middle way between realist accounts of systemic logics and revolutionist accounts that plotted the downfall of the state system as a whole. Wight's most famous protégé was Bull. He too was increasingly dissatisfied with the either/or choice between realism and idealism. The former, Bull believed, was right to puncture the utopian schemes of the idealists but wrong to rule out the idea that the inter-state order was capable of reform.

The search for a new analysis of international relations was what drove Butterfield to set up the British Committee on the Theory of International Politics (Dunne 1998; Vigezzi 2005). The committee met regularly between 1959 and 1984. The chairs of the Committee were the pivotal figures in the classical period:

Butterfield (until 1968), Wight (until 1972), Watson (until 1978), and Bull until his death in 1984. By then, the work of the Committee and those sympathetic to it was increasingly seen as being out of step with the emergence of new theories (such as postmodernism and critical theory) and sub-disciplines (such as foreign-policy analysis and international political economy). Unsurprisingly, we find that in reflections on the "state of the discipline" in the 1980s, the English School was nowhere to be seen (Banks 1984; Smith 1987); neither did it figure in early representations of the debate between neorealism and its critics. Yet, within a decade, interest in the English School had begun to rekindle. Many influential textbooks published in the 1990s began to include it as an alternative approach to the subject, placing it alongside realism, liberalism, and various critical approaches (Der Derian 1995; Brown 1997; Jackson and Sørensen 1999). Added to these, original contributions to the history and theory of international society have proliferated, all taking the English School as their point of departure (*inter alia*, Jackson 1990; 1995; Armstrong 1993; Osiander 1994; Welsh 1995; Buzan and Little 2000; Wheeler 2000; Keene 2002; Keal 2003; Clark 2005; 2007; Gonzalez-Pelaez 2005).

This sense of a resurgent paradigm was prompted in part by the recognition that it represented a distinct position that was inhospitable to the rationalist assumptions underpinning both neorealism and neoliberalism. Moreover, in terms of substantive research questions, the English School had long focused on the kind of cultural questions and normative contestations that were rising to the top of the international agenda in the 1990s. Such momentum prompted Buzan—along with Little—to seek to invigorate English School theorizing. This new phase was marked by the publication of Buzan's agenda-setting paper, "The English School: An Underexploited Resource in IR" (Buzan 2001), developed further in Buzan (2004) and followed by Linklater and Suganami's major reassessment of the School (2006).

The previous paragraphs have provided some historical and sociological context for the emergence of the English School. What follows is a focused discussion of "international society," and how this needs to be situated between the system and world society pillars of the world political system.

2 International Society: Between System and World Society

A feature of the earliest historiographical accounts of the English School is that they refer to their defense of international society being the "distinguishing power" of the School (Wilson 1989). Following Buzan (2004), I now hold the view that the School needs not only to provide a powerful account of how and why states form a society; it must also show how this domain relates to world society. Moreover, going further than Buzan, I argue that the distinguishing power of the English School is its synthetic account of how the three pillars of the world political system hang together: the system, the inter-state society, and world society.

According to Bull, the categories system, society, and world society are "elements" that exist "out there" in world politics but can be known to us only through interpretative designs. They are ideal-types, bundles of properties that highlight certain important features while minimizing that which is thought to be less relevant. By seeking to clarify the concepts that reveal patterns in world history, the English School is working with a very different notion of "theory" to that which is found in the dominant American approaches. Rather than "operationalizing" concepts and formulating "testable" hypotheses, the emphasis upon contending concepts is driven by a search for defining properties that mark the boundaries of different historical and normative orders.

It is necessary, before going any further, to consider one objection to representing English School theory as a conversation between three overlapping domains. In Andrew Linklater's view, although the School talked about international society as only one element in the complex patterns of international interactions, it was nevertheless "its central purpose" (Linklater and Suganami 2006, 119).[1] Therefore, to treat the three as being of equal significance is to misunderstand the distinctive character of English School thought. I do not doubt that one of the intellectual drivers propelling the English School into existence was a defense of a middle way between realism and idealism. I also recognize that many publications by English School advocates in the 1990s continued to privilege the societal domain, in part due to the desire to show that the English School was not just a polite form of realism, as many in the 1980s had assumed. However, neither of these points undermines the claim that the most persuasive case one can make in defense of the English School is that it is potentially more illuminating than mainstream alternatives because it seeks to provide a synthetic account of global politics that avoids the series of false dichotomies thrown up by the alternatives such as power versus norms, materialism versus idealism, anarchy versus hierarchy, reasons versus causes. Such a move requires that we situate the inter-state normative order alongside the other two ideal-types to illustrate its boundaries and constraints.

2.1 International Society: Definition, Properties, Variations

Perhaps the sharpest definition of international society is to be found on the first page of the edited collection *The Expansion of International Society*. By an international society, Bull and Watson (1984, 1) write,

---

[1] Although the Linklater and Suganami book is co-authored, the introduction clearly states which chapters were drafted by which author—hence the reference to Linklater only.

we mean a group of states (or, more generally, a group of independent political communities) which not merely form a system, in the sense that the behaviour of each is a necessary factor in the calculations of the others, but also have established by dialogue and consent common rules and institutions for the conduct of their relations, and recognize their common interest in maintaining these arrangements.

The discussion that follows scrutinizes each component of this definition.

The first key element of international society is the unique character of the membership that is confined to sovereign states. What is significant here is that actors both claim sovereignty and recognize one another's right to the same prerogatives (Wight 1977). Clearly the act of mutual recognition indicates the presence of a social practice: recognition is fundamental to an identity relationship. Recognition is the first step in the construction of an international society. If we were to doubt for a moment the social nature of the process of recognition, then this would quickly be dispelled by those peoples in history who at some time have been or continue to be denied membership of the society of states. The history of the expansion of international society is a story of a shifting boundary of inclusion and exclusion. China was denied sovereign statehood until January 1942, when Western states finally renounced the unequal treaties. Why was this the case? Membership became defined, particularly in the nineteenth century, by a "standard of civilization" that set conditions for internal governance that corresponded with European values and beliefs. What we see here is how important cultural differentiation has been to the European experience of international society. China was not recognized as a legitimate member of international society, and, therefore, was denied equal membership. If the West and China did not recognize each other as equal members, then how should we characterize their relations? Here we see how the system–society dynamic can usefully capture historical boundaries of inclusion and exclusion. There was a great deal of "interaction" between China and the West during the nineteenth and early twentieth centuries, but this was driven by strategic and economic logics. Crucially, neither side believed itself to be part of the same shared values and institutions: China, for example, long resisted the presence of European diplomats on its soil along with their claim to extraterritorial jurisdiction, which has been a long-standing rule among European powers. In the absence of accepting the rules and institutions of European international society, it makes sense to argue that from the Treaty of Nanking in 1843 to 1942 China was part of the states system but was not a member of international society (Gong 1984).

After rightful membership, the next consideration involves thinking about what it means for a state to "act." Here the English School encounters criticism from empiricists who argue that collective constructs cannot have agency. What does it mean to attribute agency to collectivities like states? One straightforward answer is that states act through the medium of their representatives or office-holders. Every state employs officials who act externally on its behalf, from the lowly consulate dealing with "nationals" who have lost their passports to the "head of state." In a narrowly empirical sense, therefore, the diplomatic and foreign-policy elite are the real agents of international society. This is the original sense in which the term "international society" came into existence in the eighteenth century. In 1736, Antoine Pecquet argued that the corps of ministers formed an "independent society" bound by a "community of privileges" (Frey and Frey 1999, 213). If we are looking for the real agents of international society, then it is to the diplomatic culture that we must look, that realm of ideas and beliefs shared by representatives of states (Der Derian 2003).

Sovereign states are the primary members of international society; however, it is important to note that they are not the *only* members. Historical anomalies have always existed, including the diplomatic network belonging to the Catholic Church and the qualified sovereign powers that were granted to nonstate actors such as the rights to make war and annex territory that were transferred to the great trading companies of the imperial era. One might also argue that influential international nongovernmental organizations (INGOs) are members insofar as they give advice to institutions such as the United Nations and on occasions participate in the drafting of significant multilateral treaties. The other important anomaly with the membership of international society is the fact that sovereign rights are often constrained for economic or security reasons. Robert Jackson (1990), a leading writer in the English School, pointed to the fact that postcolonial states are "quasi" sovereigns in that they are recognized by international society but are unable to maintain an effective government internally. A related development is the temporary suspension of sovereign prerogatives by an international institution or occupying authority, a practice that follows from a period of civil conflict or external military intervention. In the colonial period this was often described as trusteeship (Bain 2003); in contemporary international society it goes under the less politically sensitive label of a "transitional authority."

The element of mutual recognition is highly significant for English School understandings of international society, but it is not a sufficient condition for its existence. The actors must have some minimal common interests, such as trade, freedom of travel, or simply the need for stability. Here we see how aspects of the system impinge on the possibilities for a society to develop. The higher the levels of economic interdependence, the more likely it is that states will develop institutions for realizing common interests and purposes. The independence of sovereign states, however, remains an important limiting factor in the realization of common goals. For this reason, the purposes states agreed upon for most of the Westphalian era have had a fairly minimal character centered upon the survival of the system and the endurance of the dominant units within it. The condition of general war is an example of the breakdown of order, but Bull was quick to point out that, even during the Second World War, certain laws of war were respected and, perhaps more significantly, the period of total war triggered an attempt to construct a new order based largely on the same rules and institutions that had operated in the prewar era.

It was this that led him to claim that "the element of society had always existed" in the modern states system (Bull 1977, 41). Such a claim prompted disquiet from constructivists, who rightly argued that, if "society" produces order, how can it continue to exist during historical periods when order has clearly broken down (Finnemore 2001)?

2.2 Types of International Society

One answer to Finnemore's question, which the English School needs to develop more fully, is to provide clearer benchmarks that enable an evaluation of how much "society" is present in the inter-state order. At the more minimal end of the spectrum of international societies, we find an institutional arrangement that is restricted solely to the maintenance of order. In a culturally diverse world, where member states have different traditions and political systems, the only collective venture they could all agree on was the maintenance of international order. Without order, the stability of the system would be thrown into doubt and with it the survival of the units. Yet, the extent to which states formed an international society was limited and constrained by the fact of anarchy. For this reason, international society was to be equated not with a harmonious order but, rather, with a tolerable order that was better than a realist would expect but much worse than a cosmopolitan might wish for (MacMillan and Linklater 1995).

In a pluralist international society, the institutional framework is geared toward the liberty of states and the maintenance of order among them. The rules are complied with because, like rules of the road, fidelity to them is relatively cost free but the collective benefits are enormous. A good example is the elaborate rules to do with ambassadorial and diplomatic privileges. Acceptance that representatives of states were not subject to the laws of their host country is a principle that has received widespread compliance for many centuries. This is one instance among many where the rules of coexistence have come to dominate state practice. Pluralist rules and norms "provide a structure of coexistence, built on the mutual recognition of states as independent and legally equal members of society, on the unavoidable reliance on self-preservation and self-help, and on freedom to promote their own ends subject to minimal constraints" (Alderson and Hurrell 2000, 18). Fully to comprehend the pluralist order, one needs only to be reminded that great powers, limited war, and the balance of power were thought by the English School to be "institutions." By this term, Bull and his colleagues were pointing to the practices that helped to sustain order, practices that evolved over many centuries. For example, if the balance of power was essential to preserve the liberty of states, then status quo powers must be prepared to intervene forcefully to check the growing power of a state that threatens the general balance.

Are pluralist rules and institutions adequate for our contemporary world? This is a question that has provoked differing responses within the English School. On one side, traditionalists like Jackson (2000) believe that a pluralist international society is a practical institutional adaptation to human diversity: The great advantage of a society based on the norms of sovereignty and nonintervention is that such an arrangement is most likely to achieve the moral value of freedom.

Critics of pluralism charge that it is failing to deliver on its promise. The persistence of inter-state wars throughout the twentieth century suggest that sovereignty norms were not sufficient to deter predatory states. Moreover, the rule of nonintervention that was central to pluralism was enabling statist elites to violently abuse their own citizens with impunity. For these reasons, both Bull and Vincent were drawn to a different account of international society in which universal values such as human rights set limits on the exercise of state sovereignty. The guiding thought here, and one that is captured by the term solidarism, is that the ties that bind individuals to the great society of humankind are deeper than the pluralist rules and institutions that separate them.

Bull defined a solidarist international society in terms of the collective enforcement of international rules *and* the guardianship of human rights. It differs from cosmopolitanism in that the latter is agnostic as to the institutional arrangement for delivering universal values: Some cosmopolitans believe a world government is best and others would want to abandon formal political hierarchies altogether. By contrast, solidarism is an *extension* of an international society not its transformation. Like pluralism, it is defined by shared values and institutions and is held together by binding legal rules. Where it differs is in the content of the values and the character of the rules and institutions. In terms of values, in a solidarist international society individuals are entitled to basic rights. This in turn demands that sovereignty norms are modified such that there is a duty on the members of international society to intervene forcibly to protect those rights. At this point, Bull was hesitant about what was implied by solidarism. He believed that there was a danger that the enforcement of human rights principles risked undermining international order. Until there was a greater consensus on the meaning and priority to be accorded to rights claims, attempts to enforce them—what he described as "premature global solidarism"—would do more harm than good.

For much of the post-cold war period, the normative debate within the English School fractured along a pluralist/solidarist divide. On one side of the divide, Jackson (2000) made a forceful case for upholding pluralist norms, while Wheeler (2000) set out a persuasive argument in defense of a solidarist account of rights and duties. Buzan is right to argue that one of the negative consequences of the debate is that it assumed normative density was an issue primarily for the inter-state realm rather than understanding how it shapes and enables the transnational and inter-human domains.

While it is correct to argue that "pluralism versus solidarism" was one of the principal axes of difference in English School thinking after the cold war, from the vantage point of today this dispute looks increasingly like a conversation inside the normative wing of the School. Alongside the normative wing, we have seen the emergence of an analytical wing led by Buzan himself and including the work of Little. The former are drawn toward historical narratives of how the international social structure has evolved/changed (e.g. Armstrong 1993; Wheeler 2000; Bain 2003; Keal 2003; Linklater and Suganami 2006), while the latter search for analytical explanations of the various domains and sectors and how these impinge on each other (Watson 1992; Wæver 1998; Buzan and Little 2000; Little 2000; Buzan 2004).

2.3 The Elements of System and World Society

Both Wight and Bull recognized that a sophisticated analysis of world politics required a systemic component. Yet their discussion of Hobbesian dynamics in the "system" is inconsistent and unpersuasive. In my view, this vital element of the English School's theorization of world politics ought to be refined rather than discarded as Buzan (2004, 106) has argued. Bull defined the system as being an arena where there was interaction between communities but no shared rules or institutions. In order for a system to come into being, there has to be sufficient intensity of interactions to make "the behaviour of each a necessary element in the calculations of the other" (Bull 1977, 12).

The concept of a system plays three important roles in the English School's theory of world politics. First, as discussed above, the system/society distinction provides a normative benchmark for addressing the question of how far international society extends (Wight, Wight, and Porter 1991). Secondly, by looking at the formation of the system, it is possible to discern mechanisms that shape and shove international and world societies. Thirdly, the category of the system can be used to capture the basic material forces in world politics—flows of information and trade, levels of destructive capability, and capacities of actors to affect their environment. Let me examine each of these briefly in turn.

The English School's use of the category international system—or more accurately an inter-state system—shares a great deal with the use of systems theory in realist thought. What sets them apart is that the English School was interested in the system primarily for what it tells us about the history of international society. If one takes Bull's developmental insight into the relationship between system and society, then it is clear that the existence of a society presupposes the existence of a system. This can open up into an intriguing series of discussions as to when a system becomes a society—what level and type of interactions are required in order for the units to treat each other as ends in themselves? And under what circumstances might a society lapse back into a systemic order in which their actions impact upon one another but there is no mutual recognition or acceptance of a common framework of rules and institutions? In the British Committee's writings on decolonization, the emphasis is placed on the gradual inclusion of the non-Western world into a globalized society of sovereign states. It is also important to realize that systemic interactions remain a possible future arrangement if the dominant actors in international society cease to comply with the rules and act in ways that undermine international security. The hypothetical case of a major nuclear confrontation could become a reality only if the great powers acted in ways that were catastrophic for international society. As a result, the society collapses back into the system.

The idea of a states system is also useful to identify the current boundaries between members and those states that find themselves shunned by international society. It is in the dark recesses of the states system that pariah states and failed states find themselves. This does not mean pariahs are outside the framework of the rules and institutions entirely, only that their actions are subjected to far greater scrutiny. Actors in the states system can have structured interactions with members of international society—they may even comply with treaties and other rules—but these interactions remain systemic unless the parties grant each other mutual respect and inclusion into international society.

Thinking about the systemic domain also alerts us to the downward pressure exerted by the distribution of material power. In Bull's work we can find two important instances where the system impinges upon the society. First, he notes how general war is "a basic determinant of the shape the system assumes at any one time" (Bull 1977, 187). Even in the cold war, where the massive nuclear arsenals of the North Atlantic Treaty Organization and Warsaw Pact countries were not unleashed, the presence of these weapons was a crucial constraint on the two superpowers' room for maneuver. If the Soviet Union had only conventional weapons, would the United States and its allies have tolerated the "fall" of central European countries into the Soviet sphere of influence? Closely related to the phenomena of general war and destructive capacities as basic determinants of the system, one can find in the English School the view that there is logic of balancing in the states system. Under conditions of anarchy, where there is no overarching power to disarm the units and police the rules, it is in the interests of all states to prevent the emergence of a dominant or hegemonic power (Watson 1992). Those who take the balance of power seriously point to repeated instances in modern history where states with hegemonic ambition have been repelled by an alliance of powers seeking to prevent a change in the ordering principle of the system. Even if this tendency requires states to "act" in order to uphold the balance of power, it can still be persuasively argued that the survival of the states system *demands* balancing behavior from states such that it becomes an inbuilt feature of the system. This is contrasted with the institution of the balance of power in international society that is not mechanical but is rather the outcome of a deliberate policy of pursuing a strategy of self-preservation in the absence of world government (Wight 1978).

Looking through the systemic lens does not only show the ordering of the units; it also directs our attention to the levels of technology, the distribution of material power, and the interaction capacity of the units. Together, these factors tell us a great deal about the ability of units to act, and particularly their "reach" (are actors local, regional, or global?). Levels of technology can be thought of as attributes of the units; an obvious case in point is whether a state has nuclear weapons technology or not. However, it is also useful to think about technology in systemic terms, particularly in areas such as communication, transportation, and levels of destructive capacity. Compare, for example, a states system in which the dominant mode of transportation is a horse-drawn wagon, as opposed to a system in which individuals and goods can be transported by supersonic jets, high-speed rail, and ships the size of several football fields placed end-to-end. As these technologies spread, "they change the quality and character of what might be called the *interaction capacity* of the system as a whole" (Buzan, Jones, and Little 1993, 70).

What make these attributes "systemic?" They are systemic in that for the most part they fall outside the institutional arrangement developed by states to regulate order and promote justice. By way of illustration, take the place of Britain in the world from the early 1940s to the beginning of the cold war. Throughout the war, Britain was one of the "big three" great powers who were the architects of the postwar order. By 1948, the country was increasingly a policy-taker on the world stage and not a policy-maker, despite the fact that its diplomatic network remained global, its language remained dominant, and its values ascendant. None of these soft power advantages was enough to configure the system in multipolar terms. Without wanting to imply overdetermination, it is nevertheless useful to invoke the system to characterize those factors that appear immovable from the perspective of the actors, such as their geographic location, population base, and technological/economic capacity. Of course they are not immovable over the long term—even geographical "distance" can change over time, as globalization has demonstrated in recent decades.

The third element in the English School triad is world society. This concept runs in parallel to international society albeit with one key difference—it refers to the shared interests and values "linking all parts of the human community" (Bull 1977, 279). Vincent's definition of world society is something of a menu of all those entities whose moral concerns traditionally lay outside international society: the claim of individuals to human rights; the claim of indigenous peoples to autonomy; the needs of transnational corporations to penetrate the shell of sovereign states; and the claim to retrospective justice by those who speak on behalf of the former colonized powers. It is undeniable that human rights are at the center of the classical English School's conception of world society. An account of the development of human rights would need to show how the cosmopolitan culture of late modernity is shaping a new institutional arrangement in world society.

One indicator of an evolving world society is the emergence of international humanitarian law. The United Nations Charter represented an important stage in this evolution, thus indicating the dynamic interplay between the inter-state and the world society domains. Justice, rights, fundamental freedoms, were all given prominence in the Charter, and subsequently universal norms of racial equality, the prohibition on torture, and the right to development have been added (among others). Various changes in international criminal law have significantly restricted the circumstances in which state leaders can claim immunity from humanitarian crimes committed while they were in office. Similarly, the Rome Statute of the International Criminal Court adds another layer of international jurisdiction in which agents of states can be held accountable for alleged war crimes. Taken as a whole, one authority on the English School argued that they "may be interpreted as involving a clear shift from an international society to a world society" (Armstrong 1999, 549). Such a claim, however, understates the extent to which the development of world society institutions is dependent on the ideational and material support of core states in international society.

World society is not just about the growing importance of transnational values grounded in liberal notions of rights and justice. Transnational identities can be based upon ideas of hatred and intolerance. Among a significant body of world public opinion, the strongest identification is to the faith and not to the state. This generates countervailing ideologies of liberation on the part of fundamentalist Christians and holy war on the part of certain Islamist groups. In English School thinking, such dynamics can usefully be considered in the context of earlier "revolts" against Western dominance that were apparent during the struggle for decolonization.

3 THE ENGLISH SCHOOL AND ITS CRITICS

It is not unusual for proponents of a particular international relations theory to claim to be "misunderstood." From the 1970s to the early 1990s, the leading figures of English School were identified as traditionalists who bought into key realist assumptions about great-power dominance amid international anarchy. Somewhat polemically, a recent intervention by John Mearsheimer suggests the opposite: According to him, Butterfield, Wight, and Bull were "Cold War idealists" (Mearsheimer 2005, 144). This chapter has sought to show that the English School is not reducible either to realism or to idealism even if the focus on systemic forces draws insights from realism just as processes in world society—such as our widening moral sensibility—overlaps with idealism (Bull, in Hurrell and Alderson 1999).

The one theoretical position that has positively engaged with the English School is constructivism. Moreover, in the course of this conversation, constructivists have

highlighted significant sources of conceptual confusion and theoretical underdevelopment at the core of the English School's research program. In the paragraphs
below, I consider the constructivist challenge and examine the extent to which the
English School has the capacity to engage in theoretical modification as well as
remaining distinct from constructivism.

Christian Reus-Smit has written a number of articles that set out the terms of
the debate between the English School and constructivism (Reus-Smit 2002; 2005).
He rightly argues that those who wrote about the convergence in the middle 1990s
did it on the basis of a narrow reading of both paradigms. On one side, the work
of Alexander Wendt was taken to be representative of the constructivism project
overall, while, on the other, there was little effort to engage with the richness of
English School thinking beneath the standard claim that states form an international society.

Limitations on space do not permit a lengthy discussion of the faultlines between
the English School and constructivism. I nevertheless want to reflect on two significant questions that have emerged from the debate. One immediate contrast with
constructivism concerns the importance of metatheoretical correctness. Constructivists are theoretically reflective about the meaning of collective action, the status
of norms, the relative priority accorded structures and agents, and causation, and
the processes of socialization. The English School, by contrast, are more likely to
offer narratives on the evolution and contestation of norms and institutions *without*
explicit metatheoretical reflection. Part of the explanation for this divergence is the
emergence of constructivism in leading American departments of political science
where methodological rigor and epistemological awareness is an expectation for
all doctoral candidates and early career researchers. So is the need to identify—
in exclusionary ways—with one paradigm or another. Constructivism very much
emerged as an alternative to the dominant rationalist approaches to international
relations: As rationalism has never been anything other than a minority interest in
the UK, there was no need of, or desire for, metatheoretical exceptionalism on the
part of the English School.

This is not to say that leading members of the English School have avoided all
engagement with disciplinary politics. Indeed, one of the motivating factors behind
the relaunch of the English School in 2001 was precisely to take theory-building to
a new level. Buzan's agenda setting paper (2001) was published by the *Review of
International Studies*, with several authors from outside the English School asked
to comment. Martha Finnemore, writing from a constructivist standpoint, posed
a series of penetrating questions about the School's method and its theoretical
claims. While American international relations is driven by the search for causal
explanations, Finnemore (2001, 513) ruefully notes that "I am not sure that the
English School shares this interest."

Linklater and Suganami (2006), in their recent book *The English School of International Relations*, have taken up this challenge. They argue that Bull's classic text

The Anarchical Society (1977, 74–5) explicitly asks the question whether rules and institutions are a "necessary and sufficient" condition for international order to exist. The problem for Bull is that the answer cannot be clear-cut, as the dependent variable (order) is implicated in the independent variables (institutions). The same rules and institutions that "cause" international order also form part of the shared knowledge that animates social action and makes it intelligible.

What the English School needs to set out more clearly—and Buzan has begun this journey—is the way in which the ideal-types of system, society, and community can elucidate important dynamics in the international system. It is not surprising that constructivists ask for greater clarity about the status of these ideal-types and how they relate to each other. "How do you know," asks Finnemore (2001, 509), "an international society (or international system or world society) when you see one?" As I have argued elsewhere, these are analytical categories rather than entities belonging to the real world. International society "is not something you see, but an idea in light of which we can make sense of an aspect of contemporary international relations" (Linklater and Suganami 2006, 103).

Wight's work (1977) was primarily interested in showing how individuals thought and acted in ways that reinforced or altered the normative order. His project comparing international societies throughout history drew extensively on cults, practical philosophies, rhetoric, propaganda, and whatever other contextual clues he could uncover. Diplomatic treaties and legal judgments have also proved to be rich resources for those writings, revealing the prevailing understandings of the states system at any point in time (Osiander 1994; Keene 2002; Clark 2005; 2007). This attention to meaning and understanding in the history of ideas about international society is not *absent* from constructivism (particularly in Fierke 1998; Rae 2002), but it is perhaps more clearly *present* in English School writings.

The treatment of "norms" within the English School is more avowedly normative than one finds in mainstream constructivist thinking. Take, for example, the treatment of human rights by Vincent (1986) and Thomas Risse, Steve Ropp, and Kathryn Sikkink (1999). Vincent seeks to provide a normative defence of human rights. We ought, he argues, to defend the universal rights of citizens to security and subsistence; delivering this basic right to life requires rethinking the authority and legitimacy of sovereign states. The structure of Vincent's argument is classically identifiable with English School theory. Realism is dismissed for not taking duties to noncitizens seriously, while full-blown cosmopolitanism is rejected because, in the minds of domestic publics, citizens matter *more* than strangers. This leaves him to explore the complexities of human rights within contending normative conceptions of international society.

In the Risse, Ropp, and Sikkink volume, the concern is with the status of human rights norms. What impact have they had on practice? How do we account for variation? And by what processes are actors socialized into compliance with the norms? This latter question is addressed by the application of a "spiral model" that begins with repression and ends with sovereign states fully internalizing human rights norms and practices (Risse and Sikkink 1999). While it is noteworthy that the rightness of moral universalism is not openly discussed, the strength of the Risse, Ropp, and Sikkink collection is in its analysis of how international norms become domestically instantiated.

The retreat of human rights post-September 11 raises important questions for constructivist analysis, not least whether the process of socialization is reversible. An English School take on this question would, as I have suggested above, situate the institutionalization of human rights within the interplay of system, society, and community in international politics. Classical writers such as Wight and Watson believed there to be a centripetal momentum to power such that it concentrates around a single source. Once the centralization reaches a tipping point, the conditions exist to challenge the pluralist rules and institutions upon which the post-Westphalian order has been built. This line of thought goes to the heart of debates about the role of the United States (and its allies in the West) in building a world order in its own image. Aside from the emergence of an unbalanced power with global economic and military reach, the other significant systemic logic is that of "new terrorism." The willingness of coordinated Islamist terror networks to use violence against Western targets undermines international society's claim to monopolize violence and regulate its use.

Weaving together these two tendencies—the appearance of an imperial power seeking to wage pre-emptive war and a nonstate actor wielding violence outside the framework of the laws of war—we might conclude that Bull was right to be concerned that the element of international society was in decline. Set against this, just as the bell has tolled for the inter-state order many times before, it is possible that the element of society is resilient enough to resist the power of US hegemony and the challenge of transnational nihilism.

REFERENCES

ADLER, E. 2005. Barry Buzan's use of constructivism to reconstruct the English School: "not all the way down." *Millennium: Journal of International Studies*, 34: 171–82.

ALDERSON, K., and HURRELL, A. (eds.) 2000. *Hedley Bull on International Society*. Basingstoke: Macmillan.

ARMSTRONG, D. 1993. *Revolution and World Order: The Revolutionary State in International Society*. Oxford: Clarendon Press.

——1999. Law, justice and the idea of world society. *International Affairs*, 75: 547–61.

BAIN, W. 2003. *Between Anarchy and Society: Trusteeship and the Obligations of Power*. Oxford: Oxford University Press.

BANKS, M. 1984. The evolution of international relations theory. Pp. 3–21 in *Conflict in World Society: A New Perspective on International Relations*, ed. M. Banks. Brighton: Harvester.

BROWN, C. 1997. *Understanding International Relations*. New York: St Martin's Press.

BULL, H. 1977. *The Anarchical Society: A Study of Order in World Politics*. London: Macmillan.

—— and WATSON, A. (eds.) 1984. *The Expansion of International Society*. Oxford: Clarendon Press.

BURCHILL, S., DEVETAK, R., LINKLATER, A., PATERSON, M., REUS-SMIT, C., and TRUE, J. 2001. *Theories of International Relations*, 2nd edn. Basingstoke: Palgrave.

BUZAN, B. 2001. The English School: an underexploited resource in IR. *Review of International Studies*, 27: 471–88.

—— 2004. *From International to World Society? English School Theory and the Social Structure of Globalisation*. Cambridge: Cambridge University Press.

—— JONES, C. A., and LITTLE, R. 1993. *The Logic of Anarchy: Neorealism to Structural Realism*. New York: Columbia University Press.

—— and LITTLE, R. 2000. *International Systems in World History: Remaking the Study of International Relations*. Oxford: Oxford University Press.

CLARK, I. 2005. *Legitimacy in International Society*. Oxford: Oxford University Press.

—— 2007. *International Legitimacy and World Society*. Oxford: Oxford University Press.

DER DERIAN, J. (ed.) 1995. *International Theory: Critical Investigations*. Basingstoke: Macmillan.

—— 2003. Hedley Bull and the case for a post-classical approach. Pp. 61–94 in *International Relations at LSE: A History of 75 Years*, ed. H. Bauer and E. Brighi. London: Millennium.

DUNNE, T. 1998. *Inventing International Society: A History of the English School*. New York: St Martin's Press in association with St Antony's College.

—— KURKI, M., and SMITH, S. (eds.) 2007. *Theories of International Relations: Discipline and Diversity*. Oxford: Oxford University Press.

EPP, R. 1998. The English School on the frontiers of international society: a hermeneutic recollection. Pp. 47–63 in *The Eighty Years' Crisis: International Relations 1919–1999*, ed. T. Dunne, M. Cox, and K. Booth. Cambridge: Cambridge University Press.

FIERKE, K. 1998. *Changing Games, Changing Strategies: Critical Investigations in Security*. Manchester: Manchester University Press.

FINNEMORE, M. 1996. *National Interests in International Society*. Ithaca, NY: Cornell University Press.

—— 2001. Exporting the English School? *Review of International Studies*, 27: 509–13.

FREY, L. S., and FREY, M. L. 1999. *The History of Diplomatic Immunity*. Columbus: Ohio State University Press.

GONG, G. W. 1984. *The Standard of "Civilization" in International Society*. Oxford: Clarendon Press.

GONZALEZ-PELAEZ, A. 2005. *Human Rights and World Trade: Hunger in International Society*. London: Routledge.

HOFFMANN, S. 1977. An American social science: international relations. *Daedalus*, 106: 41–60.

JACKSON, R. H. 1990. *Quasi-States: Sovereignty, International Relations, and the Third World*. Cambridge: Cambridge University Press.

—— 1995. The political theory of international society. Pp. 110–28 in *International Relations Theory Today*, ed. K. Booth and S. Smith. Cambridge: Polity.

—— 2000. *The Global Covenant: Human Conduct in a World of States*. Oxford: Oxford University Press.

JACKSON, R. H., and SØRENSEN, G. 1999. *Introduction to International Relations*. Oxford: Oxford University Press.

KEAL, P. 2003. *European Conquest and the Rights of Indigenous Peoples: The Moral Backwardness of International Society*. Cambridge: Cambridge University Press.

KEENE, E. 2002. *Beyond the Anarchical Society: Grotius, Colonialism and Order in World Politics*. Cambridge: Cambridge University Press.

LINKLATER, A. 2001. Rationalism. Pp. 103–28 in Burchill et al. 2001.

—— and SUGANAMI, H. 2006. *The English School of International Relations: A Contemporary Assessment*. Cambridge: Cambridge University Press.

LITTLE, R. 2000. The English School's contribution to the study of international relations. *European Journal of International Relations*, 6: 395–422.

MEARSHEIMER, J. J. 2005. E. H. Carr vs. idealism: the battle rages on. *International Relations*, 19: 139–52.

MacMILLAN, J., and LINKLATER, A. 1995. *Boundaries in Question: New Directions in International Relations*. London: Continuum.

OSIANDER, A. 1994. *The States System of Europe, 1640–1990: Peacemaking and the Conditions of International Stability*. Oxford: Oxford University Press.

RAE, H. 2002. *State Identities and the Homogenisation of Peoples*. Cambridge: Cambridge University Press.

REUS-SMIT, C. 1999. *The Moral Purpose of the State: Culture, Social Identity, and Institutional Rationality in International Relations*. Princeton, NJ: Princeton University Press.

—— 2002. Imagining society: constructivism and the English School. *British Journal of Politics and International Relations*, 4: 487–509.

—— 2005. The constructivist challenge after September 11. Pp 81–95 in *International Society and its Critics*, ed. A. J. Bellamy. Oxford: Oxford University Press.

RISSE, T., and SIKKINK, K. 1999. The socialization of human rights norms into domestic practices: introduction. Pp. 1–38 in Risse, Ropp, and Sikkink 1999.

—— ROPP, S. C., and SIKKINK, K. (eds.) 1999. *The Power of Human Rights: International Norms and Domestic Change*. Cambridge: Cambridge University Press.

SHAPCOTT, R. 2004. IR as practical philosophy: defining a "classical approach." *British Journal of Politics and International Relations*, 6: 271–91.

SMITH, S. 1987. Paradigm dominance in international relations: the development of international relations as a social science. *Millennium: Journal of International Studies*, 16: 189–206.

VIGEZZI, B. 2005. *The British Committee on the Theory of International Politics 1945–1985: The Rediscovery of History*. Milan: Edizioni Unicopli.

VINCENT, R. J. 1986. *Human Rights and International Relations*. Cambridge: Cambridge University Press.

WÆVER, O. 1998. Four meanings of international society: a trans-atlantic dialogue. Pp. 80–144 in *International Society and the Development of International Relations Theory*, ed. B. A. Roberson. London: Pinter.

WATSON, A. 1992. *The Evolution of International Society: A Comparative Historical Analysis*. London: Routledge.

WELSH, J. M. 1995. *Edmund Burke and International Relations: The Commonwealth of Europe and the Crusade against the French Revolution*. Basingstoke: Macmillan.

WENDT, A. 1999. *Social Theory of International Politics*. Cambridge: Cambridge University Press.

WHEELER, N. J. 2000. *Saving Strangers: Humanitarian Intervention in International Society*. Oxford: Oxford University Press.

WIGHT, M. 1977. *Systems of States*, ed. H. Bull. Leicester: Leicester University Press for the London School of Economics and Political Science.

—— 1978. *Power Politics*, ed. H. Bull and C. Holbraad. Leicester: Leicester University Press.

—— WIGHT, G., and PORTER, B. 1991. *International Theory: The Three Traditions*. Leicester: Leicester University Press for the Royal Institute of International Affairs.

WILSON, P. 1989. The English School of international relations: a reply to Sheila Grader. *Review of International Studies*, 15: 49–58.

CHAPTER 16

··

THE ETHICS OF
THE ENGLISH
SCHOOL

··

MOLLY COCHRAN

THE English School understands ethics to be central to the study of world politics. However, the English School never aimed to evaluate the moral appropriateness of the choices made by statesmen. The evaluative conclusions drawn by the English School were few. For much of its history, any judgments made by these writers were limited to what they believed necessary to responsible international society management. Throughout the life of the British Committee on the Theory of International Politics, the English School's classical period from 1959 to 1985, the "good" of international society was a presumption they were unwilling and ill-equipped to pursue in any sustained fashion because of their moral skepticism.

In what Timothy Dunne calls its "post-classical phase," or second-generation English School scholarship, one sees a notable shift in the willingness of those working within this tradition to engage in moral-philosophical arguments, a willingness not seen since the British Committee's formative days. Today, English School scholars are asking whether international society is viable as a moral concern. However, in doing so, both the long shadow of moral skepticism and the School's recourse to empiricism remain. It is the argument of this chapter that the extent to which the English School tradition can demonstrate promise as an approach to international ethics will rest on whether it develops criteria for moral-philosophical judgment that are workable within the themes and concerns of English School thought.

This chapter will address the following questions: What horizon of ethical possibility exists within international society according to the English School; have these notions changed over time within the tradition; and, of the concepts of ethics employed within this tradition, one more minimal and one more maximal, which best defines the English School? In the course of this discussion, reference will also be made to the relationship of the English School to other approaches such as realism and critical theory, and their conceptions of international ethics.

1 ETHICAL POSSIBILITY? MORAL MINIMALISM VERSUS MORAL MAXIMALISM

1.1 The English School's British Committee Years

As discussed in the previous chapter, the English School has important ties with the realist tradition, but there are significant departures as well. This is no less true when one compares the two approaches on the topic of international ethics. Jack Donnelly writes in this volume that realist ethics can best be viewed as "a warning against the inappropriate application of moral standards." From its founding, the English School has issued such warnings and still does. Yet one could go further; arguably, realist ethics allows that the interests of states in survival can overlap and statesmen may act on these areas of overlap, generating a marginal degree of cooperation and responsibility between states. For many realists, this is a fragile, but not unfounded ethical possibility. For English School writers, this is a limited view of ethical possibility in world politics; instead, there exists a society of states that shares wider and deeper interests beyond survival.

For one realist, Hans Morgenthau (2005, 240–69), an international society did exist and supported moral obligations of a supranational character. It was rooted in an aristocratic culture of diplomacy that operated in Europe from the seventeenth to the nineteenth centuries, but declined with the rise of nationalism and democracy. According to Morgenthau, these aristocrats believed in and understood themselves to be members of a cosmopolitan community of humankind, and, when their diplomatic culture collapsed, so did the possibility of international ethics.

The English School challenges the realist contention that international society does not exist and that moral principles have little or no causal force in contemporary world politics. While both Morgenthau and the English School understand the concept of international society to comprise a sense of responsibility to a whole of some kind, they diverge on who or what make up that whole and the nature of the responsibilities felt therein. For Morgenthau, the members of international society were aristocratic individuals who could be held responsible for their diplomatic activity, enabling a system of personal morality, and the wider obligations owed among members stemmed from a maximal idea of ethics: that there is an "absolute barrier" to certain behaviors in international society. Arguments of expediency or interest did not hold sway without aristocratic individuals risking a loss of prestige, and thus power.

By contrast, the English School does not understand international society to be composed of aristocratic diplomatic individuals, but states. In addition, these states and their representatives, despite the rise of both democracy and nationalism, are capable of and do hold a sense of obligation to the whole that is dependent not on a shared aristocratic or cosmopolitan culture, but on common interests that over time can generate cooperation toward the building of common rules and institutions. However, at its start, the British Committee was unclear as to whether obligation in a society of states was of a lesser order in some way, and it debated whether, as Morgenthau believed, international ethics required an individual con-science acting in accordance with absolute standards along the lines of natural law or Christian belief.

The ethical discussion that took place in the earliest days of the British Commit-tee focused upon whether there was the possibility for free will and individual moral judgment to be exercised in world politics—such that the practice of international society could be directed toward the welfare of humankind—or whether an under-standing of international politics in terms of tragedy, determinism, and pessimism was more appropriate. The work of the Committee at this time was influenced by the Christian pessimist moral skepticism of Herbert Butterfield, Martin Wight, and Donald Mackinnon. What scope for progress and international ethics could there be for these Christian pessimists?

It was Mackinnon, the philosopher in the group, who laid out the problem of moral skepticism in relation to the study of international politics and ethics for the Committee. In doing so, he presented the group with two ideas of international ethics that oriented their discussions: (1) a notion of the good founded either upon ideas of natural law or upon a common way of life; and (2) a weaker notion of obligation built upon a *modus vivendi*, a balancing of interests founded upon a principle of utility.

Mackinnon argued for a concept of international ethics based on a notion of the good. He believed that international ethics required inquiry into matters of right and wrong and efforts to translate the problem of personal morality—a "conflict of the claims of justice with those of compassion"—into different terms for a new plane: the realm of the international (Mackinnon 1962a, 9). For example, Mackinnon (1960, 16) argued that, when one says an action is wrong, when one feels compelled to criticize one's leaders, then natural law "intrudes upon our consciousness," and in the name of " 'natural law' we can argue there are risks which men have no right to take with their world." While Mackinnon (1960, 19) was of the view that one should be skeptical about the possibility of metaphysics, he thought the *idea* of natural rights as "an idiom of protest" had "extraordinary resilience." Mackinnon (1962*b*, 21) wanted to discard polarizing categories altogether, and pointed to Immanuel Kant as an exemplar. "Kant knew that human life was always a curious, unexampled mutual interpenetration of ideal and actual. Where he is strong is in his insistence as a profound moralist that we do not seek any easy formula for getting rid of the problem of that interpenetration."

Whether or not the Committee was swayed by Mackinnon's reading of Kant, it was united in the belief that any concept of international ethics it adopted would have to begin from an understanding of this interpenetration. While Morgenthau's thinking about international ethics started from an either/or proposition—either you have a system of personal morality uncompromised by arguments of expediency and interest in world politics or international ethics does not exist—the Committee's thinking began from the recognition that standards of personal morality, or the ideal, and the facts of tragedy, contingency, interest, and power that are constituent parts of international practice cannot be separated.

The principle issue within the Committee was the question: *What kind of ethics is possible in the face of this interpenetration, a more maximal or more minimal one?* Mackinnon and Desmond Williams were of the view that moral limitations on state actors did exist and that the use of natural lawlike idioms was common in international practice. Butterfield and Wight disagreed. They could not invest these idioms with the same moral force that Mackinnon and Williams did (BCTIP 1960*a*, 2; 1960*b*, 8; Wight 1966, 128). Instead, the interpenetration of the ideal and the actual meant that any concept of international ethics that operated was a diminished one, but this did not compromise the possibility of international ethics altogether.

Wight's unique contribution to the English School as an ethical approach is that he was the first among its members to posit a middle-ground ethics that sat between individual or personal morality, on the one hand, and *raison d'etat* or realpolitik on the other. Wight's term for this middle-ground ethics was "political morality," and he placed it at the centre of Western values. Political morality rests on the notion that "duties are owed, not only by each government to its subjects, but by one government to another, and by one people to another" (Wight 1966, 128). Wight disputed the idea that the determinations made by statesmen within the society of states were lacking in moral value because they were, more often than not, instrumental in character. As Wight (1996, 128) wrote, "political expedience itself has to consult the moral sense of those whom it will affect, and even combines with the moral sense of the politician himself. Thus it is softened into prudence, which is a moral virtue."

Wight's *via media* understanding of international ethics did not deny the possibility of moral vetoes operating in international society, despite his skepticism. In fact, Wight (1966, 130–1) wrote that "the upholding of moral standards will in itself tend to strengthen the fabric of political life." However, consistent with a position of moral skepticism, Wight was not willing to argue for the "truth" of such standards; according to Wight (1966, 131), that is a matter of the "philosophy of history, or belief in Providence."

A pivotal change in the British Committee's thinking about ethics and world politics occurred not long after Hedley Bull joined the group; serious consideration of international ethics as an idea of the good, a more maximal ethics, fell away. While moral absolutes were not viable for Bull, he posited his own middle-ground ethics, one that drew from his pluralist conception of international society. Bull's understanding was one of international ethics as international society management: a code of practice founded upon norms of sovereignty, nonintervention, self-determination, and toleration.

In pluralist international society, states agree to "certain minimum purposes" upon the basis of their shared interest in sustaining a world of heterogeneous states and are bound in a "compact of coexistence" (Bull 1966b, 52). The very structure of coexistence "depends on norms or rules conferring rights and duties upon states" (Bull 1977, 91). In the main, these are procedural rules, rather than moral rules, built upon "the imperatives of enlightened self-interest and law," but Bull argues that notions of inter-state justice do arise amid the interests that bind states— for example, rights to sovereignty and self-determination, applied to all. Thus, the compact of coexistence is also reinforced by a "moral imperative" (Bull 1977, 81–2, 91).

However, Bull would not invest inter-state justice with a capacity to serve as a moral veto of any kind; that is, as a moral maximum that promotes anything more than the good of maintaining order within a society of states. In fact, about the only notion of a moral maximum that Bull was willing to entertain was that of academic duty, and he saw it as a dereliction of that duty to invest in the existing norms and rules of international society anything more than the consensus among a society of states could withstand (Bull 1966a).

In sum, Wight and Bull are making a similar point: There is a kind of ethics in international relations, albeit not one built upon an idea of right or wrong founded on universal moral principle. Instead, their concepts of international ethics rest on ideas of right and wrong found within a practice of states. Their reliance on this empirical ground or starting point is a product of the moral skepticism they share. Yet, a key difference in their notions of international ethical possibility—why Bull's middle-ground ethics rests more decidedly in the second of Mackinnon's two ideas of ethics than Wight's—is that Bull's moral-knowledge skepticism was altogether secular and refused any and all philosophical grounds for moral claims, whereas Wight never relinquished a foundational belief in Providence.

Nonetheless, Bull (1977, 4–5) had his own idea of a universal from which obligation in international practice could be built: a universal need for order in social life founded upon the goals of security against violence, assurance that promises will be kept, and property protections. Bull drew upon H. L. A. Hart's legal philosophy to get to something foundational—what is basic and necessary to any societal interaction—that could hold up to empirical scrutiny and sustain claims about the value of international order without recourse to philosophy. So, when Bull (1977, 97–8) would argue, as he often did, that order is a "condition of the realization of other values" and must therefore be thought of as prior, he held this not as a general rule, but as something that had to be investigated in particular cases. It is a matter of political science rather than moral-philosophical investigation.

1.2 Beyond the British Committee: Second-generation English School

For R. J. Vincent, all international orders are linked to moral principle of a kind; therefore, to study them is not to choose between the "separate enterprises" of either "asserting values or gathering facts," but involves both prescription and description (Vincent 1986, 113). Where Bull worked to avoid prescription, Vincent thought it inescapable and in his book *Human Rights and International Relations* he asserted the notion of a basic right to life understood in terms of both security and subsistence. This is a major departure, a position not taken since the earliest days of the British Committee: that is, a willingness to posit a maximalist ethics of international society.

Nonetheless, true to the tradition of moral skepticism at the heart of the British Committee, Vincent was not willing to attribute anything natural or intrinsic to his notion of this basic right. He would not presume its existence; instead, it was a "wager" he was willing to make. Rather than take the "philosopher's route of rational construction" (Vincent 1986, 54), he examined the record of human rights talk—its substantiation in international law and the degree to which it is invoked by diplomats and policy-makers—to make this claim. While he concluded that the evidence of world society was "uneven" and that power remains with states, he argued that human rights contribute to understandings of state legitimacy in international society and may yet prove to be a "midwife" to world society (Vincent 1986, 128, 150–1).

As it happened, Vincent himself served as a "midwife" to an important transition within the English School tradition: a new willingness to engage the normative underpinnings of the three international orders—system, international society, and world society—and went so far as to assert moral claims in relation to each. Unlike Bull's few, unsupported assertions that world society is the appropriate direction for world politics, Vincent (1986, 150) wrote with moral conviction that starvation across the globe was wrong and that addressing it should no longer be seen as an act of charity, but a "doctrine of human rights imposing a correlative obligation." However, it must be stressed that his moral claim is couched in pragmatic rather than moral-philosophical arguments; such a project is "a less profitless one for international society than, say, the global extension of a western concept of liberty," as it is less likely to encounter "insurmountable ideological obstacles" (Vincent 1986, 150). Vincent (1986, 87, 146) emphasized the "pre-political" quality of basic needs due to the possibility of technological, programmatic answers to such issues.

The second generation of English School scholarship is influenced by and continues to draw from both Bull's empiricism and his characterization of pluralist and solidarist international orders, and Vincent's ambition of monitoring progress beyond international society and drawing moral conclusions about the normative assumptions associated with different international orders. Today, pluralists and solidarists look for evidence within a post-cold war era either to confirm or to deny that some tipping point into a solidarist international order has been reached, and they offer arguments, often more pragmatic and empirical than moral-philosophical, as to why a society of sovereign states has moral value (Jackson 2000), why the toleration of diversity is a good (Williams 2002), or why cosmopolitan duties to strangers are owed (Wheeler 2000).

Another contributing factor to the changes within second-generation English School scholarship is the rise of normative approaches to international relations in the mid-1980s and their philosophical critique of the English School's failure to provide reasoned arguments for its prioritization of the value of order (see Frost 1996). Indeed, Andrew Linklater (1990), one of the writers who shaped normative international relations theory in this period, did so drawing upon the resources of critical theory to question the normative assumptions of pluralist international society thinking. However, Linklater, in setting out his philosophy of history of the increasing self-actualization and moral inclusion of individuals through a scale of societal forms, drew upon the societal forms of international interaction charted by the English School. Solidarists today claim Linklater as one of their own and Linklater self-identifies with the English School as well, but it remains that he argues in a way that they do not; that is, he takes, as Vincent (1986, 54) puts it, "the philosopher's route of rational construction."

Linklater does not share the moral skepticism that has long been a part of this tradition. Therefore, he does not hold the same incredulity toward knowledge claims founded in moral-philosophical argument. Also, Linklater does not hold the same faith as pluralists, and most solidarists too, in the moral standing of a society of sovereign states, and thus looks to push ethical possibility beyond a minimal ethics of coexistence. While solidarists share Linklater's aim of casting wider nets of moral obligation among persons and building more just intersocietal relationships in line with a dialogic ethic, they prefer to ground these ethical priorities in the empirical evidence of what current inter-state relations can sustain, through either the consensus measures of international law, human rights, or humanitarian intervention.

In sum, the following common traits can be found in the concepts of international ethics offered by the English School: moral skepticism; a reliance upon empirical and pragmatic rather than moral-philosophical knowledge claims; and, yet, a recognition of international ethics as an interpenetration of the ideal and the actual or the normative and the empirical. However, the divisions that emerged within this tradition centered upon the question of what kind of international ethics; that is, whether a more minimalist or prudential and practice-based ethics was all that could be hoped for or whether a more maximalist idea of the good, founded in notions of personal morality, could indeed have purchase in interest-driven world politics. This question continues to orient many of the present concerns of the English School.

2 Defining the English School as an Approach to International Ethics

How then is the English School to be defined normatively? According to the English School, this much can be agreed on the basis of the consensus that operates in world politics: International ethics arises from the situatedness of states in a wider community of states. As Nicholas Wheeler (1996, 129) has written, at the base of international society theory is "the contention that state leaders are conscious of a minimal sense of moral community." Within this community, obligations follow from a shared interest in maintaining a world of heterogeneous, sovereign states that coexist on a basis of toleration in a societal context of rules and institutions. Where pluralists and solidarists disagree is in relation to a critical judgment of just how much "society" there is. Is it enough to sustain a more maximalist sense of moral community, one founded not on an interest-based morality of a lesser, more contingent order, but something more binding and perhaps absolute?

As long as moral community is analyzed with a view to measurement rather than judgment, as an exercise in the monitoring of international consensus and what it can support, then the normative definition of the English School will continue to be an open question, since international society itself is subject to change and interpretation. However, it is important to remember that this empirical question derives from a keen normative interest on the part of the English School: the sense of responsibility it feels to ensure international order first and foremost and then, where possible and without threat to the maintenance of international society, to aspire to the establishment of cosmopolitan duties to individuals. For pluralists, moral community does not run deep and cannot be relied upon to sustain cosmopolitan duties in international society. Nonetheless, obligations of an ethical kind do obtain, a code of practice represented in an ethics of coexistence. For solidarists, there are indications that from a minimum level of moral community, more maximal ethical concerns can be brought to bear within international society without compromising the edifice of this intersocietal form.

Assessments such as these about what the level of moral community in international society can withstand do not take seriously the English School's own contention that the empirical and the normative interpenetrate. Bull (1977) acknowledged that order and justice are interlinked, but he never explored the connection in any sustained way. The moral skepticism of this tradition makes finding a standpoint for critique and evaluative judgment difficult. Default to the consensus that can be read from the status quo of actually existing international practice on the part of both pluralists and solidarists begs the question of just how much can be discerned from such a moral community-monitoring enterprise and leaves the question of what direction for its normative ambitions underdeveloped.

The shift represented in second-generation English School scholarship toward engaging with moral-philosophical argument is a promising development, but its success will depend on whether it can find tools within this tradition for combining empirical analysis with the rational construction of moral criteria.

Pluralists have to build moral as well as empirical arguments for why the kind of moral inclusion found within a code of practice among a society of states is indeed morally significant. To the extent that it can provide philosophical support for the unique middle-ground ethics espoused by Wight and Bull, contemporary normative theory will be forced to address two potential strengths of the English School's focus: (1) its understanding that ethics and interest are not necessarily at odds with each other; and (2) its respect for moral conflict and deep-running appreciation of the difficulties of building moral community at a global level.

Solidarists already share with contemporary normative theorists a high level of optimism about the possibility of expanding moral inclusion of a maximal kind in world politics. However, what is left to be seen is whether they can indeed develop such criteria in keeping with the key aspects of this tradition or whether, like Linklater, they will have to abandon its moral skepticism and its deference to state practice. If solidarists are able to combine this kind of moral-philosophical analysis with the empirical work they are doing at present, they may motivate contemporary normative theory to do more in the way of engaging in institutional, practice-based analysis.

3 CONCLUSION

To develop any promise that either its middle-ground ethics of international society or its solidarist, cosmopolitan one might hold, the English School needs to find the epistemological resources of a more maximal concept of international ethics and at least approximate standards of a common good, supported by something other than arguments like "because it makes international society possible" or "because it maintains international society." A moral-philosophical justification of the "good" that this order represents is required, but can it be done in a way that is in keeping with the moral skepticism of the tradition?

Over the history of the English School, its adherents have faced this conundrum: the recognition that international society *cannot just manage, but that it must judge and be judged,* and that a more minimal concept of ethics as a code of practice is not always up to both tasks. Despite his protests against dogmatism and the taking of ideological/political standpoints in academic inquiry, Bull grew more willing to make the occasional statement of his own in relation to the tough choices between order and justice that preoccupied his later writing (Bull 1979*a*, 86; 1979*b*, 158–9). As far back as 1961, Bull (1961, 20–1) wrote that we should not shy away from expressing moral preferences nor should we endorse policies that contradict our ideas of what is right, but we must understand that these moral preferences are parochial and that they should be put forward with humility. As it became more clear to Bull that he could no longer sidestep substantive moral questions, he proceeded in just this manner: He would state his preference for human rights, but would at the same time acknowledge its grounding in Western values and say that this is a particular moral preference upon which one is disposed and right to act, but only with a certain self-awareness.

Since the linguistic turn in philosophy, alternatives to strong foundational arguments are available that would not require the English School to abandon its moral skepticism as it works to construct rational grounds for evaluative statements. In fact, efforts such as Bull's above resemble those of Richard Rorty, in particular his argument for the expansion of a "human rights culture" (Rorty 1993; Wheeler and Dunne 1998, 50–2). Also, it should be remembered that, from the start, Mackinnon sought quasi-foundations to support his preferred concept of international ethics constructed from an idea of the good.[1] While, for Mackinnon, natural law was no longer available as grounds for moral-philosophical justification, he did believe that natural lawlike idioms operated in world politics as a restraint on state actors and that exploring sympathy and tragedy within philosophy, literature, and international history could reinforce these idioms. This line of argument in Mackinnon has similarities with the work of Rorty (1989) as well.

Perhaps the principal mis-step within this tradition was the commonly held assumption that there is necessarily a weakness or vulnerability with any interest-based ethics that a maximalist one does not possess. Today, few are willing to argue that any idea of the good commands a status of absoluteness. Thus, the idea that a pluralist ethic of international society is of a lesser order than a cosmopolitan

---

[1] For more on quasi-foundations and international ethics, see Cochran (1999).

or solidarist one because it does not stand on something we more readily associate with principle, or that it is more precarious since it is grounded upon the interests of states and subject to the vagaries of power considerations, is mistaken. Indeed, any notion of the good that might be held by solidarist or normative theorists shares this vulnerability: There is little left in the way of strong foundations on which to ground their claims. No claim in relation to the "good" is any less subject to power and interest or the particularity of time and place than a claim grounded upon a code of practice. Neither side of this debate within the English School, nor in the debate between cosmopolitans and communitarians in normative theory, has knockdown arguments available to it. Each has to accept and work within limited horizons for its ethical ambitions as it examines the requirements of justice in the context of a coercive, interest-based society of states.

References

BCTIP (British Committee on the Theory of International Politics) 1960a. Informal talk. Friday 8 Jan., 9–11 p.m. Bodleian Library, Hedley Bull papers, Box 8, file 1.

——1960b. Discussion of Mackinnon's paper. Saturday 9 Jan., 10 a.m.–12.45 p.m. Bodleian Library, Box 8, file 1.

BULL, H. 1961. *The Control of the Arms Race: Disarmament and Arms Control in the Missile Age*. New York: Praeger.

——1966a. Society and anarchy in international relations. Pp. 35–50 in *Diplomatic Investigations: Essays in the Theory of International Politics*, ed. H. Butterfield and M. Wight. London: George Allen and Unwin.

——1966b. The Grotian conception of international society. Pp. 51–73 in *Diplomatic Investigations: Essays in the Theory of International Politics*, ed. H. Butterfield and M. Wight. London: George Allen and Unwin.

——1977. *The Anarchical Society: A Study of Order in World Politics*. London: Macmillan.

——1979a. Human rights and world politics. Pp. 79–91 in *Moral Claims in World Affairs*, ed. R. Pettman. Canberra: Australian National University Press.

——1979b. The universality of human rights. *Millennium: Journal of International Studies*, 8: 155–9.

COCHRAN, M. 1999. *Normative Theory in International Relations: A Pragmatic Approach*. Cambridge: Cambridge University Press.

FROST, M. 1996. *Ethics in International Relations: A Constitutive Theory*. Cambridge: Cambridge University Press.

JACKSON, R. 2000. *The Global Covenant: Human Conduct in a World of States*. Oxford: Oxford University Press.

LINKLATER, A. 1990. *Beyond Realism and Marxism: Critical Theory and International Relations*. London: Macmillan.

MACKINNON, D. 1960. Natural law. BCTIP paper. Bodleian Library, Hedley Bull papers, Box 8, file 1.

——1962*a*. Some notes on the notion of a Christian statesman. BCTIP paper. Bodleian Library, Hedley Bull papers, Box 8, file 1.

——1962*b*. Kant: on Perpetual Peace. BCTIP paper. Bodleian Library, Hedley Bull papers, Box 8, file 1.

MORGENTHAU, H. 2005. *Politics among Nations: The Struggle for Power and Peace*, 7th edn. New York: McGraw-Hill.

RORTY, R. 1989. *Contingency, Irony, and Solidarity*. Cambridge: Cambridge University Press.

——1993. Human rights, rationality, and sentimentality. Pp. 111–34 in *On Human Rights*, ed. S. Shute and S. Hurley. New York: Basic Books.

VINCENT, R. J. 1986. *Human Rights and International Relations*. Cambridge: Cambridge University Press.

WIGHT, M. 1966. Western values in international relations. Pp. 89–131 in *Diplomatic Investigations: Essays in the Theory of International Politics*, ed. H. Butterfield and M. Wight. London: George Allen and Unwin.

WHEELER, N. 1996. Guardian angel or global gangster: a review of the ethical claims of international society. *Political Studies*, 44: 123–35.

——2000. *Saving Strangers: Humanitarian Intervention in International Society*. Oxford: Oxford University Press.

——and DUNNE, T. 1998. Hedley Bull and the idea of a universal moral community: fictional, primordial or imagined? Pp. 43–58 in *International Society and the Development of International Relations Theory*, ed. B. Roberson. London: Pinter.

WILLIAMS, J. 2002. Territorial borders, toleration and the English School. *Review of International Studies*, 28: 737–58.

C H A P T E R 17

....

CONSTRUCTIVISM

....

IAN HURD

THE basic insight behind the constructivist approach can be understood by unpacking a quick observation made by Alexander Wendt. He says that "500 British
nuclear weapons are less threatening to the United States than 5 North Korean
nuclear weapons" (Wendt 1995, 73). In this little observation are found traces of
the features that distinguish constructivism from other approaches to international
relations, including its critique of materialism, its emphasis on the social construction of interests, its relationship between structures and agents, and its multiple
logics of anarchy. On its surface, the empirical puzzle of the threat embodied by
North Korean missiles is easy to explain: As Wendt (1995, 73) says, "the British
are friends and the North Koreans are not." This of course begs an understanding
of the categories of friend and enemy, and it is through this opening that Wendt
and other constructivists have addressed both important substantive aspects of
international relations (for instance, "how do states come to see others as friends
and as enemies?") and the philosophical background it presupposes (for instance,
"how can we study social and relational phenomena like 'friend' and 'enemy' in
international relations?").

This chapter examines the features that distinguish constructivism from other
approaches to international relations and then looks at some controversies within
constructivist scholarship today and between constructivists and others. There are
many excellent short histories of the constructivist school (e.g. Barnett 2005; Reus-
Smit 2005), and my goal is to avoid repeating them and instead explain what I
think the term constructivism means in international relations. To do so, I also

For very useful comments on earlier drafts, I thank Karen Alter, Chris Reus-Smit, and Duncan
Snidal.

define other approaches, including materialism, realism, and rationalism, in order to show how constructivism differs. This involves some controversy, because the lines that separate them are not at all clear. In what follows, I take realism to be at its core about materialism (that is, the theory that states respond to *material* needs, incentives, and power) and rationalism to be about instrumentalism (that is, the theory that states pursue individual advantage by calculating costs and benefits). Constructivism, by contrast, emphasizes the *social* and *relational* construction of what states are and what they want. All these approaches might be used to focus on power politics, cooperation, conflict, or any other substantive phenomena. It is, therefore, wrong to associate a substantive interest in power exclusively with realism, because all the "paradigms" of international relations are interested in power, as either motivation, cause, or effect. I differentiate realism as a particular theory about *material* power in international relations, in contrast with constructivism's emphasis on the social meaning attached to objects or practices.[1]

In asking for an explanation of the importance in world politics of social concepts like friend and enemy, the constructivist challenge opened two paths. One was more empirical and used the tools provided by Friedrich Kratochwil (1989), Nicholas Onuf (1989), Wendt (1992), and other constructivists to explain anomalies of other approaches. The other was more conceptual and concerned how these social concepts might work in the world and how they could be studied and used in study. From constructivism's starting point as a reaction to materialism, individualism, and rationalism, the empirical branch of research was like a downstream flow; it applied the insights of constructivism to understand interesting patterns, behaviors, and puzzles. The philosophic branch went upstream—it sought to understand the reasons for, and implications of, the differences between constructivism and other approaches to social phenomena.

1 THE DISTINGUISHING FEATURES OF CONSTRUCTIVISM

This section outlines four features of constructivism that distinguish it from other approaches and show how constructivism addresses both philosophical and empirical issues that were inaccessible through the prevailing models of international relations in the 1980s. The four are not necessarily exclusive to constructivism, but each has a constructivist variant that is distinct from both the materialism of

---

[1] J. Samuel Barkin (2003), by contrast, defines realism as a concern with "power" and then notes that this is consistent with social construction. I agree that classical realists incorporated nonmaterial forces, but by my definition that makes them less "realist."

realism and the rationalism of neoliberalism, and carries distinct implications for how world politics is studied.

1.1 An Alternative to Materialism

The original insight behind constructivism is that meaning is "socially constructed." This is also the source of the label "constructivism." Wendt (1992, 396–7) says "a fundamental principle of constructivist social theory is that people act toward objects, including other actors, on the basis of the meanings that the objects have for them."[2] In a socially constructed world, the existence of patterns, cause-and-effect relationships, and even states themselves depends on webs of meaning and practices that constitute them (e.g. Kratochwil 1989). These meanings and practices might sometimes be relatively stable, but they are never fixed and should not be mistaken for permanent objects.[3] As ideas and practices vary over time or space, patterns that once looked solid and predictable may change as well. For instance, sovereignty is a social institution in the sense that a state can be sovereign only when it is seen by people and other states as a corporate actor with rights and obligations over territory and citizens (and they act accordingly). The practice of sovereignty has changed over time, and the powers and identities of actually existing states have changed as well (see, e.g., the essays in Biersteker and Weber 1996). To take a more concrete example, since 1945 the idea has spread that massive human rights violations by states against their citizens may legally justify international intervention. Sovereignty is thereby changing, and the autonomy of some rulers (that is, rights violators) is reduced while that of others (potential interveners) is increased. Sovereignty is an important organizing force in international relations that rests on the shared ideas of people and the practices people engage in.

A contrasting approach to "social construction" in world politics is the position known as "materialism," which suggests that material objects (bombs, mountains, people, oil, and so on) have a direct effect on outcomes that is unmediated by the ideas people bring to them. Neorealism and neoliberalism are explicitly materialist approaches to world politics. They seek to explain international patterns and be-haviors as the result of purely material forces, particularly the military hardware, strategic resources, and money that they see as constituting "power." For example, John Mearsheimer (1995, 91) argues that "the distribution of material capabilities among states is the key factor for understanding world politics." Among neoliberals, Joshua Goldstein and Robert Keohane (1994) identify states' material interests as distinct from people's ideas about the world, and their research on the causal effects of ideas uses as its baseline the materialist hypothesis. Neorealists and neoliberals in

[2] This insight appears also in the work of Hedley Bull and the English School as well as of some classical realists.

[3] This is the mistake of "reification."

the 1980s shared a commitment to materialism in which socially mediated beliefs were not important autonomous forces, and they argued among themselves over the likely implications of such a world for patterns such as cooperation, institution-making, arms races, and balancing (see, e.g., the essays in Baldwin 1993).

The ideas that give shape to international politics are more than just the beliefs of individuals. They include ideas that are intersubjective (that is, shared among people) and institutionalized (that is, expressed as practices and identities). Intersubjective and institutionalized forms of ideas "are not reducible to individual minds" (Wendt 1999, ch. 4; Legro 2005, 5). Jeffrey Legro (2005, 6) summarizes the constructivist understanding of ideas: "ideas are not so much mental as symbolic and organizational; they are embedded not only in human brains but also in the 'collective memories,' government procedures, educational systems, and the rhetoric of statecraft." This makes it clear that the constructivist insight is not that we replace "brute materialism" with "brute idealism" (cf. Palan 2000). Rather, constructivism suggests that material forces must be understood through the social concepts that define their meaning for human life.

A purely materialist approach has difficulty explaining why the United States should see British missiles as any less threatening than North Korean missiles. The "self-evident" friendliness of Britain toward the United States as compared to the apparent hostility of North Korea is not self-evident from a purely material perspective. After all, the physical consequences of an attack by the nuclear weapons of either country would be devastating. The brute material threat to the United States posed by a British nuclear weapon is at least comparable to, and probably much greater than, that of a North Korean weapon. The difference between the two is the conviction among many American leaders that the North Koreans are more likely to act aggressively toward the United States than are the British. This conviction is based on interpretations of history, rhetoric, and behavior, and it generates the expectation that war with North Korea is more likely than war with the British, and in turn leads to different policy strategies in response to their weapons.

For constructivists, beliefs, expectations, and interpretations are inescapable when thinking about international affairs, and their importance shows that the materialist position is untenable. While the shift from a materialist to a socially constructed view of international relations was controversial in the early 1990s, it has now been broadly accepted. The constructivist insight has been largely internalized by the discipline.[4] Even materialist theories of international relations now generally openly include at least two kinds of ideas (though mostly individual rather than collective ideas): first, "non-material" factors such as (for Mearsheimer 2001, 58) "strategy, intelligence, [and] resolve," and, secondly, socially constructed interests. However, they usually also claim that the practical importance of the social content

---

[4] Jennifer Sterling-Folker (2000) argues that this was made easier by the fact that many putatively materialist theories of international relations already incorporated social content. See also Wendt (1992); Williams (2005).

of international relations is minimal when compared to the influence of brute material factors, and so the research agendas of neorealism and neoliberalism have at once conceded the constructivist insight while maintaining their core claims.

As the socially constructed nature of world politics has been broadly accepted, it has become clear that what remains contestable between constructivists and others is *how* (not "whether") this insight affects the study of world politics, both in its methodology and in its substance. The debate over the construction of state interests and their sources follows from this debate.

1.2 The Construction of State Interests

The scholarly interest in the "national interest" has always been central to international relations and foreign-policy analysis. The constructivist approach has been productive in this area because of its focus on the *social* content involved in the production of international relations, including state interests.

While most scholars now acknowledge that state interests are at base *ideas* about needs, many nonconstructivists maintain that the *content* of those interests is for practical purposes unchanging and includes some combination of the desires for survival, power, wealth, and security. They contend that the socially constructed nature of interests does not alter the fact that the primary interests that drive states are prefigured by the material resources and situation of the states, and so states are either constructed by material forces or can be treated as if their construction is irrelevant to their interests and behavior (e.g. Brooks and Wohlforth 2007). States are "minimally constructed."

By contrast, constructivists would argue that the apparent "hostility" of North Korean missiles shows that American leaders respond to the social relationship between the United States and the military resources of others, friend or enemy, rather than to the hardware itself. These social relations are not fixed, and the American national interest therefore cannot be ascertained, let alone pursued, without considering them. The United States has an interest in resisting North Korea, because American leaders perceive a hostile relationship with it, while it has no interest in containing the UK, because it perceives a mutually beneficial relationship. Constructivists often find it useful to examine the historical construction of "national interests" (e.g. Finnemore 1996; 2003; Weldes 1999).

It is sometimes said that the difference between constructivism and other approaches is that the former is concerned with the construction of interests while the latter take interests as fixed and given (see, e.g., Goldstein 2005, 126). This is not true. Nor is it true that only constructivists suggest that state interests might be influenced by forces at the level of the international system. Constructivists do not have a monopoly on the study of how interests are made or of systemic influences on interests. Many nonconstructivists are interested in how states come to hold the interests that structure their decision-making. Andrew Moravcsik (1999), for instance, provides a liberal theory of how state interests are constructed out of the economic interests of domestic industries and coalitions. Stephen Krasner (1999) argues from a realist perspective that individual rulers present as the national interest the policies they believe will ensure their personal survival as rulers. (Both present these as "material" factors though they rest on ideas about needs.) Game theorists sometimes endogenize the formation of interests so that interests change as a result of interactions (e.g. Gerber and Jackson 1993). On system-level influences, Jon Pevehouse (2005) uses broadly rationalist tools to examine how the constitution of states is affected by their membership and participation in regional organizations.

What distinguishes a specifically *constructivist* story on interests is that the influences on interest formation are *social*. Legro (2005, 4) represents the constructivist view: "new foreign policy ideas are shaped by preexisting dominant ideas and their relationship to experienced events."[5] This follows directly from the insight on social construction above. Wendt (1992, 397) says "actors acquire identities—relatively stable, role-specific understandings and expectations about self—by participating in... collective meanings." Interests are in part products of those identities. The social constitution of interests encompasses all the ways that actors' interests and identities might be influenced by their interactions with others and with their social environment. This includes the processes of socialization and internalization (Hurd 1999), the drive for social recognition and prestige (Wendt 1999, ch. 5), the effects of social norms on interests and on behavior (including the desire to create norms that legitimize one's behavior) (Hurd 2007a), and the presence or absence of a sense of "community" (Adler and Barnett 1998).

1.3 Mutual Constitution of Structures and Agents

The constructivist attention to the social construction of interests and identities introduces the more general problem of the relationship between structures and agents. By "structures" I mean the institutions and shared meanings that make up the context of international action, and by "agents" I mean any entity that operates as an actor in that context. Returning to Wendt's illustration, the relationship of enmity that makes the United States fear North Korean nuclear weapons is not a fixed and stable fact. It is, instead, a result of ongoing interactions both between the two states and among the states and their social context. These interactions may reinforce the relation of enmity or they may change it. They may also reinforce or change the broader social structures in which the actors exist, including norms and other forms of shared meaning regarding sovereignty, threat, and interests.

---

[5] Contrast this with realism, of which Moravcsik (1999, 680, n. 6) says "the distribution of ideas and information is a function of the underlying distribution of material power resources."

The co-constitution of states and structures goes beyond recognizing that there are interaction effects between the unit and the system level. Kenneth Waltz emphasized interaction effects but in a way that maintained states as unchanging units. In *Theory of International Politics*, he suggested that two states interacting in anarchy are "not just influencing the other" by their actions; "both are being influenced by the situation their interaction creates" (Waltz 1979, 74). Consistent with his materialist premise, Waltz looked for how this changed the material incentives facing states as they weighed policy alternatives.

A constructivist approach to co-constitution, by contrast, suggests that the actions of states contribute to making the institutions and norms of international life, and these institutions and norms contribute to defining, socializing, and influencing states. Both the institutions and the actors can be redefined in the process. The recognition of mutual constitution is an important contribution to the theory of international relations, because many interesting empirical phenomena in international relations are understandable only by a methodology that avoids assuming a neat separation between agents and structures. In studying international norms, it quickly becomes clear that states are concerned simultaneously with shifting their behavior to match the rules and reconstructing the rules to condone their behavior (Hurd 2007a). For instance, when states claim they are using force only in self-defense, they cannot avoid reinforcing Articles 2(4) and 51 of the UN Charter (which forbid aggressive war) and at the same time are redefining the rules by specifying how they wish the concepts of "sovereignty," "self-defense," and "aggression" to be understood. International norms are simultaneously the products of state actions and influences upon state action. Thus, the idea that states and the international environment are mutually constituted is inherent in the constructivist approach.

1.4 Multiple Logics of Anarchy

The constructivist approach leads to a different interpretation of international anarchy from the one offered by neorealists or neoliberals, and, to the extent that the concept of anarchy organizes international life, it therefore leads to different understandings of world politics more generally.

"Anarchy" is the term used in international relations to describe a social system that lacks legitimated institutions of authority (Milner 1991). It is a formal condition of a system in the sense that it describes any system that is not organized through hierarchical structures of authority and command. Waltz (1979), in defining the neorealist school, derived from the structural condition of anarchy a set of predictions about the behavior of units, including balancing behavior, self-help strategies, and a self-interested identity. Wendt's critique of Waltz showed that these patterns did not follow simply from the structural condition of anarchy; they came from the additional assumption that units see each other as rivals over scarce goods. "Rivalry" is a social relationship that can best be understood, in international relations and elsewhere, by examining its social construction. This requires acknowledging that the relationship is not fixed, natural, or permanent. Wendt proposed a spectrum of international anarchies based on variation in the ideas that states have about themselves and others. With enmity at one end and friendship at the other, and with indifference in the middle, the formal condition of anarchy is by itself not very informative about the behavior of the units. After all, he says, "an anarchy of friends differs from one of enemies" (Wendt 1995, 78). This allows for the possibility of community (Adler and Barnett 1998; Cronin 1999), hierarchy (Simpson 2004), rivalry (Wendt 1992), and other social relations within a formally anarchic structure. Inter-state conflict is also conditioned by the social qualities of international anarchy, as illustrated by the efforts of states to appear to operate within the confines of the norms on war.[6] Such diverse behaviors, and others, are compatible with the anarchical structure of the international system, and can be addressed through the constructivist approach. (I discuss below the constructivist possibility that the system is not anarchic.)

These four elements are the distinguishing features of constructivism in international relations theory. They are related to each other in the sense that, if one adopts the first idea (that is, that world politics is partly socially constructed), then the other three logically follow as implications for studying international relations. However, each of the other three is also consistent with nonconstructivist premises. For instance, one need not be a constructivist to study the origins of national interests, nor does finding that anarchy may differ across time and place necessarily mean that one is using a constructivist approach. This has helped to generate controversy over what is and is not constructivist research in international relations. The irreducible core of constructivism for international relations is the recognition that international reality is socially constructed. This has implications for the concept of anarchy, for the agent–structure relationship, and for national interests, but all three of these areas of research are also approachable through nonconstructivist means.

2 CONTROVERSIES WITHIN CONSTRUCTIVISM

In defining constructivism in this way, widely diverse research falls within its scope. This includes work with major differences on issues such as the unit of analysis, the possibility of positivist paths to knowledge, and the nature of the international

---

[6] On shared norms that govern inter-state war, see Price and Tannenwald (1996); Price (1998); Sands (2005). On humanitarian intervention, see Welsh (2002).

system. In this section I highlight some of the controversies that arise over these issues and illustrate both the breadth of constructivist scholarship and the antagonisms it engenders among scholars.

2.1 State-centrism

The constructivist approach does not imply any particular unit of analysis as fundamental in the study of international relations. As a result, it is compatible with a kind of pluralism about the unit that has been both productive and contentious among international relations scholars.

The process of social construction cannot be understood by focusing exclusively on forces or actors at any of the three "levels of analysis" conventionally used in international relations theory (Waltz 1959; 1979). For any given puzzle in international relations, there are undoubtedly important elements of the answer to be found at all levels of analysis. In addition, one can examine how actors and structures at all levels of analysis are socially constructed. Constructivists have therefore provided interesting research on the constitution of individual state identity, on the making of meso-level norms and practices, and on the constitution of the international system (see, respectively, Lynch 1999; Shannon 2000; Reus-Smit 1999). The emphasis on forces or actors at one level over others may be defensible on pragmatic grounds given the interests of the particular scholar, but the co-constitution of actors and structures means there is no impetus in constructivism for a zero-sum debate over "which" level provides the most leverage over puzzles. There is no point in constructivist research to arguments over whether, for instance, domestic politics "matters" or not in international relations.

There is, however, room for debate over what can be taken as given by assumption at the start of a piece of empirical research. For instance, to take states as given in order to study how their interactions are structured by and contribute to a particular set of international norms implies setting aside the (prior) social construction of the state as an institution. This is potentially problematic, since the historical construction of states as sovereign may well be an important element of any story about how states interact with norms. The analytic separation of actors, practices, and structures as distinct entities can be problematic, though it may sometimes be useful. The dilemma of what to problematize and what to take as given is inherent in all research, and by focusing on the complexities of mutual constitution the constructivist approach encourages scholars to be open about what is lost by their particular choices and assumptions. This at least makes possible debate over the trade-offs implicit in these choices.

2.2 Science and Positivism

The recognition of social construction in world politics leads directly into a controversy over epistemology and the use of scientific methods in the field of international relations. This divides constructivism into a positivist and a postpos-itivist camp, distinguished by their positions on epistemological questions and the methods they believe are useful given those epistemological positions.

Positivist epistemology maintains that the socially constructed international system contains patterns that are amenable to generalization and to falsifiable hypotheses. These patterns are the product of underlying laws that govern social relations, where the laws can be identified by careful scientific research. While the methods that are appropriate to study world politics may not be those of laboratory science (for instance, controlled experiments with a strict separation between ob-server and event), the ultimate goal of the social scientific project is the same as for the physical sciences—explaining cause-and-effect relationships that are believed to exist independently of the observer's presence. Positivist constructivists are careful to include constitutive explanations among the cause–effect relations they seek to understand, but they approach the study of social constitution with the same tools of social science (e.g. Wendt 1999; 2000; Finnemore 2003; Barnett 2005).

A competing view, represented by postpositivists, is that in social life data are not fully objectifiable, observers cannot be fully autonomous of the subject under study, and social relationships cannot be separated into discrete "causes" and "effects."[7] What social "laws" a scholar might observe are, therefore, inherently contingent rather than existing naturally and objectively in the world.[8] As a result, according to David Campbell (2007, 209–10), social inquiry "has to be concerned with the social constitution of meaning, the linguistic construction of reality, and the historicity of knowledge. This reaffirms the indispensability of interpretation, and suggests that all knowledge involves a relationship with power in its mapping of the world." Claims to knowledge about world politics both reflect and act as structures of power, and there are no "Archimedean points from which to assess the validity of analytical and ethical knowledge claims" (Price and Reus-Smit 1998, 262). In this view, the purpose of theorizing is not to identify and test hypotheses about lawlike regularities. Instead, one objective for research is to interpret how social meaning and power produce the apparent stability in the social world (Devetak 2005, 169).

The epistemological divide between positivists and postpositivists runs deep and may represent a decisive fissure among constructivists, and the matter is particularly sharp over the issue of ethics. (See Price, this volume.) For postpositivists, the ethical implications of international relations theory begin immediately once a scholar adopts or argues for an interpretative stance within which claims can be made. Without the positivist's faith in an independently existing reality of world politics, the postpositivist is attentive from the start about the ethical consequences of the concepts and assumptions that frame the research. The positivist, by contrast, works from the assumption that he or she is insulated by the belief that describing

---

[7] I am grateful to Elizabeth Shakman Hurd for her comments on this section.

[8] Richard Price and Christian Reus-Smit (1998) argue for a middle position of "contingent gener-alizations." On the capacity of international relations theory to constitute the international world, see Ashley (1986); Campbell (1998); Williams (2005).

objectively existing relations makes ethical issues a separate question. For the positivist, the question of what "is" can be separated from what "ought."

The postpositivist position within constructivism is no less empirical (though not "empiricist" (Campbell 2007, 208–9)) than the positivist tradition. It is, however, empirical in a way that reflects the methods appropriate to its epistemology. For instance, Campbell's study (1998, 13) of the Bosnian wars examines how:

> the settled norms of international society—in particular, the idea that the national community requires the nexus of demarcated territory and fixed identity—were not only insufficient to enable a response to the Bosnian war, they were complicit in and necessary for the conduct of the war itself. This is because inscribing the boundaries that make the installation of the nationalist imaginary possible requires the expulsion from the resultant "domestic" space of all that comes to be regarded as alien, foreign, and dangerous.

For Campbell, the Bosnian violence was exacerbated by outsiders' insistence that there exists an underlying "law" of ethnic intolerance that counsels that the ethnic groups of Bosnia must be physically separated from each other. A more ethical response is possible, he suggests, by critiquing the assumption that individuals have unitary ethnic identities that map cleanly onto unitary territorial nation states.

2.3 Anarchy or Authority?

Constructivists disagree among themselves on the nature of the international system. This is reflected in the debate over whether the system can be characterized as an "anarchy."

Most constructivists have operated within what Ashley (1988) called the "anarchy problematique," a position that they share with neoliberals and neorealists. This view acknowledges the existence of a formal condition of anarchy among states and makes anarchy a crucial element of the international structure. It sees hierarchy as the alternative to anarchy, where hierarchy refers to a system in which the units "stand vis-à-vis each other in relations of super- and subordination" (Waltz 1979, 81). On this level, constructivists often agree with the neorealists and neoliberals that anarchy is the fundamental organizing principle of the international system, even though they may disagree with their claims about the implications of that condition for state behavior (Cronin 1999, for instance, argues that there is "community under anarchy"). They argue that the social construction of cultural content within an anarchic system produces variation in the structural constraints and opportunities for units and therefore leads to variation in outcomes and in the patterns of state behavior. As a formal condition, anarchy remains.

However, constructivism also opens the possibility that changes in the social relations among states could transform the anarchical system into something that is not anarchic (Wendt 1999, 307–8). The key concept here is authority. Authority refers to a relation of legitimated power (Ruggie 1998, 65; Barnett and Finnemore 2004, ch. 1; Hurd 2007*b*). It creates a social hierarchy within which subordinates feel an obligation to follow the directives of the authoritative rule or actor. Authority and anarchy are therefore mutually exclusive. While some constructivists have remained within the anarchy problematique, others have found empirical evidence of the existence of institutions of legitimated power. International authority can be found in international organizations, in firms, and in practices such as international law. It exists in both public and private institutions. Public forms might include the UN Secretary-General (Barnett 2001), the UN Security Council (Hurd 2007*b*), the discourses of international law (Johnstone 2005), and norms on legitimate intervention (Finnemore 2003). Private forms include the legitimated power of firms and institutions in international markets (Sinclair 1999; Hall and Biersteker 2003). In settings where states recognize a rule, institution, or actor as having the right to make authoritative decisions on their behalf, we must recognize that authority rather than anarchy exists.

Just as the epistemological disagreement among constructivists over positivism may create a fundamental disjuncture between two world-views, the controversy over the existence of anarchy defines two camps. The presence or absence of authority divides constructivists between a "conventional" strand, which shares the anarchy problematique with neorealists and neoliberals, and a "post-anarchy" strand that rejects the anarchist view on empirical grounds. The disagreement is basically empirical—that is, it is over whether authority exists or not—and so it might be more amenable to resolution than is the epistemological divide that separates positivists and postpositivists (see Hurd 2008 on the possibility of empirical "tests" of international authority). The conventional view allows that the *content* of anarchy might change (due to coordinating institutions, a shared culture, or other factors) but the basic structural *condition* of anarchy as the foundation of the international system does not. By contrast, the post-anarchy view is a fundamental challenge to the shared premise that anarchy is the continuing basis for international politics, and it has affinity with the English School, which has always been more attached to the image of an "international society" than international anarchy (see, e.g., Clark 2005).

3 CONTINUING CHALLENGES IN INTERNATIONAL RELATIONS THEORY

The rise of the constructivist approach has encouraged new strands of empirical and philosophical research in international relations, and has led to interesting problems at the boundary between constructivism and other approaches. Two strands of research, on the relations between strategic behavior and international norms and between rationalism and constructivism, serve as examples of promising research in constructivist international relations theory.

3.1 Strategic Behavior and Norms

It is a mistake to characterize constructivism as focused on norms as opposed to neorealism and neoliberalism, which are alleged to be focused on power and interests.[9] This is a common trope, and it is highly misleading. It obscures what is perhaps the most interesting and challenging puzzle in international relations theory—disentangling the relationship between strategic actors and social/normative influences. Most constructivists agree that states act in the pursuit of what they see as their interests, and all are as concerned with "power and interest" as are realists (and liberals). What differentiates these approaches are the sources that they identify for state interests, and the content of those interests. There is no reason that the study of international norms by constructivists is inherently mutually exclusive with the study of strategic behavior. The social construction of actors may well create instrumental, goal-seeking agents who pursue their goals in part by comparing costs and benefits, and their behavior cannot be understood apart from that process of construction. In other words, it is a mistake to separate the study of the logic of consequences from the logic of appropriateness (cf. March and Olsen 1998). The more strictly that separation is enforced, the less insightful is the empirical research that can result.

This conclusion is the logical consequence of my opening definitions, where I suggested that materialism, rather than rationalism, should be seen as the opposite of constructivism.[10] Constructivism generally agrees with rationalism that states perceive some needs and interests and they act in order to satisfy them. To this, constructivism adds two things: an interest in explaining how state needs and interests come to be, and the possibility that different constructions of states could lead to radically different types of states and patterns of state behavior. Constructivism problematizes states and their interests and identities, but it has no problem accepting that states generally pursue "interests." It is with materialism that constructivism has the more fundamental disagreement—there is a clear distinction between the position that actors respond directly to material incentives and the view that meaning and interpretation necessarily mediate between material forces and

---

[9] Mearsheimer (1995, 86) identifies "power and interest" as variables associated exclusively with realist theory, so that when others make reference to them he concludes that they have become realists. Fred Halliday (2005, 32–3) says that constructivist scholars "run the risk of ignoring interests and material factors, let alone old-fashioned deception and self-delusion."

[10] Michael Barnett (2005), by contrast, sees rationalism as the opposite of constructivism.

social actors. Behavior is motivated, and is studied, only through lenses acquired in and through social interaction.

3.2 Constructivism and Rationalism

The relationship between strategic behavior and international norms raises more general questions about the relationship between constructivism and rationalism, and this theme has recently received a great deal of attention. At issue are questions including whether the two stand as competitors to each other or complements, the nature of the disagreement between them, and the useful scope of each.

The two approaches are often presented as competitors to each other. There are two versions of this claim. One suggests that rationalism and constructivism predict different behaviors from states and these differences should be measurable and testable. Jeffrey Lewis (2003) takes this approach to studying EU decision-making and he performs his "test" by assuming that strategic, instrumental behavior by states is evidence in favor of rationalism, while evidence of norm internalization supports constructivism. He treats the two as mutually exclusive and zero sum. The second version of the competitive relation argues that rationalism and constructivism are based on ontological commitments that are irreconcilable. These might be about holism or individualism, inherent or constructed rationality, or social construction versus essentialism. To the extent that these are fundamental commitments about what world politics is made of, they are unbridgeable.

There are also at least two versions of the claim that rationalism and constructivism are complementary to each other. One version sees the two as asking different questions about international relations and therefore as being fundamentally uninvolved with each other. This view suggests a division of labor in which constructivism is suited to answering questions about how actors acquire their interests and identities and rationalism specializes in explaining the pursuit of interests by already constituted actors. Sterling-Folker (2000, 97; cf. March and Olsen 1998), for instance, argues that rationalist institutionalism seeks to explain "short-term behavioral cooperation in the moment," while constructivism aims to explain "its development into communal cooperation in the future." In her view, the two cannot be competitors over the same turf because they are targeted at distinct questions. This approach presumes that the real world contains separable realms that are amenable to each approach and that the two realms do not overlap. Conflicts between the two are therefore avoidable as long as the boundary between the two realms is respected. A second version sees the two as providing different views on the shared questions. Duncan Snidal and Alexander Thompson (2002, 200), for instance, examine the ways in which international institutions constrain states and, finding both rationalism and constructivism useful, conclude that the two "provide different lenses through which to view the same empirical phenomena and outcomes." On this view, the two are relevant to the same subject matter, but their different emphases allow, when combined, for greater insight into a problem than is provided by each alone.

The relationship between rationalism and constructivism is ultimately an artifact of one's definition of the two approaches. Defining either one requires also defining the other, and so the relation between them is epiphenomenal of these definitions. By categorizing constructivism as a research agenda concerned with the social construction of actors, structures, and practices in international relations, I presume from the start that there are some kinds of research that are inaccessible to rationalist methods and assumptions, and this automatically brings up aspects of the complementary view. I am therefore skeptical of the competitive versions of the constructivism–rationalism distinction. The competitive empirical tests proposed by Lewis are undermined by the fact that the behavioral distinctions between the two are extremely faint. My definition of constructivism does not support the view that strategic behavior by states is evidence for the rationalist view and against the constructivist view. As James Fearon and Wendt (2002) suggest, there may be no measurable variables in behavior that neatly differentiate the two approaches. A more substantive gap exists over the ontological questions regarding the nature of international actors and forces. A theory of ontology is unavoidable, not optional, and disagreements about ontology are real, profound, and consequential (Wight 2006). They might also, however, be best approached by setting against each other the research that follows from different ontological positions, rather than arguing for or against a theory of ontology in the abstract. It is the *consequences* (both ethical and analytical) of different ontological assumptions that are worth arguing about. Therefore, while there are indeed competing ontological positions between constructivists and others in international relations, the productive way forward would seem to be to assess the insights they generate when applied in research rather than compare them directly. This supports in practice the pluralism in research methods encouraged by the complementary views above, though it does not give up on the possibility that there are underlying differences in ontology between rationalism and constructivism.

4 Conclusion

To be a constructivist in international relations means looking at international relations with an eye open to the social construction of actors, institutions, and events. It means beginning from the assumption that how people and states think and behave in world politics is premised on their understanding of the world around them, which includes their own beliefs about the world, the identities they hold about themselves and others, and the shared understandings and practices in which they participate. It should be clear, therefore, what constructivism is *not*: It does not mean setting aside the ideas that material power is important or that actors make instrumental calculations of their interests; nor does it necessarily assume the a priori existence of sovereign states, epistemological positivism, or the anarchy problematique. Rather, it means that what goes on in these categories and concepts is constructed by social processes and interactions, and that their relevance for international relations is a function of the social construction of meaning.

One sign of constructivism's success in the past twenty years is the degree to which other approaches have come to recognize the socially constructed content of some of the concepts they use. The goods of realist competition, for instance, include status, prestige, reputation, and hegemony, all of which make sense only in terms of either legitimated power or shared understandings. They are, therefore, the stuff of constructivism as well. This has had the result of blurring the boundaries between the approaches, making them hard to define in exclusive terms, and raising the possibility that to attempt to define them creates artificial distinctions. The differences between realism, rationalism, and constructivism may be contested, but we move forward in arguing about them only by first being clear what we mean by the terms.

REFERENCES

ADLER, E., and BARNETT, M. 1998. Security communities in theoretical perspective. Pp. 3–28 in *Security Communities*, ed. E. Adler and M. Barnett. Cambridge: Cambridge University Press.

ASHLEY, R. K. 1986. The poverty of neorealism. Pp. 255–300 in *Neorealism and its Critics*, ed. R. O. Keohane. New York: Columbia University Press.

——1988. Untying the sovereign state: a double reading of the anarchy problematique. *Millennium: Journal of International Studies*, 17: 227–62.

BALDWIN, D. A. (ed.) 1993. *Neorealism and Neoliberalism: The Contemporary Debate*. New York: Columbia University Press.

BARKIN, J. S. 2003. Realist constructivism. *International Studies Review*, 5: 325–42.

BARNETT, M. 2001. Authority, intervention, and the outer limits of international relations theory. Pp. 47–68 in *Intervention and Transnationalism in Africa: Global-Local Networks of Power*, ed. T. Callaghy, R. Kassimir, and R. Latham. Cambridge: Cambridge University Press.

——2005. Social constructivism. Pp. 251–70 in *The Globalization of World Politics: An Introduction to International Relations*, 3rd edn., ed. J. Baylis and S. Smith. Oxford: Oxford University Press.

——and FINNEMORE, M. 2004. *Rules for the World: International Organizations in Global Politics*. Ithaca, NY: Cornell University Press.

BIERSTEKER, T. J., and WEBER C. 1996. *State Sovereignty as Social Construct*. Cambridge: Cambridge University Press.

BROOKS, S. G., and WOHLFORTH W. 2007. *World out of Balance: International Relations Theory and the Challenge of American Primacy*. Princeton, NJ: Princeton University Press.

CAMPBELL, D. 1998. *National Deconstruction: Violence, Identity, and Justice in Bosnia*. Minneapolis: University of Minnesota Press.

—— 2007. Poststructuralism. Pp. 203–28 in *International Relations Theories: Discipline and Diversity*, ed. T. Dunne, M. Kurki, and S. Smith. Oxford: Oxford University Press.

CLARK, I. 2005. *Legitimacy in International Society*. Oxford: Oxford University Press.

CRONIN, B. 1999. *Cooperation under Anarchy: Transnational Identity and the Evolution of Cooperation*. New York: Columbia University Press.

DEVETAK, R. 2005. Postmodernism. Pp. 161–87 in *Theories of International Relations*, 3rd edn., ed. S. Burchill et al. New York: Palgrave.

FEARON, J., and WENDT, A. 2002. Rationalism v. constructivism: a skeptical view. Pp. 52–72 in *Handbook of International Relations*, ed. W. Carlsnaes, T. Risse, and B. A. Simmons. London: Sage.

FINNEMORE, M. 1996. *National Interests in International Society*. Ithaca, NY: Cornell University Press.

—— 2003. *The Purpose of Intervention: Changing Beliefs about the Use of Force*. Ithaca, NY: Cornell University Press.

GERBER, E. R., and JACKSON, J. E. 1993. Endogenous preferences and the study of institutions. *American Political Science Review*, 87: 639–56.

GOLDSTEIN, J. S. 2005. *International Relations*, 6th edn. New York: Pearson Longman.

—— and KEOHANE, R. O. 1994. Ideas and foreign policy: an analytical framework. Pp. 3–30 in *Ideas and Foreign Policy: Beliefs, Institutions, and Political Change*, ed. J. Goldstein and R. O. Keohane. Ithaca, NY: Cornell University Press.

HALL, R. B., and BIERSTEKER, T. J. (eds.) 2003. *The Emergence of Private Authority in Global Governance*. Cambridge: Cambridge University Press.

HALLIDAY, F. 2005. *The Middle East in International Relations: Power, Politics and Ideology*. Cambridge: Cambridge University Press.

HURD, I. 1999. Legitimacy and authority in international politics. *International Organization*, 53: 379–408.

—— 2007a. Breaking and making norms: American revisionism and crises of legitimacy. *International Politics*, 44: 194–213.

—— 2007b. *After Anarchy: Legitimacy and Power in the United Nations*. Princeton, NJ: Princeton University Press.

—— 2008. Theories of international authority. In *The UN Security Council and the Politics of International Authority*, ed. B. Cronin and I. Hurd.

JOHNSTONE, I. 2005. The power of interpretive communities. Pp. 185–204 in *Power in Global Governance*, ed. M. Barnett and R. Duvall. Cambridge: Cambridge University Press.

KRASNER, S. 1999. *Sovereignty: Organized Hypocrisy*. Princeton, NJ: Princeton University Press.

KRATOCHWIL, F. V. 1989. *Rules, Norms, and Decisions: On the Conditions of Practical and Legal Reasoning in International Relations and Domestic Affairs*. Cambridge: Cambridge University Press.

LEGRO, J. 2005. *Rethinking the World: Great Power Strategies and International Order*. Ithaca, NY: Cornell University Press.

Lewis, J. 2003. Institutional environments and everyday EU decision making: rationalist or constructivist? *Comparative Political Studies*, 36: 97–124.

Lynch, M. 1999. *State Interests and Public Spheres: The International Politics of Jordan's Identity*. New York: Columbia University Press.

March, J. G., and Olsen, J. P. 1998. The institutional dynamics of international political orders. *International Organization*, 52: 943–69.

Mearsheimer, J. J. 1995. A realist reply. *International Security*, 20: 82–93.

—— 2001. *The Tragedy of the Great Powers*. New York: Norton.

Milner, H. 1991. The assumption of anarchy in international relations theory: a critique. *Review of International Studies*, 17: 67–85.

Moravcsik, A. 1999. "Is something rotten in the state of Denmark?" Constructivism and European integration. *Journal of European Public Policy*, 6: 669–81.

Onuf, N. G. 1989. *World of our Making: Rules and Rule in Social Theory and International Relations*. Columbia: University of South Carolina Press.

Palan, R. 2000. A world of their making: an evaluation of the constructivist critique in international relations. *Review of International Studies*, 26: 575–98.

Pevehouse, J. 2005. *Democracy from Above: Regional Organizations and Democratization*. Cambridge: Cambridge University Press.

Price, R. 1998. Reversing the gun sights: transnational civil society targets land mines. *International Organization*, 52: 613–44.

—— and Reus-Smit, C. 1998. Dangerous liaisons? Critical international theory and constructivism. *European Journal of International Relations*, 4: 259–94.

—— and Tannenwald, N. 1996. Norms and deterrence: the nuclear and chemical weapons taboos. Pp. 114–52 in *The Culture of National Security: Norms and Identity in World Politics*, ed. P. Katzenstein. New York: Columbia University Press.

Reus-Smit, C. 1999. *The Moral Purpose of the State: Culture, Social Identity, and Institutional Rationality in International Relations*. Princeton, NJ: Princeton University Press.

—— C. 2005. Constructivism. Pp. 188–212 in *Theories of International Relations*, 3rd edn., ed. S. Burchill et al. New York: Palgrave.

Ruggie, J. G. 1998. *Constructing the World Polity: Essays on International Institutionalization*. New York: Routledge.

Sands, P. 2005. *Lawless World: America and the Making and Breaking of Global Rules from FDR's Atlantic Charter to George W. Bush's Illegal War*. New York: Viking.

Shannon, V. P. 2000. Norms are what states make of them: the political psychology of norm violation. *International Studies Quarterly*, 44: 293–316.

Simpson, G. 2004. *Great Powers and Outlaw States: Unequal Sovereigns in the International Legal Order*. Cambridge: Cambridge University Press.

Sinclair, T. 1999. Bond-rating agencies and coordination in the global political economy. Pp. 153–67 in *Private Authority and International Affairs*, ed. A. C. Cutler, V. Haufler, and T. Porter. Buffalo: State University of New York Press.

Snidal, D., and Thompson, A. 2002. International commitments and domestic politics: institutions and actors at two levels. Pp. 197–230 in *Locating the Proper Authorities: The Interaction of Domestic and International Institutions*, ed. D. Drezner. Ann Arbor: University of Michigan Press.

Sterling-Folker, J. 2000. Competing paradigms or birds of a feather? Constructivism and neoliberal institutionalism compared. *International Studies Quarterly*, 44: 97–119.

Waltz, K. N. 1959. *Man, the State, and War: A Theoretical Analysis.* New York: Columbia University Press.

——1979. *Theory of International Politics.* Boston: Addison-Wesley.

Weldes, J. 1999. *Constructing National Interests: The United States and the Cuban Missile Crisis.* Minneapolis: University of Minnesota Press.

Welsh, J. M. 2002. From right to responsibility: humanitarian intervention and international society. *Global Governance*, 8: 503–21.

Wendt, A. 1992. Anarchy is what states make of it: the social construction of power politics. *International Organization*, 46: 391–425.

——1995. Constructing international politics. *International Security*, 20: 71–81.

——1999. *Social Theory of International Politics.* Cambridge: Cambridge University Press.

——2000. On the Via Media: a response to the critics. *Review of International Studies*, 26: 165–80.

Wight, C. 2006. *Agents, Structures and International Relations: Politics as Ontology.* Cambridge: Cambridge University Press.

Williams, M. C. 2005. *The Realist Tradition and the Limits of International Relations.* Cambridge: Cambridge University Press.

CHAPTER 18

....

THE ETHICS OF CONSTRUCTIVISM

....

RICHARD PRICE

SOCIAL constructivism has increasingly been seen as one of the chief theoretical contenders in contemporary scholarship in international relations. As a research program, one of its main substantive contributions to the field has been to show that moral norms—and thus ethics—matter in world politics. In this very agenda itself constructivist scholars have embodied ethical commitments—at its most basic level this most often has been one of challenging realist skepticism concerning the possibilities for progressive moral change. Yet the plausibility of such ethical positions has typically been defended by constructivists on rigorous empirical terms—showing that human rights norms or norms of warfare can matter, for example—rather than on comparably rigorous normative grounds (that such norms are ethically desirable). In this chapter I briefly outline the trajectory of the constructivist research program, arguing that its development and responses to its critics have now led it—and its challengers—centrally to explicit engagement with ethical questions. I then consider the extent to which constructivism can be said to entail a distinctive ethic at all, and outline its potential contributions to addressing global ethical challenges.

1 WHENCE CONSTRUCTIVISM AND ETHICS

....

Various ways of championing causes of moral progress have long been central to varieties of liberal and critical theories of international relations (as against their skeptical counterparts), even if there is hardly agreement on what would actually count as moral progress. And yet both broad camps have been the targets of persistent charges of utopianism from skeptics. Recent constructivist scholarship on the role of moral norms in international relations, I have argued elsewhere, has responded convincingly to such charges with careful empirical research that demonstrates the possibilities of moral change in world politics (Price 2003). Having successfully taken on the initial challenge of demonstrating that moral norms can matter in world politics, the constructivist agenda was pushed to a second generation of work by a comparativist/methodological critique that demanded explanations for how and why some norms mattered in some places or sometimes, but not in others (Kowert and Legro 1996; Checkel 1998). This in turn led to a plethora of work crossing the boundaries of comparative politics and international relations seeking to account for the mechanisms of variation in compliance with systemic norms, citing factors such as cultural match, domestic interests, domestic institutions, and the like.

But while it has thus opened up convincing space for taking seriously the role of moral change in the study and practice of international relations, this literature for the most part has not offered its own explicit normative or prescriptive defenses of particular changes as good. Such positions are often left more implicit rather than defended with the same kind of rigor of systematically considering alternative explanations that is typically a hallmark of constructivist empirical work.[1] One might ask, then, upon what basis are such accounts of moral change, which are presumed to be desirable, to be accepted as in fact "good?" One person's cosmopolitan victory might be another's intolerable encroachment upon the prerogatives of a self-determining cultural community. While constructivist scholarship has typically sought to demonstrate the existence and importance of intersubjective, transcommunity (systemic) norms, there is nothing in constructivism itself that inherently privileges cosmopolitan values over communitarian ones as always more just. The upshot is that empirically demonstrating, for example, that transnational activist networks have been successful in curtailing the practice of female genital cutting, by itself does not suffice to make the case that morally desirable change has occurred unless accompanied by a persuasive ethical defense that human rights ought to trump this particular cultural practice. While the challenge of having to offer a convincing defense of the ethical desirability of many international

---

[1] There are exceptions. Nicholas Wheeler (2000, 6) works from a position that takes the English School and constructivist approaches in international relations as occupying the same terrain, and offers a solidarist theory of humanitarian intervention grounded in his empirical analysis. Scholars working in the shadow of the English School tradition have tended to be less reticent than their North American colleagues in simultaneously working both the normative and the empirical terrain, though it would seem that a skepticism in American international relations that the empirical side of such work is sufficiently rigorous methodologically and theoretically has hampered the receptivity of such work.

norms—such as the abolition of slavery, apartheid, ritual sacrifice, and the like—would not exactly keep too many constructivist scholars up at night, there are thus important grounds why more explicit engagement with the question of ethics is timely for the constructivist research program.

As well, it is hardly the case that all scholars who might be considered constructivists agree on the normative desirability of various developments in world politics, as evident in cases of humanitarian intervention such as practiced in Kosovo among numerous others. Indeed, while some constructivists have argued that a variety of critical theorists, post-structuralists, and constructivists can for certain purposes be considered under one broad tent (Price and Reus-Smit 1998), other constructivists (Adler 1997) and critical scholars like David Campbell (1998) have argued that they cannot. And it is often on substantive ethical questions such as the promotion of a zone of liberal democratic peace or the justifiability of purportedly human-itarian interventions that the divides have come to the fore between the frequent liberal/cosmopolitan cast of constructivism and the more skeptical versions of critical theory, feminism, and post-structural international relations, which tend to privilege relations of domination lurking behind the embrace of such projects. In short, one cannot claim that progressive moral change is possible in world politics solely by demonstrating empirically that normative change occurs, since this presupposes that it is unproblematically accepted that such change is indeed morally desirable; thus an account of its normative appeal is also required at some point.

Besides disagreements among constructivists, an accounting of the ethics of constructivism is called for as well given the normative nature of other contem-porary challenges to constructivism. In response to a plethora of scholarly works demonstrating the importance of norms and the role of transnational advocacy networks in world politics for such developments as the Landmines Convention, and milestones in international criminal law including tribunals and the Interna-tional Criminal Court (ICC), a conservative response has emerged to challenge the normative desirability of such erstwhile progressive developments (see, e.g., Anderson 2000; Snyder and Vinjamuri 2003–4). In order to respond adequately to critics who charge that constructivist research has been beset by a normative bias in favor of "good" norms that worked, scholars ultimately must turn to some form of normative defense. To be sure, this goes both ways: Critics who make such charges can make them intelligible only on the basis of their own normative defenses of what qualifies as good or undesirable norms, or else the critique is incoherent. In either case—or better, for both reasons—normative theorizing is inescapable, and thus central to practice and intellectual discourse in international relations, even as professionally it has not been accorded pride of place in the American academy of international relations, which has been dominated by predictive and explanatory agendas that have largely excluded normative theorizing as the subjective terrain of "political theory," "normative theory," or philosophy.[2] All this has put the moral question front and center in mainstream international relations, and not just for constructivists, though that will be the focus here (see, e.g., Snyder 2003).[3]

2 BETWEEN SKEPTICISM...

In short, the trajectory of the constructivist research agenda and responses to it have led it, among other things, to ethics. But does constructivism itself entail a substantive answer to the ethical question of "what we ought to do?" Or is it better thought of as an ethically neutral analytical tool to which one may harness different substantive ethical positions? Quite to the contrary from the conservative critique that constructivism is biased toward the study of "good" norms that "worked," the opposite challenge could also be marshaled: Does constructivism entail a political or ethical position at all? It has frequently been contended that constructivism is an approach, a method, an ontology, or a social theory, but that it is not a substantive political theory or theory of international relations as such (see Ruggie 1998; Wendt 1999). This position implies the understanding that constructivism is best understood as not itself constituting a normative position, nor constituting an ethical theory as such. Is this the case? I argue here that, while constructivism does not by itself entail full-fledged normative commitments of a sort of cosmopolitanism or communitarianism, it does lend strength to a position between skepticism and utopianism.

On the one hand, the understanding of constructivism's alleged agnosticism helps explain the varieties of constructivism and how constructivism has lent itself to being harnessed to numerous more obviously substantive theories, some with no small differences between them. Thus we have so-called conventional and critical or Marxian constructivisms, "thick" and "thin" constructivisms, modernist, postmodernist, and holist constructivisms, feminist and postcolonial constructivisms, and so on. Constructivism is also agnostic, which is to say equally compatible, with either solidarist or pluralist positions on how thick the rules of international

---

[2] From a survey of what are widely regarded as the top three journals in international relations in North America—*International Organization, International Security,* and *World Politics*—over the period 1990–2006, at most four articles could be identified that are arguably characterized as engaging in normative as opposed to primarily explanatory analysis. In contrast, international relations scholarship in the UK has accorded a much more prominent place to normative theorizing. For early statements, see Brown (1992); Smith (1992). See also journals such as *Review of International Studies* and *Millennium: Journal of International Studies,* where normative theory figures prominently.

[3] It is most interesting to note the recent normative turn in the work of Robert Keohane, one of the most prominent scholars of American international relations; see, e.g., Holzgrefe and Keohane (2003); Buchanan and Keohane (2004).

society are and whether they pertain only between states or also among humanity. While it may be the case that, to this point in the English-speaking academy of international relations, a predominantly "progressivist" cast has characterized much constructivist scholarship, on this reading there is nothing to preclude realist or other illiberal constructivisms, even if constructivism to date typically has not been harnessed to such perspectives (see Barkin 2003).

At the same time, the historicist underpinnings of constructivism would seem to make its proponents hard pressed to maintain a strong view of its alleged neutrality, given the premise that all theories as cultural artifacts embody a perspective from somewhere and for something, as put famously by Robert Cox (1986). Indeed the analytic of constructivism does seem to foreclose key contentions of some substantive political theories, which inherently entail normative commitments. This is particularly the case with materialist theories, which would locate all the explanatory leverage we need in the likes of military or economic power or in unalterable givens of nature. Furthermore, constructivism's emphasis on the possibilities of social and political change that are not confined to the realm of the domestic polity does seem to preclude conservative international political theories, which as a matter of presumption discount the possibility of moral change across borders as enough of an anomaly that initiatives to those ends can be reliably dismissed as "unrealistic," though I would suggest that the relationship here is subtle.

By bringing in the centrality of power to the study of moral norms, constructivism implicitly acknowledges that the resolution of any genuine moral dilemma entails the trumping of some morally substantive visions of politics over others. The war over Kosovo involved (among numerous other things) the North Atlantic Treaty Organization's trumping of humanitarian rescue over Serbian claims of self-determination and autonomy. The dilemma between humanitarian intervention and norms of self-determination is illustrative of constructivism's relation to realist ethics. The world constructed the practice of self-determination in no small part to solve one set of moral problems, but this has now created a series of consequences (see Finnemore 2008). The dilemma we are now left with between these two international norms is not some timeless universal problem due to the anarchic system; it is not due to material power; it is not due to human nature or biological givens. Rather, it is the product of human agency, of systemic moral change, not the realm of recurrence and repetition. Constructivism's ontological granting of such developments distinguishes it crucially from important versions of realist skepticism. These dilemmas arise only if these moral norms are international social facts, which they have become. This would differentiate a constructivist ethic of moral possibility from a skepticism that would dismiss efforts toward agreement upon international moral standards as unrealistic, insofar as the analytical and ontological underpinnings of the former allows for more transcommunity shared morality in world politics than skeptical or communitarian realisms would typically be willing to concede.

This is not to say that there cannot be clashes between rival global moral visions and their sponsors, and thus realists who do take ideology, culture, and the like seriously (mostly classical realists) but see them as sources of conflict, repression, and injustice rather than the solution, can share some affinities with a constructivist emphasis on such social structures at least in that narrow sense. After all, critical constructivists point out the conflict-producing "othering" involved in establishing the liberal democratic peace or security communities, which, substantively speaking, is not too far from the logic of Samuel Huntington's clash of civilizations (though, to be sure, constructivists would typically resist the latter's essentializing, among other things). Or, as Marc Lynch (2006) has put it, Osama Bin Laden is a social constructivist.

Besides acknowledging that international social structures may clash, constructivism, as Alexander Wendt has argued, can be agnostic on the content of those intersubjective social structures—they may be what a given constructivist herself may hold to be good, like the abolition of the slave trade, or bad, like the much longer-held acceptance of slavery itself. But where constructivist international relations differs from realist skepticism is not assigning the unrealizability of international moral goods including of the cosmopolitan kind as the unchanging lot of humanity or as solely the causes rather than solutions to repetitively dire problems. Progress as defined in humanitarian terms can be had, even if in achieving it new problems and conflicts in resolving them are produced by the inherent restructuring of moral standards of possibility and impossibility that moral change itself then makes possible. But, granting this form of ever-present moral conflict at the same time denies the presumption of skepticism that meaningful moral improvement in world politics can be presumptively dismissed as ontologically implausible or inherently ethically dangerous, as a project that "sounds nice but regrettably is not the world we live in."

3 ... AND UTOPIANISM

On the other hand, the ontology and strong empirical findings of much constructivist scholarship lends strength to a normative theoretical position that accords an essential place, not just for ethical possibilities, but also for the empirical limits of ethical ideals for ultimately assessing their legitimacy and thus rightness. That is, research programs that have shown how moral norms arise and have an impact on world politics ought to be well placed to help us answer the ethical question of "what to do" insofar as it is accepted that a responsible answer to that question entails a response to the question of not just "what is just" in principle but also to some extent the question of "what might work" in practice. In that sense I would contend that constructivist scholarship in international relations on the limits and possibilities of moral change can provide a rigorous rejoinder to Immanuel Kant's rejection of the naturalist fallacy—that is, his rejection of the idea that the "ought" depends in a meaningful way upon the "is." Or, more generously, constructivism at least thrives in the small space for the "is" left open by Kant by his concession that duty requires one to enact the moral imperative unless it is demonstrably impossible to fulfill (Donaldson 1992). How do we know, constructivists might ask, what is possible or impossible morally in world politics in the absence of empirical assessments of the successes or failures of moral practice? Without presuming to deny Kantian or other idealisms to all constructivists, I would contend that, even as constructivism demonstrates the power of such idealisms in the real world, it simultaneously provides confident grounds for resisting the seductive critical skepticism born of the always available insistence of critical theory or utopianism (of the sort: "relations of power and domination are still there"/"more could have been done") at the expense of practically realizable ethics, even if it does not dictate abandonment of such critical or utopian outlooks. In short, I would argue that constructivism provides powerful grounds for an ethic that navigates between skepticism and the utopian poles of critical theory.

In response, critical scholars might respond that constructivism (or at least such a conception of constructivism) is too conservative; the celebration of what critical theorists might characterize as reformist gestures implicit in much constructivist scholarship could be condemned as an impediment to more fundamental change. Indeed, this is a challenge not easily dismissed by constructivists themselves: Given their findings on possibilities of moral action, does positing any limits for ethical possibility make sense? Implicitly or explicitly endorsing developments such as the generation of an international norm prohibiting the use of antipersonnel landmines or the creation of an ICC need not preclude what some might champion as more fundamental progressive changes such as the ending of war altogether. Indeed, until such larger international structures are in fact favorably altered, constructivists can point the way to forms of action that could claim to make a progressive difference, as opposed to falling short of much more ambitious comparisons to the ideal that, until their realization, do amount to failure. The critical position might counter that such reformist gestures simply facilitate the perpetuation of systems that are fundamentally unjust and that call for more revolutionary action. This is not an unreasonable position, particularly on constructivists' own terms, insofar as scholars documenting change and processes like learning in world politics have often emphasized the crucial importance of a "crisis" as a catalyst for major shifts. The ethical prescription that would follow is to foment the conditions for crisis rather than abate them. But this is not obviously a stronger moral position to take than judging that, if one weighs demonstrable humanitarian gains (the same causes championed by critical theorists) against the failures of an ideal, let alone making things worse in the hopes of more fundamental change, then those gains come out pretty well, especially if they cannot be demonstrably shown to render impossible or even more unlikely further progress toward more fundamental change.

The resulting ethical stance would not reject but rather would be open to efforts to reach even further for the ideal. However, at the same time this stance would approach exasperation when such a disposition is not reciprocated; that is, when criticisms from that ideal point of view target (to the point of dismissing) the smaller victories along the way that do effect meaningful change in real human lives if not whole systems, a tact that fosters a deep cynicism that undercuts moral action. This is particularly so, since constructivist scholarship's major contribution has been to demonstrate how sometimes initially small developments open wedges to wider change, from genealogical studies of unintended consequences of shifts in language to the ultimate boomerang effects of small rhetorical concessions to human rights activists. Who, really, would have thought that the Helsinki accords, routinely disparaged in the 1970s in the West as an inconsequential sell-out to the Soviets, would prove to have sowed the seeds for revolutionary peaceful change in the Soviet bloc (see Thomas 2001)? Who in 1996 (let alone weeks before its occurrence in 1998) would have really thought that the idea of Britain arresting Augusto Pinochet for his role in torture in Chile was anything but the highest flight of fancy?

4 CONCLUSION

Still, it is crucial to note that the ultimate ethical position developed here, focusing upon implications of constructivism's ontology, is contingent and open to empirical challenge. If, in fact, for example, international criminal tribunals are more decisively shown to make things worse than plausible and actually existing alternatives, then a constructivist like Kathryn Sikkink (2008) who champions them now as worthwhile progressive developments would be prepared to revise her moral support for such tribunals. This is important, and it is the ethical corollary of the explanatory agnosticism of coming down where the evidence lays, which for many constructivists has translated into a rigorous and self-reflexive working methodology of carefully weighing alternative accounts against one another. This contingency, doubled by the potential social malleability of our world in which sometimes anything does seem to be possible, ought to underscore the necessary humility in a constructivist ethic.

Humility comes also from the proposition that moral progress almost invariably does not result in simple resolution but rather comes at the price of creating new moral dilemmas. It comes further still from recognizing that the very processes diagnosed and implicitly heralded as avenues of moral progress in one context may have very different effects in another or be accompanied by simultaneously deleterious developments. Thus, the shaming techniques identified as so important for progress in human rights and other issues pushed by transnational advocacy networks can be shown to be regarded as inappropriate and likely to engender backlash in an Association of Southeast Asian Nations (ASEAN) context that trumpets an "Asian way" of consensus building and quiet diplomacy as opposed to confrontation.

Even more, humility is engendered by the historicist sensibility inherent to constructivism's focus on cultural context, which reminds us that the standards we may uphold now, we ourselves as individuals or as communities would have run afoul of in the past. As Martha Finnemore (2008) has argued, "citizens of the western states who are pushing these norms and doing most of the intervening were not able to 'self-determine' without a great deal of violence, yet we now are expecting others to do so," rarely reflecting upon "what if" such standards had been applied to their own civil wars or the colonizing of indigenous peoples. And yet, for all these reasons that constructivism would counsel an ethic of humility, constructivism at the same time provides additional rigorous grounds to act and judge in the spaces between self-fulfilling skepticism and the practical paralysis of a critical reflex unable to acknowledge practical ethical progress.

REFERENCES

ADLER, E. 1997. Seizing the middle ground: constructivism in world politics. *European Journal of International Relations*, 3: 319–63.

ANDERSON, K. 2000. The Ottawa Convention banning landmines, the role of international non-governmental organizations and the idea of international civil society. *European Journal of International Law*, 11: 91–120.

BARKIN, J. S. 2003. Realist constructivism. *International Studies Review*, 5: 325–42.

BROWN, C. 1992. *International Relations Theory: New Normative Approaches*. New York: Harvester Wheatsheaf.

BUCHANAN, A., and KEOHANE, R. O. 2004. The preventive use of force: a cosmopolitan institutional proposal. *Ethics and International Affairs*, 18: 1–22.

CAMPBELL, D. 1998. Epilogue. Pp. 207–27 in *Writing Security: United States Foreign Policy and the Politics of Identity*, rev. edn., ed. D. Campbell. Minneapolis: University of Minnesota Press.

CHECKEL, J. 1998. The constructivist turn in international relations theory. *World Politics*, 50: 324–48.

Cox, R. W. 1986. Social forces, states and world orders: beyond international relations theory. Pp. 204–54 in *Neorealism and its Critics*, ed. R. O. Keohane. New York: Columbia University Press.

DONALDSON, T. 1992. Kant's global rationalism. Pp. 136–57 in *Traditions of International Ethics*, ed. T. Nardin and D. Mapel. Cambridge: Cambridge University Press.

FINNEMORE, M. 2008. Dilemmas of humanitarian intervention. In *Moral Limit and Possibility and World Politics*, ed. R. Price. Cambridge: Cambridge University Press.

HOLZGREFE, J. L., and KEOHANE, R. O. (eds.) 2003. *Humanitarian Intervention: Ethical, Legal, and Political Dilemmas*. Cambridge: Cambridge University Press.

KOWERT, P., and LEGRO, J. 1996. Norms, identity, and their limits: a theoretical reprise. Pp. 451–97 in *The Culture of National Security: Norms and Identity in World Politics*, ed. P. Katzenstein. New York: Columbia University Press.

LYNCH, M. 2006. Al-Qaeda's constructivist turn. *Praeger Security International*, 5 May, http://psi.praeger.com/doc.aspx?d=/commentary/Lynch-20060505-Lynch-20060505.xml.

PRICE, R. 2003. Transnational civil society and advocacy in world politics. *World Politics*, 55: 579–606.

—— and REUS-SMIT, C. 1998. Dangerous liaisons? Critical international theory and constructivism. *European Journal of International Relations*, 4: 259–94.

RUGGIE, J. G. 1998. What makes the world hang together? Neo-utilitarianism and the social constructivist challenge. *International Organization*, 52: 855–85.

SIKKINK, K. 2008. The role of consequences, comparison, and counterfactuals in constructivist ethical thought. In *Moral Limit and Possibility in World Politics*, ed. R. Price. Cambridge: Cambridge University Press.

SMITH, S. 1992. The forty years' detour: the resurgence of normative theory in international relations. *Millennium: Journal of International Studies*, 21: 489–506.

SNYDER, J. 2003. "Is" and "ought:" evaluating empirical aspects of normative research. Pp. 349–77 in *Progress in International Relations Theory: Appraising the Field*, ed. C. Elman and M. F. Elman. Cambridge, Mass.: MIT Press.

—— and VINJAMURI, L. 2003–4. Trials and errors: principle and pragmatism in strategies of international justice. *International Security*, 28: 5–44.

THOMAS, D. 2001. *The Helsinki Effect: International Norms, Human Rights, and the Demise of Communism*. Princeton, NJ: Princeton University Press.

WENDT, A. 1999. *Social Theory of International Politics*. Cambridge: Cambridge University Press.

WHEELER, N. 2000. *Saving Strangers: Humanitarian Intervention in International Society*. Oxford: Oxford University Press.

CHAPTER 19

CRITICAL THEORY

RICHARD SHAPCOTT

MARTIN Wight once asked the question, "why is there no international theory?" or in other words, why is there no political theory of international relations devoted to questions of the good life and the meaning of terms such as rights, freedom, order, and justice? Why is the vocabulary of international relations dominated by words such as structure, necessity, and tragedy? Wight (1967) saw the international arena as a realm of "recurrence and repetition," where the persistence of anarchy precluded the possibility of theorizing the good life. Throughout the 1980s and early 1990s, a new generation of scholars challenged Wight's account and argued that the practice and theory of international relations had always been infused with normative content and was, therefore, amenable to the vocabulary of political theory. One of the most important sources of this new vocabulary was the intellectual project of critical theory formulated by the Frankfurt School of Social Enquiry in Weimar Germany, and later in the United States. The biggest contribution of critical theory in international relations has been to challenge Wight's vision and to prevent the question of human freedom from disappearing from the language of the study of international politics.

The Frankfurt School was inspired by Karl Marx's *Thesis on Feuerbach*, that "philosophers have only interpreted the world, in various ways; the point is to change it" (cited in Devetak 2001, 146). They sought to revive the classical idea of a "practical philosophy," a form of knowledge and inquiry that was directed toward understanding, evaluation, and practice (Shapcott 2004). In particular, they identified study of the meaning, conditions, and possibilities of human emancipation, or freedom, as the first priority of the human sciences. An interest in emancipation necessarily drives inquiry toward the investigation into possibilities for positive change that may contribute to the improvement of the conditions of human existence. In the language of Kant, this is termed enlightenment, in the language of Hegel, it is spirit or history (*Geist*), and in the language of Marx, it is emancipation. For Max Horkheimer, the use of critical reason directs us to the idea of emancipation, the good society consisted of one in which the individual could realize his or her potential for autonomy (Horkheimer 1972). Critical theory in international relations seeks to develop this project in the international context by identifying "the prospects for realising higher levels of human freedom across the world society as a whole" (Linklater 1990a, 7). Specifically, a critical theory of international relations examines "the problem of community," understood as how the members of bounded communities (states) determine the patterns of inclusion and exclusion in the international system (Linklater 1992). This project has three components, a normative inquiry into the *meaning* of emancipation and universalism, a historical sociological inquiry into the *conditions* of emancipation, and a praxeological inquiry into the *means* of emancipation in any given order, and in particular the present.

The first of these is necessary because emancipation has both positive and negative aspects and is subject to contestation. For contemporary critical theorists, emancipation means both freedom from unnecessary suffering and freedom to partake in dialogue, consent, and deliberation concerning matters that affect everybody. As a result, critical international relations theory is committed to the cosmopolitan project of achieving higher levels of inclusion in moral and political life for everyone on the planet. However, this requires a rejection of the mode of theorizing that dominates the social sciences, and international relations in particular, because it refuses the assumption of value neutrality or objectivity while remaining committed to a comprehensive research agenda. Critical theory places the normative purpose at the center of inquiry, and as a result it is necessarily interdisciplinary, engaging in both explanatory and evaluative theorizing with a practical intent. In setting out its agenda in this way, critical theorists aim to present a challenge to the discipline to provide normative as well as methodological justifications of its insights and purposes.

Critical theory is also both an interdisciplinary and a transdisciplinary inquiry. It does not aim to replace the insights of other theories but rather to incorporate them into a more "complete" and morally defensible approach. The normative and explanatory cannot be separated analytically from each other. Therefore a sociological inquiry is required because any account of any social realm is always simultaneously an account of the potential for change and freedom, as well as a reflection upon what freedom may mean in any given or possible context. For this reason it is also difficult to categorize critical theory as "a" theory of international relations as it is conventionally understood. Its place is more complex, as it incorporates both "grand theory" and more "applied" studies.

Any inquiry into critical international relations theory has to distinguish at least two central components. The first is the epistemological and methodological, what it says about theory; and the second is the normative and substantive, what it says about the world. In other words, "why do we study international relations?" and "how do we study international relations?" This chapter demonstrates why this is so by examining, first, the nature of the critical theory theoretical project and how it differs from and challenges mainstream conceptions of international relations; and secondly, the contributions that have been made by critical international relations theory so far. The chapter begins with a brief discussion of the origins of critical theory and critical international relations theory before examining the major claims and achievements.

Before proceeding further it should be noted that a common distinction is made between small "c" and large "C" critical theory, with only the latter referring to the Frankfurt School approaches. Small "c" includes approaches that are skeptical about the emancipatory project outlined by the Frankfurt School such as post-structuralism, (some) feminism, and critical realism. Some of the differences extend from different epistemologies, others from different ethical starting points. Many small "c" approaches reject their own assimilation into Andrew Linklater's project of community and have a philosophical resistance to talk of emancipation. Nonetheless, what is common to them all is a concern with power and freedom. In addition, critical theory has its own intellectual trajectory that continues outside of international relations. This chapter is concerned with large "C" critical theory in international relations.

1 THE FRANKFURT SCHOOL

Critical theory is first and foremost distinguished from "traditional," or problem-solving, theories. Traditional theory is modeled on the physical sciences and is concerned with explaining social processes from a disinterested or value-free position in order better to predict human behavior and therefore control it. As a result, traditional theory exhibits a system-maintenance bias because it takes the world as it finds it and investigates only how to manipulate it in order to achieve pre-given ends. At best it compares to what the Greeks called *technê*. Horkheimer argued that under modern conditions all reason had been reduced to technical, instrumental means–end rationality. As a result, the classical understanding of reason as giving rise to *thêoria* rather than *technê* had been forgotten or distorted. Critical theory sought to revive this deeper notion of a reason that inquired into the question of the "good." It asks not only how can good be achieved (*technê*) but what is the good? Or what is a good society? Such an inquiry is the jurisdiction of critical theory with its interest in "the experience of emancipation by means of critical insight into relationships of power" (Bernstein 1976, 189). As a result, critical theory differs from traditional theory because, in Robert Cox's words (1986, 210), it "allows for a normative choice in favour of a social and political order different from the prevailing order." It also has a substantive, but indeterminate, conception that such an order would be one in which individual destiny was "within limits determined by his [sic] own activity" (Horkheimer 1972, vii).

Horkheimer's claims were revisited thirty years later by Jürgen Habermas (1972). Like Horkheimer, Habermas was concerned by the reduction of reason to *technê* and "the attempt to attain technical mastery of history by perfecting the administration of society" (Bernstein 1976, 187). He argued that different theories provided different types of knowledge of the world and were constituted by different purposes or knowledge constitutive (cognitive) interests. The "reality" perceived by theorists is dependent on their interest. All theory helps constitute the world it claims merely to depict, and consequently the knowledge produced will be incomplete or impartial. Habermas (1972, 308) identified three such interests and three corresponding modes of theorization: "The approach of the empirical–analytic sciences incorporates a technical cognitive interest: that of the historical hermeneutic sciences incorporates a practical one; and the approach of critically oriented sciences incorporates the emancipatory cognitive interest…" Positivism, for instance, partakes of an act of wilful blindness because it contains an unacknowledged interest in the use to which its knowledge is put. The practical interest is an advance upon the technical, because it understands the intersubjective nature of social life and seeks to treat actors as participants in this world and not merely subjects of it. However, the practical interest is not enough, because it does not reflect upon the possibility of systematically distorted communication that arises from unequal power relations. This can be supplied only by a theory with an emancipatory interest. It remains disputed whether Habermas had indeed identified a fundamental cognitive relationship between theory and interests or whether he had simply provided a useful descriptive typology. Nonetheless, Habermas's framework reinforces Horkheimer's idea that a purely disinterested or detached theory, or theorist, is misleading.

Additionally, Horkheimer criticized idealist theories that ignored social contexts and realities. The inquiry into human emancipation necessarily led to a historical/sociological investigation and the material/social conditions in which reason operated. A successful critical theory must be able to provide insight into social conditions and the possibilities of freedom that can be used to inform the practice of real-world actors. To this end, Horkheimer's method was immanent critique or the analysis of the tensions within existing social arrangements and beliefs that may lead to progressive transformation. Hence, critical theory reflects upon normative and sociological, and praxeological, elements of emancipation.

The term "emancipation" necessarily invokes the question of emancipation from what? There is a good case for emancipation as an essentially contested concept and it remains one of the most difficult philosophical terms in critical theory. The term implies a privileged position for the theorist who can provide emancipating insights, and who can presumably identify when emancipation has been achieved, much like a psychiatrist. The challenge set forth by Kant, Marx, and Hegel was to use reason to reflect upon, in Kant's words, "mankind's self-incurred immaturity," and to subject social institutions to critical scrutiny in order that humankind could "actively determine its own way of life" (Horkheimer, quoted in Bernstein 1976, 181). By applying reason to social situations that were taken for granted, or appeared to be the manifestation of nature-like laws, such as gender inequality or slavery, it is possible to determine if they are in fact "lawlike." The Frankfurt School, and especially later theorists such as Habermas and Axel Honneth, argue that the obstacles to this goal lie in distorted or pathological self-understandings and forms of communication (Honneth 2004) and, in particular, in communication distorted by power and interests. Emancipation lies in the removal or correction of these distortions. However, this is a constant task; we can never be assured that our understandings are or are not distorted. So what matters is the questioning rather than any specific answer that we may arrive at. Emancipation is never realized; it is instead a motivating ideal. Furthermore, the best means we have for assessing our understandings is to test them discursively deliberatively in public—that is, with other people in free and open discussion. In this understanding, emancipation lies not so much in one's consciousness but in the creation of social and political conditions that permit one to partake in open dialogue.

2 The Critique of International Relations

If Horkheimer was influenced by the intellectual and political developments of the 1920s and 1930s, the critical turn in international relations was influenced by the legacy of the Vietnam War and the tensions created by the second cold war. Positivism was seen to be complicit in the political and moral disaster that was the American war in Vietnam and as testimony to the failure of technical reasoning in international affairs (a concern shared by some realists, notably Hans Morgenthau) and a direct result of the triumph of the idea of policy "science." Likewise, in the early 1980s, there was concern about the renewed level of tension in the superpower relationship and the nuclear arms race. Some writers asked whether the academic discipline of international relations was contributing to the problems facing the international realm. International relations scholars were challenged to reflect on Robert Cox's much quoted observation (1981, 128) that "theory is always *for* someone and *for* some purpose" (emphasis in original), and thus to reflect on their own "cognitive interests" and purposes. Critical theory's concern with emancipation was used to challenge the self-definition of international relations as "social science" and also the constitution of international relations as a distinct discipline untouched by and unrelated to others.

This self-definition was epitomized for many by the articulation of neo-, or structural, realism, in the work of Kenneth Waltz. Feminists, post-structuralists, and later constructivists all took issue with the research agenda and the philosophy of science established by neorealists. Both Richard Ashley and Cox employed Horkheimer's categories to depict neorealism as technical or problem-solving theory (while also identifying the critical potential of traditional or classical realism). By virtue of "parsimony," neorealism necessarily restricted the object of its inquiry and consequently saw only the continuities of war, great-power rivalry, and systemic reproduction, and ignored those developments that might serve to generate transformation. Not only did it filter out transformative possibilities, but it also advocated policies that conformed to its depiction of reality, thus contributing to the continuity it sought to explain. Neorealism not only endorsed the status quo of nuclear terror, but also failed to see this terror as a moral, rather than merely a technical, problem.

In addition, neorealism depicted a world in which anarchy, necessity, and sovereignty, rather than reason, determine human destiny. From the perspective of critical theory, however, humans are unemancipated so long as war and the reproduction of the international realm are seen as beyond human control and as subject to nature-like immutable laws. A critical theoretical approach to the study of war would investigate whether neorealism, and war itself, are instead ideologies exhibiting the bias of problem-solving theories in favor of the status quo.

This meta-analysis was not restricted to neorealism alone, but extended to the mainstream as a whole. In interpreting the Frankfurt School for international relations, Linklater argued that Habermas's threefold distinction corresponds with Wight's three traditions: realism, rationalism (Grotianism), and revolutionism (which he renames critical theory). Like Habermas, Linklater (1990b, 10) argued that:

a theory which analyses the language and culture of diplomatic interaction in order to promote international consensus is an advance beyond a theory of recurrent forces constituted by an interest in manipulation and control...[However] an enquiry which seeks to understand the prospects for extending the human capacity for self-determination is an even greater advance.

Hermeneutic approaches argue that language and communication give material conditions meaning for humans. These approaches understand or "recover" the meanings common to actors by interpreting and understanding the self-understanding of actors' others, rather than "explanation" of independent mechanistic process. Linklater therefore identified both liberal institutionalism and the so-called English School, or Grotian approach, with Habermas's "practical interest." Thus, while neoliberal institutionalism has a purported interest in bringing about change (see Keohane 1988)—its presuppositions are such that it is limited to change within, but not of, the international system—it likewise displays a system-maintenance bias. Liberal institutionalism is not addressed to questioning the system of states or bringing into being a different, arguably more "political," world order. The shift from a pure anarchy to a highly reflexive institutionalized or mature anarchy depicted by institutionalists represents a shift from one form of technical rationality, strategic, to another, cooperative. The international realm could, therefore, become more predictable but still not subject to "critical reasoning."

The English School is traditionally identified with the idea of an international *society* of states who not only coexist but recognize each other's right to coexist and develop rules of behavior based on this recognition. The English School therefore emphasizes communication and agreement between actors and examines the ways in which systems transform into societies, with more "civilized," rule-governed interactions between states. In forming an international society, states are able to develop a shared realm of meaning that increases the range and possibilities of moral progress. The English School has, for Linklater, an advantage because it is more inclined toward normative reflection and prescription, no matter how circumscribed (Bull 1983; Jackson 2000; Shapcott 2004).

The "practical" cognitive interest also corresponds to the *verstehen* approach of interpretative, or hermeneutic, sciences and the constructivist insight, that "anarchy is what states make it" (Wendt 1992), a realm of meaning and not just material power. Constructivism in international relations is concerned with understanding and explaining the norms that operate in the international realm and the constitution of that realm by these norms. However, from a Habermasian perspective, constructivism suffers because it retains the fact/value distinction of *verstehen* social sciences and in so doing separates questions of "is" from "ought." For the critical theorist, one of the problems associated with maintaining the distinction between fact and value is that, "while such an analysis might reveal how such norms are constituted, it lacks the intellectual resources for rational critical evaluation of these norms" (Bernstein 1976, 168). That is, it provides few, if any, criteria with which to evaluate the information it provides. For this reason, Richard Price and Christian Reus-Smit's claims (1998, 288) that constructivism is "*necessarily* 'critical' in the sense meant by Habermas..." (emphasis added) is perhaps overly optimistic. Therefore, while interpretative approaches were an advance, they remain insufficient for a suitably critical theoretical approach to develop.

The greatest contributions of the early stage of the debate lay in establishing the nature of the emancipatory research agenda and in criticizing the epistemological assumptions of the discipline. Since its inception in international relations, critical theory has faced a number of common objections—for example, that it was preoccupied with agenda setting and metatheoretical reflection but unwilling or unable to produce "substantive" work in international relations. Robert Keohane (1988) argued that "reflectivist" paradigms lacked a coherent research agenda that could structure their contribution to the discipline, and by implication provide real knowledge. John Mearsheimer's claim (1995) that critical international relations theory had failed to deliver much in the way of empirical research was later echoed by Price and Reus-Smit (1998), who compared it unfavorably to constructivism's success in this regard. However, for critical theory proper, normative and metatheoretical groundwork is fundamental, and empirical studies ought not be begun until this preparation has been laid—that is, until the project can be defended normatively. This requires an engagement with moral and philosophical traditions outside international relations. The criticisms arguably reflect the general trend toward caricature in the depictions of alternatives to the mainstream and a recurring failure to distinguish adequately between small "c" and large "C" approaches, or between critical theory and historical materialism. Arguably they also reflect the nature of the Frankfurt School challenge to mainstream international relations discipline and its resistance to doing normative and interdisciplinary theorizing.

3 CRITICAL INTERNATIONAL RELATIONS THEORY TODAY

This section sets out the major achievements in generating normatively and empirically informed theory in international relations. In addition to the distinction between small and large "c" theories, the agenda of Frankfurt School-inspired works has diversified into at least two veins. These can be broadly characterized as those that *apply* the insights of critical theory to the field of international relations; and those that aspire to develop *a* critical theory of international relations. Critical theory in the latter sense is "grand theory" seeking to provide a comprehensive account of the emancipatory potentials of the present era. Within international relations there is, at this stage, really only one contributor to this project, and that is Linklater. The following discussion uses Linklater's framework to set out his "grand theory" and to outline the principal contributions of critical international relations theory.

The most significant contributions of the first type have studied the evolution of the international system and its components (historical sociology), international political economy, or the role of gender and security in the emancipatory project. Critical theory is the natural ally of feminist thought and as a result has had a considerable influence on feminist international relations. While feminist thought in international relations has its own intellectual history that is independent of Frankfurt School theorizing, the overall thrust of feminist work is "transformative" or "critical" (J. Ann Tickner's early reading (1995) of Morgenthau could easily be read as a first piece on critical theory). Most feminist scholars are doing theory from a standpoint concerned with emancipation and the ending of unnecessary suffering for both men and women. Most obviously, feminists are concerned to denaturalize gender differences that are taken for granted and problematize many of the masculine assumptions of Frankfurt School critical theory and of Habermas in particular (see Hutchings 1996, 98). This has led Brooke Ackerly, Maria Stern, and Jacqui True (2006), for instance, to develop a critical feminist methodology. Critical security studies has sought to engage traditional thinking about the meaning and practices of security with the aim of addressing the emancipation of "those who are made insecure by the prevailing order" (Wyn Jones 1999, 118; 2001). It presents a challenge to the mainstream of international relations by undermining claims that the strategic realm is a realm apart, immune to moral progress. In denaturalizing the strategic/security realm it simultaneously demonstrates the way in which security studies makes the world in its own image and represents an interest in maintaining the status quo.

However, in beginning with an international perspective and from within the discipline of international relations, Linklater stands largely unrivalled in developing the Frankfurt School project of a "critical theory of society." At its most ambitious it deploys historical sociological insights to provide an account of a moral and political theory that aspires to give direction to the discipline as whole. What distinguishes Linklater's approach from other approaches to critical theory in international relations is the comprehensiveness of his account, its engagement with contemporary debates in social and political theory and philosophy, and the scope of his vision.

4 THE NORMATIVE PROJECT

While normative theory remains largely excluded from international relations' self-understanding (most contributions come from political theory and philosophy—for example, see Beitz 1979), there is an emerging field of international political theory, or normative international relations, that was largely absent even twenty years ago (Frost 1996; 2000; Hutchings 1996; Cochran 1999; Shapcott 2001; Brown 2002). It is no accident then that critical international relations theory has made its largest contributions in the area of systematic reflection upon the meaning of emancipation and upon normative foundations of the current order and desirable possible future orders. In keeping with the agenda of returning to political theory, Linklater (1992, 92) argued that "the normative purpose of social inquiry should be considered before all else. Clarifying the purpose of the inquiry precedes and facilitates the definition of the object of inquiry." Linklater's application of Habermas has been central to this clarification. The dialogical principle provides the basis for moral universalism and requires the "triple" transformation of political community. The goal of emancipation is understood as freedom to consent or to be included in open dialogue in relation to the actions of all others. Emancipation remains tied to universalizability, to rules that everyone could agree to under conditions of free communication (see Eckersley, this volume). Recognition of the moral quality of dialogue means that to emancipate:

is to increase the spheres of social interaction that are governed by dialogue and consent rather than power and force; to expand the number of human beings who have access to a speech community that has the potential to become universal; and to create the socioeconomic preconditions of effective, as opposed to nominal, involvement for all members of that community. (Linklater 2001, 31)

Such a project requires, at the normative level, reflection upon the nature of dialogue and consent, reflection upon the relationship between identity and difference, and between universal and particular, and reflection upon the moral significance of boundaries. By providing one of the strongest arguments for cosmopolitan ethics, Linklater and Habermas have advanced the debates about the nature and possibilities of the current international order.

At this point, critical theory meets some of its most important criticisms from anticosmopolitans skeptical of its universalism. The most important of these are that its notion of emancipation is too culturally specific, reflecting only the values of the European enlightenment. This gives rise, at the very least, to a problematic universalism that threatens to assimilate and legislate out of existence all significant differences (Hopgood 2000; Inayatullah and Blaney 2004). The contentious aspect of this account is whether or not any cosmopolitan ethics can do significant justice to difference, or whether the most significant problems occur only in the interpretation of cosmopolitan dialogue (Shapcott 2001).

In turn, Linklater has incorporated these insights by marrying Habermas's theory with a cosmopolitan harm principle (Linklater 2006). In this modification, emancipation is ultimately concerned with the prevention of unnecessary suffering, as much as with the idea of individual rationality. Emphasizing the necessity of developing cosmopolitan harm principles, which extends concern about harm to all human beings, follows from this recognition. It is also commensurate with the dialogic ethic because the interpretation of the meaning of harm and consent in relation to potentially and presently harmful practices, requires open dialogue between all those possibly affected by an action.

5 THE SOCIOLOGICAL PROJECT

The sociological dimension of critical theory is that aspect most closely related to the traditional interests in explaining and understanding the forces that shape the international order. The realist charge against idealism was that it did not take seriously the restraints of the era. Idealists and utopians underestimated the tendency of the international realm to reproduce itself and its resistance to reformist ideologies. However, because critical theory is informed by a practical goal, it studies not just the world as it is but "how it got that way," "how it ought to be," and what possibilities there may be for transforming it. The prospects for emancipation are conditional upon tendencies within the existing world order, and any change can come about only as a development of that order. Critical theory's normative agenda requires an accompanying social theory that takes the conditions of the age into account without reifying them. It has drawn upon constructivist and sociological work, on the spread of humanitarian, democratic, and human rights norms, and historical sociology of state building, thus confirming Price and Reus-Smit's claim that critical and constructivist approaches can be mutually supportive. It is worth noting that the critical theory of international relations has remained largely unconcerned with Habermas's own sociological theory, which addresses the "colonization" of the life world by technical instrumental rationality and the rationality of money and productive exchange. Such colonization provides both threats to freedom and the risk of overadministration, as well as opportunities for more universal forms of association (Weber 2005).

Marx's observation that humans make the world but not under conditions of their own choosing is the appropriate starting point for this aspect of the critical project. The mundane but profound insight that the world has not always been divided into sovereign states raises the possibility of an inquiry into how that world came to be and how it might transform in the future. This in turn involves identification of the forces that have worked in favor of and against universalism in any given order. According to Linklater, the interest in emancipation requires an investigation into how human history has witnessed different levels of commitment to universalistic practices—that is, a comparative sociology of states systems "which focuses on long-term historical approaches in which visions of the unity of the human race influence the development of states-systems" (Linklater and Suganami 2006, 231).

Elements of this type of investigation are present in the work of both Heather Rae (2002) and Paul Keal (2003). Rae addresses Theodor Adorno and Horkheimer's concern in the *Dialectic of Enlightenment* with the dark, as well as progressive, capacities of modernity and raises questions about the emancipatory possibilities of states that are premised upon violent exclusion. Rae claims that the evolution of the sovereign state with exclusive territorial jurisdiction is related to the exclusion of minority nonconformist identities from the body politic. State-builders identify sub-groups who do not conform to their ideal or whose identity is perceived to threaten their territorial authority. In the context of international competition and insecurity, many states adopt "pathological"—that is, murderous and genocidal—practices against these internal "threats," culminating, of course, in the Holocaust and Armenian genocides of the twentieth century. Rae also identifies the praxeological possibilities of a critical study of this subject by examining a recent case of potential pathological practices that was circumvented by domestic and international action.

Keal's work is informed by an emancipatory interest in understanding the way in which international society has harmed indigenous peoples by dispossessing, subordinating, or forcibly assimilating them to European practices. Fundamental to Keal's inquiry are the implications of the earlier dispossession of the indigenous peoples for the legitimacy of many states and international society today. Colonial settler states such as Australia, Canada, and the United States are vulnerable to the claim that they rest on illegitimate foundations stemming from this dispossession. The historical/empirical aspect of his work does not prevent reflection upon alternative practices that might make contemporary states and the international society of states more legitimate from the position of all those affected by them.

Preliminary work on the comparative historical sociology of states systems suggests, for Linklater, that the evolution of an international society of states provides some of the strongest evidence that the contemporary order has been uniquely successful in institutionalizing greater levels of concern for humanity as whole. He identifies the norm of national self-determination and the continuing progress in drafting and enforcing international human rights norms, in the laws of war, on the targeting of civilians, the ban on nondiscriminatory weapons such as landmines, and criminalizing of rape as a weapon of war, as indicators of cosmopolitan commitments to restrict the range of permissible harms against individuals. Universal harm conventions involve recognition of a substantive conception of humanity in which suffering is recognized as an assault on what it is to be human, individual, and autonomous. In addition, the possible "pacification" of the relations between core industrial states raises the argument that more profound transformations of inter-state relations are possible under conditions of anarchy than is often portrayed. These developments raise the possibility of an account whereby humankind progresses first from an international system to a society of states, and then from a "pluralist" to a "solidarist" international society. If this is the case, it may be possible to move from a solidarist society of states to a cosmopolitan society.

The importance of these norms should not be underestimated, as there is little evidence that cosmopolitan thought has had such an impact in the past or in other international orders. At the same time, the relative success in institutionalizing cos-mopolitan harm principles in the current international order exists in tension with the tendency of global economic relations to contribute to the suffering of the poor. However, a general decline in the tolerance of unnecessary suffering and the spread of a belief in equality may contribute to a decline in tolerance for an international economic order that is imposed by the rich upon the poorest members of humanity (Pogge 2002).

The sociological dimensions of critical theory in international relations belie the claims that it is uninterested in empirical work. More importantly, they indi-cate that it necessarily incorporates insights drawn from a variety of approaches. For instance, Marxism added the realm of production and the processes of state-building to the understanding of the state system, offering an explanation of rel-ations of material reproduction and the development of capitalism on a world scale. On the other hand, the methodological limitations of historical materialism meant that it was insufficient for the purposes of a comprehensive critical inter-national relations theory.[1] Marxism's emphasis on the capitalist "base" rendered it effectively blind to the possiblity of a separate logic of inter-state insecurity that might run counter to capitalism's universalizing potential, as depicted by realism.

Linklater (1990*b*) claims that realism identifies how the logic of geopolitics, state-building, and war contribute to the maintenance of particularistic forms of association such as tribe, nation, or state. In a threatening international en-vironment, appeals to universalism are likely to be overridden or come behind appeals to security and stability. The discourse of the "war on terror" illus-trates this tendency. Under the condition of a perceived existential and "civ-ilizational" crisis, there is pressure to retreat from universalistic norms and forms of association, including the United Nations, the Universal Declaration of Human Rights, and the Geneva Conventions. The necessity for state sur-vival in an uncertain anarchic environment therefore provides a brake on uni-versalizing forces that emerged from modernity, the Enlightenment, and later, globalization.

Likewise, realist moral skepticism also provides a useful normative contribution by focusing on the clear cases of false universalism that accompany hegemony and great power hubris. The realist critique of American foreign policy's universalist pretensions provides an appropriate illustration. The identification of American values with universal ones is misplaced and likely to meet with hostility and provoke resistance abroad. Nonetheless, both the realist and "Grotian" emphasis on the role of the great powers also reveals sources of stability in inter-state relationships.

---

[1] It is worth noting that, while it is perhaps Cox's account (1986) of the relationship between states, social forces (class, production), and world orders that is most associated with critical international relations theory, it is only marginally influenced by the Frankfurt School.

In turn, this suggests that cosmopolitanism is likely to find a more conducive environment where the great powers are in concert and committed to universalism.

The insights of a preliminary cosmopolitan sociology of states systems provide the conditions for the third part of the critical international relations theory project. The praxeology, referring to the relationship between norms and practices, or the practice of norms, requires an understanding of the social, material, and normative conditions in which the pursuit of the project of emancipation can occur. The subject of this praxis is taken up next.

6 THE PRAXEOLOGICAL PROJECT

The praxeological research program extends from understanding critical theory as a "practical philosophy" involving a normative critique of the present, a sketch of an alternative and better normative future, and a responsibility to inform praxis in the present. In other words, it involves the attempt to theorize how the cosmopolitan emancipatory values defended in the first agenda, and situated in the conditions identified in the second, can be developed or institutionalized in the present. The praxeological is perhaps the least developed aspect of critical international relations theory, in part because it is dependent upon progress in the normative and sociological realms. However, for a school that is ultimately concerned with changing the world and not just understanding it, more clearly needs to be done. The philosophical difficulty here is how to provide insight that can guide action without it turning into instrumentalism or a "program." As one commentator has observed, this very tension may prove irresolvable, making any contribution to praxis severely limited (Rengger 2001).

Critical theory is not the only tradition engaged in thinking about the practice of freedom and equality. Without a doubt, liberalism, in all its varieties, has been the most successful at putting theory into praxis. Critical theory has been successful at mounting a normative and sociological critique of liberalism but has yet to be able to equal its success in informing institutional design and political practice. Investigating how the practice of emancipation goes beyond liberalism's emphasis on positive individual human freedom remains the unfulfilled promise of critical international relations theory.

Nonetheless, several aspects of how an emancipatory interest may be played out in praxis are emerging. For Linklater, the praxis of emancipation requires "alleviating the varieties of human suffering that arise in the conditions of globalization. It involves building a global community that institutionalizes respect for the harm principle and grants all human beings the right to express their concerns and fears about injury vulnerability and suffering" (Linklater and Suganami 2006, 277). This praxis has two major concerns—identifying avenues for greater inclusion in international and global decision-making, and remedying the varieties of avoidable human suffering characterizing current global relationships.

The normative and sociological concerns of critical theory direct attention toward identification of both actors and policies or practices that help advance the "triple transformation" of community. Without a doubt, the state and, by extension, the society of states are the most important agents in this process. Therefore, among the aims of critical praxeology is an effort to identify cosmopolitan policies and practices available to states and international society. While global civil society has a role to play in emancipation of the human species, it is states, and great powers in particular, that have the greatest potential for moving the international order in a progressive direction.

The first element of such a praxis, therefore, is to raise the possibility of states as good international citizens or, in Hedley Bull's terms, local agents of the world common good who recognize that "it is wrong to promote the interest of our [sic] own society ... by exporting suffering to others, colluding in their suffering or benefiting from the ways in which others exploit the weakness of the vulnerable" (Linklater 2002a, 145). Beyond that, states are challenged to develop harm conventions in relation to three categories. First, bilateral relationships: what "we" do to "them" and vice versa. Secondly, third-party relationships: what they do to each other. Thirdly, global relationships: what we all do to each other (Linklater 2002b). Examples of the first are cases where one community "exports" damaging practices, goods, or byproducts to another. In this case, states have a duty to consider the negative effects they have on each other, as well as a duty to prevent and punish harmful actions of nonstate actors and individuals for whom they are directly responsible. An example of the second is when a state is involved in harming either members of its own community or its neighbor's, such as in cases of genocide. Third-party states and the international community also have duties to prevent, stop, or punish the perpetrators of these harms. The third relationship refers to practices to which many communities contribute, often in different proportions, such as in the case of global warming. States have a negative duty not to export harm to the world as a whole and a positive duty to contribute to the resolution of issues arising from such harms. A cosmopolitan foreign policy should be committed to the possibility of developing more universally inclusive arrangements for democratic governance of the international, regional, and national orders. The democratic project requires a democratization of the international realm in order to make it more accountable but also more representative of the interests of each and every member of the human species. In other words, good international citizens should be concerned not only to alter their own practices but also to seek to transform the institutions of international order so that they do not cause, participate in, or benefit from unnecessary suffering.

7 CONCLUSION: THE CONTRIBUTION
OF CRITICAL TEORY

The question of freedom and the relationship of the individual to humanity has been central to the discourses of political theory in Western history. Critical theory has sought to provide a further elaboration on the nature and possibilities of free- dom understood as moral universalism in the international realm. Such a defence challenges the status quo of international politics, not from the outside, but rather from within the tradition of Western enlightenment. The biggest contribution of critical international relations theory is that it keeps the question of individual human freedom and its relationship to political community from disappearing from the language of the study of international politics.

This chapter provided an overview of the most important elements of the critical theory of international relations and therefore it has not been possible to elaborate on the criticisms or problems of critical theory. However, a number of points can be noted briefly. Frankfurt School critical theory in international relations remains a fairly select group and this may or may not reflect the limits of this mode of the- orizing. It is not currently fashionable to engage in constructing "metanarratives" of emancipation; the term evokes the idea that it is the theorist's job to emancipate the enslaved and to instil a single model of the human agent. While critical theorists have done much to try to dispel this understanding, Habermas himself rejecting its use, it remains a problematic term for many. On the other hand, the vast majority of international relations continues to see normative reflection as "somebody else's business" and not what we do. Such a self-understanding clearly limits the avenues for critical international relations for many and is likely to continue to do so.

What has been emphasized are the achievements in challenging the dominant understanding of the discipline of international relations as a social science and the success in setting forth an alternative research program. Because it constitutes itself outside the mainstream understanding of social science, it appears that the contributions and insights provided by critical theory cannot count as real knowl- edge for most social scientists. However, if we take the insights of the Frankfurt School seriously, then it is the mainstream that provides "limited" or incomplete accounts both of the world and of the nature of its own insights. In particular, a challenge has been raised to mainstream and positivist approaches to provide more coherent accounts of their own methodological, epistemological, and normative positions. From a critical theory perspective, the weight of argument is against any continuation of the fact/value distinction, and as a consequence the onus of proof, so to speak, lies with the mainstream. Positivist-influenced approaches need to demonstrate either the inaccuracy of the division between traditional and critical theory, or to defend the separation of purpose from interests and the necessity and desirability of an instrumental account of reason. In addition, the force of the argument necessarily draws mainstream approaches to address normative issues, both in the substance of world politics and also insofar as they relate to underlying purposes of inquiry. Thus either they must reject the claim that their epistemology biases the status quo, or alternatively must defend that bias. Whichever way they respond, they nonetheless will be drawn to certain normative issues about the nature of social sciences and about the purposes to which they are put. Ultimately they will be drawn to the terrain of evaluative questions about the quality and nature of freedom and political community. The very structure and themes of this *Handbook* testify to the fertility and success of the critical theory of international relations in advancing this agenda.

REFERENCES

ACKERLY, B., STERN, M., and TRUE, J. (eds.) 2006. *Feminist Methodologies for International Relations.* Cambridge: Cambridge University Press.

BEITZ, C. R. 1979. *Political Theory and International Relations.* Princeton, NJ: Princeton University Press.

BERNSTEIN, R. J. 1976. *The Restructuring of Social and Political Theory.* London: Methuen.

BROWN, C. 2002. *Sovereignty, Rights, and Justice: International Political Theory Today.* Cambridge: Polity.

BULL, H. 1983. Justice in international relations. 1983–84 Hagey Lectures, University of Waterloo, 12–13 Oct.

COCHRAN, M. 1999. *Normative Theory in International Relations: A Pragmatic Approach.* Cambridge: Cambridge University Press.

COX, R. W. 1981. Social forces, states and world orders: beyond international relations theory. *Millennium: Journal of International Studies,* 10: 126–55.

—— 1983. Gramsci, hegemony and international relations: an essay in method. *Millennium: Journal of International Studies,* 12: 162–75.

—— 1986. Social forces, states and world orders: beyond international relations theory. Pp. 204–54 in *Neorealism and its Critics,* ed. R. O. Keohane. New York: Columbia University Press.

DEVETAK, R. 2001. Critical theory. Pp. 155–80 in *Theories of International Relations,* 2nd edn., S. Burchill, R. Devetak, A. Linklater, M. Paterson, C. Reus-Smit, and J. True. Houndmills: Palgrave.

FROST, M. 1996. *Ethics in International Relations: A Constitutive Theory.* Cambridge: Cambridge University Press.

—— 2000. *Constituting Human Rights: Global Civil Society and the Society of Democratic States.* New York: Routledge.

HABERMAS, J. 1972. *Knowledge and Human Interests,* trans. J. Shapiro. London: Heinemann.

HONNETH, A. 2004. A social pathology of reason: on the intellectual legacy of critical theory. Pp. 336–60 in *The Cambridge Companion to Critical Theory,* ed. F. Rush. Cambridge: Cambridge University Press.

HOPGOOD, S. 2000. Reading the small print in global civil society: the inexorable hegemony of the liberal self. *Millennium: Journal of International Studies,* 29: 1–25.

HORKHEIMER, M. 1972. *Critical Theory: Selected Essays*. New York: Continuum.

HUTCHINGS, K. 1996. *Kant, Critique and Politics*. London: Routledge.

INAYATULLAH, N., and BLANEY, D. L. 2004. *International Relations and the Problem of Difference*. New York: Routledge.

JACKSON, R. H. 2000. *The Global Covenant: Human Conduct in a World of States*. Oxford: Oxford University Press.

KEAL, P. 2003. *European Conquest and the Rights of Indigenous Peoples: The Moral Backwardness of International Society*. Cambridge: Cambridge University Press.

KEOHANE, R. O. 1988. International institutions: two approaches. *International Studies Quarterly*, 32: 379–96.

LINKLATER, A. 1990a. The problem of community in international relations. *Alternatives*, 15: 135–53.

—— 1990b. *Beyond Realism and Marxism: Critical Theory and International Relations*. London: Macmillan.

—— 1992. The question of the next stage in international relations theory: a critical-theoretical point of view. *Millennium: Journal of International Studies*, 21: 77–98.

—— 2001. The changing contours of critical international relations theory. Pp. 23–44 in *Critical Theory and World Politics*, ed. R. Wyn Jones. Boulder, Colo.: Lynne Rienner.

—— 2002a. Cosmopolitan political communities in international relations. *International Relations*, 16: 135–50.

—— 2002b. The problem of harm in world politics: implications for the sociology of states-systems. *International Affairs*, 78: 319–38.

—— 2006. The harm principle and global ethics. *Global Society*, 20: 329–43.

—— and SUGANAMI, H. 2006. *The English School of International Relations: A Contemporary Reassessment*. Cambridge: Cambridge University Press.

MEARSHEIMER, J. J. 1995. The false promise of international institutions. Pp. 332–76 in *The Perils of Anarchy: Contemporary Realism and International Security*, ed. M. E. Brown, S. M. Lynn-Jones, and S. E. Miller. Cambridge, Mass.: MIT Press.

POGGE, T. W. 2002. *World Poverty and Human Rights: Cosmopolitan Responsibilities and Reforms*. Cambridge: Polity.

PRICE, R., and REUS-SMIT, C. 1998. Dangerous liaisons? Critical international theory and constructivism. *European Journal of International Relations*, 4: 259–94.

RAE, H. 2002. *State Identities and the Homogenisation of Peoples*. New York: Cambridge University Press.

RENGGER, N. 2001. Negative dialectic? The two modes of critical theory in world politics. Pp. 91–110 in *Critical Theory and World Politics*, ed. R. Wyn Jones. Boulder, Colo.: Lynne Rienner.

SHAPCOTT, R. 2001. *Justice, Community and Dialogue in International Relations*. Cambridge: Cambridge University Press.

—— 2004. IR as practical philosophy: defining a "classical approach." *British Journal of Politics and International Relations*, 6: 271–91.

TICKNER, J. A. 1995. Hans Morgenthau's principles of political realism. Pp. 53–71 in *International Theory: Critical Investigations*, ed. J. Der Derian. New York: New York University Press.

WEBER, M. 2005. The critical social theory of the Frankfurt school, and the "social turn" in IR. *Review of International Studies*, 31: 195–209.

WENDT, A. 1992. Anarchy is what states make of it: the social construction of world politics. *International Organization*, 46: 391–425.

WIGHT, M. 1967. Why is there no international theory? Pp. 17–34 in *Diplomatic Investigations: Essays in the Theory of International Politics*, ed. M. Wight and H. Butterfield. London: George Allen and Unwin.

WYN JONES, R. 1999. *Security, Strategy, and Critical Theory*. Boulder, Colo.: Lynne Rienner.

—— (ed.) 2001. *Critical Theory and World Politics*. Boulder, Colo.: Lynne Rienner.

CHAPTER 20

THE ETHICS OF CRITICAL THEORY

ROBYN ECKERSLEY

THIS chapter offers an explication and evaluation of the ethics of critical international relations theory. Critical international relations theory is now a very broad and heterogeneous church, but this chapter will focus only on the work of those critical theorists who have sought inspiration from the work of Jürgen Habermas. The primary focus will be on the ethics of Habermas's discourse ethic; neo-Gramscian, postmodern, postcolonial, and feminist strands of critical international relations theory will not be considered.

First, what do we mean by "ethics?" If we were to accept Habermas's distinction between ethics and morality, which broadly corresponds to the distinction between the good and the right in liberal theory, then this would be a rather short chapter. This is because critical theory is not in the business of ethical inquiry if we understand this in the practical sense to mean deciding "what should be done?" or "what is the good life?" Indeed, Habermas (1993, 123) has argued that, if we are to take modern pluralism seriously, then philosophers must renounce these classical ethical questions along with the attempt to elaborate a preferred way of life. Following in the footsteps of John Rawls, Habermas considers that the task of the modern philosopher is to accept ethical pluralism as a starting point, and then to elucidate the universalizable principles of justice that ought to regulate communal life in ways that foster toleration and the accommodation of different conceptions of the good life. It is therefore *not* the task of critical theorists to offer practical, ethical judgments on particular issues or to pronounce upon "the good life" on behalf of others, since that is for citizens to decide. Whereas Rawls uses the hypothetical device of the original position to elucidate his liberal principles of justice, Habermas employs the method of "rational reconstruction" of human communication to explain and defend his discourse ethic. Through this method, he finds the universalizable principles of justice to be *already implicit* in the idealized and unavoidable presuppositions of communication, reflected in the idea of an inclusive and uncoerced discourse between free and equal partners in communication. That is, every time speakers make a claim, they also make the implicit claim that what they say is true, normatively right, and sincerely meant, and they implicitly promise that each of these claims could, if challenged, be redeemed in further argument. According to Habermas, speakers must follow these presuppositions if language is to remain meaningful and any attempt to argue to the contrary amounts to a performative contradiction.

Of course, it would be profoundly misleading to conclude from Habermas's renunciation of classical ethical inquiry that critical theory is an ethics-free zone. To illuminate the ethics of the discourse ethic I therefore propose to put Habermas's distinction between ethics and morality to one side and employ a more general framing device based on the standard distinction in philosophy between meta-ethics, normative ethics, and applied ethics (see Fieser 2006). Meta-ethics is concerned with the foundations of ethics, and how we know when something is right or valid. Normative ethics is concerned with developing general principles of good or right conduct, which may be virtue based (for example, Aristotle), deontological (for example, Kant), consequentialist (for example, Bentham), religious (Christian, Islamic, Buddhist, and so on), and so on. Applied ethics develops answers to particular ethical or political controversies (such as the problem of poverty, environmental degradation, the conduct of war, or the treatment of animals) by applying the general principles of normative ethics. Employing these distinctions, we can say that Habermasian critical theory offers a well-developed meta-ethics and a proceduralist normative ethics, but it has self-consciously refrained from developing an applied ethics. As to meta-ethics, critical theorists maintain that a claim or norm is right or valid when it has received the unforced consent of the affected constituents after full and free deliberation from all conceivable vantage points. As to normative ethics, critical theory's overriding ethical goal is to promote emancipation, or to remove constraints on human autonomy, by means of ever more inclusive and less distorted dialogue. As to applied ethics, critical theorists can only offer evaluations about the degree to which particular conversations are "distorted" or free, or exclusive or inclusive, legitimate or illegitimate according to the regulative ideal of the discourse ethic. However, they cannot pronounce upon the good life, or offer advice on what should be done, because that would usurp the role of the relevant/affected social agents to work through these questions in practical discourses in particular contexts.

The foremost critical international relations theorist working in the Habermasian tradition, Andrew Linklater, has largely followed this division of ethical labor. As Linklater (1998, 92) has explained, "discourse ethics sets out the procedures to be followed" but it "does not offer putative solutions to substantive moral debates, envisage historical end points or circulate political blueprints." Indeed, "if genuine dialogue is to exist, no particular outcome can be anticipated or presupposed" (Linklater 1998, 86).

In this chapter I seek to highlight the distinctive contribution to cosmopolitan ethical inquiry of this Habermasian branch of critical international relations theory, while also pinpointing certain unresolved ethical tensions and inadequacies associated with the discourse ethic. I show that the tensions arise, in part, from the fact that critical theory's ultimate purpose—emancipation—is not exhausted by the procedural requirements of the discourse ethics. I also critically examine critical theory's reluctance to "do ethics" in the applied sense of the term. My purpose is not to reduce the ethics of critical theory to applied ethics, nor to discount the importance of critical theory's procedural normative ethics. Rather, it is merely to suggest that, once critical theory acknowledges the extradiscursive underpinnings of its normative ethics, the door is opened to engagement in applied ethical debates.

1 THE CONTRIBUTION OF CRITICAL THEORY TO INTERNATIONAL ETHICS

The first wave of "appropriation" of critical theory by international relations theorists in the 1980s was largely concerned with the critique of traditional Marxism, realism, and positivism (see Shapcott, this volume). Critical international relations theory's major contribution to international ethics during this formative period was to question the idea of disinterested, value-free inquiry in the social sciences and to expose the unacknowledged ethical assumptions and inclinations that inevitably shape both theoretical and empirical inquiry in international relations. For example, in positing the anarchic structure of international society as fixed and unchangeable, realist theory was shown to conceal and therefore foreclose the possibility of system transformation and thereby serve as an apologist for the perpetuation of major asymmetries in power, wealth, and opportunity in the state system. In contrast, critical international relations theory embraced the task of *revealing* the possibilities for institutional transformation that would remove constraints on human autonomy. This distinguished critical theory from positivism and mere problem-solving theory, which, intended or unintended, sustained the existing order (Cox 1981).

Since the 1980s, critical international relations theory has taken many paths, one of which has been to explore the potential of Habermas's discourse ethic in international politics. At its most general and ambitious, this Habermasian stream of critical international relations theory has been concerned to explore the potential and possibilities of a world where power and force are replaced with dialogue and consent in social interaction, not only within societies but also between societies, states, and civilizations. However, by extending the discourse ethic beyond domestic society to encompass intersocietal, inter-state, and intercivilizational interaction, critical international relations theory was to venture into waters that had been only partially chartered by Habermas. Habermas's discourse ethic (1997) forms the centerpiece of a rational reconstruction of democracy, law, and legitimacy in the liberal democratic state. In what ways, then, could critical international relations theory show that the discourse ethic is relevant and ethically significant in international politics, where there is no common language or life world and where power and national interests, rather than unconstrained dialogue, have so often held sway?

There are two, mostly complementary but sometimes overlapping, streams of critical theory that have provided responses to this question. The first comprises Habermasian-inspired political theorists (along with Habermas himself) who have directed their critical attention to the democratic deficit in supranational governance, to the role of transnational or cosmopolitan public spheres, and/or to the potential of transnational democracy (e.g. Bohman 1998; Baynes 2001; Habermas 2001).

The second stream, which is the main focus of this chapter, comprises international relations theorists who have sought inspiration from Habermas in exploring the potential for new forms of political community that expand the possibilities for mutual understanding and human emancipation through uncoerced dialogue (e.g. Hoffman 1992; Haacke 1996; Linklater 1998; Wyn Jones 2001). Many constructivist theorists have also drawn on Habermas's theories of the public sphere or communicative action in empirical studies of the role of discourse and argument in international politics (e.g. Lynch 1999; Risse and Ulbert 2005). While most of these constructivist studies are primarily sociological and explanatory rather than normative, they nonetheless endorse, mostly implicitly but sometimes explicitly, the protocols of communicative action.

Both these streams of Habermasian critical theory identified above share a cosmopolitan orientation and seek to break down the distinction between the domestic and the international by extending the democratic achievements of the domestic sphere to the international sphere. Whereas political theorists (including Habermas) have primarily focused on the potential for democratic engagement in regional and international governance structures by transnational civil society actors, Habermasian international relations theorists have been preoccupied with a more macro-level analysis of different forms of exclusion and inclusion in the evolution of states and the international society of states, along with an elaboration of the dialogic protocol that is appropriate to a multicultural world. Linklater (1998, 7) has characterized critical international relations theory's quest in terms of a "triple transformation" of political community toward social relations that are more universal, less unequal, and more sensitive to cultural difference. Critical theory is a post-Marxist theory that "continues to evolve beyond the paradigm of production to a commitment to dialogic communities that are deeply sensitive about all forms of inclusion and exclusion—domestic, transnational, and international" (Linklater 2001, 25).

Linklater has laid out critical international relations theory's general research program in terms of three closely interrelated tasks that he calls the normative, the sociological, and the praxeological (Linklater 1998, 6–7; 2001). The normative task seeks to promote human emancipation by exploring how more inclusive and culturally sensitive dialogic communities may be fostered that give voice and representation to excluded groups. The sociological task is concerned with exploring the nature and evolution of political community, focusing principally on states and the society of states, and their potential to develop in more inclusive ways. For Linklater, this entails moving toward some kind of post-Westphalian order. The praxeological task is to explore the moral resources within existing social arrangements that might be harnessed for emancipatory purposes. Both the sociological and praxeological tasks are informed by the normative goal of emancipation, which provides both the ethical inspiration and the ultimate purpose of critical theory.

Now one might be forgiven for thinking that praxeology represents, or ought to represent, critical theory's study of how to "apply" the discourse ethic to practical ethical problems, and Linklater himself (2001, 37–40) has defended praxeology as producing policy-relevant insights. However, Linklater has largely deployed it as a *method* of critical inquiry or "immanent critique" with emancipatory intent. In effect, praxeology is the method by which critical theory can highlight the unfulfilled promise of the Enlightenment and draw attention to the potential for more inclusive social arrangements that expand human autonomy. For example, Linklater considers the ideal of citizenship to provide a particularly fertile moral resource that has enabled the progressive inclusion of hitherto excluded groups, classes, and peoples in the life of the political community. He has also argued that the principle "do no harm is a useful place to begin in spelling out what it means to belong to a cosmopolitan community" (Linklater 2002, 143). He has tracked the evolution of what he calls "cosmopolitan harm conventions" (such as conventions against genocide, violence against women, and torture) as examples of "moral progress" and suggested that the harm principle has the potential to do more radical work in promoting human emancipation (Linklater 2002). However, much of Linklater's praxeology has remained a relatively abstract inquiry that has focused more on the "big picture" of unfolding possibilities than on particular ethical or policy controversies. Given that what counts as "harm" is not self-evident but rather specific to particular cultures, he is concerned to search for an overlapping consensus or common ground between different communities, faiths, and cultures that might ground a global cosmopolitan ethic based on the harm principle (Linklater 2006). Nonetheless, Linklater is reasonably clear in terms of the general normative direction in which he would like to see international law and an "ethical foreign policy" evolve: toward harm reduction and avoidance (Linklater 2002; see also Shapcott, this volume). Yet, insofar as he begins to spell out more con-crete policy recommendations, such as dispensing with the principle of sovereign immunity and strengthening international criminal law (Linklater 2002), he runs foul of his acknowledgement of the contestability of the meaning of harm, and his commitment to the principle that ethical problems ought to be addressed in an open and undistorted dialogue by those who are affected by them. These tensions are addressed further below.

Against this background, Linklater's major normative ethical contribution has been to elaborate the ethics of the discourse ethic through an engagement not only with Habermas and his sympathizers but also with his feminist and postmodern critics. Linklater's commitment to dialogue (2001, 27) is driven by the insight that those who maintain or benefit from unjust forms of inclusion are unlikely to garner consent or support from the subjects of this exclusion in an unconstrained dialogue. His basic argument is that no one enjoys an "Archimedian" vantage point from which to decide moral claims or appropriate ways of life for others, and therefore submitting all claims to the test of unconstrained dialogue by all those affected (the powerful and the marginal) is the only legitimate means to negotiate collective norms. Such a dialogue would expose morally arbitrary forms of exclusion. As he explains:

all human beings have an equal right to belong to communication communities where they can protest against actions which may harm them, that all participants in ideal speech should enter dialogue with the conviction that no-one knows who will learn from whom, and that all should strive to reach agreements which rely as far as possible on the force of the better argument... (Linklater 2005, 147)

However, one of Linklater's constant worries is that the ethical universalism of the discourse ethic may threaten nonliberal and non-Western ways of life with an exclusionary liberal or Western moral framework that assumes its own superiority in advance of the dialogue. Linklater seeks to avoid this problem by defending a "thin" version of the discourse principle, and hence a "thin" cosmopolitanism, that pursues the twin aim of more universalism and more respect for difference.

2 ETHICAL TENSIONS IN THE DISCOURSE ETHIC

The discourse ethic offers an appealing regulative ideal as well as a critical vantage point from which to assess communicative contexts in international politics and identify shortfalls or distortions. However, critics have often pointed out that the discourse ethic provides very little guidance on how these shortfalls and distortions in real-world communication might be addressed. As Ricardo Blaug (1997, 102) has argued in the context of the general Habermasian debates in political theory, efforts to explore the practical intentions of the discourse ethic encounter problems of "excessive abstraction and discrimination failure." He directs the same criticisms toward Habermas's notion of the public sphere, which he suggests "never quite comes down to earth" (Blaug 1997, 112). He points out that the ideal of undistorted communication is insufficiently discriminating to guide political practice, since no weight is assigned to different elements of the ideal for comparative purposes (and he suggests it would be "preposterous" to do so). All we can do is to say of individual cases how far they are from the ideal, but there is very little crossing over into practical institutional design. Blaug (1997, 112) traces this failure to "a profound ambivalence regarding the relation of meta-theory to substantive political questions." According to Blaug (1997, 117), critical theory is caught between a fear of the coercive power of utopianism, which prevents it from acting, and a disappointment arising from its inability to act in response to suffering. The upshot is that critical theory "remains caught in a twilight zone between fear and disappointment. It has practical intentions which it knows it must not fulfil."

Blaug's critique applies with equal force to Linklater's critical international relations theory.[1] Here I want to draw attention to three tensions or inadequacies. The first concerns the tension between universality and difference, which threatens to blunt critical theory's critical edge; the second concerns the tension between the proceduralism of the discourse ethic and critical theory's overriding substantive goal of emancipation; and the third relates to critical theory's unwillingness to explore the emancipatory possibilities of strategic intervention in a world that falls far short of the communicative ideal.

2.1 Universality versus Difference?

Linklater's effort to develop a dialogic protocol that upholds greater universalism *and* greater respect for difference has forced him on to a narrow tightrope, where

---

[1] Given that Linklater is the towering figure in Habermasian international relations theory, this critique focuses largely on his work. However, it should be noted that the small number of other scholars working in this field have been relatively more engaged with applied ethics. For example, Mark Hoffman (1992) has explored third-party facilitation from a Habermasian perspective, while Deiniol Lloyd Jones (2001) has defended the idea of critical mediation based on "cosmopolitan power."

he is constantly at risk of falling one side or the other when confronted with "hard" practical ethical questions that involve a direct confrontation between these ideals. Indeed, the only way to prevent a fall is not to favor either universality or difference, which leaves critical theory unable to offer any practical resolution to hard ethical questions. This is starkly illustrated in Linklater's equivocation (2005, 153) over the practice of female circumcision, which he concedes raises "awkward questions for discourse ethics." On the one hand, he notes that victims of the practice may not be in a position freely to consent, yet outsiders who find the practice offensive are not harmed by them, and they may be guilty of foisting their Western values on a very different culture if they choose to intervene. So he leaves the matter unresolved.

Even upholding the rights of communication can run into difficulties in relation to non-Western communities, so Linklater counsels that one must also be open to different accounts of what unconstrained dialogue should mean. His general approach is to focus on how "we" in the West relate to other cultures, rather than how "they" in other cultures relate to each other. Yet this advice sits uneasily with Linklater's more general claim that the evolution of human rights is a moral achievement, which suggests that the subjects of female circumcision should be considered first and foremost as human beings (with human rights to bodily integrity and to political participation) rather than as members of a particularistic culture. More generally, as Kimberly Hutchings (2005, 161) notes in a critique of Seyla Benhabib's dialogic ethic (2002) that is equally applicable to Linklater's, the principles of universal respect and egalitarian reciprocity that are basic to the discourse ethic rule out certain identities and ethical postures in advance of the dialogue. Extending the discourse ethic to the transnational realm *necessarily* introduces a hierarchy of morals that privileges certain aspects of Western, liberal morality (Hutchings 2005, 162). It seems that *if* critical theory is to remain critical, cosmopolitan, and modernist, which includes upholding its notion of collective moral learning, then it must inevitably privilege what has been singled out as the progressive aspects of (liberal) modernity.

2.2 Procedural versus Substantive Ethics?

As we have seen, critical theory's overriding purpose is emancipation, and Linklater (1998, 7) has cashed this out in terms of a triple transformation of political community, one that is more universal, less unequal, and more sensitive to cultural difference. But is the discourse ethic always the best, or only, means for achieving this triple transformation, or emancipation in general? On the one hand, given that no particular outcome can be anticipated or presupposed in a genuinely open dialogue, then there is clearly no guarantee that dialogue would necessarily produce a transformation on any one or more of these three fronts. For example, Jürgen Haacke (1996) asks: Why should we assume that the movement toward a post-Westphalian order would necessarily flow from a free intersocietal dialogue? On the other hand, there are other paths to the alleviation of inequality or suffering, or the removal of constraints on human autonomy, than through respectful dialogue. In the international domain, these range from military intervention to prevent genocide and gross human rights abuses, to the application of criminal or economic sanctions or material inducements to recalcitrant states, and a variety of different forms of moral shaming. In short, critical theory's larger normative purpose of human emancipation is by no means exhausted by the ideal of unconstrained communication. This suggests the need for some kind of recalibration of the means–end relationship embedded in critical theory's normative ethics. Either the larger normative purpose needs to be scaled down (so that it becomes a quest for free dialogue for free dialogue's sake, rather than dialogue as the means to human emancipation), or the means for achieving the larger normative purpose are scaled up (to include, yet go beyond, dialogue).

Norman Geras (1999, 159) has highlighted this problem in rather stark terms through his thought experiment of a constituency affected by a proposed dialogue that is so famished, or so victimized by torture, as to be unable to participate in political dialogue. In this case, we would expect critical theorists to insist on the right of this constituency to participate in the dialogue, but can Linklater's thin cosmopolitanism also insist on their right to adequate nourishment or their right to freedom from physical abuse? Or must they wait until these claims are validated through a free dialogue? Now Linklater has argued with some force that these rights are *presupposed* by the discourse ethic, because they must necessarily be satisfied for individuals to engage in deliberation. As he puts it, the "discourse ethic comes fully fitted with an ethic of redistribution" (Linklater 1999, 173). The realization of the discourse ethic requires collective efforts to remove existing inequalities in wealth, income, power, and opportunity to ensure that excluded groups enjoy the substantive, and not merely formal, rights of political participation in the dialogue (Linklater 2001, 30). But must the satisfaction of these rights be conditional on whether the individuals wish to enter a dialogue? Adequate nourishment and freedom from physical abuse are both necessary conditions for human autonomy in general; participation in a political dialogue is only one facet of human autonomy.

In his reply to Geras, Linklater (1999) has reiterated his argument that respectful dialogue is the only legitimate option because there is no transcendental viewpoint from which to judge what is right or wrong. However, this defence of even the most basic right to survival operates only circuitously, via the discourse ethic, rather than independently by appeal to human reason, solidarity, or compassion. However, as Geras points out, the grounds for the thin ethical universalism defended by Linklater are moral preconditions that are assumed in advance of the dialogue and cannot be validated through dialogue: "Linklater embraces both a substantive moral principle and a procedure. But without the principle, the procedure is not worth as much as it is with it" (Geras 1999, 159). If critical theory is to maintain its critical edge and offer more than proceduralism, then it must acknowledge that there is a wider range of ways of serving its ultimate ends. Drawing out the substantive and pre-discursive normative core of critical theory also provides a normative basis from which critical theorists might engage in applied ethical debates. As it happens, much of Linklater's more recent work on cosmopolitan harm conventions and ethical foreign policy has moved in this direction, and this is an appropriate move. Critical theorists should be able to declare that torture is wrong because it represents a particularly egregious form of human domination, not because it impedes a free dialogue.

2.3 Communicative versus Strategic Action?

Given that real-world political communication in international politics typically falls well short of the critical theory's discursive ideal, then one might ask how any cultural practices, normative arguments, or even the procedural requirements of the discourse ethic itself can *ever* be properly justified to all affected? Critical theorists can only ever answer: "more or less." Yet, in the absence of some kind of strategic intervention designed to create the conditions for less distorted communication, then it is typically going to be less rather than more. We noted earlier that Linklater's embrace of dialogue rests on the insight that dominant groups are unlikely to persuade subordinate groups of the wisdom or justice of their subordination in an unconstrained dialogue. However, critical theorists have failed to show why the dominant would ever wish to enter into such a dialogue with the subordinate. Mahatma Gandhi understood this problem well in his dealings with the British, so he resorted to nonviolent civil disobedience, and related tactics such as marches and hunger strikes, to bring the colonial power to the negotiating table.

One way out of the dilemma of fear and disappointment outlined by Blaug would be for critical theory to follow Gandhi's lead and explore the possibilities of other forms of political intervention, including strategic, tactical, and symbolic intervention, which might prepare the ground for more meaningful dialogues in unjust or conflict-ridden situations. Indeed, critical theory already has the moral resources to justify such action in situations where communicative action is not feasible or when it is extremely constrained. As Haacke (1996, 279) explains, strategic action would be justifiable "only as long as it seeks to establish conditions that allow communicative rationality to unfold its potential, not insofar as it anticipates the possible outcome of praxis as discourse." This may also require some rethinking of the positivist–critical binary that seems to have disabled critical theory from offering policy-relevant ethical prescriptions for fear of somehow collaborating with, rather than critiquing, the existing order. Alexander Wendt (2001, 206) has suggested that this binary can be transcended by linking reform and transformation over different time horizons, with the former serving as a bridge to the latter, and Linklater (2001, 37) has also welcomed this approach.

In light of the foregoing, there is no reason why critical international relations theorists should not throw their hat into the ring of public ethical debates.[2] There is nothing "coercive" associated with offering an argument, given that it will either be redeemed or fail through further argument. While it would be too heroic a feat for critical theorists to take on the task of imagining a universal communication community and deciding what ethical prescriptions might flow from an unconstrained dialogue, it is quite possible for critical theorists to develop applied ethical prescriptions that would help to expand the autonomy of the least autonomous. Moreover, such prescriptions need not always be confined to preparing the ground for less distorted communication. As we have seen, the discourse ethic provides only one means toward the expansion of human autonomy, which is critical theory's ultimate normative purpose, so there is no reason why critical theorists should confine their applied ethical attention to developing culturally sensitive dialogic protocols. For example, if it is accepted that adequate nourishment and freedom from physical abuse are necessary conditions for human autonomy, then critical theorists have a basis upon which to develop applied ethical arguments against torture and in favor of much more generous aid and poverty relief (and these examples are not exhaustive).

3 CONCLUSION

Critical theory has set itself an ambitious research program of sociological, normative, and praxeological inquiry—perhaps the most ambitious research program in international relations theory—and it would be churlish to expect it to have fully realized all dimensions of this program, given the enormity of the challenges involved. Moreover, while there is room for further ethical development in critical international relations theory, it has nonetheless travelled further on this front than either of its main postpositivist cousins, constructivism and post-structuralism. Critical theory's vision of a world of social interaction that is based on dialogue and consent rather than power and force is no less appealing just because it is challenging and requires further elaboration. Nonetheless, if critical theory wishes to ensure its practical relevance to contemporary politics, then it must embrace applied ethics

---

[2] Habermas (1994) has played an increasingly prominent role in public policy debates, not only in Germany but also in Europe and the world, ranging between German unification, European integration, the Gulf War, and the asylum debate.

and explore the kinds of institutional designs *and* strategic interventions that might help to realize the dialogic ideal and, ultimately, human autonomy.

REFERENCES

BAYNES, K. 2001. Deliberative politics, the public sphere and global democracy. Pp. 161–70 in Wyn Jones 2001.

BENHABIB, S. 2002. *The Claims of Culture: Equality and Diversity in the Global Era.* Princeton, NJ: Princeton University Press.

BLAUG, R. 1997. Between fear and disappointment: critical, empirical and political uses of Habermas. *Political Studies*, 45: 100–17.

BOHMAN, J. 1998. The globalization of the public sphere: cosmopolitan publicity and the problem of cultural pluralism. *Philosophy and Social Criticism*, 24: 199–216.

COX, R. 1981. Social forces, states and world orders: beyond international relations theory. *Millennium: Journal of International Studies*, 10: 126–55.

FIESER, J. 2006. Ethics. *The Internet Encyclopedia of Philosophy*, www.iep.utm.edu/e/ethics.htm#H1.

GERAS, N. 1999. The view from everywhere. *Review of International Studies*, 25: 157–63.

HAACKE, J. 1996. Theory and praxis in international relations: Habermas, self-reflection, rational argumentation. *Millennium: Journal of International Studies*, 25: 255–89.

HABERMAS, J. 1993. *Justification and Application: Remarks on Discourse Ethics*, trans. C. Cronin. Cambridge: Polity.

——1994. *The Past as Future*. Cambridge: Polity.

——1997. *Between Facts and Norms: Contributions to a Discourse Theory of Law and Democracy*, trans. W. Rehg. Cambridge: Polity.

——2001. *The Postnational Constellation: Political Essays*, trans. M. Pensky. Cambridge: Polity.

HOFFMAN, M. 1992. Third-party mediation and conflict-resolution in the post-Cold War world. Pp. 261–86 in *Dilemmas of World Politics: International Issues in a Changing World*, ed. J. Baylis and N. J. Rengger. Oxford: Clarendon Press.

HUTCHINGS, K. 2005. Speaking and hearing: Habermasian discourse ethics, feminism and IR. *Review of International Studies*, 31: 155–65.

LINKLATER, A. 1998. *The Transformation of Political Community: Ethical Foundations of the Post-Westphalian Era*. Cambridge: Polity.

——1999. Transforming political community: a response to the critics. *Review of International Studies*, 25: 165–75.

——2001. The changing contours of critical international relations theory. Pp. 23–43 in Wyn Jones 2001.

——2002. Debate: cosmopolitan political communities in international relations. *International Relations*, 16: 135–50.

——2005. Dialogic politics and the civilising process. *Review of International Studies*, 31: 141–54.

——2006. The harm principle and global ethics. *Global Society*, 20: 329–43.

Lloyd Jones, D. 2001. Creating cosmopolitan power: international mediation as communicative action. Pp. 171–87 in Wyn Jones 2001.

Lynch, M. 1999. *State Interests and Public Spheres: The International Politics of Jordan's Identity*. New York: Columbia University Press.

Risse, T., and Ulbert, C. 2005. Deliberately changing the discourse: what does make arguing effective? *Acta Politica*, 40: 351–67.

Wendt, A. 2001. What is international relations for? Notes toward a postcritical view. Pp. 205–24 in Wyn Jones 2001.

Wyn Jones, R. (ed.) 2001. *Critical Theory and World Politics*. Boulder, Colo.: Lynne Rienner.

CHAPTER 21

....

POSTMODERNISM

....

ANTHONY BURKE

IF this chapter were a self-help book, it might be called: "Your paradigm is killing you." And if it were a placard at a demonstration: "Your paradigm is killing *us*."

By this I mean to situate postmodernism in international relations through its most fundamental and powerful characteristic: its systematic denaturalization of the real and the given, with the aim of social critique in the name of some ethical good. This it does by connecting systems of knowledge, theory, and representation with the operations of social and political power. This is how "paradigms" can kill or save—through the ways they define and impose "realities" upon a diverse and recalcitrant world. "Postmodern" or "post-structuralist" strands of critical theory in international relations have not always handled ethical or normative issues well. However, they have all been motivated by a desire to challenge existing practices and conceptualizations of international reality because of their perceived untenability or danger to human beings, societies, and ecosystems. Their aim has not been to break language free from all claims to truth—they constitute another such claim, after all—but to show how modern social structures, institutions, and events are historically bound and contingent; how they are the products, not of human nature, the laws of politics, the progress of history, or the cunning of reason, but of human action and thought in a world without stable foundations.

In this chapter I will distinguish "postmodernism" (a set of theories) from "postmodernity" (a historical period) and focus on postmodernism as a theoretical orientation and set of concerns about global politics. While some postmodernist arguments and insights have come from attempts to periodize a uniquely "postmodern" historical period and social reality—one characterized by dramatic increases in the size and speed of global movements of information, capital, and goods, and an increasingly "virtual" social environment ever more saturated by media and signification (Der Derian 1993)—this chapter reads "postmodernism" in terms of writings that have taken up insights from "post-structuralist" theory and applied them to world politics. It sees it as an *analytical orientation* inspired by a range of continental philosophers who have challenged some of the fundamental structures and concepts of Western thought.

The chapter includes some criticisms of postmodernism and a strong defense of its ongoing value and relevance. I do so (sympathetically) to push postmodern critique a little harder, and to promote internal debate over some of its claims. Critically, it argues for postmodernist currents in international relations to engage productively with sympathetic elements of other critical and traditional approaches, to gain greater clarity about their normative commitments, possibilities (and dangers), and for more work that connects theoretical innovation with specific projects and struggles that are of relevance both to policy-makers and to marginalized communities. And, in defense of postmodernism, I argue for its ethical and analytical value, and its sheer *timeliness*: its ability to diagnose and resist the bizarre nihilism of our age. In such an age of omnipresent media and political "spin," where destructive wars are launched to destroy weapons of mass destruction that do not exist and nations are bombed, occupied, and tortured in the name of freedom—an age, in short, where policy-makers claim to be able to make their own realities—the charges of relativism and nihilism launched by positivist and conservative scholars against postmodernism are brazen and perverse (Burke 2007a, 232).

What could be more nihilistic, or more relativistic, than such a politics? What could enact more perfectly Jean Baudrillard's notorious prognosis (1988) of a postmodernity that is pure surface, an endless cascade of signs and simulacra divorced from a "real" it never ceases to impersonate? It seems that the powerful are allowed to sunder words from things, to murder truth in the defense of truth, but that students of world politics are allowed neither to theorize and critique this process, nor to ponder its implications as a social phenomenon. Perhaps it is the positivists and the statesmen who are "postmodern," and the theorists merely lonely prophets on a hillside.

1 REALITY, REALISM, AND POWER

In 1994 Jim George began his book *Discourses of Global Politics* with the bold statement that "reality, it seems, is not what it used to be in international relations." The occasion was the end of the cold war in Europe, after which "patterns of thought and behaviour identified as corresponding with an enduring essence of

global existence are coming under increasing scrutiny as old ideological commitments and alliances are reformulated, territorial boundaries are hastily redrawn,
and new symbols of identity are constructed or resurrected" (George 1994, 1).
This was said in the face of an underlying "positivist–empiricist" consensus that
reality is external to the observer and can be mapped, recorded, and reduced to
a series of timeless ahistorical essences, to a system of truth from which we can
derive enduring and unchallengeable rules for politics. Groundshaking events may
occur, but the rules of the game do not, as Kenneth Waltz (2002) asserted after
11 September. In international relations theory this view was persuasively put by
Hans Morgenthau (1973, 4), who sought to develop a "scientific" theory that was
based on a view that

politics, like society in general, is governed by objective laws that have their roots in human nature...the operation of these laws being impervious to our preferences, men will
challenge them only at the risk of failure. Realism, believing as it does in the objectivity of
the laws of politics, must also believe in the possibility of developing a rational theory that
reflects, however imperfectly and one-sidedly, these objective laws. It believes also, then, in
the possibility of distinguishing in politics between truth and opinion—between what is
true objectively and rationally, supported by evidence and illuminated by reason, and what
is only a subjective judgment, divorced from the facts as they are and informed by prejudice
and wishful thinking.

The other famous "classical" realist, E. H. Carr (1966, 10), made a similar claim
that, for realism, "the function of thinking is to study a sequence of events which it
is powerless to influence or to alter."

Revisionist scholars of classical realism such as Christian Reus-Smit (2001, 578),
Michael Williams (2005, 101), and Muriel Cozette (2008) have rightly shown how
these thinkers were not as crudely positivist and amoral as they have been represented. Carr (1969, 5, 10), for example, also pointed out that "every political judgment helps to modify the facts on which it is passed," and argued for a paradigm
where realism and utopianism balance the respective "barrenness" and "exuber-
ance" of the other. Morgenthau and Carr also had the honorable aim of attempting
to counteract the dangers and complacencies of "utopian" schemas for political
change that might resolve the problem of politics once and for all. However, the
classical realists left two problematic legacies that postmodern readings of world
politics have challenged.

First, later (especially American) writers reduced their arguments to a much
narrower positivism, which allied a correspondence theory of truth and falsifica-
tionist reasoning to an "applied" model of social science, which simultaneously
denied and assumed its own normative commitments as universal. This reached its
apogee with neorealism, "a parsimonious explanatory theory...ostensibly stripped
of all normative commitments" (Reus-Smit 2001, 574). Indeed Stanley Hoffmann
(2001, 32–3) questioned the "profound conviction" of postwar Americans that "all

problems can be resolved, that the way to resolve them was to apply the scientific method—assumed to be value free, and to combine empirical investigation, hypothesis formation, and testing—and that the resort to science will yield practical applications that will bring progress."

This had the effect of lending scholarly weight to crude strategic theory that assumed that analysis could be matched with policy to produce predictable results and a controllable world: that the realities of analysis could be made to match reality as such. Hubris was one possible outcome, as was the potential for grossly immoral and destructive policy directions once the normative commitments and consequences of intellectual frameworks were denied. At the very least, the routine ability of powerful states to shape new realities—and the moral responsibilities this brought with it—was denied. This could take the resigned and tragic mode of Karl Deutsch (1968, v) (who argued that "we can neither escape from nor form the pattern of world affairs; we can only try to adjust the world while adapting to it") or the brutal geopolitics of Henry Kissinger (1969, 48), who stated in 1969 that the "scientific revolution" uniting "technology" and "managerial skills" has "removed technical limits from the exercise of power in foreign policy."

The postpositivist effort to recover the agency involved in political action has been described well by John Vasquez (1995, 220) as an effort to expose "choice posing as truth." Postmodern thinkers deny that politics possess "objective laws" or that a lawlike analysis could be based on an essentialist fiction such as "human nature," and they would point to Morgenthau's rhetorical strategies: his use of dichotomies that affirm rationality as the prime value in politics—arguably his strongest contribution to the mode of realist thinking at issue. They would challenge the way his text privileges facts over values, reason over subjectivity, and truth over opinion, obscuring the presence of opinion in every claim to truth, of subjectivity in every claim to reason, and value judgments in every assertion of fact. After Jacques Derrida, they argue that this is a *logocentric* strategy that simultaneously incorporates and silences what it cannot acknowledge in its will to truth; a "post-Enlightenment will to knowledge," writes George (1994, 32), that "has quite literally become a will to power."

Postmodern writing in international relations has arguably developed an epistemology (and a sociological analysis of power) that synthesizes key insights from the literature that developed and critiqued the semiology of Charles Pierce and Ferdinand de Saussure, the language games of Ludwig Wittgenstein, and the structuralism of Claude Lévi-Strauss, Jacques Lacan, Louis Althusser, and the early Michel Foucault. From Roland Barthes (1984), it derived arguments about the cultural power within modernity of narratives and myths about identity and existence, of the tendencies of ideology to mask its partisanship in claims to neutrality and truth, and (in his famous essay "The Death of the Author") the socially dispersed nature of interpretation such that a text's meaning cannot be fixed by the name or authority of a single origin. Derrida extended these insights with arguments that full meaning is always deferred and operates often through dichotomizing strategies that, since the ancient Greeks, have opposed speech to writing, truth to fiction, man to woman, politics to ethics, and so on, while devaluing and suppressing the lesser term. Yet Derrida (1976) reminds us that such terms depend for their meaning and effect on this structure (or play) of opposition, so that differences and discontinuities are always revealed within drives for unity, self-presence, and sameness. Deconstruction, then, claims not to be able to destroy such oppositions but seeks to show how they operate, what they disavow, and what tactics might be sought to resist or refigure them. This insight has proved enormously productive for theorists, who see such "metaphysical" tactics everywhere at work in global politics and traditional theory.

Foucault's contribution was to reinforce arguments that all reality is structured by (and only accessible from within) language, and, following a more "structuralist" phase where he focused on the way "discourses" created coherent systems of knowledge, objects, and subjects, then moved into a more dynamic analysis of the mutual constitution of power/knowledge. This introduced a model of power that was not merely repressive but productive and enabling, that relied not merely on material capacities or institutional–legal powers but ideas and norms: on "the politics of truth" (Rabinow 1984). This shift, characterized by Hubert Dreyfus and Paul Rabinow (1983, 103) as one from "archaeology" to "genealogy," has been seized upon as a powerful methodology by many international relations scholars, who use it to trace the emergence of particular ideas and practices of policy and social action, and to examine the "conditions of possibility" for particular concepts and institutions, so that space can be found for the imagination and enactment of critical alternatives.

While virtually every postmodern scholar has made powerful points in critique of rationalism, George has arguably made the most thorough analysis of its roots both in Western thought—in the philosophy of René Descartes, Francis Bacon, Thomas Hobbes, David Hume, Karl Popper, and US behavioralism—and then in its emergence at the discursive centre of mainstream international relations as a "cold war discipline." This he describes as a "positivist–empiricist metaphysic" that distils powerful elements of *modernity* as a process and structure of thought (George 1994, 41–110). This supports a major contribution of postmodern thought to international relations: its ability to show how, as historico-theoretical processes, modernity and global politics are closely intertwined and must be analyzed together.

In this, George echoed and developed early Frankfurt School critical theory, especially when discussing the modernization theory of Walt Rostow, Samuel Huntington, and others, which he describes as "an explicit celebration of Western modernity and its central sovereign figure, rational man (the user and controller of all things) ... a doctrine of utilitarian 'usefulness' and control" that "continues to inform neo-realist scholarship" and became an important knowledge form in "the power-politics of Cold War political practice." Among many other points where his critique made profound statements about policy, George also analyzed George Kennan's "long telegram" of 1946, which (notwithstanding his later nuance and dissent) did much to create the conditions for the cold war at a time when a less hostile relationship between the superpowers may have been imaginable. Instead, the text helped create "an interpretive straitjacket from which neither Western nor Soviet analysts could escape for forty years" (George 1994, 96–7, 86).

Hence, ethically, the critique of positivism has aimed to unmask the operations of power in the "knowledge" of global politics, and to uncover its formal and rhetorical structures, so as to open up suppressed choices in policy-making and bring out the voices of the marginalized and oppressed. This is to liberate and celebrate "difference," both in terms of the forms of life and culture suppressed by Western drives for hegemony, and in terms of suppressed forms of scholarship and ideology (George and Campbell 1990, 281).

2 FOUNDING GIVENS: SOVEREIGNTY, ANARCHY, AGENCY

Realist and liberal paradigms of international relations rest upon a set of core ontological givens, first among them being the normative and existential priority of the territorial nation state as a privileged container for being and a structuring fact of the international system or society. This digs its ground in two influential stories about modernity. The first is the narrative of the creation of political society we know as the "social contract," in which humans emerge from an ungoverned state of nature characterized by permanent insecurity into a unified political community known as the body politic, which enforces sameness and identity by suppressing internal differences, projecting others (such as those of indigenous societies) into a fading temporal horizon of backwardness and nature, and warding off external differences with borders, diplomacy, and weapons. The second is the appropriation of the Hobbesian metaphor to describe the international system of states—riven by differences and conflicts—as "anarchic" and thus ungovernable by laws made within state-based political communities (Der Derian 1987; Burke 2007a, 27–53).

Well before Alexander Wendt (1992) published his constructivist critique of anarchy, postmodern writers were challenging many of the most fundamental claims about sovereignty, the state, and global politics in ways that both liberal and constructivist analysis has proven reluctant to. Richard Ashley (1987; 1988; 1989), for example, used a deconstructive reading to show how realist assertions about anarchy depended on a fictive imagination of the sovereign state as a repository of the order, homogeneity, and identity that is absent outside its borders.

Important critiques of the concept of "anarchy"—as describing the division between domestic and international politics—have also come from Beate Jahn (2000) and Aaron Beers Sampson (2002). Jahn challenges the idea of the state of nature, showing how it legitimated colonialism, exploitation, and differential human rights standards by applying "different kinds of moral principles...to the different 'stages of development'." She challenges the "neutrality" of the view, developed as the Spanish pushed into the Americas, that the Amerindians were "peoples without culture"—an assumption which she argues still permeates Western foreign policies (Jahn 2000, xv). Sampson shows how Waltz's realism (*and* Wendt's constructivism) draw upon Durkheimian sociology and functionalist anthropology to portray the international system as a primitive "tropical anarchy" that "reduces possible policy responses to a simple choice: either maintain the status quo or civilize the world." Indeed, he argues that by "appropriating a theory originally intended to help colonial administrators control primitive societies" Waltz produces "an image of international politics that privileges power over progress, equilibrium over change, and preventive measures over curative ones" (Sampson 2002, 429–30).

Thus Jahn and Sampson implicitly problematize the philosophy of historical progress central to enlightenment modernity, especially when it takes the form of racist narratives of technological and civilizational superiority that legitimate hegemonic dominance. The critique of such "metanarratives" of progress—central to the work of philosophers such as Jean-François Lyotard (1989) and Agnes Heller (1999)—is strangely under-represented in postmodern international relations theory, but has been central to my own research (Burke 2007a, chs. 1, 7, 9), was the focus of a part of R. B. J. Walker's *Inside/Outside* (1993, ch. 8), and has appeared in very timely critiques of the liberal rhetoric central to George W. Bush's doctrine by Bruce Buchan (2002) and Brett Bowden (2004).

Postmodernist thought has also contributed to a more intellectually diverse effort to show how the ontological privilege granted to sovereignty has been used to deny indigenous peoples full subjectivity and rights within the institutions that govern international relations—a problem that persists and, argues the normative scholar Paul Keal (2003), gravely undermines the moral legitimacy of "international society" (see also Connolly 1995; Shapiro 1997; Shaw 2002). This critique underpins practical efforts to legitimate the struggles of indigenous peoples against miners, loggers, and security forces, and are among a number of injustices that have stimulated a deeper challenge to sovereignty as an ontology. William Connolly questions the claims of sovereignty to provide an ontological ground for being by pointing to the acts of force that enable its founding and are dissolved into acts of "forgetting." This spurs him to develop a pluralistic ethics of domestic and transnational democracy that seeks to weaken the suppression of differences within states and forge coalitions of citizens across national boundaries to work on global problems (Connolly 1995, 138; 2005; Burke 2007a, 120–38). Writers such as Cynthia Weber (1995) have likewise pointed to the constructed and "simulated" nature of sovereignty, not merely at its point of origin but in ongoing policy processes. In this sense, she argues, it is performative—of itself. Walker (1993, 129) put the assumed confluence of territory, sovereignty, and identity into question by denaturalizing the construction of space since the Renaissance, after which there was an increasing "linkage between ideas of state sovereignty and a sense of inviolable and sharply delimited space."

Statist ontologies of international reality also presuppose particular images of identity, subjectivity, and agency. Walker critiques the bounded and exclusivist political communities imagined by social contract models of sovereignty (1993, 60–7), and the way they privilege the category of the "citizen" over the "human" (1997, 71). Other writers have shown how sovereignty acts ontologically to construct subjectivity in terms of an immersion of individual identity into that of the state, giving meaning to individual lives and making them more pliable to the operations of national and corporate power (Neal 2004, 391–7; Burke 2007a). Yet, if an obvious answer would be to promote cross-border allegiances and movements that challenge dominant state and corporate hegemonies, do we have useful models of resistance with which to work? Roland Bleiker's groundbreaking work on agency addresses this problem, suggesting a need to move beyond masculine and heroic models of dissent to ones that work at the levels of discourse that support and enable domination. These he calls "discursive terrains of dissent," which are made visible by an approach that "investigates how social dynamics have been imbued with meaning and how this process of rendering them rational circumscribes the boundaries within which the transversal interaction between domination and resistance takes place" (Bleiker 2000a, 209–10).

3 SECURITY, VIOLENCE, AND THE HUMAN

The above lines of critique—of positivism, metaphysics, sovereignty, and identity—have all informed what is a significant (and in some quarters resented) postmodern contribution to security and strategic studies. Its major themes have been a deconstruction and genealogy of the idea of discourse of security in modernity, a challenge to its ontological claims and function, and an associated interrogation of sovereign violence and its relation to constructions of the human. Key early contributions came from Walker (1988; 1997), Timothy Luke (1989), Bradley Klein (1989; 1994), Simon Dalby (1990), David Campbell (1992), and Der Derian (1993). These writers put the textual and discursive strategies of military, foreign policy, strategic, and security discourse under scrutiny, refuting their claims to be objective or neutral descriptions of the realist play of deterrence and threat. Campbell in particular showed how threat constructions were central to a mutually constitutive practice of foreign policy and identity. Der Derian (1993, 95) dug more deeply into security as an ontological claim with a reading of Hobbes that located the cultural force of security in its mediation between state and citizen, and in the fact that "within the concept of security there lurks the entire history of western metaphysics ... the security of the centre has been the shifting site from which the forces of authority, order, and identity philosophically and physically kept at bay anarchy, chaos and difference"—an approach also visible in work by Michael Dillon (1996) and Walker (1997).

Walker's *One World, Many Worlds* (1988) had made a valuable contribution to popularizing human-centered policy approaches—a normatively better approach to the realist "broadening" debates of the 1980s—though scholars such as Dalby (1997) began to question how far "security" could be stretched as a meaningful signifier, given that it appeared to name very different practices and ends that were neither normatively nor politically commensurate. This focus on the practices generated by particular languages and conceptualizations of security was pursued in work by David Mutimer (2000) on weapons proliferation, and in the "securitization" arguments of Ole Wæver (in Buzan, Wæver, and de Wilde 1998), which suggested that security was a particular, intense kind of "speech act" that—when issues were subsumed under its rubric—signified them in stark terms of existential threat and legitimated actions outside the normal. However the Copenhagen School's blend of realism and post-structuralism generated normative ambiguities that have been criticized (McSweeney 1999, 75; Booth 2005).

Other approaches reject Wæver's stress on exceptionalism but see the deployment of security in Foucauldian terms as a knowledge–power formation. Such analysis locates security historically as both a metaphysic of being and a "political technology" that links sovereign and subject into a single ontological form (the "body politic" of Hobbes and John Locke), then wagers its security upon the suffering and insecurity of others (Burke 2001; 2007a). This in turn has coincided with a range of useful practical studies of "security politics," especially in relation to refugees and terrorism (Jackson 2005; McDonald 2005).

In this sense valuable work has sought to think the relation between violence and the human, as exemplified by Judith Butler's response to 11 September, *Precarious Life* (2004). Using the work of philosophers Giorgio Agamben and Emmanuel Levinas, she critiques the practices of detention, torture, and warfare mobilized in the name of the victims by asking whether grief can be memorialized in nonviolent ways, and by asking what kind of lives are "grievable" in public discourse. Grief for her holds the potential for creating new kinds of "political community ... by bringing to the fore the relational ties that have implications for theorizing fundamental dependency and ethical responsibility" (Butler 2004, 22). The ungrievable are those, like the *homo sacer* of Agamben's theory, who have been reduced to "bare lives" that can be used or killed at will, who lack fundamental status as human. Agamben's work has inspired international relations scholarship that has extended his analysis beyond concentration camps to refugee camps and policies (Puggioni 2006), the global liberal governance of Western response to complex emergencies (Dillon and Reid 2000), and the provision of famine relief and the North Atlantic Treaty Organization's care for Kosovar refugees. In this latter example, Jenny Edkins (2000) uses Agamben to make a controversial analogy between the bare life produced in the Holocaust and that mobilized in Ethiopian famine-relief camps. Her critique of the depoliticizing strategies of the camps that denied agency to refugees is very well made, but there is a vast normative and moral gulf between the genocidal strategy pursued by the Nazis and that of an enterprise, however flawed and criticizable, that aims to save and preserve life. Such a sweeping appropriation of Agamben is probably unwise, and his relevance to problems in global politics has more recently been critically appraised (Neal 2004; Puggioni 2006; Burke 2007a, 9–12).

4 (Inter)textuality, Art, and Aesthetics

Postmodern work has also impressively developed the interest in questions of textuality, language, and genre evident in early collections like *International/Intertextual Relations* (Der Derian and Shapiro 1989). This work, which has been published under various rubrics such as "art and IR" (Sylvester forthcoming), "poetic world politics," "aesthetics" (Bleiker 2000b; forthcoming), and "mediation" (Debrix and Weber 2003), transforms the scholarly practice of international relations by mixing it with art, theatre, and literary and cultural theory, bringing into question the linguistic rules of positivistic social science, which rule out the text drawing attention its own form, rhetorical strategies, and metaphors. At the same time, by encouraging more literary forms of writing, and criticism of social texts as (and via) cultural forms—of the social as a complex text—it has created space for more imaginative and challenging ways of conceiving and reconceiving world politics.

Many authors argue that this is a matter of bringing neglected empirical realities of world politics to light: As Christine Sylvester (forthcoming) argues in an important new work, *Art/Museums: International Relations where You Least Expect It*, art and museums are already part of world politics—whether this be the looting of museums in the Iraq invasion, the imperial histories underpinning the dispute over the Parthenon marbles, the symbolic politics of grief, nationalism, and capital played out in struggles over the reconstruction of the World Trade Center—and hence deserve analysis. Other cultural sites of international relations have been explored by Debbie Lisle, in the intersections between war and tourism (2000) and between airports, national signifiers, borders, and movement (2003). Other efforts to think the semiotic connections between culture and power have addressed the Zapatistas (Higgins 2000), the fall of the Berlin Wall (Bleiker 2000*b*), development (Sylvester 2000; 2003), imagings of African famine (Campbell 2003), 11 September (Weber 2003), and security practices and imaginaries (Constantinou 2000; Burke 2007*a*).

Dedicated journal issues on international relations "poetics," "dramaturgies," and art have been published by *Alternatives* (2000; 2006), *Millennium: Journal of International Studies* (2001; 2006), and *Borderlands* (2003), and collected in books by François Debrix and Weber (2003), and Bleiker (forthcoming). This work also sought to identify positive possibilities through cultural forms—such as Campbell's discussion (2003) of the photography of Sebastião Salgado, which restores agency to starving communities, Costas Costantinou's example (2000) of the poetry of Archilochus, Rumi, and Gibran, which enables us to think past security anxieties, or Richard Devetak (2005*b*), whose meditations on the sublime and 11 September light routes of escape from the politics of dread it engendered. In this way, the postmodern analytical intersection between culture and events is where some of its most hopeful normative and existential potentials emerge.

5 A FUTURE FOR POSTMODERN INTERNATIONAL RELATIONS?

What should, or could, be the future of postmodernism in international relations? It is obviously hard to make predictions, but my hunch is that its future hinges on three things: on its ability to look self-critically at its past, and respond to new ethical, political, and intellectual challenges; in doing so, on its ability to engage constructively with other strands of critical and traditional theory; and, most importantly, on the outcome of a darker struggle with forms of political theory and practice that wish to silence it. This is why it may be better to stake out clearer normative positions and commitments, engage in detail with events, and confront critics head-on rather than through strategies of displacement.

The stakes involved in this struggle became clear in 2006 when the *Australian*, a national newspaper published by Rupert Murdoch's News Corporation, published a series of articles arguing that the Australian Research Council should cease funding critical research on terrorism. While this agenda was driven by a neoconservative political lobby close to that in the United States, their charges echoed those of some leading scholars of international relations. Consider how Peter Katzenstein, Robert Keohane, and Stephen Krasner (1998, 678) justified the absence of debate between postmodernist and rationalist theory in the journal *International Organization*:

Little of this debate was published in *IO*, since *IO* has been committed to an enterprise that postmodernism denies: the use of evidence to adjudicate between truth claims. In contrast to conventional and critical constructivism, postmodernism falls clearly outside the social science enterprise, and in international relations research risks becoming self-referential and disengaged from the world, protests to the contrary notwithstanding.

There is a brazen acknowledgement of censorship and suppression in this statement about the publication history of arguably the discipline's most influential US journal. Claims that postmodernism "rejects the use of evidence" and is not social science are damaging ones echoed by Fred Halliday (1996, 320), who sweepingly conflates "various forms of relativism and postmodernism," which he argues, are characterized by "an abandonment of claims to rational analysis [and] and an affectation of language and reference ... at the expense of substantive or particular analysis." As wrong as such charges are, I fear that postmodern scholarship has not dealt with them effectively or kept them in its critical horizon.

In the last few years there has been a welcome growth in the number of works (at least partly) influenced by post-structuralism that deal in detail with historical events and empirical problems, without being positivistic (Campbell 1998; Burke 2001; 2007a; Sylvester 2002; 2003; Bleiker 2005). In this they have been joined by a number of constructivist works (see Price and Reus-Smit 1998; Reus-Smit 2005), and, in the case of Lene Hansen's important new account (2006) of how discourse analysis can be pursued and used to explain the practice of foreign policy, an empirical focus on Bosnian war diplomacy is matched by a compelling account of discourse analysis as a methodology. "It's time," she remarks, "for poststructuralism to take methodology back [from rationalism]" (Hansen 2006, 5). Perhaps ironically, it was a traditionalist "data-based" scholar, Vasquez (1995), who made one of the strongest arguments for a postpositivist approach that can use and evaluate "evidence" without slipping into relativism. Importantly, Vasquez (1995, 225–9) saw this as part of an effort to "restore normative practical theory to its rightful place within international relations discourse."

Less happily, Ashley and Walker (1990, 368–9) concluded their edited issue of *International Studies Quarterly* on dissidence in international studies by addressing a list of similar complaints about postmodern theory, including serious questions about its lack of "criteria for choosing among the multiple and competing explanations" or its failure to identify with a "'someone' on behalf of whose purposes they theorize." While much post-structuralist scholarship has implicitly refuted such claims, when given a high-visibility opportunity to address them explicitly

Ashley and Walker merely deconstructed their strategies—especially their attempts to discipline and exclude—rather than set out a persuasive and direct refutation.

At such times postmodern analysis can fail to appreciate the political stakes of its own discourse. For example, consider how Hansen (2006, 5), in the course of her brilliant defense of post-structuralism as a methodology, makes the problematic claim that it has a "non-causal epistemology." Against Keohane's view that, while "reflectivists were right in pointing to the importance of identity, culture, norms, regimes and ideas," they "needed to formulate causal hypotheses and subject them to more rigorous testing," she argues that "poststructuralism cannot be formulated as a causal theory because the relationship between identity and foreign policy is co-constitutive or performative" (Hansen 2006, 2–3).

Hansen (2006, 9–10) is right to criticize the rationalist idea of causality as too "narrowly and rigorously defined" and as enacting intellectual exclusion because "there is no scope...within the rationalist epistemological position for research projects that cannot be conceptualized in causal epistemological terms." Yet her rejection of causality *as such* neglects an opportunity both to improve causal models and to show how post-structuralist analysis can explain events and help make policy. The idea of causality is not owned by rationalism, and it is of supreme importance in how we weigh decisions and make choices when exercising the instrumental and rhetorical powers of modern politics.

Hansen's account makes any process of co-constitution of discourses and events strangely static, when surely the point of discourse theory is to show what kind of ethical and political outcomes are at stake in the performance of particular forms of identity and the mobilization of particular kinds of knowledge. How else are we to make ethical arguments about discourse and representation if not in terms of what they might cause or at least bring into the realm of the possible? *This* is how we choose between competing explanations. This point is at the heart of Maja Zehfuss's critique (2002, 250) of mainstream constructivism, which, by positing a material reality prior to norms and representations, "obscures the politics already involved in representing reality" and enables an evasion of political and ethical responsibility. Post-structuralism certainly challenges instrumental models of causation that link means and ends unproblematically—as in much strategic policy—by showing how events are subject to contradictory interpretations and are often the outcome of discourses competing for hegemony and influence (Burke 2007a, 83–5; 2007b). Yet a careful marriage of social, policy, and textual analysis can enable both historical and predictive arguments about causes.

In turning to the ethical implications of postmodern analysis, we also need to pay attention to the normative consequences of particular exercises of deconstruction. Of most concern to me in this regard are works that collapse the moral and normative distinction between war and peace (which is different from keeping the ways and purposes for which such distinctions are mobilized under scrutiny; Burke 2005, 84). For example, in her discussion of binary oppositions put into question by postmodern international relations, Donna Gregory includes the dichotomy war/peace, citing Ashley's incisive deconstruction of Stephen Walt's projection of war as chaos to fortify an image of man (and the ordering Western state) as rational (Der Derian and Shapiro 1989, xv–xvii). In *Women and War* (1995) the just war theorist and vocal supporter of the US war on terror Jean Bethke Elshtain seeks to deconstruct this opposition to discredit Kant's *Perpetual Peace*, which she describes as a "solipsistic dream" (Elshtain 1995, 255; 2005; Burke 2005). More recently, scholars have written about Foucault (2003), who, in the course of trying to recast our solely repressive and juridical models of power, inverted Carl von Clausewitz to assert that politics is a form of war by other means (Reid 2003; Neal 2004; Devetak 2005a, 165–6). Ironically, in these lectures Foucault had posed the question of whether to analyze politics and discourse in terms of "the vicissitudes of a war ... according to a grid which would be one of strategy and tactics," but refused to answer definitely yes or no (Davidson 2003, xvii–xviii).

Yet this was framed dogmatically by Arnold Davidson (2003, xviii) in his introduction to *Society Must be Defended* as "Foucault's most concentrated and detailed historical examination of the model of war as a grid for analysing politics" and a "strategic model that would allow us to reorient our conception of power." I agree with Foucault's attempt to show how power is productive, fissured by conflict, and permanently at risk, but he could have done so without making such an uncritical appropriation of Clausewitz's categories, which comes at great cost. We lose the ability to distinguish normatively between a nonviolent—if agonistic, tactical, and disciplinary—"politics," and vast exercises of strategic violence and threat that involve systematic slaughter, destruction, and chaos. Nor can we critique the dehumanizing force of a "strategic" approach that turns men and women into means, "mere machines and instruments in the hands of someone else," and seek to imagine a different kind of political image of the human (Kant 2001, 437; Burke 2007a, ch. 8).

This is where postmodernism's ability to place normative discourse under scrutiny needs to be matched with greater efforts to engage with *and make* normative argument, to argue for positive forms of change, and to suggest ways of achieving them. After all, the other of the most damning charges against postmodernism is that it is anti-Enlightenment and nihilistic (Halliday 1999). Yet such views are quite wrong, as Devetak (2002) shows when he demonstrates important affinities between the "postmodern ethics" advanced by Campbell (1998) in his book on Bosnia, and the Kantian cosmopolitan project advanced by Andrew Linklater (2001)—both of which begin from a critique of the modern state as a totalizing and exclusivist project. Michael Shapiro (1998) has pursued similar affinities. George (1994, 161–7) early on pondered a possible normative (if not analytical) synthesis between critical theory and postmodernism in international relations, sentiments more recently echoed by Linklater (2001) and Kimberley Hutchings (2001, 89) and enacted in Richard Shapcott's *Justice, Community and Dialogue* (2001). In the wake of the liberal and universalizing rhetorics of neoconservatism, the postmodern critique of universalism and the philosophy of history remains ever salient (Burke 2005; 2007a), but without a critical reconnection with Kant's hopeful vision of a universal human community, we can wonder how it will ever restore the lives made "bare" by the terrible sovereign ontologies of the twentieth century.

In some thoughts about the aims of the long-running journal *Alternatives*, its editor summed up well the possibilities of and challenges for postmodernism. The journal had, he argued, sought to pursue "debates about the possibility of alternatives... about who it is that might be able to imagine alternatives and who these alternatives might be for... about what kind of authorities might be able to respond to novel structural conditions, to new dangers, and to new opportunities... debates, in short, about what we mean when we claim to be engaging in politics" (Walker 2000, 1). Our current global politics is a time when certainty is ever invoked, imposed, and desired, but there are few certainties to be had. At such a time, postmodernism holds the unique potential of being able to navigate a world without borders and charts; to conceive worlds outside the current boundaries of the possible.

REFERENCES

ASHLEY, R. 1987. The geopolitics of geopolitical space: toward a critical social theory of international politics. *Alternatives*, 12: 403–34.

——1988. Untying the sovereign state: a double reading of the anarchy problematique. *Millennium: Journal of International Studies*, 17: 227–62.

——1989. Living on border lines: man, poststructuralism, and war. Pp. 259–321 in Der Derian and Shapiro 1989.

—— and WALKER, R. B. J. 1990. Conclusion: reading dissidence/writing the discipline: crisis and the question of sovereignty in international studies. *International Studies Quarterly*, 34: 367–416.

BARTHES, R. 1984. *Image, Music, Text*, sel. and trans. S. Heath. London: Flamingo.

BAUDRILLARD, J. 1988. Simulacra and simulation. Pp. 166–84 in *Selected Writings*, ed. M. Poster. Cambridge: Polity.

BLEIKER, R. 2000a. *Popular Dissent, Human Agency, and Global Politics*. Cambridge: Cambridge University Press.

——2000b. Stroll through the wall: everyday poetics of Cold War politics. *Alternatives*, 25: 391–408.

——2005. *Divided Korea: Toward a Culture of Reconciliation*. Minneapolis: University of Minnesota Press.

——forthcoming. *Aesthetics and World Politics*. London: Palgrave.

BOOTH, K. (ed.) 2005. *Critical Security Studies and World Politics*. Boulder, Colo.: Lynne Rienner.

BOWDEN, B. 2004. In the name of progress and peace: the "standard of civilization" and the universalizing project. *Alternatives*, 29: 43–68.

BUCHAN, B. 2002. Explaining war and peace: Kant and liberal IR theory. *Alternatives*, 27: 407–28.

BURKE, A. 2001. *In Fear of Security: Australia's Invasion Anxiety*. Annandale: Pluto Press.

—— 2005. Against the new internationalism. *Ethics and International Affairs*, 19: 73–89.

—— 2007*a*. *Beyond Security, Ethics and Violence: War against the Other*. London: Routledge.

—— 2007*b*. Cause and effect in the war on terror. Pp. 25–41 in *Security and the War on Terror*, ed. A. J. Bellamy, R. Bleiker, S. E. Davies, and R. Devetak. London: Routledge.

BUTLER, J. 2004. *Precarious Life: The Powers of Mourning and Violence*. New York: Verso.

BUZAN, B., WÆVER, O., and DE WILDE, J. 1998. *Security: A New Framework for Analysis*. Boulder, Colo.: Lynne Rienner.

CAMPBELL, D. 1992. *Writing Security: United States Foreign Policy and the Politics of Identity*. Manchester: Manchester University Press.

—— 1998. *National Deconstruction: Violence, Identity, and Justice in Bosnia*. Minneapolis: University of Minnesota Press.

—— 2003. Salgado and the Sahel: documentary photography and the imaging of famine. Pp. 69–96 in *Rituals of Mediation*, ed. F. Debrix and C. Weber. Minneapolis: University of Minnesota Press.

CARR, E. H. 1969. *The Twenty Years' Crisis, 1919–1939: An Introduction to the Study of International Relations*. New York: Harper and Row.

COSTANTINOU, C. 2000. Poetics of security. *Alternatives*, 25: 287–306.

CONNOLLY, W. E. 1995. *The Ethos of Pluralization*. Minneapolis: University of Minnesota Press.

—— 2005. *Pluralism*. Durham, NC: Duke University Press.

COZETTE, M. 2008. Reclaiming the critical dimension of realism: Hans J. Morgenthau on the ethics of scholarship. *Review of International Studies*, 34: 5–27.

DALBY, S. 1990. *Creating the Second Cold War: The Discourse of Politics*. London: Pinter.

—— 1997. Contesting an essential concept: reading the dilemmas in contemporary security discourse. Pp. 3–32 in *Critical Security Studies: Concepts and Cases*, ed. K. Krause and M. C. Williams. Minneapolis: University of Minnesota Press.

DAVIDSON, A. 2003. Introduction. Pp. xv–xxiii in Foucault 2003.

DEBRIX, F., and WEBER, C. (eds.) 2003. *Rituals of Mediation: International Politics and Social Meaning*. Minneapolis: University of Minnesota Press.

DER DERIAN, J. 1987. The value of security: Hobbes, Marx, Neitzsche and Baudrillard. Pp. 94–113 in *The Political Subject of Violence*, ed. D. Campbell and M. Dillon. Manchester: Manchester University Press.

—— 1993. The value of security: Hobbes, Marx, Nietzsche and Baudrillard. Pp. 94–113 in *The Political Subject of Violence*, ed. D. Campbell and M. Dillon. Manchester: Manchester University Press.

—— and SHAPIRO, M. (eds.) 1989. *International/Intertextual Relations: Postmodern Readings of World Politics*. Lexington: Lexington Books.

DERRIDA, J. 1976. *Of Grammatology*. Baltimore: Johns Hopkins University Press.

DEUTSCH, K. 1968. *The Analysis of International Relations*. Englewood Cliffs, NJ: Prentice Hall.

DEVETAK, R. 2002. Signs of a new enlightenment? Concepts of community and humanity after the Cold War. Pp. 164–83 in *The New Agenda for International Relations: From Polarization to Globalization in World Politics*, ed. S. Lawson. Cambridge: Polity.

——2005a. Postmodernism. Pp. 161–87 in *Theories of International Relations*, 3rd edn., S. Burchill, A. Linklater, R. Devetak, J. Donnelly, M. Paterson, C. Reus-Smit, and J. True. London: Palgrave.

——2005b. The gothic scene of international relations: ghosts, monsters, terror and the sublime after September 11. *Review of International Studies*, 31: 621–43.

DILLON, M. 1996. *Politics of Security: Towards a Political Philosophy of Continental Thought*. London: Routledge.

——and REID, J. 2000. Global governance, liberal peace and complex emergency. *Alternatives*, 25: 117–43.

DREYFUS, H., and RABINOW, P. 1983. *Michel Foucault: Beyond Structuralism and Hermeneutics*, 3rd edn. Chicago: University of Chicago Press.

EDKINS, J. 2000. Sovereign power, zones of indistinction, and the camp. *Alternatives*, 25: 3–25.

ELSHTAIN, J. B. 1995. *Women and War*. Chicago: University of Chicago Press.

——2005. Against the new utopianism: response to "Against the new internationalism." *Ethics and International Affairs*, 19: 91–5.

FOUCAULT, M. 2003. *Society Must Be Defended: Lectures at the Collège de France 1975–1976*. London: Allen Lane.

GEORGE, J. 1994. *Discourses of Global Politics: A Critical (Re)Introduction to International Relations*. Boulder, Colo.: Lynne Rienner.

——and CAMPBELL, D. 1990. Patterns of dissent and the celebration of difference: critical social theory and international relations. *International Studies Quarterly*, 34: 269–93.

HALLIDAY, F. 1996. The future of international relations: fear and hopes. Pp. 318–27 in *International Theory: Positivism and Beyond*, ed. S. Smith, K. Booth, and M. Zalewski. New York: Cambridge University Press.

——1999. The potentials of enlightenment. *Review of International Studies*, 25: 105–25.

HANSEN, L. 2006. *Security as Practice: Discourse Analysis and the Bosnian War*. New York: Routledge.

HELLER, A. 1999. *A Theory of Modernity*. London: Blackwell.

HIGGINS, N. 2000. The Zapatista uprising and the poetics of cultural resistance. *Alternatives*, 25: 359–74.

HOFFMANN, S. 2001. An American social science: international relations. Pp. 27–51 in *International Relations—Still An American Social Science? Towards Diversity in International Thought*, ed. R. Crawford and D. Jarvis. Albany, NY: State University of New York Press.

HUTCHINGS, K. 2001. The nature of critique in international relations theory. Pp. 79–90 in *Critical Theory and World Politics*, ed. R. W. Jones. Boulder, Colo.: Lynne Rienner.

JACKSON, R. 2005. *Writing the War on Terrorism: Language, Politics and Counter Terrorism*. Manchester: Manchester University Press.

JAHN, B. 2000. *The Cultural Construction of International Relations: The Invention of the State of Nature*. London: Palgrave.

KANT, I. 2001. To eternal peace. Pp. 433–75 in *Basic Writings of Kant*, ed. A. W. Wood. New York: Modern Library.

KATZENSTEIN, P. J., KEOHANE, R. O., and KRASNER, S. D. 1998. International Organization and the study of world politics. *International Organization*, 52: 645–85.

KEAL, P. 2003. *European Conquest and the Rights of Indigenous Peoples.* Cambridge: Cambridge University Press.

KISSINGER, H. 1969. *American Foreign Policy: Three Essays.* London: Weidenfeld and Nicolson.

KLEIN, B. S. 1989. The textual strategies of the military. Pp. 97–112 in Der Derian and Shapiro 1989.

—— 1994. *Strategic Studies and World Order: The Global Politics of Deterrence.* Cambridge: Cambridge University Press.

LINKLATER, A. 2001. The changing contours of critical international relations theory. Pp. 23–44 in *Critical Theory and World Politics*, ed. R. W. Jones. Boulder, Colo.: Lynne Rienner.

LISLE, D. 2000. Consuming danger: reimagining the war/tourism divide. *Alternatives*, 25: 91–115.

—— 2003. Site specific: medi(t)ations at the airport. Pp. 3–29 in Debrix and Weber 2003.

LUKE, T. W. 1989. "What's wrong with deterrence?" A semiotic interpretation of national security policy. Pp. 207–29 in Der Derian and Shapiro 1989.

LYOTARD, J.-F. 1989. *The Postmodern Condition: A Report on Knowledge.* Minneapolis: University of Minnesota Press.

MCDONALD, M. 2005. Be alarmed? Australia's anti-terrorism kit and the politics of security. *Global Change, Peace and Security*, 17: 171–89.

MCSWEENEY, B. 1999. *Security, Identity and Interests: A Sociology of International Relations.* Cambridge: Cambridge University Press.

MORGENTHAU, H. J. 1973. *Politics among Nations: The Struggle for Power and Peace.* New York: Alfred A. Knopf.

MUTIMER, D. 2000. *The Weapons State: Proliferation and the Framing of Security.* Boulder, Colo.: Lynne Rienner.

NEAL, A. 2004. Cutting off the king's head: Foucault's *Society Must be Defended* and the problem of sovereignty. *Alternatives*, 29: 373–98.

PRICE, R., and REUS-SMIT, C. 1998. Dangerous liaisons? Critical international theory and constructivism. *European Journal of International Relations*, 4: 259–94.

PUGGIONI, R. 2006. Resisting sovereign power: camps in-between exception and dissent. Pp. 68–83 in *The Politics of Protection: Sites of Insecurity and Political Agency*, ed. J. Huysmans, A. Dobson, and R. Prokhovnik. London: Routledge.

RABINOW, P. (ed.) 1984. *The Foucault Reader.* New York: Pantheon.

REID, J. 2003. Foucault on Clausewitz: conceptualizing the relationship between war and power. *Alternatives*, 28: 1–28.

REUS-SMIT, C. 2001. The strange death of liberal international theory. *European Journal of International Law*, 12: 573–93.

—— 2005. Constructivism. Pp. 188–212 in *Theories of International Relations*, 3rd edn., S. Burchill, A. Linklater, R. Devetak, J. Donnelly, M. Paterson, C. Reus-Smit, and J. True. London: Palgrave.

SAMPSON, A. B. 2002. Tropical anarchy: Waltz, Wendt, and the way we imagine international politics. *Alternatives*, 27: 429–57.

SHAPCOTT, R. 2001. *Justice, Community and Dialogue in International Relations.* Cambridge: Cambridge University Press.

SHAPIRO, M. J. 1997. *Violent Cartographies: Mapping Cultures of War.* Minneapolis: University of Minnesota Press.

——1998. The events of discourse and the ethics of global hospitality. *Millennium: Journal of International Studies*, 27: 695–713.

Shaw, K. 2002. Indigeneity and the international. *Millennium: Journal of International Studies*, 31: 55–81.

Sylvester, C. 2000. Development poetics. *Alternatives*, 25: 335–51.

——2002. *Feminist International Relations: An Unfinished Journey*. Cambridge: Cambridge University Press.

——2003. Global "development" dramaturgies/gender stagings. *Borderlands*, e-journal, 2.

——forthcoming. *Art/Museums: International Relations where You Least Expect It*. Boulder, Colo.: Paradigm.

Vasquez, J. A. 1995. The post-positivist debate: reconstructing scientific inquiry and international relations theory after enlightenment's fall. Pp. 217–40 in *International Relations Theory Today*, ed. K. Booth and S. Smith. Cambridge: Polity.

Walker, R. B. J. 1988. *One World, Many Worlds: Struggles for a Just World Peace*. Boulder, Colo.: Lynne Rienner.

——1993. *Inside/Outside: International Relations as Political Theory*. Cambridge: Cambridge University Press.

——1997. The subject of security. Pp. 61–81 in *Critical Security Studies*, ed. M. C. Williams and K. Krause. Minneapolis: University of Minnesota Press.

——2000. Editorial note: re-engaging with the political. *Alternatives*, 25: 1–2.

Waltz, K. 2002. The continuity of international politics. Pp. 348–53 in *Worlds in Collision: Terror and the Future of Global Order*, ed. K. Booth and T. Dunne. London: Palgrave.

Weber, C. 1995. *Simulating Sovereignty: Intervention, the State, and Symbolic Exchange*. Cambridge: Cambridge University Press.

——2003. Epilogue: romantic mediations of September 11. Pp. 173–88 in *Rituals of Mediation*, ed. F. Debrix and C. Weber. Minneapolis: University of Minnesota Press.

Wendt, A. 1992. Anarchy is what states make of it: the social construction of power politics. *International Organization*, 46: 391–425.

Williams, M. C. 2005. *The Realist Tradition and the Limits of International Relations*. Cambridge: Cambridge University Press.

Zehfuss, M. 2002. *Constructivism in International Relations: The Politics of Reality*. Cambridge: Cambridge University Press.

CHAPTER 22

THE ETHICS OF POSTMODERNISM

PETER LAWLER

VIEWED from the mainstream, the hallmarks of postmodern or post-structuralist[1] writing—antifoundationalism, the emphasis on the multiplicity of possible readings or interpretations, and the critique of subjectivity—seemingly rule out a meaningful contribution to debates about the ethical dimensions of international relations. Although post-structuralists do indeed reject the premises of orthodox moral theorizing, they also refute the common charge that they are merely latter-day ethical relativists or simply disinterested in the ethical dimensions of international politics. As David Campbell (2007, 225) sees it, "the overall purpose of a poststructuralist analysis is ethical and political." Indeed, Campbell's bringing-together of the terms "ethical" and "political" provides useful insight into the particular character of the nonparadigmatic treatment of ethics by post-structuralists. For many, perhaps most, the ethical impulse translates not into the laying-down of ethical prescriptions for the conduct of international politics but in the recovery of what they understand as its political dimensions. In combination with a rejection of orthodox accounts of the moral subject, it is the *political* qualities of the international that denies the possibility of a definitive international ethics, even if much post-structuralist writing is overtly concerned with the ethical dimensions of international political life.

---

[1] Writers usually identified as postmodernists rarely use the term themselves, tending to prefer post-structuralist, and this is the term used in this discussion.

1 AGAINST ORTHODOXY

The bulk of writing on the ethical dimensions of international relations centers on moral cosmopolitanism, the view that humans are members of a single moral community and any ethical principles worth their salt should be universally applicable. Cosmopolitans disagree as to how such principles should be derived, be it through, say, the application of a priori reason to discern the rightness of an action, as in the Kantian or deontological tradition, or through utilitarian calculation of the good as in consequentialism. For many philosophers, notably John Rawls, this deontological–consequentialist binary effectively exhausts moral debate. Furthermore, the boundaries between cosmopolitanism as moral philosophy or world-view and cosmopolitanism as a transnational, institutionalist political project are increasingly blurred within the post-cold war literature on the normative dimensions of international relations (Vertovec and Cohen 2002).

Within mainstream debate, the principal critics of cosmopolitanism tend to argue from some form of relativist or communitarian position that holds that our moral principles are socially created—that is, they derive in part or wholly from our cultural, customary, or historical circumstances. Seen thus, our capacities to pass judgment on the ethical principles or conduct of others in different circumstances to ourselves, variously defined, may be limited or even illegitimate. In the context of international relations, communitarianism tends to be a fellow traveler of nationalism or statism in that moral boundaries are often seen as coterminous with the boundaries of a nation or the state. What binds cosmopolitanism with its communitarian critics, however, is a shared sense that the ethical subject can be known. Both positions can be found in "thick" or "thin" versions, which, more or less, make concessions to the other side. This is in part simply a consequence of the widespread perception that the cultural, economic, and political boundaries separating human communities are increasingly porous, along with a heightened sensitivity to cultural and social contexts. Nonetheless, the prominence of rights talk in the post-1945 world attests to the power of the view that, in spite of, or perhaps because of, the myriad differences between our circumstances, the very fact that we are all humans nonetheless creates the possibility of, and perhaps the necessity for, developing universal rules applicable to all, regardless of circumstance. Quite what those rules should be is a matter of considerable and often heated dispute.

What is perhaps most unsettling about the treatment of ethics in post-structuralist international relations scholarship is that it does not operate upon the terrains of either mainstream international relations theory or orthodox moral philosophy. Although much post-structuralist writing is overtly concerned with the key moral and ethical issues of our time—in particular the forms of violence that pervade international politics—it resists orthodox ethical binaries, such as communitarianism–cosmopolitanism, as well as the distinction between the domestic and the international that has figured so large in international relations theory. The post-structuralist critique of "the sovereignty of the discourse of sovereignty," for example, suggests affinities with cosmopolitanism; the emphasis placed on context and contingency, on the other hand, resonates with communitarian and relativist concerns. Yet, because post-structuralism does not present itself as an alternative international relations theory but rather as a "critical attitude" or "ethos" (Campbell 1998a, 4–8; 2007, 203), it does not set out to offer a definitive set of moral principles that might govern human conduct. This is not to say that post-structuralists never come to conclusions that chime with a range of familiar political and ethical points of view. Rather, post-structuralism starts off by questioning the assumptions that underpin our claims to *know* the world and, by extension, our capacity to lay down authoritative principles of conduct for the various actors in it. However, there is no straightforward entry point into post-structuralism, no clear linear path to follow in order to unpack what is understood by the ethical within it, just as there is no fixed end point at which to arrive. Insofar as one can generalize about post-structuralist ethics, however, the treatment of the subject seems key.

2 THE "UNSETTLING OF THE SUBJECT"

Jenny Edkins (1999, xi) argues that post-structuralism's challenge to international relations stems from its "unsettling of the subject," a "realignment and reexamination of subjectivity that leads to a rearticulation of fundamental political questions." For Edkins, what we understand by "politics" has in many senses become "depoliticised" or "technologised." In certain respects echoing Max Weber's distinction between forms of authority, Edkins (1999, 2) argues that what various writers such as Claude Lefort, Slavoj Zizek, Jacques Derrida, and Michel Foucault have sought is the recovery of "the political"—that is, "the establishment of the very social order which sets out a particular, historically specific account of what counts as politics and defines other areas of social life as *not* politics." Particular forms of society emerge out of periods of contestation and struggle and reflect a specific representation of power and legitimacy. However, for post-structuralists the orthodox emphasis on *politics* (the state apparatus, elections, parties, leaders, and so on) serves to obscure or conceal the often violent constitution of a prevailing social world, which, in Ernesto Laclau's words, "presents itself to us, primarily, as a sedimented ensemble of social practices accepted at face value, without questioning the founding acts of their institution" (Laclau cited in Edkins 1999, 5). Furthermore, from a post-structuralist point of view, the subject does not exist prior to the formation of any social order but is inextricably bound up with the formative process. Power is productive not only in the formation of specific social orders but also in the formation of subjects: "the individual is not a pregiven entity which is seized on by the exercise of power. The individual with his identity and character-istics is the product of relations of power" (Foucault 1980, 73–4). Thus the modern notion of the autonomous sovereign individual subject, located moreover within a sovereign state-centric global political order, is seen as an invention, a fiction, but no less "real" for that. The fictive subject of politics is to be distinguished, then, from subjectivity, because the latter disappears the moment a new social and political order is in place. This account is to be distinguished from superficially similar arguments found in the constructivist literature, notably in the emphasis on the discursive constitution of identity—that is, "the reiterative and citational practice by which discourse produces the effects that it names" (Butler 1993, 2). In contrast to constructivists, post-structuralists do not see ideas and language as merely co-constituting or modifying a material world but depict the latter as know-able in thought only through "their discursive condition of emergence" (Laclau and Chantal Mouffe cited in Campbell 1998a, 25; see also Zehfuss 2002). For many post-structuralists, the unsettling of the subject means that identity and "selfhood" become intrinsically fluid, mobile, and contingent. Judith Butler (2004) in her discussion of violence and mourning in the wake of 11 September, for example, argues that "selves" are never constituted alone. Instead, we come to know who "we" are only in the context of our relationship to the social world and to the others who populate that world. When we lose our connections with others, we also lose, in this important sense, elements of who we "are" or were. Thus, Butler (2004, 22) asks: "who 'am' I without you?"

Other post-structuralists, following on Emmanuel Lévinas, argue that ethics constitutes a "first philosophy." In other words, we emerge into the social world already bound up by our obligations to others. Lévinas (1989) argues that, as soon as we stake claims for ourselves in the political world, we have already usurped someone else's place. Lévinas's ethical relation—and the formulation for which he is perhaps best known—is found in the notion of the "face to face." For Lévinas, we are drawn into the world through the facing of others. This is a departure from the Heideggerian notion of the subject walking along a progressive continuum with others at his side. In this facing, the subject is decentered by the imperative to ethical responsibility for the other. For Lévinas, ethical responsibility is such that the self, in its infinite obligation, becomes the "hostage" of the other. While arguably Lévinas cannot be understood as a post-structuralist (because of his insistence on the immutability of ethics as a prior condition), many international relations poststructuralists employ the Lévinasian face to face as a starting point for their own ethical arguments.

Campbell is perhaps one of the most notable international relations scholars to employ Lévinas and shows that the abandonment of orthodox accounts of the subject does not entail disengagement from ethics. For Campbell, the Lévinasian notion of obligation means that conflicts in other parts of the world cannot be simply dismissed on the basis of spatial or cultural distance, lack of national interest, or the like. In his exploration of the Bosnian war, Campbell (1998a, 176) draws on Lévinas's notion of infinite responsibility to argue that "there is no condition under which we could say that it was not our responsibility." However, for Campbell, the recognition that we are ethically obliged to respond to a conflict such as the war in Bosnia is coupled with a requirement to consider *how* to respond in a way that does not simply re-enact the claims put forward by ethnic nationalists. Campbell argues that the international community's exclusive engagement with nationalist political elites in Bosnia legitimated their claims to the detriment of other possibilities, which may have proven less violent and exclusionary. Support for multicultural leaders in Bosnia might have helped to decenter and delegitimize ethnically pure identities.

Other scholars, such as Michael Shapiro, also employ a Lévinasian notion of ethics in order to develop what they call an "ethic of encounter." For Shapiro (1999), the ethic of encounter evokes a radical hospitality and a welcoming of the other despite the possible risks to the security of the self and the self's identity. This radical welcoming of the other is intrinsic to the philosophical thought of Derrida, who argues that the specter of the other always already haunts the very notion of what it means to be a "self" in the first place. Concerned with the relationship between self and other, Derrida points out that the mutual constitution of identities is an ethically necessary component of what might be understood to constitute the political. For this reason, among others, Derrida argues that an ethical welcoming is made possible only by the arrival of the guest as such. Thus, our very notion of ourselves as "hosts" is reliant in the first instance on the existence of those who receive hospitality. Yet international politics is constructed, not exclusively but arguably more overtly than any other political realm, upon the allocation of sovereign rights to determine who qualifies for the receipt of our hospitality in the form of our ethical concern: "sovereignty can only be exercised by filtering, choosing and thus by excluding and doing violence. Injustice, a certain injustice . . . begins right away, from the very threshold of the right to hospitality" (Derrida 2000, 55). The call to ethics is not reducible to specific moments in international political life or a discrete area of academic inquiry but permeates the political itself and, by extension, the activity of political analysis and investigation. For many post-structuralists, perhaps John Caputo (1993) most forcefully, the pervasiveness and everydayness of our obligations to others renders impossible the laying-down of transcendental rules and criteria of qualification for the ethical without doing violence to ethics itself.

There is, of course, a universalism haunting such a position. It is not, however, a universalism that many cosmopolitans would recognize for it is hostile to universalizing moral prescription. As such, it also provides the basis for a wide-ranging critique of the core assumptions of orthodox normative international relations scholarship as well as the practical proposals for the reform of international politics contained therein. It would be mistaken, however, to confuse this with a rejection of reform per se, as many of post-structuralism's critics assume.

3 MORAL SPACES

The predominant forms of cosmopolitanism in international relations theory offer fraternal accounts of the relationship between ethics, space, and subjectivity: the elucidation of universal rules appropriate to a singular community of human subjects in a global social space. As such, they purport to provide a basis for critiquing skepticism about the very possibility of international ethics as well as varieties of spatially contained or communitarian ethics. Although post-structuralist critiques of orthodox accounts of subjectivity resonate with aspects of cosmopolitanism's disavowal of the moral significance of the political boundary and its purportedly nonexclusionary emphasis on a universal moral community, they part company with cosmopolitanism in key respects. Post-structuralists "resist the desire for *a* theory of ethics that articulates abstracted principles in a systematised manner" (Campbell and Shapiro 1999, x). Some recent explorations of a "thin cosmopolitanism" do attempt to take account of post-structuralist (and feminist) resistance to the elucidation of overly abstracted, universalist, ethical blueprints as well as the dilemmas that cultural difference raise for cosmopolitanism. This has been principally through conceptual explorations of Habermasian discourse ethics (notably in Linklater 1998), often in combination with more practical critical explorations of the reconfiguration of democracy above, below, and across national boundaries (e.g. Held 1995). However, even these revisions fall foul of post-structuralist disquiet about orthodox accounts of the rational subject and the related tendency to depict moral development as a linear movement from particularity to universality (Walker 1999), as well as a dependence upon an overly abstracted or idealized account of communication and its ethical potential. In particular, post-structuralists question the cosmopolitan tendency to move rapidly on to the exploration of novel frameworks and institutions above and below the sovereign state. In spite of their seemingly transversal implications, these are seen effectively to reify highly particularistic political and spatial conceptions of the ethical dimensions and dilemmas of contemporary world politics. For example, contemporary cosmopolitan explorations of appropriate responses to outbreaks of large-scale violence (so called new wars) are clearly intended to shift our thinking and action away from a historical preference for predominantly military solutions to the construction of new universal norms of humanitarian intervention centered upon discourses of criminality and policing (Kaldor 1999). However, the voice in which much of such exploration is conducted betrays its political and ethical connections with what Michael Dillon (1998, 545) calls "the allied processes" that collectively frame and seek to impose a highly specific model of "global liberal governance."

Campbell and Shapiro (1999) address the relationship between cosmopolitanism and post-structuralism in their identification of the "productively ambiguous" legacy of Immanuel Kant. They depict their own work and that of other key post-structuralists as "post-Kantian" in that it derives inspiration from Kant's commitment to a cosmopolitan ethos (if not an ethic) and his "resistance to ethical closure." Kant's philosophical and political writings, through both the development of principles and a commensurate legal structure, promoted a global hospitality that encouraged "solicitude to every citizen-subject, native-born or not." Nonetheless, what they term as Kant's "spatial commitments" and the geopolitical metaphors that permeate his philosophical and his more practical writings provide a basis for contextualizing and critiquing his cosmopolitanism. In Kant's controversial dualist view of the human subject, the exercise of "judgment" connects the phenomenal world with the non-natural, noumenal world of self-determination and the exercise of a moral faculty. This enables the fully developed rational–moral subject to reject the world of sense experience and embrace a cosmopolitan ethos. What Campbell and Shapiro highlight, however, is the homology between Kant's "philosophical geography" and his "practical geography." Writing during the rise of the territorial state and advocating the displacement of religious and monarchical authority by republican forms of governance, Kant depicts the fully formed universal ethico-political human agent within what is in fact a highly particularistic yet "European state-oriented political imaginary." On this view, Kant's cosmopolitanism relies ultimately upon what Derrida has called a "national philosophism" wherein one country or nation claims "the privilege of 'representing,' 'embodying,' 'identifying with,' the universal essence of man" (cited in Campbell and Shapiro 1999, xvii). As such it is inhospitable toward "oppositional practices and subjectivities that have incommensurate commitments to meaning and value" and construes moral space within a "state-oriented geographic imaginary" (Campbell and Shapiro 1999, xvii; see also Walker 1993, 71).

Campbell and Shapiro's analysis offers one example of post-structuralist questioning of the orthodox representations of global space, notably the distinction between the "inside" of the sovereign state (itself understood in a very particular Eurocentric way) and an ethically untamed "outside" where *international* politics supposedly takes place. Resistance to constitutive dualisms and their ethical implications is a well-known feature of most international relations post-structuralist writing. Although post-structuralism evinces a discomfort or even a hostility to the sovereign state as the dominant spatial resolution of the relationship between

peoples, it is equally hostile to the presumption that the only response is to invoke universal accounts of the right and the good or to presume that difference,
as expressed in the form of the bounded sovereign community, can ultimately
be dissolved into the singular human community. For R. B. J. Walker (1993, 77),
"universalism, to put it bluntly and heretically, can be understood as the problem,
not the solution." Rather than trying to resolve or transcend the sometimes violent
tensions between the many forms of human identity through the invocation of
a universalizable account of subjectivity, such as that which overtly underpins
most rights talk or, more latently, current legitimations of armed intervention,
post-structuralists tend to ask *how* those differences are constructed, expressed, and
sustained. While recognizing the seductiveness of the pursuit of secure universal
principles as the basis for resolving the dilemmas of contemporary global social life,
post-structuralists tend to see it as demanding too high a price: the loss of "politics"
itself. In exploring the "(im)possibility" of universalism, Véronique Pin-Fat offers
a more nuanced reading and cites Laclau in support of the paradox that many
post-structuralists depict as inescapable: "the impossibility of a universal ground
does not eliminate its need: it just transforms the ground into an empty place which
can be partially filled in a variety of ways (the strategies of this filling is what politics
is all about)" (Laclau cited in Pin-Fat 2000, 665).

4 MORAL PRACTICES

We live, claim Campbell and Shapiro (1999, 161), "in a time of doubt, paradox and
difference." Challenging dominant modes of ethical universalism is thus particularly apposite in the contemporary era, marked as it is by tensions between the
contemporary prominence of the moral dimensions of international politics and
the very mixed record of the international community's responses (under various
institutional guises) to them. In the post-cold war era, early enthusiasm for the
ethical potentiality of an emergent "new world order" has been sobered by the
sheer prominence of moral dilemmas both old and new. Problems such as the gross
inequalities of material wealth and life chances in a globalizing world economy,
the eruption of ethnic cleansing as a feature of contemporary large-scale conflicts
and the calls for intervention that they generate, varieties of terrorism, and the
dilemmas of increased flows of migrants and refugees have helped to generate a
voluminous, overtly normative literature.

Evident public moral disquiet about both the problems that confront us as well as
the concrete responses to them serves to provide an increasingly hospitable milieu
for the ambiguity and contingency that surround post-structuralist explorations

of ethics. The bulk of orthodox writing on contemporary ethical dilemmas of world politics focuses on both the general definition of the problems themselves, itself a source of widespread contestation, and the construction of universalizable solutions. In contrast, post-structuralist engagements with contemporary global ills are much more concerned with the constitutive relationship *between* problems and solutions. Thus they focus more on how contemporary ethical dilemmas are named and framed in the process of responding to them. This is not to suggest that post-structuralists uniformly avoid engagement with concrete ethical issues and the articulation of substantive responses to them. As noted above, Campbell's depiction of the origins and very purpose of post-structuralism overtly refutes this. Certainly much recent post-structuralist writing directly addresses the ethical dimensions of a wide range of empirical issue areas in international politics such as human rights (Pin-Fat 2000), humanitarian interventions (Campbell 1998*a*; 1998*b*; Orford 2003; Dauphinée 2007), war and its remembrance (Zehfuss 2007), the politics of development (Duffield 2001), complex emergencies (Edkins 2000), national refugee and immigration policies (Doty 2003; Edkins and Pin-Fat 2005), national security policy (Campbell 1992; Doty 1996; Weber 1995; Weldes 1999), and the war on terror (Butler 2004; Dauphinée and Masters 2007; Zehfuss 2007). Nonetheless, many post-structuralists refuse to adhere to the orthodox linear relationship between the defining and framing of an ethical issue in an intersubjectively agreed fashion and the devising of appropriate principles as the basis for designing a strategic and/or an institutional response to that issue. In particular, post-structuralism constantly invokes the political nature of both the identification and the classi-fication of the ethical dilemmas of contemporary world politics. This provides the basis for destabilizing the pervasive faith in the ultimate rationalization and instrumentalization of international politics. From this point of view, the pursuit of solutions to a whole range of ethical conundrums constantly and perhaps in-escapably generates new challenges to any comfortable sense of ourselves as ethical beings.

Central to post-structuralist doubts about the possibility of universal ethical panaceas is the constant presence of violence within the definition of the problem-atics that demand our response and the responses themselves. This is hardly a new concern; it lies at the heart of the centuries-old "just war" tradition, for example. But the idea of just war provides an acute representation of that which post-structuralism rails against: the attempt to codify, rationalize, and thus legitimate the deployment of violence, even if it is ostensibly against violence. As Zehfuss (2007) notes, just war principles may enable us rationally to justify apparently unintended civilian deaths as a consequence of going to war, but it has nothing to say about the inescapable tragedy of such deaths other than providing an elision of our responsibility for bringing them about. Thus just war thinking provides an example of the naturalization of certain kinds of violence at the same time as it endeavors to constrain violence. Ethical justifications for recourse to violence always leave a residue of ethical responsibility. For post-structuralists, the impossibility of tidy, final, ethical responses to the violence of international politics is something we cannot escape but have to live with and in. Elizabeth Dauphinée's account of her experience as a doctoral researcher in Bosnia brings out acutely the shades of grey surrounding ascriptions of victimhood and aggressor, guilty and innocent, by external observers of conflict choosing to immerse themselves in a "maze of uncertainty." For Dauphinée (2007, 28), in "the recognition that the ethical lies in the refusal to arrive at a totalising outcome or iteration, the focus of attention falls on the undecidable. For Derrida, undecidability is precisely that crisis of confidence which renders decision-making simultaneously impossible and imperative." Such formulations no doubt infuriate those pursuing moral certitude or closure. They stem, however, from both the centrality of the notion of responsibility to otherness and the challenging of orthodox accounts of scholarship and expertise, theory, and practice, that bind otherwise heterogeneous post-structuralist analyses. They do not preclude the exercise of judgment or the taking of a position, as is commonly supposed.

5 POLITICS IN PERPETUITY

Although post-structuralism originates from various currents of radical criticism of mainstream social and political thought, contemporary post-structuralist international relations scholarship does not cohere tidily with progressivist orthodoxy as developed within long-standing lines of antirealist and nonrealist thinking. Herein lies perhaps a key reason for the ongoing hostility toward post-structuralist scholarship, on ethics in particular, within the international relations field. The distinction between other strands of critical thought and post-structuralist or deconstructionist thinking arises particularly in the latter's preference for localized, contingent responses to ethically troubling cases, rather than the erection of transnational processes or institutions designed to dispense justice according to supposedly universal norms or codes of conduct (Campbell 1998a; Dillon 1998). The idea of an inescapable ethical responsibility to others certainly looms large in post-structuralist writing. However, while being global in its reach, it pointedly does not appeal to a universal conception of human subjectivity or a notion of solidarity that presumes "we [are] all potentially or imaginary citizens of a great state" (Derrida 1994, 47–8). In his study of the intersection of the global politics of development, aid, and security within still emerging "strategic complexes" of liberal global governance, Mark Duffield focuses on the relationship between aid policy and complexity. Rejecting all-encompassing notions that aid either does more harm than good or that it can produce an ultimate resolution of the development problematic, Duffield (2001, 253) instead argues that "the main consequence of aid of any form…is to change and reinforce the dominant relations and forms of discourse that it encounters and through which it flows." Aid adds to already complex situations, and such complexity does not end with its arrival or indeed its absence. For this reason, Duffield sees Western faith in the possibility of achieving steady-state outcomes or finally ending the problem of development as part of the problem itself. Framed ultimately by the wider pursuit of a liberal–capitalist global peace settlement, it is conducive to technocratic responses. Echoing Edkins's observations on depoliticization, Duffield sees these as insufficiently sensitive to always unfolding political complexities and can end up complicit in the very violence and suffering they ostensibly seek to alleviate. Campbell's analysis of the Bosnian conflict overtly expresses a preference for political concepts such as democracy, justice, and multiculturalism and identifies the failure to grant sovereignty to Bosnia as "a grave injustice." In these respects, his voice has an air of progressivist familiarity about it. Nonetheless, Campbell (1998a, 242) also emphasizes that the enactment of any political proposals has to be "*preceded* by the qualification of a 'perhaps' and *followed* by an insistent and persistent questioning. With this all-important temporal dimension, deconstructive thought calls for an ongoing political process of critique and invention that is never satisfied that a lasting solution can or has been reached."

It is through such formulations that many postmodernists or post-structuralists seek to continue the *ethos* of the Enlightenment, in contrast to the multitude of voices that depict post-structuralism as the Enlightenment's principal contemporary enemy. The post-cold war record of collective action in so many international domains in the name of ethics is such that the postmodern pursuit of an ethos appropriate to our complex contemporary global circumstances can be plausibly now cast as the principal critical alternative to either realist moral despair or a liberal moral cosmopolitanism fatally tainted by its relationship to the concrete practices of dominant Western states.

References

Butler, J. 1993. *Bodies that Matter: On the Discursive Limits of "Sex."* New York: Routledge.

——— 2004. *Precarious Life: The Powers of Mourning and Violence.* London: Verso.

Campbell, D. 1992. *Writing Security: United States Foreign Policy and the Politics of Identity.* Minneapolis: University of Minnesota Press.

——— 1998a. *National Deconstruction: Violence, Identity, and Justice in Bosnia.* Minneapolis: University of Minnesota Press.

——— 1998b. Why fight: humanitarianism, principles, and post-structuralism. *Millennium: Journal of International Studies,* 27: 497–521.

—— 2007. Poststructuralism. Pp. 203–28 in *International Relations Theories: Discipline and Diversity*, ed. T. Dunne, M. Kurki, and S. Smith. Oxford: Oxford University Press.

—— and SHAPIRO, M. J. 1999. Introduction: from ethical theory to the ethical relation. Pp. vii–xx in *Moral Spaces: Rethinking Ethics and World Politics*, ed. D. Campbell and M. J. Shapiro. Minneapolis: University of Minnesota Press.

CAPUTO, J. D. 1993. *Against Ethics: Contributions to a Poetics of Obligation with Constant Reference to Deconstruction*. Bloomington: Indiana University Press.

DAUPHINÉE, E. 2007. *The Ethics of Researching War: Looking for Bosnia (New Approaches to Conflict Analysis)*. Manchester: Manchester University Press.

—— and MASTERS, C. (eds.) 2007. *The Logics of Biopower and the War on Terror: Living, Dying, Surviving*. New York: Palgrave Macmillan.

DERRIDA, J. 1994. Nietzsche and the machine: interview with Jacques Derrida by Richard Beardsworth. *Journal of Nietzsche Studies*, 7: 7–66.

—— 2000. *Of Hospitality: Anne Dufourmantelle Invites Jacques Derrida to Respond*, trans. R. Bowlby, Stanford, Calif.: Stanford University Press.

DILLON, M. 1998. Criminalising social and political violence internationally. *Millennium: Journal of International Studies*, 27: 543–68.

DOTY, R. 1996. *Imperial Encounters: The Politics of Representation in North–South Relations*. Minneapolis: University of Minnesota Press.

—— 2003. *Anti-Immigrantism in Western Democracies: Statecraft, Desire and the Politics of Exclusion*. New York: Routledge.

DUFFIELD, M. 2001. *Global Governance and the New Wars: The Merging of Development and Strategy*. London: Zed Books.

EDKINS, J. 1999. *Poststructuralism and International Relations: Bringing the Political Back In*. Boulder, Colo.: Lynne Rienner.

—— 2000. *Whose Hunger? Concepts of Famine, Practices of Aid*. Minneapolis: University of Minnesota Press.

—— and PIN-FAT, V. 2005. Through the wire: relations of power and relations of violence. *Millennium: Journal of International Studies*, 34: 1–24.

FOUCAULT, M. 1980. *Power/Knowledge: Selected Interviews and Other Writings, 1972–1977*, ed. C. Gordon. Brighton: Harvester.

HELD, D. 1995. *Democracy and the Global Order: From the Modern State to Cosmopolitan Governance*. Cambridge: Polity.

KALDOR, M. 1999. *New and Old Wars*. Cambridge: Polity.

LÉVINAS, E. 1989. Ethics as first philosophy. Pp. 75–87 in *The Lévinas Reader*, ed. S. Hand. Oxford: Blackwell.

LINKLATER, A. 1998. *The Transformation of Political Community: Ethical Foundations of the Post-Westphalian Era*. Cambridge: Polity.

ORFORD, A. 2003. *Reading Humanitarian Intervention: Human Rights and the Use of Force in International Law*. Cambridge: Cambridge University Press.

PIN-FAT, V. 2000. (Im)possible universalism: reading human rights in world politics. *Review of International Studies*, 26: 663–74.

SHAPIRO, M. J. 1999. The ethics of encounter: unreading, unmapping the imperium. Pp. 57–91 in *Moral Spaces: Rethinking Ethics and World Politics*, ed. M. J Shapiro and D. Campbell. Minneapolis: University of Minnesota Press.

VERTOVEC, S., and COHEN, R. (eds.) 2002. *Conceiving Cosmopolitanism: Theory, Context, and Practice*. Oxford: Oxford University Press.

WALKER, R. B. J. 1993. *Inside/Outside: International Relations as Political Theory*. Cambridge: Cambridge University Press.

——1999. The hierarchicalization of political community. *Review of International Studies*, 25: 151–6.

WEBER, C. 1995. *Simulating Sovereignty: Intervention, the State, and Symbolic Exchange*. Cambridge: Cambridge University Press.

WELDES, J. 1999. *Constructing National Interests: The United States and the Cuban Missile Crisis*. Minneapolis: University of Minnesota Press.

ZEHFUSS, M. 2002. *Constructivism in International Relations: The Politics of Reality*. Cambridge: Cambridge University Press.

——2007. *Wounds of Memory: The Politics of War in Germany*. Cambridge: Cambridge University Press.

——2007. The tragedy of violent justice: the danger of Elshtain's *Just War Against Terror*. *International Relations*, 21: 493–501.

CHAPTER 23

....

FEMINISM

....

SANDRA WHITWORTH

THIS chapter will examine some of the principle tensions, but also compatibilities, between the study of international relations and feminism. It will also review briefly some of the main points of debate and controversy within feminist thinking, and the ways in which feminist insights have been taken up by global actors in world politics, such as the United Nations (UN). While much of the discussion of feminism and international relations has usefully focused on the ways in which mainstream accounts of international relations ignore its impact on gender and/or make invisible the kinds of contributions that feminist analyses can bring to processes of international relations,[1] this chapter will go in a somewhat different direction. It will examine the ways in which "gender" *does* circulate globally, and the ways in which gender has obtained something of a worldwide currency, especially in (but not limited to) questions of peace, violence, and conflict.

The global circulation of "gender" does not, however, mean that those who use gender understand it, or employ it in the way feminists intended when conceptualizing the term. Gender circulates with considerable frequency within the corridors of the UN and other mainstream institutions like the World Bank. It circulates within member states of the UN. Most of these organizations are committed to a strategy called gender mainstreaming. Although gender is used and referred to a great deal by institutions like the UN, when taken up by these international actors, gender is largely depoliticized (Whitworth 2004, ch. 5). The argument here is that the uses to which "gender" have been put globally, rather than producing a critical and politically engaged politics, have instead been part of a practice of policing

---

[1] For an excellent review of these discussions, especially as they concern questions of globalization, see Rai (2004).

knowledge production, or, in James H. Mittleman's term (2004, 223), "narrative entrapment." In short, part of the transformed "lifeways" of international relations and globalization (Mittleman 2004, 220) entails the circulation of a set of understandings about gender that removes from it any examination of the ways in which relations of power sustain (or sometimes challenge) prevailing assumptions about men and women and masculinity and femininity.

1 FEMINISM AND INTERNATIONAL RELATIONS: TENSIONS AND COMPATIBILITIES

In important ways, feminist thought and the study of international relations are very difficult and sometimes incompatible terrains to navigate. Students or scholars of international relations may use terms like states, power, and anarchy, or acronyms and abbreviations like MAD (mutual assured destruction, a way of describing nuclear-deterrence policies), IBRD (International Bank for Reconstruction and Development, or the World Bank), IMF (International Monetary Fund), and WTO (World Trade Organization). They may talk comfortably about theoretical approaches that include realism, liberal pluralism, Gramscian political economy, or critical international relations theory, and they may ask questions about the relations between states, or about nuclear deterrence, arms races, structural adjustment programs, or comparative advantage.

Feminists, by contrast, may declare themselves to be liberal feminists, or feminist postmodernists. They may talk about the importance of understanding the difference between gender and sex, and they may ask how antiracist scholarship has been incorporated into analyses of global politics. The student of international relations may profess hopes to work one day for the foreign policy bureaucracy of his or her state or may pass out flyers for an upcoming "Model UN," while the feminist student may describe volunteering at a local women's shelter or make an announcement about an upcoming "Take Back the Night" march. Feminist students and scholars who encounter international relations, and international relations students and scholars who encounter feminism, regularly report confusion, miscommunication, and in general a sense that they are operating in very different worlds from one another.[2]

[2] For an entertaining account of the "other worldly" experiences of international relations scholars, see Rosenau (1993). For a discussion about the ways in which international relations scholars "just don't understand," see Tickner (1997; 1998); Keohane (1998); Marchand (1998).

The fact is, in many ways, feminism and international relations *do* operate in very different worlds[3]—one comes out of a heritage of social movement activism and critique while the other has been located in a field of study focused largely on serving the policy needs of governments. Feminist thought, as Alison Jaggar (1983, 3) writes, has probably always existed: "as long as women have been subordinated, they have resisted that subordination. Sometimes the resistance has been collective and conscious; at other times it has been solitary and only half-conscious." Jaggar's early remarks on feminist thought signal the connection of feminism to activism and resistance. Feminist activism has been directed at an enormously varied set of goals, including involvement in anticolonial struggles, struggles for reproductive freedoms (which itself has been defined in a variety of ways), organizing around violence against women, or peace and disarmament objectives, seeking to achieve civil and political rights, organizing around sexuality issues, whether in the form of "rights" for gays and lesbians or queer and transgender activism, involvement in environmental or workers' rights movements, antiglobalization activism, and development issues, to name but a few.[4]

Not only do feminists organize around a whole variety of issues, not all of which appear on the surface to be explicitly feminist; they also organize in different ways. In some cases, feminist activism has sought to show the particular impact of phenomena such as environmental damage or reliance on nuclear weapons on women and marginalized men. In other instances, feminist activism aims at achieving specific gains for women—protective legislation, for example, or the recognition of certain rights, such as reproductive rights, equality legislation, or affirmative action programs. In other instances, women organize around issues that are seen to affect communities as a whole (colonialism, globalization, or racism), in which feminist struggle forms one part of a larger movement of resistance.

The variety of activism associated with feminism is paralleled by the variety of ways feminist theory has evolved, and the varieties of "feminisms" that have emerged as a result (see Jaggar 1983; Mohanty, Russo, and Torres 1991; Whitworth 1994; Steans 1998; Zalewski 2000). There is no single or monolithic feminist theory, any more than there is a single form of feminist activism. *Liberal feminists*, for example, argue that women must be included in areas of public life previously denied them. Liberals start from the assumption that women share the same capacity for reason as men, and so on equality grounds should not be excluded from any of the important elements of the public sphere within modern societies: higher learning, government, international institutions, business, and so on. Feminists who work from this perspective collect empirical information about women's roles, and generally find that, within governments and international institutions, women

---

[3] For a discussion that also uses the idea of different "worlds" (but in different ways from those used here), see Linklater, Carver, and Enloe (2004); Youngs (2004).

[4] For a review of only some of this activism, see, e.g., Alexander and Mohanty (1997, especially sect. III). See also Peterson and Runyan (1999, especially ch. 5).

remain highly under-represented. Where women are present, they are still largely relegated to clerical and support work, and do not figure prominently in the middle and upper management levels of institutions. As of June 2006, for example, women in the UN comprised some 60 percent of General Service employees, but less than 40 percent in the Professional categories (and only 15 percent of the highest professional category of Under Secretary General) (Office of the Special Advisor on Gender Issues and Advancement of Women 2006).

This is the kind of information that liberal feminists collect, and then they also track the reasons why women may be excluded from public or political activities. This kind of research has shown that in some cases women may be socialized away from the public sphere; or they may have differential access to educational or other opportunities needed to gain access to public life; they also may face discrimination and subtle or flagrant forms of exclusion when attempting to become more active; sometimes also the burdens of their private lives (responsibilities in the home, in the care of children or the elderly) may make it more difficult to become involved in local- or global-level political activity. For liberal feminists, the barriers to women's participation need to be identified so that they can be removed, in this way permitting those women who are interested in equal opportunity to take on the challenges of political and public life.

Radical feminists, by contrast, focus less on women's participation in the public sphere and more on the workings of patriarchy, the relations of inequality between women and men, and the ways in which—historically and to this day—men seek to control women through controlling their sexuality, their roles in reproduction, and their roles in society more generally. For radical feminists, women and men are essentially quite different from one another (and essentially quite similar to one another). Some point to biology, others point to socialization, but radical feminists tend to agree that men as a group are less able to express emotion, are more aggressive, and more competitive, while women as a group are more nurturing, more holistic, and less abstract. By this view, much of the way in which society is organized supports patriarchy and the privileging of masculine norms, which affects not only the ways in which the world actually operates, but even the ways in which we think about the world.

On questions of representation, radical feminists might agree with liberals that women ought to be represented in positions of public power, but not for the equality-rights reasons the liberals give; rather because women bring a different point of view to politics, one that is more focused on cooperation and peace. In international relations, this position is most forcefully expressed by some radical feminists who argue that, if women were in control of the world's governments, there would be no war and no conflict.[5] But radical feminists also argue that "politics" is not simply located within the traditional places that we see as political, such as government or international institutions. They argue that the separation

---

[5] Radical feminists are not alone in this position. See also Fukuyama (1998).

of the public and private spheres, in which "politics" exists only within the public, is untenable: The bedroom is political, as is the workplace, a daycare center, people's bodies—all (and more) are sites of politics. Radical feminists thus also suggest different forms of political activism than do liberal feminists, and will be involved, among other things, with creating women's shelters, organizing around reproductive freedoms, creating safe spaces for women to meet, and the like.

Radical feminists may reject the view of the world as offered by liberals (that everyone is largely the same), but they do not reject the project of defining what women and men are and how they are different from one another. This is where they differ from *feminist postmodernists*, who agree with radical feminism that "the political" exists everywhere, but take exception to the radical feminist project of defining women at all. For feminist postmodernists, any definition or standpoint will necessarily be partial, and indeed any attempt to posit a single or universal truth needs to be deconstructed (Steans 1998, 25). Deconstruction entails exploring, unravelling, and rejecting the assumed naturalness of particular understandings and relationships, and examining the impact that otherwise "taken-for-granted" assumptions and understandings have on our ability to act in the world and even to think about global politics. For feminist postmodernists, as Marysia Zalewski (2000, 26) explains, any truth claim is an assertion of power that silences or makes invisible possibilities that do not fit easily into prevailing discursive practices.

Some developments of postmodern thought have picked up on its focus on discursive practices but attempt also to focus on the material lived conditions of people's lives. *Feminist critical theory* examines prevailing assumptions about both women and men: what it is to be a man or woman, what is appropriately feminine or masculine behavior, the appropriate roles of women and men within society, within the workforce, the family, and so on. They often argue that prevailing norms associated with masculinity must also be examined, and likewise that these norms can have an enormous impact on men, particularly marginalized men (Connell 1995; Hooper 2001). Critical feminists insist also that the assumptions that exist around women and men/masculinity and femininity take place not just at the level of discourse. Gender depends in part on the real, material, lived condition of women and men in particular times and places, which includes but is not limited to the lived conditions of race, class, sexuality, ethnicity, and religion.

Postcolonial feminist theorists also draw on these insights and argue further that imperialism constitutes one of the crucial moments, or processes, through which modern identities in all their guises become established. For postcolonial theorists, although some feminists acknowledge the intersectionality of race, class, and gender, there is nonetheless "a discernible First World feminist voice" in international relations that does not sufficiently foreground the "erasures surrounding race and representation" (Chowdhry and Nair 2002, 10). Postcolonial feminist theory attempts to do precisely this, further unpacking the assumed universality of experience between women that earlier (and particularly liberal and radical) feminisms relied upon.

Methodologically, feminists are equally eclectic, and may pursue any number of strategies: Some are empirically oriented and seek to show "where the women are," while others reject more traditional notions of methodology and pursue instead postpositivist approaches to research (Ackerly, Stern, and True 2006). Feminists thus share no single goal of theorizing or activism, and can disagree vociferously among themselves about what the world looks like and how to study it.

Where feminism is, almost by definition, breathtakingly heterogeneous, international relations is usually seen as considerably more homogeneous. Part of that homogeneity results from the particular way in which the discipline of international relations emerged. Stanley Hoffmann (1977) once famously (or infamously, depending on your point of view) wrote that international relations is largely an American social science. As a distinct discipline of study, it became established within the United States in the post-Second World War era. Hoffmann did not mean that international relations was only "discovered" in the United States after the Second World War, because, of course, philosophers, historians, poets, economists, artists, and political scientists had discussed issues of relevance to global-level politics for hundreds, if not thousands, of years. Nor was Hoffmann entirely accurate in suggesting that it was in the United States that international relations became a "discipline" of study—as British scholars point out, the first Chair of International Relations was created at the University of Aberystwyth in Wales in 1919 and was held by E. H. Carr (much of the account of the discipline of international relations that follows is drawn from Hollis and Smith 1991, ch. 2).

But Hoffmann's observations were useful in describing the way in which programs of study at both the undergraduate and graduate levels, research centers, and "think tanks" devoted to the study of international relations began to proliferate within the United States in the post-Second World War period. As Hoffmann noted, the United States emerged from the Second World War the dominant Western power, but it had little available expertise to help guide those in its political and bureaucratic offices in negotiating the issues and problems that a "world leader" and "superpower" would confront. The US government poured research money and other forms of support into universities and research centers for the explicit purpose of creating that expertise.

So successful was this exercise that American scholars, and the theoretical lenses they developed to understand international relations, came to dominate the study of international relations (George 1994; Smith 2002). This led to a number of very unique, if quite peculiar, characteristics. Once the discipline had been created explicitly to help guide policy-makers, the question of what international relations theory ought to be "for," what its goals should be, appeared to be settled at the outset—it was a practical discipline aimed at influencing, and improving upon, the decisions of policy-makers. So close was the relationship between academia and policy-making that sometimes the academics and the policy-makers were one and the same people, circulating between positions within universities and positions within government. As William Wallace (1996, 302) describes it, "the distinction be-tween the academic theorist and the practical policy-maker was a matter of degree."

It was not, moreover, just any policy-makers that international relations as a discipline aimed to assist; it was, in the first instance, American policy-makers, who faced a particular set of circumstances around which they needed expert advice. The United States emerged from the Second World War the world's sole nuclear superpower, but that status would soon need to be shared with the Soviet Union—a regime largely opposed not only to the United States, but to the principles of liberalism and free market capitalism upon which it was based. The most important issues that decision-makers needed advice on, then, were those that focused on conflict and security, and in particular on the potential for nuclear confrontation between East and West.

There was also a sense that the study of international politics needed to be conducted in a rigorous and scientific manner. In part, this resulted from a rejection of idealist thought, which had prevailed prior to the Second World War. Idealism was associated with the faith that institutions like the League of Nations (created at the end of the First World War) could provide a forum in which state leaders could choose to act collectively and avoid war. But that faith was thought to have died a certain death with the outbreak of the Second World War so closely on the heels of the First. Decision-makers needed advice, by this view, based not on ideals of what humanity ought to be like, and what might be possible in world politics, but rather on what the world really was—they needed rational, objective, and realistic accounts of global politics.

The approach to the study of world politics known as realism thus came to dominate the study of international relations. Realism posited that states were the most important actors in world politics, they acted in a condition of anarchy, and they acted in the pursuit of power. Although at different points throughout the latter half of the twentieth century debates among realists erupted, in particular over quantitative as opposed to more qualitative and historical forms of analysis, the central theoretical commitments of realism (states/power and anarchy) remained largely unchanged.

From these very brief accounts it should be clear that the different worlds of femi-nism and international relations suggest very different visions of what politics looks like, how we ought to study it, and what the goals of that study should be. But this does not mean that there is no room for engagement between the worlds of femi-nism and international relations, though, admittedly, that engagement sometimes can be quite spirited. Part of the spiritedness of those discussions may come out of the ways in which feminism and international relations are of different worlds, but part of it also comes out of the many questions and concerns that international relations and feminist scholars share in *common*. For all their differences, feminist and international relations scholars are also sometimes concerned with very similar types of questions. One of the most important of these is the question of power.

Feminists are as curious about power as are international relations theorists; both want to know, for example, about the way power operates and what it takes to sustain any given set of relationships, whether between states, peoples, or institutions. But, for feminists, understanding the operations of power inevitably means examining gender (Enloe 1996, 186). For much of traditional international relations theory, concerned as it is with states, institutions, or economic processes, actual "people" enter into the picture only rarely. For feminists, by contrast, we can only understand how power operates by not simply looking at generic "people," but digging further still and examining gender. As Cynthia Enloe notes, an analysis of politics inside or between states that ignores a feminist informed analysis of gender not only underestimates power; it is "politically naïve" (Enloe 2007a, 000).

Gender is a term intended to explore the ideational, material, historical, and institutional configurations of power that together contribute to the understandings about women and men, and masculinities and femininities, that prevail in any given time or place. The ideas and assumptions that prevail about women and men in situations of armed conflict and political violence, for example, are a good way to illustrate this point (Whitworth 2004, 27). Women and men are *both* active "agents" and "victims" of conflict and political violence, but they are usually positioned quite differently: women have long been portrayed primarily as victims of conflict, while men are portrayed as actors and agents (Moser and Clark, 2001, 4). This has implications for both women and men. Women are seldom viewed as having held public power prior to the emergence of conflict, or as having served as combatants. As a result, they may experience greater freedom in organizing informal peace campaigns, but at the same time they are usually ignored when formal peace processes begin, and are normally excluded from disarmament, demobilization, and reintegration (DDR) programs, which give former combatants access to educational, training, and employment opportunities. Men, on the other hand, are presumed to have held power and decision-making authority prior to the emergence of conflict and to have been combatants and instigators of the conflict itself. This sometimes makes their motivations suspect when they become involved in efforts to bring conflict to an end. At the same time, however, it is men who are normally invited to the formal "peace table" once it has been established, and they are the ones who primarily receive the benefits of DDR and other post-conflict activities (United Nations 2002). Prevailing understandings about women and men, and the material conditions of their lives, can thus significantly shape their experiences in institutions, nations, or social processes like armed conflict.

Importantly for feminists, power does not simply operate "out there" in history, in armed conflict, in faraway places, or in large institutions. Power informs all social relations, from the most personal through to the global. As V. Spike Peterson (1997, 199) writes of gender, it is "hard to see and critique because it orders 'everything' and disrupting that order feels threatening—not only at the 'level' of institutions and global relations but also in relation to the most intimate and deeply etched beliefs/experiences of personal (but relentlessly gendered) identity." The final phrase here is important—not because it suggests the primacy of gender over other relations of inequality, but rather because it reminds us how personally powerful gender is. This matters not only insofar as it points to the ways in which gender informs and impacts the most "intimate" parts of ourselves, but also because it signals just how effective forms of exclusion organized through gender can be. This is accomplished by marginalizing the feminine, by making it unquestioned to "infantilize, ignore, trivialize, or...actively cast scorn upon what is thought to be feminized" (Enloe 2004, 5).

Feminist scholars have underscored the ways in which crises of masculinity and fears of being feminized have been not only a powerful motivator for foreign policy-makers (a traditional focus of international relations scholars) but also an effective mobilizing tool for entire populations. Maya Eichler's (2006, 497) analysis of the Russian Chechen wars, for example, demonstrates the ways in which the Russian leadership of Vladimir Putin mobilized public support for the second Chechen war "on the basis of terrorist fears and masculinized humiliation." As Eichler (2006, 498, 501) argues, the second Chechen war was seen as a way to associate the Russian state with a militarized, patriotic, and orderly form of militarized masculinity, which not only served as a form of recuperation from the humiliations associated with the economic and financial experience of Russia since the collapse of the Soviet Union and the losses in the first Chechen war, but also juxtaposed Russian masculinity with a "notion of criminal, destabilizing and aggressive Chechen masculinity." Together, these ideas became an important element in securing popular support for the war.

This example is also illustrative of one final point that feminists would want to emphasize about gender: The forms of exclusion or privilege organized through gender—the ideas that constitute specifically gendered and racialized men and women, or masculinities and femininities, or nations or institutions—are never closed or fixed; rather they are constantly being produced and reproduced. This requires, as Enloe has long noted, a "lot of work;" it does not happen automatically (Enloe 1989, ch. 1 and *passim*; 2004, introduction). This means that the "natural-ness" of some forms of exclusion or privilege is never a finished project. This is why it is important also to interrogate the ways in which gender has been put into global circulation through the formal actors of global politics.

2 WHEN GLOBAL ACTORS USE GENDER

Many formal or "mainstream" actors in international relations seem recently to have been saying some of the things that feminists have argued around gender.

Many use the term gender, and numerous states and international institutions have pursued a strategy called "gender mainstreaming," adopted in the Beijing Platform for Action from the Fourth United Nations World Conference on Women in Beijing in 1995. Though many find the term unwieldy, "mainstreaming" is intended to call attention to the importance of incorporating attention to gender through all aspects of a state's or organization's work, and to move away from simply counting the number of women who are present. Conceptually, the idea of gender mainstreaming is relatively sophisticated; it accepts the idea that gender is a social construct, not a biological fact, and that the prevailing norms and assumptions concerning both women and men will differ across time and place. Mainstreaming views gender as shaped by cultural, class, religious, and ethnic differences and recognizes the power differentials between women and men, the fluid nature of those differences, and that these differences are made manifest in a variety of ways (United Nations 2001).

Gender mainstreaming has also had some clearly identifiable impacts on various international actors. The UN, for example, passed Security Council Resolution 1325 on women, peace, and security in 2000. The Security Council is known more for establishing peacekeeping missions or sanctioning the use of force in global politics (as it did in the early 1990s with the first Gulf War, and as it refused to do in 2003 in the second Gulf War). It is the only body within the UN system that can pass resolutions that are binding on the member states of the UN. Its resolution on women, peace, and security noted that women and children account for the vast majority of those adversely affected by armed conflict and increasingly those who are targeted by combatants in those conflicts. The resolution called for the incorporation of a gender perspective into peacekeeping operations and in the negotiation of peace agreements. It also called for the greater inclusion of women in peace operations, and called upon all parties to armed conflict to find ways to protect women and girls from sexual and gender-based violence during conflict (United Nations 2000).

Another international institution, the World Bank, was created after the Second World War to provide financial assistance to help in the postwar reconstruction of European countries, then later shifted its focus to development programs within the global South. The World Bank is also one of the international financial institutions that, along with the IMF and the WTO, has been targeted by antiglobalization activists for protests since the late 1990s. The World Bank has issued a variety of studies in which it insists that gender plays an important role in economic growth, poverty reduction, and development. In a 2002 report, the Bank writes: "Gender equality is a matter of development effectiveness, not just a matter of political correctness or kindness to women" (World Bank 2002, 1).

Even state leaders increasingly invoke discussions of gender, or at least women, when explaining or justifying foreign-policy decisions. US President George W. Bush, for example, has done this numerous times during his term of office, in particular when discussing the US-led interventions into both Afghanistan in 2001 after the attacks on the United States and then Iraq in 2003 in search of weapons of mass destruction. On Afghanistan, Bush (2002b) commented that "the Taliban used violence and fear to deny Afghan women access to education, health care, mobility and the right to vote. Our coalition has liberated Afghanistan and restored fundamental human rights and freedoms to Afghan women ... " The US intervention, in short, had not only sought to address the sources of terrorist attacks against the United States; it had made women's lives better in Afghanistan. Bush (2002a) made the same promise when it came to Iraq: Saddam Hussein, he said, had ordered the systematic rape of the wives and mothers of political opponents, and a US intervention would bring an end to both the Hussein regime and these kinds of practices.

Thus, although feminist interventions into the field of international relations are relatively recent, and sometimes resisted by scholars of international relations, they seem to have had an impact on the way in which many of the formal actors in international relations—like the UN, the World Bank, and even the President of the United States—think through, and use, notions of gender. The question for many feminists, however, is *how* these actors use gender, and there is considerable concern and suspicion about the ends to which such discussions are aimed.

Krista Hunt (2002; Hunt and Rygiel 2006), for example, points out that the sudden interest of the United States, and the West, in the plight of Afghan women after the 11 September attacks on the United States was, at best, suspicious. There had long been information available about the systematic abuse of women in Afghanistan—much of it raised by the Revolutionary Association of the Women of Afghanistan—which until 11 September had been largely ignored by Western governments and the international media. For Hunt, this meant not only that women's bodies were being "written" in a way that justified particular forms of military response, but, moreover, that the enormous impact on women that resulted from that military response was rendered, if not invisible, at least "justified."

Mainstream uses of gender, in fact, regularly seem intended to justify or accommodate existing policies or practices, not to transform them. When organizations like the UN or World Bank focus on gender, their concern is often increasing the efficiency of existing policies. Anne Orford (2002, 281; 2003) writes that, when used in this way, "a 'gender perspective' can be mapped onto existing ways of doing business" without questioning the bases of that business in the first place. The UN Security Council Resolution on women, peace, and security, for example, does not seek to alter militarized responses to conflict but asks only that the impact of conflict on women and girls receive greater attention and that women have greater opportunities to participate in formal peace-building and peacemaking processes. As noted above, for the World Bank, the relationship between gender and development is relatively straightforward: Gender equality increases economic efficiency and productivity, two goals that the Bank seeks to achieve.

Increased efficiency is a common argument used by international actors when discussing gender, and regularly both feminist activists and international bureaucrats use this kind of language when making the case for or speaking to the advantages of gender mainstreaming. As one nongovernmental organization brief argues regarding peacekeeping, "gender mainstreaming is possible and can improve the effectiveness of operations" (International Alert 2002, 1). This approach has several consequences, the most important of which is that it turns a critical term such as "gender" into an instrument for problem-solving goals (Whitworth 2004, 120). Once the purpose of using gender becomes helping international actors become more effective in their work, a whole series of questions are ruled out of bounds; for example, whether institutions like the UN or World Bank are engaged in imperial practices through their aid-giving practices, their peace operations, and their humanitarian interventions. When used in this way, gender does not transform what mainstream international actors do; rather the use to which it is put is to contribute to helping these institutions "do better" what they already do. A focus on power is thus eliminated and the term gender is depoliticized.

3 IF NOT INTERNATIONAL INSTITUTIONS, WHO?

The argument thus far has been that global institutions like the UN or World Bank regularly use the term gender, but do not actually understand gender in the way feminists intended. If this group of international actors use gender but do not understand it, who does? Disturbingly, one set of actors that does seem to understand gender as a site around which power is constituted is the military intelligence people who conduct interrogations at Abu Ghraib and Guantanamo Bay. *They* understand gender. Those who planned the sexual torture and humiliation techniques used against prisoners understand that we can discover (and in their cases, manipulate) the deeply felt expectations associated with prevailing conceptions of masculinity. The interrogations involved a systematic assault on conceptions of appropriately masculine behavior: smearing fake menstrual blood on prisoner's faces, forcing them to masturbate or simulate and/or perform oral and anal sex on one another, to disrobe in one another's presence, to touch one another, to touch women, and to be photographed in these and other positions (Highman and Stephens 2004). It is a racist and heterosexist understanding of masculinity, to be sure, but it is one that "understands" gender. Alarmingly, the people who interrogated prisoners at Guantanamo Bay and Abu Ghraib probably never use the term gender, but they do understand it.

Zillah Eisenstein (2004) has written of the "gender confusions" at Abu Ghraib. She means by this the ways in which gender swapping (the sexual torture and humiliation of Muslim men perpetrated by white American women) and the gender confusions associated with it were used as a cover for hyperimperialist masculinity.[6] But it is important to be clear that gender confusion should not signal that those who used these torture techniques were confused about what they were doing. As many feminists have argued, militaries have long been in the business of manipulating gender. The creation of soldiers has always involved rituals and myths that focus on messages about masculinity, manliness, race, and belonging. Soldiers in most national militaries are constituted through often violently misogynist, racist, and homophobic messages delivered through basic training, initiation, and indoctrination exercises. As Judith Stiehm (1989, 226) has written, "all militaries have ... regularly been rooted in the psychological coercion of young men through appeals to their (uncertain) manliness." What militaries do is replace that uncertainty with a hegemonic representation of idealized norms of masculinity that privilege the tough, stoic, emotionless warrior, capable and willing to employ violence to achieve whatever ends he may be ordered into. Militaries work hard to fix the identities of young men in these terms, and have worked equally hard to deny the fragility of this construction (Whitworth 2004, 172). That militaries are also quite capable of manipulating the fragilities and uncertainties of masculinity, to play into sexist, racialized, and heterosexist fears to disrupt the norms of masculinity is another component of the production of militarized men in a globalized world.

The observation that militaries and military intelligence interrogators better understand gender than apparently more benign neoliberal institutions like the UN or World Bank should cause some concern. Feminists could despair that the only actors who seem to understand gender are militaries, and that their understanding is used to accomplish violent, racist, and imperialist ends. But appreciating the ways in which militaries understand gender might also point us in the direction of trying to uncover why organizations like the UN or World Bank so persistently refuse to understand it, and indeed persistently circulate depoliticized visions of gender as part of the "lifeways" of contemporary global politics. What militaries understand is that relations of power work through gender. This is the very idea that liberal institutions such as the UN or World Bank actively resist—gender in this context is a variable ("women") that may impact and be impacted on by events in global politics and policies pursued by these institutions. Women and men may be impacted on by those events or policies in unequal ways, but recognizing this does not see "gender" as the constitution of relations of power through exclusions and privileges associated with masculinity and femininity, the very point that feminists have tried to make in using the term gender.

---

[6] For further feminist discussions of Abu Ghraib see articles by Melanie Richter-Montpetit (2007), Liz Philipose (2007), and Laura Sjoberg (2007) in a special section of *International Feminist Journal of Politics* entitled "Feminist readings on Abu Ghraib" (Enloe 2007b).

Militaries understand gender as relations of power in part because, within the current era of globalization, what Arundhati Roy (2004) calls the "new imperialism," militaries are the only actors who deal in power in its most explicitly and openly violent forms. There is no contradiction for militaries openly to embrace violence and at the same time clearly "understand" gender as relations of power (even if they may never openly acknowledge that understanding). But such a position would be fundamentally contradictory for institutions and organizations like the UN or the World Bank that exercise power in much more subtle and less explicitly and openly violent forms. Representations of otherwise critical ideas like gender as depoliticized is necessary because it is the only approach that is not, for liberal institutions, contradictory. Seeing gender means seeing power—this is something that militaries have long relied on in the creation of soldiers but that liberal institutions have ignored through their conceptions of power as largely benign. For liberal institutions, truly understanding gender would require, in their case, transformation; for militaries, it is already in keeping with existing practices. Clearly one further way in which feminist activists will remain focused will be to push for precisely this kind of transformation, so that militaries do not hold a monopoly on the global circulation of ideas about gender that understand it as one of the means through which power is constituted, and that neoliberal institutions do not continue to make this relationship invisible through its circulation of understandings about gender that reduce it to simply a "variable."

4 CONCLUSIONS

As Enloe (2001, 111) has observed, "A funny thing has happened on the way to international political consciousness: 'gender' has become a safe idea." What Enloe is flagging in this statement is that the consequence of using "gender" without simultaneously exploring relations of power and inequality deprives us of some of the most important insights feminist thinking has to offer international relations (see also Sjoberg 2007). It is in its concern with power that feminism most "shares" a focus with scholars of international relations, but what should be clear from this chapter is that the way power is analyzed by feminists is dramatically different from most traditional international relations scholarship. What should also be clear from the above analysis is that feminist thinking was never intended to be "safe"—it has opened up new questions and new ways of looking at global politics that were supposed to make traditional analysts and observers rethink and unpack taken-for-granted assumptions about international relations. Feminism is supposed to make us uncomfortable, but by doing so its aim is to promote critical engagement with very difficult contemporary political issues, and, more than this, to motivate and inspire us to act upon those issues.

REFERENCES

ACKERLY, B. A., STERN, M., and TRUE, J. (eds.) 2006. *Feminist Methodologies for International Relations*. Cambridge: Cambridge University Press.

ALEXANDER, M. J., and MOHANTY, C. T. (eds.) 1997. *Feminist Genealogies, Colonial Legacies, Democratic Futures*. New York: Routledge.

BUSH, G. W. 2002a. President Bush outlines Iraqi threat. Oct. www.whitehouse.gov/news/releases/2002/10/20021007-8.html.

—— 2002b. Women's equality day. Proclamation 7584, 23 Aug. www.whitehouse.gov/ogc.

CHOWDHRY, G., and NAIR, S. 2002. Power in a postcolonial world: race, gender, and class in international relations. Pp. 10–32 in *Power, Postcolonialism and International Relations: Reading Race, Gender, and Class*, ed. G. Chowdhry and S. Nair. London: Routledge.

CONNELL, R. W. 1995. *Masculinities*. Berkeley: University of California Press.

EICHLER, M. 2006. Russia's post-communist transformation: a gendered analysis of the Chechen wars. *International Feminist Journal of Politics*, 8: 486–511.

EISENSTEIN, Z. 2004. Sexual humiliation, gender confusion and the horrors at Abu Ghraib. PeaceWomen, June. www.peacewomen.org/news/Iraq/June04/abughraib.html.

ENLOE, C. 1989. *Bananas, Beaches and Bases: Making Feminist Sense of International Politics*. London: Pandora.

—— 1996. Margins, silences and bottom rungs: how to overcome the underestimation of power in the study of international relations. Pp. 186–202 in *International Theory: Positivism and Beyond*, ed. S. Smith, K. Booth, and M. Zalewski. Cambridge: Cambridge University Press.

—— 2001. Closing remarks. Pp. 111–13 in *Women and International Peacekeeping*, ed. L. Olsson and T. L. Tryggestad. London: Frank Cass.

—— 2004. *The Curious Feminist: Searching for Women in a New Age of Empire*. Berkeley: University of California Press.

—— 2007a. Feminist international relations: how to do it; what we gain. Pp. 000 in *International Relations Theory for the 21st Century*, ed. M. Griffiths. New York: Routledge.

—— 2007b. Feminist readings on Abu Ghraib: introduction. *International Feminist Journal of Politics*, 9: 35–7.

FUKUYAMA, F. 1998. Women and the evolution of world politics. *Foreign Affairs*, 77: 24–40.

GEORGE, J. 1994. *Discourses of Global Politics: A Critical (Re)Introduction to International Relations*. Boulder, Colo.: Lynne Rienner.

HIGHMAN, S., and STEPHENS, J. 2004. New details of prison abuse emerge: Abu Ghraib detainees' statements describe sexual humiliation and savage beatings. *Washington Post*, 21 May: A01.

HOFFMANN, S. 1977. An American social science: international relations. *Daedalus*, 106: 41–60.

HOLLIS, M., and SMITH, S. 1991. *Explaining and Understanding International Relations*. Oxford: Clarendon Press.

HOOPER, C. 2001. *Manly States: Masculinities, International Relations, and Gender Politics.* New York: Columbia University Press.

HUNT, K. 2002. The strategic co-optation of women's rights: discourse in the "war on terrorism." *International Feminist Journal of Politics,* 4: 116–21.

——and RYGIEL, K. (eds.) 2006. *(En)Gendering the War on Terror: War Stories and Camouflaged Politics.* Aldershot: Ashgate.

INTERNATIONAL ALERT 2002. Gender mainstreaming in peace support operations: moving beyond rhetoric to practice. July. www.international-alert.org/pdfs/Gender_ Mainstreaming_in_PSO_Beyond_Rhetoric_to_Practice.pdf.

JAGGAR, A. M. 1983. *Feminist Politics and Human Nature.* Lanham, Md.: Rowman and Littlefield.

KEOHANE, R. O. 1998. Beyond dichotomy: conversations between international relations and feminist theory. *International Studies Quarterly,* 42: 193–7.

LINKLATER, A., CARVER, T., and ENLOE, C. 2004. Three commentaries on Gillian Youngs' "Feminist International Relations." *International Affairs,* 80: 89–97.

MARCHAND, M. 1998. Different communities/different realities/different encounters: a reply to J. Ann Tickner. *International Studies Quarterly,* 42: 199–204.

MITTLEMAN, J. H. 2004. What is critical globalization studies? *International Studies Perspectives,* 53: 219–30.

MOHANTY, C. T., RUSSO, A., and TORRES, L. (eds.) 1991. *Third World Women and the Politics of Feminism.* Bloomington: Indiana University Press.

MOSER, C. O. N., and CLARK, F. C. 2001. *Victims, Perpetrators or Actors? Gender, Armed Conflict and Political Violence.* London: Zed Books.

Office of the Special Advisor on Gender Issues and Advancement of Women 2006. The Status of Women in the United Nations System (OHRM data from 31 Dec. 2003 to 31 Dec. 2004) and in the Secretariat (OHRM data from 1 July 2004 to 30 June 2006). www.un.org/womenwatch/osagi/pdf/Fact%20sheet%2028%20september.pdf.

ORFORD, A. 2002. Feminism, imperialism and the mission of international law. *Nordic Journal of International Law,* 71: 275–96.

——2003. *Reading Humanitarian Intervention: Human Rights and the Use of Force in International Law.* Cambridge: Cambridge University Press.

PETERSON, V. S. 1997. Whose crisis? Early and post-modern masculinism. Pp. 185–201 in *Innovation and Transformation in International Studies,* ed. S. Gill and J. H. Mittleman. Cambridge: Cambridge University Press.

——and RUNYAN, A. S. 1999. *Global Gender Issues,* 2nd edn. Boulder, Colo.: Westview.

PHILIPOSE, L. 2007. The politics of pain and the end of empire. *International Feminist Journal of Politics,* 9: 60–81.

RAI, S. M. 2004. Gendering global governance. *International Feminist Journal of Politics,* 6: 579–601.

RICHTER-MONTPETIT, M. 2007. Empire, desire and violence: a queer transnational feminist reading of the prisoner "abuse" in Abu Ghraib and the question of "gender equality." *International Feminist Journal of Politics,* 9: 38–59.

ROSENAU, J. N. (ed.) 1993. *Global Voices: Dialogues in International Relations.* Boulder, Colo.: Westview.

ROY, A. 2004. The new American century. *The Nation,* 9 Feb.

SJOBERG, L. 2007. Agency, militarized femininity and enemy others: observations from the war in Iraq. *International Feminist Journal of Politics,* 9: 82–101.

SMITH, S. 2002. The United States and the discipline of international relations: "hegemonic country, hegemonic discipline." *International Studies Review*, 4: 67–85.

STEANS, J. 1998. *Gender and International Relations: An Introduction*. Piscataway, NJ: Rutgers University Press.

STIEHM, J. H. 1989. *Arms and the Enlisted Woman*. Philadelphia: Temple University Press.

TICKNER, J. A. 1997. You just don't understand: troubled engagements between feminists and IR theorists. *International Studies Quarterly*, 41: 611–32.

—— 1998. Continuing the conversation. *International Studies Quarterly*, 42: 205–10.

UNITED NATIONS 2000. Security Council Resolution 1325, S/RES/1325 (2000). www.un.org/events/res_1325e.pdf.

—— 2001. Gender mainstreaming: an overview. New York: Office of the Special Advisor on Gender Issues and Advancement of Women, United Nations, www.un.org/womenwatch/osagi/pdf/e65237.pdf.

—— 2002. Women, peace and security. Study submitted by the Secretary-General. New York: United Nations, www.un.org/womenwatch/daw/public/eWPS.pdf.

WALLACE, W. 1996. Truth and power, monks and technocrats: theory and practice in international relations. *Review of International Studies*, 22: 301–21.

WHITWORTH, S. 1994. *Feminism and International Relations: Towards a Political Economy of Gender in Interstate and Non-Governmental Institutions*. Basingstoke: Macmillan.

—— 2004. *Men, Militarism, and UN Peacekeeping: A Gendered Analysis*. Boulder, Colo.: Lynne Rienner.

WORLD BANK 2002. Integrating gender into the World Bank's work: a strategy for action. Washington: World Bank, Jan., http://siteresources.worldbank.org/INTGENDER/Resources/strategypaper.pdf.

YOUNGS, G. 2004. Feminist international relations: a contradiction in terms? Or: why women and gender are essential to understanding the world "we" live in. *International Affairs*, 80: 75–87.

ZALEWSKI, M. 2000. *Feminism after Postmodernism: Theorising through Practice*. London: Routledge.

CHAPTER 24

···

THE ETHICS OF FEMINISM

···

JACQUI TRUE

FEMINIST perspectives on international relations are explicitly and positively normative. Together with feminists in other fields, international relations feminists seek to understand existing gender relations—the dominance of masculinities over femininities—in order to transform how they work at all levels of social, political, and economic life. Within international relations, feminist scholars have drawn on the experiences of marginalized and oppressed peoples, including women, in order to challenge and revision the conventional foundations of the field. They have interrogated gender bias inherent in rationalist ways of knowing and embedded in the core concepts and concerns of international relations, such as states, sovereignty, power, security, international conflict, and global governance. More recently, feminists have given an explicit account of their alternative methodological approaches to research on global politics. However, the axiological dimension of feminist international relations is still relatively underdeveloped. In particular, there is little scholarship that translates feminist theory into guidelines for ethical conduct by state and nonstate actors in international relations.

International relations feminists share a praxis-oriented normative theory—consciously building theory from practice and to guide political practice—but

I would like to thank Brooke Ackerly and Elisabeth Prügl for their comments and the many insights I have drawn from conversations with them and their respective scholarship. I would also like to thank the editors for their extremely helpful feedback and engagement with the arguments presented here. See True (2005) for a more comprehensive review of feminist approaches to international relations.

their normative approaches are plural. They differ over the philosophical grounds for their knowledge of gendered international reality, the theoretical location and centrality of gender as an analytic category in the study of international relations, and, on the basis of these, their prescriptions for ethical conduct. This chapter explores these differences among international relations feminisms and their significance for international relations theory. As well, it considers the debates between feminist and other international relations perspectives, often construed as one-way conversations.

1 DEFINING FEMINISM

Contrary to some recent claims, feminism's normative commitments are not what distinguish it from mainstream theories of international relations. Like critical international relations theorist Robert Cox (1981, 128), feminists argue, "theory is always for someone, and for some purpose" (and thus that all perspectives on international relations are inherently normative, whether consciously or not). *Rather, it is ethical commitments to inclusivity and self-reflexivity, and attentiveness to relational power, that distinguish most feminist perspectives on international relations* (see Ackerly and True 2006). Despite the normative variations within feminist international relations, these forms of ethical commitment are strongly evident within the diverse range of international relations feminist scholarship. They are akin to what Ann Tickner (2006) has broadly termed feminist practices of responsible scholarship.

Guided by the commitment to be inclusive of the multiple vantage points on international relations and self-reflexive about potential exclusions, feminists are acutely sensitive to power, relationships, and politics in all places within and beyond the boundaries of states and international public spheres. This leads them to ask questions not only about the powerful but also about their relationship to the powerless. For instance, feminists draw theoretical connections between the plight of prostitutes and the practices of peacekeepers on foreign military bases and UN missions to show how international relations are dependent on particular constructions of masculinity and femininity (Moon 1997). Moreover, the norm of inclusivity leads feminists to "study up," as international relations scholars have conventionally done, and to "study down." For example, feminist research on globalization examines the perspectives of international institutions, state agencies, and elites in promoting capital mobility as well as the perspectives of female migrant domestic servants, micro-entrepreneurs, and women trafficked for prostitution who cross borders to facilitate global production and reproduction (Marchand and

Runyan 2000). Moreover, feminists analyzing the gendered politics in international conflict zones tend to conduct their research on both sides of the conflict in order to understand its identity dynamics and the alternative possibilities for conflict resolution (Jacoby 2006).

If the norm of inclusivity helps feminists to correct some of the biases of international relations scholarship that does not consult a wide range of perspectives, elite and marginalized, then the norm of self-reflexivity assists feminists in discovering their own exclusions and biases. Generated within and through collective scholarship, this self-reflexive norm helps feminist scholars to be more conscious of the exclusions that result from their normative purposes, choices of research subject, and methodology, and to be responsible for these exclusions. Carol Cohn and Sara Ruddick's feminist analysis (2004) of weapons of mass destruction illustrates this ethical commitment to relational understanding; that we are always implicated in the global subjects that we study. They argue that staking out a normative position as "anti-war feminists" means opposing the development, proliferation, and use of all weapons of mass destruction. However, they also recognize that this feminist position tends to deny the social and political realities of women and men living in less powerful states and to reinforce the dominant perspective of Western possessor states. Demonstrating their self-reflexivity about the political implication of their argument, they explicitly state: "As citizens of the most highly-armed possessor state [and anti-war feminists], our credibility ... will be contingent upon our committed efforts to bring about nuclear disarmament in our own state, and our own efforts to redress the worldwide inequalities that are underwritten by our military superiority" (Cohn and Ruddick 2004, 424).

2 FEMINISM GENEALOGIES

Feminist perspectives have developed alongside some impressive power shifts in contemporary international relations. Feminist international relations like most contemporary feminist scholarship is indebted to the second wave of women's movements that thrived all over the world in the 1960s and 1970s. These movements were the harbingers of feminist theories that analyzed sex and gender as social constructions to be transformed rather than facts of nature to be taken for granted. Feminist scholars shaped by their activist experiences considered it a moral imperative to include women's voices and to change both the subjects and the objects of study (Tickner 2006). Many feminist scholars trace their interest in international relations as an area of study to their involvement in cold war peace movements and in feminist peace politics that go back to the First World War (Rupp 1997).

Not surprisingly, in the late 1980s the first feminist contributions to the international relations field were highly controversial, since the field was at the time one of the most male dominated and had as its central focus inter-state diplomacy and war, both on the face of it near exclusive masculine affairs. But the sudden collapse of Communism and with it the bipolar international system had far-reaching implications for the international relations field. Dominant realist theories singularly focused on power politics among states did not anticipate this transformation. Nor could they explain it. This glaring impoverishment of theories of international relations opened the way for new approaches to understanding global politics, including critical, and explicitly normative, perspectives such as feminism.

2.1 Post-Cold War Feminism

The end of the cold war also had a profound impact on the political opportunities available for principled, nonstate actors to participate in global politics and put nontraditional issues on global policy agendas. At the same time as feminist perspectives began to challenge the norms of international relations scholarship, women's movements gained a foothold in the United Nations (UN) and began to use that international institution to mobilize global alliances of Western and non-Western women activists, scholars, and policy-makers. A feminist epistemic network that included international relations feminists emerged through the UN and other international conferences in the 1990s. The 1990s also heralded two successful global campaigns to get women's rights recognized as human rights in international law and to address a range of egregious practices, often state and culturally sanctioned, as forms of "violence against women." Transnational feminist networks used their substantive expertise on gender relations—through both critical argumentation and evidence-based research—to engage institutional power (True and Mintrom 2001).

By the end of the millennium it looked as if feminists had had more success in engaging international institutions than in influencing the discipline of international relations. Antiwar feminists collaborated to get the UN Security Council to pass Resolution 1325 securing women's rights to participate in international peace negotiations and operations, while feminists critical of neoliberal globalization and the disproportionate impact of structural adjustment policies on poor women made inroads into the World Bank and other international development agencies. At the same time, the European Union formally adopted gender mainstreaming as a methodology for paying attention to gender inequalities and differences across all policy domains and areas of competency. Feminist scholarship mirrored the focus of global women's movements, more so than the statist theoretical concerns of the mainstream international relations discipline, by developing gendered analyses of nationalism and ethnic conflict, democratization, and economic globalization. Tickner (2001) observed that mainstream American international relations, in particular, was focused narrowly on its own paradigmatic research questions, marginalizing the more popular questions that dominated the global public realm in the 1990s. She and other international relations feminists regretted mainstream international relations' lack of engagement with feminist perspectives yet noted the intellectual gulf between their different approaches (Tickner 1997).

2.2 Post-11 September Feminism

Whereas the post-cold war era allowed many political opportunities for feminist and other critical international relations perspectives to shape the international relations research agenda, the events of 11 September changed this relatively propitious environment. Like other perspectives on international relations responding to the changed global political context, the emphasis of feminist analysis shifted after 11 September to focus more on international security. However, feminist analyses have sought to understand the gendered roots of terrorism in underlying political and economic inequalities and in constructions of masculinity in Western and non-Western contexts that contribute to global insecurities (see Agathangelou and Ling 2004).

3 DIFFERENCES WITHIN FEMINISM

Despite some of the difficult encounters between feminist and nonfeminist international relations, feminism has thrived over the past decade, as evidenced by the many and varied feminist contributions to the international relations field. At the same time, international relations feminists have had rich debates among themselves. This chapter puts me in the ironic position of defining a normative field that not only is plural, but eschews definition. Feminism is difficult to classify precisely because, as Christine Sylvester (2000, 269) articulates, it "has many types and shifting forms. It is non-uniform and non-consensual; it is a complex matter with many internal debates."

Here I explore three major differences within feminism in the international relations field. These differences revolve around epistemological stance, ontologies, and theoretical understandings of gender relations and prescriptions for ethical conduct. Guided by the ethical attentiveness to inclusivity, power, relationships, and self-reflexivity, feminists are continually conversing, and contesting the norms of international relations, accepting the ironies of self-definition, and the differences among them (see Ackerly, Stern, and True 2006).

3.1 Epistemological Differences

The first salient debate within international relations feminism concerns the philosophical foundations for feminist normative claims. Much emphasis has been placed on the distinction between the feminist standpoint and postmodern epistemologies. Following Marxism, the feminist standpoint asserts that a stronger, more objective perspective on social reality can be gained from taking the standpoint of marginalized political subjects, historically women, who by virtue of their dominated position tend to be less ideologically vested in maintaining the status quo. This feminist standpoint is counterposed to a postmodern feminist stance, which is suspicious of any claims to a better vantage point on the truth of social and international reality.

Postmodern feminism problematizes the feminist standpoint assumption that women's experience of oppression in social hierarchies can constitute the basis for critical knowledge. Postmodernists argue that such a standpoint tends to homogenize differences among women and reinforce gender stereotypes. Although oversimplified, this epistemological distinction among feminisms remains relevant in analyzing international relations debates. Influenced by Third World, postcolonial, postmodern, Black, and lesbian feminist critiques, some international relations feminists posit a *plural* rather than a singular feminist standpoint. But they retain the belief in the value of a feminist perspective from the political margins that begins by asking questions about excluded women's lives—that is, the work women do and the material structures of gender inequality (although it does not stop there) (see Tickner 1997; Enloe 2000).

Postmodern feminists dispute even provisional, diversified, feminist standpoints. They shift the attention away from the subject of women or the perspective of gender difference in international relations. Employing strategies of deconstruction, including the strategic use of woman or the feminine, postmodern feminists aim to destabilize both international relations' and feminism's philosophical and epistemological grounds (Zalewski 2006). Roland Bleiker (1997) recommends, for instance, that feminists and other postpositivists "forget IR" in their theoretical or empirical research to avoid creating the very same totalizing knowledges and exclusionary political effects as mainstream perspectives.

Rather than deconstruction, some international relations feminists have advocated a dialogic approach. This approach critically scrutinizes the conditions of exclusion in all fields of knowledge in order to bring about the emancipation of all subjects, feminist and nonfeminist. It also deploys a destabilizing epistemology to the extent that it assumes the grounds for knowledge claims, feminist politics, and transnational alliances are always shifting. Yet dialogic feminists seek to overcome postcolonial and postmodern critiques through an ethical stance that involves entering into constructive conversation and seeking common albeit contested ground with marginalized others (see Porter 2000). For example, Brooke Ackerly (2008) builds a feminist universalist theory of human rights that is sensitive to local, cultural struggles and the social contexts of rights by listening to as well as analyzing the partial perspectives of Third World women human rights activists. Such a feminist approach involves an ethical commitment to deconstructing one's own position of privilege while actively working to transform the power relations that support that position.

3.2 Ontologies of Gender

Feminists differ in their normative views of how the category of gender can be applied to international relations. The majority of international relations feminists conceive of gender as the relational construction of masculine and feminine identities, where masculine identities are preferred over feminine ones, and are a signifier for power relations of domination and subordination among individuals and collectivities generally. In these dual senses of the term, gender is seen as infusing all aspects of international relations and, therefore, is a highly relevant category of analysis. For example, feminist scholars use gender analysis to critique gendered identities and security discourses in the post-11 September global "war on terror." They deconstruct US conceptions of security that look for "real men" to protect "us" from "them" and blame feminism and homosexuality for weakening the resolve of the West (Agathangelou and Ling 2004). They also scrutinize the gendered discourses in the Islamic fundamentalist groups behind the terrorist acts of violence against the West and among the US occupation forces in Iraq and the greater Middle East (Kaufman-Osborn 2005). These discourses perceive Western sexual and gender equality, and the supposed imprisonment and abuse of Muslim women by non-Muslim men (or vice versa), as threatening Islamic culture and, as such, they are used both to incite and to justify violence.

By contrast with this use of gender as an analytical tool to theoretically challenge mainstream international relations concepts of security, some feminists deploy gender as a variable in empirical research. Feminist empiricism views gender relations as relevant to international relations analysis because patterns of gender inequality exist at every level of state and global politics (although the extent of gender inequality differs across states and regions; see Gray, Kittilson, and Sandholtz 2006, 294). Thus, for example, feminist scholars use gender to explain state behavior in an anarchic system (Caprioli 2004). Their research shows that states with the greatest domestic inequality between men and women are more likely to go to war or to engage in state-sanctioned violence (Goldstein 2001), whereas those states with near gender equality tend to be the most pacific in their inter-state relations, and more generous international aid donors. Feminist empiricism is potentially radical, since it can highlight the relevance of gender to the study of even the most conventional international relations questions, and, with the use of statistical methods, such research can show the demonstrable impact of gender inequality and feminist actors in global politics.

Another feminist variation with respect to ontology concerns the treatment of gender relative to other categories of oppression such as race, ethnicity, nationality, class, and sexuality. Progressively, international relations feminists have moved away from binary conceptions of gender to explore plural masculinities and femininities in global politics. For example, Charlotte Hooper (2001) argues that multiple masculinities exist across ethnicity, class, sexuality, nationality, and so on and that changes in dominant masculine identities underpin (and indeed can help to explain) shifts in world order, such as the contemporary globalization of political economies. More recently, some feminists have located gender at the intersection of various forms of subordination, marking a paradigm shift away from the monolithic representation of gender relations, as the patriarchal domination of women by men without regard to oppression based on race, ethnicity, sexuality, and colonial hierarchy (Han and Ling 1998; Stern 2006). Feminist knowledge about the diversity of women's experiences and contexts leads them to appreciate the inter-related character of social hierarchies and their influence on oppression (D'Costa 2006). This intersectional approach takes account of poor, minority, migrant, and refugee women and girls, who often fall through the categories of feminist and international relations theories, global policy, and international law. It has normative implications for both feminist and nonfeminist efforts to understand complex identities and differences within international relations.

International relations feminists also differ in how they understand the construction of gender relations. Although most feminists conceive of gender relations as involving elements of structure and agency, feminists influenced by neo-Marxism understand gender as an ideological and structural hierarchy, that is primarily rooted in the material divisions created by patriarchal capitalism, such as the globalized, gender division of labor, reinforced by international organizations and the ideologies of globalization (Steans 1998). However, feminists influenced by constructivist theories of the rules of discourse within language tend to see gender as a hegemonic discourse of difference that is reproduced through institutionalized norms and identities rather than material structures (Prügl 1999). Efforts to transform gender domination depend greatly on how its existence is understood or explained. Thus, these theoretical differences have normative import within international relations and feminism. Consider their implications for feminist agency: If gender hierarchies are rooted in material structures, then feminist strategies for transformation will probably be oppositional to states and international organizations insofar as they seek structural change in the organization and regulation of political economies. But if gender hegemonies are located in discourse, then feminist strategies for transformation will involve struggles over the meanings of women and gender embedded in rules and norms, and will probably require institutional engagement with states and international organizations to disrupt and/or change their practices.

3.3 Practical Ethics

In addition to epistemological and ontological differences, feminists differ on the implications for ethical conduct they draw from their theory. Some feminists assert the political value of the ethic of care in international relations, whereas other feminists suggest a postmodern form of feminist ethics that recognizes the plurality of the self and is responsive to its constitutive other (Jabri 1999). Joan Tronto (1993, 145) argues that "care is not solely private or parochial; it can concern institutions, societies, even global levels of thinking." Although it is derived from a normative context of the feminine against the masculine, the private against the public, the ethic of care is not associated exclusively with women nor does it rely on an essentialist conception of woman. It offers a "distinct moral perspective that is gender-focused but not exclusively 'woman-centered'," that seeks to understand, reflect on, and possibly transform gendered patterns of moral relations rather than construct universal, generalizable, moral principles (Robinson 2006, 228, 231). By contrast, the postmodern feminist "care of self" ethic subverts categorical gendered identities through a performative, stylized celebration of difference. It is self-critical with respect to all efforts to assimilate the other or develop a discourse with global application (see also Hutchings 2004).

Unlike the postmodern ethic of the self, the ethic of care perspective is no longer defined as an epistemological stance but as an ontological claim about "the central role of care and other relational moral practices in the everyday lives of people in all settings" (Robinson 2006, 225). It recognizes global divisions of caring labor and the power relations among women due to social hierarchies. Moreover, care ethics is an axiological approach that develops ethical guidelines from feminist theory for humanitarian intervention, multilateral peacekeeping, development aid, foreign security policy, and human rights protection among other practical global issues and dilemmas (see Hutchings 2000, 122–3). For example, Tronto (2006) analyzes the normative framework supporting multilateral peacekeeping from a feminist perspective. She stresses that the shift from "the right to intervene" in a sovereign state to a "responsibility to protect" citizens not protected by their own state is a shift from liberal to care ethics, from the masculine assumption of an autonomous self—sovereign man or state—to the assumption of a relational self with responsibilities to others.

4 Encounters between Feminist and Nonfeminist International Relations

Some feminist perspectives embrace a dialogical approach to knowledge and ethical conduct, whereas other feminist perspectives are more wary of engagement with dominant theories and institutions, and of losing feminism's critical perspective and destabilizing epistemology. Like any other approach to inquiry, however, feminism must itself be evaluated in terms of its ability to respond to critical scrutiny from other perspectives. International relations feminism has evolved in both relation and reaction to mainstream international relations and its insistence that feminism set out and defend its theoretical approach and research agenda.

Many international relations feminists are skeptical of rationalist approaches, preferring a relational epistemology and ontology, and narrative-based, interpretative, and/or ethnographic methods that stress the social, constitutive aspects of world politics. Yet feminists are also eclectic with respect to methodology, as the earlier discussion about gender analysis versus gender as a variable noted. Indeed, Mary Caprioli (2004) contends that the empirical analysis of gender and state behavior may be better than critical, interpretative feminist approaches at delivering the goals of social justice and women's empowerment.

Increasingly feminist research is adapting nonfeminist research questions on state behavior, international norms and law, and global civil society, and nonfeminist methodologies such as quantitative analysis, institutional analysis, and constructivist analysis. Birgit Locher and Elisabeth Prügl (2001) contend that feminism and constructivism share an "ontology of becoming." But they also argue that constructivist scholars tend to use concepts of socially constructed identities, ideas, and norms empirically and analytically to examine aspects of international relations without explicitly addressing their normative content. For feminist constructivists, such an approach reproduces masculinist ways of knowing, denying the scholars' own normative position and relationship to their research subjects.

Nonfeminist research on international relations also increasingly utilizes feminist theory in developing its conceptual analysis. For example, Michael Barnett and Raymond Duvall (2005, 20) argue that the analysis of power must consider gender as one of the normative structures and discourses that generate differential social capacities for actors to define and pursue their interests and ideals and that constitute the possible, the natural, what counts as a problem, as legitimate knowledge, and whose voices are marginalized. Gender is not merely an additive to international relations research designs but a form of *productive* power. Employing this feminist constructivist approach, Helen Kinsella (2005, 253) explores how the ostensibly gender-neutral distinction between civilians and combatants in the laws of war is produced by discourses that naturalize sex and gender difference. The categorical distinction has contradictory effects on the treatment of male civilians in war, who are by definition assumed to be combatants, and on the treatment of women civilians, who are considered always already to be victims (see also Sjoberg 2006). The normative implication of this analysis is that, by (re)producing the civilian/combatant dichotomy, international law inscribes gender hegemonies within domestic (familial) and international (civilized) orders (Barnett and Duvall 2005, 31).

Critical theory and postmodern approaches have often been seen by feminists as the most fruitful international relations perspectives with which to engage, since they share the view that knowledge is socially constructed on the basis of specific interests and normative purposes. Indeed, feminists have developed the sociological analysis that is fundamental to a critical international relations theory by illuminating the multiple dynamics of inclusion and exclusion that prevent the realization of a just and equitable global society (see Ackerly and True 2006, 249–52). By contrast, nonfeminist critical theorists have failed to take up questions about multiple, intersecting oppressions in a systematic way because they address ethical questions within the dichotomous communitarian versus cosmopolitan framework, which is based on the assumption of a male subject (Cochran 1999).

Feminists have also shown themselves to be more praxis-oriented than nonfeminist critical theorists. They scrutinize the normative assumptions of a perspective by evaluating their practical import for the struggles of women and men located in varied social contexts and, within those contexts, in a myriad of intersecting power relations. Despite the apparent affinities between feminist and critical theory international relations perspectives, feminists judge critical theorists' neglect of the gender dimensions of injustice and the possibilities for transformation to be a demonstrable weakness for the practical application of their normative theory.

5 CONCLUSION

Normative commitments infuse not only feminist questions, interpretations, and claims to know international relations but also how feminists do their work. There are many differences among feminisms, but the ethics of inclusivity, self-reflexivity, and attentiveness to power and relational subjects distinguish most feminist approaches to international relations. These norms guide feminists to put into practice their own critical theories, epistemologies, and explicit normative commitments. Thus, rather than a source of division, the contestations among international relations feminisms about the grounds for feminist knowledge, the ontology of gender, and the appropriate ethical stance in a globalizing albeit grossly unequal world are a source of their strength. With a normative commitment to ongoing dialogue rather than to a particular ideal world, feminisms can appreciate and even celebrate internal diversities and multidimensional identities. "Feminist IR is avant-garde," a movement showing what is to come and that offers innovative methods to get there (Sylvester 2000, 269).

Given these strengths, how can feminist perspectives position themselves to make a greater contribution to normative debate in international relations? There are several promising avenues for the future of feminism that involve closer engagement with other international relations perspectives. Tickner (2006) has suggested that feminist efforts to broker conversations across differences present a potential way forward for responsible practices of international relations scholarship. Consistent with this, a critical feminist approach involves bringing the insights of feminist praxis to bear on discussions of universal human rights, social justice, economic globalization, democratization, and peace processes. Within feminist collective practice there are resources for building a normative theory about the possibility for global dialogue respectful of differences—and for determining the form that it could and should take.

Another avenue for feminism is to explore the normative approaches of multilateral economic institutions to justice and equity. This might involve examining the meanings of gender as they are institutionalized in new rules and hegemonies, and critically scrutinizing them in terms of feminist goals and criteria for a more gender-just world order. Such a feminist normative approach to institutions could allow for greater synthesis between feminism and international political economy, feminism and neoliberal institutionalism, for instance. Lastly, a future feminist research agenda would not be self-reflexive or attentive to relational power if it did not leave room for feminist deconstruction and displacement. Postmodern feminism is crucial to critical analysis of post-11 September security discourses and practices of statecraft, since falsely universalizing assumptions about the boundaries of gender shape the strategies of so-called terrorists and foreign policy elites alike.

Feminism does not merely add another perspective to international relations. Rather, its ethical attentiveness to inclusivity and relationships opens international relations to feminist criticism from inside the discipline, as feminists draw on marginalized actors and subjects to challenge conventional international relations theories, while self-reflexivity and attentiveness to power opens international relations to feminist criticism from outside in feminist interdisciplinary studies and social movements. As a result, feminist contributions not only deepen our normative theories; they improve the "strong objectivity" and methodological rigor of international relations theories, subjecting them to ongoing, critical scrutiny (Harding 1991; Ackerly, Stern, and True 2006).

References

ACKERLY, B. A. 2008. *Universal Human Rights in a World of Difference*. Cambridge: Cambridge University Press.

—— STERN, M., and TRUE, J. (eds.) 2006. *Feminist Methodologies for International Relations*. Cambridge: Cambridge University Press.

—— and TRUE, J. 2006. Studying the struggles and wishes of the age: feminist theoretical methodology and feminist theoretical methods. Pp. 241–60 in Ackerly, Stern, and True 2006.

AGATHANGELOU, A. M., and LING, L. H. M. 2004. Power, borders, security, wealth: lessons of violence and desire from September 11. *International Studies Quarterly*, 48: 517–38.

BARNETT, M., and DUVALL, R. (eds.) 2005. Power in global governance. Pp. 1–32 in *Power in Global Governance*, ed. M. Barnett and R. Duvall. Cambridge: Cambridge University Press.

BLEIKER, R. 1997. Forget IR theory. *Alternatives*, 22: 57–85.

CAPRIOLI, M. 2004. Feminist IR theory and quantitative methodology: a critical analysis. *International Studies Review*, 6: 253–69.

COCHRAN, M. 1999. *Normative Theory in International Relations: A Pragmatic Approach*. Cambridge: Cambridge University Press.

COHN, C., and RUDDICK, S. 2004. A feminist ethical perspective on weapons of mass destruction. Pp. 405–35 in *Ethics and Weapons of Mass Destruction: Religious and Secular Perspectives*, ed. S. H. Hashmi and S. P. Lee. Cambridge: Cambridge University Press.

COX, R. W. 1981. Social forces, states and world orders: beyond international relations theory. *Millennium: Journal of International Studies*, 10: 126–55.

D'COSTA, B. 2006. Marginalized identity: new frontier of research for IR? Pp. 129–52 in Ackerly, Stern, and True 2006.

ENLOE, C. 2000. *Maneuvers: The International Politics of Militarizing Women's Lives*. Berkeley: University of California Press.

GOLDSTEIN, J. 2001. *War and Gender: How Gender Shapes the War System and Vice Versa*. Cambridge: Cambridge University Press.

GRAY, M. M., KITTILSON, M. C., and SANDHOLTZ, W. 2006. Women and globalization: a study of 180 countries, 1975–2000. *International Organization*, 60: 293–333.

HAN, J., and LING, L. H. M. 1998. Authoritarianism in the hypermasculinized state: hybridity, patriarchy, and capitalism in Korea. *International Studies Quarterly*, 42: 53–78.

HARDING, S. 1991. *Whose Science? Whose Knowledge? Thinking from Women's Lives*. Ithaca, NY: Cornell University Press.

HOOPER, C. 2001. *Manly States: Masculinities, International Relations, and Gender Politics*. New York: Columbia University Press.

HUTCHINGS, K. 2000. Towards a feminist international ethics. *Review of International Studies*, 26: 111–30.

—— 2004. From morality to politics and back again: feminist international ethics and the civil-society argument. *Alternatives*, 29: 239–64.

JABRI, V. 1999. Explorations of differences in normative international relations. Pp. 42–54 in *Women, Culture, and International Relations*, ed. V. Jabri and E. O'Gorman. Boulder, Colo.: Lynne Rienner.

JACOBY, T. 2006. From the trenches: dilemmas of feminist IR fieldwork. Pp. 153–73 in Ackerly, Stern, and True 2006.

KAUFMAN-OSBORN, T. 2005. Gender trouble at Abu-Ghraib? *Politics and Gender*, 1: 597–619.

KINSELLA, H. M. 2005. Securing the civilian: sex and gender in the laws of war. Pp. 249–72 in *Power in Global Governance*, ed. M. Barnett and R. Duvall. Cambridge: Cambridge University Press.

LOCHER, B., and PRÜGL, E. 2001. Feminism and constructivism: worlds apart or sharing the middle ground? *International Studies Quarterly*, 45: 111–29.

MARCHAND, M., and RUNYAN, A. S. (eds.) 2000. *Gender and Global Restructuring: Sightings, Sites and Resistances*. New York: Routledge.

MOON, K. 1997. *Sex among Allies: Military Prostitution in US–Korea Relations*. New York: Columbia University Press.

PORTER, E. 2000. Risks and responsibilities: creating dialogical spaces in Northern Ireland. *International Feminist Journal of Politics*, 2: 163–84.

PRÜGL, E. 1999. *The Global Construction of Gender: Home-based Work in the Political Economy of the 20th Century*. New York: Columbia University Press.

ROBINSON, F. 2006. Methods of feminist normative theory: a political ethic of care for international relations. Pp. 221–40 in Ackerly, Stern, and True 2006.

RUPP, L. 1997. *Worlds of Women: The Making of an International Women's Movement*. Princeton, NJ: Princeton University Press.

SJOBERG, L. 2006. Gendered realities of the immunity principle: why gender analysis needs feminism. *International Studies Quarterly*, 50: 889–910.

STEANS, J. 1998. *Gender and International Relations: An Introduction*. Cambridge: Polity.

STERN, M. 2006. Racism, sexism, classism, and much more: reading security-identity in marginalized sites. Pp. 174–97 in Ackerly, Stern, and True 2006.

SYLVESTER, C. 2000. *Feminist International Relations: An Unfinished Journey*. Cambridge: Cambridge University Press.

TICKNER, J. A. 1997. You just don't understand: troubled engagements between feminists and IR theorists. *International Studies Quarterly*, 41: 611–32.

—— 2001. *Gendering World Politics: Issues and Approaches in the Post-Cold War Era*. New York: Columbia University Press.

—— 2006. On the frontlines or sidelines of knowledge and power? Feminist practices of responsible scholarship. *International Studies Review*, 8: 383–95.

TRONTO, J. 1993. *Moral Boundaries: A Political Argument for an Ethic of Care*. New York: Routledge.

—— 2006. Is peacekeeping care work? Presented at the Canadian Political Science Association Conference, Vancouver, June.

TRUE, J. 2005. Feminism. Pp. 213–34 in *Theories of International Relations*, 3rd edn., S. Burchill, A. Linklater, R. Devetak, J. Donnelly, M. Paterson, C. Reus-Smit, and J. True. Basingstoke: Palgrave Macmillan.

—— and MINTROM, M. 2001. Transnational networks and policy diffusion: the case of gender mainstreaming. *International Studies Quarterly*, 45: 27–57.

ZALEWSKI, M. 2006. Distracted reflections on the production, narration, and refusal of feminist knowledge in international relations. Pp. 42–61 in Ackerly, Stern, and True 2006.

PART IV

THE QUESTION
OF METHOD

CHAPTER 25

METHODOLOGICAL INDIVIDUALISM AND RATIONAL CHOICE

ANDREW H. KYDD

METHODOLOGICAL individualism and rational choice (MIRC) theory are intellectual offshoots of two august intellectual traditions. The first is liberalism, the struggle for freedom and democracy dating back to the Enlightenment, the Protestant Reformation, and in some sense to the ancient Greeks. The second is science, the attempt to understand the world through close observation and mathematical models, dating back to the European Renaissance and before that to the development of mathematics and astronomy by the ancient civilizations. If society is composed of free individuals acting to pursue their individual and shared interests, and the world is understood by creating mathematical models that shed light on its inner workings, then it stands to reason that society should be investigated by studying mathematical models of individual choosers, acting in isolation, in small groups and in large numbers. In this sense, rational choice theory is the science of freedom, or at least the science of liberalism (Gay 1996). The strength and prestige of liberalism and science and the intellectual coherence of the approach lend tremendous support to MIRC across the social sciences. In international relations, there is a thriving research tradition of mathematical models of rational choosers applied to war, arms competition, crisis bargaining, international trade and cooperation, and other topics. This work has greatly improved our theoretical understanding of international relations, although systematic empirical confirmation remains somewhat scarce, as it does for all international relations theory. Even for researchers who depart from the assumptions of MIRC, it is increasingly difficult to advance the state of knowledge theoretically or empirically without a good understanding of what MIRC has contributed to the topic.

1 Defining the Approach

For the sake of this chapter I will treat MIRC as an acronymizable unity, because in the field of international relations there is a fairly unified approach that can be reasonably identified with these labels. However, the concepts have varying origins and interpretations in different fields, and the boundaries of the approach are becoming increasingly unclear. In part this reflects the dreaded rational choice imperialism by which formal modelers extend the scope of their endeavor to cover topics once thought to be the province of other approaches. It also reflects the adoption of mathematical modeling techniques to explore assumptions antithetical to the rationalist tradition, such as nonrational decision-making and the evolution of actors in response to systemic forces.

At the core of the approach are actors, defined as entities that make choices. Actors can be thought of as endowed with six attributes, assumptions about which will serve to differentiate the approach from its alternatives, as illustrated in Figure 25.1. First is a decision-making style, which can be rational, imperfectly

Attributes	Approaches			
	MIRC	Evolutionary	Psychology	Constructivism
Decision-making style	Rational	Automatic	Imperfectly rational	
Identity and preferences	Fixed	Changeable via differential reproduction	Changeable via learning, emulation, and socialization	
Positive beliefs	Rationally updated		Imperfectly updated	
Normative beliefs		Not central	Somewhat important	Very important
Action set		Fixed	Open ended	

Fig. 25.1. Actor characteristics in international relations theories

(or boundedly) rational, or automatic. Second is an identity, which can be thought of as a membership in a social category (social identity) as well as a continuing existence that can be held accountable for past behavior or used to predict future behavior (individual identity). Third, the actor has a set of preferences over the outcomes in the domain of inquiry, such as the possible outcomes of a war. Fourth, it has a set of positive beliefs about the state of the world and the other actors in it. Fifth, the actor has a set of normative beliefs about what is good and bad, as well as appropriate or inappropriate behavior given the actor's identity and the situation. Sixth, it has a set of possible actions that can be combined into strategies for dealing with other actors in the situation under examination. MIRC, for example, assumes that actors make rational decisions, have fixed identities and preferences,[1] change their positive beliefs rationally in response to new information, downplay normative considerations (although these can be folded into preferences for normatively appropriate behavior if need be), and face a fixed and known set of options, not an open-ended process subject to discovery or innovation.

Methodological individualism began as the assumption that the actors in the above story are human beings, and that the goal of social inquiry is to understand their behavior and to explain larger-scale social phenomena, such as poverty or war, in terms of individual behavior (Weber 1968, 4–15; Elster 1982). At one level this seems trivial, since societies are made up of people. However, societies are also made up of families, clans, tribes, companies, nations, and other groups, organized and unorganized, which could equally serve as units of analysis. The fact that the individual is privileged over these other groups seems an obvious product of the Enlightenment and liberalism, with their emphasis on the rights of the individual, though the assumption is sometimes said to be value neutral. In addition, there are more abstract subjects of study, such as general concepts like the interest rate or divorce rate. Macroeconomists can study the interest rate without reference to the decisions of individual borrowers and lenders—for instance, by identifying statistical correlations with other cyclical phenomena like the weather. The methodological individualist, however, argues that such explanations need to be grounded in "microfoundations" that explain how the behavior of the relevant individuals aggregates up to produce the macro-level phenomenon of interest.

A related understanding of methodological individualism is that it traces causality from the individual to larger social phenomena rather than from the structure to the individual (Fearon and Wendt 2002, 56). The actor, human or state, is taken as exogenous to the explanation (MacDonald 2003, 558). This conception assumes that the actor's identity and preferences are fixed and denies or ignores any process of socialization.

---

[1] A small rational choice literature explores the idea of identities that are chosen instrumentally (Rabushka and Shepsle 1972).

An important question for methodological individualists in international relations is whether or under what conditions to treat the state as an individual
(Wolfers 1962, 3–24). Max Weber (1968, 13, 14) explicitly rejects this equation, but
it has enduring popularity especially in the study of war. The tradition of political
realism in international relations is often said to make the "unitary rational actor"
assumption and attempts to explain state behavior without reference to how states
are internally constituted (Mearsheimer 2001, 17–18). Many game theoretic models
also make this assumption; states are represented by unitary actors with coherent
preferences that make rational decisions.

The most powerful theoretical critique of the unitary actor assumption stems
from Kenneth Arrow's work on preference aggregation. Arrow (1970) proved that
no voting rule will always produce a coherent preference ordering over three or
more alternatives from a group of individuals with heterogeneous preferences. This
result raised doubts about whether one could even theoretically posit a "national
interest" to be pursued by the state on behalf of its citizens, echoing an earlier
philosophical debate on the "general will" (Wolfers 1962, 147–65; Krasner 1978, 10–
17; Rousseau 1997).

Two broad responses have been made to this problem. First, one can argue
that states are organizations designed specifically to enable large groups to act in
a unitary fashion in accordance with the preferences of the national leader. For
instance, Bruce Bueno de Mesquita (1981, 27) argues that decisions about war
and peace are made by a single strong leader so that the state's preferences are
simply the leader's preferences. In autocracies this assumption has natural appeal,
and even in democracies, presidents and prime ministers tend to assume greater
powers during wartime. This *l'état, c'est moi* solution reconciles methodological
individualism with the state as unitary rational actor assumption in the simplest
way. However, it has obvious limitations in policy areas where the state is permeable to outside forces, such as tariff policy, not to mention for weak states
that simply lack the organizational coherence to transmit the leader's will into
policy.

Secondly, one can abandon the unitary rational actor assumption at the state
level, and directly model domestic politics along with international relations. States
have legislatures and executives, each having specific powers, which enable them to
take or block action on specific issues. These institutional features can be modeled
in the context of an international decision to look for equilibrium results. This
insight has led to a large literature that incorporates domestic political institutions
into models of international relations (e.g. Putnam 1988; Iida 1993*a*; Schultz 2001;
Bueno de Mesquita et al. 2003). Of course, many of the actors in such models—
"Congress," the "electorate," and so on—are not themselves unitary, so we have
not really satisfied strict methodological individualism. In fact, some of them
are less unitary than a state led by a strong executive. However, these models

allow a better understanding of how domestic political concerns, especially the desire to remain in office, affect international decision-making and so have been very fruitful.[2]

This debate has never been fully resolved, and, in the end, methodological individualism is employed somewhat loosely in international relations. Theorists generate models of unitary actors making choices. The actors in these models are variously thought of as states, political leaders, and median voters in legislatures or populations, without much concern about whether the model satisfies a strict construction of methodological individualism that would insist on studying only the behavior of individual human beings.

Rational choice theory is a subset of methodological individualism in which the actor's decision-making style is assumed to be rational. Actors are assumed to have preferences over the various possible outcomes in any situation and so can rank them in terms of their desirability. They then choose whatever strategy or course of action makes the better outcomes most likely, or maximizes the actor's "utility" or happiness. For the actor to qualify as rational, the preferences must be transitive, meaning that, if I prefer victory to a stalemate and a stalemate to defeat, I must prefer victory to defeat. In addition, rational actors must process information correctly. Specifically, they are assumed to update their beliefs about the likelihood of uncertain events in response to new information according to the laws of probability—namely Bayes's rule, hence the term "Bayesian rational actor." For example, if expansionist states escalate in an arms race with certainty, while security-seekers have only a 50 percent chance of escalating, and our prior belief is that the opponent we face has a 50 percent chance of being an expansionist, after we observe the opponent escalate, we will think there is a two-thirds likelihood that it is an expansionist.[3]

Although rational choice theory can be done in a nonformal way, sometimes called "soft" rational choice, it lends itself to mathematical models of decision-making, and only such models can provide rigorous deductive support to the propositions or hypotheses of any rational choice analysis. Models that focus on a single decision-maker in isolation are the province of decision theory, game theory focuses on small groups of actors interacting strategically with each other, and market models or perfect competition models (the bulk of traditional economic theory) focus on mass behavior where the individuals can ignore strategic interaction and take other parties' behavior as given.[4]

---

[2] A related approach focuses on bureaucratic bargaining (Allison 1971; Downs and Rocke 1990, 92–100).

[3] Bayes's rule specifies that the posterior likelihood of A obtaining after observing B is $p(B|A)p(A)/[p(B|A)p(A) + p(B|\neg A)p(\neg A)]$, so if B is "the opponent escalated" and A is "the opponent is an expansionist" we have $1^*0.5/[1^*0.5 + 0.5^*0.5]$ or 2/3.

[4] An introduction to modern rational choice theory is Mas-Colell, Whinston, and Green (1995).

A great deal of evidence has accumulated from experimental work demonstrating that people fail to act rationally, particularly when it comes to updating beliefs in accordance with Bayes's rule and making judgments in the face of uncertainty (Kahneman, Slovic, and Tversky 1982; Camerer 2003). This has led to some debate on what role the rationality assumption actually serves. Paul MacDonald (2003) has argued that two epistemologies are used to justify rational choice. Instrumentalist empiricism is primarily interested in deducing hypotheses and testing them, and does not care about the "accuracy" of assumptions in the model (Friedman 1952). Scientific realism, on the other hand, believes scientific theory helps understand the inner workings of reality, and hence must be founded on accurate mechanisms and assumptions.

Although some practitioners seem to lean toward instrumentalist empiricism (Fearon and Wendt 2002), the weight of opinion is probably with a pragmatic scientific realist perspective. All theory makes simplifying assumptions. The goal is to come up with simplifications that are good enough in certain domains; simplifications that reasonably well characterize the entities and mechanisms involved, and produce predictions that are better than what we were capable of before. From a pragmatic scientific realist perspective, evidence for the irrationality of human behavior is troubling but not lethal for rational choice theory, and it calls for two responses. The first is to investigate when people act more or less rationally. It could be that in some circumstances people behave more rationally than in others, which limits the domain of the theory. The second is to investigate models of bounded rationality. Such models may illuminate when structural conditions lead boundedly rational actors to act "as if" they were rational (shades of instrumentalist empiricism), and when they do not, both of which should refine our understanding of human behavior.

The normative stance and biases of MIRC are those of its parent ideology, liberalism. MIRC generates models of intelligent actors freely choosing among their available options. As a result, policy advice based on methodological individualism contains an inherent degree of respect for the individuals concerned. In the MIRC world, one can alter one's own behavior, and strive to alter the constraints and opportunities facing other actors, and their beliefs, but one cannot fundamentally alter their preferences and identities. One must take them as they are and try to cope with them. The rationality assumption in MIRC reinforces this respect for the subject of study. The rationality assumption means that the actor is assumed to be intelligent and know what he or she is doing. The job of the analyst is to figure out what the actor already knows, at least at an intuitive level, and to deduce some consequences of intelligent purposive behavior that may not be generally known.

MIRC's primary normative criterion is efficiency. This can be defined abstractly as Pareto efficiency, approving changes that make everyone concerned better off, or more concretely as efficiency of production or trade, which maximizes wealth but may create losers in the short run unless they are compensated in some fashion. By both criteria, MIRC generally opposes war, revolution, and other forms of violence, which destroy goods in an effort to redistribute them. This is often considered a very weak normative criterion, although it does rule out many objectionable practices.

This weakness generates a key tension between MIRC and its parent ideology over the issue of freedom, human rights, and the absence of coercion. Liberalism endorses individual freedoms on which democratic constitutions and international agreements, from the eighteenth-century US Bill of Rights to the 1948 Universal Declaration of Human Rights, are based. The ideal society is one in which, provided they obey mutually beneficial laws, individuals are free to do as they please. Liberalism could therefore endorse a war or revolution designed to overthrow tyranny and establish a liberal regime. To attain the ideal society, sacrifices must be made; freedom is not free. MIRC, however, can easily model interactions that involve coercion, power disparities, and gross human rights violations, and contains no inherent normative bias against them. In an interaction between Nazi Germany and its East European satellites, MIRC endorses only outcomes that make Germany and its client states better off; liberalism advocates the overthrow of Nazi tyranny. A benefit of this tension, however, is that it makes MIRC a better social scientific tool for international relations, where rights are often ignored and coercion across power disparities is a central focus of study.

For the international political economy, MIRC favors free trade and globalization. Let capital flow to where it can be most efficiently used, let goods be produced where the cost is lowest, and let the world be tied together in one big happy productive economy. In all models of the international economy, global free trade maximizes the efficiency of production. Even when models of optimal tariffs and industries featuring increasing returns to scale indicate that states can maximize their own welfare by imposing trade restrictions, economists are quick to minimize these implications and endorse free trade (Helpman and Krugman 1985).

Although its parent ideology is biased against political interference with individual choice, MIRC is not libertarian; it does see a positive role for governmental institutions that restrict individual freedom. Much of the game theoretic revolution in economics and its application to political science, in fact, highlights the existence of suboptimal equilibria that leave everyone worse off than they might be. These suboptimal equilibria are a product of several factors, including lack of information, short time horizons, disparities of power, and changes in relative power. George Akerlof (1970) inaugurated the literature on asymmetric information by arguing that some markets, such as for used cars, may be inefficient because sellers know the quality of their goods but buyers do not. Douglass North and Barry Weingast (1989) argued that the state must establish the rule of law to protect private property-holders from the state and encourage them to invest. Equally, the state must protect weak private property-holders from strong ones, who would otherwise engage in predation. In international relations, institutions that provide information or otherwise shape incentives or beliefs so as to enable more cooperative behavior are viewed positively (Koremenos, Lipson, and Snidal 2001).

2 Applications to International Relations

MIRC has a long and fruitful history in the study of international relations. Thucydides explained the onset of the Peloponnesian War by arguing that Sparta attacked preventively to stem the rise in Athenian power (Thucydides 1972, 49). A good methodological individualist, he focuses quite closely on decision-making by generals, statesmen, and representative bodies in explaining key decisions such as the Spartan declaration of war (Thucydides 1972, 72–87). Thucydides' concept of preventive war has become a staple of realist thought, influencing modern analyses of the origins of war and becoming enshrined in US national security strategy (Gilpin 1981; Copeland 2000; Bush 2002). The mechanism he identifies, changes in relative power that cause the declining side to attack preventively, turns out to be one of the few fully rationalist explanations of war and generalizes to many settings where changing power creates commitment problems (Fearon 1995; Powell 2004a).

Thomas Hobbes and Jean-Jacques Rousseau pioneered another cornerstone of international relations theory: the security dilemma. Hobbes argued that individuals in the state of nature without a government to regulate their behavior will attack each other even if they are not themselves aggressively motivated. The fact that others may be aggressively motivated and can attack without warning implies that one should strike out and subdue threats pre-emptively (Hobbes 1968, 184). Rousseau employed the metaphor of a group hunt for a deer. If every member of the group cooperates, the deer will be trapped and all will dine well. If an individual chases after a rabbit, the deer will escape through the gap and the others will suffer (Rousseau 1997, 163). The general idea that actors in anarchy will be competitive, suspicious, and violent toward each other became a central theme of international relations theory (Hertz 1950; Butterfield 1951; Waltz 1954, 167). Robert Jervis (1978) introduced elementary game theory to the study of the security dilemma by discussing the Prisoner's Dilemma and Stag Hunt games, the latter named after Rousseau's fable.[5] More recent analyses of trust in international relations have built upon this foundation by using modern incomplete information game theory to study the impact of anarchy on competition and mistrust (Kydd 2005).

---

[5] Kenneth Waltz's widely read formulation of structural realism rested essentially on the security dilemma as well (Waltz 1979).

A third general area to which methodological individualism and rational choice theory have contributed is the relationship between bargaining and war. The subject first became prominent in the discussion of nuclear deterrence, and Thomas Schelling (1960) embodied the thinking of the 1950s and 1960s on how commitments could be made credible and how the willingness to run risks of annihilation could provide a state with leverage in international bargaining. Glenn Snyder and Paul Diesing (1977) applied simple two-by-two normal form games to the crisis bargaining context, but a proper game theoretic analysis of the subject awaited the development of bargaining theory in the 1980s. Robert Powell (1990) applied modern incomplete information game theory to nuclear deterrence and international bargaining and resolved a number of issues left over from the earlier literature.

In the 1990s, this literature burgeoned and became one of the most central and progressive in the field (Powell 2002). James Fearon made two influential contributions. First, he argued that during international crises states risk suffering domestic "audience costs" in the event that they back down after making a commitment to attain a certain goal (Fearon 1994). This enables them to commit to fight credibly rather than abandon their aims, which in turn may convince the other side to give in. The greater a state's ability to incur audience costs, the more leverage it has in international crises. In another paper, Fearon argued (1995) that war can result between rational actors only if (*a*) the issue over which they are negotiating is indivisible, (*b*) they have private information about their preferences or relative power, or (*c*) they face a commitment problem, such as changing relative power, which makes it impossible for them to abide by a deal that they might currently both prefer to war. This argument set the course for much subsequent theorizing on war initiation in US international relations theory. Currently, the focus in the bargaining and war issue has shifted to bargaining during war, and how war termination arises from forces internal to the war (Goemans 2000; Slantchev 2003; Powell 2004*b*).

Another important area of application for MIRC in international relations theory has been the topic of cooperation and collective action. The core model here is the Prisoner's Dilemma, used in its n-person form to study collective action and in its two-person repeated form to study cooperation over time. The n-person Prisoner's Dilemma and related public goods games have been used to study hegemony, international cooperation, and international regimes (Olson 1965; Kindleberger 1973; Snidal 1985; Pahre 1999). While the verbal literature tended to argue that hegemons were necessary for international cooperation, game theoretic analyses tended to find that they were neither necessary nor sufficient. In the 1980s, the repeated Prisoner's Dilemma game became the generic representation of bilateral cooperation (Oye 1986). This owed much to Robert Axelrod's pathbreaking computer tournament analysis of the game (1984), which I will discuss further below. Versions of the game were later applied to arms control, international trade, and other issue areas (e.g. Downs and Rocke 1990).

3 Related and Alternative Approaches

There is a spectrum of related and alternative approaches to MIRC, which depart from it in varying ways, as illustrated in Figure 25.1. The boundaries between these approaches are fluid and populated by transitional models, so these must be taken as ideal types.

3.1 Evolutionary Approaches

Evolutionary models assume a population of actors interacting over time and study the pattern of behavior that emerges and is resistant to alternative strategies. Actors make decisions automatically and do not think about other actors much, but incorporate some ideas about the population they face in their strategies. Actors pursuing suboptimal strategies die out and are replaced by actors pursuing better ones. Kenneth Waltz made use of evolutionary arguments to explain why less than rational states would nonetheless be found to obey the dictates of a rational pursuit of survival under anarchy. He argues that if they did not, they would be eliminated from the system by military competition from other states (Waltz 1979, 127–8).

Axelrod (1984) developed the most influential evolutionary argument using a computer tournament to simulate an evolutionary process in which actors who pursued ineffective strategies in the Prisoner's Dilemma would gradually be supplanted by those pursuing more effective ones.[6] The strategy called Tit for Tat, which consists of starting by cooperating and then reciprocating whatever the other side does, had the advantage that it did quite well against itself and other similar strategies, but also did not do too badly against different, more exploitative strategies. The more exploitative strategies did badly against each other, and so tended to lower each other's scores. This could explain an evolutionary drift toward strategies like Tit for Tat. This approach has evolved into the study of "agent-based models" (Axelrod 1997). These are more detailed computer models in which spatially located actors endowed with certain resources and an automatic decision rule interact over time (Cederman 1997). States evolve and grow by conquering other states and the composition of the international system varies as certain types of state die out and others supplant them. Lars-Erik Cederman (2001) has applied this style of analysis to explain the prevalence of democracies today, as a result of their alliance and war-making strategies.

---

[6] Evolutionary and learning models have been popular in economics as well. See Weibull (1995); Fudenberg and Levine (1998).

Evolutionary models featuring state death by conquest as the selection mechanism may be appropriate for questions covering the long sweep of international history. Over this timeframe, states did indeed die out in large numbers, and so evolutionary pressure could be severe. However, since 1945, state death has become quite rare (Fazal 2004). A more common selection mechanism in the modern era would be regime change, or even simple elections, in which leaders pursuing suboptimal strategies are replaced by those promising better ones. Such models border on psychological learning and diffusion models in which the identity of the actor is fixed but its positive beliefs about how the world works are affected by new information gleaned from observing the experience of others and imperfectly processed (Reiter 1996; Bennett 1999; Simmons and Elkins 2004).[7]

The normative implications of evolutionary theory have themselves evolved over time. Nineteenth-century social Darwinists used evolutionary theory to justify expansion by conquest and colonization as the natural order of things. The fate of states, such as Hitler's Germany, that took these ideas seriously, along with the subsequent collapse of imperialism, indicated that a more nuanced view of evolutionary forces was in order. Indeed, evolutionary models by Axelrod and Cederman demonstrate the survival value of more cooperative ideas and strategies. The approach endorses experimentation and empiricism, acknowledging our limited ability to understand the world with theory alone. One could even deduce an endorsement of decentralization and limits on central authority, so that local policy experimentation is not unduly hampered by central regulations.

3.2 Psychology

Psychological theories in international relations take their inspiration from the experimental literature in psychology.[8] Psychological theories depart from MIRC by assuming that actors are imperfectly rational, may have fluid identities and preferences influenced by groupthink (Janis 1972), update via prospect theory or other less than rational approaches, and face open-ended problems that require creativity and a search for solutions. The approach is surveyed by James Goldgeier and Philip Tetlock (this volume), so I will mention only two works to convey the feel.

Jervis's landmark contribution (1976) identified several mechanisms by which people fall short of the rational standard. For instance, he argued that decision-makers are unduly attached to past beliefs and unwilling adequately to change their

---

[7] Another evolutionary approach focuses on the biological evolution of human beings and looks for clues to present behavior in evolutionary pressure on human ancestors (Thayer 2000; Johnson 2004). This approach is more closely allied with psychological approaches, since it focuses on understanding human nature.

[8] Stephen Peter Rosen (2005) looks to modern neuroscience for insights into human nature and behavior during war.

beliefs in response to new information. Also, new information will be interpreted to suit old beliefs: A hostile act from an enemy will be interpreted as further confirmation of its evil intentions, while the same act from a friend will be interpreted as a mistake. Rose McDermott (1998) applied prospect theory, Daniel Kahneman and Amos Tversky's empirically based alternative to rational choice, to international relations. Prospect theory argues that people's attitude toward risk depends on how the problem is framed. People are generally cautious in the face of potential gains, but risk acceptant if they seek to avoid loss. Given that the same situation can be portrayed as an opportunity for gain or a chance to avoid loss, this introduces an important role for rhetoric and persuasion.

The normative stance of psychological theory can be thought of as theraputic. Bad things happen in international relations because leaders suffer from biases that they fail to recognize and compensate for. Accurate diagnosis can lead to better decision-making and presumably less conflict. Institutions should be designed to select less biased leaders and to compensate for the remaining biases. From the MIRC perspective, this diagnostic approach sometimes errs on the side of presuming irrationality on the part of the subject of study when it has not been demonstrated, and so can border on the patronizing.

3.3 Constructivism

Constructivism is the latest oppositional movement to fix its critical sights on intellectual orthodoxy in international relations. It departs from MIRC in every category of Figure 25.1, emphasizing not fully rational individuals engaged in socialization and facing open-ended problems. Its main departure from psychological theory is in its emphasis on normative beliefs and argument, and in its origins in European social theory rather than experimental psychology. It is, in fact, split on science, with some constructivists rejecting scientific method in favor of interpretivism or postmodernism, and others pursuing a scientific study of identity (Abdelal 2001; Fearon and Wendt 2002, 57; Abdelal et al. 2006; Hymans 2006).

Rejecting MIRC's focus on the individual, constructivism embraces social theory, or "holism," the idea that individuals cannot be understood apart from the collectivities of which they are a part (Wendt 1999, 29). The identities and preferences of the actors are said to result from socialization by groups to which they belong. Socialization is most clearly seen in childhood, when individuals form identities by interacting with parents, schools, and other children. Constructivists argue that a similar process of socialization takes place among adults and between states. Some constructivists also make what they consider a deeper argument about holism under the heading of "constitutive" theory. They argue that what it means to be a certain kind of actor depends on shared understandings of that actor's role in relation to other actors, and that investigating these understandings enables one to identify the "conditions of possibility" for certain "modes of subjectivity." In practical terms, this seems to mean that actors are constrained in their behavior by the expectations of others about what their proper role is.[9]

A further argument made by constructivists is that normative beliefs and normative argumentation are important in international relations. Martha Finnemore and Kathryn Sikkink (1998) provide a model of how international normative change occurs that argues that normative beliefs influence behavior, and states and nongovernmental organizations influence each other's normative beliefs through argument and persuasion. A remarkable recent example of large-scale rapid normative change in international security politics is the 1997 Ottawa treaty banning antipersonnel landmines. In the space of a single decade landmines went from a perfectly normal weapon of war found in every state arsenal in the world to an internationally proscribed weapon restricted to around forty, albeit important, holdout states (Price 1998). The change was driven by an alliance of nongovernmental organizations and a few key national leaders.

The normative or political stance of constructivism tends to be of the left, or "progressive," which for some means desiring not just to understand but to change (see Cox, this volume). Though it shares much with social theory, constructivism departs from neo-Marxist approaches in its rejection of structural (economically deterministic) explanations, and it has little in common with Marxism's utopianism, or Leninism's faith in social engineering and thirst for violent revolution.[10] However, constructivism retains a general oppositional stance, focusing on power relations, favoring the weak over the strong, and emphasizing the role of shared ideas and socially based change to reduce disparities of power and wealth. From the MIRC perspective, holism and the attendant de-emphasis of individual agency can get a bit scary if taken too far, as in talk of "problematizing" the individual, and showing how actors are "constructed" by abstract forces like modernity or Christianity (Fearon and Wendt 2002, 57; Meyer and Jepperson 2000, 110). However, most constructivists do not pursue holism to the point of negating agency, and indeed often have a focal role for normative or identity entrepreneurs (Checkel 1993; Risse 2000).

3.4 The Usefulness of a Rationalist Baseline

Even for those who view decision-making as imperfectly rational, identities as fluid, and norms as important, it is often critical to know what a model adhering to MIRC

[9] An example, which Alexander Wendt uses with strange frequency, is the master–slave relationship; one cannot define "master" without defining "slave," and vice versa (Fearon and Wendt 2002, 58, 66). However, it is difficult to think of a relationship in which shared ideas are less important in comparison to violent coercion and straightforward self-interest.

[10] However, in Wendt (2003) it would seem, the old utopian fires still burn brightly.

has to contribute to a given research problem. This is because it is difficult to know what results from cognitive limits if we do not know what rational actors would do, and it is difficult to deduce the impact of norms without knowing what selfishness leads to. In general, a rationalist baseline will often be useful for non-MIRC research projects. Models of learning and evolution most clearly make use of a rationalist baseline. The evolutionary game theory literature often explicitly solves for fully rationalist equilibria and then examines under what conditions boundedly rational actors will approximate this ideal. Psychological learning models at least implicitly have a Bayesian updating understanding of rational learning in the background as the ideal, and assess how real-life learning approximates or falls short of this norm.

Constructivists can also make use of a rationalist baseline. A great example is the debate over the role of material conditions versus ideas at the end of the cold war. Because the Soviet retreat at the end of the cold war seemed antithetical to its previous governing ideology, constructivists sought to explain it as a product of ideational change. Stephen Brooks and William Wohlforth (2000–1) countered with an analysis showing how much worse Soviet economic prospects were in the 1980s than had been previously known, and argued that even "old thinkers" supported retrenchment. The resulting debate is a model of productive interaction across paradigmatic boundaries.[11] In another example, in Wendt's argument (2003, 525) on behalf of a world state, he writes: "If the choice is between a world of growing threats as a result of refusing to recognize Others versus a world in which their desires for recognition are satisfied, it seems clear which decision a rational Great Power should make." If so, it can only be because of prior strategic analysis of great powers and rational recognition-seeking states.

4 FUTURE PROSPECTS

MIRC is a well-established research program moving forward on a broad front. I will sketch only two areas of especially interesting trends.

One promising area of advance for MIRC is models that focus on uncertainty about the state of the world. Heretofore, most models featuring incomplete information have focused on private information about a state's characteristics that might affect its behavior in a crisis or in war (Powell 2002). An alternative form of uncertainty is about how the world works in general. Is global warming happening, and if so why and how fast? How will the wars of the future be fought, and how will

[11] See *Journal of Cold War Studies*, 7(2), special issue (2005), for an overview of the debate and citations to other contributions.

current technological or social trends affect them? Who is to blame for tragedies of uncertain authorship, such as the terrorist attacks of 11 September, al-Qaeda or Mossad? Different people have different beliefs and theories about such matters, and they affect behavior, including people's ability to communicate effectively and learn from each other. While this type of uncertainty has been explored in the past (Iida 1993b; Morrow 1994), it is of increasing relevance today as the issues facing national leaders and mass publics grow ever more complex. Work in this area raises interesting methodological issues, such as whether to retain the "common prior" assumption, and will have great substantive importance as well (Smith and Stam 2004; Fey and Ramsay 2006).

A second area of increasing importance is the link to empirical testing. MIRC has been criticized for the rarity, poor quality, and boring findings of its efforts at empirical testing (Walt 1999). The link with statistical testing has received increased attention recently, which makes sense given the common mathematical framework underlying both approaches (Signorino 1999; Bueno de Mesquita et al. 2003; Lewis and Schultz 2003). There are also efforts to do more case-study and historical research in conjunction with formal theory, beyond the usual one illustrative example per article (Kydd 2005). The increasing popularity of the book/dissertation containing a model, quantitative chapter, and case study or two (for example, Sartori 2005) is likely to continue, despite the difficulty of doing all three well.

5 Conclusion

Methodological individualism and rational choice strive to explain international events by positing individuals, states, or substate actors, with fixed preferences and identities, who rationally adjust their beliefs and strategies in response to the information they receive and the strategies pursued by other actors. MIRC derives tremendous legitimacy from its relationship to the two strongest belief structures in the world today, liberalism in the normative sphere and science in the positive sphere. It draws further strength because it presents a unified (at the level of assumptions) body of theory that can be generalized and extended to new issue areas with relative ease. Ironically, for a scientific movement, it is on weakest grounds empirically; confirmation of its findings has been difficult. However, nontrivial empirical regularities have proved very difficult to find for any theory in international relations; typically the more precise and falsifiable the theory, the more resoundingly falsified it is. Given the difficulty in establishing robust lawlike findings in international relations, strong theoretical frameworks such as MIRC will continue to be useful in the discipline.

References

ABDELAL, R. 2001. *National Purpose in the World Economy: Post-Soviet States in Comparative Perspective*. Ithaca, NY: Cornell University Press.

——HERRERA, Y. M., JOHNSTON, A. I., and McDERMOTT, R. 2006. Identity as a variable. *Perspectives on Politics*, 4: 695–711.

AKERLOF, G. A. 1970. The market for "lemons:" quality uncertainty and the market mechanism. *Quarterly Journal of Economics*, 84: 488–500.

ALLISON, G. T. 1971. *Essence of Decision: Explaining the Cuban Missile Crisis*. Boston: Little, Brown.

ARROW, K. J. 1970. *Social Choice and Individual Values*, 2nd edn. New Haven, Conn.: Yale University Press.

AXELROD, R. 1984. *The Evolution of Cooperation*. New York: Basic Books.

——1997. *The Complexity of Cooperation: Agent-Based Models of Competition and Collaboration*. Princeton, NJ: Princeton University Press.

BENNETT, A. 1999. *Condemned to Repetition? The Rise, Fall, and Reprise of Soviet–Russian Military Interventionism, 1973–1996*. Cambridge, Mass.: MIT Press.

BROOKS, S. G., and WOHLFORTH, W. C. 2000–1. Power, globalization, and the end of the Cold War: reevaluating a landmark case for ideas. *International Security*, 25: 5–53.

BUENO DE MESQUITA, B. 1981. *The War Trap*. New Haven, Conn.: Yale University Press.

——SMITH, A., SIVERSON, R. M., and MORROW, J. D. 2003. *The Logic of Political Survival*. Cambridge, Mass.: MIT Press.

BUSH, G. W. 2002. *The National Security Strategy of the United States of America*. Washington, DC: White House.

BUTTERFIELD, H. 1951. *History and Human Relations*. London: Collins.

CAMERER, C. F. 2003. *Behavioral Game Theory: Experiments in Strategic Interaction*. Princeton, NJ: Princeton University Press.

CEDERMAN, L.-E. 1997. *Emergent Actors in World Politics: How States and Nations Develop and Dissolve*. Princeton, NJ: Princeton University Press.

——2001. Modeling the democratic peace as a Kantian selection process. *Journal of Conflict Resolution*, 45: 470–502.

CHECKEL, J. 1993. Ideas, institutions, and the Gorbachev foreign policy revolution. *World Politics*, 45: 271–300.

COPELAND, D. C. 2000. *The Origins of Major War*. Ithaca, NY: Cornell University Press.

DOWNS, G. W., and ROCKE, D. M. 1990. *Tacit Bargaining, Arms Races, and Arms Control*. Ann Arbor: University of Michigan Press.

ELSTER, J. 1982. The case for methodological individualism. *Theory and Society*, 11: 453–82.

FAZAL, T. M. 2004. State death in the international system. *International Organization*, 58: 311–44.

FEARON, J. D. 1994. Domestic political audiences and the escalation of international disputes. *American Political Science Review*, 88: 577–92.

——1995. Rationalist explanations for war. *International Organization*, 49: 379–414.

——and WENDT, A. 2002. Rationalism v. constructivism: a skeptical view. Pp. 52–72 in *Handbook of International Relations*, ed. W. Carlsnaes, T. Risse, and B. A. Simmons. London: Sage.

FEY, M., and RAMSAY, K. W. 2006. The common priors assumption: a comment on "Bargaining and the nature of war." *Journal of Conflict Resolution*, 50: 607–13.

FINNEMORE, M., and SIKKINK, K. 1998. International norm dynamics and political change. *International Organization*, 52: 887–917.

FRIEDMAN, M. 1952. The methodology of positive economics. Pp. 3–43 in *Essays on Positive Economics*, M. Friedman. Chicago: University of Chicago Press.

FUDENBERG, D., and LEVINE, D. K. 1998. *The Theory of Learning in Games*. Cambridge, Mass.: MIT Press.

GAY, P. 1996. *The Enlightenment: The Science of Freedom*. New York: W. W. Norton.

GILPIN, R. 1981. *War and Change in World Politics*. Cambridge: Cambridge University Press.

GOEMANS, H. E. 2000. *War and Punishment: The Causes of War Termination and the First World War*. Princeton, NJ: Princeton University Press.

HELPMAN, E., and KRUGMAN, P. 1985. *Market Structure and Foreign Trade: Increasing Returns, Imperfect Competition, and the International Economy*. Cambridge, Mass.: MIT Press.

HERZ, J. H. 1950. Idealist internationalism and the security dilemma. *World Politics*, 2: 157–80.

HOBBES, T. 1968. *Leviathan*. New York: Penguin; originally published 1651.

HYMANS, J. E. C. 2006. *The Psychology of Nuclear Proliferation: Identity, Emotions, and Foreign Policy*. Cambridge: Cambridge University Press.

IIDA, K. 1993a. When and how do domestic constraints matter? Two-level games with uncertainty. *Journal of Conflict Resolution*, 37: 403–26.

——1993b. Analytic uncertainty and international cooperation: theory and application to international economic policy coordination. *International Studies Quarterly*, 37: 431–57.

JANIS, I. L. 1972. *Victims of Groupthink: A Psychological Study of Foreign-Policy Decisions and Fiascoes*. Boston: Houghton Mifflin.

JERVIS, R. 1976. *Perception and Misperception in International Politics*. Princeton, NJ: Princeton University Press.

——1978. Cooperation under the security dilemma. *World Politics*, 30: 167–214.

JOHNSON, D. D. P. 2004. *Overconfidence and War: The Havoc and Glory of Positive Illusions*. Cambridge, Mass.: Harvard University Press.

KAHNEMAN, D., SLOVIC, P., and TVERSKY, A. (eds.) 1982. *Judgment under Uncertainty: Heuristics and Biases*. Cambridge: Cambridge University Press.

KINDLEBERGER, C. 1973. *The World in Depression, 1929–1939*. Berkeley: University of California Press.

KOREMENOS, B., LIPSON, C., and SNIDAL, D. 2001. The rational design of international institutions. *International Organization*, 55: 761–99.

KRASNER, S. 1978. *Defending the National Interest: Raw Materials Investments and US Foreign Policy*. Princeton, NJ: Princeton University Press.

KYDD, A. H. 2005. *Trust and Mistrust in International Relations*. Princeton, NJ: Princeton University Press.

LEWIS, J. B., and SCHULTZ, K. A. 2003. Revealing preferences: empirical estimation of a crisis bargaining game with incomplete information. *Political Analysis*, 11: 345–67.

MacDonald, P. K. 2003. Useful fiction or miracle maker: the competing epistemological foundations of rational choice theory. *American Political Science Review*, 97: 551–65.

McDermott, R. 1998. *Risk-Taking in International Politics: Prospect Theory in American Foreign Policy*. Ann Arbor: University of Michigan Press.

Mas-Colell, A., Whinston, M. D., and Green, J. R. 1995. *Microeconomic Theory*. Oxford: Oxford University Press.

Mearsheimer, J. J. 2001. *The Tragedy of Great Power Politics*. New York: Norton.

Meyer, J. W., and Jepperson, R. L. 2000. The "actors" of modern society: the cultural construction of social agency. *Sociological Theory*, 18: 100–20.

Morrow, J. D. 1994. Modeling the forms of international cooperation: distribution versus information. *International Organization*, 48: 387–423.

North, D. C., and Weingast, B. R. 1989. Constitutions and commitment: the evolution of institutions governing public choice in seventeenth-century England. *Journal of Economic History*, 49: 803–32.

Olson, M. 1965. *The Logic of Collective Action: Public Goods and the Theory of Groups*. Cambridge, Mass.: Harvard University Press.

Oye, K. A. (ed.) 1986. *Cooperation under Anarchy*. Princeton, NJ: Princeton University Press.

Pahre, R. 1999. *Leading Questions: How Hegemony Affects the International Political Economy*. Ann Arbor: University of Michigan Press.

Powell, R. 1990. *Nuclear Deterrence Theory: The Search for Credibility*. Cambridge: Cambridge University Press.

—— 2002. Bargaining theory and international conflict. *Annual Review of Political Science*, 5: 1–30.

—— 2004a. The inefficient use of power: costly conflict with complete information. *American Political Science Review*, 98: 231–41.

—— 2004b. Bargaining and learning while fighting. *American Journal of Political Science*, 48: 344–61.

Price, R. 1998. Reversing the gun sights: transnational civil society targets land mines. *International Organization*, 52: 613–44.

Putnam, R. D. 1988. Diplomacy and domestic politics: the logic of two-level games. *International Organization*, 42: 427–60.

Rabushka, A., and Shepsle, K. A. 1972. *Politics in Plural Societies: A Theory of Democratic Instability*. Columbus, Ohio: Merrill.

Reiter, D. 1996. *Crucible of Beliefs: Learning, Alliances, and World Wars*. Ithaca, NY: Cornell University Press.

Risse, T. 2000. "Lets argue!": communicative action in world politics. *International Organization*, 54: 1–39.

Rosen, S. P. 2005. *War and Human Nature*. Princeton, NJ: Princeton University Press.

Rousseau, J.-J. 1997. *The Social Contract and Other Later Political Writings*, ed. and trans. V. Gourevitch. Cambridge: Cambridge University Press.

Sartori, A. E. 2005. *Deterrence by Diplomacy*. Princeton, NJ: Princeton University Press.

Schelling, T. C. 1960. *The Strategy of Conflict*. Cambridge, Mass.: Harvard University Press.

Schultz, K. A. 2001. *Democracy and Coercive Diplomacy*. Cambridge: Cambridge University Press.

Signorino, C. S. 1999. Strategic interaction and the statistical analysis of international conflict. *American Political Science Review*, 93: 279–97.

SIMMONS, B. A., and ELKINS, Z. 2004. The globalization of liberalization: policy diffusion in the international political economy. *American Political Science Review*, 98: 171–89.

SLANTCHEV, B. L. 2003. The principle of convergence in wartime negotiations. *American Political Science Review*, 97: 621–32.

SMITH, A., and STAM, A. C. 2004. Bargaining and the nature of war. *Journal of Conflict Resolution*, 48: 783–813.

SNIDAL, D. 1985. The limits of hegemonic stability theory. *International Organization*, 39: 579–614.

SNYDER, G. H., and DIESING, P. 1977. *Conflict among Nations: Bargaining, Decision Making, and System Structure in International Crises*. Princeton, NJ: Princeton University Press.

THAYER, B. A. 2000. Bringing in Darwin: evolutionary theory, realism, and international politics. *International Security*, 25: 124–51.

THUCYDIDES 1972. *History of the Peloponnesian War*, trans. R. Warner. London: Penguin.

WALT, S. M. 1999. Rigor or rigor mortis? Rational choice and security studies. *International Security*, 23: 5–48.

WALTZ, K. 1954. *Man, the State and War*. New York: Columbia University Press.

—— 1979. *Theory of International Politics*. New York: Random House.

WEBER, M. 1968. *Economy and Society*. Berkeley: University of California Press.

WENDT, A. 1999. *Social Theory of International Politics*. Cambridge: Cambridge University Press.

—— 2003. Why a world state is inevitable. *European Journal of International Relations*, 9: 491–542.

WEIBULL, J. 1995. *Evolutionary Game Theory*. Cambridge, Mass.: MIT Press.

WOLFERS, A. 1962. *Discord and Collaboration: Essays on International Politics*. Baltimore: Johns Hopkins University Press.

CHAPTER 26

....

SOCIOLOGICAL
APPROACHES

....

FRIEDRICH KRATOCHWIL

THE fact that peoples and states live in permanent anarchy has been the dominant paradigmatic assumption of most of post-Second World War international
relations analysis. Despite its foundational claims, however, these assumptions are
open to several theoretical and empirical challenges. One, of course, is that the
relationship between nations and states is problematic but remains largely outside
the scope of realist inquiry. The second is simply that the centralization of force is
not *eo ipso* a guarantee for peace: *vide* insurrections, civil wars, and so on. Therefore,
the existence of central decision-making institutions is at best a facilitating factor
of "peace" whose historical contingency ought to be empirically investigated, rather
than solved by assumption. Thirdly, contrary to the Hobbesian assertion, in virtually all well-ordered political systems, power is deliberately "separated" rather than
"hierarchically" arranged. As thinkers in the "republican" tradition (Deudney 1995;
Onuf 1998) have pointed out, creating viable political institutions requires dealing
with two dilemmas simultaneously: preventing anarchy *and* tyranny, rather than
simply subordinating oneself to a Hobbesian sovereign, who promises to provide
the collective good of security.

Fourthly, from the first and third objection follows: that crucial for the functioning of social systems are not only the palpable "capabilities" of coercion but
shared beliefs, such as who is the "we"—that is, whom do we protect and accept
as a member, and which exercises of power are legitimate. After all, politics comes
from *polis*, and *polis* is derived from *polizo* ("building a wall"), which points to the
issues both of security and of membership as the crucial dimensions of politics.

While realism has centered on the provision of security, the other two areas—that of legitimacy and that of membership and identity—were usually neglected and do not figure prominently in the liberal paradigm either (Rawls 1971). These omissions lead then at best to a rather restricted set of interesting questions, and, when combined with the ideal of "parsimony," to a rather barren "theory" of international politics. Issues of solidarity and questions of the self-understanding of the actors concerning the game they are involved in are systematically excluded, since the "anarchical" structure and the objective capabilities (Waltz 1979) rather than the actions, purposes, and shared ideas serve as the major *explanans*. While one might be inclined to accept such an Occam's razor in the expectation of a more elegant, coherent, and explanatory (or even predictive) theory, such hopes are ill founded for logical as well as practical reasons.

Logically, we have to realize that nothing follows from the existence of a "structure" alone, unless one reduces actors to mere "throughputs" and negates the problem of choice in the first place. The simple reason is that we cannot get from the assertion of a possibility to some more determinate *probability* without introducing additional, more substantive "variables" into our theoretical constructs. Thus we have to open up the "theory," for now not only structure, but also preferences, play a role. We also have to understand how issues of uncertainty are handled *in practice*. Here institutional arrangements as well as "ideas" provide guide posts in a world that otherwise would become incalculable. In addition, "history" also matters not only in that choices made earlier constrain later developments—an argument that has been made about the path-dependency of evolution in both biology and social science—but in cases of transformative change, such as when revolutions (violent or silent) change the nature of the international game (Koslowski and Kratochwil 1994). As Jervis (1985) and Ikenberry (2001) have shown, through the creation of institutions in the aftermath of system-wide wars, the fears as well as the opportunistic behavior, otherwise fueling noncooperative behavior, can be alleviated.

Some realists, less impressed by the promise of a structural theory, have, of course, pointed out that much of the dynamics of the international system depends on the nature of its members—that is, on whether they are revisionist (either in a territorial or in an ideological fashion), or status-quo-oriented (Kissinger 1964; Schweller and Priess 1997). Even Hobbes himself suggested that the alleged state of nature among "persons of sovereign authority" is far more benign than the state of nature "among individual men." States are not as vulnerable as natural persons, thus alleviating the security dilemma. They also provide the basis for "commodious living" by "upholding the industry of their subjects" (Hobbes 1985, ch. 11). Thus, in a way, Hobbes contradicts his own analogy between the state of nature and the description of international politics, where the sovereigns are in a permanent posture of war, thereby underlining that the transition from the *possibility* to the *probability* of war requires a far more extended analysis.

Historically, of course, the important corrections were provided by authors like Hume (1964), who showed that security need not be provided by governments alone, as other devices such as alliances, the balance of power, or diplomacy can sometimes substitute for a central government. Furthermore, he underlined that the emergence of such arrangements is historically variable and not simply the outcome of interactions among independent actors in a system, all functionalist or systemic "requirements" notwithstanding. Finally, security does not *always* trump all other state goals. Consequently, we both have to take different and multidimensional interests into account when we debate issues of the national or common interest, and have to be aware that the articulation of those interests occurs in civil society (Locke 1980) rather than within the state machinery alone. This fact belies the fixity of interests as well their identification with the state. Finally Kant (1970) suggested that the project of the *Rechtsstaat*—that is, the rule of law and the protection of rights—cannot be effectively procured if states do not form a league based on the renunciation of force and on binding dispute settlement.

Aside from their particular projects, all three thinkers raise the issue of the *constitution* of the international system (Reus-Smit 1997). Here, of course, the old adage *ubi societas ibi ius* ("wherever there is a society there is law") provides continuity with the old conception of a universal order based on "natural law." However, the predominant legal paradigm is now based on *contract* and on the extension of institutions of Roman private law to the international system (Lauterpacht 1970). Thus, the loose assembly of contracts and practices that accrues by happenstance rather than by wilful constitutional design points to the importance of history and change for understanding the international "game" and its reproduction. Since the international system is not "natural" but entirely artificial, it is based on certain shared understandings that bring about what they seemingly only describe (Searle 1995). As we will see, this problem of self-reference has important implications for theorizing about the social world, for the methods we choose, for the nature of "proofs" or tests, and for what "counts" as an explanation.

In the next sections I organize my discussion around the following points. After a clarification of the concept of society, I examine whether we can meaningfully speak of a "world society." Finally (Section 3), I address some methodological issues that are crucial for approaches that focus on social action, be it in the internal or the external arena.

1 The Issue of Society and its Constitution

To think of international relations in "social" terms requires some unlearning of deeply ingrained assumptions, as well as the development of an alternative positive heuristic. Thus, while we are, for example, prone to identify the "social" with macro-phenomena (as opposed to individual or singular actions or events) and while we think that the "big" phenomena have to be explained in terms of aggregation of micro-phenomena, a closer inspection shows the problematic nature of these assumptions. Similarly, even if we grant a connection between law and "society," the historically close identification of a "society" with the state (in the sense that we talk about a French, German, or American "society"), and of "law" with the "command of the sovereign" (Austin 1995), sends us right back to what Ashley (1984) has called the *anarchy problematique*. Consequently, there cannot be anything like "international law," and hence no "constitution" either.

But there are good reasons not to dispose of these problems by definitions. As Weber (1964) has shown, the "social" is not a descriptive term for mass phenomena. While hundreds of people leaving their office and opening their umbrella might be an example of the latter, it is not a "social" phenomenon. Rather the crucial "social" element is that *actions of agents are meaningfully oriented toward each other.* Here Weber uses the example of two bicyclists who are approaching a narrow bridge and want to avoid a collision. Aside from understanding the strategic aspect of the situation, they can prevent an accident only if they also know the rules of the road—that is, keep right! Thus, we need not only take the "subjective" point of view (that is, an actor's perspective) and the actors' "interests" (avoiding a collision) into account; we also have to understand that only through the existence of some inter-subjectively shared norms does the coordination of their respective actions become possible.

This conceptualization of the "social" has several corollaries. It shows the importance of "norms" for the coordination of action and for the "reproduction" of social order. Consequently, when investigating these "constitutive" effects of norms, we need not focus on "sanctions" and "enforcement" in order to explain how rules and norms "work." Furthermore, the reproduction of social order is possible because rules and norms have a powerful "prospective" ordering function in that they inform the actors what to do in certain situations. Even punishment and sanctions derive their effectiveness not from the *ex post* retribution but mainly from the "signal" they send to others preventing defection *ex ante*. No social order can be built on "enforcement" or on "sanctions," as the latter can be effective only when it is clear what a "violation" is that deserves "punishment." Otherwise we would perceive just acts of violence against which we could try to shield ourselves, but which could not fulfil the broader mission of facilitating social reproduction.

As the Iraq example shows, there is certainly a lot of force and "enforcement," but even the military admit that things are out of hand and that the "society" is coming apart. It also becomes clear that the impact of norms cannot be explained in terms of simple coincidence of interest, or of an aggregation of individually rational actions. After all, only the antecedent collective understanding of the rules of the road makes the individually rational action possible (keeping right). Thus, even if we face simple issues of coordination, where everyone has an interest in finding a solution, aside from "interests," we also need "norms." Therefore, we might not care whether we send our radio transmissions at 800 or 810 kiloherz, but we must have a norm that allocates the radio spectrum.

In short, the shift in focus away from enforcement and punishment to the constitutive and enabling function of norms allows for a much more fine-grained analysis of social order, as it no longer considers institutions specifically associated with the state as a precondition for social interaction. It thus breaks through the "domestic analogy" (Suganami 1989) of conceiving of international relations and politics only in negative terms (the absence of central institutions, the absence of enforcement, and so on), and also rectifies the myopia that the fragility of the international order could be remedied by simply creating more "laws" (always a favorite of legalists in both the domestic and the international arena) and statelike institutions.

It is here that the contribution of the English School can be appreciated (Buzan 1993; Dunne 1998). Basing their research program not on a priori assumptions, but delving into the rich historical heritage of the Empire that had exposed the metropolitan center to different social formations (rather than only states) and to great variations in "systems of states" (Wight 1977), the loose group of scholars forming that school was attentive both to the cultural embeddedness of societies in wider structures of meaning, and to the great historical variability of a-cephalic ("head-less") social orders. By using a comparative method, they compared the institutions of several systems. This comparison, in turn, allowed them to draw a clearer picture of the European system that was based on a status conception of sovereignty, and on diplomacy, alliances, certain maxims (balance of power), on congresses, and on a common recognition that the relations between the "equal" sovereigns was based on customary and contractual law.

Analytically perhaps the most articulate counter-proposal to realism was, therefore, Hedley Bull's *Anarchical Society* (1977). Basing his analysis on Hume, he spelled out the preconditions for the reproduction of social systems in general. All social systems must regulate the resort to force, establish the presumption that promises will be kept, and make provisions for the acquisition and transfer of titles. In the international arena, the rules of warfare (*ius ad bellum* and *in bello*) attempted such a regulation in regard to force, the presumption that promises were to be kept was reflected in the norm of *pacta sunt servanda*, and the acquisition of titles and transfer of rights was enshrined in different entitlements to territory, provisions for state responsibility, state succession, and so on. Although Bull's and the English School's work on the specific character of a "society of states" was an important contribution, it was already at odds with contemporary political practice. Here human rights, claims for self-determination, and the "rights of (non-state) peoples" showed that the exclusive focus on states had become problematic (Brown 2001).

The growth of international interdependencies (Keohane and Nye 1977) and the increasing differentiation of domestic societies not only demonstrated that the focus on the "state" or the political system as a "steering mechanism" was increasingly at odds with the sensitivities and vulnerabilities created by complex interdependence, and by the complex "corporate" form of internal and external governance that emerged. It was at first experienced as a "loss of control" by state institutions. Some authors, such as Cox (1981), tried to capture this new complexity by an argument about the "internationalization of the state," but the growth of transnational law that foreshadowed complex forms of governance in which public and private actors take over regulatory and distributive functions (Hall and Biersteker 2002) raised serious questions as to whether the traditional categories, derived from the state and state-building project, were still adequate. We encountered failed states, which subsequently often transformed into warlordism, kleptocracies, and strange partnerships with international crime networks. But we also noticed that the decline of the United States as a hegemonic power—which supposedly set and enforced the rules—did not lead to anarchy, or even to the highly problematic interwar policies, where states had tried to create some order by resorting to unilateral "beggar thy neighbor" policies (Ruggie 1983).

The ensuing discussion about *regimes* moved away from the traditional agenda of international politics that had focused nearly exclusively on power and security by now also including economic and environmental issues. This shift engendered an intense discussion about the methodologies that were considered appropriate for the assessment of how norms matter—that is, influence choices. The "consensus definition" of regimes treating them as "intervening variables" seemed to provide a compromise between the traditional emphasis on power (as capabilities) and that of ideas. Furthermore, given the difficulties in showing that ideas or norms had efficient "causal powers" since they shape choices in a different fashion, as Kratochwil and Ruggie (1986) pointed out, much of the debate generated more heat than enlightenment. This led to a nearly hypertrophic concern with epistemological issues, precisely at a time at which the history of science and sociology (Knorr-Cetina 1981; Fuller 1988) had shown that the old epistemological project had failed. "Science" was no longer a self-justificatory enterprise showing us how the "world out there" really is, but had to be conceived as a social enterprise of knowledge production in which the community of practitioners is deeply involved in the construction of the very problems they investigate.

Here "constructivism," going back to Kant and having experienced a more radical revival in modern biology, challenged the positivist notion that science creates warranted knowledge by simply "discovering" a ready-made world. Precisely because we never test against "nature" directly—not even in the natural sciences—but only against other theories, "nature" itself can hardly "answer" us, even if "asked" in experiments, unless it uses, so to speak, our language, and that means that debates about the "weight" of evidence and "translations" from one theory to another become necessary. Notwithstanding considerable disagreements in this respect, the regime debate engendered some detailed studies of the working regimes, particularly in the environmental (Young 1999) but also in the security realm (Katzenstein 1996), to which positivists and constructivists alike contributed.

The ensuing pluralism also explains why the larger epistemological and methodological issues originally raised by constructivism have recently receded into the background. There are several reasons for this shift. One has to do with the fact that, as soon as constructivism had been more or less accepted as a legitimate approach, research could focus on "normal science" rather than paradigmatic challenges and their justification. After all, many issues can be analyzed without engaging in epistemological debates. As in the case of a skipper who charts his course by "shooting" the stars, the "truth" of various theories of the solar system is rather irrelevant for his purposes and our explanations of his actions. The fact that he proceeds more or less with the same practices as countless generations before him does not mean that the theoretical debates between Ptolemeans, Copernicans, Newtonians, and adherents of Einstein have been meaningless, but indicates that not all issues have to be raised for all purposes. We can "go on" and solve (at least some) of our problems even if our explanations rely on problematic, perhaps even false assumptions. Furthermore, given that most actions and events are overdetermined, our theoretical assertions, emphasizing different factors, cannot claim to have found the unique "fitting" explanation. Rather, in most debates, the issues center on what should be taken as the null-hypothesis and what the burden of proof is, as well as the sociology of knowledge-based questions where different authors "fit" in the larger enterprise of international relations or political science.

Even more important is a second reason. Precisely because the social world does not consists of "natural facts" but is an artifice based on shared concepts and understandings, the "explanations" we give cannot be reduced to one single form, such as some demonstrative procedure based on a particular method, or some logical inference. We give and require explanations in a variety of contexts, and a sociological approach has to be particularly sensitive to this problem. Thus, in explaining why Mrs Brown died, there will be different answers from the coroner and the district attorney. For the former the blood clot resulting from a stab with a knife is the "cause," for the latter it is that her husband had a mistress and, having taken out a big life insurance on his wife, he wanted to ride with his new love (and the money) into the sunset. This set of circumstances establishes the "motive" that explains what happened when Mr Brown encountered his wife on the day of the killing.

As this example shows, holding on to the conviction that only explanations based on "efficient" causes are acceptable because of their "scientific" status is based on a misconception of the social world and of science alike. When we explain actions, for example, we often use "final" causes as an *explanans*—that is, the actor's future goal rather than independently specified antecedent conditions, as required by efficient causal explanations. Furthermore, as the discussion by Wendt (1999) has shown, "constitutive" explanations, which are again different from efficient cause explanations, abound both in the hard and in the social sciences. Finally, when structural or productive power are used (see Barnett and Duvall 2005), they function as "formal" causes in the Aristotelian sense. However, few of us would reject such explanations because they do not utilize efficient causes.

While the above discussion suggests that the conceptualization of regimes as an "intervening" variable was unfortunate and needlessly narrow, the other part of the regime definition concerning the issue was probably too amorphous, lumping together organizations, decisional processes, norms, and so on. Nevertheless, this "imprecision" provided rather fertile ground for further exploration. The focus on rule and informal understandings liberated the analysis from the legalistic prejudice of normativity being an "all or nothing property" made of one cloth. As in the case of legitimacy, where notions of input and output legitimacy compete with each other and also with the fact that "coherence" among norms might have a certain legitimizing function, different types of norms impact on and shape choices. Furthermore, the focus on an "issue area" of a regime engendered investigations of how such areas are constructed and become accepted. R. B. Haas (1975) showed, for example, how the "ocean," seemingly a simple designation of a part of the "world out there," became, in the United Nations Conference on the Law of the Sea (UNCLOS) III, a new "whole" that not only united formerly distinct regimes but whose construction involved significant normative and cognitive shifts. Such research paved the way for studies of "learning" and cognitive evolutions (Adler 1991) and the role of the transnationally active scientific communities (R. B. Haas 1992; Risse 1995).

But different from former functionalist arguments where experts "ended" politics by letting (scientific or technical) "truth" speak to power, the newer literature on epistemic communities realized that "science" is rife with controversies, and thus with politics, and that the "expertocracy" of international organizations can create serious problems, in terms both of organizational pathologies and of legitimacy (Stiglitz 2002). These problems were particularly raised in the context of the European Union and the international financial institutions. It also turned our attention to domestic social structures, which crucially enable or disable the (trans)national flow of ideas and knowledge and their impact on decisions. As opposed to these approaches, the work on norm diffusion through transnational activist networks (Finnemore and Sikkink 1998) suffers a bit from the simplicity of a stage model of norm development, which remains largely silent on why, when, and how we advance from one stage to the other.

In addition, the listing of several organizational forms within the regime definition encouraged both the analysis beyond the barren dichotomy of hierarchy and anarchy and pointed to the embeddedness of these organizational forms in wider understandings (social episteme). Here Ruggie's study (1993) on multilateralism as a specific organizational form and his argument about the embedded liberalism of the post-Second World War international economic order (Ruggie 1983) are good examples. They provided a far richer account of the Bretton Woods institutions than the usual arguments about "hegemony" and the provisions of public goods (never mind that neither "free trade" nor "protection" (security) is, on the international level, a simple nonexclusionary public good!). That the conditions underlying the Bretton Woods settlement no longer prevail, as the liberal trading order was then predicated on firm capital controls, designed to prevent speculative flows, need not be rehearsed here, as it has been addressed by the globalization literature.

2 FRAGMENTATION OR THE EMERGENCE OF GLOBAL SOCIETY?

These considerations lead us back to the "constitutional" issues. The existence of many free-standing regimes (Teubner 1996), some of which are even furnished with rather effective compulsory settlement procedures (World Trade Organization), raises the issue that has been discussed in international law under the rubric of the "fragmentation" of the international (legal) order (Koskenniemi and Leino 2002). Unless we make the heroic assumption that all regimes fit like hand in glove, issues of "priorities" and of incoherence of the existing arrangement arise. What may make for good trade policies might be bad for environmental protection or even human rights. The multiplicity of courts ranging from the International Court of Justice to international tribunals, the International Criminal Court, the Law of the Sea Court, and arbitration panels might indeed be a mixed blessing. It is likely to produce widely differing rulings, encourage forum-shopping, and fail, therefore, to send clear signals for the "prospective ordering" in a complex globalized world. Thus different from former times, where "cheating" seemed the main impediment to cooperation, the present predicament is one in which we face, aside from cheating, the categorical rejection of the entire statist project by fundamentalist leaders and predatory power-holders, but in which we also suffer, strangely enough, from an embarrassment of riches.

The last remarks raise some important issues about whether, through the eradication of both the "internal" and the "external," and the "private" and the "public" spheres (Walker 1993), something like a "world society" is in the offing. Here several caveats are in order. On the one hand, the universal acceptance of the Western model seems to suggest that, if not politically, at least in terms of the cultural forms and in the construction of meaning, a world civilization has been created. Thus the appeal of human rights, the seemingly near universal acceptance of "democracy," the introduction of "best practices" and accountability by states and international organizations, and the new public–private partnerships that have taken over important governance functions, all seem to support this interpretation. Here the work of the Stanford School has shown in impressive detail the thorough impact of Western forms of organization on other societies (Meyer et al. 1997). But, different from former *efficiency* arguments, familiar from Weber and the adherents of "political development," this spread is better explained by the greater *legitimacy* of the political project for which these organizations stand.

On the other hand, we have to acknowledge that this "hegemony" of ideas does not frequently translate into direct practice. Consequently, the adoption of the Western model is not only quite uneven, but often far removed from the actual way in which people interact and solve their individual and collective problems. We have not only "failed" and "rogue" states; efforts of "reforming" states through surveillance (filing reports, meeting benchmarks, and so on) by reaching deep into the respective societies hardly ever meet expectations. Here the experiences of Haiti, Afghanistan, Timor, or Kosovo provide sobering evidence. The reason for these failures is that people are not cultural dopes, who directly translate prescriptions into practice, especially when the forms are unfamiliar and the processes of translation are not "owned." Consequently, "democratization" efforts are likely to engender resistance, as the challenges by fundamentalists demonstrate. Furthermore, the implementers (aid, United Nations, officials, or staff of nongovernmental organizations) are often unable to remain "neutral professionals," who, like "doctors," can treat a patient because of their detachment. Precisely because they distribute resources, they create new political processes, and they also become, in a way, dependent on their "clients." After all, as Hegel pointed out, you can only be master if a servant recognizes you as such. Indeed, in the case of nongovernmental organizations where activities depend to a significant amount on "customer satisfaction" at contract renewal, this dependency is quite visible (Cooley and Ron 2002).

Similar criticism can be levelled against all too optimistic assessments of the communications revolution. True, the "reachability" (Albrow 1997) of people has dramatically increased, new networks have formed, and chat rooms unite people in cyberspace and make it possible to debate, even "vote," on issues. Similarly, the enormously increased risks that transcend calculability and localization—such as, for example, Chernobyl or global warming—might make us aware of the "global" context in which we live. But is this enough to speak of a world risk society (Beck 1999)? True, this awareness is necessary for a "public space" in which new forms of politics and democratic participation could emerge (Archibugi and Held 1995).

Here transnational social movements come to mind. Some Marxists (Hardt and Negri 2000) put their faith in the "multitude" of the exploited, which is becoming a "class for itself." The question remains, nevertheless, how even organized movements can, aside from performing spectacular protests, provide effective levers for action. Here "reachability" is not enough, as *access* and wherewithal are crucial. The fact that all of Manhattan had more telephones than sub-Saharan Africa (Everard 2000, 34) clearly indicates the distorted picture of a new global public sphere.

Finally, as Sunstein (2001) pointed out, the information overload leads to new problems of selection, effectively impairing the discussion of "public" issues, precisely because the requisite variety of opinions, crucial for the vetting function of a "public," is usually missing in cyberspace. There people can switch in and out and usually prefer to talk only to those who are like-minded. In short, the point is not that people can now register their preferences in more ways, but that in a public space existential issues of war and peace, of justice, welfare, and identity, need to be deliberated and decided on. Here it has to be settled who can speak and must be heard, and who has to abide by the final decision even if it is not to his or her liking. Thus, while markets function through entry and exit, the question remains whether for a "society" both voice and loyalty are necessary or whether "exit" and "voice" indeed are enough (Hirschman 1970).

The last remarks also suggest that a decision as to whether a world society exists, or emerges, is not one of a simple match between a concept and the "world out there." The term does not function as a simple "label" but serves as a yardstick for appraisal, and this involves operations quite different from simply looking at empirical facts. Significantly Weber (1964, pt. 1, ch. 1, Basic Sociological Concepts) had no entry for "society" in his definitional section. He mentioned only two processes of *Vergesellschaftung* ("association"), based on different patterns of solidarity, a division that goes back to Ferdinand Toennies and Émile Durkheim. The missing noun in Weber's vocabulary suggests that we should think of society not as a "thing" but as a set of processes in which various differentiations occur. Instead of the usual notions in which the objects of investigation are brought under a concept, we should focus on the *processes of drawing the boundaries* that constitute the objects, such as nations, markets, states, and so on. In that case not only would "solidarity" provide the criterion for making distinctions, but a wide variety of "codes" would determine the bounds of sense, facilitate interaction, and enable us to go on. Thus the "economy" goes as far as we have "prices," the province of law would be delineated when we consider actions under the aspect of legal/illegal, "religion" would be constituted by the code of the "sacred/profane," and so on. Such a conception of "society" has been proposed by Luhmann (1972; 1999), and in this sense we, of course, "are" in a world society, even if it is quite different from the familiar notions of a "state" beyond the state, of the emergence of a world public sphere, or of a world "community."

3 A Note on Method

As the above discussion suggests, the main difference between sociological and other approaches consists of how to treat "social" facts, whether they can be treated like "natural" ones or not. Quite clearly this is a far wider issue than the discussion on "methods" or even on "science." Behind it looms the larger problem of what our "concepts," which are part of our theories, do; whether they simply match a preexisting reality—which is therefore susceptible to "one" correct description—or whether our concepts are implicated in the constitution of the very entities and problems we study. Here scientific realists, on the one hand, and conventionalists, constructivists, and so on, on the other, face each other in all disciplines, the hard sciences as well as the social sciences. The scientific realist position is based on the belief that, if the concepts were not really matching the "world," then the success of science would be a miracle.

But this at first very convincing argument is undermined by two powerful counter-arguments, one logical, the other empirical. Logically, the miracle argument has the same structure as one of the "proofs" of the existence of God (when the perfect designs that we find in nature are attributed to a designer), an illicit inference, as Kant pointed out in his first critique. The empirical objection concerns the history of science. Although many past theories were based on near universal acceptance, they were later abandoned, as some of the crucial theoretical terms, such as ether, caloric, phlogiston, and so on, did not "correspond" to anything in "the world." It is, therefore, likely that crucial terms that are part of our present ontology of science will share the same fate. Strangely enough, the "success" of science—engendering the industrial and technological revolutions—were based on theories that have been proved "wrong" (for example, the ether-based electromagnetic theory). Both arguments seem to suggest that the "miracle" argument in favor of "realism" is less than convincing.

Be that as it may. The fact remains that many of the interests and problems in the social sciences concern issues of agency, ascription of status (for example, who is recognized as an actor), responsibility (which we can attribute only if we believe that the actions are not determined by causal necessity), and identity (the historical contingencies of groups). As we have seen, these issues can be addressed only if we are attentive to issues of meaning and the constitutive function of values, and that means we have to broaden our conception of "explanation." Focusing, therefore, on communication and meaning, rather than on "material" capabilities or "interest," has important methodological implications.

First, we cut in at the level of the intersubjective understandings that enable and constrain the actors "to go on," rather than on the level of the actor and his "motives," or on that of "systemic" structures. We can do this because action explanations, I maintain, are always based on "attributions" rather than on the exploration of the actor's "mind." In a way, we provide an "externalist" account rather than one based on "private" motives, precisely because we do not have access to the actor's "mind," and even the actor might not be clear about his actual motives. Cognitive and motivated biases might cloud the picture, and the multiplicity of "reasons" for action might be difficult to reduce to one single motive. This is the point Weber (1954) makes against "empathy" and in favor of "understanding." To have explained an action is to have made it intelligible, having put it in a context, and shown that the attributions make sense according to intersubjectively shared standards. Thus, when we query someone why, for example, he paid a large sum of money to someone else, and he answers that it was a "promise" or a contract, we have the action explained, although no law, or "causal mechanism," or even identifiable "desire" of the actor à la Hume was involved.

Secondly, attempts to "cleanse" the language of certain value considerations in deference to scientific objectivity are essentially misguided, because they are "pointless." Thus, when we use terms like "he abandoned her," instead of simply stating that "he left," we want to characterize an action and ascribe responsibility, or blame. Rather than treating this action like an "event" that just happened, but that was beyond anybody's control (like an earthquake), we want to make a point that is of interest to us (Connolly 1983). Thus, reducing everything to a presumably "objective" language is fundamentally at odds with the problems of the world of *practice*, leading to an impoverished research agenda. As Weber suggested, values are *constitutive* of our interests and cannot be eliminated, even if we accept that their validity cannot be *proved* by "scientific" inferences. That is why he thought that the "honesty" befitting a scientist required making these values explicit. But it would be a total misconstruction of his argument if we ascribed to him a position of "cleansing" the inquiry of any value traces in accordance with a mistaken notion of methodological purity.

These are rather elemental observations, but they are helpful in clarifying some hotly contested issues—for example, of the agent–structure debate. Here, the argument that structures do not determine choices has been made by some rational choice adherents and constructivists alike, but the latter also insisted that just adding preferences is not enough. Both their genesis and the constitution of the actors through action has to be endogenized into the theory instead of being dealt with by assumption. But, in examining the debate, Doty (1997) correctly points out that, despite the theoretical manifesto of explaining the "co-constitution" of agents (Giddens 1979; Archer 1982) and structures, actual research still favors either structures over agents or vice versa. The reason is rather simple: As long as we take the paradigm of efficient causes as our yardstick, the dilemma is insoluble, since one element *has* to be prior to the other. It disappears only when it is circumvented—that is, when other forms of "causality" are admitted, such as, for example, Aristotelian formal causes.

Another issue concerns the status of unobservable elements in both nature and the field of practice, and the inference that they work in the same fashion, as, for example, Waltz (1979, ch. 5) suggested. True, while both "black holes" and the international system are not directly observable, there is nevertheless a significant difference in how they produce their effects. "Black holes" can be inferred because their effects obtain whether or not they are observed. If they are observed, they do not require a change in the description we use for natural facts. If I say, however, this is a "paperweight" rather than a mere stone, then my description is in a way "observer-relative" (Searle 2001). "Seeing" a paperweight requires an observer and familiarity with the particular cultural practices in a society, rather than a simple reference to a brute fact (even though such observer-relative "descriptions" are not arbitrary or idiosyncratic). So much for the "scientific realist" argument of "rump materialism" (Wendt 1999) that assumes what things are can be settled by one "correct" description!

Things get even more complicated if we deal with institutional facts. When I say "this is money," I am not so much referring to the object, or token, because it does not "work" in virtue of its intrinsic properties (such as "weight") to which a function was ascribed, as in the case of the paperweight. After all, in the latter case, I could also have used a marmalade jar or an ash-tray. But, in the case of money, the meaning of the term is virtually entirely determined by shared conventions. We see this most clearly in the case of "electronic" cash, in which even the tokens of paper or plastic have disappeared and only informational digits in cyberspace indicate a transaction. Furthermore, the concept is self-referential, because something can be money only if it is believed to be money. Thus the content of that belief is the shared belief that something serves among a group of actors as money and engenders actions that would not be possible without it. Similarly, when we "appoint" someone to be ambassador, or marry two people, we create by a "speech act" (indicated by a formula and a "hereby") virtually *ex nihilo* a new situation and endow a person with new rights and capacities. Finally, the international system also exists only insofar as actors share an assembly of practices based on institutional rules, such as treaties, diplomacy, alliances, and so on, and create and reproduce thereby the system.

Here constructivists of various stripes have provided important contributions to international relations analysis, whereby the main distinction among those constructivists is between those who focus on language, and those who want to understand society more in terms of an interactionist model, or according to more mainstream approaches (Zehfuss 2002). Wendt, for example, is influenced by the symbolic interactionism of Mead (1954) and attempts to build bridges to the dominant neorealist school in international relations and to rational choice theory. It was Onuf (1989) who perhaps most consistently emphasized language and tried to apply the speech-act theory of Austin (1962) and Searle (1979) to politics, while Kratochwil (1989) focused on the function of "rules" and their enabling and constraining effects. Precisely because rules have to be interpreted, they cannot be understood in terms of identical effects, as is presupposed by causal analysis. While rules serve to stabilize expectations and thus create some observable general patterns, their more important function is their *internal* aspect—that is, the

enabling (or regulative) capacity that allows actors "to go on." Here social reproduction does not consist of the iteration of identical exemplars, but implies always
change, through "deviance" (working "around" the rules), contestation (arguing
that a situation requires a different rule, as we have, for example, in the case of
humanitarian intervention, when "sovereignty" is abridged in the name of human
rights), or extension to new areas (as, for example, treating services like goods, or
intellectual achievements like "property").

This view that emphasizes the importance of "ideas" (or rather of concepts and
language) "all the way down" engenders, of course, resistance, as "reality" (understood as the palpable things that surround us) seems to disappear right before our
eyes. Arguments that such an approach fosters "relativism," mistakes rhetoric for
reality, and is likely to end up in a "denial of truth" are therefore common, even
though they are confused. First, it is quite clear that "truth" cannot be a property
of things, because "true" can only be *assertions about* things. Consequently, truth
is always a function in a semantic system and "relative" to it, even though this
relativity is neither arbitrary nor idiosyncratic. Secondly, the naive notion that
the "world out there" is like a furniture store has been thoroughly discredited by
modern physics and biology alike. There are no "ultimate" givens such as essences
or even (indivisible) atoms or genera and species (unless you are a creationist). Precisely because the "nature" consists of fields and processes rather than ready-made
ultimate "things," reification and the assumption that proper conceptualizations
consist of matching operations between "words" and "things" are the *result of a
particular philosophical tradition* and not of "nature" or the "world."

Finally, from the recognition that all we have are "constructs" rather than "things,
as they are," it does not follow that anything is possible, as it does not follow from
my conception of a perfect being that it also exists (Descartes notwithstanding). As
we all know, dilemmas are real, even if they are not "natural," and social reality is
difficult to change because of collective action problems, ideological hegemonies,
or determined opposition. Thus, it is not hard to demonstrate that (national)
identities are not fixed, but it is much harder to show how they can be changed,
since we are not dealing here with a simple "membership" problem that arises in
bowling clubs or "interest groups." Precisely because man is a social animal, politics
matters, and the brotherhood of man is an aspiration and ethical demand rather
than an institutionalized practice.

References

ADLER, E. 1991. Cognitive evolution: a dynamic approach for the study of international
    relations and their progress. Pp. 43–88 in *Progress in Postwar International Relations*, ed.
    E. Adler and B. Crawford. New York: Columbia University Press.

ALBROW, M. 1997. *The Global Age: State and Society beyond Modernity*. Stanford, Calif.: Stanford University Press.

ARCHER, M. S. 1982. Morphogenesis versus structuration: on combining structure and action. *British Journal of Sociology*, 33: 455–83.

ARCHIBUGI, D., and HELD, D. (eds.) 1995. *Cosmopolitan Democracy: An Agenda for a New World Order*. Cambridge: Polity.

ASHLEY, R. 1984. The poverty of neorealism. *International Organization*, 38: 225–86.

AUSTIN, J. 1962 *How to do Things with Words*. Cambridge, Mass.: Harvard University Press.

——1995. *The Province of Jurisprudence Determined*, ed. W. Rumble. Cambridge: Cambridge University Press; originally published 1832.

BARNETT, M., and DUVALL, R. 2005. Power in international politics. *International Organization*, 59: 39–75.

BECK, U. 1999. *World Risk Society*. Cambridge: Polity.

BOLI, J., and THOMAS, G. (eds). 1999. *Constructing World Culture: International Nongovernmental Organizations since 1875*. Stanford, Calif.: Stanford University Press.

BROWN, C. 2001. World society and the English School: an "international society" perspective on world society. *European Journal of International Relations*, 7: 423–41.

BULL, H. 1977. *The Anarchical Society: A Study of Order in World Politics*. New York: Columbia University Press.

BUZAN, B. 1993. From international system to international society: structural realism and regime theory meet the English School. *International Organization*, 47: 327–52.

CONNOLLY, J. 1983. *The Terms of Political Discourse*, 2nd edn. Princeton, NJ: Princeton University Press.

COOLEY, A., and RON, J. 2002. The NGO scramble: organizational insecurity and the political economy of transnational action. *International Security*, 27: 5–39.

COX, R. W. 1981. Social forces, states and world orders: beyond international relations theory. *Millennium: Journal of International Studies*, 10: 126–55.

DEUDNEY, D. 1995. The Philadelphia system: sovereignty, arms control, and balance of power in the American states-union, circa 1787–1861. *International Organization*, 49: 191–228.

DOTY, R. L. 1997. Aporia: a critical examination of the agent–structure problematique in international relations theory. *European Journal of International Relations*, 3: 365–92.

DUNNE, T. 1998. *Inventing International Society: A History of the English School*. New York: St Martin's Press.

EVERARD, J. 2000. *Virtual States: The Internet and the Boundaries of the Nation-State*. London: Routledge.

FINNEMORE, M., and SIKKINK, K. 1998. International norm dynamics and political change. *International Organization*, 52: 887–917.

FULLER, S. 1988. *Social Epistemology*. Bloomington: Indiana University Press.

GIDDENS, A. 1979. *Central Problems in Social Theory: Action, Structure and Contradiction in Social Analysis*. Berkeley: University of California Press.

HAAS, E. B. 1975. Is there a hole in the whole? Knowledge, technology, interdependence, and the construction of international regimes. *International Organization*, 29: 827–76.

HAAS, P. M. 1992. Introduction: epistemic communities and international policy coordination. *International Organization*, 46: 1–35.

HALL, R., and BIERSTEKER, T. (eds.) 2002. *The Emergence of Private Authority in Global Governance*. Cambridge: Cambridge University Press.

HARDT, M., and NEGRI, A. 2000. *Empire*. Cambridge, Mass.: Harvard University Press.

HIRSCHMAN, A. 1970. *Exit, Voice, and Loyalty: Responses to Decline in Firms, Organizations, and States*. Cambridge, Mass.: Harvard University Press.

HOBBES, T. 1985. *Leviathan*, ed. C. B. Macpherson. Harmondsworth: Penguin; originally published 1651.

HUME, D. 1964. Of the balance of power. Pp. 339–48 in *Essays: Moral, Political and Literary*, D. Hume. London: Oxford University Press.

IKENBERRY, J. 2001. *After Victory: Institutions, Strategic Restraint, and the Rebuilding of Order after Major Wars*. Princeton, NJ: Princeton University Press.

JERVIS, R. 1985. From balance to concert: a study of international security cooperation. *World Politics*, 38: 58–79.

KANT, I. 1970. Perpetual peace. Pp. 93–130 in *Kant's Political Writings*, ed. H. Reiss, trans. H. S. Nisbet. Cambridge: Cambridge University Press; originally published 1795.

KATZENSTEIN, P. (ed.) 1996. *The Culture of National Security: Norms and Identity in World Politics*. New York: Columbia University Press.

KEOHANE, R., and NYE, J. 1977. *Power and Interdependence*. Boston: Little, Brown.

KISSINGER, H. 1964. *A World Restored*. New York: Grosset and Dunlap.

KNORR-CETINA, K. D. 1981. *The Manufacture of Knowledge: An Essay on the Constructivist and Contextual Nature of Science*. Oxford: Pergamon.

KOSKENNIEMI, M., and LEINO, P. 2002. Fragmentation of international law? Postmodern anxieties. *Leiden Journal of International Law*, 15: 553–79.

KOSLOWSKI, R., and KRATOCHWIL, F. 1994. Understanding change in international politics: the Soviet empire's demise and the international system. *International Organization*, 48: 215–47.

KRATOCHWIL, F. 1989. *Rules, Norms, and Decisions: On the Conditions of Practical and Legal Reasoning in International Relations and Domestic Affairs*. Cambridge: Cambridge University Press.

——and RUGGIE, J. G. 1986. International organization: a state of the art on an art of the state. *International Organization*, 40: 753–75.

LAUTERPACHT, H., SIR 1970. *Private Law Sources and Analogies of International Law, with Special Reference to International Arbitration*. Hamden, Conn.: Archon.

LOCKE, J. 1980. *The Second Treatise of Government*, ed. C. B. Macpherson. Indianapolis: Hackett; originally published 1690.

LUHMANN, N. 1972. Die Weltgesellschaft. *Archiv für Rechts- und Sozialphilosophie*, 57: 1–34.

——1999. *Die Gesellschaft der Gesellschaft*, 2 vols. Frankfurt: Suhrkamp.

MEAD, G. H. 1954. *Mind, Self and Society*. Chicago: University of Chicago Press.

MEYER, J., BOLI, J., THOMAS, G. M., and RAMIREZ, F. O. 1997. World society and the nation-state. *American Journal of Sociology*, 103: 144–81.

ONUF, N. 1989. *World of Our Making: Rules and Rule in Social Theory and International Relations*. Columbia: University of South Carolina Press.

——1998. *The Republican Legacy in International Thought*. Cambridge: Cambridge University Press.

RAWLS, J. 1971. *A Theory of Justice*. Cambridge Mass.: Harvard University Press.

REUS-SMIT, C. 1997. The constitutional structure of international society and the nature of fundamental institutions. *International Organization*, 51: 55–89.

RISSE, T. 1995. *Bringing Transnational Relations Back In: Non-state Actors, Domestic Structures, and International Institutions*. Cambridge: Cambridge University Press.

RUGGIE, J. 1983. International regimes, transactions and change. Pp. 195–232 in *International Regimes*, ed. S. Krasner. Ithaca, NY: Cornell University Press.

——(ed.) 1993. *Multilateralism Matters: The Theory and Praxis of an Institutional Forum.* New York: Columbia University Press.

SCHWELLER, R. L., and PRIESS, D. 1997. A tale of two realisms: expanding the institutions debate. *Mershon International Studies Review*, 41: 1–32.

SEARLE, J. 1979. *Expression and Meaning: Studies in the Theory of Speech Acts.* Cambridge: Cambridge University Press.

——1995. *The Construction of Social Reality.* London: Penguin.

——2001. *Rationality in Action.* Cambridge, Mass.: MIT Press.

STIGLITZ, J. 2002. *Globalization and its Discontent.* New York: Norton

SUGANAMI, H. 1989. *The Domestic Analogy and World Order Proposals.* Cambridge: Cambridge University Press.

SUNSTEIN, C. 2001. *Republic.com.* Princeton, NJ: Princeton University Press.

TEUBNER, G. 1996. *Globale Bukowina: Zur Emergenz eines transnationalen Rechtspluralismus.* Basel: Basel University Press.

WALKER, R. 1993. *Inside Outside: International Relations as Political Theory.* Cambridge: Cambridge University Press.

WALTZ, K. 1979. *Theory of International Politics.* Reading, Mass.: Addison-Wesley.

WEBER, M. 1954. *Gesammelte Aufsätze zur Wissenschaftslehre*, ed. J. Winckelmann. Tübingen: C. B. Mohr.

——1964. *Wirtschaft und Gesellschaft*, ed. J. Winckelmann. Cologne: Kiepenheuer and Witsch.

WENDT, A. 1999. *Social Theory of International Politics.* Cambridge: Cambridge University Press.

WIGHT, M. 1977. *Systems of States.* Leicester: Leicester University Press.

YOUNG, O. (ed.) 1999. *The Effectiveness of International Environmental Regimes: Causal Connections and Behavioral Mechanisms.* Cambridge, Mass.: MIT Press.

ZEHFUSS, M. 2002. *Constructivism in International Relations: The Politics of Reality.* Cambridge: Cambridge University Press.

CHAPTER 27

....

PSYCHOLOGICAL APPROACHES

....

JAMES GOLDGEIER

PHILIP TETLOCK

DEBATES over whether international relations theories are reducible—in some mysterious metaphysical sense—to psychology should have faded long ago into intellectual history (Waltz 1959). As we have noted in earlier essays (Tetlock and Goldgeier 2000; Goldgeier and Tetlock 2001) and as others have patiently pointed out over the last few decades (Kelman and Bloom 1973; Jervis 1976; George 1980), the right question is more nuanced and less polarizing: under what conditions, in what ways, and to what degree should various strands of theorizing at the international level—structural realism, institutionalism, constructivism—incorporate various categories of psychological theory?

   With this as our starting point, our goal in this chapter is to sample the diverse ways in which such interweaving of levels of analysis has either already begun or could be readily initiated given recent empirical and theoretical developments. We organize the most promising candidates for conceptual integration into four broad categories: (1) identifying the appropriate boundary conditions for the applicability of clashing hypotheses within the structural–realist tradition (for example, when and why do states pursue more or less risk-seeking security policies?); (2) identifying the factors that facilitate and impede the creation of international institutions and norm enforcement mechanisms within the institutionalist tradition (for example, when and why do states make commitments that apparently reduce their sovereignty and freedom of action?); (3) identifying the factors that determine whether policy-makers and epistemic communities frame issues in terms of the logic of consequential action or the logic of obligatory action within the constructivist tradition (for example, when and why do powerful norms—such as the taboos against using nuclear and chemical weapons—take hold?); and (4) highlighting the price that international relations theorists pay for placing a hedgehog-style premium on theoretical parsimony and the value of adopting a more flexible, foxlike, contextualist style in future theory-building exercises (for example, when and why are expert observers most vulnerable to contingency blindness?).

Before launching this exercise, we should, however, reassure readers who worry that psychology is too fragmented—insufficiently paradigmatic—to be a reliable guide for revising international relations theories. To be sure, the most relevant fields of psychology—cognition, social, personality—have their controversies. Disagreements persist on basic issues such as the degree to which human behavior is under the control of stable personality dispositions or shifting situational cues (Mischel 1999) or whether alleged cognitive biases represent departures from rationality or adaptive responses to the environment (Gigerenzer and Goldstein 1996; Kahneman and Tversky 2000; Gigerenzer and Selten 2001). But we take no extreme theoretical stands here and see little disagreement on the circumscribed and well-replicated findings that we import into our analysis. And, in view of past borrowing practices in international relations theory (Waltz 1979), we suspect that future historians of ideas will find it curious if international relations theorists should now prove choosier about feeder disciplines than microeconomists who have already made extensive use of many of the findings we highlight (Rabin 1998; Camerer 2003; Fehr, Fischbacher, and Kosfeld 2005).

1 REALISM

Thanks partly to Jervis (1976) and partly to the high costs associated with miscalculations over war and peace issues, psychological approaches have made greater inroads into realist thinking than in the other major international relations traditions. Often these works are implicit in their use of psychology, relying on an unspecified notion of "perceptions" to fill in gaps in realist thinking—for example, Walt's transformation (1987) of balance-of-power theory into balance-of-threat theory or Christensen and Snyder's efforts (1990) using perceptions of the offense–defense balance to explain when states tie themselves too closely to the fate of other states as opposed to when they fail to do enough to assist others in the international system.

A recent attempt to marry explicit psychological theorizing with realist theory is Taliaferro (2004), who draws heavily on prospect theory to explain why great powers often initiate risky ventures in peripheral areas and persist even as prospects for victory dim and costs escalate.

Prospect theory, developed by Kahneman and Tversky (1979; 2000) and their collaborators, shows that individuals make decisions under risk differently depending on whether they confront prospective gains or losses, and that individuals are much more risk acceptant when faced with losses and risk averse in the domain of gains. Problems that are logically equivalent but framed differently (for example, number of lives saved versus numbers lost) are treated sharply differently by respondents. Experimental evidence shows that prospective losses hurt more than gains gratify by roughly two to one, and much more than that when the endowments are charged with moral and emotional symbolism (McGraw, Tetlock, and Kristel 2003).

Behavioral economists (e.g. Rabin 1998; Thaler 2000; Camerer 2003) have embraced prospect theory's findings to reshape their field. Not so political scientists, even though, as McDermott (1998; 2004) notes, the theory is based not on personality predispositions but on situationally activated response tendencies, which should appeal to structural theorists in international relations. Indeed, recent work has shown that people think about costs and benefits with different parts of their brain, rather than making a single calculation as utility theorists would assume (Cowen 2006), thus providing a neurological substrate for prospect theory and underscoring how far certain lines of reductionist inquiry can be taken.

Applications of prospect theory to international relations have grown (e.g. Levy 1992; Farnham 1994; McDermott 1998; 2004; Taliaferro 2004; Mercer 2005), although skeptics have stressed the difficulty of specifying in a nontautological fashion decision-makers' reference points and their calculations of gains and losses (Tetlock 1999b). Taliaferro (2004) focuses on aversion to losses in states' relative power, international status, or prestige as driving the risky behavior, thereby combining prospect theory's emphasis on framing with defensive realism's emphasis on relative power, and ducking the complexities of gauging the role of domestic politics in shaping how leaders frame problems as prospective gains or losses.

Prospect theory applies directly to a central debate within realism—that between the defensive realists (Waltz 1979) and the offensive realists (Mearsheimer 2001). Waltz and his followers have argued that states seek to maximize their security in an anarchic state system that requires them to practice balance-of-power politics. Their main goal is to assure their survival, which requires accruing power by either building military might or finding allies, but states can become satisfied with the status quo if they feel sufficiently powerful vis-à-vis other states. For Mearsheimer, no power advantage can ever be big enough, and thus states can be modeled as power maximizers pursuing hegemonic aspirations. In either case, states have to form accurate representations of the world and respond to the actions of other powers in a timely manner, which makes them deeply suspicious and receptive to worse-case assumptions about the motives of other states in the system.

Waltzian states can become satisfied with their position in the system. Such states will be loss averse and disinclined to pursue expansionist policies that might trigger counterbalancing by other states. In Mearsheimer's world, states are never satisfied short of hegemony. Prospect theory would suggest that Waltz is more correct when states are faced with prospective gains; Mearsheimer when states are facing losses. The United States was reluctant to suffer casualties in interventions abroad in the 1990s (Haiti, Somalia, Bosnia, Kosovo) as it sat confidently atop the international system, and acted in a highly risk-averse manner, as Waltz would predict. But, in the wake of the attacks of 11 September, it became more willing to take risks. To invoke much more extreme examples, in which regime type and leader personalities also play powerful roles, Nazi Germany in 1939 and Imperial Japan in 1941 were willing to roll the dice in environments in which they had either incurred steep losses or faced the prospect of such losses and pursued high-risk efforts to reverse or avoid those fates, as Mearsheimer would predict. Rather than seeing the feud within realism as one that can be definitively resolved in favor of one approach or another, psychology helps us to reconnoiter boundary conditions: to appreciate that defensive realism is more likely to apply when decision-makers frame problems as potential gains, and offensive realism is more likely to apply when states confront potential losses.

Prospect theory and associated work on the endowment effect (the increase in value one places on something once one possesses it) also explains a major difference between deterrence and compellence—namely, that it is far more difficult to induce a state to give up something that it already possesses than to prevent it from taking something that it does not possess (Schelling 1967). The Clinton administration should have paid heed in the 1990s. Bosnia was not part of Serbia, and Slobodan Milošević was willing to negotiate a settlement over something he did not possess in 1995. Believing the lesson from that case was that he could be shaken by a brief demonstration of force, the Clinton administration thought in 1999 that it would not take much to get him to cease and desist in Kosovo. But Kosovo was part of Serbia, and Milosevic was willing to take much higher risks to keep something in his possession than he had been to acquire new territory (Chollet and Goldgeier 2002). Similarly, the United States was willing to use force when the North Koreans attacked the South in 1950 in order to ensure the viability of containment but was not willing to roll-back Communism to liberate Hungary in 1956. Psychologists will predict that deterrence is roughly twice as easy as compellence in analogous situations—with two key exceptions: (1) when the target state feels a deep emotional attachment to the territory in question, in which case compellence becomes many orders of magnitude more difficult than deterrence; and (2) when the target state has not internalized the territory as part of its self-definition (its "endowment"), in which case compellence may not be appreciably more difficult than deterrence.

Given the widespread influence of prospect theory in economics, it is curious that the theory has not had comparable impact in political science, particularly in international relations. Mercer (2005) has noted that of the 2,000 most recent citations to Kahneman and Tversky's article (1979) on prospect theory, half come from economics and related fields, one-third from psychology, and only one-twentieth from political science; the article received a mere eight citations in the *American Political Science Review* between 1985 and 2003. Mercer (2005, 18) reasons that choices made by decision-makers in the world of international relations are not the same as choices between gambles in the lab, but he also concludes that, given how well the theory has been utilized in economics, "it seems likely that the resistance is to the discipline of psychology rather than to problems unique to prospect theory."

2 INSTITUTIONALISM

The institutionalist challenge arose in response to the realists' pessimistic appraisal of the prospects for cooperation in an anarchic international system. The micro-economic variant of institutionalism articulated by Keohane (1984) accepted that the international system is anarchic and populated by unitary, egoistic actors, but argued that those actors can create institutional frameworks that, by lowering their fear of being exploited by free riders, permit them to secure the gains obtainable through cooperation.

In the neoliberal variant of the institutionalist model, when actors recognize that they confront a repeated play situation and that the transaction costs for continuing to improvise ad hoc solutions are high, they quite rationally enter into binding compacts that can persist despite shifting balances of power among member states. Psychology has something to say about when and why states seek to create institutions in the first place, when and why states abide by institutional norms and principles, and whether and when institutions can over time transform how decision-makers view their own state's interests.

A key psychological element in the formation of institutions is transparency, which includes both the ability to discern basic facts and the ability to draw sound causal inferences. Epistemic communities (Haas 1997) can both advance and re-flect causal transparency. At one end of the transparency continuum are policies shaped by epistemic communities possessing great authority and prestige by virtue of their scientific achievements in teasing apart cause–effect relationships. This is especially likely in domains where investigators can test theoretical hypotheses in controlled and replicable experiments (and there is minimal reliance on what

Tetlock and Belkin (1996) call speculative counterfactual control groups). Examples include the near consensus among biomedical specialists on the right strategies (or methods of developing strategies) for coping with transnational epidemics, among climatologists on the effect of chlorofluorocarbons (CFCs) on the ozone layer of the atmosphere, or among physicists and engineers on the prerequisites for nuclear proliferation. Political elites in the advanced countries are usually disinclined to question advice emanating from these communities on their issues of expertise.

But this deference does not hold in those policy domains in which the epistemic communities are either deeply divided or relatively undeveloped, as was the case with respect to the sources, scope, pace, and effects of global warming until recently. But, as evidence mounts, and fears that a tipping point may be closer than previously recognized, just as has been the case in the policy domains mentioned above, even political elites who dislike regulation are becoming less willing to dismiss scientists who present evidence that global warming requires coordinated international action (Hansen 2006).

Realists often argue that institutions typically come about because the most powerful state in the system decides to create them as a means of pursuing its interests with greater legitimacy and/or efficiency. But we should also expect that, for psychological reasons, institutions are more likely to be created in those domains where there is a consensus among experts with epistemic authority, and that in the absence of such consensus, political obstacles to the formation of international institutions will often be insurmountable.

Once institutions are created, questions arise about why states comply with the demands of the institutions and whether over time institutions can transform how decision-makers view their state's interests (Simmons 1998). Here we think it useful to posit a social influence continuum that runs from compliance to internalization (Kelman 1958). At the compliance end, decision-makers abide by the rules of the institution based purely on utilitarian calculations of rewards and punishment. Institutions in which compliance is the likely source of rule-following include military alliances formed to counter direct threats and the World Trade Organization, which lowers trade barriers for members and provides sanctioning mechanisms to punish norm and rule violators.

Toward the middle of the continuum are decision-makers who do what is expected of them because they seek to establish particular social identities in the eyes of domestic or international audiences whose opinion they value, and because they are unwilling to bear the reputation costs of defecting. This form of social influence—sometimes called identification by social psychologists—should be less context specific than mere compliance. Identification should persist even when it is materially inconvenient, but it still falls short of full-fledged internalization because it will not persist when the policy ceases to serve its function of enhancing a desired social identity. Examples include states with dubious civil liberties practices or suspect environmental records signing human rights or environmental agreements in order to be part of the "civilized" international community—decisions that can produce normative entanglements with real political consequences (for example, the 1975 Helsinki Accords basket three provisions for protecting human rights that the Soviet Union and its Warsaw Pact allies signed).

As we continue toward the internalization end of the continuum, we find states doing the right thing for what they perceive to be the right reasons. The calculation is no longer utilitarian but guided by moral, religious, or ideological ideals—in other words, decision-makers are following a logic of appropriate action rather than the logic of consequential action (March and Olsen 1998). The humanitarian assistance efforts of Scandinavian countries come to mind here.

Psychology can help delineate the conditions under which decision-makers are likely to go from compliance to internalization. Cognitive dissonance and self-perception research using forced-compliance paradigms suggest that decision-makers are especially likely to internalize attitudes consistent with their behavior when they believe they had some elements of free choice (see Bem 1967; Larson 1985). Most psychologists would agree that political actors (psychopaths excluded) are likely to internalize the norms of fair play implicit in international institutions, and these norms can become autonomous from the original interest-based actions. This internalization process should be especially reliable in democracies, in which leaders must justify departures from widely held norms of fair play to their constituents.

Rational choice approaches to norm enforcement stress the problem of free-riding; in the absence of a sovereign, no single party wants to incur the costs of punishing norm violators, so defectors escape sanction (Coleman 1990). A growing body of work in experimental social psychology and microeconomics has revealed, however, that people are often willing to make substantial sacrifices to punish cheaters—and those who fail to punish cheaters (Fehr and Schmidt 1999)—and that this self-sacrificial behavior is driven, in part, by moralistic anger (desire for retribution) aimed at those who violate shared foundational values (Tetlock et al. 2007). Indeed, brain-imaging studies have shown that people derive pleasure from inflicting pain on norm violators (Fehr, Fischbacher, and Kosfeld 2005). From this standpoint, international institutions built on shared values of distributive and procedural justice should be able to perpetuate themselves in the absence of strong central authority as long as members perceive the specific norms and norm-enforcement agencies to be anchored in those shared values. Psychology does not tell us this will be easy; there will be many occasions when the human tendency to engage in motivated reasoning causes participants to "see" evidence of wrong-doing that the alleged wrong-doers do not see (Kunda 1999) and delicate mediational and perspective-taking exercises will be required (Rouhana and Kelman 1994). Nonetheless, putting the complexities of establishing and maintaining legitimacy to the side, the more egregious the normative transgression, the more willing people will be to punish both transgressors and those who fail to punish transgressors (Axelrod 1984; Coleman 1990; Crawford 2000).

3 CONSTRUCTIVISM

For constructivists, actors often make decisions not using the logic of consequential action, the cost–benefit analyses of realists and institutionalists, but rather using the logic of obligatory action, the normative guidelines for legitimating conduct that are specified by a given social order that is itself the emergent byproduct of interactions among actors in the system (Wendt 1999). Examples of norm-following logics include the demise of dueling and slave trading (Mueller 1989); the rise of human rights norms, including the sensitivity to racism (Risse, Ropp, and Sikkink 1999); the nonuse of weapons of mass destruction and other constraints on the conduct of war (Legro 1995; Price 1997; Tannenwald 1999); and the changing purpose of military intervention over time (Finnemore 2003).

From a constructivist perspective, every policy debate carries a social-identity subtext: What kind of people are we, the advocates of this policy, claiming to be—and what kind of people do they, the opponents of this policy, portray us to be? In the case of the ferocious debate over the wisdom of invading Iraq in 2003, many advocates laid claim to the following identities: principled enforcers of international law, prudent defenders of national interests, and even heroic liberators of the Middle East. By contrast, opponents depicted proponents as neocolonialists interested only in oil and geopolitical leverage or, somewhat more charitably, as irrational and overly emotional Americans whose judgment has been clouded by the trauma of 11 September. These identity claims were, of course, just the initial moves: Each side would do its best—in response to events and moves of the other side—to bolster its own credibility and dismantle the other side's credibility.

From a psychological perspective, debates over the "true motives" underlying policies are generally rather fruitless: People have, at best, a shaky introspective grasp of the factors driving their own behavior—and there is not much reason for supposing that people are better at divining the true drivers of the behavior of others (Bargh and Williams 2006).

In short, psychology is likely to be unhelpful in determining which masters of political spin are closer to the "truth." The competition for the social-identity high ground in debates will be with us into the indefinite future. Psychology can, however, be helpful in determining which masters of political spin are more likely to prevail in particular battles for the identity high ground. For instance, psychological research on the implicit theories of leadership suggests that, *ceteris paribus*, people associate leadership with firmly upholding principles and staying the course more than they do with flexibility and midcourse corrections (Staw 1980; Tetlock 1999a), which gave George W. Bush an advantage in his 2004 re-election campaign against John Kerry.

Another realm in which psychology can help to determine who has the rhetorical advantage is that of trade-off reasoning. There is a profound disjuncture between constructivism and the more rationalist strands of international relations theory (realism and institutionalism) in how they approach trade-off reasoning (Katzenstein, Keohane, and Krasner 1998; Ruggie 1998). Realists and institutionalists expect states rationally to measure costs and benefits. By contrast, there are large classes of issues for which constructivists should expect trade-off reasoning to be extremely difficult and politically toxic. Indeed, the very willingness to consider certain categories of trade-offs is taken as a sign in many political cultures that one is not adequately committed to core cultural values and identities.

A key issue in many identity contests is how people "frame" the various types of trade-offs underlying policy options: routine, taboo, and tragic. A routine trade-off is the type of reasoning one uses when shopping and comparing the relative importance of secular values. A trade-off is taboo if it pits a secular value such as money against a sacred value such as protection of human rights or ecosystems—a value that members in good standing of moral communities are supposed to treat as beyond monetization. Finally, a trade-off is tragic if it pits two sacred values against each other—for example, protection of endangered species against protection of indigenous cultures (Tetlock 2003).

Decision-makers caught making taboo trade-offs are often ostracized by their moral communities, and thus they go to great lengths to portray their decision process as free of any taint of taboo trade-offs; their adversaries meanwhile attempt to convince key constituencies that the boundaries of the thinkable have been breached. We can observe this dynamic process at work in debates as disparate as those over Israeli withdrawal from parts of the West Bank and the sacred city of Jerusalem, Pakistani and Indian willingness to compromise over Kashmir, or, in the United States, the solvency of Social Security or Medicare or the wisdom of drilling in the Arctic National Wildlife Refuge in Alaska.

As a general psychological proposition, adversaries should be able to block compromise whenever they can plausibly portray the policy they oppose as implicating taboo trade-offs that degrade sacred values by mixing them with secular values of money, comfort, and convenience. Those in the position of defending policies that opponents characterize as involving taboo trade-offs must work hard to claim the social identities of flexible and reasonable while avoiding the identities of immoral and unprincipled. Those in the position of opposing these policies must work hard to claim the social identities of resolute and principled while avoiding the identities of dogmatic and fanatical. All other things being equal, the advantage falls to the opponents of taboo trade-offs. The exceptions arise when political leaders with unusually solid credentials as defenders of the sacred value decisively change sides—as in the resolute anticommunist President Richard Nixon establishing relations with China (and abandoning a trusted ally, Taiwan) or the Israeli hardline Prime Minister Ariel Sharon withdrawing from Gaza.

From a realist or institutionalist standpoint, resistance to making taboo trade-offs (among the mass public and sometimes among policy elites as well) is an unwelcome complication. Instead of adjusting in a timely fashion to the geopolitical or economic realities of the moment—for example, compromising on security policy or agricultural price supports—states may appear to outsiders to be displaying an ostrich-like obliviousness to trade-offs. But one theorist's bothersome anomaly can be another theorist's productive obsession.

4 THE NEED FOR A FOURTH PERSPECTIVE: REFLEXIVISM (THEORIZING ABOUT THE THEORISTS)

Seizing on an enigmatic epigram from the classical Greek poet Archilocus, Isaiah Berlin (1953) divided thinkers into two admittedly crude categories: the hedgehogs who know one big thing and the foxes who know many things. Crossing that classification with our threefold discussion of international relations theorists yields a six-category system: hedgehog and fox realists, institutionalists, and constructivists.

We suspect that few international relations scholars qualify as true hedgehogs—so wedded to their favorite framework that they eschew anything that smacks of foxlike opportunism or borrowing from other frameworks. From a psychological perspective, cognitive styles are a matter of degree, not kind (Kruglanski 1996; Suedfeld and Tetlock 2001). Some of us are closer to the ideal-type hedgehog, faithful to our vision, and some of us closer to the ideal-type fox, prepared to improvise whatever patchwork quilt of ideas best fits the peculiarities of the current situation. And there is good reason to suppose that, just as cognitive stylistic orientations shape how people think in other domains, so they also influence professional observers of world politics.

Tetlock (2005) underscores just how applicable psychological research on cognitive styles and biases is to the judgments that professional observers make of possible pasts and futures in world politics. Drawing on a sample of almost 300, mostly Ph.D.-level professionals, he assessed the following variables: (*a*) theoretical allegiances to various schools of thought in social science (including realism and institutionalism); (*b*) cognitive styles (including the hedgehog–fox index that gauged the value that respondents placed on parsimony, comprehensiveness, and explanatory closure); (*c*) plausibility judgments of historical counterfactuals that undercut, reinforced, or were irrelevant to theoretical allegiances; (*d*) probability judgments of possible futures conditional on their theoretical understanding of the underlying forces at work being correct or conditional on alternative views being correct; (*e*) willingness to change one's mind in a roughly Bayesian fashion in response to learning that relatively expected or unexpected events either did or did not transpire.

Turning first to judgments of historical counterfactuals, we find evidence for some basic cognitive processes in theoretical reasoning about international relations. Cognitive theory leads us to expect that, confronted by the quirkily complex, path-dependent meanderings of history (Pierson 2004), even experts need to resort to simplifying strategies. One obvious strategy is to rely on one's causal schemata to impose order by portraying what we all know did happen as the inevitable, or at least highly probable, result of the operation of one's favorite covering laws on well-defined antecedent conditions (such as a bipolar or multipolar world)—in the process ruling out large classes of alternative outcomes (historical counterfactuals) as impossible, or at least highly improbable. Many experts do exactly that. For instance, experts sympathetic to structural realism and to nuclear-deterrence theory are more likely to dismiss dissonant counterfactual scenarios that imply that the cold war could easily have become a hot war. In their view, structural realism and nuclear-deterrence theories are well positioned to explain the general pattern of observed outcomes: the bipolar stability of the cold war and the reluctance of the superpowers to provoke each other in regional contests.

This fit provides support for the theory only insofar as we are prepared to grant that, if we could rerun the history of the cold war hundreds of times, each time manipulating theoretically trivial background conditions such as the location of American and Soviet ships during the Cuban missile crisis, we would get pretty much the same pattern of outcomes. Perhaps the theoretically committed observers are right and this proposition is true, but no one has devised the time machinery necessary for checking on the veridicality of such claims, either in the affirmative (yes, history would have come back on to roughly the same trajectory) or in the negative (no, history would have diverged dramatically from what we know as international reality).

Experts vary in the degree to which they find parsimony attractive—and ambiguity aversive (hedgehogs more so than foxes in both cases). It follows that hedgehogs should be especially inclined to dismiss historical counterfactuals that mess up their causal models of the past, whatever those models might be. Again, the prediction holds. For instance, structural realists with hedgehog epistemological preferences are more likely than their fox colleagues to dismiss counterfactuals that imply that the First World War (some kind of major war among European powers in the early twentieth century) could easily have been averted by manipulating theoretically trivial antecedent conditions, such as whether Archduke Franz Ferdinand's carriage driver had not made a fateful wrong turn after the initial assassination attempt had failed.

We suspect much the same would be true for institutionalist hedgehogs and foxes confronted by counterfactuals that imply the European Union could easily have never emerged or could have come undone. We are less confident about constructivists, because the symbolic interactionist fluidity of much of their theorizing would seem more compatible with accepting indeterminacy in historical outcomes. But it would be worth checking whether hedgehog versus fox constructivists differ markedly in their openness to the possibility that basic features of the normative landscape of world politics today could easily have been undone by tweaking coincidences from the past. For instance, would the nuclear taboo be as taboo as it is if the United States had used such weapons in Korea, as Dwight Eisenhower seriously considered?

The term "theory" carries deterministic connotations: a framework that allows us to deduce a relatively immutable chain of causality from first premises. It is, therefore, discomfiting to contemplate how much international relations theory depends on contingency, on speculative counterfactual judgments of what was or was not once historically possible—and on what, looking forward, might now be possible. What should happen to our confidence in international relations theories if it turns out that many aspects of the international landscape that they are well positioned to explain could easily have worked out otherwise, but for minor accidents of personalities and timing? Or, more modestly, what should happen to our confidence in these theories if it turns out that we just do not know whether these supposedly stable aspects of the landscape really are stable?

Shifting from experts' judgments of possible pasts to possible futures, we can derive a strikingly similar series of predictions from cognitive theory. For instance, we should expect the greater hedgehog aversion to ambiguity to manifest itself in imposing greater theoretical order on the long-range future than foxes are inclined to impose (or than, for that matter, may be justified given the inherent unpredictability of politics). Looking at a broad range of forecasts, Tetlock found evidence that hedgehog forecasters were indeed systematically more overconfident than were foxes in their longer-range predictions. Perhaps most serious, Tetlock also found that hedgehog forecasters were less inclined to acknowledge mistakes and more inclined to resist changing their minds as much as they should according to Bayesian benchmarks of belief updating. Tetlock documents in detail the dissonance-reduction strategies that experts—especially hedgehogs making longer-range forecasts—tended to invoke when the relatively unexpected happened. For instance, experts who were most surprised by the demise of the Soviet Union were also most inclined to embrace the close-call counterfactual defense that the disintegration of the Soviet state was the result of the odd or reckless (from an orthodox Communist point of view) liberalization policies pursued by Mikhail

Gorbachev—and that the disintegration of the state could have been prevented even as late as the coup attempt of August 1991 (if the coup plotters had been more resolute and less intoxicated, they just might have prevailed in reinstalling the old regime).

Some international theorists may believe it is inappropriate to use psychological theory to explain the behavior of theorists—bordering on the *ad hominem*. But from a cognitive perspective, theorists are human beings attempting to make sense of a bizarrely complicated world that forces each and every one of us to rely on speculative counterfactual thought experiments to infer causality. Under such conditions, we have no alternative but to resort to simplifying strategies. Psychology can shed light on what types of strategies we use—and on whether we may be at risk of overusing them, as arguably many of the hedgehogs in the Tetlock sample seem to do.

5 THE INFLUENCE OF THE REAL WORLD—AND EFFORTS TO INFLUENCE IT

Like other international relations theorists, those drawing heavily on psychological approaches have often been influenced by the central issues of contemporary international politics. During the cold war, for example, policy-makers and scholars alike most feared the miscalculation that might result in nuclear conflagration, particularly after the Cuban Missile Crisis, when President Kennedy opined that the chances of a nuclear exchange had been between one in three and even. The Nixon–Kissinger détente policy was predicated on the notion that the US–Soviet competition had to be bounded in some way so that conflicts did not escalate even while each side vied for advantage vis-à-vis the other.

Given the dangers, those using psychology to understand international relations during the cold war focused their attention on the US–Soviet relationship and particularly on crisis bargaining (e.g. Snyder and Diesing 1978; Lebow 1981; George 1983; Goldgeier 1994). Crises lend themselves to psychological approaches quite well. Decision-makers are pressed for time, they are under tremendous stress, and they have to sort through voluminous and ambiguous information. They are prone to using analogies that might or might not be appropriate (Khong 1992), to falling prey to wishful thinking about how things might turn out, and to discounting information that does not fit with their preconceptions of the adversary (Larson 1985). During the cold war, leaders often found themselves having to make decisions that carried great risks, both to their political futures and to their country's survival. And so many who studied cold war decision-making used psychological approaches, particularly in explaining why crises over Korea and Taiwan, Cuba, and the Middle East turned out the way they did.

Among the most influential scholars of the cold war period, Alexander George sought to use theory to inform and improve policy on a range of topics such as coercive diplomacy (1971), deterrence (with Smoke 1974), and the organization of presidential advisory systems (1980). His work on the most important topics of the cold war was infused with an effort to understand how leaders' belief systems shaped their approach to politics, how value trade-offs got resolved psychologically, and the reasons why distortions were introduced into the policy process. His pioneering work on qualitative methods that continued into the post-cold war era (George and Bennett 2005) was never an end in itself but rather a means by which one could use the careful study of historical examples to provide guidance in current and future policy problems of a similar nature.

As the cold war ended, and Yugoslavia erupted in violence and the Soviet Union broke apart along ethnic lines, there was an increasing emphasis on identity issues, and thus a resurgence of work utilizing social identity theory and work on in-groups and out-groups (Mercer 1995; Goldgeier 1997). How do individuals learn to distinguish themselves as part of a group that is dissimilar to another, even in cases where to outsiders there is hardly any basis for understanding why deep divisions should occur?

During the cold war, we discussed how best to convey credible commitments in order to ensure effective deterrence, and the psychological problems included ensuring that signals were sent and received clearly and that decision-makers had sufficient reputations to be believed by their audience. After 11 September, the question is whether suicide bombers can be deterred, with some arguing they are the ultimate irrational actors, whereas other scholars are suggesting that deterrence is possible even with respect to terrorists, and thus many of the old theories of deterrence developed during the cold war remain relevant (Lebovic 2006).

Finally, let us consider the decision to go to war in Iraq in the context of psychological theories of error and bias. Over the past three decades, we have learned a lot in experimental social psychology and behavioral economics about the social and market forces that can either amplify or attenuate deviations from rationality. Many experimental researchers assume that the root cause of error and bias is widespread over-reliance on simple, easy-to-execute heuristics that give people unjustifiable confidence in their judgments and decisions. If correct, then social, political, and economic systems that encourage actors to engage in more self-critical and reflective forms of information processing should have the net effect of attenuating bias. Conversely, social, political, and economic systems that encourage mindless conformity, defensiveness, and the perpetuation of shared misconceptions should have the net effect of amplifying bias.

Competitive market pressures can also reduce error and bias. Certain classes of error and biases—especially breakdowns in consistency and transitivity produced by reliance on simple (lexicographic) decision rules—can be corrected when the choice process moves into open and transparent market settings that provide for repeated play, interaction with attentive competitors, and rapid, unequivocal feedback on the consequences of one's choices (Kagel and Roth 1995; Camerer and Hogarth 1999).

It is now possible to identify an ideal set of conditions under which the error-and-bias portrait of the decision-maker should be of minimal predictive usefulness. The inner advisory group deliberates under the norms of multiple advocacy, is accountable to the institutions of a self-correcting democratic polity, and is making decisions in a policy domain in which critical information is readily available. Mistakes are quickly and publicly punished.

Although the full story of the 2003 Bush administration's decision to go to war in Iraq remains to be told, we know enough to suspect that the conditions for eliminating error and bias were not present. Complaints have abounded, particularly from senior officials at the State Department (Wilkerson 2006), that a "cabal" led by Vice-President Dick Cheney and Secretary of Defense Donald Rumsfeld overrode any objections to the rosy scenarios they painted regarding the war and its subsequent occupation. The US Congress barely debated the authorization to use force, and failed to ask the tough questions that mark ideal domestic accountability networks. And, in terms of available information, we now know that the core of Secretary of State Colin Powell's presentation to the United Nations regarding the intelligence information on weapons of mass destruction programs was hardly robust in its definitiveness. It was nowhere near the "slam dunk" described to the president by CIA director George Tenet (Woodward 2004), and as the story is now being told, was based on evidence provided by a mentally unstable Iraqi engineer, codenamed Curveball. In the war's aftermath, mistakes were neither quickly nor publicly punished, even as casualties tragically mounted, as the president effectively painted his critics as soft on terror.

6 Closing Remarks: Beyond Reductionism

Psychological explanations work best when seamlessly integrated into more macro-organizational, societal, economic, and systemic approaches to international relations. Properly integrated, psychological explanations fill logical holes in existing theoretical coverage and offer salutary reminders of the dangers of passionate hedgehog-style theoretical commitments and the benefits of detached foxlike eclecticism. Parsimony is not a trump value: Theories should be as simple as possible, but no simpler.

REFERENCES

AXELROD, R. M. 1984. *The Evolution of Cooperation*. New York: Basic Books.

BARGH, J. A., and WILLIAMS, E. L. 2006. The automacity of social life. *Current Directions in Psychological Science*, 15: 94–8.

BEM, D. 1967. Self-perception: an alternative interpretation of cognitive dissonance phenomenon. *Psychological Review*, 74: 183–200.

BERLIN, I. 1953. *The Hedgehog and the Fox: An Essay on Tolstoy's View of History*. New York: Simon and Schuster.

CAMERER, C. F. 2003. *Behavioral Game Theory: Experiments in Strategic Interaction*. Princeton, NJ: Princeton University Press.

—— and HOGARTH, R. M. 1999. The effects of financial incentives in experiments: a review and capital-labor-production framework. *Journal of Risk and Uncertainty*, 19: 1–3, 7–42.

CHOLLET, D., and GOLDGEIER, J. 2002. The scholarship of decision-making: do we know how we decide? Pp. 153–80 in *Foreign Policy Decision-Making (Revisited)*, Richard C. Snyder et al. New York: Palgrave.

CHRISTENSEN, T. J., and SNYDER, J. 1990. Chain gangs and passed bucks: predicting alliance patterns in multipolarity. *International Organization*, 44: 137–68.

COLEMAN, J. S. 1990. *Foundations of Social Theory*. Cambridge, Mass.: Belknap Press.

COWEN, T. 2006. Enter the neuro-economists: why do investors do what they do. *New York Times*, 20 Apr.: C3.

CRAWFORD, N. C. 2000. The passion of world politics: propositions on emotion and emotional relationships. *International Security*, 24: 116–56.

FARNHAM, B. R. 1994. *Avoiding Losses/Taking Risks: Prospect Theory and International Conflict*. Ann Arbor: University of Michigan Press.

FEHR, E., FISCHBACHER, U., and KOSFELD, M. 2005. Neuroeconomic foundations of trust and social preferences. *American Economic Review*, 95: 346–51.

—— and SCHMIDT, K. 1999. A theory of fairness, competition, and cooperation. *Quarterly Journal of Economics*, 114: 817–68.

FINNEMORE, M. 2003. *The Purpose of Intervention: Changing Beliefs about the Use of Force*. Ithaca, NY: Cornell University Press.

GEORGE, A. L. 1971. *Limits of Coercive Diplomacy*. New York: Little, Brown.

—— 1980. *Presidential Decisionmaking in Foreign Policy: The Effective Use of Information and Advice*. Boulder, Colo.: Westview.

—— 1983. *Managing US–Soviet Rivalry: Problems of Crisis Prevention*. Boulder, Colo.: Westview.

—— and BENNETT, A. 2005. *Case Studies and Theory Development in the Social Sciences*. Cambridge, Mass.: MIT Press.

—— and SMOKE, R. 1974. *Deterrence in American Foreign Policy*. New York: Columbia University Press.

GIGERENZER, G., and GOLDSTEIN, D. G. 1996. Reasoning the fast and frugal way: models of bounded rationality. *Psychological Review*, 103: 650–69.

—— and SELTEN, R. (eds.) 2001. *Bounded Rationality: The Adaptive Toolbox*. Cambridge, Mass.: MIT Press.

GOLDGEIER, J. M. 1994. *Leadership Style and Soviet Foreign Policy: Stalin, Khrushchev, Brezhnev, Gorbachev*. Baltimore: Johns Hopkins University Press.

—— 1997. Psychology and security. *Security Studies*, 6: 137–66.

—— and TETLOCK, P. E. 2001. Psychology and international relations theory. *Annual Review of Political Science*, 4: 67–92.

HANSEN, J. 2006. The threat to the planet. *New York Review of Books*, 53: 12–16.

HAAS, P. M. (ed.) 1997. *Knowledge, Power and International Policy Coordination*. Columbia: University of South Carolina Press.

JERVIS, R. 1976. *Perception and Misperception in International Politics*. Princeton, NJ: Princeton University Press.

KAGEL, J. H., and ROTH, A. E. 1995. *The Handbook of Experimental Economics*. Princeton, NJ: Princeton University Press.

KAHNEMAN, D., and TVERSKY, A. 1979. Prospect theory: an analysis of decision under risk. *Econometrica*, 47: 263–91.

—— —— (eds.) 2000. *Choices, Values, and Frames*. New York: Cambridge University Press.

KATZENSTEIN, P. J., KEOHANE, R. O., and KRASNER, S. D. 1998. International organization and the study of world politics. *International Organization*, 52: 645–85.

KELMAN, H. C. 1958. Compliance, identification, and internalization: three processes of attitude change. *Journal of Conflict Resolution*, 2: 51–60.

—— and BLOOM, A. 1973. Assumptive frameworks in international politics. Pp. 261–95 in *Handbook of Political Psychology*, ed. J. Knutson. San Francisco: Jossey-Bass.

KEOHANE, R. O. 1984. *After Hegemony: Cooperation and Discord in the World Political Economy*. Princeton, NJ: Princeton University Press.

KHONG, Y. F. 1992. *Analogies at War: Korea, Munich, Dien Bien Phu and the Vietnam Decisions of 1965*. Princeton, NJ: Princeton University Press.

KRUGLANSKI, A. 1996. Motivated freezing of the mind: seizing and freezing. *Psychological Review*, 103: 263–83.

KUNDA, Z. 1999. *Social Cognition: Making Sense of People*. Cambridge, Mass.: MIT Press.

LARSON, D. W. 1985. *Origins of Containment*. Princeton, NJ: Princeton University Press.

LEBOVIC, J. 2006. *Deterring International Terrorism: US National Security Policy after 9/11*. New York: Routledge.

LEBOW, R. N. 1981. *Between Peace and War: The Nature of International Crisis*. Baltimore: Johns Hopkins University Press.

LEGRO, J. W. 1995. *Cooperation under Fire: Anglo-German Restraint during World War II*. Ithaca, NY: Cornell University Press.

LEVY, J. 1992. Prospect theory and international relations: theoretical applications and analytical problems. *Political Psychology*, 13: 283–310.

MARCH, J. G., and OLSEN, J. P. 1998. The institutional dynamics of international political orders. *International Organization*, 52: 943–70.

McDERMOTT, R. 1998. *Risk-taking in International Politics: Prospect Theory in American Foreign Policy*. Ann Arbor: University of Michigan Press.

—— 2004. Prospect theory in political science: gains and losses from the first decade. *Political Psychology*, 25: 289–312.

McGRAW, P., TETLOCK, P. E., and KRISTEL, O. 2003. The limits of fungibility: relational schemata and the value of things. *Journal of Consumer Research*, 30: 219–29.

MEARSHEIMER, J. J. 2001. *The Tragedy of Great Power Politics*. New York: Norton.

MERCER, J. 1995. Anarchy and identity. *International Organization*, 49: 229–52.

—— 2005. Prospect theory and political science. *Annual Review of Political Science*, 8: 1–21.

MISCHEL, W. 1999. Implications of person-situation interaction: getting over the field's borderline personality. *European Journal of Personality (special issue)*, 13: 455–61.

MUELLER, J. 1989. *Retreat from Doomsday: The Obsolescence of Major War*. New York: Basic Books.

PIERSON, P. 2004. *Politics in Time: History, Institution, and Social Analysis*. Princeton, NJ: Princeton University Press.

PRICE, R. 1997. *The Chemical Weapons Taboo*. Ithaca, NY: Cornell University Press.

RABIN, M. 1998. Psychology and economics. *Journal of Economic Literature*, 36: 11–46.

RISSE, T., ROPP, S. C., and SIKKINK, K. (eds.) 1999. *The Power of Human Rights: International Norms and Domestic Change*. New York: Cambridge University Press.

ROUHANA, N. N., and KELMAN, H. C. 1994. Non-official interaction processes in the resolution of international conflicts: promoting joint Israeli–Palestinian thinking through a continuing workshop. *Journal of Social Issues*, 50: 157–78.

RUGGIE, J. G. 1998. *Constructing the World Polity: Essays on International Institutionalization*. London: Routledge.

SCHELLING, T. C. 1967. *Arms and Influence*. New Haven, Conn.: Yale University Press.

SIMMONS, B. A. 1998. Compliance with international agreements. *Annual Review of Political Science*, 1: 75–93.

SNYDER, G. H., and DIESING, P. D. 1978. *Conflict among Nations: Bargaining, Decision Making, and System Structure in International Crises*. Princeton, NJ: Princeton University Press.

STAW, B. M. 1980. Rationality and justification in organizational life. Pp. 45–80 in *Research in Organizational Behavior*, vol. ii, ed. B. M. Staw and L. Cummings. Greenwich, Conn.: JAI Press.

SUEDFELD, P., and TETLOCK, P. E. 2001. Individual differences in information processing. Pp. 284–304 in *Blackwell International Handbook of Social Psychology: Intraindividual Processes*, vol. i, ed. A. Tesser and N. Schwartz. London: Blackwell.

TALIAFERRO, J. 2004. *Balancing Risks: Great Power Intervention in the Periphery*. Ithaca, NY: Cornell University Press.

TANNENWALD, N. 1999. The nuclear taboo: the United States and the normative basis of nuclear non-use. *International Organization*, 53: 433–68.

TETLOCK, P. E. 1999a. Theory-driven reasoning about possible pasts and probable futures: are we prisoners of our preconceptions? *American Journal of Political Science*, 43: 335–66.

—— 1999b. Prospecting for evidence for prospect theory. Review of R. McDermott, *Risk-taking in International Politics: Prospect Theory in American Foreign Policy. Contemporary Psychology*, 44: 399–401.

—— 2003. Thinking about the unthinkable: coping with secular encroachments on sacred values. *Trends in Cognitive Science*, 7: 320–4.

—— 2005. *Expert Political Judgment: How Good Is It? How Can We Know?* Princeton, NJ: Princeton University Press.

—— and BELKIN, A. (eds.) 1996. *Counterfactual Thought Experiments in World Politics*. Princeton, NJ: Princeton University Press.

TETLOCK, P. E., and GOLDGEIER, J. 2000. Human nature and world politics: cognition, influence, and identity. *International Journal of Psychology*, 35: 87–96.

——VISSER, P., SINGH, R., POLIFRONI, M., SCOTT, A., ELSON, B., MAZZOCCO, P., and RESCOBER, P. 2007. People as intuitive prosecutors: the impact of social-control motives on attributions of responsibility. *Journal of Experimental Social Psychology*, 43: 195–209.

THALER, R. H. 2000. From homo economicus to homo sapiens. *Journal of Economic Perspectives*, 14: 133–41.

WALT, S. M. 1987. *The Origins of Alliances*. Ithaca, NY: Cornell University Press.

WALTZ, K. N. 1959. *Man, the State and War*. New York: Columbia University Press.

——1979. *Theory of International Politics*. Reading, Mass.: Addison-Wesley.

WENDT, A. 1999. *Social Theory of International Politics*. New York: Cambridge University Press.

WILKERSON, L. 2006. Weighing the uniqueness of the Bush administration's national security decision-making process: boon or danger to American democracy? The New America Foundation, at www.thewashingtonnote.com.

WOODWARD, B. 2004. *Plan of Attack*. New York: Simon and Schuster.

CHAPTER 28

....

QUANTITATIVE APPROACHES

....

EDWARD D. MANSFIELD

JON C. PEVEHOUSE

OVER the past half-century, there has been a substantial rise in the amount of quantitative research conducted in the field of international relations. The range of issue areas covered in this research has also expanded. Whereas early statistical research in international relations focused primarily on international security—especially the causes and consequences of war—more recent work has addressed a remarkably wide array of topics and has shed considerable light on (as well as generated) some of the most heated debates in the field.

The purpose of this chapter is to survey quantitative research on international relations, tracking its development and assessing the contribution that this body of literature has made. We make no pretense of offering a comprehensive survey of this literature; nor do we attempt to explain particular statistical techniques. Rather, we aim to analyze how quantitative work has informed some key debates in the field of international relations.

1 WHY USE QUANTITATIVE TECHNIQUES TO STUDY INTERNATIONAL RELATIONS?

....

There are a variety of general reasons why researchers have relied on statistical techniques to study international relations (on these issues see, e.g., Bueno de

Mesquita 1985; Braumoeller and Sartori 2004). First, these techniques are especially useful when analyzing a large number of observations. Many key questions in international relations involve comparisons across the global system at different points in time; others involve comparisons across different regions or countries. Consequently, empirical research in international relations often entails the analysis of large data-sets. Secondly, scholars often wish to make generalizations about global affairs based on a set of cases. Statistical research facilitates these inferences about the broader population through the analysis of representative samples and the laws of probability.

Thirdly, various statistical techniques allow researchers to assess the direction and the strength of relationships. For the purposes of testing theories, it is obviously important to understand whether the key independent variable(s) specified by a theory covary with the dependent variable. Quantitative techniques can help researchers gauge the extent of such covariation. These techniques can also help address the directionality of causation between an independent variable and the dependent variable, ensuring that any observed effect of an independent variable on the dependent variables does not actually stem from the dependent variable's influence on the independent variable. Furthermore, these techniques can shed light on the magnitude of an independent variable's impact on the dependent variable, a very important issue that is often given short shrift. Fourthly, and related, certain quantitative methods are well suited to testing competing explanations of a given outcome. Multivariate models, for example, allow researchers to compare the effects of factors emphasized in competing theories. These models also allow researchers to account for the effects of variables that could be related to both the core independent variable(s) and the dependent variable, thereby reducing the likelihood of observing a spurious correlation between them.

Despite these and other advantages, however, quantitative methods also have well-known limitations. Critics have charged that the variables included in statistical models sometimes lack internal or external validity. They have argued that existing measures of some central concepts—such as political power, conflict, interests, and preferences—are crude at best and inaccurate at worst. Others contend that important variables in certain international relations theories—for example, norms or ideas—cannot be measured at all, thus rendering quantitative tests of these theories impossible. Critics also charge that quantitative tests in the field of international relations sometimes violate key statistical assumptions, thereby casting doubt on the results generated by these tests. Finally, various observers maintain that some quantitative studies are not firmly grounded in international relations theories, and that they focus too heavily on establishing whether variables are correlated without paying enough attention to the underlying causes of any such correlation.

Over time, researchers have paid increasing attention to many of these critiques, attempting to improve measurement techniques, conduct sensitivity analyses, and better link theory to statistical models. Moreover, while researchers should always be sensitive to measurement issues, these are not concerns relevant only to quantitative research. All empirical analysis, whether quantitative or qualitative, requires the operationalization and measurement of concepts and variables. One advantage of quantitative research is that judgments about measurement tend to be especially transparent and replicable. If a scholar disagrees with a coding or measurement scheme, he or she can readily replicate and adjust that scheme accordingly.

2 QUANTITATIVE RESEARCH ON INTERNATIONAL RELATIONS DURING THE COLD WAR

Quantitative research in the field of international relations has been characterized by a number of trends. First, most of the early quantitative work in the field focused on international security, largely as a result of the discipline's preoccupation with issues involving the cold war. More recently, quantitative research has covered a much broader array of topics, particularly those related to the international political economy and international institutions. Secondly, much of the initial quantitative literature was systemic in orientation: It treated states as unitary actors and paid little attention to domestic politics. Both of these trends began to change near the end of the cold war, an event that contributed to broadening the range of issues that have been analyzed using quantitative techniques.

Until about a half-century ago, quantitative research on international relations was virtually nonexistent. That changed with Karl Deutsch's pioneering work on integration and other topics (e.g. Deutsch et al. 1957) and with the advent of J. David Singer's Correlates of War (COW) Project. The latter research effort was launched in the early 1960s. Since then, it has spawned hundreds of quantitative studies of international relations. During the first few decades of its existence, the COW Project relied on relatively simple bivariate and multivariate techniques to uncover patterns in war, as well as other aspects of international security. The history of this project and its contributions to the study of international relations have been documented elsewhere, so we will not address these issues here (Vasquez 1987; Singer 1990). Nevertheless, it is worth noting that many of the studies we take up in this chapter rely on data generated by the COW Project.

Much of this research project focused on testing hypotheses drawn from realist theories of international relations (on realist theories, see Waltz 1979; Jervis 1999).

In keeping with this realist focus, quantitative research during the cold war was largely systemic in orientation and tended to treat states as unitary actors.[1] Within this literature, analyses of arms racing were particularly influential. Indeed, one of the pioneering quantitative works in the field of international relations addressed the link between arms races and war. In *Statistics of Deadly Quarrels*, Lewis Richardson (1960)—a meteorologist by training—attempted to model the circumstances under which countries engage in arms races that spiral out of control and the conditions under which countries grow weary of such competition, resulting in a peaceful resolution. Spurred by interest in the growing pace and intensity of the cold war arms race, scholars produced a sizeable body of statistical work that adapted Richardson's basic model to investigate military spending as well as more general patterns of conflict and cooperation among the major powers (Goldstein and Freeman 1990).

Many systemic theories argue that patterns of global outcomes are shaped by the structure of the international system and that variations in this structure occur when the global distribution of power changes. Owing in part to the influential work of Kenneth Waltz (1979), quantitative researchers often measure the global distribution of power in terms of polarity—that is, whether one (hegemonic or unipolar), two (bipolar), or more than two (multipolar) particularly powerful states exist. A large portion of the quantitative work on this issue has focused on resolving long-standing debates about whether polarity influences the outbreak of international war. However, quantitative studies have generated no consensus on either the strength or the nature of this relationship (Levy 1984; Hopf 1991; Mansfield 1994). In part, these disagreements stem from differences in how polarity is defined and measured, illustrating why it is important to pay careful attention to whether empirical results are sensitive to the measurement and operationalization of key variables.

Polarity, however, is not the only dimension of the system's structure. Another dimension is the concentration of power in the system, which is determined by the number of major powers and the relative inequality of power among these states (Singer, Bremer, and Stuckey 1972). Focusing on concentration rather than polarity has a number of advantages (Mansfield 1994), and various efforts have been made to assess the relationship between concentration and the outbreak of war. In a review of this literature, Randolph Siverson and Michael Sullivan (1983) suggest that a low level of concentration (that is, a more uniform distribution of power) is associated with more conflict. More recently, Edward Mansfield (1994) has found the relationship to have an inverted

---

[1] Of course, there were various exceptions to this tendency. For example, a large quantitative literature emerged on internal–external conflict linkages. Partially inspired by an interest in the diversionary theory of war, scholars attempted to determine whether domestic strife gave rise to international conflict and vice versa (Wilkenfeld 1972). The studies, however, found little evidence of this type of relationship.

U-shape: at both low and high levels of concentration, major-power war is least likely to occur. At intermediate levels of concentration, such wars occur most frequently.

In addition to the system's structure, realist theories have placed a heavy emphasis on political–military alliances. Numerous cold war-era quantitative studies attempted to link the creation, operation, cohesiveness, and dissolution of alliances to inter-state conflict. In one of the first studies of this sort, J. David Singer and Melvin Small (1968) concluded that the relationship between alliances and war was conditional on the time period analyzed—increases in the number of alliances correlated with peace in the nineteenth century, but with war in the twentieth century. Later research by Siverson and Sullivan (1983) found that the effects of alliances on war depend on whether the focus is on major or minor powers. In a review of research conducted in the COW Project, John Vasquez (1987) argues that alliances seem to be associated with war, but not causally. The latest wave of quantitative research on this topic has distinguished between different types of alliances. Brett Ashley Leeds (2003), for example, shows that whether the alliance agreement provides for the defense of members, increases an aggressive member's offensive capabilities, or guarantees neutrality in the event of hostilities influences whether it deters or encourages aggression. Defense pacts tend to inhibit conflict, whereas offensive and neutrality agreements tend to promote belligerence.

While this review is not meant to be exhaustive, it does suggest some features of the early quantitative literature: acceptance of the unitary actor assumption, an emphasis on structural theories, and a focus on security concerns. Moreover, in each of these areas of research, initial results yielded considerable debate. These disagreements led researchers to refine the measures and tests that were used, and to focus on the particular conditions under which a theory holds. In this way, quantitative analysis has advanced various theoretical debates in the field.

2.1 International Political Economy

While many quantitative studies during the cold war addressed security issues, a handful of studies began to analyze systemic theories of the international political economy. Part of that literature focused on testing hegemonic stability theory, which holds that the relatively liberal international economy that existed during much of the nineteenth century and after the Second World War is attributable to the power preponderance of Great Britain during the former era and the United States during the latter (Kindleberger 1973; Gilpin 1987).

In an effort to test this theory, a number of statistical studies have been conducted, but the results have been far from uniform. John Conybeare (1983), for example, evaluated the relationship between the international distribution of power and nominal tariff levels on manufactured goods in 1902 and in 1971, controlling for a host of economic, political, and military factors. He found little evidence that power relations affect national tariff levels, and therefore concluded that hegemonic stability theory does not provide an adequate explanation of trade policy. Similarly, Timothy McKeown (1991) conducted a time-series analysis of the relationship between variables associated with hegemony and the ratio of imports to national income for a set of advanced industrial states during the period from 1880 to 1989. Measuring the distribution of power using several variables, McKeown found only a modest influence of these measures on the ratio of imports to national income, leading him to share Conybeare's skepticism about the explanatory power of hegemony stability theory.

Other studies, however, have found more support for the view that hegemony affects the global trading system. For example, Robert Pahre (1999) distinguishes between periods of benevolent and malevolent hegemony. He finds that hegemony generally has a malign effect on the international political economy. In addition, hegemons having more foes than friends tend to be benevolent, but malevolent hegemony can induce cooperative behavior on the part of the remaining states in the international system.

Finally, Mansfield (1994) analyzes the effects of hegemony and the concentration of capabilities on the level of global trade as a percentage of total global production from 1850 to 1965. He finds that whether hegemony promotes global trade depends heavily on how it is defined and measured. Furthermore, there is a U-shaped relationship between the concentration of capabilities and global trade. The ratio of global trade to global production is highest when the level of concentration is both relatively high and relatively low, whereas this ratio is lowest when concentration is at an intermediate level.

In addition to analyzing the effects of hegemony, quantitative research on the international political economy during the cold war and its immediate aftermath also focused on the political economy of national security. One strand of research addressed the influence of political–military alliances on trade patterns. Central to the effects of alliances on trade are the efficiency gains from overseas commerce, which increase each trade partner's national income and can be used to augment each state's military power. Joanne Gowa (1994) argues that states can address the security implications of foreign commerce by trading more freely with their allies than with their (actual or potential) adversaries. To test these arguments, Gowa and Mansfield (1993; Gowa 1994) conducted a statistical analysis of the effects of alliances on trade flows between major powers during the twentieth century. They find strong evidence that allies trade more extensively than other states. A number of subsequent studies have largely confirmed this finding, while covering a wider range of countries and years, and using statistical techniques designed for data that are both cross-sectional and time series (Morrow, Siverson, and Tabares 1998; 1999; Gowa and Mansfield 2004).

A related strand of work centers on the influence of political–military conflict on trade. One set of studies focuses on the effects of political cooperation and conflict on bilateral trade flows. In two influential articles, Brian Pollins (1989*a*; 1989*b*) found that cooperative political relations significantly increased the flow of trade. A second set of studies considers the effects of political–military conflict on trade. Some research finds that wars significantly reduce trade, both globally and between combatants (Gowa 1994; Mansfield 1994). However, other studies have concluded that conflicts—a category that includes wars as well as other less intense political disputes—have little influence on trade patterns, since traders may anticipate conflict and adjust their overseas business relations accordingly (Morrow, Siverson, and Tabares 1998; 1999).

3 QUANTITATIVE RESEARCH ON INTERNATIONAL RELATIONS SINCE THE MID-1990S

Since the mid-1990s, there have been a number of dramatic changes in quantitative international relations research. First, it has grown more pervasive. A recent survey, for example, found that the portion of articles in the leading international relations journals that rely on statistical analysis rose from about 25 percent in the late 1970s to almost 45 percent by the late 1990s (Sprinz and Wolinsky-Nahmias 2004, 7). Secondly, this work has become increasingly sophisticated, involving a wider range of techniques. Whereas earlier work relied heavily on simple bivariate correlations or ordinary least-squares regression models, recent research has taken advantage of the many innovations that have been made in statistical analysis over the past few decades. Thirdly, contemporary studies cover a much broader array of substantive topics than before. Rather than focusing primarily on testing systemic theories, much of the more recent quantitative work analyzes how domestic politics affects international relations. Furthermore, contemporary statistical research that does focus on systemic theories is often designed to test neoliberal institutional and even constructivist approaches, rather than realist theories. Fourthly, and closely related, recent quantitative studies span a variety of issue areas that received little attention in statistical research during the cold war, including economic sanctions, monetary policy, human rights, and environmental politics.

What explains the rapid proliferation of quantitative research in the field of international relations over the past decade or so? We suspect a handful of forces are at play. An increasing emphasis on quantitative methods training in Ph.D.

programs, the growing amount of quantitative work in other subfields of political science (such as American politics and political economy), the decline in computing costs and the simultaneous rise in computation power to estimate more complex models, and more readily available data-sets (especially over the internet) have each contributed to the proliferation of quantitative work in the field.

Not only has the amount of quantitative research expanded, but the range of methods has expanded too. This development stems from a number of sources. First, important advances have been made in related fields, especially economics and sociology, including improvements in time-series modeling and duration models; the analysis of rare events, simultaneous relationships, endogeneity, and nonrandom selection; and the analysis of data that are both a time series and cross-sectional.

Secondly, the field of international relations underwent an important theoretical shift soon after the end of the cold war, placing less emphasis on realist and neorealist models. Realism, of course, has not been abandoned. There continues to be much research conducted in this theoretical tradition, and much of the statistical research conducted in other traditions is careful to account for variables emphasized by realists. However, the end of the cold war led many observers to question whether realism was the most appropriate theoretical lens through which to view international relations.

Researchers began turning to other approaches with increasing frequency. Among systemic theories, the contemporary era has been marked by the rise of constructivism and by heightened interest in neoliberal institutionalism.[2] Among alternative approaches, this era has been marked by the rapid growth of work on the links between domestic politics and international relations (Milner 1997). Furthermore, whereas research in the field of international relations—quantitative and qualitative—focused largely on international security during the cold war, the end of this period stimulated rising interest in international political economy, international institutions, and various other substantive issues. These developments have had important implications for statistical research in the field.

3.1 The Liberal Peace

Shifting theoretical tides in the aftermath of the cold war led to the creation of various data-sets that were both cross-sectional and time series. Usually, the cross-sectional units were countries (a "monadic" research design) or pairs of countries (a "dyadic" design). In almost all cases, data on issues of interest to international

---

[2] For an overview of constructivism, see Ruggie (1998). For an overview of neoliberal institutionalism, see Keohane and Martin (1995).

relations scholars are reported on an annual basis; as such, the temporal units are generally years. Consider, for example, the voluminous literature that has been produced on the democratic peace. During the late 1980s, scholars displayed growing interest in the proposition that relations between democracies are particularly cooperative and peaceful (Doyle 1986). Indeed, Jack Levy (1989) went so far as to characterize the argument that democracies rarely if ever fight each other as the closest thing that the field of international relations has to a law. Although a few scattered tests of this proposition had been conducted earlier, the 1990s and early 2000s were marked by an enormous amount of research on this topic, most of it statistical (e.g. Russett 1993; Russett and Oneal 2001).

Quantitative studies of the democratic peace typically rely on a dyadic research design. Data are compiled on pairs of states over the longest available period of time, usually the post-Second World War era, but (depending on data availability) sometimes the entire nineteenth and twentieth centuries. The dependent variable in these studies is the outbreak of conflict, usually defined as a militarized inter-state dispute (Jones, Bremer, and Singer 1996), but sometimes defined as war.

During the course of the 1990s, interest in the democratic peace grew broader. Bruce Russett and John Oneal (2001), for example, analyzed whether there was a more general liberal peace. Drawing on long-standing arguments by Immanuel Kant and others, they hypothesized that democracy, high levels of economic interdependence, and participation in international organizations combine to inhibit inter-state conflict. These developments led to models of conflict in which the key independent variables were not just regime type, but also the flow of trade between the states in each dyad (usually normalized by their national incomes to construct a measure of interdependence) and the extent to which they participated in intergovernmental organizations (Russett and Oneal 2001; Pevehouse and Russett 2006).

Initial statistical studies provided considerable support for the democratic peace and for a more general liberal peace, yet these studies also provoked various criticisms. Some observers questioned whether the democratic peace might be a function of chance alone (Spiro 1994), while others charged that the effects of democracy grew out of the similar interests and preferences that democracies share about international affairs (Gartzke 1998; Gowa 1999). Still others challenged the statistical techniques that were being used to test the liberal peace. What should be done to address the temporal dependence that exists in these data-sets (Beck, Katz, and Tucker 1998), the fact that there may be unmeasured heterogeneity in the data stemming from factors such as history or culture that are specific to a particular country or dyad (Green, Kim, and Yoon 1998), or the fact that inter-state conflict is a rare event (King and Zeng 2001)? These concerns have led researchers to use a variety of different techniques and have cast doubt on some aspects of the liberal peace, although most studies confirm that democratic dyads are less likely to fight than other country pairs.[3]

One key issue in research on the liberal peace is whether international trade affects the outbreak of political–military conflict. The bulk of the available evidence indicates that heightened interdependence inhibits conflict (Russett and Oneal 2001), a result that accords with arguments advanced by commercial liberals. Most of these studies use the ratio of international trade to national income as a measure of interdependence. However, a number of studies using alternative measures of interdependence have found little support for the liberal position (e.g. Barbieri 2005). Equally, while most studies of this topic treat interdependence as exogenous, some recent research argues that it is endogenous. When interdependence is treated in this way, the evidence that it is inversely related to conflict is far weaker (Keshk, Pollins, and Reuveny 2004).

Partially as a result of these inconclusive findings, some scholars have investigated the particular conditions under which heightened interdependence inhibits hostilities. For example, Mansfield and Pevehouse (2000) argue that extensive trade ties dampen conflict only when the trade partners belong to the same preferential trading arrangement. Joseph Grieco and Christopher Gelpi (2003) contend that the relationship is mediated by the regime type of the states involved: Because democratic governments are more sensitive than other governments to political pressure exerted by private traders, the pacific influence of heightened trade will be felt more strongly in democratic than in nondemocratic states. Thus, the effects of interdependence may be more complex than suggested by earlier theoretical or empirical work.

The links between domestic politics and international security have also been studied in the quantitative literature on the use of military force by the United States. Although this literature emerged in the latter part of the cold war (Ostrom and Job 1986), the bulk of this research has been conducted more recently and has focused on how domestic processes influence the incentives of US presidents to use force. As with nearly every area of literature reviewed here, disagreements and discontinuities have emerged. Initial contributors to this literature suggested that domestic economic conditions directly shaped a leader's incentives to engage in conflict (Ostrom and Job 1986). More recently, however, some contributors have argued that the domestic environment influences only perceptions of threat (Fordham 1998); others have argued that domestic factors play no role in the process (Gowa 1998). In addition, debates have emerged as to whether particular domestic institutions, such as Congress, directly influence the propensity to use force (Howell and Pevehouse 2005). Methodological debates have ensued as well, including a suggestion that existing models suffer from selection on the dependent variable

---

[3] Furthermore, these modeling issues have influenced related work on democratic transitions and the outbreak of conflict (Mansfield and Snyder 2005).

(Meernik 1994) and pay insufficient attention to time-series dynamics (Mitchell and Moore 2002).

In each of these newer research areas, debates over measurement, boundary conditions, and estimation techniques have both theoretical and empirical implications. In essence, these debates are more about what a theory predicts, the conditions under which we expect the theory to hold, and whether competing theories offer more compelling accounts of the evidence. While it might be easy to dismiss debates in these literatures as solely statistical in nature, they are essential to how we reformulate theories in light of evidence, a topic we return to in the conclusion.

3.2 Domestic Politics, International Institutions, and International Political Economy

Interest in how domestic politics affects international affairs has not been limited to the study of international security. On the contrary, there is a burgeoning quantitative literature on the influence of domestic factors on trade and monetary relations, foreign direct investment (FDI), foreign aid, and economic sanctions. William Bernhard and David Leblang (2006), for example, study the links between domestic politics and market behavior, placing particular emphasis on how democratic competition promotes change in currency, bond, and equity markets, and on how such change influences the ability of democratic politicians to retain office. Equally, a sizable number of quantitative studies have analyzed how partisanship, the number of "veto points" in government, a country's regime type, and other domestic political factors influence foreign trade relations (Lohmann and O'Halloran 1994; Mansfield, Milner, and Rosendorff 2000; 2002; Milner and Judkins 2004; Henisz and Mansfield 2006).

In addition, recent statistical work has addressed the effects of domestic politics on FDI. Quan Li and Adam Resnick (2003), for example, find that democracy has a mixed effect on FDI in developing countries. Strong property rights promote FDI and these rights are stronger in democracies than other countries. However, the direct effect of democracy is different: Holding constant the strength of property rights, democracies received less FDI than other countries during the last few decades of the twentieth century. Conversely, Nathan Jensen (2006) finds that democracies attract more FDI than other states, based on an analysis of both developed and developing countries covering roughly the same period of time. Additional quantitative research on the links between domestic institutions and FDI is likely to refine these findings and to specify the conditions under which these empirical relationships hold.

Quantitative work on the domestic politics of foreign economic relations has also focused on sanctions. Lisa Martin (2000, ch. 4) examines how partisanship affects the decision to impose sanctions. She finds that, in the United States, the executive branch typically takes the lead in wielding sanctions when the government is "unified" (that is, when the executive and legislative branches are controlled by the same party), whereas Congress typically does so when the government is "divided" (that is, when these branches are controlled by different parties).

A number of other quantitative studies of economic sanctions have considered the impact of nonrandom selection, an issue that has attracted attention throughout the field of international relations. In one study, T. Clifton Morgan and Valerie Schwebach (1997) examine the conditions under which sanctions lead a target country to change policy without the state sending the sanctions resorting to force. They use Gary Hufbauer, Jeffrey Schott, and Kimberly Ann Elliott's data (1990) on sanctions to test their argument, but recognize that relying solely on these data could introduce a selection bias if the same factors that affect whether states become involved in sanctions also influence the outcome of sanctions. For this reason, they supplement the sanctions data with a set of inter-state crises in which sanctions were not imposed. Morgan and Schwebach find that sanctions have neither a statistically significant nor a substantively large effect on the outcome of such disputes; nor do they influence which crises escalate to war.

In a related study, Daniel Drezner (2000) argues that many observers fail to appreciate the usefulness of sanctions, because a selection bias is at work. The most successful sanctions, Drezner argues, are the ones that are threatened but never implemented, since sanctions impose costs on both the sending country and the target state. Drezner uses statistical methods to show that a large number of sanctions attempts end when sanctions are threatened and before they are imposed, because the targets of these actions comply with the senders' demands. Equally, these cases generate more concessions on the part of targets than cases in which sanctions are actually imposed, providing evidence of a selection effect to which researchers need to pay careful attention.

Selection effects are hardly limited to economic sanctions. James Vreeland (2003), for example, analyzes whether International Monetary Fund (IMF) programs succeed in promoting growth, a topic of considerable importance and one marked by substantial disagreement. He argues that existing empirical studies of this topic are flawed because they fail to account for both the factors prompting governments to enter into agreements with the IMF and the subsequent effects of these agreements on growth. Vreeland develops a model to account for nonrandom selection and then uses it to assess the effects of IMF agreements. He finds that governments turn to the IMF when their foreign reserve position is weak, but also to help offset domestic opposition to reform programs. Moreover, Vreeland finds that, when controlling for conditions that drive states to the Fund, IMF programs reduce economic growth and that participation in these programs exacerbates incomes inequalities within states.

Over the past decade, the issue of nonrandom selection has also generated increasing attention outside the area of international political economy. Studies of international security, for example, began emphasizing the distinction between the onset of conflict and the escalation of conflict. Moreover, scholars recognized that some of the same factors would probably influence both outcomes, creating a source of potential bias. To address this issue, William Reed (2000), Paul Huth and Todd Allee (2003), and others have used selection models that account for the possibility that factors affecting whether countries become embroiled in a dispute might also affect whether the dispute escalates. In some cases, the effects of variables when these two stages of conflict are modeled independently change when these stages are analyzed using a unified selection model. For example, Reed (2000, 88) finds that regime type has a statistically significant impact on the escalation of hostilities until one controls for its influence on the onset of conflict. This avenue of inquiry has contributed to a broader methodological argument concerning the need to account for selection processes in the field of international relations.[4]

Most recently, researchers have analyzed whether there are selection effects in the formation and implementation of international agreements. Inspired by theoretical debates in the literature on compliance with international institutions (Downs, Rocke, and Barsoom 1996), scholars started examining whether the states that choose to enter international agreements do so because they intend to comply with those agreements. If so, then the agreements may have little independent effect on compliance or other aspects of state behavior. In a recent quantitative study, Jana von Stein (2005) finds that the states that enter into IMF agreements are predisposed to take steps that are in accord with these agreements. In her view, this evidence suggests that international institutions help to distinguish "compliant" from "noncompliant" types of states. As such, participating in an international institution helps a state to signal its willingness to abide by its overseas commitments.[5]

More generally, there has been considerable debate in the field of international relations over whether international institutions are endogenous. There are various well-known statistical techniques (including instrumental variables regression and other related two-stage estimators) that can be used to examine whether institutions are actually endogenous and, if so, to model institutions as endogenous when assessing their impact on international relations. The methodological concerns discussed in this section are more than worries over statistical nuance. In fact, they are central to the theoretical debates in the field, reflecting a concern about exactly what theories predict and how to test those predictions adequately.

---

[4] For a review of selection models and instances where alternatives to these models may be superior, see Signorino (2002).

[5] Recently, Koremenos (2005) has linked questions of regime design and flexibility to issues of enforcement, opening a new avenue of quantitative research on international organizations.

4 CONCLUSIONS

In this chapter, we have reviewed some of the burgeoning literature in the field of international relations that utilizes quantitative techniques. We conclude with three observations about the use of these methods. First, as is obvious even to the casual observer, quantitative analyses are now increasingly common in the field. The use of statistical techniques started during the cold war, but the end of the superpower rivalry corresponded with a sharp increase in both the amount of quantitative research and the topics on which this research focused. Both trends seem likely to persist.

Secondly, concomitant to the general rise of statistical approaches in the discipline and the end of the cold war, researchers became increasingly interested in the roles of domestic politics and international institutions in shaping global outcomes. Also, the scope of questions analyzed with quantitative analyses has continued to expand. Recent quantitative work on international security, for example, has placed considerable emphasis on state failure (Goldstone et al. 2002), civil wars and genocide (Valentino, Huth, and Balch-Lindsay 2004; Doyle and Sambanis 2006), human rights (Poe and Tate 1994; Poe, Tate, and Keith 1999; Hafner-Burton and Tsutsui 2005), and the environment (Midlarsky 1998; Neumayer 2002).

Thirdly, and most importantly, while some continue to criticize quantitative approaches as atheoretical, statistical work in the field of international relations has advanced our empirical understanding and has pushed theoretical boundaries. It is difficult to imagine current theorizing regarding liberalism, neoclassical realism, or human security without taking into account the knowledge generated by large-n studies. More than simply confirming preconceived notions about the relationship posited by theory, quantitative studies have generated new insights while helping to specify conditions under which relationships hold.

The rise in quantitative work has had important implications for the field of international relations. Some critics of quantitative analysis point to inconsistent findings, measurement problems, and problems of operationalization as weaknesses of statistical approaches. However, while empirical investigation (quantitative or qualitative) must be informed by theory, debates over measurement, operationalization, and method force scholars to think about theory. Exactly what does a given theory predict? What variables are crucial to the theory's prediction? Is the predicted relationship direct or conditional? Good theory informs good empirical analysis, but good empirical analysis is needed to update and refine theories. Quantitative techniques are powerful and valuable tools of empirical analysis, and the field of international relations is far richer for their heightened use.

References

BARBIERI, K. 2005. *The Liberal Illusion: Does Trade Promote Peace?* Ann Arbor: University of Michigan Press.

BECK, N., KATZ, J., and TUCKER, R. 1998. Taking time seriously: time-series-cross-section analysis with a binary dependent variable. *American Journal of Political Science*, 42: 1260–88.

BERNHARD, W., and LEBLANG, D. 2006. *Democratic Processes and Financial Markets: Pricing Politics.* New York: Cambridge University Press.

BRAUMOELLER, B., and SARTORI, A. 2004. The promise and perils of statistics in international relations. Pp. 129–51 in *Models, Numbers, and Cases: Methods for Studying International Relations,* ed. D. Sprinz and Y. Wolinsky-Nahamias. Ann Arbor: University of Michigan Press.

BUENO DE MESQUITA, B. 1985. Towards a scientific understanding of international conflict: a personal view. *International Studies Quarterly*, 29: 121–36.

CONYBEARE, J. A. C. 1983. Tariff protection in developed and developing countries: a cross-sectional and longitudinal analysis. *International Organization*, 37: 441–67.

DEUTSCH, K. W., BURRELL, S. A., KANN, R. A., MAURICE LEE, M., LICHTERMAN, R. E. L., LOWENHEIM, F. L., and VAN WAGENEN, R. W. 1957. *Political Community and the North Atlantic Area: International Organization in the Light of Historical Experience.* Princeton, NJ: Princeton University Press.

DOWNS, G. W., ROCKE, D. M., and BARSOOM, P. N. 1996. Is the good news about compliance good news about cooperation? *International Organization*, 50: 379–406.

DOYLE, M. W. 1986. Liberalism and world politics. *American Political Science Review*, 80: 1151–69.

—— and SAMBANIS, N. 2006. *Making War and Building Peace: United Nations Peace Operations.* Princeton, NJ: Princeton University Press.

DREZNER, D. 2000. Bargaining, enforcement, and multilateral sanctions: when is cooperation counterproductive? *International Organization*, 54: 73–102.

FORDHAM, B. 1998. The politics of threat perception and the use of force: a political economy model of US uses of force, 1949–1994. *International Studies Quarterly*, 42: 567–90.

GARTZKE, E. 1998. Kant we all just get along? Opportunity, willingness, and the origins of the democratic peace. *American Journal of Political Science*, 42: 1–27.

GILPIN, R. 1987. *The Political Economy of International Relations.* Princeton, NJ: Princeton University Press.

GOLDSTEIN, J., and FREEMAN, J. 1990. *Three Way Street: Strategic Reciprocity in World Politics.* Chicago: University of Chicago Press.

GOLDSTONE, J., GURR, T. R., HARFF, B., LEVY, M., MARSHALL, M., BATES, R., EPSTEIN, D., KAHL, C., WOODWARD, M., SURKO, P., and UNGER, A. 2002. *State Failure Task Force Report: Phase III Findings.* McLean, Va.: Science Applications International Corporation.

GOWA, J. 1994. *Allies, Adversaries, and International Trade.* Princeton, NJ: Princeton University Press.

—— 1998. Politics at the water's edge: parties, voters, and the use of force abroad. *International Organization*, 52: 307–24.

—— 1999. *Ballots and Bullets: The Elusive Democratic Peace.* Princeton, NJ: Princeton University Press.

GOWA, J., and MANSFIELD, E. D. 1993. Power politics and international trade. *American Political Science Review*, 87: 408–20.

———— 2004. Alliances, imperfect markets, and major-power trade. *International Organization*, 58: 775–805.

GREEN, D. P., KIM, S. Y., and YOON, D. 1998. Dirty pool. *International Organization*, 55: 441–68.

GRIECO, J., and GELPI, C. 2003. Economic interdependence, the democratic state, and the liberal peace. Pp. 44–59 in *Economic Interdependence and International Conflict: New Perspectives on an Enduring Debate*, ed. E. D. Mansfield and B. M. Pollins. Ann Arbor: University of Michigan Press.

HAFNER-BURTON, E. M., and TSUTSUI, K. 2005. Human rights in a globalizing world: the paradox of empty promises. *American Journal of Sociology*, 110: 1373–411.

HENISZ, W. J., and MANSFIELD, E. D. 2006. Votes and vetoes: the political determinants of commercial openness. *International Studies Quarterly*, 50: 189–211.

HOPF, T. 1991. Polarity, the offense defense balance, and war. *American Political Science Review*, 85: 475–93.

HOWELL, W., and PEVEHOUSE, J. 2005. Presidents, Congress, and the use of force. *International Organization*, 59: 209–32.

HUFBAUER, G., SCHOTT, J., and ELLIOT, K. A. 1990. *Economic Sanctions Reconsidered: History and Current Policy*. Washington, DC: Institute of International Economics.

HUTH, P., and ALLEE, T. 2003. *The Democratic Peace and Territorial Conflict in the Twentieth Century*. Cambridge: Cambridge University Press.

JENSEN, N. M. 2006. *Nation-States and the Multinational Corporation: A Political Economy of Foreign Direct Investment*. Princeton, NJ: Princeton University Press.

JERVIS, R. 1999. Realism, neoliberalism, and cooperation: understanding the debate. *International Security*, 24: 42–63.

JONES, D. M., BREMER, S. A., and SINGER, J. D. 1996. Militarized interstate disputes, 1816–1992: rationale, coding rules, and empirical patterns. *Conflict Management and Peace Science*, 15: 163–213.

KEOHANE, R. O., and MARTIN, L. L. 1995. The promise of institutionalist theory. *International Security*, 20: 39–51.

KESHK, O., POLLINS, B., and REUVENY, R. 2004. Trade still follows the flag: the primacy of politics in a simultaneous model of interdependence and armed conflict. *Journal of Politics*, 66: 1155–79.

KINDLEBERGER, C. 1973. *The World in Depression, 1929–1939*. Berkeley: University of California Press.

KING, G., and ZENG, L. 2001. Explaining rare events in international relations. *International Organization*, 55: 693–715.

KOREMENOS, B. 2005. Contracting around international uncertainty. *American Political Science Review*, 99: 549–65.

LEEDS, B. A. 2003. Do alliances deter aggression? The influence of military alliances on the initiation of militarized interstate disputes. *American Journal of Political Science*, 47: 427–39.

LEVY, J. 1984. Size and stability in the modern great power system. *International Interactions*, 10: 341–58.

———— 1989. The causes of war: a review of theories and evidence. Pp. 209–313 in *Behavior, Society, and Nuclear War*, vol. i., ed. P. E. Tetlock, J. L. Husbands, R. Jervis, P. C. Stern, and C. Tilly. New York: Oxford University Press.

Li, Q., and Resnick, A. 2003. Reversal of fortunes: democratic institutions and foreign direct investment inflows to developing countries. *International Organization*, 57: 175–211.

Lohmann, S., and O'Halloran, S. 1994. Divided government and US trade policy: theory and evidence. *International Organization*, 48: 595–632.

McKeown, T. 1991. A liberal trade order? The long-run pattern of imports to the advanced capitalist states. *International Studies Quarterly*, 35: 151–72.

Mansfield, E. D. 1994. *Power, Trade, and War*. Princeton, NJ: Princeton University Press.

—— Milner, H. V., and Rosendorff, B. P. 2000. Free to trade: democracies, autocracies, and international trade. *American Political Science Review*, 94: 305–21.

—— —— —— 2002. Why democracies cooperate more: electoral control and international trade agreements. *International Organization*, 56: 477–513.

—— and Pevehouse, J. 2000. Trade blocs, trade flows, and international conflict. *International Organization*, 54: 775–808.

—— and Snyder, J. 2005. *Electing to Fight: Why Emerging Democracies Go to War*. Cambridge, Mass.: MIT Press.

Martin, L. 2000. *Democratic Commitments: Legislatures and International Cooperation*. Princeton, NJ: Princeton University Press.

Meernik, J. 1994. Presidential decision making and the political use of military force. *International Studies Quarterly*, 38: 121–38.

Midlarsky, M. 1998. Democracy and the environment: an empirical assessment. *Journal of Peace Research*, 35: 341–61.

Milner, H. V. 1997. *Interests, Institutions, and Information: Domestic Politics and International Relations*. Princeton, NJ: Princeton University Press.

—— and Judkins, B. 2004. Partisanship, trade policy, and globalization: is there a left–right divide on trade policy? *International Studies Quarterly*, 48: 95–119.

Mitchell, S., and Moore, W. 2002. Presidential uses of force during the cold war: aggregation, truncation, and temporal dynamics. *American Journal of Political Science*, 46: 438–52.

Morgan, T. C., and Schwebach, V. 1997. Fools suffer gladly: the use of economic sanctions in international crises. *International Studies Quarterly*, 41: 27–50.

Morrow, J., Siverson, R., and Tabares, T. 1998. The political determinants of international trade: the major powers, 1907–90. *American Political Science Review*, 92: 649–61.

—— —— —— 1999. Correction to "The political determinants of international trade." *American Political Science Review*, 93: 931–3.

Neumayer, E. 2002. Do democracies exhibit stronger international environmental commitment? A cross-country analysis. *Journal of Peace Research*, 39: 139–64.

Ostrom, C., and Job, B. 1986. The president and the political use of force. *American Political Science Review*, 80: 541–66.

Pahre, R. 1999. *Leading Questions: How Hegemony Affects the International Political Economy*. Ann Arbor: University of Michigan Press.

Pevehouse, J., and Russett, B. 2006. Democratic international governmental organizations promote peace. *International Organization*, 60: 969–1000.

Poe, S. C., and Tate, C. N. 1994. Repression of human rights to personal integrity in the 1980s: a global analysis. *American Political Science Review*, 88: 853–72.

—— —— and Keith, L. C. 1999. Repression of the human right to personal integrity revisited: a global cross-national study covering the years 1976–1993. *International Studies Quarterly*, 43: 291–313.

POLLINS, B. 1989*a*. Does trade still follow the flag? *American Political Science Review*, 83: 465–80.

——1989*b*. Conflict, cooperation, and commerce: the effect of international political inter-actions on bilateral trade flows. *American Journal of Political Science*, 33: 737–61.

REED, W. 2000. A unified statistical model of conflict onset and escalation. *American Journal of Political Science*, 44: 84–93.

RICHARDSON, L. F. 1960. *Statistics of Deadly Quarrels*, ed. Q. Wright and C. C. Lienau. Pacific Grove, Calif.: Boxwood.

RUGGIE, J. 1998. *Constructing the World Polity: Essays on International Institutionalization*. London: Routledge.

RUSSETT, B. 1993. *Grasping the Democratic Peace*. Princeton, NJ: Princeton University Press.

——and ONEAL, J. R. 2001. *Triangulating Peace: Democracy, Interdependence, and International Organizations*. New York: Norton.

SIGNORINO, C. 2002. Strategy and selection in international relations. *International Interactions*, 28: 93–115.

SINGER, J. D. 1990. One man's view: a personal history of the Correlates of War Project. Pp. 11–28 in *Prisoners of War? Nation-States in the Modern Era*, ed. C. Gochman and A. Sabrosky. Lexington, Mass.: Lexington Books.

——BREMER, S., and STUCKEY, J. 1972. Capability distribution, uncertainty, and major power war, 1820–1965. Pp. 19–48 in *Peace, War, and Numbers*, ed. B. Russett. Beverly Hills, Calif.: Sage.

——and SMALL, M. 1968. Alliance aggregation and the onset of war, 1815–1914. Pp. 247–86 in *Quantitative International Politics: Insights and Evidence*, ed. J. D. Singer. New York: Free Press.

SIVERSON, R., and SULLIVAN, M. 1983. The distribution of power and the onset of war. *Journal of Conflict Resolution*, 27: 473–94.

SPIRO, D. 1994. The insignificance of the liberal peace. *International Security*, 19: 50–86.

SPRINZ, D., and WOLINKSY-NAHMIAS, Y. 2004. Methodology in international relations research. Pp. 1–17 in *Models, Numbers, and Cases: Methods for Studying International Relations*, ed. D. Sprinz and Y. Wolinsky-Nahamias. Ann Arbor: University of Michigan Press.

VALENTINO, B., HUTH, P., and BALCH-LINDSAY, D. 2004. "Draining the sea:" mass killing and guerilla warfare. *International Organization*, 58: 375–407.

VASQUEZ, J. 1987. The steps to war: toward a scientific explanation of Correlates of War findings. *World Politics*, 40: 108–45.

VON STEIN, J. 2005. Do treaties constrain or screen? Selection bias and treaty compliance. *American Political Science Review*, 99: 611–22.

VREELAND, J. 2003. *The IMF and Economic Development*. New York: Cambridge University Press.

WALTZ, K. 1979. *Theory of International Politics*. Reading, Mass.: Addison-Wesley.

WILKENFELD, J. 1972. Models for the analysis of foreign conflict behavior of states. Pp. 275–98 in *Peace, War, and Numbers*, ed. B. Russett. Beverly Hills, Calif.: Sage.

....

CHAPTER 29

CASE STUDY
METHODS

....

ANDREW BENNETT
COLIN ELMAN

As we have noted elsewhere (Bennett and Elman 2007*a*), qualitative research methods are currently enjoying an almost unprecedented popularity and vitality in both the international relations and the comparative politics subfields. To be sure, this renaissance has not been fully reflected in contemporary studies of American politics, which continue to emphasize statistical analysis and formal modeling (Bennett, Barth, and Rutherford 2003; Bennett and Elman 2007*b*; Mahoney 2007; Pierson 2007). Nevertheless, in the international relations subfield, qualitative methods are indisputably prominent, if not pre-eminent. In a 2007 survey, 95 percent of US international relations scholars reported that qualitative analysis is their primary or secondary methodology, compared with 55 percent for quantitative analysis and 16 percent for formal modeling (Maliniak et al. 2007, 37). Substantively, qualitative research has contributed to essentially every research program in international relations, including those on international political economy (Odell 2004), the democratic peace (George and Bennett 2005, 37–59), ethnic and civil conflicts (Sambanis 2004; Bennett and Elman 2007*b*), the end of the cold war (Wohlforth 1998), international environmental politics (Mitchell and Bernauer 2004), and security studies (Katzenstein 1996; Kacowicz 2004).

The present resurgence in qualitative research methods owes a significant debt to two previous generations of ground-breaking scholars. A first generation of post-Second World War case study methods made important contributions but eventually came to be seen as being too atheoretical, lacking in methodological rigor, and not conducive to cumulative theory-building (George 1979). A second generation of scholars developed more systematic procedures for qualitative research from the 1970s through the early 1990s, including Adam Przeworski and Henry Teune (1970), Arend Lijphart (1971), Harry Eckstein (1975), Neil Smelser (1976), Alexander George (1979), Timothy McKeown (George and McKeown 1985), Charles Ragin (1987), and David Collier (1993).

We focus in this chapter on a third generation of qualitative methods research. We argue that this third generation constitutes a renaissance in qualitative methods that has clarified their procedures, grounded them more firmly in the contemporary philosophy of science, illuminated their comparative advantages relative to quantitative and formal methods, and expanded the repertoire of qualitative techniques on conceptualization and measurement, case selection, and comparative and within-case analysis. Qualitative methods have also become more deeply institutionalized than in prior periods. In 2003, the American Political Science Association (APSA) formed the Qualitative Methods section. Subsequently renamed Qualitative and Multi-Method Research, as of February 2008 it was the second-largest of APSA's thirty-seven sections. In addition, the Consortium for Qualitative Research Methods (CQRM) was founded in 2001, and in 2007–8 it had roughly sixty member departments and research institutes. By January 2008 it had co-organized seven Institutes for Qualitative and Multi-Method Research, training more than 600 graduate students and faculty in state-of-the-art qualitative methods (Collier and Elman 2008).[1]

An important dimension of the recent development of qualitative research methods has been the emergence of more pluralistic attitudes toward methodology. This pluralism is clearest in the increasing use of sophisticated multi-method research designs. It is also evident within the qualitative research methods community itself, which has grown in size and variety to the point that it now incorporates a diverse range of views. One school of thought, influenced by quantitative research techniques, suggests that "the same underlying logic provides the framework for each research approach [statistical and qualitative]. This logic tends to be explicated and formalized clearly in discussions of quantitative research methods" (King, Keohane, and Verba 1994, 3). In contrast to this single-logic-of-inference approach, advocates of what we have termed the third generation of qualitative research argue that there are alternative ways to make inferences. These scholars often use within-case methods to establish the presence of particular causal mechanisms and the conditions under which they operate.[2] The third-generation group also emphasizes the value

---

[1] In 2007, the institute name was changed from the Institute for Qualitative Research Methods.

[2] International relations scholars may already be familiar with some of the third-generation works centrally located in their subfield—e.g. Tetlock and Belkin (1996); George and Bennett (2005)— but the larger canon also includes works by Bates et al. (1998); Ragin (2000); Elman and Elman (2001;

of theory development, as well as theory testing; and of historical explanation of individual cases, as well as generalized statements about causal mechanisms. In the view of third-generation qualitative methodologists, different methods have different strengths and weaknesses, and they should be used with those trade-offs in mind. From this perspective, quantitative methods are very useful and powerful, but they are not always the best choice for all inferential goals, even when many cases exist.

The qualitative research methods community also includes a variety of scholars engaged in interpretative approaches. Interpretivism involves an extraordinary range of modes of analysis,[3] as well as difficult issues arising from the variety of philosophical and linguistic traditions in which interpretative approaches have their roots. We find useful in the international relations subfield John Ruggie's distinction (1998) among neoclassical, postmodernist, and naturalistic constructivists. Neoclassical constructivists, among whom Ruggie counts himself, follow a pragmatic epistemology and are committed to the idea of a pluralistic social science even if its results are time-bound and culturally contingent. Naturalistic constructivists, such as Alexander Wendt (1999) and David Dessler (1999; Dessler and Owen 2005), aspire to make valid inferences on the causal mechanisms that underlie social life, and see much in common between the epistemologies of the social and natural sciences. These two groups' approach to methods are largely consistent with those of third-generation qualitative researchers.[4] For instance, Peter Katzenstein's neoclassical constructivism (2005, x–xi, 40) is open to an analytically eclectic combination of interpretative and other methods. In contrast, Ruggie's final category of postmodernist constructivists take a much more skeptical view. This group, which grounds its works in the writings of Friedrich Nietzsche, Michel Foucault, and Jacques Derrida, focuses on the linguistic construction of social reality. They "make a decisive epistemic break with the precepts and practices of modernism" (Ruggie 1998, 881) and hence are pessimistic about the prospects for a legitimate social science or for justifiable causal inferences.[5]

2003); Gerring (2001; 2007a); Goertz and Starr (2002); Mahoney and Rueschemeyer (2003); Brady and Collier (2004); Pierson (2004); Goertz (2006); and Goertz and Levy (2007).

[3] See, e. g., the list of thirty-five varieties of interpretative research methods listed in table 1 in the introduction to Yanow and Schwartz-Shea (2006).

[4] There is a substantial overlap here with scholars whom Christian Reus-Smit (2002, 495) identifies as "methodological conventionalists." These two categories also roughly coincide with what Andrew Hurd (this volume) identifies as "positivists," though in our view many international relations scholars, whether constructivist or not, are methodologically conventional but do not subscribe to traditional positivist notions of "laws" and "falsifiability."

[5] See also Yanow (2006, 6), and Yanow and Schwartz-Shea (2006, xxxvi, n. 15). Similarly, Friedrich Kratochwil (this volume) raises several hermeneutic critiques of the most ambitious form of scientific realism, specifically the claim that theories in some sense "refer" in progressively more accurate ways to underlying "realities." Kratochwil does not go so far as suggesting, however, that there is no basis

Third-generation qualitative methods have the potential to occupy a pivotal position in the discourses among different qualitative approaches. In some respects they can be seen as providing a unique bridge between the single-logic-of-inference and interpretivist communities. Accepting comparison and intuitive regression as part of its underlying justification, the third-generation case study approach is readily compatible with large-n studies, as well as being accepting of many of the claims of the comparative advantages offered by quantitative methods. On the other hand, its close attention to detail, narrative, and context gives the third generation a close compatibility with interpretative approaches, especially with the pragmatist and naturalist branches. For the rest of the chapter, we consider some of the ways in which the third generation has developed and suggest potentially fruitful directions for future research. We focus on some key innovations in third-generation qualitative methods over the last decade regarding within-case analysis, comparative case studies, case selection, concepts and measurement, counterfactual analysis, typological theorizing, and Fuzzy Set analysis. We conclude with a discussion of promising avenues for future developments in qualitative methods, including ways of combining qualitative methods with statistical and/or formal methods, means of assessing theories involving various forms of complexity, ways of adapting qualitative methods to address common inferential biases uncovered by cognitive research, means of increasing the replicability and accessibility of qualitative data and using qualitative knowledge to improve codings in statistical databases, and ways of generalizing from case studies.

1 Innovations in Third-Generation Qualitative Methods

....

Third-generation qualitative scholars have over the last fifteen years revised or added to essentially every aspect of traditional case study research methods.[6] Although these new and updated methods vary along more than one dimension, Figure 29.1 presents them along a spectrum from methods of within-case analysis

for judging some interpretations to be superior to others, and it is not clear whether he objects as well to more modest forms of scientific realism that do not presume science is always progressive (for an analysis of different varieties of scientific realism, see Chernoff 2002).

[6] The discussion below draws upon and further develops our previous separate and joint writings on qualitative methods, including George and Bennett (2005); and Bennett and Elman (2006a; 2006b; 2007a; 2007b).

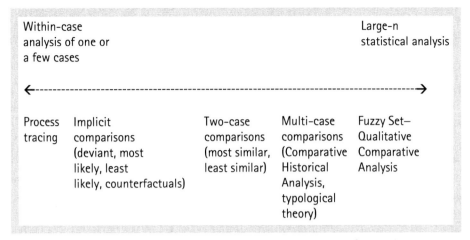

Fig. 29.1. Qualitative methods by numbers of cases and modes of analysis

of single cases at the left end, through methods of implicit comparison and small-n comparison in the middle, to multi-case comparisons and Fuzzy Set/Qualitative Comparative Analysis (FS/QCA) on the right. We very briefly discuss each of these methods in turn below.

1.1 Process Tracing

Methods of within-case analysis have a long pedigree, but scholars have recently clarified their procedures and illuminated their foundations in the contemporary philosophy of science. A central method of within-case analysis, termed process tracing (George 1979; George and Bennett 2005), involves the close examination of the observable implications of alternative hypothesized explanations for a historical case.[7] The researcher using process tracing continually asks "if this explanation is accurate in this case, what else must be true about the processes through which the hypothesized causal mechanisms unfolded in this case?" The investigator then tests these hypothesized intervening variables against evidence from the case. With its emphasis on testing hypothesized causal mechanisms, often at a lower or more detailed level of analysis than the independent and dependent variables, process tracing is consistent with the "scientific realism" school of thought in the philosophy of science (George and Bennett 2005).

Process tracing can involve both inductive analysis to generate hypotheses about a case and deductive tests of potential explanations of a case. A hypothesis can

---

[7] See also Collier, Brady, and Seawright's discussion (2004, 252–5) of causal process observations.

even be developed in a case and tested in that same case if it is tested against evidence that is in some way independent of the evidence that gave rise to it. In these regards, process tracing is closely analogous to traditional historical methods, as well as methods of developing and testing explanations of individual cases in epidemiology, pathology, geology, evolutionary biology, and detective work. Good process tracing requires giving attention to alternative hypotheses and their observable implications, taking into account potential biases in the available evidence, incorporating diverse sources of information, and providing as continuous as possible an explanation of the key sequential steps in a hypothesized process.

The logic of process tracing is quite similar to that of Bayesian inference (Bennett 2007).[8] Like Bayesian inference, process tracing uses evidence to affirm some explanations and to cast into doubt, through eliminative induction, explanations that do not fit the evidence. Although there can be a problem of indeterminacy if there is no accessible evidence to discriminate between two competing and incompatible explanations of a case, it is also possible for one or a few pieces of evidence strongly to increase confidence in one explanation while also calling into question many others. Hence, in contrast to the single-logic-of-inference approach to qualitative methods, the third-generation view is that, to the extent that case studies rely on within-case methods, they are not necessarily vulnerable to the "degrees of freedom critique." This is because within-case methods provide evidence that bears on multiple testable implications of alternative theories within a single case (George and Bennett 2005, 28–9; see also Campbell 1975). Although case studies (and indeed all methods) are vulnerable to the more general problem of underdetermination of theories by evidence, the presence and severity of this problem in any particular case study research design depends, not on the number of variables or cases, but on whether the evidence from the cases is suitable for discriminating between alternative explanations. There is thus no inherent "degrees of freedom" problem in using process tracing to test several potential explanations in a single case.

---

[8]   The Bayesian approach to theory testing focuses on updating degrees of belief in the truth of alternative explanations. In other words, Bayesians treat statistical parameters probabilistically, attaching subjective probabilities to the likelihood that hypotheses are true and then updating these probabilities in the light of new evidence. In contrast, frequentist statistics attaches probabilities to the likelihood of getting similar results from repeated sampling of a population. Bayesian inference can apply to one or a few cases or pieces of evidence, whereas frequentist statistical analysis needs a higher number of cases to allow inferences, although the two forms of inference should converge on similar results as the number of cases or pieces of evidence grows. Process tracing follows a logic that is very similar to Bayesian reasoning, updating degrees of belief in alternative explanations of a case in light of evidence generated from within that case. For further discussion of the similarities between process tracing and Bayesian inference, see Bennett (2007).

1.2 Implicit Comparisons: Deviant, Most-likely, Least-likely, Crucial, and Counterfactual Cases

Just as language and concepts are inherently comparative, all single case studies, even when not explicitly comparative, are implicitly so. Case studies that are at least implicitly comparative include deviant, most-likely, least-likely, crucial, and counterfactual cases. Methodologists have clarified the uses of each of these kinds of case study in the last decade. Deviant cases are cases whose outcomes either do not conform to theoretical expectations or do not fit the empirical patterns observed in a population of cases of which the deviant case is considered to be a member. Prior statistical work can be useful in identifying deviant cases through these cases' high error term (Seawright and Gerring 2006). Deviant cases are often useful for generating new hypotheses through inductive process tracing (Eckstein 1975; George and Bennett 2005). A hypothesis generated from a deviant case may prove to be applicable to that case only, or to broad populations of cases. It is impossible to predict how generalizable the explanation for a deviant case might be until one has studied the case, developed an explanation, and considered the conditions under which the newly hypothesized underlying mechanisms might apply.

Most-likely cases are those in which a theory is likely to provide a good explanation if it applies to any cases at all, and least-likely cases are "tough test" cases in which the theory in question is unlikely to provide a good explanation. A theory that fails to fit a most-likely case is strongly impugned, while a theory that fits even a case in which it is least likely gains confidence. A "crucial" case is a tough test in both senses: It must fit one explanation if the explanation is true, and it must not fit any other explanations. Harry Eckstein (1975) developed the ideas of crucial, most-likely, and least-likely cases in the 1970s, but scholars have more recently clarified that whether a case is most likely or least likely for a theory should be judged, not just by its values on the variables of that theory, but on the values of variables pointed to by alternative theories as well (George and Bennett 2005; see also Gerring 2007b).

Counterfactual analysis is another form of implicit comparison, one in which the researcher compares an extant case with a counterfactual case that differs in one or more key respects. Philip Tetlock and Aaron Belkin have devised a number of standards for judging counterfactuals, including the "miminal re-write rule" (changing as few variables as possible to construct the counterfactual) and the prescription that to the extent possible counterfactuals should include projectible and testable implications for the real world (Tetlock and Belkin 1996). Counterfactual reasoning also serves as a useful test of consistency in a researcher's thinking, as every causal or explanatory claim about the world has a logically equivalent counterfactual claim. If a researcher finds a causal claim convincing, but does not find the logically equivalent counterfactual claim equally convincing, the researcher needs to consider whether there are asymmetries or faults in their theorizing about a case (Lebow 2000; George and Bennett 2005; for applications to international relations cases, see Goertz and Levy 2007).

1.3 Small-n Comparisons: Most-similar and Least-similar Cases, Comparative Historical Analysis

Methodologists have updated two forms of pairwise comparison that have a long pedigree: most-similar and least-similar case comparisons. In a most-similar case comparison, two cases are similar in all but one independent variable, and differ on the outcome variable. In a least-similar case comparison, two cases are similar on only one independent variable and have the same value on the dependent variable. These comparisons draw, respectively, on John Stuart Mill's "method of difference" and "method of agreement" (the seeming confusion of the terms arises from the fact Mill named his methods for the cases' difference or agreement on the dependent variable, while the contemporary labels correspond to similarity or lack thereof on the independent variables).

As Mill himself noted, inferences from these kinds of comparisons are potentially flawed for a variety of reasons: cases rarely differ in only one or all but one variable, there may be alternative paths to the same outcome (equifinality), some variables may be left out from the comparison, or there may be measurement error. More recently, methodologists have reaffirmed these potential threats to inferences in pairwise comparisons, but at the same time they have emphasized that process tracing helps reduce the likelihood of these problems (George and Bennett 2005). In a most-similar cases design, for example, process tracing can supplement the comparative analysis by using within-case analysis to test whether the independent variable that differs between the two cases is related to the outcome through the hypothesized processes. Researchers can also use process tracing in this design to test whether other residual differences in the two cases' independent variables are related to the differences in the cases' outcomes.

Several of the innovations discussed in this chapter have been developed and/or deployed in the comparative historical analysis tradition, which straddles the disciplines of both political science and sociology. It has a particularly strong following in the subfields of comparative politics and American political development. James Mahoney and Dietrich Rueschemeyer (2003, 6) suggest that the comparative historical analysis approach addresses substantially important outcomes, and is defined by "a concern with causal analysis, an emphasis on process over time, and the use of systematic and contextualized comparison." Uncomfortable with either universal generalizations or idiographic explanations, comparative historical analysis typically focuses on configurational analysis and on making contingent generalizations.

1.4 Typological Theorizing

Typological theorizing often involves a number of cross-case comparisons within a single research design. Such theorizing uses a combination of these comparisons and within-case analysis to develop theories about different configurations of variables and the outcomes to which they lead. One of the distinctive features of such theories is that they treat cases inherently as configurations of variables (Ragin 1987; George and Bennett 2005), thereby allowing for the possibility of different multivariate interaction effects within each configuration.

Depending on the state of development of theories on the phenomenon of interest, the development of a typological theory can begin with established theories or it can proceed more inductively from individual case studies. In either event, the researcher usually iterates between evidence from cases and development of the theoretical framework, seeking with each iteration to uncover "new facts" to guard against the dangers of post hoc anomaly-solving (Lakatos 1970; Elman and Elman 2002). To build a typological theory, the investigator begins with the variables earlier research has identified (if any) on the phenomenon of interest. Using categorical measures of these variables, often dichotomous or trichotomous ones, the researcher outlines the "typological space" (termed a "truth table" in philosophy) of all the possible combinations of the variables. If, for example, there are four dichotomous independent variables and a dichotomous dependent variable, there will be two to the power of five or thirty-two potential combinations or types.

Next, the researcher arrays the cases from the relevant population into the types that they best fit based on preliminary knowledge of the values of the variables in each case. This process can contribute to changes to the theoretical framework. If there are cases classified in the same type that the researcher thinks of as being dissimilar cases in important respects, for example, this can stimulate further consideration of the differences between the cases, and of any associated variables that might need to be added to the typological space to separate the cases into different types. Similarly, if cases with the same combination of independent variables have different outcomes, this poses a potential anomaly that merits attention.

Even after the apparent anomalies have been resolved to the extent possible using preliminary knowledge about the cases, at this point the typological space can be complex and seemingly unwieldy. Fortunately, there are several ways to reduce the typological space (Elman 2005). First, the variables can be rescaled to a less detailed level of measurement if fine-grained distinctions are not essential to the theory. Secondly, variables might be indexed, or aggregated into composite variables. Thirdly, the researcher can use logical compression to eliminate any empirically empty cells that are theoretically unlikely ever to include actual cases. A fourth option is empirical compression, eliminating empty cells whether or not they seem unlikely. A fifth route is pragmatic compression of adjacent types when their division serves no theoretical purpose. A sixth is to set aside from further and more detailed analysis types of cases whose outcomes appear to be theoretically overdetermined and whose empirical examples do not deviate from the expected outcomes. Finally, the researcher can decide to focus on a more narrowly circumscribed set of specific cells or subtypes of the phenomenon of interest.

Alternatively, if the typological space appears to be oversimplified, a researcher can use expansion (sometimes called "substruction") to add variables and/or more finely grained distinctions back into the theory. Once the typological space has been reduced or expanded to the desired degree, it can contribute directly to the selection of cases that serve alternative research designs. Cases in adjacent cells that differ in one independent variable and in the dependent variable, for example, can be used for most-similar comparisons, and cases with different outcomes from those of the other cases within the same cell constitute deviant cases that might be examined to try to identify left-out variables. Examples of typological theories include those on burden-sharing in ad hoc security coalitions (Bennett, Lepgold, and Unger 1997), military occupations (Edelstein 2008), status quo and revisionist regimes (Schweller 1994; 1998), and types of federalist states (Ziblatt 2006).

1.5 Fuzzy Set Analysis

Fuzzy Set (FS) analysis is another recent innovation in qualitative methods, one that typically includes studies of about ten to fifty cases (Ragin and Rihoux 2004). A full explication of FS is beyond present purposes (see Ragin 2000), and we focus only on a few of its features and its comparative advantages vis-à-vis other qualitative methods.

FS methods are a variation on Charles Ragin's (1987) Qualitative Comparative Analysis (QCA), which uses "crisp" categorical variables and Boolean algebra to reduce populations of cases in truth tables to logical statements of necessity and sufficiency consistent with these cases. In contrast to crisp set QCA, FS methods assign "degree of membership" values between zero and one to cases based on the extent to which they are "fully in" a specified concept or collection of attributes. For example, a state that is "fully in" the conceptually defined set of "democracies" would be assigned a score of 1.0, a state whose attributes place it "mostly in" this set might have a score of 0.75, one that is "more in than out" might be a 0.5, and so on. After a researcher has assigned FS values to the cases in a study, he or she can use statistical tests to assess whether the outcomes of a particular type of case are consistent enough to sustain a claim of (near) necessity or sufficiency (in contrast to QCA, FS methods can use probabilistic statements).

FS analysis is a comparative method that does not necessarily rely on within-case analysis of individual cases, although it does require sufficient information about each case to assign it an FS value, and it is not incompatible with within-case analysis. FS analysis differs from typological theorizing in that it tends to assume that outlier cases can arise by chance, whereas typological theorizing typically uses a default assumption that deviant cases are potential sources for identifying left-out variables. In addition, FS analysis is best suited to subjects for which prior theories are well established, for which diversity of cases is not sharply limited, and for the goal of testing claims of necessity or sufficiency rather than that of generating new theories (Bennett and Elman 2006a). Typological theorizing, on the other hand, can be used both for testing and generating theories and for explaining individual cases.

1.6 Innovations in Conceptual Analysis, Two-level Theories, and Case Selection

There are three other important sets of recent innovations in case study methods that do not fit neatly on the spectrum from single to multiple case study designs but are applicable to many of these designs. First, methodologists have clarified the role and procedures of developing and refining concepts. Robert Adcock and David Collier (2001) have outlined the relationships among background concepts, systematized concepts, indicators, and scores on individual cases, noting that there are often iterative changes from one level to another in the course of research. Collier and Stephen Levitsky (1997) have pointed out the prevalence and uses of "diminished subtypes," or conceptual categories that lack one or more of the attributes of full examples of the phenomenon in question. Collier, Hidalgo, and Maciuceanu (2006) have unpacked and updated the debate over essentially contested concepts. John Gerring (2001; Gerring and Barresi 2003) has clarified the trade-offs among different desiderata of qualitative concepts and measures, as well as suggested guidelines for concept formation. Gary Goertz (2006) has distinguished between necessary/sufficient concepts, or concepts for which some component is necessary or sufficient, and family resemblance concepts, for which membership in a conceptual category is determined by having a specified minimal level of several substitutable attributes.

Secondly, Goertz and Mahoney (2005) have identified "two-level theories" as an important pattern of theorizing common to many qualitative studies. Two-level theories can combine elements of necessity at one level that interact with family resemblance relationships at another level. Goertz and Mahoney illustrate this with Theda Skocpol's famous theory (1979) on social revolutions, in which state breakdown and peasant revolt are both necessary for social revolution, but either of these conditions can be achieved through several different substitutable routes. There are many possible kinds of two-level theories, which can be depicted either as a flowchart diagram or as a typological space (for an example showing the correspondence of these two forms of presentation, see Bennett 1999, 109–10).

Thirdly, several methodologists have clarified the problems of case selection and selection bias in case study research designs. Proponents of a single logic of inference level strong criticisms at qualitative methods undertaken without a proper appreciation for what they consider to be universally applicable quantitative rules of inference. One common critique is that case study research designs often involve the investigator selecting cases for study based on prior knowledge of these cases' outcomes. The most common form of this critique is that the selection of cases on the basis of values of the dependent variable leads to an underestimation of the effects of the independent variable (King, Keohane, and Verba 1994; Geddes 2003, 87).

Third-generation methodologists, however, argue that the challenge of case selection in qualitative research is often misunderstood when it is viewed through the prism of case selection biases in observational statistical studies. Properly understood, case selection procedures in qualitative research designs could in some instances be more damaging to causal inference than the standard statistical critique suggests, but often these procedures are in fact well adapted to the inferential purposes for which qualitative researchers use them. Selection on the dependent-variable and no-variance designs have important uses in case study research. A single deviant case, for example, can prove fruitful in identifying a new variable, even though such a case is selected on the dependent variable. As noted above, although a deviant case is seemingly a "no-variance" design, it is chosen for implicit or explicit comparison to a theoretical or empirical pattern from which it varies. Moreover, no-variance single cases selected on the dependent variable can test claims of necessity or sufficiency (Dion 1998).

In addition, the statistical selection bias critique assumes a preconstituted population, but if the researcher has no such population in mind and is trying to learn more about similarities among positive cases before identifying the relevant underlying population, selection on the dependent variable is justifiable. Otherwise, "addressing the question of selection bias before establishing an appropriate population puts the cart before the horse" (Collier, Mahoney, and Seawright 2004, 88). In addition, the selection bias critique does not apply to process tracing in the same way that it does to cross-case comparative methods, as process tracing does not rely on cross-case covariation (Collier and Mahoney 1996; Collier, Mahoney, and Seawright 2004, 96). As noted above, even comparative cases research designs, such as the most-similar cases design, draw much of their inferential power from process tracing. In short, although variance on the independent and dependent variables is essential for many kinds of case study research designs and inferential goals, it is not necessary or even useful for all such designs and goals.

Another area of innovation regarding case selection concerns an important issue that researchers using both qualitative and quantitative methods often overlook: the problem of defining and selecting negative cases of a phenomenon, or contexts in which the outcome of interest could have happened but did not. The inclusion of irrelevant cases in a statistical study, such as including in a study of inter-state wars dyads of far distant countries with no capability or motivation to fight one another, can make a theory look stronger than it actually is. Mahoney and Goertz (2004) have suggested a "possibility principle" for identifying relevant cases by a "rule of inclusion," in which cases are included if the value of at least one independent variable points to the outcome of interest, and a "rule of exclusion," through which cases are excluded if they have a variable at a value known through previous studies to make the outcome of interest impossible. These authors note that these rules are in part theory dependent and should not be applied mechanically, and in fact there may be many variants on these rules depending on the nature of prior knowledge of the phenomenon in question. Whatever criteria one chooses for identifying negative cases, the task of identifying them as rigorously as possible is important for many studies.

2 NEW FRONTIERS IN QUALITATIVE METHODS

Innovations in qualitative methods are ongoing, and five areas in particular deserve mention as current or potential subjects for further development. First, the development of multi-method research designs is already well under way, led by empirical research examples rather than by systematic analyses by methodologists of alternative ways of combining different methods. There are several excellent examples of international relations research designs combining case study methods with formal models, statistical analysis or both. Other methods, including experiments and ethnographic research, can be combined with case studies as well. The great advantage of combining methods is that each approach offers the potential for at least partly offsetting the limitations of another. The challenge of multi-method research, particularly for graduate students, is that a great deal of time and skill are required to develop expertise in more than one method and to gather the evidence each method requires. Scholars have only just begun addressing the question of how to combine methods more generally (Lieberman 2005; Seawright and Gerring

2006; Bennett and Elman 2007*b*), and much more work on this subject remains to be done.

Secondly, qualitative methodologists have begun focusing on how to assess theories that involve different forms of complexity. Several have investigated issues related to path dependence and ways in which qualitative methods can address them (Mahoney 2000; Bennett and Elman 2006*b*). Goertz and Mahoney (2005) address a different form of complexity in their work on various combinations of necessity and family resemblance relations in two-level theories. Fuzzy Set analysis and typological theorizing are ways of addressing the related challenge of multivariate interaction effects. There is potential for further advances in these and other areas of complexity theory, perhaps drawing on work from other sciences that have confronted the problems of complexity, such as evolutionary biology.

Thirdly, qualitative methods need to keep pace with developments in the cognitive sciences. One role for rigorous methodological procedures is to safeguard against our own cognitive biases. Many procedures in both qualitative and quantitative methods, for example, are geared to guard against the dangers of confirmation bias, which have been amply demonstrated in laboratory experiments. Research in cognitive psychology and behavioral economics has pointed to many other kinds of inferential biases (Kahneman, Slovic, and Tversky 1982), and studies in political psychology have demonstrated that political scientists are vulnerable to such biases (Tetlock 2005). Recent work suggests that a few simple procedures, such as asking individuals to think counterfactually about the conditions under which their predictions might be proved wrong, can improve performance at inferential tasks like Bayesian updating (Herrmann and Choi 2007). Qualitative methodologists, and methodologists more generally, need to mine the large and growing literature on cognitive biases and systematically develop procedures for addressing them.

A fourth area for further development is that of improving the access to and replicability of qualitative evidence. Qualitative researchers can make much greater use of improved technologies for gathering and storing audio and visual data and making these data web-accessible. Field notes, audio and videotapes of interviews and events, photographs of symbols and artifacts, and other kinds of qualitative data can be made accessible and linked to publications. As more such evidence becomes available online, research organizations like the National Science Foundation need to address the question of whether they can play a role in providing storage space for such information, and to consider whether existing open-source search engines are adequate for the task of enabling users easily to find what they need. Methodologists and communities of scholars also need to devise standards and protocols on the presentation and replicability of such qualitative data. There is a role as well for qualitative researchers with regional and functional expertise to contribute to the improvement of quantitative databases, and cumulatively to apply their knowledge toward making the codings in such databases more accurate (Bowman, Lehoucq, and Mahoney 2005). Web-based means of soliciting and vetting community input, similar to the process used by Wikipedia, may prove helpful here.

Finally, qualitative methodologists need to renew their focus on the challenge of generalizing from individual and comparative case studies. The findings of studies of deviant cases, and of studies that affirm a theory in a least-likely case or undermine it in a most-likely case, may be widely generalizable, or they may prove to be limited only to the case studied. The standards for assessing the generalizability of findings from such cases need to be clarified, and researchers need to be more precise in stating whether they think their findings apply only to the case under study, to some type or category of configurative cases of which it is member, or to broad populations sharing only one or a few features of the case studied. Put another way, qualitative researchers need to clarify the conditions under which they can claim different kinds of scope conditions for their theories based on the cases they study (Goertz and Mahoney 2006). These five tasks pose important and potentially fruitful challenges for the next generation of qualitative researchers and methodologists.

References

ADCOCK, R., and COLLIER, D. 2001. Measurement validity: a shared standard for qualitative and quantitative research. *American Political Science Review*, 95: 529–46.
BATES, R. H., GRIEF, A., LEVI, M., ROSENTHAL, J. L., and WEINGAST, B. R. 1998. *Analytic Narratives*. Princeton, NJ: Princeton University Press.
BENNETT, A. 1999. *Condemned to Repetition? The Rise, Fall, and Reprise of Soviet-Russian Military Interventionism, 1973–1996*. Cambridge, Mass.: MIT Press.
—— 2007. Process tracing: a Bayesian approach. Presented at the American Political Science Association Annual Conference, Chicago, 1 Sept.
—— BARTH, A., and RUTHERFORD, K. 2003. Do we preach what we practice? A survey of methods in political science journals and curricula. *PS: Political Science and Politics*, 36: 373–8.
—— and ELMAN, C. 2006a. Qualitative research: recent developments in case study methods. *Annual Review of Political Science*, 9: 455–76.
—— —— 2006b. Complex causal relations and case study methods: the example of path dependence. *Political Analysis*, 14: 250–67.
—— —— 2007a. Qualitative methods: the view from the subfields. *Comparative Political Studies*, 40: 111–21.
—— —— 2007b. Case study methods in the international relations subfield. *Comparative Political Studies*, 40: 170–95.
—— LEPGOLD, J., and UNGER, D. (eds.) 1997. *Friends in Need: Burden Sharing in the Gulf War*. Basingstoke: Macmillan.

BOWMAN, K., LEHOUCQ, F., and MAHONEY, J. 2005. Measuring political democracy: case expertise, data adequacy, and Central America. *Comparative Political Studies*, 38: 939–70.

BRADY, H. E., and COLLIER, D. (eds.) 2004. *Rethinking Social Inquiry: Diverse Tools, Shared Standards*. Lanham, Md.: Rowman and Littlefield.

CAMPBELL, D. 1975. "Degrees of freedom" and the case study. *Comparative Political Studies*, 8: 178–85.

CHERNOFF, F. 2002. Scientific realism as a meta-theory of international politics. *International Studies Quarterly*, 46: 189–207.

COLLIER, D. 1993. The comparative method. Pp. 105–20 in *Political Science: The State of the Discipline II*, ed. A. W. Finifter. Washington, DC: American Political Science Association.

—— BRADY, H. E., and SEAWRIGHT, J. 2004. Sources of leverage in causal inference: toward an alternative view of methodology. Pp. 229–66 in Brady and Collier 2004.

—— and ELMAN, C. 2008. Qualitative and multi-method research: organizations, publication, and reflections on integration. In *Oxford Handbook of Political Methodology*, ed. J. Box-Steffensmeier, H. E. Brady, and D. Collier. Oxford: Oxford University Press.

—— HIDALGO, F. D., and MACIUCEANU, A. O. 2006. Essentially contested concepts: debates and applications. *Journal of Political Ideologies*, 11: 211–46.

—— and LEVITSKY, S. 1997. Democracy with adjectives: conceptual innovation in comparative research. *World Politics*, 49: 430–51.

—— and MAHONEY, J. 1996. Insights and pitfalls: selection bias in qualitative research. *World Politics*, 49: 56–91.

——— and SEAWRIGHT, J. 2004. Claiming too much: warnings about selection bias. Pp. 85–102 in Brady and Collier 2004.

DESSLER, D. 1999. Constructivism within a positivist social science. *Review of International Studies*, 25: 123–37.

—— and OWEN, J. 2005. Constructivism and the problem of explanation: a review article. *Perspectives on Politics*, 3: 597–610.

DION, D. 1998. Evidence and inference in the comparative case study. *Comparative Politics*, 30: 127–45.

ECKSTEIN, H. 1975. Case study and theory in political science. Pp. 79–137 in *Handbook of Political Science*, vol. vii. *Strategies of Inquiry*, ed. F. I. Greenstein and N. W. Polsby. Reading, Mass.: Addison-Wesley.

EDELSTEIN, D. M. 2008. *Occupational Hazards: Success and Failure in Military Occupation*. Ithaca, NY: Cornell University Press.

ELMAN, C. 2005. Explanatory typologies in qualitative studies of international politics. *International Organization*, 59: 293–326.

—— and ELMAN, M. F. (eds.) 2001. *Bridges and Boundaries: Historians, Political Scientists, and the Study of International Relations*. Cambridge, Mass.: MIT Press.

——— 2002. How not to be Lakatos intolerant: appraising progress in IR research. *International Studies Quarterly*, 46: 231–62.

——— (eds.) 2003. *Progress in international relations Theory: Appraising the Field*. Cambridge, Mass.: MIT Press.

GEDDES, B. 2003. *Paradigms and Sand Castles: Theory Building and Research Design in Comparative Politics*. Ann Arbor: University of Michigan Press.

GEORGE, A. 1979. Case studies and theory development: the method of structured, focused comparison. Pp. 43–68 in *Diplomacy: New Approaches in History, Theory, and Policy*, ed. G. Lauren. New York: Free Press.

——and Bennett, A. 2005. *Case Studies and Theory Development in the Social Sciences*. Cambridge, Mass.: MIT Press.

——and McKeown, T. J. 1985. Case studies and theories of organizational decision making. Pp. 21–58 in *Advances in Information Processing in Organizations*, vol. ii, ed. R. F. Coulam and R. A. Smith. Greenwich, Conn.: JAI Press.

Gerring, J. 2001. *Social Science Methodology: A Criterial Framework*. Cambridge: Cambridge University Press.

——2007a. *Case Study Research: Principles and Practices*. Cambridge: Cambridge University Press.

——2007b. Is there a (viable) crucial-case method? *Comparative Political Studies*, 40: 231–53.

——and Barresi, P. A. 2003. Putting ordinary language to work: a min-max strategy of concept formation in the social sciences. *Journal of Theoretical Politics*, 15: 201–32.

Goertz, G. 2006. *Social Science Concepts: A User's Guide*. Princeton, NJ: Princeton University Press.

——and Levy, J. (eds.) 2007. *Explaining War and Peace: Case Studies and Necessary Condition Counterfactuals*. London: Routledge.

——and Mahoney, J. 2005. Two-level theories and Fuzzy-Set analysis. *Sociological Methods and Research*, 33: 497–538.

————2006. Scope in case study research. Presented at the American Political Science Association annual conference, Philadelphia, 31 Aug.

——and Starr, H. (eds.) 2002. *Necessary Conditions: Theory, Methodology, and Applications*. Lanham, Md.: Rowman and Littlefield.

Herrmann, R., and Choi, J. K. 2007. From prediction to learning: opening experts' minds to unfolding history. *International Security*, 31: 132–61.

Kacowicz, A. M. 2004. Case study methods in international security studies. Pp. 107–28 in *Models, Numbers and Cases: Methods for Studying International Relations*, ed. D. F. Sprinz and Y. Wolinsky-Nahmias. Ann Arbor: University of Michigan Press.

Kahneman, D., Slovic, P., and Tversky, A. 1982. *Judgment under Uncertainty: Heuristics and Biases*. Cambridge: Cambridge University Press.

Katzenstein, P. (ed.) 1996. *The Culture of National Security: Norms and Identity in World Politics*. New York: Columbia University Press.

——2005. *A World of Regions: Asia and Europe in the American Imperium*. Ithaca, NY: Cornell University Press.

King, G., Keohane, R. O., and Verba, S. 1994. *Designing Social Inquiry: Scientific Inference in Qualitative Research*. Princeton, NJ: Princeton University Press.

Lakatos, I. 1970. Falsification and the methodology of scientific research programmes. Pp. 91–196 in *Criticism and the Growth of Knowledge*, ed. I. Lakatos and A. Musgrave. New York: Cambridge University Press.

Lebow, R. N. 2000. What's so different about a counterfactual? *World Politics*, 52: 550–85.

Lieberman, E. 2005. Nested analysis as a mixed-method strategy for comparative research. *American Political Science Review*, 99: 435–52.

Lijphart, A. 1971. Comparative politics and the comparative method. *American Political Science Review*, 65: 682–93.

Mahoney, J. 2000. Path dependence in historical sociology. *Theory and Society*, 29: 507–48.

MAHONEY, J. 2007. Qualitative methodology and comparative politics. *Comparative Political Studies*, 40: 122–44.

——— and GOERTZ, G. 2004. The possibility principle: choosing negative cases in comparative research. *American Political Science Review*, 98: 653–69.

——— and RUESCHEMEYER, D. (eds.) 2003. *Comparative Historical Analysis in the Social Sciences*. Cambridge: Cambridge University Press.

MALINIAK, D., OAKES, A., PETERSON, S., and TIERNEY, M. 2007. The view from the ivory tower: TRIP survey of international relations faculty in the United States and Canada. Program on the Theory and Practice of International Relations, College of William and Mary, Williamsburg, Va., Feb.

MITCHELL, R., and BERNAUER, T. 2004. Beyond story-telling: designing case study research in international environmental policy. Pp. 81–106 in *Models, Numbers and Cases: Methods for Studying International Relations*, ed. D. F. Sprinz and Y. Wolinsky-Nahmias. Ann Arbor: University of Michigan Press.

ODELL, J. S. 2004. Case study methods in international political economy. Pp. 56–80 in *Models, Numbers and Cases: Methods for Studying International Relations*, ed. D. F. Sprinz and Y. Wolinsky-Nahmias. Ann Arbor: University of Michigan Press.

PIERSON, P. 2004. *Politics in Time: History, Institutions, and Social Analysis*. Princeton, NJ: Princeton University Press.

——— 2007. The costs of marginalization: qualitative methods in the study of American politics. *Comparative Political Studies*, 40: 145–69.

PRZEWORKSI, A., and TEUNE, H. 1970. *The Logic of Comparative Social Inquiry*. New York: Wiley Interscience.

RAGIN, C. C. 1987. *The Comparative Method: Moving beyond Qualitative and Quantitative Strategies*. Berkeley: University of California Press.

——— 2000. *Fuzzy-Set Social Science*. Chicago: University of Chicago Press.

——— and RIHOUX, B. 2004. Qualitative comparative analysis (QCA): state of the art and prospects. *Qualitative Methods: Newsletter of the American Political Science Association Organized Section on Qualitative Methods*, 2: 3–13.

REUS-SMIT, C. 2002. Imagining society: constructivism and the English School. *British Journal of Politics and International Relations*, 4: 487–509.

RUGGIE, J. G. 1998. What makes the world hang together? Neo-utilitarianism and the social constructivist challenge. *International Organization*, 52: 855–85.

SAMBANIS, N. 2004. Using case studies to expand economic models of civil war. *Perspectives on Politics*, 2: 259–79.

SCHWELLER, R. L. 1994. Bandwagoning for profit: bringing the revisionist state back in. *International Security*, 19: 72–107.

——— 1998. *Deadly Imbalances: Tripolarity and Hitler's Strategy of World Conquest*. New York: Columbia University Press.

SEAWRIGHT, J., and GERRING, J. 2006. Case-selection techniques in case study research: a menu of qualitative and quantitative options. Unpublished typescript, University of California at Berkeley.

SKOCPOL, T. 1979. *States and Social Revolutions: A Comparative Analysis of France, Russia, and China*. Cambridge: Cambridge University Press.

SMELSER, N. J. 1976. *Comparative Methods in the Social Sciences*. Englewood Cliffs, NJ: Prentice Hall.

TETLOCK, P. E. 2005. *Expert Political Judgment: How Good Is It? How Can We Know?* Princeton, NJ: Princeton University Press.

—— and BELKIN, A. (eds.) 1996. *Counterfactual Thought Experiments in World Politics: Logical, Methodological, and Psychological Perspectives.* Princeton, NJ: Princeton University Press.

WENDT, A. 1999. *Social Theory of International Politics.* Cambridge: Cambridge University Press.

WOHLFORTH, W. 1998. Reality check: revising theories of international politics in response to the end of the Cold War. *World Politics,* 50: 650–80.

YANOW, D. 2006a. Thinking interpretively: philosophical presuppositions and the human sciences. Pp. 5–26 in Yanow and Schwartz-Shea 2006b.

—— and SCHWARTZ-SHEA, P. (eds.) 2006b. *Interpretation and Method: Empirical Research Methods and the Interpretive Turn.* Armonk, NY: M. E. Sharpe.

ZIBLATT, D. 2006. *Structuring the State: The Formation of Italy and Germany and the Puzzle of Federalism.* Princeton, NJ: Princeton University Press.

CHAPTER 30

HISTORICAL METHODS

JOEL QUIRK

For most international relations scholars, historical inquiry is not simply (or even primarily) an end in itself, but also serves as an essential platform for the advancement of a range of theoretical goals. This self-conscious orientation extends to the study of both international and intellectual history. It not only plays a decisive role when it comes to the methods adopted by scholars from various schools, but also helps to ensure that historical projects are routinely organized around the demands of modern theoretical arguments. In this intellectual environment, the importance attached to making a theoretical contribution can be both an asset and an obstacle. International relations scholars have marshaled an arsenal of valuable tools, techniques, and templates, offering important insights into many vital questions, but these contributions can also come at the price of historical depth, with complex, multicausal issues ending up as testing grounds for partisan efforts to corroborate abstract theoretical models.

Historical inquiry is often identified as a neglected area in international relations circles (Teschke 2003, 14; Keene 2005, 1–3). This might have been true in the past, but it is no longer true today, as research into both international and intellectual history has flourished in recent times. Although silences and problem areas remain, especially when it comes to long-standing Eurocentrism, there has nonetheless been tremendous growth over the last two decades. In this chapter I highlight a number of recent contributions, paying particular attention to the relationship between history, theory, and method. This project is organized into five distinct sections. The first section offers a brief sketch of the vagaries of history as a field of study.

The second section is concerned with the search for universal models, and the relationship between rationalist theories, radical simplification, and international history. The third section is concerned with critical responses to the historical limitations of radical simplification, and allied attempts to come to terms with questions of contingency and complexity. The fourth section explores more recent developments in rationalist theory. Using innovations in realist theory as an explicatory focal point, I examine a number of recent contributions that have placed rationalist approaches on a stronger historical footing. The main focus throughout this discussion is the origin and operation of the state system, which has long been a premier site for historical inquiry in international relations circles. The final section of the chapter takes up the parallel field of intellectual history, exploring how recent works on the history of ideas have been shaped around contemporary agendas.

1 On History

In his famous work *What is History?*, E. H. Carr (1962, 6) observes that "the belief in a hard core of historical facts existing objectively and independently of the interpretation of the historian is a preposterous fallacy, but one which it is very hard to eradicate." It is not necessary to be a postmodernist to recognize the merits of this position. Many different forms of interpretation are involved in the complex relationship between historical events and their contemporary representation. The recollections of relevant participants will not always point in a single direction. Many competing factors, both proximate and long term, will necessarily be involved. Subsequent records are unlikely to be complete, and those that are available will inevitably reflect parochial orientations and preoccupations. Other key issues include the selection of events that become "history," rather than falling by the wayside, and the level of importance that ends up being attached to any number of potentially relevant factors. It is also clear, moreover, that the vagaries of historical inquiry also extend to contemporary orientations and agendas, where it is not unusual for people to "study history less for what they might learn than for what they want to prove" (Hinsley 1963, 13). The classical example here is the "Whig interpretation" of history, which refers to a long-standing tendency among Anglo-Saxon historians to "emphasise certain principles of progress in the past and to produce a story which is the ratification if not the glorification of the present" (Butterfield 1965, v). This represents the most well-known manifestation of a much larger conundrum, as contemporary preoccupations can end up influencing how the historical record is represented in a variety of ways.

These considerations apply to all forms of historical inquiry. When we focus our attention upon international relations, a number of additional issues come to light, starting with differences between history and international relations (as a form of social or political science). This issue is complicated by internal variations within disciplines, which make it difficult to speak of anything more than general tendencies. There is widespread agreement, however, that the two disciplines ultimately favor different approaches. One synopsis comes from Jack Levy (1997, 32), who maintains "that the distinctive difference between history and political science is that historians describe and explain the connections between a series of events, whereas political scientists formulate and test general theoretical propositions about relationships between variables or classes of events." Another reading comes from John Gaddis (2002, 62–3), who observes that all forms of social inquiry inevitably involve generalizations, but that historians tend to embed generalizations within narratives, while social scientists tend to embed narratives within generalizations. Academic international relations' attachment to general theoretical propositions has also ensured that international relations theorists are often heavily reliant upon the works of historians for information. This widespread dependence on secondary sources raises difficult methodological questions, which are rarely explicitly addressed. Historians may not always make their underlying assumptions explicit, but this does not mean that they simply compile historical data, detached from theoretical or methodological commitments (Lustick 1996; Kratochwil 2006; Roberts 2006). This has led to a slightly odd situation where international relations theorists draw extensively upon the often painstaking research conducted by historians, yet regularly disconnect these contributions from the nuanced, case-specific, and typically multicausal approach that most historians favor.

The main point at issue here is the close relationship between history, theory, and method. In order fully to understand the various ways in which the historical record has been conceptualized and discussed amongst international relations scholars one must first interrogate both the theoretical aspirations involved, and the methods utilized to advance these goals. This is particularly important when it comes to more recent works, as modern scholars typically end up structuring their arguments around the strengths and weaknesses of previous contributions. Many disciplines tackle "big picture," macro-historical projects, yet these projects tend to be organized on very different lines to equivalent projects in academic international relations. These projects may end up exploring similar historical topics, but they remain embedded within different academic discourses. In the case of international relations, this has both positive and negative dimensions. International relations scholars have offered valuable insights into many important questions, yet theorists can sometimes lose sight of history as a distinctive field of study, with its own methodological and interpretative challenges (see Pierson 2004; Trachtenberg 2006). Theory will always need history, since past events offer an indispensable platform against which various models come to be formulated and evaluated, but there will always be a danger of theory becoming an end in itself, rather than a valuable tool.

2 RATIONAL ACTION, MATERIALISM, AND FUNCTIONALISM

In any given sequence of international events, an extraordinary number of factors will be in play. These factors can be evaluated inductively, by taking into account a range of competing influences, but as more issues are taken into account it invariably becomes harder to move beyond case-specific idiosyncrasies and thereby identify unambiguous causal patterns or universal models. Modern social scientists have sought to resolve this dilemma through various forms of radical simplification. This has chiefly been expressed in three overlapping strategies: rational action, materialism, and functionalism. Each of these strategies comes with considerable intellectual baggage. In this setting, I am primarily concerned with their theoretical dimensions and methodological rationale.

Rational action is designed to cut through the vagaries of human behavior by treating individuals as atomized utility maximizers. For some detractors, this constitutes "a caricature of the human condition" (Jackson 2000, 47), yet this objection loses some of its force if we view rational action as a qualified methodological move, rather than a totalizing ontological stance. The key point at issue is not whether every actor operates according to a hyper-rational calculus, but whether it is heuristically useful to structure theoretical inquiry around this universal behavioral model. Rational action is commonly coupled with various forms of materialism, building upon the underlying notion that the organization and distribution of material capabilities ultimately define the structural context within which political actors pursue their strategic interests. Material properties do not always exist in isolation, but often gain depth and definition through the ideational orientations that surround them, yet it can still be useful to operate *as if* material forces were entirely separate. The final component in this theoretical triad is functionalism, which often serves as a bridge between rational action and materialism, as the origin and operation of various institutional forms is explained by their strategic functions, or utilitarian purposes. Functionalism can operate on multiple levels. On the one hand, we have institutional arrangements between political communities, such as regimes or international organizations, which are said to reflect strategic interests in developing institutions that serve favorable political and economic functions. On the other, we have institutional arrangements within communities, as the genesis and subsequent development of various political and economic complexes can be traced to utilitarian responses to competition amongst powerful vested interests.

This triad has been central to an ongoing theoretical quest for universal models, clear causal connections, and definitive predictions. From this standpoint, it is difficult to imagine a more effective set of tools. Rational action cuts through the vagaries of human behavior, materialism delineates both interests and capabilities, and functionalism provides an explanation for the origin and operation of various institutional forms. The primary goal is not to blend together a range of considerations, but to specify a small number of key mechanisms that clearly account for variations across multiple cases. This has in turn given rise to two overlapping axes of theoretical contention. The first axis is defined by wide-ranging disputes over the application of these overlapping strategies, as theorists of various persuasions share an underlying commitment (albeit with some modifications or additions) to rational action, materialism, and functionalism, yet disagree over their substantive ramifications. This dynamic has been central to debates amongst neorealists and neoliberal institutionalists. It also extends to differences among many exponents of rational choice theory, neoclassical realism, the new liberalism, and other theories that draw inspiration from economic models. Not all rationalist theories are universal in scope. Some theories become applicable only in particular circumstances, such as international negotiations, leading to sophisticated debates over the specific consequences of universal behavioral models operating within narrowly defined parameters. The second axis of contention revolves around a host of issues, actions, and idiosyncrasies that have frequently been marginalized as part of a methodological commitment to radical simplification. This dynamic is chiefly concerned with questions of identity, ideology, epistemology, and contingency. It is also especially relevant to the study of international history, as the search for enduring axioms has frequently overshadowed the distinctive qualities of less familiar historical settings.

In order to illustrate these themes, I turn to a familiar point of departure: Kenneth Waltz's outstanding *Theory of International Politics* (1979). The main features of Waltz's theory are well known, starting with the state-centric character of the international system and the enduring effects of anarchy, both institutional (like-units, functional adaptation) and behavioral (self-help, rational action), and then extending to the structural dimensions of relative material capabilities, and more specific points regarding bipolarity and economic interdependence. In many ways, the path Waltz takes is more interesting than his ultimate destination. Rejecting the "inductivist route," Waltz (1979, 4, 7) argues that "explanatory power...is gained by moving away from 'reality', not by staying close to it." A theorist must cut through complexity by identifying a bounded realm of activity, within which generalizable patterns become explicable through the integration of a small number of heuristically powerful, ruthlessly simplified mechanisms. This means embracing a systemic approach that excludes domestic politics, or regime type, not because they are irrelevant, but because they can force us "back to the descriptive level," unduly complicating our grasp of "big, important, and enduring patterns" stem-ming from international anarchy (Waltz 1979, 65, 70). This ruthless strategy ends up "bracketing out" a tremendous range of issues. Of particular importance here is Waltz's static approach to international history, which is encapsulated in his claim that "the texture of international politics remains highly constant, patterns recur, and events repeat themselves endlessly. The relations that prevail internationally seldom shift rapidly in type or in quality" (Waltz 1979, 66).

Waltz's theory has played a central role in numerous debates. His main con-tribution to the study of international history has been as a critical foil. In this context, his work has been regularly presented as an emblem of the more general historical shortcomings of "mainstream" approaches. This association may not be entirely fair, since Waltz is not necessarily the strongest example available, but it has nonetheless served as an important starting point for a range of historical projects. While these projects differ in many important respects, they can be loosely integrated around a shared critique of the historical limitations of radical simpli-fication. From here, the theoretical quest for universal essences has given way to a more qualified focus upon contingent properties, as scholars have (re)turned to a range of issues previously marginalized on methodological grounds.

3 Historical Complexity and Contemporary Theory

For theorists like Waltz, the current status quo is best viewed as an unbroken exten-sion of enduring axioms. This totalizing stance has provoked a sustained barrage of historically oriented critique. One of the main objections to this perspective is that it ends up incorrectly projecting recent innovations backward through time, thereby elevating contingent structures and orientations to the status of transhistorical essences. This line of argument is nicely summarized by John Hobson (2002), who argues that international relations scholarship often suffers from two distinct modes of ahistoricism: chronofetishism and tempocentrism. The former is said to denote "a 'sealing off' of the present such that it appears as an autonomous, natural, spontaneous and immutable entity." The latter refers to the extrapolation of this "naturalized" present "backwards through time such that *discontinuous* ruptures and *differences* between historical epochs and states systems are smoothed over and consequentially obscured" (Hobson 2002, 9).

One of the key points at issue here is the relationship between theoretical par-simony and historical complexity. The main advantage of radical simplification is that it enables theorists to cut through complexity, making it possible to speak of definitive, universal causes that unite otherwise disparate cases, yet this source of strength can also be a source of weakness, as the search for transhistorical essences has also tended to "smooth over" both distinctive historical features and fundamental differences. This trade-off is especially acute in the cases of neorealism and neoliberal institutionalism, which both played major roles within theoretical debates during the 1980s and 1990s, and thus regularly served as focal points for historical and theoretical critique. Among the many strategies that have been employed here, three main impulses can be identified: (1) a concerted effort to catalogue the historical shortcomings of rational action, materialism, and functionalism; (2) a concerted effort to interrogate the complexities and idiosyncrasies that have shaped particular historical milieux; and (3) a concerted effort to challenge aspects of contemporary life that might otherwise appear natural, or immutable.

From this vantage point, an important point of departure is provided by John Ruggie (1993). Expressing profound frustration with a widespread inability to conceptualize meaningful challenges to the modern state system, Ruggie famously looks to the transition from medieval to modern forms of political rule for guidance. This transition poses severe problems for Waltz, who posits a sharp, consistent demarcation between domestic and international. This image is difficult to reconcile with medieval history, where political life was organized around a heteronomous order of cross-cutting jurisdictions, both religious and secular, together with a significant level of functional differentiation (non-like-units). If political life has been organized on fundamentally different terms, how did the states system arise? For Ruggie (1993, 151), modern statehood is defined by a commitment to "territoriality defined, fixed, and mutually exclusive enclaves of legitimate dominion." This unique model is said to have emerged within a relatively short timeframe, with a range of cumulative factors paving the way for a decisive moment of radical disjuncture in the sixteenth and seventeenth centuries, which Ruggie tentatively frames in terms of epochal change, or a form of punctuated equilibrium.

In making this argument, Ruggie (1993, 141) is explicit about the inherent limitations of his project, observing that much of his work is limited to searching "for a vocabulary and . . . research agenda by means of which we can start to ask systematic questions about the possibility of fundamental international transformation today." His case is strongest when it comes to substantive differences between medieval and modern, but his explanation of the transformation from one order to the other remains fairly suggestive. On this point, a theoretically more rigorous argument has recently been advanced by Daniel Philpott. According to Philpott (2001, 4), the constitutional structure of our current global order can be traced to two seminal revolutions in sovereignty, the Treaty of Westphalia and colonial independence, which in turn reflect "prior revolutions in ideas about justice and political authority." To substantiate these claims, he identifies two distinct roles played by ideas in shaping these momentous events. The first role is concerned with identities, as ideas are said to persuade actors to take on new forms of identification through reason of reflection. The second role is concerned with social power, as ideas are said to "alter the costs and benefits facing those who are in a position to promote or hinder the policies that the ideas demand" (Philpott 2001, 58). Ideas do not operate in isolation from other factors, but neither are they reducible to material structures or strategic calculations.

Philpott's argument is well suited to decolonization (see also Jackson 1990; Crawford 2002), but has proved to be more contentious when it comes to Westphalia. Like Ruggie, Philpott favors a decisive moment of radical disjuncture, but this formula has been challenged on several fronts. Some scholars accept Westphalia as a key turning point, but also identify a further transformation from absolutist sovereignty to sovereign nationhood (Reus-Smit 1998; Hall 1999). Others question its status as a decisive moment (Osiander 2001). On this front, several neo-Marxist scholars have developed an alternative methodological approach to historical transformation. In one pioneering contribution, Justin Rosenberg favors a quite different form of "structural discontinuity," which separates pre-capitalist orders from the modern capitalist system. This emerges from a strident critique of realism, as the widely held notion of an essential continuity in relations between states is discarded in favor of a comparative approach that connects variations in geopolitical behavior to underlying forms of political and economic organization. In this model, the distinctive qualities of the modern state system are said to correspond to the unique social structures of capitalist society (Rosenberg 1994). This line of argument has recently been expanded and further refined by Benno Teschke (2003), who charts a staggered progression through medieval, absolutist, and modern capitalist politics. In developing his argument, Teschke is careful to balance historical complexity and theoretical parsimony, giving due consideration to uneven development while nonetheless making a strong case for the role of property regimes in (re)structuring the identities of political communities. In this context, "the decisive shift towards modern international relations is not marked by the Peace of Westphalia, but comes with the rise of the first modern state: post-revolutionary England" (Teschke 2003, 249).

Interest in sovereignty and modernity has not been limited to international history, but also extends to intellectual history. A complex amalgam of these two related fields can be found in the work of Jens Bartelson. Focusing on the relationship between sovereignty and knowledge, Bartelson offers a genealogical history that spans the Renaissance, the "Classical Age," and Modernity. The genealogical method has become increasingly popular in recent times. Commonly associated with Friedrich Nietzsche and Michel Foucault, a genealogy "is strategically aimed at that which looks unproblematic and is held to be timeless; its task is to explain how these present traits, in all their vigour and truth, were formed out of the past" (Bartelson 1995, 73). For Bartelson, this translates into an episodic narrative that builds upon a series of textual exemplars, as impromptu shifts in political discourse are traced to mutations in the epistemic and ontological foundations of intellectual inquiry. Another prominent exponent of a discursive approach to sovereignty is Cynthia Weber (1995), who focuses upon changing boundaries between sovereignty and intervention. Instead of stabilizing the definition of sovereignty (or intervention), and evaluating substantive historical practices against an abstract standard, Weber contends that individual states are "written," or constituted, according to logics of representation and simulation. To be sovereign, a state needs to "organize its affairs in such a way that its foundation of sovereign authority is authorized to speak for its particular domestic community in international affairs" (Weber 1995, 124). Through a series of case studies, she connects ruptures in this symbolic relationship to a range of interventionary practices, demonstrating that claims about (true) sovereign authority are not always incompatible with intervention, but have also been invoked to validate incursions that transgress conventional notions of territorial demarcation.

The genesis, operation, and ongoing evolution of the state system is now firmly established as a premier focal point for historical research in international relations circles. It is here that tremendous progress has been made over the years, yet this heavy concentration upon one historical milieu, however important, also opens the door to charges of Eurocentrism. On this front, academic international relations remains shamefully weak, yet is slowly improving. Of particular significance here is the macro-historical work of Barry Buzan, Charles Jones, and Richard Little. For these scholars, Waltz's theory remains a useful starting point, but is unnecessarily restrictive. Moving beyond a static association between anarchy and like-units, they identify four possible combinations of political units and international structure: (1) hierarchy and like-units, (2) anarchy and like-units, (3) hierarchy and un-like-units, and (4) anarchy and un-like-units (Buzan, Jones, and Little 1993, 37–47). These variations serve dramatically to undercut "the Westphalian Straightjacket" (Buzan and Little 2001, 25), giving pride of place to different forms of organization, from empires and suzerain networks, to tribal orders and city states (see also Watson 1992; Buzan and Little 2000). This perspective also reflects a substantial debt to the expansive approach of prominent "English School" figures such as Martin Wight and Hedley Bull (Wight 1977; Bull and Watson 1984). This debt is shared by many modern scholars, most notably when it comes to the theory and practice of international society. Historical discussion of international society usually begins with the premise that there are different *kinds* of society, which have evolved over time in response to various dynamics. This theoretical starting point has been successfully applied to a range of historical cases, proving to be especially valuable as a framework for evaluating relationships between European and non-European peoples (Keene 2002).

The approaches outlined above are loosely bound together by a shared rejection of radical simplification. Once we move beyond this common affinity we quickly encounter significant variations. This is partially a question of the specific strategies and orientations that particular approaches favor, and partially a question of the overarching goals to which they aspire. For many scholars, the main purpose of historical inquiry is to provide a more compelling explanation of particular events, and/or persuasive theoretical argument. This can translate into "thick description," various forms of causal and constitutive analysis, or more traditional historical narratives. For other scholars, the primary purpose of historical inquiry is to shatter prevailing orthodoxies into both complicit and contestable fragments, paving the way for either modernist reform or postmodern resistance.

4 RENEWING RATIONALISM

The various works considered in the previous section collectively pose a fundamental challenge to rationalist theories of international relations. In most cases, the main axis of contention is not metaphysical, but empirical, as critics have repeatedly documented the difficulties involved in reconciling various historical experiences with rational action, materialism, and/or functionalism. In response to this ongoing challenge, rationalist scholars from various schools have recently offered a range of innovative theoretical models and historical elaborations, while striving to uphold the overall tenor of the social scientific project. These works may not convince every critic, but they collectively go a considerable way in reinvigorating the historical credentials of rationalist approaches. In this context, Waltz once again occupies a key position. This has both negative and positive dimensions. In the case of the former, more nuanced works can end up being indirectly overshadowed, as Waltz's shortcomings are often held to epitomize rationalist shortcomings more generally. This is problematic, as other projects frequently have more to offer (Gilpin 1981; Doyle 1986). Many forms of historical analysis, such as debates over the "democratic peace" or the obsolescence of major war, have chiefly taken place amongst rationalists of various stripes, with relatively limited external input. It is also clear, however, that Waltz continues to serve as a major historical and theoretical foil. This is particularly evident when it comes to realist theory, where more recent scholarship has cautiously returned to some of the key issues and developments that Waltz deliberately excluded.

In this context, two pioneering contributions have come from Stephen Walt (1987), who highlights the role of intentions, and Jack Synder (1991), who focuses on domestic politics. Walt offers a sophisticated, policy-driven analysis of the formation of international alliances, both formal and informal. His primary empirical evidence comes from the diplomatic history of the Middle East between 1955 and 1979, where he identifies thirty-six alliances, both bilateral and multilateral, which involve eighty-six national decisions. This evidence is marshaled to evaluate a number of interlinked hypotheses, revolving around the prevalence of balancing and bandwagoning, the role of ideology, foreign aid, and transnational penetration. Walt's major contribution (1987, 172) emerges out of a compelling critique of traditional notions of the balance of power, where he concludes that "examining the impact of several distinct sources of threat can provide a more persuasive account of alliance formation than can solely focusing on the distribution of aggregate capabilities." Balance-of-threat theory gives considerable weight to material resources, an essential component of Waltz's theory, but introduces an additional set of considerations, based upon the intentions of the actors involved. Another influential reformulation of realist theory comes from Synder (1991, 19), who argues that "realism must be recaptured from those who look only at politics between societies, ignoring what goes on within societies." This model is expressed in a case-study driven analysis of imperial overexpansion. Building upon an analysis of the evolving policies of Germany, Japan, Britain, the USSR and the United States, Snyder argues that imprudent, counter-productive expansionary policies can be chiefly traced to domestic coalition-making and ideological mythmaking. While expansion may not be in the national interest, or the interests of the general population, logrolling domestic coalitions are held to have successfully mobilized various institutional and ideological resources to advance their parochial interests.

These works represent early examples of a larger trend, as realist theory has experienced a renaissance in the aftermath of the cold war. Echoing Walt and Synder, this new generation of realist scholarship has regularly ended up "sacrificing some of Waltz's parsimony" (Schweller 1998, 10) in the pursuit of greater theoretical precision and historical sophistication. The best example here is arguably Dale Copeland (2000, 3), whose theory of dynamic differentials seeks to explain the causes of major war, integrating "power differentials, polarity, and declining power trends into one cohesive logic." This innovative synthesis is then tested against a series of empirically rich case studies from the twentieth century, followed by a more limited survey of earlier cases within Europe, as Copeland argues that declining yet still dominant great powers are most likely to initiate (or risk) major war. In this model, estimations of the inevitability and severity of decline are mediated by international polarity, sustaining enduring systemic pressures that tend to overshadow, but not entirely eliminate, unit-level dynamics. This reformulation of systemic theory constitutes one of two main avenues of recent inquiry (see also Schweller 1998; Mearsheimer 2001). Other contributions have followed Snyder in taking up internal factors such as elite behavior and (mis)perceptions, or a combination of internal and international dynamics (Wohlforth 1993; Van Evera 1999). Some of these moves have proved controversial (Legro and Moravcsik 1999), but they have also enhanced the explanatory power of realism on multiple fronts. Historical inquiry has been an essential part of this equation, as theorists have sought to validate their preferred approach using detailed case studies, measures, and models. Rather than rejecting rational action, materialism, and functionalism, the underlying impulse has instead been to formulate strategies to place these models on a stronger historical footing.

In keeping with larger trends, these works have been primarily organized around debates within rationalist circles. Those involved are well versed with larger critiques, but have here concentrated their energies upon getting their own house in order. This does not mean, of course, that there have been no explicit rejoinders. Especially prominent here is Stephen Krasner's work on sovereignty, which is organized around the idea that logics of consequences, based upon strategic calculations, have consistently trumped logics of appropriateness, based upon rules and identities (Krasner 1999, 5–6). The history of sovereignty, a premier site for rationalist critics, is framed in terms of "organized hypocrisy," as states are said to have routinely deviated from prevailing norms, decoupling political behavior from institutional scripts. This argument finds expression in thematic studies of minority rights, human rights, sovereign lending, and state creation from the nineteenth century onwards. In this model, ideas are not entirely irrelevant, but material power and strategic interests remain the decisive arbiter.

The preceding discussion is by no means exhaustive. As other chapters in this volume can attest, realism is by no means the only theory available here. I would argue, however, that the trajectory of realist theory reveals a great deal about the evolving relationship between rationalist methods and historical research. From the 1950s onwards, academic international relations attached considerable importance to parsimonious, universal models, leading to various forms of radical simplification. This reached its most influential expression in the work of Waltz, who ruthlessly sacrificed historical detail in the pursuit of theoretical elegance, introducing a focal point for critique in which questions of historical contingency emerged as vital issues. In the face of this challenge, more recent scholarship has favored a higher degree of theoretical precision and empirical rigor, furnishing realism with a stronger historical foundation. It is also worth noting, however, that the various works identified above continue to assume, rather than explain, the existence of the state, thereby largely sidestepping Ruggie's concern with epochal change. It is not that rationalist theories have little to offer here (see Spruyt 1994), but when it comes to the ongoing search for universal models, this could very well be one major historical variable too many.

5 INTELLECTUAL HISTORY AND CONTEMPORARY THEORY

In each of the approaches outlined above, the content of historical inquiry is primarily structured around the requirements of modern conceptions of the nature and purpose of theoretical endeavor. A similar dynamic also applies to the closely related field of intellectual history, where various aspects of the history of ideas have been consistently called upon to validate a range of contemporary causes and theoretical positions. The relationship between intellectual history and international history is not always easy to pin down. There have recently been some innovative attempts to combine the two realms (Johnston 1995; Hopf 2002), but it is also not unusual to see textual sources being presented as major influences, or historical exemplars, without direct verification of the impact of their often esoteric content on parallel historical developments. In this context, discussion of the history of ideas can end up as an unacknowledged substitute for detailed research into international history.

The main point at issue here, however, is the relationship between intellectual history and contemporary theory. Intellectual inquiry into international relations was not consistently differentiated from the study of law, philosophy, history, economics, and/or religion until the twentieth century. A key component in the development of this modern innovation has been a cumulative, retroactive effort to forge genealogical links with earlier intellectual endeavors, resulting in a range of mainly European scholars being recruited to a range of theoretical causes. This widespread practice raises several methodological issues, which have not always been explicitly addressed (Schmidt 2002a, 6–7). Much like the study of international history, the study of intellectual history has flourished in recent times. Three main areas of inquiry can be identified here: (1) the composition of the realist tradition, (2) the integration of political and international theory, and (3) the early history of the international relations discipline.

The search for universal templates is not confined to international history, but also extends to intellectual history, where canonical figures have been routinely presented as exemplars of timeless ideas or eternal conversations. This approach has been comprehensively challenged in other disciplines, but remains popular within international relations circles, with the two most prominent exponents being the realist tradition (Gilpin 1984) and Martin Wight's expansive differentiation (1991) between realism, rationalism, and revolutionism. Both schemes project modern categories backward through time, with the realist tradition placing luminaries such as Thucydides, Niccolò Machiavelli, Thomas Hobbes, and Jean-Jacques Rousseau alongside more recent innovations. Modern realists have regularly invoked this pedigree to bolster various theoretical claims, provoking two main lines of critique. The first line of critique questions the attribution of a realist persona to various scholars, leading to charges that those involved should not be caricatured as realists (George 1994, 70–4; Walker 1993, 26–47). The second (sometimes tentatively) accepts that these figures belong to an identifiable tradition, and instead uses their vaunted status to interrogate modern conceptions of realist theory (Haslam 2002; Williams 2005). The best example of this approach arguably comes from Richard Lebow, who bases his work upon detailed, contextual case studies of Thucydides,

Carl von Clausewitz, and Hans Morgenthau. This serves as a platform from which to re-evaluate modern conceptions of realism, supporting Lebow's contention (2003, 58) that "the modern academy has introduced a false dichotomy between political and moral behavior and political and moral theorizing."

This line of argument resonates with recent moves to integrate political and international thought. Early international relations scholarship presented political and international theory as discrete categories, with the scarcity of the latter being unfavorably contrasted with the bounty of the former (Wight 1966). Recent scholarship has challenged this formulation, embracing an integrated framework under the rubric of international political theory. This forms part of the rapid growth of normative theorizing during the 1990s (Schmidt 2002b). In this context, the history of ideas has once again been called upon to bolster contemporary agendas, as scholars have sought out compelling antecedents for more recent endeavors. One influential approach comes from Chris Brown (1992), who organizes the history of ideas into cosmopolitan and communitarian strands, with Immanuel Kant exemplifying the former and Georg Hegel exemplifying the latter. Another comes from David Boucher (1998), who bases his expansive historical survey upon a tripartite division between empirical realism, universal moral order, and historical reason. In both of these frameworks dominant conceptions of value-neutral explanation give way to an explicitly normative orientation. This also extends to recent works on "classical" theory (Clark and Neumann 1996; Jahn 2006), which are similarly organized around tensions between past and present intellectual models (see also Jackson 2000). Some contributions have provided variations on the timeless ideas framework. Others have concentrated upon key differences between historical milieux. In the case of the latter, the goal is to "illuminate our contemporary intellectual situation by establishing *contrasts* rather than affinities with the past, to call attention to the fact that at different times thinkers have conceptualized international politics ... in quite different ways" (Keene 2005, 17). This line of argument shares many features in common with Hobson's indictment of academic international relations' widespread tendency to "smooth over" underlying historical differences.

The final focal point for recent research into intellectual history has been the early development of academic international relations, where there has been a concerted effort to move beyond perfunctory treatments of immature idealism (Long and Wilson 1995; Long and Schmidt 2005). This has found expression in a stream of detailed critiques, as scholars have argued that conventional narratives offer a grossly distorted picture of the intellectual history of the early twentieth century, most notably when it comes to the story of a "first great debate" (Wilson 1998; Quirk and Vigneswaran 2005). Many eminent figures from this period have also been subject to critical reappraisal, including realist icon Carr (Jones 1998; Cox 2000). The best example from this now extensive literature arguably comes from Brian Schmidt, who contends that international relations scholars have routinely confused retroactive analytical constructs for authentic traditions, and thereby incorrectly elevated the historiographical (by)products of current agendas to the status of historical realities. Schmidt instead embraces an alternative methodological approach, which he describes as a critical internal discursive history, that strives to "reconstruct as accurately as possible the history of the conversation that has been constitutive of academic international relations" (Schmidt 1998, 37).

The eclectic contributions outlined here can be loosely grouped together around two main impulses. On the one hand, we have a common desire to offer a distinctive account of the intellectual contribution of particular authors and/or eras. In many cases, this is primarily a question of offering a more detailed account than those currently available, and thereby deflating problematic representations. On the other hand, we have a common desire to utilize the history of ideas as an authoritative platform from which to speak to contemporary theoretical debates. In many cases, this translates into attempts to open space for different models of intellectual inquiry, as earlier authors and eras are held to have operated in quite different ways from current theoretical conventions. Beyond these overarching impulses we encounter considerable variation. While the timeless ideas framework remains popular, recent scholarship has continued a now long-standing practice of looking outside academic international relations for inspiration, drawing upon scholars such as John Gunnell (1993) and Quentin Skinner (2002).

6 Concluding Remarks

All forms of historical inquiry invariably have important normative and praxeo-logical dimensions. For theorists who view history as a realm of recurrence and repetition, the key point at issue is effective management. By exploring cyclic historical patterns, they cautiously seek to identify ways of mitigating the worst effects of enduring structural forces. For theorists who view history as a realm of contingency and complexity, the key point at issue is fundamental change. By exploring historical ruptures and essential differences, they cautiously seek to identify nascent potentials within contemporary life that point to ways of reorienting international order. This perspective does not necessarily translate into historical determinism, since future cataclysms are always possible, but it does suggest that aspects of the current status quo that otherwise appear natural, or immutable, are best understood as contingent expressions of a long-term process of historical contestation. Within both these perspectives we encounter further variation, as scholars regularly offer divergent accounts of the strategies and orientations that are required to promote and/or evaluate either effective management or fundamental change.

International relations theory has served as a common medium through which these differences have been conceptualized and discussed, helping to provide purpose and structure to an eclectic array of historical projects. On this front, the main axis of contention has been an ongoing search for universal models, clear causal connections, and definitive predictions. This has been chiefly expressed in various forms of radical simplification, based upon rational action, materialism, and functionalism. The most influential example of this approach has been the work of Kenneth Waltz. More recent contributions have introduced powerful modifications of Waltz's abstract vision, offering a higher degree of historical rigor and theoretical precision while remaining committed to social scientific ideals. These contributions have gone against the grain of recent trends in historical research within international relations circles, which have been heavily populated by critics of rationalist approaches. The search for transhistorical essences that operate across various time periods and regions will always be tremendously challenging. It is easy to be overly critical when scholars fall short in pursuing such a difficult theoretical task. The real sticking point, however, has less do with individual shortcomings than with the uncertain wisdom of the overall exercise. As we have seen, this has often translated into a referendum on the merits of radical simplification, and the relative importance of various issues and idiosyncrasies that have been marginalized in the pursuit of theoretical parsimony. Both international and intellectual history have been central to this often fractious debate, as scholars have highlighted historical developments and intellectual contributions that do not conform with prevailing models. This central relationship between history, theory, and method has ultimately ensured that historical research within academic international relations is not so much an end in itself as an expansive platform for the advancement of various contemporary goals.

REFERENCES

BARTELSON, J. 1995. *A Genealogy of Sovereignty*. Cambridge: Cambridge University Press.

BOUCHER, D. 1998. *Political Theories of International Relations: From Thucydides to the Present*. Oxford: Oxford University Press.

BROWN, C. 1992. *International Relations Theory: New Normative Approaches*. New York: Harvester Wheatsheaf.

BULL, H., and WATSON, A. (eds.) 1984. *The Expansion of International Society*. Oxford: Clarendon Press.

BUTTERFIELD, H. 1965. *The Whig Interpretation of History*. New York: W. W. Norton.

BUZAN, B., JONES, C., and LITTLE, R. 1993. *The Logic of Anarchy: Neorealism to Structural Realism*. New York: Columbia University Press.

——and LITTLE, R. 2000. *International Systems in World History: Remaking the Study of International Relations*. Oxford: Oxford University Press.

BUZAN, B., and LITTLE, R. 2001. Why international relations has failed as an intellectual project and what to do about it. *Millennium: Journal of International Studies*, 30: 19–39.

CARR, E. H. 1962. *What is History?* London: Macmillan; originally published 1961.

CLARK, I., and NEUMANN, I. (eds.) 1996. *Classical Theories of International Relations*. London: Macmillan.

COPELAND, D. 2000. *The Origins of Major War*. Ithaca, NY: Cornell University Press.

COX, M. (ed.) 2000. *E. H. Carr: A Critical Appraisal*. Hampshire: Palgrave.

CRAWFORD, N. 2002. *Argument and Change in World Politics: Ethics, Decolonization, and Humanitarian Intervention*. Cambridge: Cambridge University Press.

DOYLE, M. 1986. *Empires*. Ithaca, NY: Cornell University Press.

GADDIS, J. 2002. *The Landscape of History: How Historians Map the Past*. Oxford: Oxford University Press.

GEORGE, J. 1994. *Discourses of Global Politics: A Critical (Re)Introduction to International Relations*. Boulder, Colo.: Lynne Rienner.

GILPIN, R. 1981. *War and Change in World Politics*. Cambridge: Cambridge University Press.

——1984. The richness of the tradition of political realism. *International Organization*, 38: 287–304.

GUNNELL, J. 1993. *The Descent of Political Theory: The Genealogy of an American Vocation*. Chicago: University of Chicago Press.

HALL, R. 1999. *National Collective Identity: Social Constructs and International Systems*. New York: Columbia University Press.

HASLAM, J. 2002. *No Virtue Like Necessity: Realist Thought in International Relations since Machiavelli*. New Haven, Conn.: Yale University Press.

HINSLEY, F. H. 1963. *Power and the Pursuit of Peace: Theory and Practice in the History of Relations between States*. Cambridge: Cambridge University Press.

HOBSON, J. 2002. What's at stake in "bringing historical sociology back into international relations?" Transcending "chronofetishism" and "tempocentrism" in international relations. Pp. 3–41 in *Historical Sociology of International Relations*, ed. S. Hobden and J. Hobson. Cambridge: Cambridge University Press.

HOPF, T. 2002. *Social Construction of International Politics: Identities and Foreign Policies, Moscow, 1955 and 1999*. Ithaca, NY: Cornell University Press.

JACKSON, R. 1990. *Quasi-States: Sovereignty, International Relations, and the Third World*. Cambridge: Cambridge University Press.

——2000. *The Global Covenant: Human Conduct in a World of States*. Oxford: Oxford University Press.

JAHN, B. (ed.) 2006. *Classical Theory in International Relations*. Cambridge: Cambridge University Press.

JOHNSTON, A. 1995. *Cultural Realism: Strategic Culture and Grand Strategy in Chinese History*. Princeton, NJ: Princeton University Press.

JONES, C. 1998. *E. H. Carr and International Relations: A Duty to Lie*. Cambridge: Cambridge University Press.

KEENE, E. 2002. *Beyond the Anarchical Society: Grotius, Colonialism and Order in World Politics*. Cambridge: Cambridge University Press.

——2005. *International Political Thought: A Historical Introduction*. Cambridge: Polity.

KRASNER, S. 1999. *Sovereignty: Organized Hypocrisy*. Princeton, NJ: Princeton University Press.

KRATOCHWIL, F. 2006. History, action and identity: revisiting the "second" great debate and assessing its importance for social theory. *European Journal of International Relations*, 12: 5–29.

LEBOW, R. 2003. *The Tragic Vision of Politics: Ethics, Interests, and Orders*. Cambridge: Cambridge University Press.

LEGRO, J., and MORAVCSIK, A. 1999. Is anybody still a realist? *International Security*, 24: 5–55.

LEVY, J. 1997. Too important to leave to the other: history and political science in the study of international relations. *International Security*, 22: 22–33.

LONG, D., and SCHMIDT, B. (eds.) 2005. *Imperialism and Internationalism in the Discipline of International Relations*. New York: State University of New York Press.

—— and WILSON, P. (eds.) 1995. *Thinkers of the Twenty Years' Crisis: Inter-War Idealism Reassessed*. Oxford: Clarendon Press.

LUSTICK, I. 1996. History, historiography, and political science: multiple historical records and the problem of selection bias. *American Political Science Review*, 90: 605–18.

MEARSHEIMER, J. 2001. *The Tragedy of Great Power Politics*. New York: W. W. Norton.

OSIANDER, A. 2001. Sovereignty, international relations, and the Westphalian myth. *International Organization*, 55: 251–87.

PHILPOTT, D. 2001. *Revolutions in Sovereignty: How Ideas Shaped Modern International Relations*. Princeton, NJ: Princeton University Press.

PIERSON, P. 2004. *Politics in Time: History, Institutions, and Social Analysis*. Princeton, NJ: Princeton University Press.

QUIRK, J., and VIGNESWARAN, D. 2005. The construction of an edifice: the story of a first great debate. *Review of International Studies*, 31: 89–107.

REUS-SMIT, C. 1998. *The Moral Purpose of the State: Culture, Social Identity, and Institutional Rationality in International Relations*. Princeton, NJ: Princeton University Press.

ROBERTS, G. 2006. History, theory and the narrative turn in IR. *Review of International Studies*, 32: 703–14.

ROSENBERG, J. 1994. *The Empire of Civil Society: A Critique of the Realist Theory of International Relations*. London: Verso.

RUGGIE, J. 1993. Territoriality and beyond: problematizing modernity in international relations. *International Organization*, 47: 139–74.

SCHMIDT, B. 1998. *The Political Discourse of Anarchy: A Disciplinary History of International Relations*. Albany, NY: State University of New York Press.

—— 2002a. On the history and historiography of international relations. Pp. 3–22 in *Handbook of International Relations*, ed. W. Carlsnaes, T. Risse, and B. Simmons. London: Sage.

—— 2002b. Together again: reuniting political theory and international relations theory. *British Journal of Politics and International Relations*, 4: 115–40.

SCHWELLER, R. 1998. *Deadly Imbalances: Tripolarity and Hitler's Strategy of World Conquest*. New York: Columbia University Press.

SKINNER, Q. 2002. *Visions of Politics, Vol. i. Regarding Method*. Cambridge: Cambridge University Press.

SPRUYT, H. 1994. *The Sovereign State and its Competitors: An Analysis of Systems Change*. Princeton, NJ: Princeton University Press.

SYNDER, J. 1991. *Myths of Empire: Domestic Politics and International Ambition*. Ithaca, NY: Cornell University Press.

TESCHKE, B. 2003. *The Myth of 1648: Class, Geopolitics, and the Making of Modern International Relations*. London: Verso.

TRACHTENBERG, M. 2006. *The Craft of International History: A Guide to Method*. Princeton, NJ: Princeton University Press.

VAN EVERA, S. 1999. *Causes of War: Power and the Roots of Conflict*. Ithaca, NY: Cornell University Press.

WALKER, R. B. J. 1993. *Inside/Outside: International Relations as Political Theory*. Cambridge: Cambridge University Press.

WALT, S. 1987. *The Origins of Alliances*. Ithaca, NY: Cornell University Press.

WALTZ, K. 1979. *Theory of International Politics*. Reading, Mass.: Addison-Wesley.

WATSON, A. 1992. *The Evolution of International Society: A Comparative Historical Analysis*. London: Routledge.

WEBER, C. 1995. *Simulating Sovereignty: Intervention, the State, and Symbolic Exchange*. Cambridge: Cambridge University Press.

WIGHT, M. 1966. Why is there no international theory? Pp. 17–34 in *Diplomatic Investigations: Essays in the Theory of International Politics*, ed. H. Butterfield and M. Wight. London: George Allen and Unwin.

—— 1977. *Systems of States*. Leicester: Leicester University Press.

—— 1991. *International Theory: The Three Traditions*. Leicester: Leicester University Press.

WILSON, P. 1998. The myth of the "first great debate." *Review of International Studies*, 24: 1–15.

WILLIAMS, M. 2005. *The Realist Tradition and the Limits of International Relations*. Cambridge: Cambridge University Press.

WOHLFORTH, W. 1993. *The Elusive Balance: Power and Perceptions during the Cold War*. Ithaca, NY: Cornell University Press.

PART V

BRIDGING THE
SUBFIELD
BOUNDARIES

CHAPTER 31

INTERNATIONAL POLITICAL ECONOMY

JOHN RAVENHILL

The whole point of studying international political economy rather than international relations is to extend more widely the conventional limits of the study of politics, and the conventional concepts of who engages in politics, and of how and by whom power is exercised to influence outcomes. Far from being a subdiscipline of international relations, IPE should claim that international relations are a subdiscipline of IPE.

(Strange 1994, 218)

1 THE EMERGENCE OF IPE

INTERNATIONAL political economy (IPE) emerged as a significant field of study in the early 1970s. As often happens in the study of international relations, the

I am grateful to the editors, Benjamin J. Cohen, Anthony Payne, Nicola Phillips, and Len Seabrooke for comments on a July 2006 draft of this chapter. I have benefited from reading draft chapters from Benjamin J. Cohen's forthcoming Princeton University Press book, *Building Bridges: The Construction of International Political Economy*, which promises to be the definitive history of the early development of the field.

appearance of a new field was a response to developments in the real world that existing theories appeared not well equipped to explain. The context was the growth of economic interdependence that had occurred following the completion of Western Europe's and Japan's recovery from wartime devastation, dramatic increases in foreign direct investment—initially in response to the formation of the European Common Market—and the transformation of the structure of international trade away from the historically dominant exchange of manufactures for raw materials to one increasingly characterized by intra-industry trade.

From the perspective of many observers, however, it would be more accurate to state that IPE *re*-emerged as a significant field of study in the 1970s. For them, its lineage can (and *should*—because this is very much a prescription for the future directions the field should take) be traced back to the classical economists (Adam Smith, David Ricardo, John Stuart Mill, and so on), the nineteenth-century theorists of social change (Karl Marx, Émile Durkheim, and so on), and the institutional economists and anthropologists (Thorstein Veblen, Karl Polanyi, and so on) of the late nineteenth century and first half of the twentieth century (for such a perspective see, e.g., Gamble et al. 1996; Underhill 2000; Watson 2005). Others with a narrower conception of the field would nonetheless acknowledge significant contributions before the late 1960s, notably Albert Hirschman's pioneering study (1945) of asymmetrical economic relations, and Jacob Viner's examination (1948) of mercantilism. And, as early as 1951, the business economist and economic historian Charles P. Kindleberger, whose work was to be particularly influential in the resurrection of IPE in the 1970s, had written about the Bretton Woods institutions in *International Organization* (Kindleberger 1951).

The trigger for the field's revival and rapid expansion was the trade and payments problems experienced by the United States in the second half of the 1960s, which culminated in the Nixon administration's decision in August 1971 to devalue the dollar and to end the gold-exchange standard that had provided the foundation for the Bretton Woods international monetary regime. As J. Lawrence Broz and Jeffry Frieden (2001, 317) note, this dramatic action ended the "tedious predictability of currency values under Bretton Woods" that had "lulled most scholars into inattention." The new "turbulence" that ensued in the global economy was exacerbated by the success of the Organization of Petroleum Exporting Countries (OPEC) in dramatically pushing up the price of oil following the outbreak of the 1973 Middle East war, the consequent "stagflation" that emerged in industrialized economies, their fears over the future security of supply of raw materials, and demands by less developed economies for a "New International Economic Order" (NIEO).

These developments challenged the then-dominant approaches to international relations on several dimensions. In particular, they posed a challenge to the ontology of realism. Realists had never considered economic interactions to be significant in international relations save in their role as a component of national power (Knorr 1973; 1975). Moreover, the new literature suggested that realism's favorite instrument, military force, was of limited utility in resolving some of the most prominent issues currently in contention among the industrialized economies, and between them and less developed countries. An equally fundamental challenge to realism's ontology was the emphasis that the new IPE literature placed on nonstate actors. One element of this was the attention given to the multinational corporation, drawing on work done primarily by business economists, work that had theorized the activities of corporations from a very different perspective to that of neoclassical economics (Penrose 1959; Vernon 1966; 1971; Kindleberger 1969; 1970; Hymer 1976; for an early work from an IPE perspective, see Gilpin 1975). But the rebirth of IPE coincided with a new interest in a much broader variety of nonstate actors, the seminal collection being the special issue of *International Organization* edited by Robert Keohane and Joseph S. Nye (25 (1971)) (subsequently published as Keohane and Nye 1972).

If the then-dominant approach to the study of international relations was not well equipped to address the new significance of international economic interactions, neither was the discipline of economics itself (although it is important to acknowledge that one of the key works that stimulated new thinking about the political consequences of increasing economic interdependence was written by an economist, Richard N. Cooper 1968). In its efforts to emulate the natural sciences, mainstream economics had become increasingly mathematical in its orientation, and its modeling of behavior reflected a commitment to methodological individualism. Whereas the study of economic institutions and economic history used to be part of the core undergraduate training in economics, by the second half of the 1960s it had all but disappeared from the curriculum. And development economics—that branch of the discipline that had the greatest affinity with political economy—came increasingly under attack. Economists in the neoclassical mainstream perceived its emphasis on the role of the state and on the necessity of conceptualizing the problems faced by less developed countries differently from those of the industrialized world as standing in the way of a unified science. The attack on the ontology and methodology of economics and the discipline's consequent inability to pursue a "realist" approach (that is, one that could account for the role of power) in the study of international economic relations was spelled out most strongly in a pioneering article by Susan Strange (1970). Such views, however, were by no means confined to European writing—see, for instance, Robert Gilpin's magisterial introduction to the field, *The Political Economy of International Relations* (1987). It was no coincidence that some of the pioneers of IPE were refugees from the economics profession—including Strange herself, and Benjamin J. Cohen.

Students of international relations had challenged realism in the 1950s and 1960s primarily through studies that focused on the experience of European integration as an exemplar of how one might move "beyond the nation state" (Haas 1958; 1964; Deutsch et al. 1957). These approaches, especially neofunctionalism, were to provide the intellectual foundation on which much early work in IPE in the United States would build (and their implicit if not explicit constructivism would provide some of the inspiration for a new generation of IPE scholars in the 1990s—see Ruggie 1998, 862). Yet, while the emphasis in neofunctionalism on economic interactions, on institutions, on ideas, on interest groups, and on the creative role of intellectual and policy entrepreneurs sat well with the ontology of the fledgling field of IPE, neofunctionalist approaches themselves were not well placed to explain the new turbulence in international economic relations. By the end of the 1960s, disillusionment had set in among neofunctional theorists. This disappointment arose because of the lack of consensus on identifying dependent variables (for instance, what would the end point of integration be?), and their relationship with a proliferation of independent variables (a problem exacerbated when neofunctionalist theorists turned their attention to non-Western regional schemes).

Moreover, the real world was not behaving as neofunctionalists had expected. Recalcitrant political leaders had slowed the process of integration in Western Europe (Hoffmann 1966). Meanwhile, the growth in significance of economic independence with extraregional actors seemed to cast doubt not only on the prospects for successful regionalism but also on the utility of theorizing that attempted to explain these processes—leading to Ernst Haas's famous conclusion (1975) regarding the "obsolescence" of regional integration theory. In the United States, those who previously had been prominently involved in studies of regionalism broadened their approach to focus on global interdependence, and made this the main organizing principle for the new IPE literature. Particularly significant in illustrating these links is the essay on international interdependence and integration by Keohane and Nye (1975).

2 WHAT IS IPE?

On one issue, most students of IPE have always agreed: IPE is a field defined by its subject matter. In itself, such a definition suggests that the field should reflect a tolerance for eclecticism in theoretical approaches, methodologies, and ontology. It stands in contrast to, for example, the study of political economy in neoclassical economics, especially the Chicago school approach, or to Marxist political economy.

It is the economic component of IPE that distinguishes the field from other areas of international relations (and the international dimension that distinguishes it from studies of the politics of "purely" domestic economic policies). IPE is thus a field that embraces "all work for which international economic factors are an important cause or consequence" (Frieden and Martin 2003, 118). Gilpin's succinct statement (1987) that IPE encompasses the study of the interaction of "state and market," and thus of politics and economics, was used for many years as a shorthand definition of the field (see also Strange 1988). This definition remains popular (e.g. Grieco and Ikenberry 2003) even though in his later work Gilpin (2001) himself abandoned the phrase because of its failure to capture the significance of nonstate actors in the field.

An insistence on the economic component in defining IPE moves one away from impossibly broad conceptions that see IPE as comprising all nonsecurity aspects of international relations (Milner 2002). The subject matter of IPE may have been the most significant site in the last three decades for the development of certain concepts and approaches—perhaps the most prominent of which is the neoinstitutional approach to international regimes—that were subsequently applied to the study of other areas of international relations. Equally, students of IPE have been omnivores in borrowing concepts from other fields of international relations (from security studies, for instance—see Jervis 1998, 989, n. 59) and more broadly from other disciplines—most prominently in recent years from economics, but also from law, history, and sociology. But if IPE is to have any coherence as a field of inquiry, then it needs to be separated from the broader study of international institutions.

On both sides of the Atlantic, proponents of the new field of IPE viewed it as a component of the study of international relations. Strange's pioneering article (1970), for instance, was a clarion call for students of international relations to pay attention to economics (in later work, reflected in the epigraph to this chapter, she saw international relations as a component of IPE rather than vice versa—but in large part because she was critical of the tendency of "mainstream" international relations scholars, especially those based in the United States, to confine their analysis to relations among states).

Very different conceptions of international relations—and hence of how the new field of IPE should be constructed—existed between the United States and the UK in particular, however, and these conditioned the future development of the field. Whereas scholars in the United States have typically conceived of international relations as part of the discipline of political science, the tradition in many universities in the UK has been to view it as a multidisciplinary enterprise—a divergence whose consequences are examined later in this chapter.

3 THE EARLY YEARS

Given the apparent destabilizing consequences of increased interdependence that had prompted the new interest in international economic relations, much of the early work in IPE was devoted to issues of how to restore collaboration among key players in the global economy. In giving priority to this topic, analysts did not eschew the normative: It was not just a matter of attempting to identify the conditions under which cooperation might occur but also one of a clear preference (frequently stated explicitly) for restoring order. Similarly, in dealing with relations between industrialized and less developed economies, analysts were usually explicit in their calls for either a positive or a negative response to Southern demands for systemic change.

International monetary relations were a particular focus of early work, with Strange (1976) leading the call for the US hegemon to pursue policies that were more responsible (see also Cohen 1977). The focus soon broadened to the more general issue of how to sustain international economic cooperation in a situation where the relative power of the United States had declined—at least in comparison with the relatively brief period from 1944 onwards when the winning wartime coalition negotiated the framework for the postwar global economic regimes. And, after a diversion into what proved to be a theoretical dead end—the theory of hegemonic stability—the focus was broadened still further to ask how international regimes might help promote cooperation by changing actors' incentives, and the circumstances in which international institutions make a difference to outcomes (see below).

Considerable variance in the success of industrialized economies in coping with the challenges of oil price increases and with the threat of stagflation prompted a second major line of inquiry. The differential capacity of industrialized economies to cope with crises proved to be a subject where significant overlap existed with the interests of students of comparative political economy and of sociology—and some fruitful collaborative projects resulted (e.g. Hirsch and Goldthorpe 1978; Lindberg, Maier, and Barry 1985). This debate reflected a broader research agenda that embraced investigation of how the characteristics of states and their position in the international system conditioned governments' choice of foreign economic policies, and in turn how developments in the global economy affected domestic economic interests (Zysman 1977; Gourevitch 1978; 1986; Katzenstein 1985; Castles 1988).

Another area that received attention during the early years of IPE, consistent with the desire to move beyond realism's emphasis on military force, was the role of economic instruments of foreign policy, especially economic sanctions. Again, real-world developments stimulated this interest, with sanctions and boycotts figuring in the Middle East war of 1973 and in debates within the British Commonwealth in the 1970s on how to pressure South Africa to end its apartheid policies. Such instruments again came to prominence following the Soviet invasion of Afghanistan in 1979 (Doxey 1971; Hufbauer, Schott, and Elliott 1983).

The initial success of OPEC and the subsequent demands by less developed economies for an NIEO stimulated research on relations between industrialized and less developed economies, and the conditions under which producer associations might overcome collective action problems (Bergsten 1974*a*; 1974*b*; Krasner 1974; 1985; Mikdashi 1974; Rothstein 1979; Ravenhill 1985). These topics again linked into the concerns and approaches of other fields of study—most notably development economics. And it was in this context that mainstream IPE engaged (albeit temporarily and usually from a critical perspective) most closely with Marxist and various structuralist perspectives on relations between industrialized and developing economies—particularly the literature on underdevelopment and dependency (Frank 1967; Wallerstein 1974; Cardoso and Faletto 1979; see also Cohen 1974, which provides a critical assessment).

While students of IPE attempted to move beyond what they perceived as realism's excessively narrow ontology, few of the studies—even those from a "radical" perspective—strayed from a commitment to elements of positivism, at least minimally—that is, in the sense of empirically based analysis. One reason arguably was the character of the field's subject matter, which lent itself to a relatively easy identification of interests and the strategies various actors deployed to pursue them. Positivist approaches were dominant in US political science; moreover, the two leading critics of "conventional" IPE—Robert Cox and Strange—were both disdainful of postmodern approaches, which, alongside those of Marxism and feminism, Strange characterized with typical bluntness as "woolly."

In the early years, the main dividing lines within IPE corresponded with the broader "inter-paradigm" debate in international relations. Dividing the field into "liberal," "Marxist," and "mercantilist/statist" approaches became a convenient device for organizing introductory courses for students; the presentation of theoretical approaches as a trichotomy continued to be popular in textbooks long after its limited utility for classifying contemporary research in IPE became obvious. The principal vehicle through which the inter-paradigm clash was initially expressed in IPE was the debate over "hegemonic stability," which combined elements of realism with arguments on the logic of collective action (for the realist variant, see Gilpin 1975; 1981; and Krasner 1976; while Kindleberger 1973 provides the classic statement from a public goods perspective). It soon became clear, however, that the hegemonic stability hypothesis was lacking in both empirical and theoretical support (Keohane 1997 provides an overview of the debate on hegemonic stability; see also Cohen forthcoming, ch. 3).

The clash between "institutionalists" and "realists" within IPE then broadened into a debate over the role of international regimes, and how they might affect the prospects for collaboration. The concept of international regime, originally introduced into the IPE literature by John Ruggie (1975), was popularized by Keohane and Nye's *Power and Interdependence* (1977). As Cohen (forthcoming, ch. 4) notes: "Rarely has a new concept, once introduced, caught on so swiftly in scholarly circles." In the decade and a half after the publication of a special issue of *International Organization* (36 (1982)) devoted to the subject, the factors determining the demand for and supply of international regimes became the dominant feature of IPE research (not just in the United States but also in parts of Europe—despite trenchant criticism from Strange 1982, who saw the concept as merely an unproductive diversion prompted by American concerns about the seeming decline of US hegemony: for European approaches, see Rittberger with the assistance of Mayer 1993; Hasenclever, Mayer, and Rittberger 1997). The inter-paradigm debate on regimes focused primarily on the issue of whether states' pre-occupation with relative gains would prevent cooperation from being realized. This again proved to be an argument that lacked a convincing theoretical foundation (Grieco 1988; 1993; Powell 1991; 1993; Snidal 1991a; 1991b; 1993).

The concept of international regime was intended to move analysis beyond a focus solely on formal international organizations, and on states as the only significant actors in the global economy. While the former objective continued to be pursued as the debate on regimes unfolded, the primacy of the state was reinstated in most studies of IPE in the United States when IPE, like other areas of international relations, was profoundly affected by the publication of Kenneth Waltz's *Theory of International Politics* (1979). This contained the most elaborate statement of Waltz's criticisms of arguments about the constraining effects of in-terdependence on great powers, and his reaffirmation of the continuing centrality of the state in all *significant* dimensions of international relations. Waltz's book was also a call for the discipline to become more scientific in its approach, em-ulating that of economics (from which, of course, his arguments about the logic of state behavior were drawn—Waltz was another refugee from the economics profession).

Following the publication of Waltz's work, a substantial convergence of views among many US students of IPE occurred around what became known as the "neo-neo" synthesis (Wæver 1996), a reconciliation of neorealist and neoinstitutionalist views. Crucial to this reconciliation was the adoption by neoinstitutionalists of at least a "soft" rational choice approach in which analysts again gave primacy to states, but which they now viewed as rational egoistic actors that were able without any great difficulty to identify their interests. The application of game-theoretic approaches played a significant role in advancing this agenda (Axelrod 1981; 1984; Keohane 1984; Aggarwal 1985; 1996). The consequence was a marked narrowing of ontology: Nonstate actors, such as the transnational corporation, largely disappeared from the analysis; and the role of ideas was largely reduced to "information." The significance of structures, emphasized not only by Strange but also by those such as Gilpin who followed more conventional realist analysis, disap-peared from the neoutilitarians' horizons. Debates revolving around principals and agents replaced those on agency and structure. Normative concerns were deemed to be incompatible with the more "scientific" approach that was sought. Subsequently, the field of IPE appeared increasingly polarized between the "hard" rational choice analysis utilized by many US scholars, and what they often termed less "rigorous" methodologies applied by scholars elsewhere.

4 BEYOND DUBIOUS DICHOTOMIES

Over the years, it has been commonplace in discussions of the evolution of the field to draw a distinction between how IPE evolved in the United States in contrast to other parts of the world. Commentators have applied a diversity of labels, with various degrees of dyslogy, to this dichotomy. "Rationalist," "mainstream," "orthodox," "hegemonic," "conventional," the "*International Organization* school," "American," and most cutely, "*Ratiosaurus Rex*" (Dickins 2006) are all labels that have been used to describe what is perceived as the dominant approach to IPE amongst US-based academics. The antonyms have included "reflectivist," "radical," "progressive," "heterodox," "nonhegemonic," and "British." Because critics of the "American" approach have usually drawn up these dichotomies, it is perhaps not surprising that the latter group of terms generally have a far more positive connotation. While these critics are like a group of terriers snapping at the heels of the best-known American IPE specialists, their regular fate is simply to be treated with regal disdain in surveys of the field conducted by those they label "mainstream."

Pointing to differences in the way IPE is studied within and outside the United States builds on a substantial literature that portrays international relations as a "divided discipline" (Holsti 1985; Wæver 1998; Smith 2000). And, at one level of generality, such dichotomous treatments do resonate with differences in the methodologies and ontologies of the majority of IPE scholars in the United States as opposed to the preponderance of those in Europe. One finds few scholars committed to "hard" rational choice approaches outside the United States; similarly, one finds *relatively* few students of IPE within the United States who embrace perspectives informed by critical theory or postmodernism. Beyond this rather superficial level, however, the US–British dichotomy tends to obscure more than it illuminates. It is more useful to conceive of a spectrum of approaches to the study of IPE, where hard rational choice and post-structuralist/postmodern treatments represent the two extremities. In between is a "missing middle" where there is a far greater overlap between scholarship inside and outside the United States than simple dichotomies suggest.

The "disciplinarians" occupy one end of the spectrum. They conceive of IPE as a subfield of political science, and draw extensively less from work in other areas of international relations than from political science more generally and especially from economics, which many seem to regard as the "master discipline." As they have borrowed increasingly from the literature of economics, and economists themselves have applied techniques drawn from their discipline to the study of policy-making on economic issues (notable examples include Grossman and Helpman 1995; Bagwell and Staiger 1999; Irwin and Kroszner 1999), some have argued that the application of economic theory will provide a foundation for a unified social science. Their commitment is to a "scientific" approach to the study of IPE characterized by "rigorous theory" and "systematic empirical testing" (Frieden and Lake

2005). Their methodological individualism reflects the dominant approach of neo-classical economics. States may still be primary in their ontology of international relations, but much of their work focuses on opening the "black box" of the state—that is, in identifying the interests that determine the policies that states pursue.

The principal focus of this work has been on trade policies, although increasingly these methods are being applied to international finance (see the overview presented in Broz and Frieden 2001). They acknowledge institutions insofar as these shape the opportunities various interests have to influence policy—but have doubts as to whether institutions can be studied systematically, given problems of endogeneity and selection bias (Frieden and Martin 2003). Generally, however, the emphasis is on individuals rather than social aggregates: The median voter is more important than are social classes. Nonstate actors rarely figure in their analysis of the international dimensions of economic relations. They eschew normative approaches as inconsistent with a commitment to science. Similarly, they see little value in approaches beyond their own because of the lack of scientific validity in these alternatives.

At the other end of the spectrum are those who embrace critical theory and/or postmodern or post-structuralist perspectives, a much smaller group that typically is similarly intolerant of those who do not share their world-views. Authors writing from these perspectives deny that it is possible to construct a social science, that "objective" knowledge is impossible (building on Cox's aphorism that all theory is for someone and for some purpose), that observers do (and should aim to) change reality through their work; they typically favor hermeneutic approaches.

Yet it is a caricature to suggest that the study of IPE within and outside the United States is captured by these two poles. Critics often present the "hard" form of rational choice analysis—that is, the formal modeling and reductionism associated with the discipline of economics—as *the* "American", *the* "mainstream", or *the* "*International Organization*" approach. Yet, despite the growing popularity of rational choice methods in political science departments in US universities, these are by no means the only methods employed in the contemporary study of IPE in the United States. It was the case that, while *International Organization* was under the editorship of Lisa Martin, an increase occurred in the share of articles that employed "hard" rational choice methods. Nonetheless, the journal continued to reflect a substantial variety of the theoretical perspectives and methodologies used by students of IPE—and the share of articles that used formal modeling in *International Organization* was still much lower than that in most other political science journals published in the United States (Murphy and Nelson 2001). It was the case, however, that the *International Organization* of 2005 was a very different beast from that of 1985 and 1995 (and there is a certain irony that the leading figures in the "*International Organization* school" against which early critics, notably Murphy and Tooze 1991, railed—the very individuals identified by Cohen (forthcoming) as the founding fathers of the discipline: Peter Katzenstein, Robert Keohane, Stephen Krasner, Robert

Gilpin—display little enthusiasm for the turn to hard rational choice seen in the journal in recent years).

IPE, like other fields of political science, is particularly prone to fads—and there is nothing in its history to lead one to think that the field will not at some point turn away from rational choice methods once the easy gains assimilated by borrowing ideas from economics have been exhausted. A new editorial team, which assumed responsibility for *International Organization* in 2007, based for the first time outside the United States, can be expected to move the field's leading journal in a different direction.

The category of "British" school is equally unhelpful: The geographic reference is misleading, given that some of the leading critics of rationalist approaches to IPE are based not in the UK but in Canada (Cox, Stephen Gill) or in the United States itself (Craig Murphy). Moreover, while many IPE scholars outside the United States are happy to appropriate the label of "critical," it is, as Chris Brown (2001) points out, the criticism of the disaffected rather than critical theory as conventionally understood in the social sciences. Unless one equates non-American approaches with critical theory (which would make for a very small "school"), the diversity of approaches—a residual after subtracting the supposedly hard rational choice perspective of *International Organization*—makes any application of a single label (such as the "British" school) of dubious utility. There is no sensible parallel to be drawn here with the "English School" of international relations, where one can write credibly of a reasonably coherent body of thought.

Even outside the United States, relatively little work has been published on IPE using reflectivist epistemologies; indeed, the enthusiasm afforded such approaches in non-US surveys of the field has been disproportionate to their use in the study of IPE. With the exception of Gill (2003), van der Pijl (1998), and Murphy (2005), few have attempted to develop the agenda that Cox initiated. Even rarer is any reference to the Frankfurt School, influential in critical theorizing in other areas of international relations, or to the ideas of Michel Foucault. Although many IPE specialists outside the United States profess themselves open to a variety of theoretical, methodological, and indeed disciplinary approaches, few cross the dividing line between rationalism and reflectivism.

Their criticism of their American counterparts is typically of the narrowness of the ontology of neoutilitarian and rational choice approaches, often coupled with an expression of normative concerns over the distributive consequences of the current economic order. The plea is for an expansion of the scope of the agenda of IPE research, seen, for instance, in much of the feminist work on IPE, rather than for an adoption of post-positivist approaches (Ling 2000 and Whitworth 2000 provide rare calls for postmodernist feminist IPE). In this respect, many of the "critics" are not dramatically different in their views from one of the favorite targets of early critics of the United States "mainstream"—Gilpin. He, too, is disparaging of what he terms "economic imperialism," the increasing application in the study of IPE of the methodological individualism of neoclassical economics, and argues for more attention to be paid to recent developments in economic theorizing, such as the new growth and trade theories, and the literature on economic geography, as well as arguing for the importance of structures and of nonstate actors in the contemporary global economy (see especially Gilpin 2001). Of course, few scholars outside the United States would embrace the label of "realist" that Gilpin proudly wears, and there are differences in emphasis, especially on the subjects that individuals believe should be high priority for investigation, and on the significance of various social forces. But we see here an example of how the "US–British" dichotomy is misleading in suggesting that the contributors on the two sides of the Atlantic are poles (or worlds) apart.

A careful examination of IPE scholarship outside the United States would indicate that the bulk of it consists of "midlevel theories, contingent propositions, and empirically grounded generalizations drawn from the intense study of particular cases" (Frieden and Lake 2005, 137). Contributions from outside the United States have been particularly strong on regionalism (especially but not exclusively the European Union), on the impact of globalization on states, on development issues, and in the Katzenstein–Gourevitch tradition on the domestic sources of economic policies. This work may not constitute what Frieden and Lake regard as the way forward if the field is to become more scientific, but nonetheless is very firmly rooted in empirical analysis that can be subjected to falsification.

There is clearly a "missing middle" in crude dichotomies, a middle ground that provides the basis for bridge-building across the mythical Atlantic divide. A cursory glance at the so-called British IPE journals shows many instances of overlap in the work of scholars on both sides of the Atlantic. And there is, of course, a long tradition of non-US scholars working with their counterparts in the United States on collaborative projects across the various areas of IPE (some notable recent examples include Andrews, Henning, and Pauly 2002; Odell 2006).

Another potential bridge among those located in the middle of the spectrum is an increasing interest in normative issues—particularly on the part of neoinstitutionalist scholars in the United States. In particular, there is a new focus on questions of legitimacy—relating to global governance generally, including the role of nongovernmental organizations and other private actors. Concerns that in the last two decades have been left primarily to political philosophers with interests in international relations, such as Thomas Pogge (2002), are being reintegrated into the IPE mainstream (for further discussion, see Dickins 2006; a review article by Helen Milner 2005 combines an explicit normative approach with analysis of the impact of international financial institutions on less developed economies).

The single most important development in international relations theorizing since the early 1990s—the emergence of constructivist theorizing—has until recently found little resonance in the study of IPE. In the last few years, however, new research, particularly in international finance, has highlighted the importance of uncertainty and ambiguity in IPE, often in contexts where "appropriate" action depends upon the actions of others. Constructivist approaches address a central issue of concern to many in the missing middle: when and how ideas and norms matter (examples of the new constructivism in IPE include Best 2005; Sinclair 2005; Seabrooke 2006; and Seabrooke 2007 is a review essay on recent contributions to economic constructivism).

5 AND NE'ER THE TWAIN SHALL MEET?

Most students of IPE agree on one matter: The range of topics covered by the field to date has been excessively narrow. The majority of the research has focused on international trade issues; global finance has been the second-most significant issue area but has received less attention than trade, while—despite their importance in a globalizing economy—issues relating to foreign direct investment and the reorganization of production have been left largely to management studies and to sociologists (e.g. Gereffi 1996; Gereffi, Humphrey, and Sturgeon 2005; Rugman 2005). The concern over the field's limited perspective has been over not just the range of topics investigated but also the actors that have been the principal focus of study. Despite the origins of IPE in a rejection of the state-centric ontology of realism, states continue to occupy the central place in most IPE analysis. Only a limited universe of states, that is. Less developed economies have rarely featured since the demise of the NIEO debate at the end of the 1970s, save as the objects of the policies of the international financial institutions or the industrialized economies—a reflection both of the difficulties experienced in Latin America and East Asia as a consequence of financial crises, and of the triumphalism of the West following the end of the cold war (Narlikar 2003 provides a rare exception).

Efforts to broaden IPE as a field of study have included work on the application of IPE theories to less developed economies and to development more generally (Payne 2005; Phillips 2005). Most commentators agree on the need to give greater attention to private actors. But to which actors is a matter of contention. For rational choice theorists, it is a matter of extending the approaches used to derive the preference of actors in trade policy formation to other areas—for instance, foreign direct investment (Frieden and Martin 2003). For others, the focus should be on the role of private actors in significant areas of governance, building on work done in other areas of international relations (e.g. Cutler, Haufler, and Porter 1999; Hall and Biersteker 2002; Underhill 1995 is an early example of work within IPE that focuses on private actors' roles in the governance of the global economy; Timothy Sinclair's study of credit rating agencies (2005) provides a recent example). For still others, the objective is to widen the agenda in a manner similar to that advocated by many feminist scholars—to examine "everyday" actors previously overlooked (e.g. Hobson and Seabrooke 2007). Such differences in focus influence the choice of literatures/disciplines with which analysts seek to engage. For "hard" rational choice theorists, it is less with other areas of international relations than with the literature on US domestic politics, and of course with that of the economics discipline. For many others, the road ahead lies not necessarily in closer engagement with other areas of international relations but with political economy approaches either in other subfields of political science—notably comparative politics—or with those of classical economics. No one would pretend that the diversity of approaches current in the study of IPE can easily be unified—and many would not believe that this would be a desirable development.

What progress has been made in understanding the global political economy in the three and a half decades since the field of IPE came into being? Cohen's answer is unequivocal. He writes: "If knowledge is measured by our ability to make definitive statements—to generalize without fear of dispute—the field's success may be rated as negligible at best" (Cohen forthcoming, ch. 6). The field has seen plenty of excursions into what proved to be theoretical dead ends—whether the theory of hegemonic stability or the debate over relative gains. But as Cohen himself argues, to judge progress in IPE by whether or not students have produced a general theory is to set the hurdle unrealistically high. Even the excursions into dead ends did generate new understandings—for instance, of when considerations of relative gains might be more likely to come to the fore in states' deliberations on whether or not to collaborate. We may not, for instance, have an approach that can enable us in all circumstances to deduce what actors' preferences on trade or financial liberalization will be, but we do have a better understanding of when the alternative Stolper–Samuelson and Ricardo–Viner models are more likely to apply (Hiscox 2002). It is such middle-range, contextually specific theorizing that has been most fruitful in the development of IPE.

REFERENCES

AGGARWAL, V. K. 1985. *Liberal Protectionism: The International Politics of Organized Textile Trade.* Berkeley: University of California Press.
——1996. *Debt Games: Strategic Interaction in International Debt Rescheduling.* Cambridge: Cambridge University Press.
ANDREWS, D. M., HENNING, C. R., and PAULY, L. W. (eds.) 2002. *Governing the World's Money.* Ithaca, NY: Cornell University Press.
AXELROD, R. 1981. The emergence of cooperation among egoists. *American Political Science Review,* 75: 306–18.
——1984. *The Evolution of Cooperation.* New York: Basic Books.

BAGWELL, K., and STAIGER, R. W. 1999. An economic theory of GATT. *American Economic Review*, 89: 215–48.

BERGSTEN, C. F. 1974*a*. The threat from the Third World. *Foreign Policy*, 11: 102–24.

—— 1974*b*. The threat is real. *Foreign Policy*, 14: 84–90.

BEST, J. 2005. *The Limits of Transparency: Ambiguity and the History of International Finance*. Ithaca, NY: Cornell University Press.

BROWN, C. 2001. "Our side?" Critical theory and international relations. Pp. 191–203 in *Critical Theory and World Politics*, ed. R. W. Jones. Boulder, Colo.: Lynne Rienner.

BROZ, J. L., and FRIEDEN, J. A. 2001. The political economy of international monetary relations. *Annual Review of Political Science*, 4: 317–43.

CARDOSO, F. H., and FALETTO, E. 1979. *Dependency and Development in Latin America*. Berkeley: University of California Press.

CASTLES, F. G. 1988. *Australian Public Policy and Economic Vulnerability: A Comparative and Historical Perspective*. Sydney: Allen and Unwin.

COHEN, B. J. 1974. *The Question of Imperialism: The Political Economy of Dominance and Dependence*. London: Macmillan.

—— 1977. *Organizing the World's Money: The Political Economy of International Monetary Relations*. New York: Basic Books.

—— forthcoming. *Building Bridges: The Construction of International Political Economy*. Princeton, NJ: Princeton University Press.

COOPER, R. N. 1968. *The Economics of Interdependence: Economic Policy in the Atlantic Community*. New York: Columbia University Press.

CUTLER, A. C., HAUFLER, V., and PORTER, T. (eds.) 1999. *Private Authority and International Affairs*. Albany, NY: State University of New York Press.

DEUTSCH, K. W., BURRELL, S. A., KANN, R. A., LEE, M., LICHTERMAN, M., LINDGREN, R. E., LOWENHEIM, F. L., and WAGENEN, R. W. V. 1957. *Political Community and the North Atlantic Area: International Organization in the Light of Historical Experience*. Princeton, NJ: Princeton University Press.

DICKINS, A. 2006. The evolution of international political economy. *International Affairs*, 82: 479–92.

DOXEY, M. P. 1971. *Economic Sanctions and International Enforcement*. London: Oxford University Press for the Royal Institute of International Affairs.

FRANK, A. G. 1967. *Capitalism and Underdevelopment in Latin America: Historical Studies of Chile and Brazil*. New York: Monthly Review Press.

FRIEDEN, J. A., and LAKE, D. A. 2005. International relations as a social science: rigor and relevance. *Annals of the American Academy of Political and Social Science*, 600: 136–56.

—— and MARTIN, L. L. 2003. International political economy: global and domestic interactions. Pp. 118–46 in *Political Science: The State of the Discipline*, ed. I. Katznelson and H. V. Milner. New York: W. W. Norton.

GAMBLE, A., PAYNE, A., DIETRICH, M., HOOGVELT, A., and KENNY, M. 1996. Editorial: new political economy. *New Political Economy*, 1: 1–12.

GEREFFI, G. 1996. Global commodity chains: new forms of coordination and control among nations and firms in international industries. *Competition and Change*, 4: 427–39.

—— HUMPHREY, J., and STURGEON, T. 2005. The governance of global value chains. *Review of International Political Economy*, 12: 78–104.

GILL, S. 2003. *Power and Resistance in the New World Order*. Basingstoke: Palgrave Macmillan.

GILPIN, R. 1975. *US Power and the Multinational Corporation: The Political Economy of Foreign Direct Investment*. New York: Basic Books.

—— 1981. *War and Change in World Politics*. Cambridge: Cambridge University Press.

—— 1987. *The Political Economy of International Relations*. Princeton, NJ: Princeton University Press.

—— 2001. *Global Political Economy: Understanding the International Economic Order*. Princeton, NJ: Princeton University Press.

GOUREVITCH, P. 1978. The second image reversed: the international sources of domestic politics. *International Organization*, 32: 881–912.

—— 1986. *Politics in Hard Times: Comparative Responses to International Economic Crises*. Ithaca, NY: Cornell University Press.

GRIECO, J. M. 1988. Realist theory and the problem of international cooperation: analysis with an amended Prisoner's Dilemma model. *Journal of Politics*, 50: 600–24.

—— 1993. The relative-gains problem for international cooperation: comment. *American Political Science Review*, 87: 729–35.

—— and IKENBERRY, G. J. 2003. *State Power and World Markets: The International Political Economy*, 1st edn. New York: W. W. Norton.

GROSSMAN, G. M., and HELPMAN, E. 1995. The politics of free-trade agreements. *American Economic Review*, 85: 667–90.

HAAS, E. B. 1958. *The Uniting of Europe: Political, Social, and Economic Forces, 1950–1957*. Stanford, Calif.: Stanford University Press.

—— 1964. *Beyond the Nation-State: Functionalism and International Organization*. Stanford, Calif.: Stanford University Press.

—— 1975. *The Obsolescence of Regional Integration Theory*. Berkeley: Institute of International Studies, University of California.

HALL, R. B., and BIERSTEKER, T. J. (eds.) 2002. *The Emergence of Private Authority in Global Governance*. Cambridge: Cambridge University Press.

HASENCLEVER, A., MAYER, P., and RITTBERGER, V. 1997. *Theories of International Regimes*. Cambridge: Cambridge University Press.

HIRSCH, F., and GOLDTHORPE, J. H. (eds.) 1978. *The Political Economy of Inflation*. Cambridge, Mass.: Harvard University Press.

HIRSCHMAN, A. O. 1945. *National Power and the Structure of Foreign Trade*. Berkeley: University of California Press.

HISCOX, M. J. 2002. *International Trade and Political Conflict: Commerce, Coalitions, and Mobility*. Princeton, NJ: Princeton University Press.

HOBSON, J. M., and SEABROOKE, L. (eds.) 2007. *Everyday Politics of the World Economy*. Cambridge: Cambridge University Press.

HOFFMANN, S. 1966. Obstinate or obsolete? The fate of the nation-state in Europe. *Daedalus*, 95: 862–915.

HOLSTI, K. J. 1985. *The Dividing Discipline: Hegemony and Diversity in International Theory*. Boston: Allen and Unwin.

HUFBAUER, G. C., SCHOTT, J. J., and ELLIOTT, K. A. 1983. *Economic Sanctions in Support of Foreign Policy Goals*. Washington, DC: Institute for International Economics.

HYMER, S. H. 1976. *The International Operations of National Firms: A Study of Direct Foreign Investment*. Cambridge, Mass.: MIT Press.

IRWIN, D., and KROSZNER, R. 1999. Interests, institutions, and ideology in securing policy change: the Republican conversion to trade liberalization after Smoot–Hawley. *Journal of Law and Economics*, 42: 643–73.

JERVIS, R. 1998. Realism in the study of world politics. *International Organization*, 52: 971–91.

KATZENSTEIN, P. J. 1985. *Small States in World Markets: Industrial Policy in Europe*. Ithaca, NY: Cornell University Press.

KEOHANE, R. O. 1984. *After Hegemony: Cooperation and Discord in the World Political Economy*. Princeton, NJ: Princeton University Press.

——1997. Problematic lucidity: Stephen Krasner's "State power and the structure of international trade." *World Politics*, 50: 150–70.

——and NYE, J. S. (eds.) 1972. *Transnational Relations and World Politics*. Cambridge, Mass.: Harvard University Press.

————1975. International interdependence and integration. Pp. 363–414 in *Handbook of Political Science*, vol. viii. *International Politics*, ed. F. I. Greenstein and N. W. Polsby. Reading, Mass.: Addison-Wesley.

————1977. *Power and Interdependence: World Politics in Transition*. Boston: Little, Brown.

KINDLEBERGER, C. P. 1951. Bretton Woods reappraised. *International Organization*, 5: 32–47.

——1969. *American Business Abroad: Six Lectures on Direct Investment*. New Haven, Conn.: Yale University Press.

——(ed.) 1970. *The International Corporation: A Symposium*. Cambridge, Mass.: MIT Press.

——1973. *The World in Depression, 1929–1939*. Berkeley: University of California Press.

KNORR, K. E. 1973. *Power and Wealth: The Political Economy of International Power*. New York: Basic Books.

——1975. *The Power of Nations: The Political Economy of International Relations*. New York: Basic Books.

KRASNER, S. D. 1974. Oil is the exception. *Foreign Policy*, 14: 68–84.

——1976. State power and the structure of international trade. *World Politics*, 28: 317–47.

——1985. *Structural Conflict: The Third World against Global Liberalism*. Berkeley: University of California Press.

LINDBERG, L. N., MAIER, C. S., and BARRY, B. M. (eds.) 1985. *The Politics of Inflation and Economic Stagnation: Theoretical Approaches and International Case Studies*. Washington, DC: Brookings Institution.

LING, L. H. M. 2000. Global passions within global interests: race, gender, and culture in our postcolonial order. Pp. 242–55 in *Global Political Economy: Contemporary Theories*, ed. R. Palan. London: Routledge.

MIKDASHI, Z. 1974. Collusion could work. *Foreign Policy*, 14: 57–68.

MILNER, H. 2002. Reflections on the field of international political economy. Pp. 207–23 in *Conflict, Security, Foreign Policy, and International Political Economy: Past Paths and Future Directions in International Studies*, ed. M. Brecher and F. P. Harvey. Ann Arbor: University of Michigan Press.

——2005. Globalization, development, and international institutions: normative and positive perspectives. *Perspectives on Politics*, 3: 833–54.

MURPHY, C. N. 2005. *Global Institutions, Marginalization, and Development*. London: Routledge.

——and NELSON, D. R. 2001. International political economy: a tale of two heterodoxies. *British Journal of Politics and International Relations*, 3: 393–412.

——and TOOZE, R. 1991. Getting beyond the "common sense" of the IPE orthodoxy. Pp. 11–31 in *The New International Political Economy*, ed. C. N. Murphy and R. Tooze. Boulder, Colo.: Lynne Rienner.

NARLIKAR, A. 2003. *International Trade and Developing Countries: Bargaining Coalitions in the GATT and WTO*. London: Routledge.

ODELL, J. S. (ed.) 2006. *Negotiating Trade: Developing Countries in the WTO and NAFTA*. Cambridge: Cambridge University Press.

PAYNE, A. 2005. *The Global Politics of Unequal Development*. Basingstoke: Palgrave Macmillan.

PENROSE, E. T. 1959. *The Theory of the Growth of the Firm*. Oxford: Blackwell.

PHILLIPS, N. (ed.) 2005. *Globalizing International Political Economy*. Basingstoke: Palgrave.

POGGE, T. W. M. 2002. *World Poverty and Human Rights: Cosmopolitan Responsibilities and Reforms*. Cambridge: Polity.

POWELL, R. 1991. Absolute and relative gains in international relations theory. *American Political Science Review*, 85: 1303–20.

——1993. The relative-gains problem for international cooperation: response. *American Political Science Review*, 87: 735–7.

RAVENHILL, J. 1985. *Collective Clientelism: The Lomé Conventions and North–South Relations*. New York: Columbia University Press.

RITTBERGER, V., with the assistance of MAYER, P. (eds.) 1993. *Regime Theory and International Relations*. Oxford: Clarendon Press.

ROTHSTEIN, R. L. 1979. *Global Bargaining: UNCTAD and the Quest for a New International Economic Order*. Princeton, NJ: Princeton University Press.

RUGGIE, J. G. 1975. International responses to technology: concepts and trends. *International Organization*, 29: 557–83.

——1998. What makes the world hang together? Neo-utilitarianism and the social constructivist challenge. *International Organization*, 52: 855–85.

RUGMAN, A. M. 2005. *The Regional Multinationals: MNEs and "Global" Strategic Management*. Cambridge: Cambridge University Press.

SEABROOKE, L. 2006. *The Social Sources of Financial Power: Domestic Legitimacy and International Financial Orders*. Ithaca, NY: Cornell University Press.

——2007. Varieties of economic constructivism in political economy: uncertain times call for disparate measures. *Review of International Political Economy*, 14: 371–85.

SINCLAIR, T. J. 2005. *The New Masters of Capital: American Bond Rating Agencies and the Politics of Creditworthiness*. Ithaca, NY: Cornell University Press.

SMITH, S. 2000. The discipline of international relations: still an American social science? *British Journal of Politics and International Relations*, 2: 374–402.

SNIDAL, D. 1991a. International cooperation among relative gains maximizers. *International Studies Quarterly*, 35: 387–402.

——1991b. Relative gains and the pattern of international cooperation. *American Political Science Review*, 85: 701–26.

——1993. The relative-gains problem for international cooperation: response. *American Political Science Review*, 87: 738–42.

STRANGE, S. 1970. International economics and international relations: a case of mutual neglect. *International Affairs*, 46: 304–15.

——1976. *International Monetary Relations*. London: Oxford University Press for the Royal Institute of International Affairs.

——1982. *Cave! hic dragones*: a critique of regime analysis. *International Organization*, 36: 479–96.

——1988. *States and Markets*. London: Pinter.

——1994. Wake up, Krasner! The world *has* changed. *Review of International Political Economy*, 1: 209–19.

UNDERHILL, G. R. D. 1995. Keeping governments out of politics: transnational securities markets, regulatory cooperation, and political legitimacy. *Review of International Studies*, 21: 251–78.

——2000. State, market, and global political economy: genealogy of an (inter-?) discipline. *International Affairs*, 76: 805–24.

VAN DER PIJL, K. 1998. *Transnational Classes and International Relations*. London: Routledge.

VERNON, R. 1966. International investment and international trade in the product cycle. *Quarterly Journal of Economics*, 80: 190–207.

——1971. *Sovereignty at Bay: The Multinational Spread of US Enterprises*. New York: Basic Books.

VINER, J. 1948. Power versus plenty as objectives of foreign policy in the seventeenth and eighteenth centuries. *World Politics*, 1: 1–29.

WÆVER, O. 1996. The rise and fall of the inter-paradigm debate. Pp. 149–85 in *International Theory: Positivism and Beyond*, ed. S. Smith, K. Booth, and M. Zalewski. Cambridge: Cambridge University Press.

——1998. The sociology of a not so international discipline: American and European developments in international relations. *International Organization*, 52: 687–727.

WALLERSTEIN, I. M. 1974. *The Modern World-System*. New York: Academic Press.

WALTZ, K. N. 1979. *Theory of International Politics*. Reading, Mass.: Addison-Wesley.

WATSON, M. 2005. *Foundations of International Political Economy*. Basingstoke: Palgrave Macmillan.

WHITWORTH, S. 2000. Theory and exclusion: gender, masculinity, and international political economy. Pp. 91–101 in *Political Economy and the Changing Global Order*, 2nd edn., ed. R. Stubbs and G. R. D. Underhill. Oxford: Oxford University Press.

ZYSMAN, J. 1977. *Political Strategies for Industrial Order: State, Market, and Industry in France*. Berkeley: University of California Press.

CHAPTER 32

....

STRATEGIC
STUDIES

....

ROBERT AYSON

SCHOLARS contemplating strategic studies as a subfield of international relations may wish to think twice about granting admission to this potentially unruly resident. This comment may sound odd, because strategic studies focuses on the role of armed force in international politics. Moreover, issues of war and peace were central in the arrival of international relations as a fully-fledged academic discipline, symbolized after the First World War by the establishment of the Woodrow Wilson Chair of International Politics at University College of Wales in Aberystwyth.

But some of the preoccupations that make strategic studies such a fascinating subject—how states and other political actors utilize force to advance their wider objectives, how their interactions can become heated, and how these violent confrontations might be shaped—are potentially troubling for students of international relations. The issues that animate strategic studies reflect an overdeveloped interest in practice rather than in theory, and betray assumptions that some international relations scholars may find questionable and unreflective. The stubborn amorality of strategic studies also seems to clash with the rising tide of ideational considerations in contemporary international relations thinking.

Because it deals with an event posing the greatest challenge to the international system—armed conflict that may threaten its key units or the overall system itself—strategic studies cannot be ignored by students of international relations. But, as the following analysis suggests, it might be best to consider strategic studies as a somewhat competitive sibling, rather than a subset, of international relations, both of whom belong to the extended family we call political science. In recent years the growth of security studies as a subdiscipline of international relations, incorporating wider perspectives such as human and environmental security, has been offered as a broad church into which strategic studies might be placed. But strategic studies still deserves to be considered as a subject in its own right. With its emphasis on the interaction between self-interested actors engaged in the politics of force, strategic studies has strong claims to make sense of the supposedly novel challenges generated in an era of global terrorism, nuclear proliferation, and failing states.

1 UNDERSTANDING STRATEGIC STUDIES

It is axiomatic that strategic studies involves the study of strategy, but this realization does not necessarily help us determine its origins as an academic subject with its own conceptual underpinnings. Strategy comes to Western thought from the Greek *strategos*, meaning generalship. But a focus on warfare itself, and its treatment as an art form that can be learned and mastered, is not really the genius behind the modern study of strategy. Instead, its subject matter consists of the political origins, applications, and implications of organized violence in times of both war and peace.

This modern understanding can be linked above all to the early nineteenth-century thinking of the Prussian philosopher of war Carl von Clausewitz, whose commentary on the enduringly political nature of war helps us understand strategy as the connecting ligament between war and politics (Gray 1999, 17). His one major work (Clausewitz 1976), first published posthumously in 1832, encourages the view that the use of force is subordinate to the interests of policy (a notion that scholars were also to find in Sun Tzu's *Art of War*, written in China millennia before). If understood as a military means to a political end, warfare is less likely to be viewed as an end in itself, a danger that became all too tempting for the excessively optimistic military thinking in Europe on the outbreak of an eventually catastrophic war in 1914.

This end–means logic in Clausewitz could be applied in environments other than the land-based wars of the Napoleonic age. Its echoes are found in the maritime strategy of Alfred Thayer Mahan in the last decade of the nineteenth century and in Giulio Douhet's exaggerated projections in the 1920s of the political impact of aerial bombardment. It could be extended to the organization of a full range of nonmilitary as well as military resources for the purposes of the state—a notion wrapped up in the idea of "grand strategy." This inclusion of "economic, psychological, moral, political, and technological" factors (Earle 1943, viii), which was especially relevant to the all-encompassing conflict of the Second World War, intensified the relationship between strategy and international politics. But it could still allow for an excessively instrumental view of military power where organized violence is viewed as easily customized for the circumscribed policy aims of a particular government. This tendency is sometimes found in the teaching of strategy in defense staff colleges where military power is treated as one of the many tools in the state's toolbox, as if it could be picked up and put away with the ease and precision available to a mechanic or carpenter.

An antidote to this simplistic logic is offered by the comment from Clausewitz (1976, 87) himself that "war is not merely an act of policy, but a true political instrument, a continuation of political intercourse." War is inherently political—it has the capacity both to reflect and to intensify the often messy and fiery relationships of power. These features became supremely important as the Second World War ended with the most stunningly violent use of force for political purposes—the atomic bombing of Hiroshima and Nagasaki. The big challenge now lay in what to do with this immensely destructive power, which seemed eminently capable of exceeding any reasonable political boundaries.

On the whole a new subject had to be fashioned. A good deal of the existing study of war consisted of military history, and the law and philosophy of the use of armed force. Moreover, in many Western circles the trauma of the First World War had discouraged the treatment of warfare as a political act that needed to be understood, as opposed to a nasty disease that needed to be eradicated. As the French strategic thinker André Beaufre (1965, 20) later wrote: "The static warfare of 1914–18 was held to be proof of the 'bankruptcy of strategy', whereas in fact it demonstrated only the bankruptcy of one particular strategy." This tendency not only had an impact on interwar international relations thinking. It also haunted the perspectives of some of the few people writing directly about strategy. One such figure, the British strategist and former army officer Basil Liddell Hart, regarded Clausewitz as a prophet of annihilation.

Unlike Liddell Hart and many of his contemporaries, most of the students of strategy in the new cold war age were civilian intellectuals (Bull 1968, 594). Their methodologies, which had often been shaped by industrial-scale efforts to apply force in the century's second global conflict, owed as much to the burgeoning social and decision sciences as they did to the humanities and the military arts. Some, like the hugely influential Bernard Brodie, were able to draw on backgrounds in political science and history, but others were economists like Thomas Schelling and mathematicians like Albert Wohlstetter (Baylis and Wirtz 2002, 4). Many of them spent time at the RAND Corporation in California, which offered a stimulating venue for studying the problems of strategy in the nuclear age, often from unusual interdisciplinary perspectives. The establishment of this original "think tank" in 1948 as a government-funded, but intellectually inventive, research hothouse marks the beginning of strategic studies as an identifiable subject.

These scholars and their colleagues did not tend to set up university departments of strategic studies as such (Betts 1997, 23). Instead they helped provide a strongly strategic flavor to new units such as Columbia University's Institute of War and Peace, founded in 1951, and Harvard University's Center for International Affairs, which opened seven years later. It was in London where the more direct use of the term was to be found in the establishment in 1958 of the Institute for Strategic Studies (which later added the prefix "International" to become the IISS). King's College London had preferred the much less opaque phrase "War Studies" when a department under that name was set up in 1953 under the leadership of Michael Howard, the eminent historian of European armed conflict. By the mid-1960s the Australian National University had its own Strategic and Defence Studies Centre, the first of its type designed to deal with strategic challenges in the Asia–Pacific region.

Despite this increasingly international feel of strategic studies, there was no doubt that the American thinkers were the doyens of this new field. Their work flowered as the problems of strategy in an age of even more destructive thermonuclear weapons (which arrived in the early 1950s) became urgent and all-consuming priorities. This gave rise to a so-called golden age of nuclear strategy from the mid-1950s to the mid-1960s (Gray 1982, 15). The ideas and concepts developed in such modern classics as Brodie's *Strategy in the Missile Age* (1959) and Schelling's *The Strategy of Conflict* (1960) laid out the standard operating procedures of the subject writ large. Strategy as a genus was defined and dominated by its nuclear species, whose peculiar challenges dominated international relations thinking as well.

2 THE PREOCCUPATIONS OF STRATEGIC STUDIES

Many of the main preoccupations, concepts, and oversights that characterized strategic studies in these early decades of the nuclear age remain discernible in the subject today. One important feature was a heightened sensitivity to the implications of almost any decision made about the use of force. This involved a much wider ambit than the fighting of wars per se. Especially in a nuclear age, it might be preferable to exploit the coercive potential of armed force by communicating credible threats regarding the military action that one might reluctantly need to carry out (Schelling 1966). The mere build-up of armed forces could signal important intentions and, hopefully, condition the responses of the other side without requiring the resort to violence itself.

As Hedley Bull (1968, 593) noted in his brilliant review of strategic studies at the cold war's halfway point: "Attention has shifted away from war as an instrument of actual policy toward the threat of war." Deterrence became the central concept (Freedman 2004, 1), defined classically by Glenn Snyder (1961, 3) as "discouraging the enemy from taking military action by posing for him a prospect of cost and risk outweighing his prospective gain." Theoretically this extended to preventing escalation beyond the initial use of nuclear weapons as well as the deterrence of any nuclear use at all. But any confidence in the capacity to control the nuclear blaze once it had broken out, raised in a famous study authored by Henry Kissinger (1957), proved difficult to sustain. This debate resumed in the early 1980s when renewed interest in Washington about prevailing in a limited nuclear war was attacked as unrealistic if not utterly dangerous (Ball 1981).

Deterrence thinking assumed that governments would want to avoid excessive harm out of a sense of national interest. This understanding treated strategic behavior as a branch of rational activity. It did not mean strategic actors were regarded as incapable of making poor decisions (Garnett 1987, 18) or that deterrence was foolproof. But this proposition could, in the words of Schelling (1960, 4), be "potent... for the production of theory." The assumption of rational, purposeful activity is also reflected in the very aims of the subject. For example, Lawrence Freedman (1998, 15) defines strategy as "the search for the optimum relationship between political ends and the means available for obtaining them." There would be little sense of striving for optima if strategic actors were regarded as irrational. But strategic studies could not escape the Jekyll and Hyde paradox where the use of military force was subject to deliberate and rational control and at the same time was an inherently volatile and inflammable agent. Some strategic thinkers stretched that paradox to breaking point by arguing that the risks due to the volatility of force could themselves be exploited for intimidatory purposes.

These considerations also reflected a strong emphasis on the interdependence of strategic behavior; another rediscovery of Clausewitzian logic. Rather than a simple relationship between ends and means, strategy could be understood as the interaction between two or more purposeful actors whose "best course of action" depended upon "what the other players do" (Schelling 1960, 3 n). This was highlighted by an age of increasingly global vulnerability to devastation where strategic action had inherently intercontinental consequences.

At times this lent itself to a rather simplistic appreciation of strategic interaction as a rather crude action–reaction process, revealed especially in concern about arms races and their implications. But even more sophisticated appreciations of strategic interaction revealed a close interest in the impact that military technological change could have on strategic decisions. This has not been without its problems. Howard (1979, 982) has argued that "works about nuclear war and deterrence normally treat their topic as an activity taking place almost entirely in the technological dimension."

Nonetheless, strategic thinkers have needed to understand the weapons systems of their time and to watch for new developments and their implications for the military balance between potential adversaries. (The flagship publication of the IISS since the late 1950s has been an annual review entitled *The Military Balance*.) As something of a vaccination against the hazards of military technological change, the theory of arms control emerged by the early 1960s essentially as a byproduct of strategic studies. The classic works on that subject (Bull 1961; Schelling and Halperin 1961) took a markedly pragmatic line. In contrast to the more radical, abolitionist aims of disarmament, the objective was to restrain the more dangerous elements of armaments competition rather than to remove competition entirely, and thus to stabilize rather than outlaw strategies of deterrence. The need to manage the military sector was also reflected in an endorsement of civilian control—a not uncontroversial approach to civil–military relations, given the desire among military leaders for a free hand (Cohen 2002, 3). It was also a reflection of the civilian analysts' own sense of their place in things, modesty not being one of the main hallmarks of strategic studies.

There also emerged within strategic studies a keen interest in understanding the dynamics of crises where the normally cool-headed and rational judgments of political leaders might be spoiled by the pressures of the moment. Of the available case studies, the 1962 Cuban Missile Crisis was utilized to highlight an influential bureaucratic politics model of decision-making (Allison 1971) that raised serious questions about single-actor models of rational action. But there was also some recognition that states could choose to use force in the cool light of day. Here the classical case was Japan's 1941 attack on Pearl Harbor, which encouraged some strategic thinkers to emphasize the possibilities of strategic surprise (Wohlstetter 1962). Israel's pre-emptive strike on Egypt in 1967 offered something of an in-between case.

On the whole, though, the nuclear strategists had few real case studies to draw from, a fact for which we should all be grateful. This encouraged the speculative side of strategy, which at times could get rather too colourful, as witnessed in the almost surreal speculations of a larger than life figure such as Herman Kahn (1960). But this also reveals the prominence of uncertainty in strategy that no amount of military history can shift. One reason here is Clausewitz's concept of friction, where anything that could go wrong in war usually does (Luttwak 1987, 11). As Colin Gray (1999, 5) argues: "statesmen in peacetime, and even generals and admirals in peacetime, can rarely be confident about the probable performance of their military instruments in war." This also applies to the peacetime application of threats of violence.

This uncertainty left some interesting conceptual questions that the civilian analysts were keen to address. In the US community, there was a noticeable use of formal methods to examine strategic behavior. These included game theory, whose inspiration derives from the interdependent relationships between purposeful actors, and which as Duncan Snidal (1985, 25) notes, highlights the possibilities for cooperation as well as conflict. The formal methods deployed also included varieties of systems analysis and operations research, whose tendency to quantify strategic problems can be as much a hazard as an advantage. In response, John Garnett (1987, 27) has argued that many strategic thinkers (especially in the British analytical narrative tradition) have studiously avoided the treatment of their subject as a science. Brodie (1973, 474), once an advocate of economic methods in strategy, came to regard systems analysis in particular as problematic because it could not see the forest of political considerations for the trees of cost-effectiveness.

But these formal techniques found use in an age where decisions over defense-force structure and the allocation of resources could easily run into billions. And the civilian strategists seemed to have the analytical tools to make a difference in public policy. However, their first major move into government positions, which occurred in the early 1960s under the John F. Kennedy administration, was followed by the obvious defeat of many of their ideas in the Vietnam War. Hanoi's evident immunity to the application of carefully calculated quanta of violence indicated the vulnerability of strategic studies as an applied academic subject. Its assumptions and conclusions seemed to run aground against a relatively small conflict that by most measures ought to have been easily won.

3 UNDER SIEGE? NEW CHALLENGES AND OPPORTUNITIES

The Vietnam experience caused a crisis of confidence for strategic studies, especially in the United States. It seemed to confirm the exaggerated criticisms that the civilian analysts were dangerously misguided in their assumptions and impervious to moral considerations in their application of formal theory (Rapoport 1964; Green 1966). Perhaps the most valuable point in this attack was that Western strategic thinkers were mirroring their own assumptions on to the strategic reasoning on the other side of the cold war divide. The sense that the civilian analysts might be blind to different strategic cultures was later reflected in powerful claims of "strategic ethnocentrism" (Booth 1979).

But these more introspective moments did not stop strategic studies in its tracks. As Richard Betts (1997, 8) has argued, the 1970s and 1980s saw important empirical work being undertaken on issues such as the role of intelligence and conventional (nonnuclear) strategy. For Stephen Walt (1991), this inductive scholarship generated a veritable renaissance, more than filling the gaps left by the deductive theorizing of the 1950s and 1960s. Additional layers were added to the understanding of strategic crises and the mutual perceptions that drove them, the origins of military doctrine, and the decision-making processes of the major powers. But it is open to question whether this scholarship helped answer Lenin's famously strategic question: "what is to be done?"

The international turbulence of the period also had its impact. For example, the use of terrorism by nationalist movements in the 1970s stimulated a mini-boom in studies of politically motivated violence by substate actors (Wardlaw 1982). Yet the strategic studies community's capacity to make sense of messy internal conflicts was limited by its state-centric tendencies. These were only strengthened as the short-lived period of détente was replaced by a revival of cold war tensions that renewed interest in strategic studies (Baldwin 1995, 125) and the central nuclear balance. But the civilian strategists were not as visible as they once had been, and the assumptions behind their deterrence logic were subjected to ever closer scrutiny (Jervis, Lebow, and Stein 1985). The realization that the nuclear shadow was not as powerful as it once had seemed had already raised the profile of armed forces as strategic actors in their own right, rebalancing the ends–means relationship (Summers 1982) and encouraging a rediscovery of Clausewitz as a theorist of conventional warfare.

The biggest questions about the future of strategic studies were to come with the end of the cold war. Was a subject preoccupied with the use of force relevant when the risk of major inter-state warfare seemed so low? There have been at least two varieties of this interrogation. First there is the argument that use-of-force questions are increasingly marginalized in a world of more broadly based threats and challenges. In the 1990s nontraditional security issues such as environmental degradation and disease (which were in fact rather old concerns) and ideas of geoeconomics rather than geopolitics seemed poised to dominate the agenda. Some were prepared to discount these challenges because they did not emanate from the conscious decisions of another actor and would therefore not involve strategic interaction. Others, however, have viewed these issues as a lifeline for a broadening discipline of strategic studies itself—and valid academically because these challenges might well threaten the survival of nation states.

A middle-range position, as noted by Alan Dupont (2001, 14–15), suggests that nonmilitary challenges should be taken into account if they nonetheless increase the prospects of armed conflict. Examples could include armed conflict between neighboring states over increasingly rare natural resources such as clean water or the exacerbation of internal conflict by environmental damage. Of course the early 1990s witnessed the continuing role of an older and more direct nexus between resources and armed violence—the energy considerations that were a factor in Iraq's invasion of Kuwait in 1990 and in the US-led response.

The second criticism from the post-cold war era is that, even if use-of-force issues were allowed to remain dominant within strategic studies, the model of inter-state symmetric warfare was now obsolete. The Israeli military historian

Martin van Creveld (1991) argued that there was little life remaining in what he regarded as the Clausewitzian universe of large, state-based armed forces in an age of unconventional wars fought by nonstate actors. This theme was an attractive one, but it took the September 2001 attacks on the United States to bring the analysis of nonstate groups and networks toward the forefront of strategic studies.

These sudden events raised questions about the supposed rationality of nonstate actors who were ready to use force, and about their willingness to limit that force in line with reasonable political aspirations. Yet, while some studies have emphasized the potentially catastrophic reach of terrorism (Allison 2004), others, including the account of suicide terrorism by Robert Pape (2005), have indicated the continuing relevance of viewing strategy as violence associated with particular (and sometimes quite limited) political aspirations. Moreover, while the terrorism question challenged prevailing assumptions about the specific origins of threats, it has to some extent reinforced the old bias toward use-of-force issues. There is also growing recognition that the state's demise as a strategic actor in a globalizing world has been exaggerated, as has the irrelevance of strategies of deterrence (Morgan 2006, xix).

These supposedly obsolete features of international strategy have been reinforced as the United States and its allies have taken on "rogue states" and addressed their concerns about the proliferation of weapons of mass destruction. As force has been employed with these ends in mind, the importance of military technological change has again been highlighted, although the results have not always been promising. For instance, while some scholars have been cautious about the degree to which military technology can enhance fighting power and strategic influence (Biddle 2004), others have been much more willing to endorse notions of an information-age revolution in military affairs. In an example of the perils of strategic studies in action, the more optimistic argument helped feed the Pentagon's notion of defense transformation, which came unstuck in Iraq after the 2003 invasion. This experience helped invigorate interest in the analysis of asymmetric conflict, where the weak seem so often to have advantages over the strong. But this has done less to revolutionize strategy than to emphasize hard power relationships between different sets of actors.

In sum, the evolving focus of strategic studies is shaped as much by the political conditions in which threats arise and are dealt with as by their material basis. In Clausewitz's time, Napoleon's failed bid for European hegemony focused attention on the political uses of armed force by the great powers of that day. Following the Second World War, the arrival of the United States and the Soviet Union as superpowers placed a premium on managing their competition in a hazardous nuclear era. The end of the cold war contest gave the international community room to consider the use of force for more humanitarian purposes, reflected in the spate of literature on peace operations. It allowed a dominant United States space to intervene militarily, stimulated by fears that the weak had become its main adversaries. This power imbalance also gave the weak an obvious target upon which to concentrate their frustrations. As these political conditions evolve, so will the focus of strategic studies. As a new multipolar order approaches, and as the global balance shifts in the direction of Asia, the contest between the new mix of great powers will increasingly shape the strategic studies agenda.

4 EMPIRICAL, NORMATIVE, AND THEORETICAL ELEMENTS

It is hard to deny the strong, empirical, and positivist elements of strategic studies. Peter Paret (1986, 3) has noted that "strategic thought is inevitably highly pragmatic. It is dependent on the realities of geography, society, economics, and politics, as well as on other, often fleeting factors that give rise to the issues and conflicts war is meant to resolve." This is associated with an obvious bias toward material understandings of power in international politics, not least because of the importance of physical military capabilities, and the operational demands placed on them in varying land, maritime, and aerospace environments. The audiences for strategic studies also merit consideration. The many scholars of the subject who have been asked to provide strategic advice to politicians or media commentary on unfolding crises will be aware that there is a limited appetite in these circles for intricate and self-reflective theoretical disposition.

Students of strategy generally treat armed conflict as an underlying, and sometimes unavoidable, reality of the international system (Garnett 1987, 10). Cynics might say their academic livelihood depends on this debatable position: War is to strategic studies what crime is to the fictional barrister Rumpole of the Bailey. But the obsolescence of force is quite genuinely seen as a pipe dream in a world where risks can be managed but rarely transcended. This helps make realism a natural partner of strategic studies, in terms of its emphasis on the material basis of power and the competition for influence and security within a largely anarchic international system. Realist assumptions offer students of strategy a common language and make their work especially accessible to the policy community. But they can also produce a self-reinforcing logic that exaggerates the role of force in international politics.

This is not to suggest a complete absence of links with other schools of international relations thinking. For example, by the early 1960s there were arguments in the strategic studies community that nuclear weapons had generated a non-zero-sum relationship between the superpowers that could be managed by exploiting their common interests. This is similar to the liberal institutionalist emphasis on cooperation, and a scholar such as Schelling might be thought of as a pioneer of some of the arguments used later in regime theory. The strategic culture literature that examines the influence of particular national preferences on strategic decision-making (Johnston 1995) can bear a striking resemblance to the constructivist accounts of the role of ideas and culture in international relations, which has been applied to the politics of national security-making (Katzenstein 1996). Freedman (2007, 365) argues that it may help if "the practical strategist" is a constructivist, because "effective strategy requires a clear sense of the dynamic relationship between ends and means, knowing that how ends are defined in the first place is critical to whether available means will be adequate." Similarly, the limitations of realist explanations have been highlighted by use of organizational theory to understand strategic decision-making (Sagan 1993) and in studies of the domestic origins of grand strategy (Rosecrance and Stein 1993).

Aside from the linkages with international relations theory per se, there is something that resembles a distinct theory of strategy. This can be found above all in the Clausewitzian framework. There are, however, no indigenous "isms" in strategic studies. There remains what Gray (1982, 13) calls an "ambivalence" within the subject on the right relation between theory and practice. For much of the strategic studies community, and especially for those closest to policy-making, the debates are eminently practical ones; whether the international community should use force to remove a particular country's nuclear weapons program; what approach to the use of force works best (and worst) in interventions; whether a particular government should plan for regional missions or global roles; or whether the United States lost the war in Vietnam because it was unwinnable or because the generals had their hands tied by their political masters.

This style of thinking has its critics. Barry Buzan (1991, 10) argues that "Strategic Studies is . . . both empirically bound and constrained not to wander much beyond the imperatives of the national policy level." But this is probably more a strength of strategic studies than a weakness. As Paret (1986, 3) declares: "The history of strategic thought is a history not of pure but of applied reason." Yet this raises a further area of contestation, as many within the strategic studies community end up proffering advice about what governments ought to do. Down the years this has created some discomfort for some within the discipline, and even more so from those outside, about the academic credibility of strategic studies. Are students of strategy more interested in advocacy and in newspaper headlines than in scholarship? Gray (1982, 106) observes that "most strategists are unable to refrain from effecting the transition from analysis to recommendation."

This is evidence of a significant *normative* tradition within strategic studies. But that normative streak does not often extend to moral concerns. As Garnett (1987, 12) argues, "many contemporary strategists have failed to allocate priority to the moral aspects of strategic policy, and as a result much contemporary strategic writing has an air of moral neutrality about it." By implying that political interests can be advanced by the deliberate use of violence, strategic studies has been understood by some critics as incorporating a dangerously amoral (if not outright immoral) approach to human affairs.

This criticism applied much more during the heady days of the cold war. But it can still be argued that strategic studies tends to emphasize what states can physically and psychologically do to one another (and to nonstate actors) rather than what they are morally or legally obliged to do. These latter considerations may be limitations that need to be recognized (and at times exploited), but they are not necessarily seen as ends in themselves. The dichotomy in Clausewitz is revealing here: War is subordinate to policy but also has a logic of its own (Howard 1983, 59). Isolating the second of these points allows the leading ethicist of war Michael Walzer (1977, 24) to argue that "the social and historical conditions that 'modify' war are not to be considered as accidental or external to war itself, for war is a social creation." The coercive statecraft that students of strategy examine, assume, and sometimes endorse is rather similar to practices that are normally outlawed in domestic society. As a result, students of strategy are especially vulnerable to the double-standards charge that has been leveled at many realists.

Even though many within the strategic studies community highlight problems associated with the use of force, its treatment as a purposeful instrument of statecraft offends some consciences. For some, as Garnett (1987, 14) notes, this justifies violence as acceptable and perhaps even necessary. The argument by Betts (1997, 8) that strategic studies "focuses on the essential Clausewitzian problem: how to make force a rational instrument of policy rather than mindless murder" provides little improvement to those for whom any use of force is still plain wrong. A similar criticism might be made of the citation by Edward Luttwak (1987, 3) of the paradoxical dictum "*Si vis pacem, para bellum* (If you want peace, prepare war)." The role of "peace studies" as an attempted antidote to the assumptions of strategic and war studies (Teriff et al. 1999, 71–5) is further evidence of the criticism that students of war tend to risk encouraging their objectionable subject. As a consequence, some parts of the academy have not always been happy at the presence of strategic studies in their institutions, especially when these scholars are undertaking work on military issues (or when their work is sponsored by defense organizations).

It must be admitted that students of strategy have not always been the quickest to latch on to attempts to humanize the study of relationships of power. They have been somewhat resistant to the growing tradition of human security, which seeks to emphasize the security interests of individual citizens (Paris 2001) and which has helped motivate a growing tradition of humanitarian intervention. Neither have they been especially attracted to the charms of critical theory. While used to some effect by Bradley Klein (1994), this approach may seem too self-reflexive for an action discipline and may raise unanswerable questions about the discourses of power from which students of strategy might benefit. And the impact of gendered accounts of security and gendered critiques of strategic studies, while generating a good degree of debate in the 1980s, can probably be best described as fleeting.

As a general rule, the comfort levels within strategic studies tend to diminish the further the discussion moves away from use-of-force issues. This resistance is not shared, however, by security studies, even when this subfield of international relations is understood to house strategic studies as its most difficult resident. In comparison to the theory of action provided by strategic studies—which lends itself to emphasizing what states can rather than ought to do—security studies tends to focus on the conditions of existence within the international system. Security studies focuses on challenges to what Arnold Wolfers (1952) famously called "acquired values." As more recent scholarship has emphasized, these can be held by a particular state, or group of states, or some nonstate entity. These make for a wide range of "referent objects" that security studies incorporates alongside a similarly catholic assessment of what can count as threats to these various consumers of security (Buzan 1991, 116–34; Terriff et al. 1999, 18–22).

Security studies brings into play an implicit normative assumption that greater security (and thus fewer threats) is better than less, even though there may be a trade-off between security and other interests (C. A. Snyder 1999, 8). There is also an implied sense of responsibility among security studies academics to discover those things that enhance the security conditions of existence—or at least to hold that security is a positive attribute. The same feature does not translate as well for strategic studies. It is not so apparent whether we are better off when there is more strategy or when there is less. Since strategy often involves the use of force, some may well say the latter. Indeed, in an environment of absolute security, strategy may no longer be necessary. Since international relations owes so much of its origins as a formal academic discipline to the interwar quest for the abolition of armed conflict, there is a much better fit within its ranks for the aspirations of security studies than for the pessimism of strategic studies. The latter is an especially unhappy hunting ground for those seeking a commitment to emancipation.

5 STRATEGIC STUDIES, SECURITY STUDIES, AND INTERNATIONAL RELATIONS

By now it should be clear that strategic studies enjoys a complicated relationship with international relations and that part of the latter discipline known as security studies. This relationship has long been contested. For Bull (1968, 596), a rare scholar in terms of his capacity to straddle the divide, it was not "desirable to separate strategic studies from the wider study of international relations." This was in large part because of the political veins that run through the body of strategic studies: once separated, the latter risked becoming a desiccated military end in itself. Similar sentiment is evident in the warning from Garnett (1987, 5) that "strategic thought is so inextricably entwined with international politics that it would be misleading and dangerous to try to separate the two subjects."

In more recent times, however, it has become something of a convention to argue, not so much that strategic studies and international relations are inseparable, but that strategic studies is a subfield of international relations. The inclusion of the current chapter in this *Handbook* may be taken as further evidence of this argument. There is much to support such a linkage. The overviews of Baylis and Wirtz (2002, 12), and Betts (1997, 9), suggest that strategic studies is a specialized portion of security studies, which is itself a subfield of international relations. The last is a field of the broader discipline of political science. Enthusiastic support for this approach comes from Buzan (1987, 2–3), who sees strategic studies as "embedded within the broader field of international relations...similar to that of a major organ within a living body." As a subfield that specializes in the "military aspects of international relations," strategic studies is, when compared to security studies, "the much narrower subject" (Buzan 1991, 23, 25).

This elegant taxonomy would seem to make a good deal of sense. First, it can be argued that strategic studies deals with a particular *subset* of security concerns—those where threats arise from the use and potential use of armed force, normally by states. Security studies becomes the wider subject that encapsulates all harmful challenges, including but going well beyond those emanating from state-based military activity. Secondly, security studies is undoubtedly an integral part of international relations, relying heavily on international relations theory for its main bearings. As Terry Terriff et al. (1999, 12) argue, treating security studies as a "sub-field of IR...means that an approach to security ought to be defined by the central theoretical perspective on IR that is being employed." Thirdly, international relations is the international dimension of political science as reflected in the tendency to treat international relations and international politics as synonyms. We can combine these steps by saying that *strategic* studies has been focused primarily on the role of armed force in the context of *security* challenges that arise from the nature of the *international* system of *political* relations.

But strategic studies actually deserves to stand alongside international relations as a direct subfield of political science. First, strategy is not so much a subset of security as its interactive partner. Students of strategy focus on the responses of states and other actors to the international security environment: If security is the condition, strategy is the reaction (Ayson 2006, 18). Strategic action in turn affects the security conditions faced by other actors; again security is the condition, but strategy can also be the cause. It can be the independent variable. The use of force often has a major bearing on the security conditions faced by other actors (and by the user of the force themselves); it can quite easily give rise, for example, to the security dilemmas analyzed so skilfully by Robert Jervis (1978). There is at the very least an interactive relationship between strategic studies and security studies.

Security studies is at times the more passive side of the coin—a study of the conditions of the international security system and theories on the nature of that system. Strategic studies has a stronger interest in action and decision—what are states and other actors doing as they interact strategically, what choices do they face, and what choices ought they take? As Brodie (1973, 452) once noted: "Strategic thinking, or 'theory' if one prefers, is nothing if not pragmatic. Strategy is a 'how to do it' study, a guide to accomplishing something and doing it efficiently... Above all strategic theory is a theory for action." Rather than a subset of security studies, strategic studies is more like an intersecting set with some common ground but also its own agenda.

That distinct agenda emphasizes the political purposes motivating organized violence. The emphasis on force makes strategic studies "narrower" than security studies, which has come to mean just about anything, as almost every challenge to human happiness is subjected to what Buzan, Ole Wæver, and Jaap de Wilde (1998) call "securitization." But understanding force in its political context gives strategic studies the direct connection to political science that an increasingly inclusive security studies may lack. One prominent attempt to limit security studies to "the study of the nature, causes, effects, and the prevention of war," which does not explicitly refer to the force-politics nexus of strategy, ironically argues that security studies should be abolished as a subfield of international relations because it risks divorcing the study of war from the study of political life (Baldwin 1995, 119, 136).

The prospect of a more natural linkage between strategic studies and political science is apparent in the comment by Bull (1968, 596) that strategic studies "compares very favorably with some other branches of political science both in its moral and social relevance and as an intellectual discipline." The emphasis on the overwhelmingly political context in which strategic decisions occur remains its core business. Clausewitz, the philosopher of that relationship, is in a sense the Thomas Hobbes of strategic studies. Portions of strategic studies can be regarded as a branch of political philosophy and theory.

As a result, strategic studies fits only partially within the rubric of international relations. The parts of strategic studies that do not fit (especially those that deal with strategic decisions) deserve to be treated as more direct components of political science, without the mediation of international relations, or its subfield security studies. Indeed, as strategic studies came into its own in the 1950s and 1960s, it was not immediately clear that it had been spawned by international relations. For a few years at least, what Howard (1983, 36) calls "the strategic approach to international relations" behaved more like the parent than the offspring.

REFERENCES

ALLISON, G. 1971. *Essence of Decision: Explaining the Cuban Missile Crisis*. Boston: Little, Brown.

—— 2004. *Nuclear Terrorism: The Ultimate Preventable Catastrophe*. New York: Owl Books.

AYSON, R. 2006. Concepts for strategy and security. Pp. 10–24 in *Strategy and Security in the Asia Pacific*, ed. R. Ayson and D. Ball. Crows Nest: Allen and Unwin.

BALDWIN, D. A. 1995. Security studies and the end of the Cold War. *World Politics*, 48: 117–41.

BALL, D. 1981. Can nuclear war be controlled? *Adelphi Papers*, No. 169. London: International Institute for Strategic Studies.

BAYLIS, J., and WIRTZ, J. J. 2002. Introduction. Pp. 1–14 in *Strategy in the Contemporary World: An Introduction to Strategic Studies*, ed. J. Baylis, J. Wirtz, E. Cohen, and C. S. Gray. Oxford: Oxford University Press.

BEAUFRE, A. 1965. *An Introduction to Strategy*, trans R. H. Barry. London: Faber and Faber.

BETTS, R. K. 1997. Should strategic studies survive? *World Politics*, 50: 7–33.

BIDDLE, S. 2004. *Military Power: Explaining Victory and Defeat in Modern Battle*. Princeton, NJ: Princeton University Press.

BOOTH, K. 1979. *Strategy and Ethnocentrism*. London: Croom Helm.

BRODIE, B. 1959. *Strategy in the Missile Age*. Princeton, NJ: Princeton University Press.

—— 1973. *War and Politics*. New York: Macmillan.

BULL, H. 1961. *The Control of the Arms Race: Disarmament and Arms Control in the Missile Age*. London: Weidenfeld and Nicolson for the Institute for Strategic Studies.

—— 1968. Strategic studies and its critics. *World Politics*, 20: 593–605.

BUZAN, B. 1987. *An Introduction to Strategic Studies: Military Technology and International Relations*. Basingstoke: Macmillan.

—— 1991. *People, States and Fear: An Agenda for International Security Studies in the Post-Cold War Era*, 2nd edn. New York: Harvester Wheatsheaf.

—— WÆVER, O., and DE WILDE, J. 1998. *Security: A New Framework for Analysis*. Boulder, Colo.: Lynne Rienner.

CLAUSEWITZ, C. VON 1976. *On War*, ed. and trans. M. Howard and P. Paret. Princeton, NJ: Princeton University Press; originally published 1832.

COHEN, E. A. 2002. *Supreme Command: Soldiers, Statesmen, and Leadership in Wartime*. New York: Free Press.

DUPONT, A. 2001. *East Asia Imperilled: Transnational Challenges to Security*. Cambridge: Cambridge University Press.

EARLE, E. M. 1943. Introduction. Pp. v–xi in *Makers of Modern Strategy: Military Thought from Machiavelli to Hitler*, ed. E. M. Earle with G. A. Craig and F. Gilbert. Princeton, NJ: Princeton University Press.

FREEDMAN, L. 1998. Strategic coercion. Pp. 15–38 in *Strategic Coercion: Concepts and Cases*, ed. L. Freedman. Oxford: Oxford University Press.

—— 2004. *Deterrence*. Cambridge: Polity.

—— 2007. The future of strategic studies. Pp. 356–70 in *Strategy in the Contemporary World: An Introduction to Strategic Studies*, 2nd edn, ed. J. Baylis, J. Wirtz, C. S. Gray, and E. Cohen. Oxford: Oxford University Press.

GARNETT, J. 1987. Strategic studies and its assumptions. Pp. 3–29 in *Contemporary Strategy I: Theories and Concepts*, 2nd edn, ed. J. Baylis, K. Booth, J. Garnett, and P. Williams. London: Croom Helm.

GRAY, C. S. 1982. *Strategic Studies: A Critical Assessment*. Westport, Conn.: Greenwood Press.

—— 1999. *Modern Strategy*. Oxford: Oxford University Press.

GREEN, P. 1966. *Deadly Logic: The Theory of Nuclear Deterrence*. Columbus: Ohio State University Press.

HOWARD, M. 1979. The forgotten dimensions of strategy. *Foreign Affairs*, 57: 975–86.

—— 1983. *The Causes of War and Other Essays*. Cambridge, Mass.: Harvard University Press.

JERVIS, R. 1978. Cooperation under the security dilemma. *World Politics*, 30: 167–214.

—— LEBOW, R. N., and STEIN, J. G. 1985. *Psychology and Deterrence*. Baltimore: Johns Hopkins University Press.

JOHNSTON, A. I. 1995. Thinking about strategic culture. *International Security*, 19: 32–64.

KAHN, H. 1960. *On Thermonuclear War*. Princeton, NJ: Princeton University Press.

KATZENSTEIN, P. J. 1996. *The Culture of National Security: Norms and Identity in World Politics*. New York: Columbia University Press.

KISSINGER, H. 1957. *Nuclear Weapons and Foreign Policy*. New York: Harper and Brothers.

KLEIN, B. S. 1994. *Strategic Studies and World Order: The Global Politics of Deterrence*. Cambridge: Cambridge University Press.

LUTTWAK, E. N. 1987. *Strategy: The Logic of War and Peace*. Cambridge, Mass.: Belknap Press.

MORGAN, P. M. 2006. *Deterrence Now*. Cambridge: Cambridge University Press.

PAPE, R. A. 2005. *Dying to Win: The Strategic Logic of Suicide Terrorism*. New York: Random House.

PARET, P. 1986. Introduction. Pp. 3–8 in *Makers of Modern Strategy from Machiavelli to the Nuclear Age*, ed. P. Paret. Princeton, NJ: Princeton University Press.

PARIS, R. 2001. Human security: paradigm shift or hot air? *International Security*, 26: 87–102.

RAPOPORT, A. 1964. *Strategy and Conscience*. New York: Harper and Row.

ROSECRANCE, R., and STEIN, A. A. (eds.) 1993. *The Domestic Bases of Grand Strategy*. Ithaca, NY: Cornell University Press.

SAGAN, S. 1993. *The Limits of Safety: Organizations, Accidents, and Nuclear Weapons*. Princeton, NJ: Princeton University Press.

SCHELLING, T. C. 1960. *The Strategy of Conflict*. Cambridge, Mass.: Harvard University Press.

—— 1966. *Arms and Influence*. London: Yale University Press.

—— and HALPERIN, M. H. 1961. *Strategy and Arms Control*. New York: Twentieth Century Fund.

SNIDAL, D. 1985. The game theory of international politics. *World Politics*, 38: 25–57.

SNYDER, C. A. 1999. Contemporary security and strategy. Pp. 1–12 in *Contemporary Security and Strategy*, ed. C. A. Snyder. Basingstoke: Macmillan.

SNYDER, G. 1961. *Deterrence and Defense: Toward a Theory of National Security*. Princeton, NJ: Princeton University Press.

SUMMERS, H. 1982. *On Strategy: The Vietnam War in Context*. Novato, Calif.: Presidio.

TERRIFF, T., CROFT, S., JAMES, L., and MORGAN, P. M. 1999. *Security Studies Today*. Cambridge: Polity.

VAN CREVELD, M. 1991. *On Future War*. London: Brassey's.

WALT, S. M. 1991. The renaissance of security studies. *International Studies Quarterly*, 35: 211–39.

WALZER, M. 1977. *Just and Unjust Wars: A Moral Argument with Historical Illustrations*. New York: Basic Books.

WARDLAW, G. 1982. *Political Terrorism: Theory, Tactics, and Countermeasures*. Cambridge: Cambridge University Press.

WOHLSTETTER, R. 1962. *Pearl Harbor: Warning and Decision*. Stanford, Calif.: Stanford University Press.

WOLFERS, A. 1952. "National security" as an ambiguous symbol. *Political Science Quarterly*, 67: 481–502.

....

FOREIGN-POLICY DECISION-MAKING

....

DOUGLAS T. STUART

THE subfield of foreign-policy decision-making takes as its starting point the dependent variable—a specific foreign-policy choice by an international actor—and then seeks to explain how this choice was arrived at by the agents (individuals, groups, organizations) involved in the decisional process. Because of its explicit focus on human decisional behavior in all its complexity and contingency, the study of foreign-policy decision-making is the most ambitious and multifaceted subfield of international relations. It is also one of the most popular subfields of international relations, for five reasons in particular.

The first reason is that foreign-policy decision-making is intrinsically interesting. Students are attracted to this subfield because they want to know how and why portentous decisions are (or at least, were) reached. The fact that the decision-makers themselves are in many cases fascinating individuals certainly contributes to the attraction.

The second advantage that foreign-policy decision-making has over other subfields of international relations is its explicitly interdisciplinary nature. It is enriched by, and in turn enriches, most social science disciplines. Four social science fields have been particularly important sources of insight for students of foreign-policy decision-making: political science (power), sociology (bureaucracy and authority), public administration (planning, implementation, and agency), and psychology (motives, personality types, group dynamics, perception, and cognition). Foreign-policy decision-making also provides researchers with numerous opportunities for productive engagement with new fields of study, such as neuroscience and evolutionary psychology.

The third advantage of the study of foreign-policy decision-making is that it tends to orient researchers toward "theories of the middle range." According to sociologist Robert Merton, middle-range theories have the advantage of being grounded in manageable slices of empirical reality. They avoid both excessive abstraction and narrow empiricism. They also encourage theory construction by means of bridge-building between clusters of systematically observed phenomena (Sztompka 1996).

The fourth advantage of the study of foreign-policy decision-making is that it is a particularly protean subfield of international relations, which has proven to be very adaptable to changes in the international system and in the discipline of international relations. The first generation of researchers interested in foreign-policy decision-making recognized that their subject matter was "at the hinge" of domestic politics and international relations (Hill 2003, 23). Thus it was ideally suited for research that engaged all three of Kenneth Waltz's well-known levels of analysis (the individual, the state, and the international system). Over time, however, as world politics became more complex and the state-centric model began to lose its pre-eminent position within the field of international relations, students of foreign-policy decision-making did not experience an identity crisis. Because the concept of the decision has universal applicability, students of foreign-policy decision-making have been able to adapt their methodologies and their theoretical assumptions to the study of nonstate, subnational, and transnational, actors, without having to abandon their traditional interest in the international behavior of sovereign states.

Finally, the study of foreign-policy decision-making provides researchers with numerous opportunities for "bridging the gap" between academia and the policy-making community (George 1993). By contrast to most subfields of international relations, which developed in the academy and have been viewed with suspicion or disdain by policy-makers, foreign-policy decision-making actually has its roots in both the scholarly and the policy communities, and the two groups have been engaged in a continuous dialogue ever since. I will discuss the evolution and implications of this relationship in the next section of this chapter.

Students interested in the field of foreign-policy analysis should also be forewarned about three research problems that are endemic to this subfield of international relations. First, for precisely the reasons mentioned above, the study of foreign-policy decision-making is the most inchoate subfield of international relations, and the most challenging from the point of view of research design. At times the complex and rapidly changing characteristics of a foreign-policy decision-making situation can seem to students like both a "tar baby" and a "briar patch"—a field of study that is easy to get trapped in, and impossible to maneuver through. This is precisely why students interested in the study of foreign-policy decision-making should begin with some clearly articulated and testable assumptions about the relative potency of the variables in their research design.

Research relating to foreign-policy decision-making is also uniquely vulnerable to problems of discrimination. One of the greatest challenges for scholars interested in the systematic study of foreign-policy decision-making is to distinguish between self-serving memoirs by former political insiders and reliable sources of information about high-level decision-making. Researchers are well advised to bring to the study of such individuals the kind of skepticism exhibited by one of Otto von Bismarck's biographers, who quipped that the Chancellor "believes firmly and deeply in a God who has the remarkable faculty of always agreeing with him" (quoted in Craig and George 1983, 259).

Finally, because the study of foreign-policy decision-making sometimes brings academics into regular contact with members of the policy-making community on issues of contemporary importance, researchers in this subfield are also particularly prone to the temptation to engage in punditry. They may also fall prey to co-optation, or at least to a confusion of roles and responsibilities, as they move back and forth between the scholarly community, the policy-making community, and the think-tank community. The challenge for individuals who find themselves in this situation is to maintain an appreciation of the difference between bridging the gap and crossing the line.

This chapter will begin with some background information on the development of the subfield of foreign-policy decision-making, with a particular emphasis on why and how this subfield took root in the United States in the interwar period. I will then survey some of the important orienting statements by pioneers in the subfield of foreign-policy decision-making. Next, I will focus on the independent, intervening, and dependent variables that have received most of the scholarly attention over the last five decades. I will conclude with some comments on the state of the subfield today, and the challenges and opportunities that are likely to confront students of foreign-policy decision-making during the next few years.

1 BACKGROUND: THE INTERACTION OF GOVERNMENT AND ACADEMIA

Although European experts like Max Weber, Herbert Spencer, and Émile Durkheim played an indispensable role in the development of those social science disciplines that have informed the study of foreign-policy decision-making, the literature in this subfield has been dominated by Americans. This section will trace the development of that literature, with special emphasis on the interaction between government and academia.

Foreign-policy decision-making was traditionally the domain of diplomatic historians and political biographers. For the most part, these scholars chose to study the decisions of political leaders precisely because these leaders appeared to be so intriguingly idiosyncratic and resistant to comparison. During the late nineteenth century, however, American scholars such as Woodrow Wilson began to press the case for the scientific study of decision-making and policy implementation, as a way of coping with the challenges of modernity (Wilson 1887, 201). Governmental interest in "management science" began to take on a new urgency in the mid-1930s, as the Washington policy community struggled to pull the nation out of a seemingly intractable economic depression and to make the United States competitive with the growing number of totalitarian regimes.

In the years immediately following the Second World War, as Americans adjusted to the reality of "Buck Rogers weapons" (nuclear bombs, long-range aircraft, and missiles), rational decision-making and control over foreign-policy behavior came to be viewed as indispensable for national security. As early as 1946 scholars like Bernard Brodie (1946) were studying the circumstances under which rational decision-making would lead to predictable policy choices and outcomes in situations of nuclear confrontation. With its parsimonious, elegant, and seemingly rational approach to the study of a particular type of foreign-policy decision-making, the literature relating to nuclear deterrence became extraordinarily popular and influential over the following decades. Inevitably, however, these nuclear strategists were criticized by international relations scholars on the grounds that they were so far removed from the realities of the nuclear confrontations that they routinely envisioned that they were dangerously misleading and morally bankrupt. Anatol Rapoport (1964, xxi–xxii) went so far as to compare the underlying premises of the nuclear-deterrence literature to the economic assumptions that Jonathan Swift attacked in his scathing eighteenth-century satirical essay, A Modest Proposal. Swift followed these economic arguments to their seemingly logical conclusion—that Irish farmers should sell their children as a cash crop.

As the cold war evolved, depictions of nuclear strategists as morally and intellectually "aloof" (Rapoport 1964, xviii) and attacks on the underlying premises of nuclear deterrence became familiar themes in popular culture (Dr Strangelove Failsafe). The subfield of strategic studies nonetheless continued to expand, in part because of active and sustained government sponsorship and in part because of developments in the fields of communication and automated information-processing that made it possible to envision increasingly complex scenarios for brinkmanship and the management of nuclear/conventional conflicts. The assumptions of rationality, control, and predictability that were associated with this influential literature also contributed to the development of other approaches to the study of foreign-policy decision-making, including game theory, simulation, and rational choice.

As the need for crisis management and control became more and more apparent to cold war policy-makers, the US government also began to sponsor research on the psychological and personality characteristics of foreign leaders, in order to prepare American policy-makers for future confrontations. One significant initiative was the establishment in the mid-1960s of the Center for the Analysis of Personality and Political Behavior (CAPPB) within the Central Intelligence Agency. Drawing upon insights from the social sciences and the various subfields of psychology and psychiatry, these researchers developed in-depth profiles of heads of state, with particular emphasis upon their probable decisional behaviors during international negotiations and crisis situations (Post 2003, 51–61).

At the same time that scholars and policy-makers were imagining increasingly complex nuclear scenarios and developing new methodologies for the systematic study of political leaders, the academic literature was challenging some of Brodie's foundational assumptions, in particular the assumptions that foreign-policy decision-making was managed by unitary and rational actors. It should come as no surprise that American researchers became interested in these questions during the late 1960s and early 1970s, a period when the nation was obsessed with the "quagmire" of Vietnam and looking for someone or something to blame. Fueled by the release of government documents like *The Pentagon Papers*, researchers began to focus on concepts like bureaucratic politics, organizational culture, and role socialization as determinants of foreign-policy decision-making in general, and suboptimal decision-making in particular.

2 ORIENTING STATEMENTS

The study of foreign-policy decision-making is so complex and multifaceted that it is especially dependent on general orienting statements to guide students in their decisions about the scope and method of inquiry. Fortunately, some excellent guidance is available. As early as 1954, Richard Snyder, H. W. Bruck, and Burton Sapin provided foundational insights regarding what they called the "decision making approach" to the study of international relations. Perhaps their most important contribution was their convincing argument for shifting the focus of international relations research away from the reified nation state and toward "those whose authoritative acts are, to all intents and purposes, the acts of the state. *State action is the action taken by those acting in the name of the state.* Hence, the state is its decision-makers" (Snyder, Bruck, and Sapin 1954, 36–7). The authors also articulated a number of assumptions that have guided much of the research on foreign-policy decision-making for the last five decades. Among their most important assumptions were:

- the need to focus on the "decisional unit," which is pursuing a specific objective;
- that decision-making is a process ("planful action") that is influenced by both the internal and external settings, as these are "selectively perceived and evaluated" by the decision-makers;
- that various factors impose limits on decision-making; these include uncertainty, time constraints, and competing objectives and motives.

It is a testament to the enduring value of Snyder, Bruck, and Sapin's monograph that it was recently reprinted as a guide for the next generation of scholars interested in the systematic study of foreign-policy decision-making (Snyder, Bruck, and Sapin 2002).

Snyder, Bruck, and Sapin's pioneering work was followed during the 1960s by James Rosenau's development of the concept of the "pre-theory" to guide research on foreign-policy decision-making. Rosenau (1971) argued that, in the absence of widely accepted theories of foreign-policy causation, scholars should at least be explicit about their initial assumptions when they undertake the study of a decisional situation. This meant not only listing the variables that one believes to be determinative, but also ranking these variables in terms of their assumed "relative potency" for the particular decisional situation. He also provided students with some preliminary guidance about the circumstances under which one variable was likely to have greater relative potency than another, depending upon the "issue area" (type of decisional situation) and the degree to which the nation under study was "penetrated" by external influences.

Rosenau's pretheoretical arguments generated considerable excitement among students, and served as the cornerstone for the development of an ambitious new approach to the study of foreign-policy decision-making, called Comparative Foreign-Policy (CFP). In accordance with the premises of middle-range theorizing, CFP explicitly accepted the fact that foreign-policy decisions are the product of interaction among a large number of variables. At the same time, however, CFP assumed that these variables could (and should) be testable and replicable, and that the middle-range theories that these variables were employed to test could (and should) ultimately contribute to the development of a general theory of foreign-policy causation. Critics of CFP are correct that the approach was too ambitious, and that in many cases the most important independent, intervening, and dependent variables were resistant to quantification (see, in particular, Hudson and Vore 1995; Hudson 2005). On the other hand, these critics do not give CFP enough credit for generating and sustaining scholarly interest in the systematic study of the determinants of foreign-policy decisions during the 1970s and 1980s. Furthermore, by explicitly incorporating individual, societal, and systemic variables in their studies, CFP conceived of international relations not in terms of three distinct and competing levels of analysis but rather in terms of the interaction *among* these levels of analysis. In so doing, the contributors to the CFP approach set the precedent for a number of newer approaches to the study of international relations (constructivism, poliheuristic theory), which seek to engage all three levels of analysis while maintaining the focus on foreign-policy decision-making (Wendt 1992: Mintz 2005).

It is generally assumed that the relative potency of various factors involved in a foreign-policy decision (that is, the independent variables) and the process by which the decision is arrived at (that is, the intervening variable) will differ according to the type of decisional situation. Several scholars have developed typologies of decisional situations. David Braybrooke and Charles Lindblom (1963) differentiated between decision-making situations according to the degree of importance (defined as change) accorded to the decision and the degree of uncertainty associated with the decision. They also introduced the concept of "disjointed incrementalism" to illustrate the characteristic adjustive behavior associated with "small change" situations. Charles Hermann (1969) has also provided students with a useful typology of decisional situations—ranging from crises to administrative situations—based on high or low threat to national values, short or long decision time, and the degree to which the decision-makers were surprised by the event.

It is worth reminding readers at this point of the distinction developed by Harold and Margaret Sprout between the psychological and the operational milieu. The important insight provided by the Sprouts is that both the agents involved in a particular decision and the process that ultimately leads to the policy decision will be determined by the psychological milieu—the way that the situation is defined by the key decision-makers. On the other hand, the outcome of the decisional process—the success or failure of a foreign-policy—will be determined by objective reality, which the Sprouts refer to as the operational milieu (Sprout and Sprout 1965).

Most of the literature on decisional situations has divided according to these two tracks. Several significant studies have focused on the operational milieu. One approach that bears special mention is the effort by Charles McClelland and his colleagues to use events data systematically to categorize bilateral and multilateral interactions along a continuum from complete friendship to all-out war, which laid the foundation for follow-on research on the international contexts of foreign-policy decision-making (McClelland and Hoggard 1969). Events data have been used by various government agencies, including the Department of Defense and the National Security Council, to help prepare policy-makers for international crises. Events data-sets also continue to be used by academics in imaginative ways, both to generate and to test hypotheses (Schrodt 1995).

A much larger community of scholars has pursued the alternative path envisioned by the Sprouts—the study of the psychological milieu. These researchers have developed orienting statements about the circumstances under which a policy-maker or group is predisposed to interpret an international event in a particular way. This literature, which focuses on the definition of the situation as a determinant of subsequent decision-making behavior, borrows heavily from cognitive psychology. Robert Jervis's research (1976; 1985) on the effects of a leader's cognitive predispositions (evoked set, perceptual readiness, and so on) on his or her interpretative and decisional behaviors bears special mention in this regard.

Arguably the most famous example of the impact that a leader's cognitive bias can have on his or her definition of the situation is Ole Holsti's demonstration of the "inherent bad faith" model. Holsti's ambitious study (1962) of the belief system of John Foster Dulles illustrated that the Secretary of State was so fundamentally suspicious of Soviet intentions that he could not accept nonthreatening Soviet behaviors at face value. Rather, he explained away such behaviors as indicators of Moscow's weakness. This logic led Dulles to recommend that the United States respond to apparently nonthreatening Soviet actions by increasing the pressure on the Kremlin.

Other scholars have focused on the way in which an entire national society can be predisposed to define, and then respond to, international events. Drawing on insights from systems theory, Rosenau (1981) argued that national societies can be classified according to four modes of adaptation: acquiescent, intransigent, promotive, and preservative. The four modes differ in terms of the priority that a national society accords to demands from its internal and external environments. Rosenau was primarily interested in developing hypotheses about the characteristic behaviors associated with each of the four adaptive orientations and the circumstances under which each mode of adaptation will be effective or ineffective.

Researchers have also employed the concept of ideology to explain the priorities and predispositions of national societies. In his study of the role of ideology in American foreign-policy, Michael Hunt (1987) demonstrated both the persistence of key ideological elements over time, and their importance in determining the way successive US administrations defined complex international situations. He also demonstrated a historian's sensitivity to the fact that leaders use ideology both as an epistemological and heuristic guide and as a rhetorical device for selling a particular policy.

A small but influential group of researchers has attempted to reconcile the Sprouts' operational and psychological milieux, by combining realist assumptions about the causal influence of the international system with in-depth analysis of the beliefs and preferences of the individuals and groups involved in foreign-policy decision-making. Gideon Rose asserts that these scholars, whom he calls neoclassical realists, assume that systemic pressures are always important, but that these pressures are "neither Hobbesian nor benign but murky and difficult to read." Under these circumstances, neoclassical realists recognize the need to shift their focus to the individuals and groups involved in the decisional situations in order to ascertain their specific views on the international situation. Rose commends neoclassical realist writers, whom he describes as occupying "a middle ground between pure structural theorists and constructivists," for their contributions to our understanding of foreign-policy decision-making. He nonetheless recognizes that most of their research to date has taken the form of case studies, and concludes that "future work in this vein should therefore focus on continuing to specify the ways that intervening unit-level variables can deflect foreign-policy from what pure structural theorists might predict" (Rose 1998, 152, 166, 168).

3 INDEPENDENT VARIABLES: AGENCY

In her indispensable survey article, Valerie Hudson (2005, 1) argues that not only the subfield of foreign-policy analysis, but also the social sciences in general are "grounded in human decision makers acting singly or in groups." This section will begin with some comments on the study of the individual decision-maker and then discuss the ways in which the concept of agency has been made more complex over time by the incorporation of group and organizational variables. Most contemporary students of international relations were introduced to all three of these clusters of variables by Graham Allison's pioneering study, *Essence of Decision* (1971). Allison's "three cuts" at the Cuban Missile Crisis is not only an excellent example of a theoretically informed case study. It is also a source of pretheoretical guidance, which illustrates that the conceptual model that a researcher implicitly or explicitly applies to a particular decisional situation will determine "what the analyst finds puzzling, how he formulates his question, where he looks for evidence, and what he produces as an answer" (Allison 1971, 245).

Explicit claims about the centrality of the leader in foreign-policy decision-making can be traced back to Thomas Carlyle's familiar assertion (1995, 1) that "the history of what man has accomplished in this world, is at bottom the History of the Great Men who have worked here." Carlyle's assumptions about the indispensability of leaders have been refined by contemporary students of foreign-policy decision-making. Margaret Hermann proposed three types of situation that are likely to enhance a leader's personal influence over policy: when the decisional situation is ambiguous, when the circumstances demand authoritative action (crises, cases of personal diplomacy, and so on), and "when the political leader assumes office through dramatic means" (Hermann and Milburn 1977, 20–1). Related concepts have been developed by James MacGregor Burns (1978) (the simple but useful distinction between transactional and transformative leadership) and by Jean Blondel (1987) (authority and *auctoritas* as sources of a leader's power).

The likelihood that a leader will play a decisive role in foreign-policy decision-making is also a function of his or her "will to power." As early as 1948, Harold Lasswell (1948, 57) developed the concept of the political personality based on the need for power. Since that time, extensive research has been conducted on motivational (that is, need-based) sources of leader behavior. Other scholars have classified and compared leaders according to the related concept of traits, defined by David Winter (2003, 31) as "the public, visible, stylistic (or adverbial) aspects of personality." He has identified five traits that are widely interpreted by personality psychologists as important: "extraversion ... agreeableness, conscientiousness, emotional stability, and openness to experience." These and other personality traits have been used by international relations scholars to predict and explain the ways that leaders have defined international situations, managed negotiations, and made decisions.

Students interested in developing a comprehensive and synthetic understanding of a leader's personality are well advised to begin by reading the in-depth psychobiographical study of Woodrow Wilson by Alexander and Juliette George. It is a model of scholarly sensitivity and empathy, which never loses sight of the humanity of its subject. The Georges also provide students with excellent guidance on the risks and rewards associated with the application of psychoanalytic theory to the study of political leaders (George and George 1956; 1998).

Alexander George must also be credited for his pioneering work in the development of a systematic procedure for the content analysis of the statements and speeches of leaders. Most studies of individual decision-makers rely upon these types of artifacts, but all too often such studies do not follow clearly articulated guidelines for the systematic coding and comparison of a subject's written and spoken words. George and his colleagues responded to this problem by developing the "operational code" approach, which is designed to categorize and compare individuals according to certain politically salient beliefs that are assumed to have a direct impact on the way that an individual views the world and makes foreign-policy decisions (George 1969). Over the last four decades several scholars have contributed to a rich repertoire of operational code studies of such individuals as John F. Kennedy, Henry Kissinger, George H. W. Bush, and Bill Clinton (Stuart and Starr 1981–2; Schafer and Walker 2006). The operational code methodology is also being used by scholars to test hypotheses relating to international conflict behavior and the circumstances under which liberalism or realism will serve as a better predictor of state behavior (Schafer, Robison, and Aldrich 2006).

The study of groups has served as both an enrichment of, and an alternative to, the study of individual leaders. Foreign-policy decisions are often the product of deliberations among a small group of political insiders, many of whom are *ex officio* representatives of government agencies. Morton Halperin's various writings (1974) on bureaucratic politics provide interesting illustrations of the tensions inherent in this situation. Halperin argues that bureaucracies, and the individuals who represent them, accord a high priority to the protection and advancement of four institutional interests: missions, capabilities, influence, and essence.

Role socialization is the process by which an individual's behavior and attitudes change when he or she becomes the spokesperson for a particular institution. Rosenau (1968) was one of the first international relations scholars to emphasize the significance of role factors in foreign-policy decision-making. Subsequent research on role socialization has attempted to explain not only the process by which specific role-related beliefs are acquired, but also the ways in which individuals manage dual identities—as *ex officio* spokespersons for a particular agency, and as individuals who are responsible for giving the leader the best quality advice under the circumstances.

It stands to reason that virtually every leader seeks to design his or her advisory system in order to control and/or exploit intra-group competition. Richard Johnson (1974) has identified three management styles (formalistic, collegial, and competitive) employed by US presidents to achieve this goal. The guiding premise in the research on presidential management styles is that leaders adapt their advisory and administrative machinery to match their personalities, their levels of interest in, and their expertise relating to, foreign affairs.

As Allison, Halperin, and others have observed, organizations also influence decision-making—by their standard operating procedures, their habits of information processing, their institutionalized world-views, and their distinct and competing priorities. There is still a great deal of work to be done, both empirically and theoretically, on the processes by which institutions develop distinctive identities and characteristic modes of behaving. The new institutionalism literature in public administration is a valuable source of insights in this regard (Powell and DiMaggio 1991). Students can also consult recent studies of the creation and functioning of key agencies in the US national security bureaucracy (Zegart 1999; 2005; Stuart 2008).

As mentioned earlier in this chapter, various scholars have focused on other actors and factors as influential independent variables in foreign-policy decision-making. Holsti (1996) has engaged in imaginative research on mass and elite public opinion. Other writers have emphasized the role played by the media, both as a determinant of public opinion and as a direct influence on the policy-making process (Strobel 1997). Researchers must develop their own clearly articulated guidelines for judging the relative potency of these and other independent variables. As a general rule, it makes sense to begin with an understanding of how the situation is defined by the key decision-makers, as this will affect both the membership and the relative importance of the participants in the decision-making group. It will also help to determine the process by which the final decision is reached. We turn now to this concept of process, presented here as the intervening variable in the study of foreign-policy decision-making.

4 THE INTERVENING VARIABLE: PROCESS

Students of foreign-policy decision-making often run into their most serious research problems after they have identified the agents involved in a specific decisional situation and rank-ordered these agents according to their presumed relative potency. This is the point at which they must use whatever methodologies are appropriate in order to obtain reliable information about who said or did what, when, and to what effect. Transcripts of high-level decision-making situations are rarely available, and when they are available they rarely tell the whole story. In cases of small-group decision-making, it is sometimes the nonverbal communications of key individuals that steer discussions. Silence on the part of a leader may be interpreted as consent by one member of a decisional unit and as lack of support by someone else in the group. The "real" decision may be made after the meeting was adjourned, or it may have been made before the meeting even started.

Moving from the independent to the intervening variable also forces the researcher to confront more directly issues of time and change. The decisional process is by definition dynamic, often requiring the researcher to treat a decision as a series of specific stages. One interesting approach that treats foreign-policy decision-making as a two-stage process is poliheuristic theory, which assumes that leaders "first simplify the decision problem by the use of cognitive short-cuts (heuristics). They then evaluate remaining alternatives using analytical calculations" (Mintz 2005, 94). As I will have occasion to discuss later in this chapter, other experts question any approach that assumes that foreign-policy decision-making will be either linear or cumulative.

Problems of research design and causal inference have been made somewhat more manageable thanks to scholars who have developed guidelines and procedures for the systematic analysis of small-group decisional processes. George (1979) introduced the concept of "structured and focused comparison" to guide the selection of case studies of foreign-policy decision-making. He has also provided students with a checklist of "procedural malfunctions" in the foreign-policy decision-making process (George 1980, 121–36).

Irving Janis's *Victims of Groupthink* (1972) is still the best example of how the systematic study of the process of group decision-making can be used to test an important theoretical insight—that concurrence seeking behavior can be detrimental to the quality of decision-making in a small, cohesive group. The groupthink hypothesis has been the subject of considerable scholarly debate and the source of numerous empirical studies. More research still needs to be done, however, on the circumstances under which group cohesion changes from an asset to a liability in a particular decision-making situation. Paul t'Hart (1990, 282) has also recommended that research on groupthink should be placed in a "more integrated model, drawing on both social–psychological and political–administrative concepts, theories, and research findings."

International relations experts have been particularly interested in the way that leaders and their advisers manage the process of decision-making during international crises. Students interested in how an in-depth case study of a specific crisis can generate testable hypotheses should refer to Glenn Paige's pioneering analysis (1968) of the Truman administration's decision to enter the Korean War. Many of his findings, and several other hypotheses relating to the systematic effects of high threat, short decision time, and stress, were subsequently tested by Michael Brecher (1975, 518–81) in his study of Israeli decision-making. Richard Ned Lebow has also contributed to this literature by his useful distinction between three types of crises (justification of hostility, spinoff, and brinkmanship), which he has tested against a rich panoply of historical cases in order to assess the likelihood that each type will lead to war. He concludes that "successful crisis management is . . . a function of cultural, organizational, and personal behavioral patterns established long before the onset of any crisis" (Lebow 1981, 335).

Much of the literature relating to crisis decision-making has evolved as a reaction to the aforementioned nuclear-deterrence literature, with its highly optimistic assumptions about crisis stability and brinkmanship. Lebow has been a particularly effective critic of this literature, citing the ways in which miscommunication and stress can result in loss of control in situations of international crisis. He is led to conclude that "the final and most important objective of policies aimed at war prevention must be to prevent acute crises altogether" (Lebow 1987, 167). Lebow and his colleagues have done a service to both the academic and the policy communities by their cautionary reminders of the risks of mismanagement during international crises.

5 DEPENDENT VARIABLE

It is not a coincidence that this chapter begins and ends with the dependent variable—the foreign-policy decision. As Brecher and others have observed, most decisions can be properly understood only as part of a continuous cycle of interaction between a nation and its environment. Using a systems approach, Brecher (1975) illustrated the ways in which specific Israeli foreign-policy decisions led to actions that triggered responses that in turn became new issues for interpretation and decision-making. Brecher's emphasis on the dynamic and iterative nature of many foreign-policy decision-making situations has encouraged a new generation of international relations scholars to study foreign-policy decisions sequentially. Binnur Ozkececi-Taner (2006. 545) argues that "most, if not all, foreign-policy problems continue over an extended period of time and are revisited numerous times before finally being resolved." Ranan Kuperman (2006, 539) concurs with this argument and recommends that "the first step in the analysis of foreign-policy decisions should be to identify a series of decision episodes around specific problems and then determine whether or not each episode is an isolated event or whether there is some dependency of one episode on the others." This emphasis upon the dynamic nature of many foreign-policy decision-making situations represents a valuable enrichment of our understanding of how foreign-policy decision-making actually works in many instances. But it also presents students with new problems of research design and operationalization, in a field of study that is already extremely complex and challenging.

Brecher also reminds us that most foreign-policy decisions cannot be isolated from the process of policy implementation. This is the point at which the psychological milieu (the world as it is viewed by the decision-makers) collides with the operational milieu (the world as it is) with either gratifying or disappointing results. This is also the point at which Herbert Simon's well-known distinction (1976) between substantive and procedural rationality comes into play. A scrupulously managed decision-making process, which passes Alexander George's procedural tests for the acquisition and management of information, for effective consultation, and for empathy, cannot guarantee good results. On the other hand, failure to follow these procedural guidelines will make it much more likely that the desired results will not be achieved.

Philip Tetlock (2005, 230) also reminds us that, in any decisional situation, "there will always be wiggle room for arguing over who got it right." A researcher can reduce the "wiggle room," however, by beginning with a clear sense of what the decision-makers were trying to accomplish. Arnold Wolfers's distinctions (1962, 67, 80) between "milieu and possession goals," "intermediate and ultimate goals," and "direct and indirect interests" can serve as a useful starting point.

Judgments about the success or failure of a specific decision should also take into account the constraints imposed upon the decision-makers. George (1980, 2–3) reminds us that decision-makers frequently confront "tradeoff dilemmas" between the quest for high-quality decisions, the prudent management of time, energy, and staff, and the need for consensus. These and other sources of "bounded rationality" can become especially acute in cases of international crisis. Unfortunately, as Lebow and many others remind us, in an age when decisional errors can result in catastrophically destructive conflicts, there is no such thing as an acceptable mistake.

6 CONCLUSION

In her inaugural essay for the launching of the journal *Foreign-Policy Analysis*, Hudson (2005, 21) observed that "foreign-policy analysis is situated at the intersection of all social science and policy fields as they relate to international affairs." This statement highlights both the great strengths and the great weaknesses of the subfield of foreign-policy analysis. Understanding how and why foreign-policy decisions are made is of indisputable importance for the development of a comprehensive theory of international relations. But the subject matter can be excrutiatingly resistant to systematic analysis—more "cloudlike" than "clocklike," to borrow Karl Popper's familiar distinction (Almond and Genco 1977, 489–90). Furthermore, a researcher can easily lose focus as a result of the temptation to borrow and combine theories and insights from other subfields of international relations or from other social sciences. This chapter has nonetheless attempted to demonstrate that there has been substantive progress in the subfield of foreign-policy decision-making since Snyder, Bruck, and Sapin introduced students to their foundational assumptions over four decades ago.

This chapter has also demonstrated that prior to the end of the cold war the subfield of foreign-policy decision-making was dominated by American scholars studying US foreign-policy decisions. The good news is that the next generation of international relations scholars has taken up the obvious challenge to enrich our empirical and theoretical understanding of foreign-policy decision-making in other countries and cultures. A few scholars have also gone a step further, by studying the interactions of representatives of different "knowledge regimes" (Jin 2001).

The fact that the study of foreign-policy decision-making is becoming more international, multicultural, and interdisciplinary is certainly good news. On the other hand, these trends exacerbate serious problems of research design in a field that has become increasingly complex and porous. The situation is made even more challenging by changes in the international system that have increased the salience of transnational, subnational, and nongovernmental agents whose decisions and actions must be taken into account.

This is why the most important challenge for the next generation of experts interested in the study of foreign-policy decision-making is to develop new orienting statements and pretheoretical guidelines appropriate to the changed circumstances of the twenty-first century. Criticisms of the attempts by Rosenau and others to develop the subfield of Comparative Foreign-Policy notwithstanding, the next generation of scholars cannot lose sight of the need for systematic analysis, cumulation, and theory-building (Neack, Hey, and Haney 1995). In the meantime, students of international relations should continue to develop new middle-range theories of foreign-policy decision-making, which, while taking account of Aristotle's familiar dictum to "look for precision in each class of thing just so far as the nature of the thing admits," do not fall prey to "narrow empiricism."

References

ALMOND, G., and GENCO, S. 1977. Clouds, clocks, and the study of politics. *World Politics*, 29: 489–522.

ALLISON, G. 1971. *Essence of Decision: Explaining the Cuban Missile Crisis*. Boston: Little, Brown.

BLONDEL, J. 1987. *Political Leadership: Towards a General Analysis*. London: Sage.

BRAYBROOKE, D., and LINDBLOM, C. 1963. *A Strategy of Decision: Policy Evaluation as a Social Process*. New York: Free Press.

BRECHER, M. 1975. *Decisions in Israel's Foreign Policy*. New York: Free Press.

BRODIE, B. (ed.) 1946. *The Absolute Weapon: Atomic Power and World Order*. New York: Harcourt, Brace.

BURNS, J. M. 1978. *Leadership*. New York: Harper and Row.

CARLYLE, T. 1995. *On Great Men*. New York: Penguin; originally published 1841.

CRAIG, G., and GEORGE, A. 1983. *Force and Statecraft: Diplomatic Problems of our Time*. New York: Oxford University Press.

GEORGE, A. 1969. The "operational code:" a neglected approach to the study of political leaders and decision-making. *International Studies Quarterly*, 13: 190–222.

——1979. Case studies and theory development: the method of structured, focused comparison. Pp. 43–68 in *Diplomacy: New Approaches in History, Theory, and Policy*, ed. P. Lauren. New York: Free Press.

——1980. *Presidential Decisionmaking in Foreign-Policy: The Effective Use of Information and Advice*. Boulder, Colo.: Westview.

——1993. *Bridging the Gap: Theory and Practice in Foreign Policy*. Washington, DC: United States Institute of Peace Press.

——and GEORGE, J. 1956. *Woodrow Wilson and Colonel House: A Personality Study*. New York: John Day.

————1998. *Presidential Personality and Performance*. Boulder, Colo.: Westview.

HALPERIN, M. 1974. *Bureaucratic Politics and Foreign Policy*. Washington, DC: Brookings Institution.

HERMANN, C. 1969. International crisis as a situational variable. Pp. 409–21 in *International Politics and Foreign Policy: A Reader in Research and Policy*, ed. J. Rosenau. New York: Free Press.

HERMANN, M., and MILBURN, T. (eds.) 1977. *A Psychological Examination of Political Leaders*. New York: Free Press.

HILL, C. 2003. *The Changing Politics of Foreign Policy*. Basingstoke: Palgrave Macmillan.

HOLSTI, O. 1962. The belief system and national images: a case study. *Journal of Conflict Resolution*, 6: 244–52.

——1996. *Public Opinion and American Foreign Policy*. Ann Arbor: University of Michigan Press.

HUDSON, V. 2005. Foreign policy analysis: actor-specific theory and the ground of international relations. *Foreign Policy Analysis*, 1: 1–30.

——and VORE, C. 1995. Foreign policy analysis yesterday, today, and tomorrow. *Mershon International Studies Review*, 39: 209–38.

HUNT, M. 1987. *Ideology and US Foreign Policy*. New Haven, Conn.: Yale University Press.

JANIS, I. 1972. *Victims of Groupthink: A Psychological Study of Foreign Policy Decisions and Fiascoes*. Boston: Houghton-Mifflin.

JERVIS, R. 1976. *Perception and Misperception in International Politics*. Princeton, NJ: Princeton University Press.

——1985. Perceiving and coping with threat. Pp. 13–33 in *Psychology and Deterrence*, ed. R. Jervis, R. N. Lebow, and J. Stein. Baltimore: Johns Hopkins University Press.

JIN, D. 2001. *The Dynamics of Knowledge Regimes: Technology, Culture and National Competitiveness in the USA and Japan*. New York: Continuum.

JOHNSON, R. 1974. *Managing the White House: An Intimate Study of the Presidency*. New York: Harper and Row.

KUPERMAN, R. 2006. Making research on foreign policy decision making more dynamic: a dynamic framework for analyzing foreign policy decision making. *International Studies Review*, 8: 537–44.

LASSWELL, H. 1948. *Power and Personality*. New York: Viking.

LEBOW, R. N. 1981. *Between Peace and War: The Nature of International Crises*. Baltimore: Johns Hopkins University Press.

——1987. *Nuclear Crisis Management: A Dangerous Illusion*. Ithaca, NY: Cornell University Press.

McCLELLAND, C., and HOGGARD, G. D. 1969. Conflict patterns in the interactions among nations. Pp. 711–24 in *International Politics and Foreign Policy: A Reader in Research and Theory*, ed. J. Rosenau. New York: Free Press.

MINTZ, A. 2005. Applied decision analysis: utilizing poliheuristic theory to explain and predict foreign policy and national security decisions. *International Studies Perspectives*, 6: 94–8.

NEACK, L., HEY, J., and HANEY, P. (eds.) 1995. *Foreign Policy Analysis: Continuity and Change in its Second Generation*. Englewood Cliffs, NJ: Prentice Hall.

OZKECECI-TANER, B. 2006. Reviewing the literature on sequential/dynamic foreign policy decision making. *International Studies Review*, 8: 545–54.

PAIGE, G. 1968. *The Korean Decision, June 24–30, 1950*. New York: Free Press.

POST, J. (ed.) 2003. *The Psychological Assessment of Political Leaders: With Profiles of Saddam Hussein and Bill Clinton*. Ann Arbor: University of Michigan Press.

POWELL, W., and DiMAGGIO, P. (eds.) 1991. *The New Institutionalism in Organizational Analysis*. Chicago: University of Chicago Press.

RAPOPORT, A. 1964. *Strategy and Conscience*. New York: Schocken.

ROSE, G. 1998. Neoclassical realism and theories of foreign policy. *World Politics*, 51: 144–72.

ROSENAU, J. 1968. Private preferences and political responsibilities: the relative potency of individual and role variables in the behavior of US senators. Pp. 17–50 in *Quantitative International Politics: Insights and Evidence*, ed. J. D. Singer. New York: Free Press.

——1971. Pre-theories and theories of foreign policy. Pp. 95–149 in *The Scientific Study of Foreign Policy*, ed. J. Rosenau. New York: Free Press.

——1981. *The Study of Political Adaptation*. London: Frances Pinter.

SCHAFER, M., ROBISON, S., and ALDRICH, B. 2006. Operational codes and the 1916 Easter rising in Ireland: a test of the frustration–aggression hypothesis. *Foreign Policy Analysis*, 2: 63–82.

——and WALKER, S. (eds.) 2006. *Beliefs and Leadership in World Politics: Methods and Applications of Operational Code Analysis*. New York: Palgrave.

SCHRODT, P. 1995. Event data in foreign policy analysis. Pp. 145–66 in Neack, Hey, and Haney 1995.

SIMON, H. 1976. From substantive to procedural rationality. Pp. 129–48 in *Method and Appraisal in Economics*, ed. S. J. Latsis. Cambridge: Cambridge University Press.

SNYDER, R., BRUCK, H. W., and SAPIN, B. (eds.) 1954. *Decision-Making as an Approach to the Study of International Politics*. Princeton, NJ: Princeton University, Foreign Policy Analysis Project, Foreign Policy Analysis Series No. 3.

————— (eds.) 2002. *Foreign Policy Decision-Making (Revisited)*. New York: Palgrave Macmillan.

SPROUT, H., and SPROUT, M. 1965. *The Ecological Perspective on Human Affairs, with Special Reference to International Politics*. Princeton, NJ: Princeton University Press.

STROBEL, W. 1997. *Late-Breaking Foreign-Policy: The News Media's Influence on Peace Operations*. Washington, DC: US Institute of Peace Press.

STUART, D. 2008. *Creating the National Security State: A History of the Law that Transformed America*. Princeton, NJ: Princeton University Press.

——and STARR, H. 1981–2. The "inherent bad faith model" reconsidered: Dulles, Kennedy and Kissinger. *Political Psychology*, 3: 1–33.

SZTOMPKA, P. (ed.) 1996. *On Social Structure and Science*. Chicago: University of Chicago Press.

TETLOCK, P. 2005. *Expert Political Judgment: How Good is it? How Can We Know?* Princeton, NJ: Princeton University Press.

T'HART, P. 1990. *Groupthink in Government: A Study of Small Groups and Policy Failure*. Baltimore: Johns Hopkins University Press.

WENDT, A. 1992. Anarchy is what states make of it: the social construction of power politics. *International Organization*, 46: 391–425.

WILSON, W. 1887. The study of administration. *Political Science Quarterly*, 2: 197–222.

WINTER, D. 2003. Assessing leaders' personalities: a historical survey of academic research studies. Pp. 11–38 in Post 2003.

WOLFERS, A. 1962. *Discord and Collaboration: Essays on International Politics*. Baltimore: Johns Hopkins University Press.

ZEGART, A. 1999. *Flawed by Design: The Evolution of the CIA, the JCS, and NSC*. Stanford, Calif.: Stanford University Press.

——2005. September 11 and the adaptation failure of US intelligence agencies. *International Security*, 29: 78–111.

CHAPTER 34

INTERNATIONAL ETHICS

TERRY NARDIN

My aim in this chapter is to provide both an overview of the field of international ethics and an argument for rethinking its identity and foundations. I begin with its present identity as a branch of applied ethics and consider some disadvantages of that identity, which invites too easy a transition from the realm of personal morality to the realm of politics, and which alternative labels such as "global" or "cosmopolitan" ethics do little to overcome (Section 1). I then take up the question of foundations, arguing that a coherent theory of international ethics that acknowledges the claims of politics must rest on the idea of *justice* as properly enforceable obligations—a claim I defend by examining the ideas of interest, agreement, rights, and morality as foundational alternatives to the idea of justice (Section 2). Next, I use this conception of justice to illuminate some key topics in international ethics: the *pluralism* of a world divided not only into legally autonomous states but also along religious, ethnic, and other lines; the *inequalities* of a world divided between rich and poor; and the *insecurity* of a world in which war remains endemic and inescapable (Sections 3, 4, and 5). I end (Section 6) by suggesting how attention to the history of political thought and comparative ethics can make the study of international ethics more critical and autonomous. Focusing on justice as enforceable obligations can help the field move past dead-end debates over cosmopolitanism to acquire a coherent identity as concerned with freedom, coercion, law, and politics.

1 THE QUESTION OF DEFINITION

Within the field of international relations, international ethics is a relative new-comer. The first influential book to bear the title *International Ethics* was a collection of articles from the journal *Philosophy and Public Affairs* (Beitz et al. 1985); a succession of books with similar titles soon followed (Nardin and Mapel 1992; Frost 1996; Graham 1997; Amstutz 1999). These volumes helped to consolidate a literature that had begun to accumulate in response to events outside the academy, such as the war in Vietnam and famine in Africa (Wasserstrom 1970; Cohen, Nagel, and Scanlon 1974; Held, Morgenbesser, and Nagel 1974), and that eventually led to book-length studies of the morality of war, foreign aid, and other issues (Walzer 1977; Shue 1980; O'Neill 1986). Moral philosophy, which for decades had focused on conceptual analysis, was once again asking substantive questions. *Philosophy and Public Affairs* announced in its first issue (1971) that its mission was to contribute to clarifying *and resolving* issues of public concern, and the Carnegie Council on Ethics and International Affairs, whose journal *Ethics and International Affairs* helped to institutionalize the field, recently adopted "The Voice for Ethics in International Policy" as its motto. International ethics has become, like medical or business ethics, a branch of "applied ethics." This view of international ethics has several disadvantages, however.

First, applied ethics assumes that public policy should be guided and judged by the same principles that govern individual conduct. Many philosophers of the past would have found this an odd view of the matter. Aristotle, for example, distinguished concerns bearing on individual conduct from those bearing on public affairs, devoting his *Ethics* to the former and his *Politics* to the latter. And Immanuel Kant based his theory of politics on grounds quite distinct from those of ethical theory: Politics, he thought, rests on principles of public right ("justice"), not on those of personal virtue ("ethics"). Were we to acknowledge a distinction between the ethical and the political, we might call the subfield "international political theory," not "international ethics"—and that, in fact, is a common alternative name for it (Beitz 1979; Brown 2002).

Secondly, applied ethics suggests that the activity to which moral principles are applied lacks adequate principles of its own. Instead of basing the ethics of international relations on principles of diplomacy, just war, and international law, it uses principles from outside that realm to answer questions inside it. This reinforces the impression that ethics is separate from and inherently at odds with those principles. It turns international ethics into a technical subject and awards priority to philosophers as possessors of the relevant expertise. The result is what Bernard Williams (2005) calls "political moralism"—the view that political philosophy is a mere extension of moral philosophy without distinctive concerns of its own.

Thirdly, the applied ethics model misleads by suggesting that the aim of scholarship in international ethics is to prescribe rather than to understand. Treating the field itself, and not merely its subject matter, as "normative" confuses a subject of inquiry with that inquiry, obscuring the distinction between practice and theory. Conceiving international ethics as applied ethics excludes inquiries aimed not at action but at understanding and denies it the advantages of theoretical detachment.

Further issues are raised by the phrase "global ethics," which has caught on as part of the discourse of globalization (Dower 1998; Singer 2002). Those who favor it believe that globalization is eroding the autonomy of international relations, and that the study of international ethics must broaden its focus from relations between states to relations between individuals and groups both within and across national boundaries. But on this definition it is hard to see how one can distinguish between "global ethics" and "ethics" itself, without the qualifying adjective. The same can be said of "global justice" and "global political theory" (Shapiro and Brilmayer 1999; Pogge 2001; Caney 2005). These expressions do not expand international ethics; they erase it. Martha Nussbaum (2006, 92), for example, uses "global justice" to signal an extension of the scope of justice not only to foreigners but also to persons with disabilities and animals. For her, "global" means universal or general, in contrast to local or particular. But issues of universal ethics are issues of ethics as such, not something helpfully designated as global.

The argument that justice must be universal, not international, goes too far in at least two ways. First, "universal" and "international" are not mutually exclusive words: some international obligations may be universal, others not, and vice versa. Secondly, even in a globalizing world, states continue to exist and to have relations with one another. So a theory of global justice must still concern itself with their rights and duties. Global justice can replace international justice only by claiming that states are not a proper locus for discussions of justice. But accepting that claim would exclude foreign policy from the realm of moral judgment. A more prudent approach to the problem of global justice would be to begin by asking, as Thomas Nagel (2005, 113) does, what justice on a world scale might mean, treating the relationship between the global and the international as a question to be investigated. The case for global justice, on this approach, is that its concerns—human rights, global inequality, transnational democracy, environmental justice, and the like— need to be added to the traditional concerns of international justice if we are to have a comprehensive theory of justice above the level of the state.

Another word that creates more problems than it solves is "cosmopolitanism." In normal usage, a cosmopolitan is someone who is free of local prejudices and therefore tolerant of moral differences. Many of today's cosmopolitan moralists are the reverse of this, since they posit a single standard of right and wrong for everyone (Moellendorf 2002; Hayden 2005). The word's etymology—*kosmos* (world) and *polis* (state)—implies a single body of world law, but as used today its force is ethical, not legal: Cosmopolitans argue that there is a *moral* law that binds all human beings regardless of country or faith. Many ethical systems make such a claim, including traditional (Catholic) and modern (Protestant) natural law, Kantian ethics, utilitarianism, and even the teachings of Islam, Christianity, and other religions that address themselves to all humanity. The adjective "cosmopolitan" therefore does not pick out a particular set of prescriptions—any such set, if universal in scope, counts as cosmopolitan. A cosmopolitan ethic might rest on reason or revelation; it might be teleological, prescribing ends to be pursued, or deontological, prescribing limits on that pursuit; and it might claim jurisdiction over all areas of life or only over some. Philosophers therefore distinguish different cosmopolitanisms: moral versus institutional, weak (or thin) versus strong (or thick), extreme (exclusive) versus moderate (nonexclusive), and so forth (Tan 2004, 10–12). Cosmopolitanism, in short, is not itself an ethical system but a class of systems. For that reason, the word has been made to bear far too much weight in recent discussions of international ethics. About the crucial questions—Is ethics a matter of interests, rights, or duties? Do people have *some* obligations to foreigners, or the *same* obligations to foreigners as to fellow nationals?—the label equivocates, more often obscuring than advancing the debate.

To summarize: Given its disadvantages, "international ethics" has outlived its usefulness as a name for the field. It obscures the distinction between personal conduct and public policy. At the same time, it awards moral expertise to philosophers, who become the mandarins from whom others are supposed to take instruction. It confuses understanding with prescription, suggesting that anything one might say about normative discourse is itself normative. In doing so, it leaves little room for those whose aim is to understand rather than to prescribe. Expressions such as "global" or "cosmopolitan" ethics do little to remedy these defects while introducing new problems of their own.

2 THE CENTRALITY OF JUSTICE

The advantage of justice as a foundational idea is that it connects ethics with politics and law. I want to suggest some reasons why it is superior to several other ideas that theorists have used to bring coherence to the subject: the ideas of *interest*, *agreement*, *rights*, and *morality*.

2.1 Interest

When Thrasymachus in book I of Plato's *Republic* defines justice as the interest of the stronger, his point is that to view right as independent of might is to embrace either illusion or hypocrisy. Many who find his realist claim exaggerated within the state think it does apply between states—that foreign policy, at least, is determined by interest and power, not by justice, morality, rights, or any other "ethical" idea. But there is a tension within realism between ethical skepticism, which denies ethics entirely, and the view that interest *should* determine policy, which is itself an ethical claim of sorts. In making it, realism invites the charge that reason of state scarcely qualifies as an ethic. Someone who offers maxims of prudence when asked for moral guidance can be accused of not understanding what is being asked for.

An alternative to realism, for those who want to make interest foundational, is utilitarianism. Utilitarians hold that pursuing interests is ethical when those interests are everyone's interests. Yet they fare no better than realists when they propose utility as the basis of morality. They have been fighting a rearguard action against critics who attack them for confusing the right and the good, for not taking seriously the distinction between persons, for having a theory of ethics but no ethic in the sense of an identifiable system of precepts, and for being without a criterion for deciding whether utility is defined by pleasure or other goods, or by actual preferences or rational ones. Like realism, the critics argue, utilitarianism confuses morality, which prescribes limits on the pursuit of interests, with prudence in that pursuit.

Some theorists, drawing on Aristotle and St Thomas Aquinas, take account of such objections by connecting morality ("natural law") with certain human interests ("basic goods") as proper ends, arguing that these goods are to be understood not as outcomes of action but as values to be respected in acting. In Aristotelian terms, they are internal rather than external goods. Instead of postulating an undifferentiated utility, they identify specific goods such as friendship, knowledge, and religion that people must respect in making choices (Finnis, Boyle, and Grisez 1987, 277–84). A Kantian would find this an odd use of the word "respect," however. Kantian ethics rests on respecting the autonomy of rational beings, not on a theory of human goods. The problem with the Aristotelian–Thomistic strategy, from a Kantian perspective, is not that it is openly consequentialist but that its teleological character obscures the distinction between goods and constraints. It expands the moral by enriching it with other values, which yields a morality that expresses a particular way of life rather than one that prescribes obligations to persons following different ways of life. Catholic philosophers from Vitoria and Suarez on down have, nonetheless, provided a nuanced and robust system of moral principles for international relations, especially on issues of war and peace (Anscombe 1981; Finnis 1996; Boyle 2006). Thomists who adhere to the idea of natural law agree significantly with Kantians on the principles of a just international order while continuing to disagree on the foundation of those principles, the former basing them on a substantive theory of good and the latter on a formal theory of right.

2.2 Agreement

That moralists often reach similar results from different premises has led some theorists to suggest that foundations matter less than agreement, or more radically, that agreement itself is the true foundation of ethics. Agreement can be theorized as an explicit or implicit act of will, as in social contract theory, or as inherent in a way of life, as in Hegelian, communitarian, and pragmatist theories. But agreement offers less than first appears. From the standpoint of realism or utilitarianism, agreement is defective because it collapses under the pressure of self-interest; hence the instability of treaties and other contracts. From the standpoint of natural law, agreement is defective because people agree to things that are morally indefensible. They agreed for millennia that slavery is permissible, but slavery is and always has been morally wrong. The idea of moral truth implies a distinction between conventional and critical morality. The critical moralist's aim is to extract from a body of moral beliefs, many of them false, those that are true and universally binding. Agreement contributes to this project by means of an imagined contract: We know what is morally right when we know what people would agree to if they were rational. The conditions of agreement are supposed to guarantee impartiality and therefore the ethical character of what is agreed to. John Rawls's theory of justice is an example of this approach. Notoriously, however, the thought experiment on which it rests generates not one set of principles but many, depending on how it is conducted, and the problem is compounded at the international level. Rawls's failure is not surprising: Substantive indeterminacy is inherent in all procedural ideas, from the social contract to deliberative democracy.

2.3 Rights

The standard objection to utilitarianism is that it justifies acts that violate people's rights. This, together with the rejection of social contract theory, has led some to make rights the foundation of international ethics (Shue 1980; Jones 1999). That strategy has the advantage of meshing with the prominence of human rights in everyday discourse about international affairs. But that prominence is not matched by clarity in formulating specific obligations. It is said, for example, that states must respect human rights. This means not only that governments must refrain from violating human rights but also that they are responsible for protecting human rights. This, in turn, has been taken to mean states have a collective responsibility to protect people everywhere from violence and even to ensure their material well-being. But the duty to respect human rights in acting and the duty to promote human rights as a consequence of action are distinct. Moreover, if human rights provide a basis for criticizing existing law, they must be moral and not merely legal rights, although incorporating these rights into law may help to secure them. Laws and policies are unjust if they violate basic rights.

But which rights are basic? The language of rights is vulnerable to inflation as interests are promoted to rights. If that language is construed in a self-consistent way, it drives a wide range of prescriptions from the realm of duty into the realm of discretion (Hart 1955; O'Neill 1996). Nor in the absence of moral principles can rights discourse provide a reliable way of navigating between rival rights claims. But, if the idea of rights requires a foundation, it cannot itself be foundational—a set of moral principles from which both rights and duties are derived.

2.4 Morality

It seems, then, that international ethics cannot do without the theory of morality. Such a theory is needed to give a coherent account of goods, rights, duties, and justice. It would distinguish rights from interests and legal from moral rights. It would explain why some rights take priority over others and how rights are related to duties. Moral concerns that are voiced today in the language of human rights are also expressed in the languages of natural law and other moral traditions that offer a rational and universal system of precepts—a "common morality" binding on all (Donagan 1977, 1–9). Such traditions distinguish principles that prescribe obligations for every human being from those that are based on the conventions of particular communities and bind only their members. Principles of common morality are in that sense global or cosmopolitan. They pertain to international relations because they apply to corporate as well as natural persons. The premise that states can behave immorally has shaped moral discourse on international affairs throughout the modern period. That discourse does not exclude the pursuit of collective interests, but it does require that those interests, like all interests, be pursued in morally permissible ways. Common moral principles are the basis of law, civil and international. They explain why institutions such as family, contract, property, and civil society can be justifiable; help to distinguish just from unjust governments; and provide grounds for resisting governments that are seriously unjust through revolution, war, or intervention.

To bring coherence to the eclectic field of international ethics, a theory of morality must show how interest, rights, duty, and law are related to one another. It must also explain why moral considerations are not always suitable to be included as part of a legal order. Law is coercive in the sense that its obligations can, if necessary, be enforced. But coercion should not be used to enforce legal obligations that it would be morally wrong or effectively impossible to compel people to observe. A theory of morality must be sensitive to the requirements of legal order, domestically and internationally. It must be a theory of *justice*.

2.5 Justice

As often used, the word "just" is merely a synonym for "morally justified." But "justice" can be given a narrower meaning as concerned with enforceable duties toward others, and therefore as excluding not only duties to oneself but also duties to others that are not enforceable for one reason or another. Principles of justice comprise a subset of moral principles. On this definition of justice, there is a distinction between justice and beneficence. Beneficence is a duty, but it is not always an *enforceable* duty and therefore not a duty of justice. Duties of justice are duties people could reasonably be compelled to observe. That they *have* moral duties does not mean they should be *compelled to perform* those duties. Some moral duties require a proper motive and for that reason cannot be enforced. Others cannot be turned into legal duties because their enforcement would be impractical. The discourse of justice, then, is about duties that could be enforced without moral impropriety and without inviting certain failure or incurring excessive costs. It is a discourse not about what is in fact lawful within a given legal order but about what moral prescriptions it would be proper to make legal. It is also a discourse about prescriptions that could properly justify extralegal coercion in situations where laws are unjust or ineffective. Principles of international justice are principles for determining the grounds and limits of coercion at the level of international relations. From the perspective of such principles, matters that are usually treated separately—sovereignty and its limits, the morality of international law, cultural pluralism, economic inequality, and the use of force—can be brought within an integrated theoretical framework (Nardin 2005; 2006). In this way, the idea of justice as morally justifiable coercion can bring coherence to the field of international ethics. In the next three sections, I sketch how this might be done.

3 JUSTICE AND PLURALISM

For better or worse, much of the debate about global justice has centered on the ideas of Rawls. Rawls's main concern, after the publication of *A Theory of Justice* (1971), was to articulate principles of justice for a multicultural society. People who belong to different religious or other communities—who hold different "comprehensive moral doctrines"—must within broad limits accept their differences as legitimate. If they are to live together under just laws, those laws must be consistent with principles of "public reason" that respect their differences. Rawls's aim in *The Law of Peoples* (1999) was to explore the implications of these ideas at the international level.

If the idea of public reason requires that we accept reasonable pluralism *within* liberal societies, it should also apply *between* such societies. An international society composed of liberal democratic states would therefore permit reasonable diversity among peoples, each of which has its own values and traditions. The basic principles of justice within a liberal state are modeled by an ideal social contract, as explained in *A Theory of Justice*. But principles of *international* justice are modeled by a second ideal contract in which representatives of liberal peoples choose a "law of peoples" for a society of liberal states. These representatives do not know the identity of their own country, or its size or wealth. They know it has liberal institutions, but they ignore the comprehensive moral doctrines of its citizens because, in a liberal state, only citizens, not the state itself, can have such a doctrine (Rawls 1999, 34). The chosen principles govern the transactions of liberal states with one another and, in most circumstances, with nonliberal states as well. States must respect one another's independence, observe treaty obligations, use force only in self-defense, observe limits on war, and respect human rights. In addition, they are obligated to assist societies whose economic situation prevents their enjoying just institutions. Like Descartes, who got Catholic orthodoxy out of the *cogito*, Rawls uses the two-stage contract to generate traditional principles of international morality.

Simplifying Rawls a bit, we can think of states as being of three kinds: liberal, quasi-liberal, and antiliberal. Liberal and quasi-liberal states can coexist within a society of states, but antiliberal states behave differently and have to be treated differently. By coexisting peacefully with quasi-liberal states, liberal states can nurture an expanding confederation whose members are peaceful and law-abiding, even if not all are liberal democracies. But antiliberal ("outlaw") states cannot participate in this confederation because they are violent internally or externally. Liberal and quasi-liberal states are permitted to protect themselves by force if necessary against aggression. And they have the right, even a duty, to intervene to prevent gross human rights abuses, like genocide and ethnic cleansing. The pluralism that remains when aggressors have been repelled and oppressors overthrown is the pluralism of a just, if still morally imperfect, international society.

These conclusions might seem obvious to the point of banality, but they have not gone down well with cosmopolitan theorists, who object that the law of peoples requires liberal states to tolerate nonliberal ones because quasi-liberal states are not liberal. If the principles of liberal democracy are sound, they argue, every state should be a liberal democracy. Liberal states may have to tolerate quasi-liberal ones for practical reasons, but they should not—as Rawls maintains—tolerate them in principle. To tolerate quasi-liberal societies is to recognize them as equal members of the society of peoples. In extending that recognition, liberals violate their own commitment to liberal principles (Tan 2004, 79–80). Rawls thinks that objections of this sort confuse liberalism as a comprehensive doctrine with liberalism based on principles of public reason ("political liberalism"). Just as citizens in a liberal society must respect one another's right to reach their own conclusions, so must states as members of a society of states. Liberals do *not* violate their own principles in supporting coexistence between liberal and nonliberal states, provided the latter are not aggressive externally or oppressive internally, any more than they do when they recognize nonliberal persons in their own country as fellow citizens. Tolerance is a liberal, not an illiberal, value.

Why not imagine a global contract, as many of Rawls's critics propose? Because to insist on such a contract is to insist that everyone must "have the equal liberal rights of citizens in a constitutional democracy" (Rawls 1999, 82). It is to insist that everyone live according to the same comprehensive moral doctrine. The argument does not respect diversity, domestically or globally. It assumes that only liberal societies have a right to exist, prejudging the question of whether there are morally legitimate states that are not Western constitutional democracies. The problem with many self-styled "cosmopolitan" theories of global justice is that they are the reverse of cosmopolitan. They do not take pluralism seriously. They betray their own premise because pluralism is the outcome of the individualism that cosmopolitans take as axiomatic when they say that individuals are the basic units of concern. A genuine concern for individuals means concern for their *individuality*, for their capacity and right to make their own choices. The belief that this concern rules out the choice to be associated in different kinds of community, so that the only morally legitimate community is a liberal democracy, reveals a failure to appreciate the implications of the idea of the person that cosmopolitans think they are embracing.

If these conclusions are sound, they reinforce the case for investigating the moral basis of international order as requiring states to coexist within a common framework of international law (Nardin 1983; Koskenniemi 2001; Cohen 2004). International law sets properly, if not always effectively, enforceable limits on the freedom of states. Such an investigation will seem especially appropriate to those—mainly internationalists rather than realists or cosmopolitans—who are more interested in understanding or reforming the world we actually inhabit than in advocating for an ideal world order.

4 JUSTICE AND INEQUALITY

Rawls had proposed a principle of distributive justice in *A Theory of Justice*: Economic inequalities within a society are unjust unless they benefit everyone, including the least advantaged (the "difference principle"). But he did not apply the principle internationally. Critics of that book objected that the absence of an international difference principle makes international redistribution a matter of charity or humanity, not justice, and allows extreme global inequalities (Barry 1991).

A correct interpretation of Rawls's theory, they argued, would prescribe a universal system of distributive justice—a *global* difference principle, not an *international* one (Barry 1973; Hayden 2002, 111–13). States are not analogous to individual persons, not basic units of moral concern. And a principle that prescribes a more equal distribution of wealth between states says nothing about how wealth should be distributed inside each state. So, the critics insist, the relevant principles of distributive justice are global, not international. The only principles that make sense as law *between states* are principles of mutual respect and limited mutual aid.

In *The Law of Peoples*, Rawls responded by arguing that representatives of liberal states in an ideal contract situation would not choose global principles of distributive justice because they are required—by public reason—to respect the differences that distinguish liberal and quasi-liberal states. Public reason at the international level demands that peoples address one another as peoples, in terms of common principles, not comprehensive moral doctrines, which in any case they do not hold *as liberal peoples,* even if individual citizens embrace such doctrines. Underlying Rawls's argument is a theory of justice as properly enforceable prescriptions, though he does not make that theory explicit. A global difference principle would improperly impose liberal doctrine on nonliberal states. Liberals can reasonably demand change in states that grossly violate human rights, but many nonliberal states are not oppressive on this scale. Insisting that they accept specific redistributive principles would be a kind of intolerance: a refusal to recognize the right of other people to live by principles of their own, even though those principles are illiberal. Those principles must not permit violation of the most basic human rights, however.

This disagreement between the leading contemporary theorist of justice and his critics is a sign of the disorder in our understanding of distributive justice. Before the modern age, distributive justice meant distribution according to merit or desert; only recently has it come to mean distribution without regard to merit (Fleischacker 2004). Ideas now taken for granted, such as that economic inequality can be unjust whatever its cause and that governments should reallocate wealth to rectify unjust inequalities, were not prominent before the eighteenth century. An early modern state was not seen as a single society whose members shared a common fate but as an aggregate of distinct societies—ethnic groups, faiths, and social classes—having little in common. Governments in any case had neither resources to distribute nor the capacity to distribute them. The question whether a state is one society or many, and what this might mean for how we understand economic inequality, is now being replayed at the global level, pushing the question of the moral significance of national boundaries to the forefront of debate.

When moral philosophers write about global inequality, their proposals are often utopian. The tone of these writings is sometimes like that of the celebrity who said about African poverty: "Something must be done; anything must be done, whether it works or not" (Easterly 2006, 17). The point of development assistance, it seems, is to assuage guilt, not relieve poverty. Advocates for global redistribution might reply that uncertainty about whether assistance will help is not a reason for not trying to help. That is true, but duties of assistance do depend on assessments of efficacy and cost. If ought implies can, uncertainty undermines obligation. Inquiry is not advanced when scholars skeptical of development aid are attacked as heartless reactionaries (Tucker 1977; Bauer 1981). Because philosophy is properly concerned with principles, not contingencies, we might charitably conclude that philosophers who argue for foreign aid are assuming it can be effective and leaving the details to others. When Peter Singer (1972) famously proposed that the global rich should give away most of their assets to end famine, he did so on the premise that such a transfer would actually make a difference. Efforts to define economic injustice should not be confused with specific proposals for ameliorating it.

The question for international ethics is not whether economic inequality can be remedied but whether it is unjust. Does global poverty in fact raise the issue of justice, and if so should we be concerned with absolute or relative poverty? Famine relief is premised on an absolute standard: If people are starving, there is a moral obligation to respond. The duty here is one of beneficence: We should give aid if we can do so without disproportionate cost. But arguments about economic justice sometimes presuppose a relative standard. When moralists condemn as unjust disparities between rich and poor, they condemn the inequality, not the poverty. There would be no injustice were everyone equally rich—or equally poor. Singer's utilitarianism, as many have observed, requires not only that the rich give up luxuries so the poor can survive, but that everyone's wealth be redistributed until all have more or less the same, even if they are equally poor. It does not take account of how that wealth was acquired, how it is used, the diversity of human activities it enables, or any other consideration besides marginal utility. Rawls's difference principle, which justifies inequalities that increase the well-being of the least advantaged, adds a reasonable qualification to utilitarian equality. But it too is arbitrary, insensitive to history, and incompatible with pluralism.

This is not to dismiss the idea of global distributive justice, only to say that critics of the leading theory—Rawls's law of peoples—have yet to provide a decisive refutation of his conclusion that the principles of a just global order are those that do not dismiss the international. Those principles provide a basis for reforming international law to protect people everywhere from violence and exploitation. Because the necessary policies have to be financed, the debate over distributive justice will increasingly be a debate over tax policy, and that in turn is a debate over just and unjust coercion. The most promising alternatives to Rawlsian theorizing, such as that justice is a matter of realizing human capabilities (Sen 1999), are unlikely to erase traditional understandings of international justice. Because they give primacy to the idea of freedom, the traditional understandings leave room for a world in which people value communal allegiances. That world requires coercive limits on freedom for the sake of freedom and invites an argument about justice that can define those limits. Just war theory suggests how the argument might go.

5 JUSTICE AND WAR

Just war theory is the most systematic and stable branch of international ethics, and it illustrates more clearly than does the discourse of distributive justice the idea of justice as properly enforceable obligations. Because it deals directly with the grounds for justifiable coercion, it is the core of a theory of international justice.

Just war discourse had existed for centuries when, in the mid-thirteenth century, Aquinas devised his famous synthesis distilling a host of just war criteria down to three: just cause, proper authority, and right intention. The essential modern text, much disputed but not yet displaced, is Michael Walzer's *Just and Unjust Wars* (1977). Walzer bases the justification of armed force—*jus ad bellum*—on a state's rights to political sovereignty and territorial integrity, which he explicates by analogy with the human rights of personal independence and bodily integrity. This strategy has invited criticism from those who find it misleading. One complaint is that, by awarding states a right of autonomy, it puts foreign policy beyond moral criticism. But this is a mistake: If we can criticize individual conduct, we can criticize state conduct. Autonomy is the idea that agents make choices, not the idea that choices cannot be criticized. Another objection is that states are not agents. This, too, is a mistake: Any group organized to make decisions can be said to act and can be held responsible for its actions. Where the domestic analogy goes astray is in being used to generate conclusions about international affairs from what are wrongly presumed to be relevantly similar interpersonal situations: for example, that, because a person may have a duty to intervene to prevent a crime or rescue a drowning child, a state must intervene to halt a massacre or end a famine. Such inferences ignore factual and moral disanalogies between individual and collective responsibility that can distort our conclusions about what is required at the international level (Graham 1997, 41). To put it in the vocabulary of the present chapter, they ignore the political.

David Rodin (2002) emphasizes these disanalogies in his discussion of self-defense. At the interpersonal level, the right to use coercion is based on the principle that liberty can be defended provided it is not misused. If a person misuses his liberty to violate another's moral rights, he becomes an "aggressor" and loses his immunity to coercion by, among others, the victims of his aggression, who are free to resist it forcibly. But national self-defense is not a straightforward extension of this individual right to resist aggression, because the nation that defends its rights is not identical with the individuals who compose it. Clearly, actions that count as personal self-defense for soldiers are distinct from those that count as self-defense for states. So, Rodin argues, we need a just war theory that goes beyond the domestic analogy, one that pays attention to multiple levels of relationship between states and persons. To do that, we must challenge the traditional assumption (defended by Walzer) that *jus in bello* considerations, which pertain to the conduct of war, are independent of those of *jus ad bellum*. We may excuse soldiers who serve an aggressive state from responsibility and blame, but we cannot see their violence as morally permissible (McMahan 2004, 79). A paradoxical result of this reasoning is that soldiers fighting in an aggressive war may be innocent attackers, and, if they cannot be blamed, it is hard to see on what grounds they can be killed. One answer is that, though not morally culpable, they are not innocent from the standpoint of objective injustice or material harm (Finnis 1996, 26–7; Mapel 2004, 82–3).

Rodin finds just war theory incoherent because it combines traditions with distinct rationales: *jus ad bellum* was aimed by lawyers and theologians at rulers contemplating war, whereas *jus in bello* emerged from codes of military honor. The result is paradoxical because the first tradition is asymmetrical (only one side can have just cause), the second symmetrical (soldiers on both sides fight justly if they observe the laws of war). A state might violate *jus ad bellum* while its agents, soldiers, dutifully respect *jus in bello* (Rodin 2002, 167), or it might meet *jus ad bellum* criteria while its soldiers commit war crimes. The resulting war is both just and unjust, depending on how you look at it. But this is confused. The agent to which a war is imputed is a state, not its soldiers. And the war it fights must meet both *ad bellum* and *in bello* criteria. If its soldiers grossly misbehave, a state fights an unjust war even if its cause is just. The relevant principle is that good ends must not be pursued by impermissible means.

Rodin's book has provoked a new round of debate on the moral basis of war. But despite references in this debate to "traditional" just war theory, there is no such thing if by traditional we mean an unchanging consensus: In the past we find a debate as wide-ranging and vigorous as our own, not settled doctrine. And among the propositions questioned both today and in the past is that self-defense is the core of just war theory. From one point of view it is not: What counts is that people should be protected from violence, and perpetrators of violence resisted. Self-defense is a special case of resisting violence in which those attacked protect themselves. But a state may resist violence on behalf of other states. It is, moreover, permissible for one state to intervene within the territory of another when the government of the latter perpetrates or permits atrocities against its own people. In some cases, acting to thwart violence may be a duty as well as a right, and, if that is the case, those who stand idly by can be blamed for failing to intervene. Such "humanitarian" intervention is always controversial, but it has been a topic in just war theory for centuries.

Current research on just war theory explores these and many other issues, including those of *jus post bellum* (surrender, accountability, and reconciliation) and issues raised by terrorism and religious violence. If terrorism and civil war are replacing war between states, as some probably shortsighted observers maintain, this in no way undermines the continued relevance of just war theory, because that theory pre-dates the states system. Paying attention to the history of just war theory, and making its principles theoretically coherent, can help us to detach its basic principles from present contingencies.

6 Issues and Agendas

The ethics of coercion is central to just war theory, but, if the argument of this chapter is correct, it is also central (in ways that have yet to be adequately worked out) to theories of pluralism and distributive justice, which must address global differences while remaining sensitive to the demands of freedom and the limits of permissible coercion. International ethics cannot ignore the political. And this means, among other things, that international law still has a place in world affairs despite changes brought about by globalization, transnational ideologies and allegiances, and other challenges to inherited patterns of international relations. Even if there is now a global civil society shaped by economic and other associations, or a new world order based on transnational governance networks, there remains a place for rules governing relations between states. To say this is not to defend the international legal order as desirable; it is simply to suggest that the dichotomy between international and global order is an abstraction that fails to capture what is actually going on. The dismissal of international relations gratuitously predicts an event—the emergence of a single system of world law—that may not occur.

Considered as an academic subfield, international ethics provides a snapshot of an ongoing discourse. Thinking of it as a historical tradition—a conversation in time—offers a corrective by reminding us that the present has the past as its context. Much is written by those who know little of earlier debates, creating an illusion of progress when there is only repetition. History is also a good antidote to dogmatism, inviting us to imagine our descendants questioning our notions as we question those of our predecessors. But paying attention to the past means doing more than reading Thucydides, Machiavelli, and Kant. It involves inquiry into the ideas of lesser figures and into the discourses that provide the context for those ideas. Efforts to recover forgotten debates can shed new light on the relationship between changing mores and enduring moral principles. And contextual inquiry can overturn received interpretations, revealing (for example) surprising continuities between Grotius and Hobbes, who are usually thought to be on opposite sides of a moralist–realist divide (Tuck 1999). From Aquinas to Suarez, and again from Grotius to Kant, philosophers have articulated systematic and nuanced theories of international justice. Certainly there are problems with these theories, but they have resources that ignorance and present-mindedness have led recent generations to overlook.

The field can also learn from comparative ethics. Comparative inquiry can help Western scholars to become less parochial and to deepen their theoretical understanding. Comparison need not be driven by a search for common ground. Differences are as important as similarities. Different traditions do not offer different answers to the same questions; they ask different questions. To understand a statement, one must first understand the question it purports to answer. Its meaning is determined by the presuppositions that shape a given discourse of question and answer (Collingwood 1939, 36–40). Only then can we decide whether someone's answers are reasonable answers to *their* questions. A proposition that looks wrong as an answer to *our* questions may make sense as an answer to someone else's. Comparative inquiry, which is always to some extent both historical and cross-cultural, offers a route toward understanding such differences.

Historical and comparative inquiry can help us gain perspective on current issues. But no matter how important these issues are, practically speaking, addressing them cannot substitute for considering questions whose significance is theoretical. Basic research has legitimate claims, as does applied research, and those claims are not limited to its long-term utility. Ethical theory has its place beside applied ethics and political theory beside politics. We should acknowledge the autonomy of theory and avoid reducing everything to advocacy. We should also resist exaggerating the significance of current affairs, recognizing that, although issues change, principles are seldom novel. And we should remember that ethics can make an independent contribution to policy debates only if moral considerations are kept distinct from those of economics, strategy, and prudence.

REFERENCES

AMSTUTZ, M. R. 1999. *International Ethics: Concepts, Theories, and Cases in Global Politics.* Lanham, Md.: Rowman and Littlefield.

ANSCOMBE, G. E. M. 1981. *Ethics, Religion, and Politics.* Minneapolis: University of Minnesota Press.

BARRY, B. 1973. *The Liberal Theory of Justice: A Critical Examination of the Principal Doctrines in* A Theory of Justice *by John Rawls.* Oxford: Oxford University Press.

——1991. Humanity and justice in global perspective. Pp. 182–210 in *Liberty and Justice,* B. Barry. Oxford: Oxford University Press.

BAUER, P. T. 1981. *Equality, the Third World, and Economic Delusion.* London: Weidenfeld and Nicolson.

BEITZ, C. R. 1979. *Political Theory and International Relations.* Princeton, NJ: Princeton University Press.

——COHEN, M., SCANLON, T., and SIMMONS, A. J. (eds.) 1985. *International Ethics.* Princeton, NJ: Princeton University Press.

BOYLE, J. 2006. Traditional just war theory and humanitarian intervention. Pp. 31–57 in *Humanitarian Intervention*, ed. T. Nardin and M. S. Williams. New York: New York University Press.

BROWN, C. 2002. *Sovereignty, Rights, and Justice: International Political Theory Today*. Cambridge: Polity.

CANEY, S. 2005. *Justice beyond Borders: A Global Political Theory*. Oxford: Oxford University Press.

COHEN, J. L. 2004. Whose sovereignty? Empire versus international law. *Ethics and International Affairs*, 18: 1–24.

COHEN, M., NAGEL, T., and SCANLON, T. (eds.) 1974. *War and Moral Responsibility*. Princeton, NJ: Princeton University Press.

COLLINGWOOD, R. G. 1939. *An Autobiography*. Oxford: Oxford University Press.

DONAGAN, A. 1977. *The Theory of Morality*. Chicago: University of Chicago Press.

DOWER, N. 1998. *World Ethics: The New Agenda*. Edinburgh: Edinburgh University Press.

EASTERLY, W. 2006. *The White Man's Burden: Why the West's Efforts to Aid the Rest Have Done So Much Ill and So Little Good*. New York: Penguin.

FINNIS, J. 1996. The ethics of war and peace in the Catholic natural law tradition. Pp. 15–39 in *The Ethics of War and Peace: Religious and Secular Perspectives*, ed. T. Nardin. Princeton, NJ: Princeton University Press.

—— BOYLE, J. M., and GRISEZ, G. 1987. *Nuclear Deterrence, Morality, and Realism*. Oxford: Oxford University Press.

FLEISCHACKER, S. 2004. *A Short History of Distributive Justice*. Cambridge, Mass.: Harvard University Press.

FROST, M. 1996. *Ethics in International Relations: A Constitutive Theory*. Cambridge: Cambridge University Press.

GRAHAM, G. 1997. *Ethics and International Relations*. Oxford: Blackwell.

HART, H. L. A. 1955. Are there any natural rights? *Philosophical Review*, 64: 175–91.

HAYDEN, P. 2002. *John Rawls: Towards a Just World Order*. Cardiff: University of Wales Press.

—— 2005. *Cosmopolitan Global Politics*. Aldershot: Ashgate.

HELD, V., MORGENBESSER, S., and NAGEL, T. (eds.) 1974. *Philosophy, Morality, and International Affairs*. New York: Oxford University Press.

JONES, C. 1999. *Global Justice: Defending Cosmopolitanism*. Oxford: Oxford University Press.

KOSKENNIEMI, M. 2001. *The Gentle Civilizer of Nations: The Rise and Fall of International Law, 1870–1960*. Cambridge: Cambridge University Press.

McMAHAN, J. 2004. War as self-defense. *Ethics and International Affairs*, 18: 75–80.

MAPEL, D. 2004. Innocent attackers and rights of self-defense. *Ethics and International Affairs*, 18: 81–6.

MOELLENDORF, D. 2002. *Cosmopolitan Justice*. Boulder, Colo.: Westview.

NAGEL, T. 2005. The problem of global justice. *Philosophy and Public Affairs*, 33: 113–47.

NARDIN, T. 1983. *Law, Morality, and the Relations of States*. Princeton, NJ: Princeton University Press.

—— 2005. Justice and coercion. Pp. 247–63 in *International Society and its Critics*, ed. A. J. Bellamy. Oxford: Oxford University Press.

—— 2006. International political theory and the question of justice. *International Affairs*, 82: 449–65.

——and MAPEL, D. R. 1992. *Traditions of International Ethics*. Cambridge: Cambridge University Press.

NUSSBAUM, M. C. 2006. *Frontiers of Justice: Disability, Nationality, Species Membership*. Cambridge, Mass.: Harvard University Press.

O'NEILL, O. 1986. *Faces of Hunger: An Essay on Poverty, Justice, and Development*. London: Allen and Unwin.

——1996. *Towards Justice and Virtue: A Constructive Account of Practical Reasoning*. Cambridge: Cambridge University Press.

POGGE, T. W. (ed.) 2001. *Global Justice*. Oxford: Blackwell.

RAWLS, J. 1971. *A Theory of Justice*. Cambridge, Mass.: Harvard University Press.

——1999. *The Law of Peoples: With, the Idea of Public Reason Revisited*. Cambridge, Mass.: Harvard University Press.

RODIN, D. 2002. *War and Self-Defense*. Oxford: Oxford University Press.

SEN, A. 1999. *Development as Freedom*. New York: Random House.

SHAPIRO, I., and BRILMAYER, L. (eds.) 1999. *Global Justice*. New York: New York University Press.

SHUE, H. 1980. *Basic Rights: Subsistence, Affluence, and US Foreign Policy*. Princeton, NJ: Princeton University Press.

SINGER, P. 1972. Famine, affluence, and morality. *Philosophy and Public Affairs*, 1: 229–43.

——2002. *One World: The Ethics of Globalization*. New Haven, Conn.: Yale University Press.

TAN, K.-C. 2004. *Justice without Borders: Cosmopolitanism, Nationalism, and Patriotism*. Cambridge: Cambridge University Press.

TUCK, R. 1999. *The Rights of War and Peace: Political Thought and the International Order from Grotius to Kant*. Oxford: Oxford University Press.

TUCKER, R. W. 1977. *The Inequality of Nations*. New York: Basic Books.

WALZER, M. 1977. *Just and Unjust Wars: A Moral Argument with Historical Illustrations*. New York: Basic Books.

WASSERSTROM, R. A. (ed.) 1970. *War and Morality*. Belmont, Calif.: Wadsworth.

WILLIAMS, B. 2005. *In the Beginning Was the Deed: Realism and Moralism in Political Argument*. Princeton, NJ: Princeton University Press.

CHAPTER 35

....

INTERNATIONAL LAW

....

MICHAEL BYERS

THE international legal system is a centuries-old matrix of treaties, customary rules, general principles, judicial precedents, and scholarly opinions. International law is part and parcel of diplomacy, whether in the context of the United Nations, economic relations, or environmental protection. International rules—and respect for the commitments they represent—enable people to send emails and fly airplanes across borders, to enjoy exotic foods, and to share technological innovations. They protect human rights and help to allocate territory.

We call politicians "lawmakers" because politics and law are intrinsically related. At the international level, statesmen and diplomats are the principal lawmakers, with international organizations, transnational corporations, and nongovernmental organizations playing subsidiary roles. In certain areas, such as war and peace, international law may seem peripheral. In others, such as the protection of foreign investments, patents, and copyrights, it is indisputably central. Like an iceberg, only the most weathered portions of the international legal system are regularly scrutinized.

Despite its ubiquity, international law has received relatively little attention from scholars of international relations. And, despite the intrinsic relationship between politics and law, scholars of international law have devoted relatively little attention to international politics. A rapprochement is slowly taking place, but is far from complete. This chapter traces the history of theorizing at the border between international law and international relations in a chronological manner. It concludes by suggesting that one particular area—international lawmaking—offers rich territory for new analysis.

1 REALISM VERSUS POSITIVISM

The discipline of international relations emerged out of a split between two groups of Anglo-American international lawyers during the 1930s and 1940s. On the international relations side were the "realists," who saw states engaged in a self-interested struggle for power. They considered international law to be an epiphenomenon, subject to short-term change at the will of power-applying states. E. H. Carr's comments (1946, 170) were representative: "International law differs from the municipal law of modern states in being the law of an undeveloped and not fully integrated community. It lacks three institutions which are essential parts of any developed system of municipal law: a judicature, an executive and a legislature."

On the international law side were the "positivists," who sought to identify rules based upon measured assessments of the "sources" of international law. Over time, the positivist approach was reinforced by the expanding case law of international courts, the "codification" work of the UN International Law Commission, and literally thousands of treaties.

Positivism remains dominant in international law today. International lawyers practicing as advocates, judges, and arbitrators have little choice. International courts are modeled on their domestic counterparts: They hear contesting arguments based upon traditional sources and accord weight to precedent. Positivists deny their approach is theoretical, but the denial of theory is itself a theory—in this case, one that defines international law as a set of objectively determinable rules devoid of moral content and applicable to states solely on the basis of their consent (Ago 1984).

2 FUNCTIONALISM AND THE NEW HAVEN SCHOOL

Not all practicing international lawyers focus on litigation. Many advise governments, not just on the existence and content of rules, but on their application, the consequences of noncompliance, scope for new interpretations, and—perhaps most importantly—the making or changing of rules. In the early 1960s, Richard Bilder (1962, 638) explained that most lawyers working in foreign ministries are "heavily involved in high-level policy questions having legal implications." Abram Chayes later recalled how international law played a functional role in the Cuban Missile Crisis, helping to steer US decision-makers toward a blockade rather than air strikes and influencing their choice of justification (Chayes 1974). The functionalist approach was best represented by Francis Boyle's work on how international law can be relevant to crises, and how crises can prompt legal change. He argued that the lawyer's role was to "analyze the ability of international law . . . to contribute to the successful management of international crises and the peaceful resolution of the underlying disputes" (Boyle 1985, 131).

Around the same time, Harold Lasswell and Myres McDougal took a social science methodology developed by Lasswell for domestic politics and applied it to international law. The "New Haven School" of legal process theory rejected "the notion of law merely as the impartial application of rules" and recast it as "the entire decision-making process" (Reisman 1992). International rules were simply the products of decision-making, with decision-makers being those individuals whose decisions turned out to be "authorizing and controlling." Had Lasswell and McDougal stopped there, the approach might have been labeled legal realism. However, they insisted that decisions should be made on the basis of values (power, entitlement, wealth, skill, well-being, affection, respect, rectitude), leading to common interests or goals such as the furtherance of human dignity. These criteria introduced an element of subjectivity whenever the New Haven School addressed real-world situations. For example, McDougal (1955, 361), without even considering the opinions or actions of other countries, determined that the United States could legally engage in atmospheric nuclear tests "in preparation for the defense of itself and its allies and of all the values of a free world society." Despite its usefulness as a justification for US foreign policy, international law was accorded no independent influence. In expanding the ambit of analysis to include a plethora of nonlegal factors, Lasswell and McDougal left the *specificity* of international law behind.

3 REGIME THEORY AND INSTITUTIONALISM

"Regime theorists" were among the first international relations scholars to accept that normative structures influence states. Drawing on rational choice theory—an economics-based approach that assumes individuals calculate their actions with a view to achieving goals—they defined regimes as "sets of implicit or explicit principles, norms, rules, and decision-making procedures around which actors' expectations converge in a given area of international relations" (Krasner 1983, 2). Recognizing the impossibility of explaining all state behavior solely on the basis of power and short-term calculations of interest, they asserted that regimes could acquire a life of their own, controlling or at least qualifying applications of state power. Regime theory flourished during the late 1970s and 1980s before evolving into "institutionalism."

For Robert Keohane (1989, 3), institutions included all "persistent and connected sets of rules (formal and informal) that prescribe behavioral roles, constrain activity, and shape expectations." For Oran Young (1989, 81), all social institutions, including international ones, were created as a result of "the conjunction of behavioral regularities and convergent expectations." This "commonly produces identifiable social conventions, which actors conform to without making elaborate calculations on a case-by-case basis" (Young 1989, 82). Yet, while these definitions suggest that institutions have independent influence, Keohane and Young continued to treat them as dependent variables. Young (1989, 205) argued that institutions change "in response to an array of political, economic, technological, sociocultural, and even moral developments"—in short, changes that affect the interests and relative power of different states. Keohane (1988, 381), for his part, defended a continued reliance on rationalism: "Even though the assumption of substantive rationality does not compel a particular set of conclusions about the nature or evolution of international institutions, it has been used in fruitful ways to explain behavior, including institutionalized behavior, in international relations."

Power might take the shape of pressure to cooperate in institutions, but this did not entail the abandonment of rationalism. As Daniel Warner (1998, 322) explains:

Keohane is concerned with how States interact in the United Nations or World Bank. In this sense, as a neo-institutionalist, he focuses on why States cooperate in certain situations as well as how the institution has a life of its own which can compel States to act in certain ways. Keohane is not himself reflective because his focus on cooperation treats it as a separate phenomenon that needs to be explained, as opposed to a natural, organic relationship. By isolating cooperation, Keohane implies that there is no natural cooperation in international relations.

The rationalist focus on deliberately structured cooperation is apparent in Keohane's work on international law. At first glance, the following passage accords considerable weight to normative influences. On closer reading, it becomes clear that these influences develop within, and are shaped by, institutions that are rationally designed to promote power and interests through subsidiary, seemingly nonrational means:

Interests are changeable, responding to changes in descriptive information, causal beliefs, and principled beliefs. Hence norms matter for interests. So do beliefs about others' beliefs; that is, reputation. Concern for reputation can be a means of reconciling instrumentalist prescriptions with normative ones. However, this reconciliation only takes place reliably within the context of highly valued institutions, which align material and extramaterial incentives. Institutions are especially important for the way in which they can alter beliefs, can sometimes influence what we want or do, and can always affect how others will behave if they have any impact at all. If I am right, much depends in world politics not only on material interests and on normative views but on how institutions are designed.

(Keohane 1997, 501)

The assumption that normative structures are, at root, still about power and calculations of interest helps explain why these scholars have shown relatively little interest in how institutions are formed. They believe that institutions are created at the will of the powerful, and so their concerns have focused on the resilience and qualifying effects of these structures, and how to design better ones.

4 Liberal Theory

Andrew Moravcsik (1997) and other "liberal" theorists have added context by arguing that the interests and demands of domestic constituencies are what generate state preferences, as expressed internationally. For instance, Moravcsik (2000, 219) examines the negotiation of the European Convention of Human Rights and finds that "the primary proponents of binding international human rights commitments" were the governments of newly established democracies, and not the great powers ("as realist theory would have it") or governments and transnational groups based in long-established liberal democracies ("as the ideational account would have it"). He concludes that "creating a quasi-independent judicial body is a tactic used by governments to 'lock in' and consolidate democratic institutions, thereby enhancing their credibility and stability vis-à-vis nondemocratic political threats" (Moravcsik 2000, 220).

Anne-Marie Slaughter has drawn on Moravcsik's work to advance an approach to international law that focuses on the regulative activity of "transnational networks" of state, substate, and nonstate actors (Slaughter Burley 1993; Slaughter 2000; 2004). She argues that domestic institutions, including domestic courts, are (and should be) the principal means by which international rules are developed and applied. Today, nobody doubts that transnational networks play a role. Disagreements with Slaughter's analysis focus on: (1) her early (and since muted) suggestion that, since these networks are most common among Western liberal democracies, much international law is limited to that sphere (Simpson 2001); and (2) her reluctance to acknowledge the potential for applications of power within the networks (Marks 2000, 87–92; Alvarez 2001; Mills and Stephens 2005, 28).

Martti Koskenniemi has gone so far as to cast Slaughter's work as a threat to "valid," nonfunctionalist international law:

Ann-Marie Slaughter has drawn a broad picture of (the real) new world order in which sovereign States are disaggregating while formal diplomacy and formal international organizations are being replaced by "transnational networks"...within which judges, government officials, company executives, and members of governmental and non-governmental organizations and interest groups meet to co-ordinate their policies and enhance the enforcement of laws in a fashion which, by comparison to formal inter-State co-operation, is "fast, flexible, and effective". Her vision of the "end-of-State" sociology is nuanced and moderate but still conceives of statehood and sovereign equality as formalistic obstacles to the realization of the dynamic embedded in "real life". An absolutely central aspect of this sociology is the fact that it is normatively tinged. [It] does away with the image of valid law and thus leads lawyers to contemplate an agenda that is posed to them by an academic intelligentsia that has been thoroughly committed to smoothening the paths of the hegemon.   (Koskenniemi 2000, 33–4, quoting Slaughter 1997, 193–7)

Clearly, when there is any proposal for new forms of lawmaking, the potential political consequences must be considered. New forms might be more responsive to the interests of some actors while diminishing the influence of others. If new forms of lawmaking benefit some actors more than others, the possibility that they are being strategically advanced cannot be denied.

5 RATIONAL CHOICE THEORY

From the mid-1990s, some scholars began to apply rational choice theory explicitly to international law. John Setear (1996) explained the increasing degrees of commitment sometimes apparent in the different phases of treaty-making on the basis of multiple plays of a "game." He concluded that treaties are based on states' calculations that their long-term interests are best served through the cooperative creation of normative structures.

Andrew Guzman explained why developing states, which had united in the UN General Assembly to reject a rule requiring "prompt, adequate and effective" compensation for expropriated foreign-owned property, accepted that standard when later negotiating bilateral investment treaties with developed states (Guzman 1998). The answer lay in the Prisoner's Dilemma, since a state negotiating bilaterally finds itself in a very different position from when it is voting in the company of other states. Any developing state that refused to conclude a treaty containing the "prompt, adequate and effective" standard risked being placed at a disadvantage if other, similarly placed states agreed to do so—a risk exacerbated by the opaque character of most bilateral negotiations, which made it difficult to ascertain whether other developing states were holding fast to the previously united position.

Guzman (2002) later sought to explain how the entire international legal system operates. Central to his argument was the assertion that states manifest their self-interest primarily as reputation. A good record of obeying international law has, as its payoff, an increased willingness on the part of other states to cooperate. As a result: "We can no longer be satisfied with the simple conclusion that 'treaties are to be obeyed'" (Guzman 2002, 1887). Instead, states deliberately build and then leverage reputation in pursuit of their goals.

Jack Goldsmith and Eric Posner (1997) reached for rational choice theory as part of an effort to distinguish between "traditional" international law (law of the sea, diplomatic immunity) and "modern" international law (human rights, international criminal law); they then claimed that only the former areas count as real international law, which binds the United States. Later, in a book-length treatment, they argued that "international law emerges from states acting rationally to maximize their interests, given their perceptions of the interests of other states and the distribution of state power" (Goldsmith and Posner 2005, 3). At the same time, they excluded a preference for obeying international law from the composite of state preferences from which they inferred interests, on the basis that it was "unenlightening" to explain compliance in these terms, and because a preference for compliance was dependent upon what citizens and leaders were "willing to pay in terms of other things that they care about," such as security and economic growth. Goldsmith and Posner (2005, 10) asserted that people "care about these latter goods more intensely than they do about international law compliance."

Several criticisms can be made of these applications of rational choice theory to international law. First, some of the conclusions—such as Setear's—simply reinforce accepted wisdom. Secondly, the approach has been applied in a manner that treats states as the only actors in international affairs. This, as Jan Klabbers (2004–5, 40) points out, strengthens dated assumptions by "firmly locating law-making in the international community as the prerogative of states, and states alone." And "stronger states are bound to benefit more from this bolstering of sovereignty and statehood than their weaker counterparts." Thirdly, these rational choice theorists ignore the specificity of international law, which is rooted in obligation. By consenting to a treaty or rule of customary international law, a state binds itself to behave in a certain manner *even if* it subsequently changes its mind about the desirability of that conduct. Moreover, states consent, not just to the specific rules, but also to the general processes through which the rules develop and change. Finally, those scholars who have applied rational choice theory to international law assume that rational decision-makers are selfish decision-makers. They expect— and manifest—no concern for the welfare of people in other countries. But, as Jon Elster (1989, 23–4) points out, we can only say that a person "acts so as to maximize utility, as long as we keep in mind that this is nothing but a convenient way of saying that he does what he most prefers. There is no implication of hedonism."

6 RATIONAL DESIGN THEORY

Some international relations scholars have adapted rational choice methods to explain why states have created international institutions—including treaties and other rules—in particular forms. Proponents of "rational design theory," including Barbara Koremenos, Charles Lipson, and Duncan Snidal (2001, 762), argue that the design of international institutions is the result of "rational, purposive inter- actions among states and other international actors to solve specific problems." This rationality is "forward looking as states use diplomacy and conferences to select institutional features to further their individual and collective goals, both by creating new institutions and modifying existing ones" (Koremenos, Lipson, and Snidal 2001, 766).

Although Koremenos et al. do not claim that all institutional change is the prod- uct of conscious design, they consider it the "overriding mechanism guiding the development of international institutions" (Koremenos, Lipson, and Snidal 2001, 766–7). They identify five key dimensions in which institutions vary—membership, scope of issues covered, degree of centralization, rules for controlling the institu- tion, flexibility of arrangements—and, on this basis, make a series of conjectures, such as "restrictive membership increases with the severity of the enforcement problem" (Koremenos, Lipson, and Snidal 2001, 783) and "flexibility increases with uncertainty about the state of the world" (Koremenos, Lipson, and Snidal 2001, 793).

Although rational design theory offers important insights, its proponents have so far paid little attention to the ways in which states might seek strategically to outmaneuver, manipulate, or co-opt each other when designing institutions. Since the creation of institutions is a political process, competitive behavior al- most certainly takes place. In addition, Alexander Wendt (2001, 1025–6) suggests that "normative logics" could compete with rational explanations of institutional design, for instance, by "supplying desiderata for institutions that make little sense on consequentialist grounds," such as the norms of universal membership and democratic control that operate in many international institutions. Logics of appro- priateness may complicate things further by "taking design options that might be instrumentally attractive off the table as 'normative prohibitions', and by affecting the modalities used to design institutions, thus rendering them historically specific" (Wendt 2001, 1026). These latter considerations would seem particularly relevant when the institutions in question are rules of international law.

7 CONSTRUCTIVISM

Led by Wendt and Friedrich Kratochwil, another group of international relations scholars developed an approach known as "constructivism" (Kratochwil 1989; Wendt 1995; 1999). As Christian Reus-Smit (2004, 3) explains, they argue:

International politics, like all politics, is an inherently social activity. Through politics states and other actors constitute their social and material lives, determining not only "who gets what when and how", but also who will be accepted as a legitimate actor and what will pass as rightful conduct. International politics takes place within a framework of rules and norms, and states and other actors define and redefine these understandings through their discursive practices.

A number of scholars at the interface between international law and international relations have seized upon constructivist approaches—for instance, by considering how evolving identities feed into the formation and content of rules. Constructivist approaches are well suited to explaining morally infused developments such as the Ottawa Landmines Convention (Price 1998), or those forms of "soft law" that do not involve binding obligations (Brunnée and Toope 1997; Abbott and Snidal 2000).

Richard Price (1997) has traced the development of the prohibition on chemical weapons from the nineteenth century. These weapons came to be thought of differently from other equally or even more destructive weapons and gradually attracted a unique moral opprobrium that eventually led to a "taboo." Price (1997, 7–8) argues that this development must be understood from a "genealogical" perspective that sees any moral structure as rooted in a "marriage of chance occurrences, fortuitous connections, and reinterpretations." Crucial elements included an early linkage between the ban on chemical weapons and a broader discourse on "civilization," the absence of any recourse to such weapons against civilians in the First World War (which prevented societies from "getting used to" them), and an "overzealous" postwar lobbying effort by chemical companies that "crystallized the public's attention on chemical weapons as a special threat to civilians about which something had to be done" (Price 1997, 12).

Ellen Lutz and Kathryn Sikkink (2001) have applied a similar approach to the spread of human rights in Latin America. The origins of many international rules are found, "not solely in preexisting state or societal interests but in strongly held principled ideas (ideas about right and wrong)." These ideas play a central role in shaping a state's perceptions of its identity and interests, and therefore its policies. Lutz and Sikkink (2001, 5–6) regard the international system as a "society" that includes nonstate actors that "may have transnational identities and overlapping loyalties." Along with state actors, they bring political pressure to bear, express community norms, and confer collective legitimacy through a variety of "vehicles," including international law. Legal standards are both consequences and causes within this complex social world.

The constructivist movement is especially relevant to those areas where shared conceptions are clearly essential to, and wrapped up with, rules and other normative structures. It is difficult to explain *opinio juris*, the subjective element of customary international law, without recourse to concepts akin to constructivist thought (Haggenmacher 1986; Byers 1999). The same is true of international humanitarian law, which is informed by the "Martens Clause" and its reference to the "requirements of the public conscience" (Skordas 2003, 317).

Again, as Warner (1998, 323) explains:

Today we are witnessing a movement in IR theory toward social constructivism only because the rationalist position took International Relations away from any historical or sociological grounding. International Relations is going back to international relations. However, international law never left international relations since one of its main sources—if not the main source—is customary practice. International law is by its very nature situated within the practices of international relations since it describes and prescribes norms, rules, and procedures that are crystallising or emerging from social practice.

Some constructivists have begun to consider how international law "feeds back" into politics "through its discourse of institutional autonomy, language and practice of justification, multilateral form of legislation, and structure of obligation" (Reus-Smit 2004, 5). Nicholas Wheeler examines the role played by international humanitarian law in the targeting decisions taken during the 1999 Kosovo War. He explains how the North Atlantic Treaty Organization (NATO) felt compelled to limit and justify its actions in accordance with the expectations of domestic and international public opinion. And "it was only possible to have a conversation between NATO and its critics because each side shared a common normative language that constituted the givens of the legal discourse" (Wheeler 2004).

8 RATIONALISM AND CONSTRUCTIVISM CONVERGE

Recently, some scholars have blended rationalism and constructivism, on the basis that the explanatory power of the two approaches is complementary. Kenneth Abbott and Snidal (2002, S142) argue that "international law and legal institutions depend on the deeply intertwined interaction of 'values' and 'interests'" and that "normative and rationalist accounts must therefore be joined to understand the creation and impact of legalized arrangements." Moreover, values and interests "become ever more tightly intertwined as legalization deepens," with the consequence that the two motivations are difficult to discern separately "in highly developed legal arrangements." This leads Abbott and Snidal (2002, S143) to focus on the "creation and development of international legal arrangements" with a view to providing a "clearer window into the underlying motivations for legalization, while also offering insights into the operations of legal regimes." They examine the creation of the 1997 OECD Anti-Bribery Convention and find that changing attitudes toward corruption combined with—and were deliberately promoted by—unilateral US action and civil society activism. This complex of factors led to the achievement of the strongest possible outcome: a multilateral treaty requiring criminalization of corruption in the domestic laws of ratifying states.

Caroline Fehl (2004, 360) combines rationalist and constructivist approaches when explaining the development of the International Criminal Court (ICC):

From a rationalist point of view, the ICC's establishment can be explained with a cooperation problem in criminal justice among national courts, and with the high costs of existing UN tribunals. The first argument can be "deepened" by a constructivist analysis of normative developments in the field of human rights that explain the consensual *identification* of the problem in international criminal justice by the international community. The second argument can be complemented by an alternative constructivist explanation that focuses on legitimacy deficits of UN tribunals. Regarding institutional design, hypotheses put forth by rational design theory help explain the crucial institutional design tradeoff between an independent court and US support that the participants of the Rome Conference faced. Yet a constructivist argument—emphasizing the role of "norm entrepreneurs" and international norms of treaty-making—is a necessary complement that explains which particular point was eventually picked on this tradeoff curve.

Keohane (2002, S314) now expresses a preference for "rational choice theories that are embedded in a rich contextual and historical analysis and that take into account both strategic calculations and other relevant conditions." A deeper and broader consideration, he argues, better enables us to explain the behavior of "value activists" as well as the role of socially constructed "understandings of reality"—such as the fact that only some pieces of paper carry monetary value. He concludes: "The common knowledge produced by social processes provides a point of complementarity between constructivist thinking, which seeks to explain common knowledge or common conjectures, and game [i.e. rational choice] theory, which relies on it to solve games of strategic interaction" (Keohane 2002, S316).

But why limit the theoretical synthesis to rationalism and constructivism? Other approaches, such as bureaucratic politics and critical legal studies, may at times provide explanatory value. Abbott (2004–5, 27–8), for one, has begun to extend his theoretical reach, arguing that a "richer institutionalism" is needed, one that "brings to bear liberal insights into the role of NSAs [nonstate actors], government agencies and domestic politics, constructivist insights into the role of values, norms and identities, and processes such as shaming, persuasion and socialization, and realist (and other) insights into the role of power."

Peter Katzenstein and Nobuo Okawara advocate an analytically "eclectic" approach that is open to drawing from any variety of theories. They reject "the privileging of parsimony that has become the hallmark of paradigmatic debates," on the basis that:

Strict formulations of realism, liberalism, and constructivism sacrifice explanatory power in the interest of analytical purity. Yet in understanding political problems, we typically need to weigh the causal importance of different types of factors, for example, material and ideal, international and domestic. Eclectic theorizing, not the insistence on received paradigms, helps us understand inherently complex social and political processes.

(Katzenstein and Okawara 2001–2, 167; see also Katzenstein and Rudra Sil, this volume)

With respect to international law, the key point is that there is no a priori relationship between structure and agent, or the material and ideational. In some instances, law might be influencing politics; in other instances, politics might be influencing law. In most instances, they are probably influencing each other, often in intensely complex ways.

For instance, an eclectic approach may help to redress the fact that some of the scholars who have applied constructivist approaches to international law have failed to consider whether ideational factors are ever deliberately deployed and manipulated by *state* actors. In other words, there has been relatively little inquiry into whether, and how, rules and other normative structures might strategically be "constructed" through a combination of state power, principled persuasion, and moral suasion. Which raises the question: Are the social, nonrationalist elements of international relations—the changing identities, interests, and shared understandings described by constructivists—any more immune to political manipulation than those elements of international relations traditionally examined by rationalists? And if so, to what degree?

Jutta Brunnée and Stephen Toope (2000, 65) draw on constructivism to advance an "interactional theory of international law" whereby "law is constructed through rhetorical activity producing increasingly influential mutual expectations or shared understandings of actors." Law is "persuasive" when "it is viewed as legitimate, largely in terms of internal process values, and when, as a result of the existence of basic social understandings, it can call upon reasoned argument, particularly analogy, to justify its processes and its broad substantive ends, thereby creating shared rhetorical knowledge" (Brunnée and Toope 2000, 65). Their work is remarkably optimistic: "Although built in the spirit of aspiration, law acts in shaping human conduct partly through a morality of duty. The primary test for the existence of law is not in hierarchy or in sources, but in fidelity to internal values and rhetorical practices and thick acceptances of reasons that make law—and respect for law—possible" (2000, 69).

Brunnée and Toope regard the roots of international law as largely distinct from, and uninfluenced by, state power. Indeed Toope (2003), in a sole-authored essay, argues that constructivist elements are so significant that they might prevent *any* state from "persistently objecting" to (and thus avoiding the obligations imposed by) a new rule of customary international law. Brunnée and Toope thus fail to address what Wayne Sandholtz and Alec Stone Sweet (2004, 242) identify as the "basic epistemological question" raised by constructivist approaches: "pursuant to some observable alteration of the institutional environment, is a given, stable shift in the observable behaviour of any actor or set of actors best explained by (1) a change in the actors' preferences or identities, or (2) a change in actors' strategies (with preferences fixed)?"

Nearly three decades ago, Brigitte Stern (1981, 479) argued that *opinio juris* involves two kinds of will, depending on each individual state's "position of power within the international order." Some states will feel bound because they freely consented to be, while other states "will feel bound because they cannot not want to be, because the rule is imposed upon them;" as a result, "the customary international rule is the one which is considered to be such by the will of those states which are able to impose their point of view." Stern (1981, 479) concluded that *opinio juris* "thus represents the dominant ideology of international society, taken up by all, even though it may be wanted by some and endured by others." If her analysis is correct, and applies to other shared conceptions, perspectives, and identities, some constructivists might be overlooking an important way in which state power influences international law.

To be fair, constructivists are careful not to claim a comprehensive explanation, and Stern's analysis works only because it explores the role of power within a context that would today be described as constructivist. My point is simply that, when dealing with international law, the constructivist ambit requires broadening, deepening, and a degree of disillusioning.

9 ORIGINS OF OBLIGATION

Some international relations scholars have broadened the ambit by probing the deepest foundations of international law. Shirley Scott (2004–5, 49) locates "the power of international law in an interrelated set of assumptions regarding the nature of international law" (see also Scott 1994). In this approach, which she labels "international law as ideology", Scott draws "on the proposition that within every socio-political structure of power there is one principle or small set of interrelated principles, which can be referred to as an ideology, integral to the distribution of power." This set of ideas "plays a key role within that socio-political structure, stabilizing the set of power relations, defining who is a member of that socio-political order, and why those who are not are not." Scott (2004–5, 54) argues that international law derives its political power from a core idea: "that international law is ultimately distinguishable from, and superior to, politics. This image of international law is conveyed by legal positivist writing, which eschews arguments based on philosophy, theology, science, or morality in favour of an argument founded on the contents of the formal sources of international law."

Reus-Smit (2003, 591) considers how international law is deeply embedded in its social context. He acknowledges that states comply with international rules for a number of reasons, including self-interest, concerns for reputation and therefore their capacity to pursue their interests in other issue areas, and an increasing number of formal sanctioning mechanisms. At the same time:

> Most states recognize an obligation to observe the rules of international law; that is, they consider it right to comply with those rules and norms deemed legal . . . This sense of obligation is a crucial factor in explaining both the attraction of international law as a regulatory institution, as well as the lengths some states will go to avoid legal entanglements.
>
> (Reus-Smit 2003, 592)

Rationalist assumptions may help explain why states take on legal obligations, but they "tell us little about the deeper question of why states regard legal rules as obligating." The problem, Reus-Smit (2003, 592) explains, is one of "interiority," which arises "when the source of obligation is located within an aspect of a particular normative system, but where the theory in question lacks the theoretical recourses to account for the existence or legitimacy of the system as a whole." In response, he proposes an "interstitial" conception that "locates politics at the intersections of idiographic, purposive, ethical and instrumental forms of reason and action" and thus "provides a window on why states and other actors attach legitimacy to particular institutional forms, including the modern system of international law." This approach "suggests that a satisfactory account of international legal obligation must ultimately be historical-sociological in nature" (Reus-Smit 2003, 594). This reinforces what international lawyers have insisted for centuries—namely, that rules have a specificity that distinguishes them from other, nonlegal factors in international affairs.

10 INTERNATIONAL LAWMAKING

International lawmaking is a near-constant activity, partly because of what Sandholtz and Stone Sweet (2004, 258) refer to as the "cycle of normative change:"

In a given normative structure, actions trigger disputes. Argument ensues, grounded in analogies with previous cases. The outcome of these discourses (which also include the deployment of power) modify the rules, whether by making them stronger or weaker, clearer or more ambiguous. The cycle returns to its starting point, the normative structure, but the normative structure has changed. The altered norms establish the context for subsequent actions, disputes, and discourses.

As a result, whenever states (and nonstate actors) engage in action (or inaction in the face of action by others), they probably consider the consequences for making, changing, strengthening, or weakening rules of international law.

Abbott and Snidal (2002, S143) recognize the strategic potential inherent in decisions about lawmaking: "Actors who seek or resist international legalization do so because they have an understanding of how international law and legal institutions affect behavior. Anticipation of these effects shapes both actors' political strategies and the particular forms of legalization they seek." And a little later: "The anticorruption case is particularly instructive in demonstrating that values and interests are not simply motivations for individual actors but also have an important impact on strategies chosen in the process of legalization and on the design of legal regimes" (Abbott and Snidal 2002, S144).

When we combine an appreciation of the role played by constructed identities and shared understandings with an awareness that these social aspects are themselves to some degree political, the result is a complexity of power, normative structures, identities, interests, and understandings that, when it undergoes change, does so in a manner that is contingent and therefore susceptible to deliberate manipulation.

Those who deliberately seek to make and change international law are engaged in a "game" that is deeply embedded in the existing international legal system. As David Wippman (2004, 158–9) has recognized:

The establishment of new legal rules and judicial bodies does not take place in a vacuum, where everything is up for bargaining and all outcomes are controlled by the distribution of power among the protagonists. Instead, law-making takes place against a backdrop of existing legal norms and institutions, which condition and limit the range of options viewed by the participants in the process as possible, and which simultaneously shape the process itself.

International actors make strategic moves based upon their understanding of the existing legal system's constraining and facilitating effects, whether existing or potential. For example, a putative rule in one area of international law might be framed in such a way as to enable the drawing of analogies with existing rules elsewhere. New rules of customary international law might be advanced by either underclaiming or overclaiming, in order to engage the principle of reciprocity and thus generate more widespread support (Byers 1999, 88–105). Sometimes, lawmakers will invoke concepts of legitimacy and fairness—and advance putative rules calibrated to connect with them—knowing that the international legal system is grounded, at least to some degree, on deeply rooted shared understandings of justice (Anghie 2004, 232–3).

Although often highly resistant to change, the preexisting rules, institutions, and understandings are not themselves immutable. And so, sophisticated, strategically oriented international actors will sometimes seek to modify the "rules of the game." The mutability of existing rules, institutions, and associated understandings and their importance to efforts at constructing new rules mean that strategic thinking about international lawmaking cannot easily be analogized to a game of billiards or chess, at least not unless one considers the design of the table or board to itself be part of the game, and the game itself, as well as the preferences of the players, to be constantly undergoing (or at least open to) change.

Complicating things further is the fact that different motivations propel the individuals who strategize on behalf of states. Each and every foreign ministry lawyer will have multiple interests and identities, serving multiple clients (foreign minister, government, state, the international community) and being part of a tightly knit epistemic community with its own professional language, shared understandings, rewards, and sanctions, both international *and* national (Schachter 1977). Strategic thinking about lawmaking is a game that defies simple explanations: Playing it well requires not only knowledge and thought but also an ongoing adaptability—a "feel for the game." Soccer, with all of its innovation and fluidity, is perhaps the best—though still an inadequate—sporting metaphor.

Martin Hollis and Steve Smith (1990, 179) have argued that efforts at explaining international relations frequently encounter a tension between "individualism" and "holism." Individualism lends itself to "self-contained" games such as chess or life in a monastery, where "all motives could be read off in terms of the proper conduct of the game." Holism, on the other hand, lends itself to a view of international relations as a "socially constructed" game. Nearly two decades ago, they took the view that "international anarchy remains too firmly the starting point of the international game for an analogy with fully constituted and self-contained games to be plausible" (Hollis and Smith 1990, 179–80). Yet they agreed that "interesting similarities" existed:

Unless some kind of international society had been constructed, there could be no United Nations, with its Assembly and its fragile but often effective agencies. The more the constructed arena of international diplomacy matters for what nations are enabled and constrained to do, the more it is worth thinking of the arena as a place where Wittgensteinian games are played. (1990, 179–80)

Some areas of international relations are more socially constructed than others. The international legal system is one such area, and today, in the early twenty-first century, it would seem to have acquired sufficient normative depth and breadth to provide for precisely this kind of socially constructed game.

But again, explaining how such a complex game actually works requires recourse to a variety of theoretical approaches. Some strategic decisions, such as those between different lawmaking forums, mechanisms, and types of legal instruments, are readily amenable to rational choice theory. Others, such as the allocation of decisional powers to an independent court or tribunal, or recourse to preexisting rules and institutions as analogies or models, might best be explained through insights drawn from institutionalism. Yet further decisions, such as the deliberate invocation of shared concepts of justice and legitimacy, are usefully seen through the lens of constructivism. The diversity of tools and the complex interaction of law and politics involved in international lawmaking make this an area that requires an "eclectic" approach to theory that is interdisciplinary both across *and* within disciplines.

Making an "eclectic" approach work here will not be easy, but the rewards are potentially great. Stanley Hoffmann (1963, 33) certainly thought so, more than four decades ago: "Since every Power wants to turn its interests, ideas and gains into law, a study of the 'legal strategies' of the various units, i.e., of what kinds of norms they try to promote, and through what techniques, may be as fruitful for the political scientist as a study of more purely diplomatic, military or economic strategies." After decades of effort, international law and international relations scholars have only scratched the surface of the rich interface between their disciplines. There is much work to be done.

References

ABBOTT, K. 2004–5. Toward a richer institutionalism for international law and policy. *Journal of International Law and International Relations*, 1: 9–34.

—— and SNIDAL, D. 2000. Hard and soft law in international governance. *International Organization*, 54: 421–56.

—— —— 2002. Values and interests: international legalization in the fight against corruption. *Journal of Legal Studies*, 31: S141–78.

AGO, R. 1984. Positivism. Pp. 385–93 in *Encyclopedia of Public International Law*, vol. vii, ed. R. Bernhardt. Amsterdam: North-Holland.

ALVAREZ, J. 2001. Do liberal states behave better? A critique of Slaughter's liberal theory. *European Journal of International Law*, 12: 183–246.

ANGHIE, A. 2004. International financial institutions. Pp. 217–37 in Reus-Smit 2004.

BILDER, R. 1962. The office of the legal adviser: the state department lawyer and foreign affairs. *American Journal of International Law*, 56: 633–84.

BOYLE, F. 1985. *World Politics and International Law*. Durham, NC: Duke University Press.

BRUNNÉE, J., and TOOPE, S. 1997. Environmental security and freshwater resources: ecosystem regime building. *American Journal of International Law*, 91: 26–59.

—— —— 2000. International law and constructivism: elements of an interactional theory of international law. *Columbia Journal of Transnational Law*, 39: 19–74.

BYERS, M. 1999. *Custom, Power and the Power of Rules: International Relations and Customary International Law*. Cambridge: Cambridge University Press.

CARR, E. H. 1946. *The Twenty Years' Crisis, 1919–1939: An Introduction to the Study of International Relations*. London: Macmillan.

CHAYES, A. 1974. *The Cuban Missile Crisis*. London: Oxford University Press.

ELSTER, J. 1989. *Nuts and Bolts for the Social Sciences*. Cambridge: Cambridge University Press.

FEHL, C. 2004. Explaining the International Criminal Court: a "practice test" for rationalist and constructivist approaches. *European Journal of International Relations*, 10: 357–94.

GOLDSMITH, J., and POSNER, E. 1999. A theory of customary international law. *University of Chicago Law Review*, 66: 1113–77.

—————— 2005. *The Limits of International Law*. Oxford: Oxford University Press.

GUZMAN, A. 1998. Why LDCs sign treaties that hurt them: explaining the popularity of bilateral investment treaties. *Virginia Journal of International Law*, 38: 639–88.

—— 2002. A compliance-based theory of international law. *California Law Review*, 90: 1823–87.

HAGGENMACHER, P. 1986. La doctrine des deux éléments du droit coutumier dans la pratique de la cour internationale. *Revue générale de droit international public*, 90: 5–125.

HOFFMANN, S. 1963. The study of international law and the theory of international relations. *American Society of International Law Proceedings*, 57: 26–35.

HOLLIS, M., and SMITH, S. 1990. *Explaining and Understanding International Relations*. Oxford: Clarendon Press.

KATZENSTEIN, P., and OKAWARA, N. 2001–2. Japan, Asian-Pacific Security, and the case for analytical eclecticism. *International Security*, 26: 153–85.

KEOHANE, R. O. 1988. International institutions: two approaches. *International Studies Quarterly*, 32: 379–96.

—— 1989. Neoliberal institutionalism: a perspective on world politics. Pp. 1–20 in *International Institutions and State Power*, R. O. Keohane. Boulder, Colo.: Westview.

—— 1997. International relations and international law: two optics. *Harvard International Law Journal*, 38: 487–502.

—— 2002. Rational choice theory and international law: insights and limitations. *Journal of Legal Studies*, 31: S307–19.

KLABBERS, J. 2004–5. The relative autonomy of international law or the forgotten politics of interdisciplinarity. *Journal of International Law and International Relations*, 1: 35–48.

KOREMENOS, B., LIPSON, C., and SNIDAL, D. 2001. The rational design of international institutions. *International Organization*, 55: 761–99.

KOSKENNIEMI, M. 2000. Carl Schmitt, Hans Morgenthau, and the image of law in international relations. Pp. 17–34 in *The Role of Law in International Politics*, ed. M. Byers. Oxford: Oxford University Press.

KRASNER, S. 1983. Structural causes and regime consequences: regimes as intervening variables. Pp. 1–22 in *International Regimes*, ed. S. Krasner. Ithaca, NY: Cornell University Press.

KRATOCHWIL, F. 1989. *Rules, Norms, and Decisions: On the Conditions of Practical and Legal Reasoning in International Relations and Domestic Affairs*. Cambridge: Cambridge University Press.

LUTZ, E., and SIKKINK, K. 2001. The justice cascade: the evolution and impact of foreign human rights trials in Latin America. *Chicago Journal of International Law*, 2: 1–34.

McDougal, M. 1955. The hydrogen bomb tests and the international law of the sea. *American Journal of International Law*, 49: 356–61.

Marks, S. 2000. *The Riddle of All Constitutions: International Law, Democracy, and the Critique of Ideology*. Oxford: Oxford University Press.

Mills, A., and Stephens, T. 2005. Challenging the role of judges in Slaughter's liberal theory of international law. *Leiden Journal of International Law*, 18: 1–30.

Moravcsik, A. 1997. Taking preferences seriously: a liberal theory of international politics. *International Organization*, 51: 513–53.

—— 2000. The origins of human rights regimes: democratic delegation in postwar Europe. *International Organization*, 54: 217–52.

Price, R. 1997. *The Chemical Weapons Taboo*. Ithaca, NY: Cornell University Press.

—— 1998. Reversing the gun sights: transnational civil society targets land mines. *International Organization*, 52: 613–44.

Reisman, M. 1992. The view from the New Haven School of International Law. *American Society of International Law Proceedings*, 86: 118–24.

Reus-Smit, C. 2003. Politics and international legal obligation. *European Journal of International Relations*, 9: 591–625.

—— (ed.) 2004. *The Politics of International Law*. Cambridge: Cambridge University Press.

Sandholtz, W., and Stone Sweet, A. 2004. Law, politics, and international governance. Pp. 238–71 in Reus-Smit 2004.

Schachter, O. 1977. The invisible college of international lawyers. *Northwestern University Law Review*, 72: 217–26.

Scott, S. 1994. International law as ideology: theorizing the relationship between international law and international politics. *European Journal of International Law*, 5: 313–27.

—— 2004–5. Identifying the source and nature of a state's political obligation towards international law. *Journal of International Law and International Relations*, 1: 49–60.

Setear, J. 1996. An iterative perspective on treaties: a synthesis of international relations theory and international law. *Harvard International Law Journal*, 37: 139–229.

Simpson, G. 2001. Two liberalisms. *European Journal of International Law*, 12: 537–71.

Skordas, A. 2003. Hegemonic custom? Pp. 317–47 in *United States Hegemony and the Foundations of International Law*, ed. M. Byers and G. Nolte. Cambridge: Cambridge University Press.

Slaughter, A.-M. 1997. The real new world order. *Foreign Affairs*, 76: 183–97.

—— 2000. Governing the global economy through government networks. Pp. 177–206 in *The Role of Law in International Politics*, ed. M. Byers. Oxford: Oxford University Press.

—— 2004. *A New World Order*. Princeton, NJ: Princeton University Press.

Slaughter Burley, A.-M. 1993. International law and international relations theory: a dual agenda. *American Journal of International Law*, 87: 205–39.

Stern, B. 1981. La coutume au coeur du droit international. Pp. 479–99 in *Mélanges offerts à Paul Reuter*, B. Stern. Paris: Pedone. Approved English translation in *Duke Journal of Comparative and International Law*, 11 (2001): 89–109.

Toope, S. 2003. Powerful but unpersuasive? The role of the USA in the evolution of customary international law. Pp. 287–316 in *United States Hegemony and the Foundations of International Law*, ed. M. Byers and G. Nolte. Cambridge: Cambridge University Press.

Warner, D. 1998. The nuclear weapons decision by the International Court of Justice: locating the *raison* behind *raison d'état*. *Millennium: Journal of International Studies*, 27: 299–324.

WENDT, A. 1995. Constructing international politics. *International Security*, 20: 71–81.

—— 1999. *Social Theory of International Politics*. Cambridge: Cambridge University Press.

—— 2001. Driving with the rearview mirror: on the rational science of institutional design. *International Organization*, 55: 1019–49.

WHEELER, N. 2004. The Kosovo bombing campaign. Pp. 189–216 in Reus-Smit 2004.

WIPPMAN, D. 2004. The International Criminal Court. Pp. 151–88 in Reus-Smit 2004.

YOUNG, O. 1989. *International Cooperation: Building Regimes for Natural Resources and the Environment*. Ithaca, NY: Cornell University Press.

PART VI

··

THE SCHOLAR
AND THE
POLICY-MAKER

··

CHAPTER 36

SCHOLARSHIP AND POLICY-MAKING: WHO SPEAKS TRUTH TO WHOM?

HENRY R. NAU

Is the true test of academic scholarship whether it works in the policy-making world? The quick answer is no. On the other hand, does academic scholarship "speak truth to power" and pass final judgment on policy-making, as traditional Quaker thought expressed it? Again the quick answer is no. Too many academics comfort themselves with the thought that academic research provides the ultimate test or critique of policy decisions. This position is not only self-serving; it is damaging to good scholarship because it obscures the social and historical context of all scholarship. New academic ideas have come out of public service as often as academic ideas have influenced policy-making. Think of the postwar generation of foreign policy scholars, economists and political scientists, who served in the US and British governments during the Second World War and dominated academic scholarship after it. On the other hand, remember the famous comment of John Maynard Keynes, the British economist and government negotiator, that "practical men, who believe themselves to be quite exempt from any intellectual influences, are usually the slaves of some defunct economist" (Keynes 1936, 383). Scholarship and statesmanship, theory and practice, the academy and policy worlds, while they are different, are nevertheless joined at the hip, and neither can succeed, even within its own realm, without the other.

The split between scholarship and statesmanship has grown wider since the Second World War. Today it is rare, if not inconceivable, that leading academics incubate in government service, as many postwar scholars did, or that top government officials lead the academy, as Woodrow Wilson did as president of Princeton University. John F. Kennedy was not an academic, but his administration may have represented the high-water mark of happy intercourse between scholars and government. Thereafter, Vietnam, an era of conservative rather than liberal political leaders in both the presidency and Congress (even Democratic presidents, such as Jimmy Carter and Bill Clinton, were more centrist than liberal), and a more competitive and partisan political process soured the relationship. Most academics, who are liberal (see below), deplore the conservative turn in American politics, and recent administrations, which are conservative, spurn the advice of liberal academics in favor of think tanks and other policy institutes that ask questions the academy overlooks.[1]

The divorce between scholarship and policy-making has gone too far.[2] In what follows, I make three arguments that the two professions in fact depend upon one another. First, neither profession can make a superior claim to social knowledge. Social knowledge is not primarily objective such that scholars speak truth to power, nor is it primarily intersubjective such that consensus or policy success dictates truth. Rather social knowledge is primarily evolutionary. It is a product of the interaction between the study of policy and the making of policy, which leads over time to social change in directions that scholars discern and dispute. Secondly, while scholars and policy-makers pursue different types of knowledge, both types are necessary to achieve progress, especially when social knowledge is understood as evolutionary. Scholars seek to know *why* events occur and pursue general explanations that abstract from the policy process. Policy-makers seek to know *how* events occur and pursue knowledge specific to the policy process. Because the social world, unlike the natural world, is created as well as discovered, both scholarship and policy-makers make essential contributions to knowledge. Thirdly, both scholars and policy-makers make political commitments in pursuing their respective tasks. Scholars choose academic over practical pursuits for, among other things, the desire to change the world indirectly through the knowledge they develop; and policy-makers forsake political detachment for partisan politics for, among other things, the chance to change the world directly and make history. The types of political commitment differ, but the consequences do not. Academics who evaluate history have political preferences over outcomes. And policy-makers who

---

[1]   On the alienation of the academy from conservative politics, see Tickner (2006). On the marginalization of conservatives in academe, see Bauerlein (2006).

[2]   Other scholars have made the same point. See Jentleson (2002) and Anderson (2003).

make history have political stakes in outcomes. Each needs the other to balance judgments. Social knowledge, which is evolutionary, is the product of an inevitable partnership between scholarship and policy-making.

1 NATURE OF TRUTH AND KNOWLEDGE

If the academic world has the obligation to speak truth to power, we have to ask, as the Roman governor Herod once did, what is truth? Is knowledge true or is it just not false? And if it is just not false, is it relative? Is it, in short, a product of the selective questions we ask and explore in a specific community at a given time and place, and thus not only likely but destined to change in a different community, time, and place? Take even the natural science of physics. Newtonian mechanics is not false for large-scale planetary phenomena. Quantum mechanics is not false for subatomic particle phenomena. But the worlds these two theories posit are completely incompatible versions of reality. One is based on fixed bodies in time and space, the other on probabilities and relative time and space. Maybe a third version of reality embraces both. Albert Einstein worked most of his life, unsuccessfully, to find a "unified" field theory. String theory, some scientists believe, may be the answer. But even if string theory succeeds, it may not account for further anomalies in the future. Meanwhile, we do not know what the true version of the universe is, just which versions are not false.

Let us look at three different understandings of truth: objective, subjective, and evolutionary.[3]

Most academics, especially social and political scientists, cling to the notion that scholarship is or should strive to be objective. As Gabriel Almond (1990, 29) expresses it, "we need to have a deep-rooted and unshakable firmness in our commitment to the search for objectivity." This commitment to objectivity means that social scientists, like many natural scientists such as Einstein, share the conviction that God does not roll dice. The social like the physical world must be orderly, and the purpose of the academy is to discover that order. If this is so, the academic world has much to teach the policy world. As Hans Morgenthau (1970, 17) tells us during his bitter confrontation with the US government over

---

[3] I vastly oversimplify here. All understandings of truth combine the three characteristics, but they nonetheless differ in emphasis. Positivists emphasize objectivity, constructivists and critical theorists intersubjectivity, and Marxist and other teleological versions of truth historical materialism and sociology. For helpful discussions, see Smith, Booth, and Zalewski (1996).

Vietnam, the academy not only can but "must...speak truth to power."[4] Because the academy in this view seeks objective truth, it stands above the policy community, which often manipulates truth as a means to political ends.[5] As Morgenthau (1970, 14, 5) adds, "the intellectual seeks truth; the politician, power..." and "power positions do not yield to arguments but only to superior power..." Eventually knowledge developed by the academy will bring the policy community and society into accord with the underlying order of the social and natural universe. This commitment to truth as objective is admirable, but it is also exceedingly ambitious and self-serving. It demeans policy-making and obscures the inherent uncertainty of truth.[6] And it is only one way of understanding the nature of truth.

In affirming his commitment to objectivity, Almond (1990, 29) rejects two alternative versions of truth, one subjective, the other evolutionary. As he sees it, "the critical and Marxist schools throw in the professional sponge." The critical or historicist school sees all knowledge constrained by social and historical circumstances. Knowledge is not objective but subjective or, more precisely, intersubjective. It is constructed by an epistemic community of scholars embedded in a particular social and historical period. It is not the product of the orderly nature of society that exists objectively across time and place. Rather it is contingent and relative. Thomas Kuhn (1970, 3), who studied *The Structure of Scientific Revolutions*, concluded that "an apparently arbitrary element, compounded of personal and historical accident, is always a formative ingredient of the beliefs espoused by a given scientific community at a given time" (Kuhn 1970, 3).

According to this view of truth, even the physical sciences cannot escape the social and political context of their time. The real world may still be objective, but we can never know it as such. We can know only if our inference or interpretation from observable data is consistent with the real world. We can know, in short, if our inference is not false but not if it is true. This is so because, as Kuhn (1970,

---

[4] In this book, Morgenthau recants his earlier view (1946, see further discussion above) that truth is in the eye of the observer and never tells us why the intellectual, as only one observer, suddenly acquires a special claim on truth.

[5] As Noam Chomsky (1967, 325), Morgenthau's ally on Vietnam, put it, "it is the responsibility of intellectuals to speak the truth and to expose lies." The proclivity of scholars to assume the mantle of "truth," even in a secular world of uncertain knowledge, is puzzling. As Edward Shils (1969, 41) tells us, it may come from the earliest origins of scholarship in the seminary: "the tradition of awesome respect and of serious striving for contact with the sacred...or the ultimate ground of thought and experience...[which] is perhaps the first, the most comprehensive and the most important tradition of the intellectuals."

[6] A popular contemporary primer on social science inquiry makes this commitment to objective knowledge but emphasizes its many assumptions and uncertainty: "we sidestep many issues in the philosophy of science...[and]...assume it is possible to have knowledge of the external world but that such knowledge is always uncertain" (King, Keohane, and Verba 1994, 6).

76) further tells us, "philosophers of science have repeatedly demonstrated that more than one theoretical construction can always be placed on a given collection of data." Thus the truth or theoretical perspective that prevails is a construction of social consensus, not an imprint of physical reality (Katzenstein 1996; Wendt 1999).

As some see it, this constructivist view of truth applies *a fortiori* to the social sciences, which not only work in epistemic communities like the natural sciences but study changing social and human conditions, not unchanging physical phenomena. Natural scientists cannot alter physical realities. Social scientists can alter social realities. Hedley Bull (1972, 263) captured this difference succinctly: "The student of politics is related to his subject matter not only as a subject to object but also as cause to effect."[7] The interventions of social scientists change their subject matter in a way physical scientists cannot. The Heisenberg principle in physics suggests that the attempt to locate a particle disturbs the particle, but it does not say that it causes the particle to behave differently in the future. By contrast, human subjects are both educable and creative. They absorb the knowledge developed by social scientists and change their behavior in unpredictable ways.

Is all truth then socially relative? If so, the academy itself is part of the policy process and cannot claim to speak truth to power. "The truth of the social sciences," Morgenthau (1946, 167) tells us before his confrontation with the US government, "is truth only under the particular perspective of the observer." Social context defines the arbitrary element (personal and historical accident, according to Kuhn) of academic research no less than that of policy-making. The academy is not neutral toward power but part of the social and political fabric that justifies and criticizes power. From this perspective, Morgenthau (1970, 434) called universities "gigantic and indispensable service stations for the powers-that-be, both public and private" (see also Parsons 1969). Now the academic world is demeaned. American political science serves American politics and social elites (Oren 2003, 5). As Kenneth Prewitt (2002, 6) put it in a study for the Social Science Research Council, "our claims to universal truths are, empirically, very much about the experience of this society in this historical period."

The Marxist school, however, suggests a third possibility. What if truth is embedded in history and unfolds as history progresses? Although knowledge is temporal, it evolves in ways that lead cumulatively to outcomes across historical periods. And because social knowledge involves creative human beings not just inanimate physical objects, policy-making and social action contribute to this evolution. Academics, like Karl Marx, discover historical patterns. But policy-makers, like

---

[7] Lisa Anderson (2003, 12) offers a similar formulation: "what social scientists study is shaped by their own imaginative construction..."

Vladimir Lenin, expedite or even create them. Now the question becomes: Toward what end or truth do these patterns evolve? Here social scientists are influenced by political preferences in ways that natural scientists are not (since the latter cannot change the outcomes of the natural world). Marx thought that the direction of history was toward communism. Western liberals think it is toward pluralism or democracy. Western conservatives, like Leo Strauss, think it is toward the more complete revelation of what is already known through classical wisdom (Melzer 2006). Theologians see the direction of history in eschatological terms such as the second coming. And modernists see it in terms of the development of a richer, more educated, and more technologically sophisticated world in which natural and social scientists learn progressively more about the universe they inhabit.[8]

If truth is evolutionary rather than objective or relative, the academy and policy community may be joined at the hip. Policy-makers create history, and history unfolds in directions that scholars discover and debate. Being in the policy arena, as Theodore Roosevelt urged, is a principal way to seek the truth. Sitting above or outside the policy process, as the academy might do under an objective understanding of truth, is no longer superior to policy-making. The two are complementary. Scholars discover and debate historical patterns, influenced by the social constraints and preferences of their scientific communities, while policy-makers shape events through more explicit partisan engagement.

Curiously, almost all American and Western social scientists buy into this notion of evolutionary knowledge, even when they insist that social knowledge is or should be objective.[9] They believe that the objective knowledge scholars discover can and should be used to create a better world—better meaning, in general, more prosperous, peaceful, and humane, if not democratic. Two paragraphs after he says that political science "cannot imply a political commitment to a particular course of action," Almond (1990, 29) writes: "we have made important contributions to an age-old, worldwide effort to bring the power of knowledge to bear on the tragic dilemmas of the world of politics." If applying knowledge to tragic world problems does not involve political engagement, what does? *Social science is not just about discovery; it is also about social change.* John Gunnell (2005, 608) makes the point emphatically: "the pursuit of science as well as the critique of that pursuit have [*sic*] never been disjoined from the search for the criteria and realization of democracy."

---

[8] Ernst Haas (1990, 190) offers an example of the modernist view: "I am persuaded that human endeavors, roughly after 1600, acquired a qualitatively new content…[and] that collective decisions intended to improve health, wealth, welfare, and peace became really practical. It took another two hundred years before they became commonplace."

[9] As Anderson (2003, 15) observes, "from the very outset, social science in the United States was justified by and celebrated for its…devotion to moral improvement and the liberal purposes so characteristic of American public policy."

2 RELATIONSHIP BETWEEN ACADEMIC AND POLICY KNOWLEDGE

If social knowledge is evolutionary and scholars and policy-makers both contribute to it, what is the type of knowledge each develops and how do these different types of knowledge relate to one another?

Scientists, it is said, seek laws to explain events, policy-makers leverage to shape them. Scientists want verification and proof to explain repetitive outcomes, policy-makers timely advice to achieve novel outcomes. In this sense the two groups use knowledge at opposite ends of the spectrum. Academics pursue *general* knowledge that goes beyond what is directly observed.[10] Policy-makers seek *specific* knowledge that helps them achieve what may have never been observed. For example, they confront the need to manage peace in a nuclear age and look for unfamiliar policies of deterrence that use force short of war.

For academics, as knowledge matures (or science becomes normal), laws and theories become more abstract and esoteric. Scholars are expected to publish in academic journals that interest a few specialists in their discipline rather than in policy journals that may catch the attention of policy-makers. Academic research is pulled away from the policy world.

Policy-makers, by contrast, have little use for abstract knowledge unless it helps them build policy consensus and meet policy needs. President Clinton, for example, drew on the theory of the democratic peace to establish the broad premises of his foreign policy, "democratic enlargement and economic engagement." But, when this policy overtaxed resources and weakened consensus, he pulled back—for example, from Somalia and Rwanda. Knowledge (assuming in this example that democratic peace qualifies as knowledge) is not enough; it has to be useful to policy-makers and, in a democracy, backed by majority support. As Alexander George (1993) tells us, the policy-maker needs information of a different kind—about substantive trade-offs necessary to gain consensus, side effects or opportunity costs of different policy decisions, and the risks and timing of policy decisions.

Scholarship cannot bend to politics, as academics see it. We do not take a vote on whether the sun rises (although the International Astronomical Union did vote in 2006 to disqualify Pluto as a planet—not, however, as a fact). But, as policy-makers see it, neither can politics just bend to science. If science enters the policy arena with proposals that are not subject to debate, it shrinks the questioning and freedom on which its own development depends. The science of global warming, for example, cannot dictate policy outcomes, because all knowledge is uncertain especially when

---

[10] Positivists work from observations to descriptive and causal inference, constructivists from narratives to constitutive and interpretative meanings.

it deals with creative human beings, democracies depend on persuading majorities, and no practical system has resources to cover all risks. On the other hand, politics is not immune to the consequences of nature. Storms happen whether we forecast and prepare for them or not.

Still predictable (academic) and practical (policy-making) knowledge depend upon one another in crucial ways. As Robert Rothstein (1972, 121) observes, "involvement with practical problems is *theoretically* fruitful." To use Kuhn's terms, practice spews up puzzles that confound normal science and spark new departures or revolutionary science. Engineers confront anomalies that natural scientists cannot explain. Policy-makers encounter real-world experiences that social scientists cannot explain. Practice sets limits on scholarly self-absorption.

On the other hand, experience and judgment are pure bias unless they are informed by theory and substantive knowledge (Renshon and Larson 2003). Policy-makers do not usually think of their cognitive skills in terms of theory, but they decide all the time what facts and policy options they can consider because they can never consider all the facts and policy options. The policy-maker needs some lens to define and choose a problem before he or she collects facts and evaluates them. Why is something a problem, why is it important, and what policy choices might affect it? Perspectives if not theories guide these policy choices.[11] As both Rothstein and George agree, academic knowledge is most useful and perhaps even essential in the diagnosis of policy problems. Policy knowledge or judgment may be more useful in choosing policy options.

3 POLITICAL CONSTRAINTS OF ACADEMIC AND POLICY KNOWLEDGE

If social knowledge is evolutionary, there is no socially unconstrained knowledge. Scholars are not detached and uncommitted, and policy-makers are not immune from the judgment of objective patterns of history discerned by a more detached scholarly community.

Think of all the ways in which a scholar is involved in politics, whether he or she ever has any direct connection with the governmental sector. As Gunnell pointed out, most of us are committed to democracy, a specific political ideology,

---

[11] Nau (2006) explores the role of theories in explaining historical as well as contemporary controversies among scholars and policy-makers, even when they consider the same facts.

because without it we would have less academic freedom. We choose a profession in education over business or religion, and not surprisingly a large majority of academics are sharply critical of religious beliefs and market economics (see Lipset 1996, ch. 6). We choose a particular discipline, in our case political science, which is clearly more engaged in politics than physics or medicine. We choose topics to study based on what we consider most important, influenced in considerable measure by our political preferences.[12] We create ideas that others use in politics, and thereby become partly responsible for the policies that flow from those ideas. Finally, we participate actively as citizens in partisan political activities, joining parties, contributing money to campaigns, advising candidates, and so on.

What is more, scholars are anything but neutral or balanced in their support of partisan activities. To be neutral, one might expect natural and social scientists to be registered as independents in the political process. Scholars could pursue their obligations as citizens but do so independently of partisan political organizations in their society. Short of that ideal, one might expect them to be balanced—that is, divide up equally across the relevant political parties in their society. However, the academic world in the United States is anything but independent or evenly divided between the two major parties. Democratic scholars outnumber Republican scholars by ratios of seven to one in the humanities and social sciences and to an even higher degree in the natural sciences (Tierney 2004; Young 2005).[13] The social science ratio is more than twice as lopsided as it was thirty years ago and is projected to increase further in the future because younger scholars being hired are more consistently Democratic than older ones retiring. Whatever the reasons for this lack of political diversity (self-selection, intentional or unintentional discrimination, and so on), the American academy cannot claim to be impartial toward partisan American politics.[14]

Remember that all these forms of political participation precede any active involvement in government. Since most scholars believe that good research requires as much detachment as possible from the policy world, one might expect them to be acutely aware of the partisan nature of their commitments as

[12] As Anderson (2003, 12) points out, "even the most disengaged technicians in the ranks of the social sciences exhibit the influence of the social world on them in their choice of research terrains and problems."

[13] In 2004 employees at the Universities of California and Harvard gave $19 to the John Kerry campaign for every $1 to the George W. Bush campaign.

[14] This is true of the US media as well, where over 85% of journalists are registered Democrats. As John Tierney points out, "the problem isn't so much the stories that appear in the media as the ones that no one thinks to do" (*New York Times*, Oct. 2005, 23). In the academy, few scholars ask how to use rather than regulate markets or how to strengthen individual self-reliance rather than community institutions, and as a consequence, conservative politicians turn to think tanks and other institutions for answers.

citizens. But, to be frank, few are or choose to be. Most simply contend that their partisan political activities, short of direct service in government, do not affect their scholarship. They can separate their politics from their research. They say to the public, in effect, "trust us." Within the scholarly fraternity, most of us do trust our colleagues because we know them and study their work carefully. But the public at large needs more than the slogan "trust us." At a minimum, scholars should engage in "political truth in academic advertising." We should declare and explain to the public what our political preferences are, so that readers and users of our knowledge can make a judgment for themselves as to our objectivity.[15]

Once scholars cross over and participate directly in the government sector, political attachments become more evident. Scholars lose their academic virginity. The reasons seem to be twofold. First, the scholar policy-maker gives up the commitment to listen to and criticize all policy choices. Relative to the detached atmosphere of the university, policy-making seeks to close off debate, narrow options, and overcome opposition. Partisanship facilitates rather than corrupts this process. By going through the scrutiny of elections and daily public debate, policy-makers earn the right to set an agenda and exclude certain assumptions and options. Scholars can criticize such partisanship, but they should also recognize that history cannot be made without it.

Secondly, when scholars go into government, they acquire a stake in the interpretation of the history they make. When they return to the academic world, they are not in the same position as their colleagues to evaluate that history. It is appropriate therefore to discount their self-interested analysis.[16] But it goes too far when scholars who have served at the highest levels in government are not welcomed back into the academic fold. This fate befell Democratic policy-making scholars such as McGeorge Bundy, Walter Rostow, and Zbigniew Brzezinski as well as Republican scholars such as Henry Kissinger and Jeane Kirkpatrick.[17] These individuals are still the same qualified scholars they were before they went into government service, and they bring back to the academic world exactly what it lacks, a better understanding of how partisanship shapes history and furthers social knowledge.

[15] Samuel Huntington (2004, xvii) provides a prototype of this kind of political honesty: "The motives of patriotism and of scholarship...may conflict. Recognizing this problem, I attempt to engage in as detached and thorough analysis of the evidence as I can, warning the reader that my selection and presentation of that evidence may well be influenced by my patriotic desire to find meaning and virtue in America's past and in its possible future."

[16] For this reason, I acknowledge explicitly in my book about the Reagan administration in which I served that "academic colleagues may argue that my ideas have lost some of their objectivity..." (Nau 1990, ix).

[17] One of the few exceptions was the historian Arthur Schlesinger, a policy adviser in the Kennedy administration, who after returning to academe wrote extensively and favorably about the administration he had served, for the most part with broad approval from his academic colleagues.

4 CONCLUSION

The relationship between scholarship and policy engagement depends on how one understands the nature of knowledge or truth, the relationship between different types of knowledge, and the political constraints that affect both scholarship and policy-making.

If knowledge is mostly objective, scholarship is the true test of policy-making. If it is mostly intersubjective, both activities are socially contingent, and neither speaks truth to the other. If knowledge is evolutionary, scholarship and policy-making share in the quest for truth. Scholarship discovers patterns that inform the actions and choices of policy-making, while policy-making encounters anomalies and creates unexpected historical outcomes. History evolves in cumulative directions, but since these directions are open to various interpretations, scholarship and practice are uniquely interdependent. Scholarship tells us what *can* be known by rigorous methods of scientific inquiry; policy-making tells us what *needs* to be known to influence the course of history.

If knowledge is evolutionary, we do not have to give up our commitments to politics (policy-making) or science (truth). Bull (1972, 262–3) offers a timeless synthesis:

I...would defend a posture of political objectivity or detachment, at least as a goal of our endeavours...But...there is, of course, no such thing as a "value-free" inquiry into International Relations or any other social subject. The most one can hope to do is to be aware of one's moral and political premises, to formulate them explicitly if one is employing arguments that derive from them, and (this above all) to be critical about them, to treat the investigation of moral and political premises as part of the subject...Nor should I wish to argue that commitment, in the sense of firm belief in certain moral and political goals, together with willingness to work for them...is incompatible with scholarly inquiry in the field of politics. One can, after all, be critical and open-minded about moral and political premises, and yet be able to reach certain conclusions and act on them. I should even argue that in some cases intense commitment to one side in a political conflict provides an insight into the character of the other side, which otherwise would not be achieved.

In the last sentence, Bull affirms the positive role of political commitment in policy-making, just as, in the first sentence, he affirms the positive role of detachment in social science scholarship. He calls for a happier coexistence of the academic and policy-maker. Above all, he warns scholars to be aware and critical of their moral and political premises and formulate them explicitly in their arguments. Too many scholars forget the uncertainties of their knowledge and speak too glibly about truth.[18] An academy so disproportionately committed to one side of the political spectrum, as it is in America, is not an impartial one. This political bias at

---

[18] Max Weber (1949, 54) noted this tendency in his time: "It is true that in our sciences, personal value-judgments have tended to influence scientific arguments without being explicitly admitted."

the very least should be questioned, and not dismissed as of little consequence for "objective" academic scholarship. As Bull (1972, 263) further observes, "a danger less easy to recognise [than where scholarly values have been subordinated to political ones] is the case where scholarly values are observed, and indeed great intellectual rigour may be displayed, yet within a moral and political framework that is left unquestioned."

REFERENCES

ALMOND, G. A., 1990. *A Discipline Divided: Schools and Sects in Political Science*. New York: Sage.

ANDERSON, L. 2003. *Pursuing Truth, Exercising Power: Social Science and Public Policy in the Twenty-First Century*. New York: Columbia University Press.

BAUERLEIN, M. 2006. How academe shortchanges conservative thinking. *Chronicle Review*, 53, 15 Dec.: B6.

BULL, H. 1972. International relations as an academic pursuit. *Australian Outlook*, 26: 251–65.

CHOMSKY, N. 1967. *American Power and the New Mandarins*. New York: Pantheon.

GEORGE, A. L. 1993. *Bridging the Gap: Theory and Practice in Foreign Policy*. Washington, DC: United States Institute of Peace Press.

GUNNELL, J. G. 2005. Political science on the cusp: recovering a discipline's past. *American Political Science Review*, 99: 597–609.

HAAS, E. B. 1990. *When Knowledge is Power: Three Models of Change in International Organizations*. Berkeley: University of California Press.

HUNTINGTON, S. 2004. *Who Are We? The Challenges to America's National Identity*. New York: Simon and Schuster.

JENTLESON, B. W. 2002. The need for praxis: bringing policy relevance back in. *International Security*, 26: 169–83.

KATZENSTEIN, P. (ed.) 1996. *The Culture of National Security: Norms and Identity in World Politics*. New York: Columbia University Press.

KEYNES, J. M. 1936. *The General Theory of Employment, Interest and Money*. London: Macmillan.

KING, G., KEOHANE, R. O., and VERBA, S. 1994. *Designing Social Inquiry: Scientific Inference in Qualitative Research*. Princeton, NJ: Princeton University Press.

KUHN, T. S. 1970. *The Structure of Scientific Revolutions*, 2nd enl. edn. Chicago: University of Chicago Press.

LIPSET, S. M. 1996. *American Exceptionalism: A Double-Edged Sword*. New York: W. W. Norton.

MELZER, A. M. 2006. Esotericism and the critique of historicism. *American Political Science Review*, 100: 279–95.

MORGENTHAU, H. J. 1946. *Scientific Man vs. Power Politics*. Chicago: University of Chicago Press.

——1970. *Truth and Power: Essays of a Decade, 1960–70*. New York: Praeger.

NAU, H. R. 1990. *The Myth of America's Decline: Leading the World Economy into the 1990s.* New York: Oxford University Press.

——2006. *Perspectives on International Relations: Power, Institutions, and Ideas.* Washington, DC: CQ Press.

OREN, I. 2003. *Our Enemies and US: America's Rivalries and the Making of Political Science.* Ithaca, NY: Cornell University Press.

PARSONS, T. 1969. "The intellectual:" a social role category. Pp. 3–25 in *On Intellectuals: Theoretical Studies, Case Studies*, ed. P. Rieff. New York: Doubleday.

PREWITT, K. 2002. The social science project: then, now and next. *Items and Issues*, 3: 5–9.

RENSHON, S. A., and LARSON, D. W. (eds.) 2003. *Good Judgment in Foreign Policy: Theory and Application.* Lanham, Md.: Rowman and Littlefield.

ROTHSTEIN, R. L. 1972. *Planning, Prediction, and Policymaking in Foreign Affairs: Theory and Practice.* Boston: Little, Brown.

SHILS, E. 1969. The intellectuals and the powers: some perspectives for comparative analysis. Pp. 25–48 in *On Intellectuals: Theoretical Studies, Case Studies*, ed. P. Rieff. New York: Doubleday.

SMITH, S., BOOTH, K., and ZALEWSKI, M. (eds.) 1996. *International Theory: Positivism and Beyond.* Cambridge: Cambridge University Press.

TICKNER, J. A. 2006. On the frontlines or sidelines of knowledge and power? Feminist practices of responsible scholarship. *International Studies Review*, 8: 383–95.

TIERNEY, J. 2004. Republicans outnumbered in academia, studies find. *New York Times*, 18 Nov.: 23.

WEBER, M. 1949. *The Methodology of the Social Sciences*, trans. and ed. E. A. Shils and H. A. Finch. Glencoe, Ill.: Free Press.

WENDT, A. 1999. *Social Theory of International Politics.* Cambridge: Cambridge University Press.

YOUNG, C. 2005. Liberal bias in the ivory tower. *Boston Globe*, 11 Apr.: A–15.

CHAPTER 37

INTERNATIONAL RELATIONS: THE RELEVANCE OF THEORY TO PRACTICE

JOSEPH S. NYE, JR.

IN practice, theory is unavoidable. In order to achieve objectives, one needs at least a primitive sense of cause and effect, as well as a means to simplify and interpret reality. If I ask you to describe what happened to you in the last hour, you have to simplify or else you would reproduce sixty minutes of detail. And if I ask you to get something, you would need some idea of what actions would produce results. This is the basic wisdom that underlies John M. Keynes's oft-cited statement (1936, 383) that "practical men, who believe themselves to be quite exempt from any intellectual influences, are usually the slaves of some defunct economist." The question is not whether theory is relevant to practice, but which theories and how aware practical people are of the origins and limitations of the theories they inevitably use.

Theory, understood as a set of generalizable causal propositions, varies greatly in its scope, parsimony, explanatory value, and normative and prescriptive

I would like to thank Bruce Jentleson, Peter Katzenstein, Robert O. Keohane, John Owen, Duncan Snidal, and Stephen Walt for helpful comments.

implications. Some theories focus on the international system, some on states, some at the level of individuals. Some focus on substance, some on process. Some theories are quite abstract and general, others fill in mid-level explanations, and some are quite narrow in scope (George 1993; Walt 2005, 26 ff; see also Lepgold 2000, 363). Because simplification is inevitable, some bias is inevitable in the selection of what is relevant and what to discard. It is important to be aware of our biases.

As Stanley Hoffmann (2006, 4) pointed out three decades ago, contemporary international relations theory has a heavily American orientation. "With the single exception of the 'British school' founded on a notion of the international system that takes into account political philosophy, history, and normative concerns and which integrates elements of realism and Grotian liberalism, the discipline remains imbued with American scientism." For example, nine of the top ten journals in international relations are published in the United States, and a recent survey of 1,084 scholars found males from East Coast American institutions disproportionately represented among the twenty-five most influential scholars (Peterson, Tierney, and Maliniak 2005, 62; see also Wœver 1998).

Given these figures, one might suppose that at least American policy-makers would welcome interaction with theorists, but that is rarely the case. As Alexander George (1993) noted, mentioning theory is often a sure way to make policy-makers' eyes glaze over. Paul Nitze (1993, 3), a relatively intellectual policy-maker, once observed that "most of what has been written and taught under the heading of 'political science' by Americans since World War II has been contrary to experience and to common sense. It has also been of limited value, if not counterproductive, as a guide to the actual conduct of policy." And the situation is no better in other countries, where the gap is often greater. A number of observers have noted a growing gulf between theorists and practitioners. Joseph Lepgold and Miroslav Nincic (2001, 3) argue that "the professional gap between academics and practitioners has widened in recent years. Many scholars no longer try to reach beyond the Ivory Tower, and officials seem increasingly content to ignore it." Or, as Bruce Jentleson (2002, 169) reports, "the problem is not just the gap between theory and policy but its chasmlike widening in recent years" (see also Kruzel 1994; Newsom 1995–6).

The United States has a tradition of political appointments that is more amenable to what Richard Neustadt termed "in and out" circulation between government and academia than is true in Europe, Japan, or other places with a strong civil service tradition (Bok 2003). Notwithstanding the policy relevance of the "British school," academic theorists in the British tradition have even less direct access to policy than in the United States. While a number of important American scholars such as Henry Kissinger and Zbigniew Brzezinski have entered high-level foreign policy positions in the past, that path has tended to become a one-way street. Not many first-rate scholars are currently going into government, and even fewer return to contribute to academic theory. Of the twenty-five most influential scholars listed by *Foreign Policy*, only four have held top-level policy positions, two in the US government and two in the United Nations. Theory may be unavoidable in practice, but most practitioners, in the United States and elsewhere, seem to avoid direct contact with academic theory.

1 Is the Gap a Problem?

Some academics celebrate the appropriateness of the gap. After all, academic theorists and policy-makers fill different roles in society. A British scholar, Christopher Hill (1994, 16), has argued that, if scholars seek "policy relevance, even if only to justify our existence in the eyes of society at large, the more difficult it becomes to maintain intellectual integrity." As Niccolò Machiavelli discovered four centuries ago, it is risky to try to speak truth to power when you are in the midst of the struggle for power. Not only is there a danger of academics trimming their political sails to accommodate prevailing political winds (the "corruption-relevance trade-off"), but there is a more subtle risk that the search for short-term relevance will lead theorists to forgo levels of abstraction and elegance that may sometimes be essential to academic progress (the "rigor-relevance trade-off") (I am indebted to Stephen Walt for this distinction). From this perspective, the isolation of the ivory tower serves as a buffer against these temptations and encourages a useful division of labor.

There is much to be said for the view that universities are unique institutions, but the imagined trade-off between corruption and relevance need not be so acute. An intermediate position on the appropriateness issue is what I call the "balanced portfolio" approach. But the portfolio analogy works best when there are a number of people who have occupied both positions in the division of labor at different times and are able to act as bridges. As the above cited evidence suggests, however, "in and outers" who contribute to both practice and theory are increasingly rare.

In the past, academics have made useful contributions to policy, either directly or at arm's length. A few decades ago, academics like Arnold Wolfers, Carl Friedrich, McGeorge Bundy, Thomas Schelling, and others felt it proper to be engaged with the policy process. As Randolph Siverson (2000) has pointed out, some academic ideas have been quite significant in framing policy. Through a combination of writing and consulting, Schelling, Bernard Brodie, Albert Wohlstetter, William Kaufman, and others developed and refined theories of nuclear strategy and arms control that were widely used by practitioners in the cold war. More recently, Michael Doyle, Rudolph Rummel, Anthony Lake, Bruce Russett, and others helped to update Kant's theory of the democratic peace ("liberal democracies tend not to fight each other") and it has entered into popular political discourse and policy.

In addition to such large ideas, academics have provided many middle-level theories, and generalizations that are based upon specific functional or regional knowledge and have proved useful to policy-makers (on examples of regional expertise, see Lieberthal 2006). Theories about deterrence, balance of terror, interdependence, and bipolarity have helped shape the vocabulary that policy-makers depend upon. Historical analogies are a frequent form of ideas used by policy-makers, often in a crude and misleading way. Academics can help to discipline the use and misuse of such analogies (Neustadt and May 1986). As Ernest J. Wilson III (2000, 122) argues, academics can also help the public and policy-makers by framing, mapping, and raising questions even when they do not provide answers.

From a normative perspective, this record can be used to bolster the argument that academics, as citizens, have an obligation to help to improve policy ideas when they can. Moreover, such engagement in the policy debates can enhance and enrich academic work, and thus the ability of academics to teach the next generation. As David D. Newsom (1995–6, 64–5) has written:

the growing withdrawal of university scholars behind curtains of theory and modeling would not have wider significance if this trend did not raise questions regarding the preparation of new generations and the future influence of the academic community on public and official perceptions of international issues and events. Teachers plant seeds that shape the thinking of each new generation; this is probably the academic world's most lasting contribution.

Alternatively, one can argue that, while the gap between theory and policy has grown in recent decades and may have costs for policy, the growing gap has produced better political theory, and that is more important than whether it is relevant.

2 THE IMPACT OF THE REAL WORLD ON ACADEMIC THEORY

Regardless of one's normative views about the correct relationship of academia to policy, the field of international relations is not nearly so distant from the influences of the practical world as some scholars like to think. To paraphrase Keynes, academic theorists, who believe themselves to be quite exempt from any practical influence, are usually slaves of unseen larger world events. At times, academics trends and fads have proved to be *too* influenced by events.

Theoretical trends in the field have always been strongly influenced by the outside world. According to Steve Smith and John Baylis (2005, 4), "the separate academic discipline of International Politics was formed in 1919 when the Department of International Politics was set up at Aberystwyth" by a Welsh industrialist who saw its purpose as preventing war such as Europe had just suffered. Much of the writing in the interwar period was in a liberal legalistic, idealist mode influenced by Woodrow Wilson and efforts to sustain the League of Nations. With the Second World War and the cold war, classical realism represented by theorists such as E. H. Carr and Hans Morgenthau became predominant. Many of the most influential theorists in the United States had European backgrounds and reflected European viewpoints. Indeed, after asserting almost as a law of nature that states act on interests defined in terms of power, Morgenthau had to chide Americans for failing to follow the assumptions of his theory.

Several events in the 1960s and early 1970s temporarily dethroned the hegemony of realist theory. The progress of the European Common Market led scholars such as Ernst Haas and Karl W. Deutsch to develop theories of integration that focused on functionalism and communications. At the same time, transnational relations were increasing. The recovery of global trade and finance led to pressure on the dollar, and the United States could no longer afford to redeem dollars into gold. The Vietnam War became highly unpopular and generated protests in the United States and around the world. Most strikingly, the Organization of Petroleum Exporting Countries (OPEC) oil embargo of 1973 led to a dramatic redistribution of power in the energy arena, and serious economic dislocations ("stagflation") in wealthy countries. Poor countries called for "a new world economic order." Morgenthau (1974, 56) called the changes "an historically unprecedented severing of the functional relationship between political, military, and economic power." These circumstances gave rise to a new wave of theorizing about the politics of economic relations, and more generally about power and interdependence (see Keohane and Nye 1977). For example, the field of international organization (and the journal of that name) began to focus less on the collective security role of the United Nations and more on transnational relations, the new subfield of international political economy, and neoliberal theories.

The decline of détente, the Soviet invasion of Afghanistan, and the election of Ronald Reagan in the United States returned attention to the security agenda in the "little cold war" of the 1980s. Fears of nuclear war escalated and mass demonstrations around the world demanded a "nuclear freeze." Foundations began to fund programs in security studies and peace studies, and journals sought more articles on security than on international political economy. Theorists split into two subfields, with security studies dominant. Kenneth Waltz's *Theory of International Politics* (1979) provided a parsimonious structural neorealism that stripped away much of the content of classical realism. Neoliberals such as Robert Keohane (1986) replied with a sparse variant of liberalism that stripped away much of the context of classical liberalism in order to be able to respond to the neorealists on their own rationalist grounds (see also Nye 1988). As Miles Kahler (1997, 38) has written, with the "neo-neo" debates of the 1980s "the theoretical contest that might have been was reduced to relatively narrow disagreements within one state-centric rationalist model of international relations."

At the end of the cold war, the focus of international relations theory changed again. Both neorealism and neoliberalism were criticized as static and unable to anticipate or explain one of the most important changes in international relations in recent history. Some observers questioned whether events had proven international relations theory to be irrelevant. A diverse group of theorists loosely called constructivists focused on the importance of ideas in shaping both the reality and the discourse of international politics. They refused to take existing preferences for granted. Instead they raised important questions about how identities, norms, culture, national interests, and governance are shaped and change. Constructivism has sometimes been called an approach rather than a causal theory, but it has become an important supplement to the two major theories of realism and liberalism (see Finnemore and Sikkink 2001).

There is always a dialectic between theory and reality. International relations is not a laboratory science, and history is the closest it comes, but of course without controls. Thus theories would be bound to change and evolve, even if there were no trends in daily politics, fads in foundation funding, or changing conventional wisdom in journal editors' preferences. Thus Waltz's title, *Theory of International Politics*, today appears as a hubristic claim for what really was a parsimonious structural analysis of a now past bipolar era. Today, efforts to describe the post-cold war era in terms of structural polarities have to take into account unipolarity in military affairs, multipolarity in economic relations among states, and a chaotic distribution of power at the transnational level. Structural realists who dismissed transnational relations as epiphenomenal in a world of great powers now face a world in which a surprise attack by a nonstate network killed more people in 2001 than did the government of Japan at Pearl Harbor in 1941. As historians have long known, history is rewritten by each age, because the world looks different, and each generation asks new questions. Much the same can be said of the relation of the outside world to international relations theory. To rephrase my opening line: In theory, practice is inescapable.

3 EXPLAINING THE GROWING GAP

That a gap exists between academia and the policy world is both natural and a good thing up to a point, assuming that some efforts are made to bridge it. But in recent years, the gap has been widening and bridging efforts have become more difficult. The growing specialization of knowledge, the increasing scientific methodological orientation of academic disciplines, and development of new institutional transmission belts help to account for the change.

Some aspects of the gap, however, are not new. The world of the academic theorist and the world of the policy practitioner have always involved very different cultures. As an academic going into a policy position at the State Department three decades ago, I was struck by the fact that bureaucracy is a huge machine for turning out reams of paper, but the top policy world is really an oral culture. As I wrote of that experience, "the pace did not permit wide reading or detailed contemplation. I was often bemused by colleagues who sent me thirty- or forty-page articles they thought would be helpful. It was all I could do to get through the parts of the intelligence briefings and government papers that my various special assistants underlined for the hour or two of reading possible on a good day" (Nye 1989, 206). As a result, effective policy memos are often one or two pages long, and concise oral briefings are often more influential than memos. As Ezra Vogel (2006, 33) reports from his experience as an academic in government in the 1990s, "generally speaking...academic books and articles are useless for policymakers. Even if they were not filled with what policymakers consider arcane theories and esoteric details written solely for other academics, these publications are simply too lengthy for policymakers to go through the haystack looking for the needle they might use."

A premium on time is a major difference between the two cultures. For the academic, time is a secondary consideration, while accuracy and elegance are primary. For practitioners, timing is everything. A "B" quality memo written to brief the president for his meeting with a foreign dignitary at 3 p.m. is a success, while an "A" memo that arrives at 4 p.m. is a total failure. In the university, these priorities are (properly) reversed. Another difference is the importance of group work as opposed to individual creativity. In the university, plagiarism is a cardinal sin. In government policy work, ideas are a public good and it is often most effective not to attribute credit. Finally, in the academy, the highest value is to ignore politics and speak truth to power, while in the policy world some political trimming and appreciation of "applied truth" may be essential for effectiveness. It is not always easy to straddle these two cultures. I used fiction to dramatize some of the moral dilemmas that arise in *The Power Game: A Washington Novel* (Nye 2004).

But the inherent culture gap has grown wider in recent years largely because of trends in academic disciplines and in the institutions of foreign policy. As Stephen Walt (2005, 26, 38) explains, the incentive structures and professional ethos of the academic world have changed, and the trickle-down model linking theory and policy has weakened as a transmission belt. In his view, "the prevailing norms of academic life have increasingly discouraged scholars from doing work that would be directly relevant to policy makers." General theories such as structural realism and liberal institutionalism have become more abstract, and some rational choice models, while stimulating to theorists, often reflect what Hoffmann (2006, 4) has called "economics envy." Middle-range generalizations, historical cases, and regional expertise—the types of theory most accessible and most useful to practice—are accorded less prestige in the disciplinary pecking order. Methodology reinforces the trend. As Jentleson (2002, 178) argues, "dominant approaches to methodology give short shrift to policy analysis, to the analytic skills for addressing questions of strategy and for assessing policy options. It is one thing to train Ph.D.s primarily for academic careers; it is another to have this be virtually the only purpose of most major international relations/political science Ph.D. programs. The job market for new Ph.D.s operationalizes this incentive structure" (see also Zelikow 1994). Professors spend most of their energies reproducing little professors.

The problem is further compounded by the use of academic jargon and the lack of interest in communicating in plain language to a policy public. As George (1993, 7) put it, "not a few policy specialists exposed to the scholarly literature have concluded that most university professors seem to write largely for one another and have little inclination or ability to communicate their knowledge in terms comprehensible to policy makers." Young scholars are rated and promoted by their contributions to refereed academic journals and citations by other scholars in those same journals where there is little premium on writing in clear and accessible English. They get little credit for contributions to policy journals edited for a broader audience.

In institutional terms, the transmission belts between academia and government have also changed. Universities are less dominant sources of policy ideas than in the past. In the traditional model, professors produced theories that would trickle down (or out) to the policy world through the articles they wrote and the students they taught. As Walt (2005, 40) describes it, "the trickle-down model assumes that new ideas emerge from academic 'ivory towers' (i.e., as abstract theory), gradually filter down into the work of applied analysts (and especially people working in public policy 'think tanks'), and finally reach the perceptions and actions of policy makers... In practice, however, the process by which ideas come to shape policy is far more idiosyncratic and haphazard." Or, as Jentleson (2002, 181) writes, "whereas thirty or forty years ago academics were the main if not sole cohort of experts on international affairs outside of government and international institutions, today's world is a more competitive marketplace of ideas and expertise."

Even when academics supplement the trickle-down approach with articles in policy journals, op-eds in newspapers, blogs, and consultancy for candidates or officials, they find many more competitors for attention. Some of these transmission belts serve as translators and additional outlets for academic ideas, but many add a bias provided by their founders and funders. There are more than 1,200 think tanks in the United States alone and they are very heterogeneous in scope, funding, ideology, and location, but universities generally offer a more neutral viewpoint. The think tanks provide not only ideas but also experts ready to comment or consult at a moment's notice (Haass 2002). In addition, journalists, public intellectuals, nongovernmental organizations, trade associations, private contractors, and others are involved in providing policy ideas. As Wilson III (2007) points out, while the pluralism of institutional pathways may be good for democracy, many of the nonuniversity institutions have narrow interests and tailor their policy advice to fit particular agendas. The policy process in democracies is diminished by the withdrawal of an academic community, which has broader agendas and more rigorous intellectual standards.

One of the most effective transmission belts for ideas to travel from the academy to government might be called "embedded capital" in the minds of "in and out-ers" (a mechanism that Walt largely ignores.) As Kissinger once pointed out, the pressure on time that bears upon policy-makers means that they rely on ideas and intellectual capital created before they entered the maelstrom. I found this to be true in my own experience, and will illustrate with two examples.

In the 1970s I was responsible for the Carter administration's policy on non-proliferation of nuclear weapons. Our policies of discouraging breeder reactors and the commercial use of plutonium were condemned at international meetings such as one in Persepolis, Iran, in 1977. Because of my academic theorizing about transnational relations, I saw this, not as a representative meeting, but as a transnational coalition that empowered a particular traditional pro-nuclear point of view. It seemed important to provide an alternative focal point for discourse that would involve more foreign ministry and security officials. (This might be considered constructivism in practice well before the term was invented.) By creating a multi-year International Nuclear Fuel Cycle Evaluation, the United States was able to create an alternative forum for information and a transgovernmental network of security officials to accompany it (for a more detailed account, see Nye 1981).

The second example comes from my experience as Assistant Secretary of Defense in the 1990s when I was responsible for designing an East Asian security strategy. There was a great deal of concern about the rise of Chinese power, and some voices advocated a policy of containment before China became too strong. In my view, such an approach would guarantee Chinese enmity and unnecessarily discount possible benign futures. Yet treating China as a friend would not guarantee friendship. We designed a strategy that drew upon both realism and liberalism. By reestablishing the security relationship with Japan, we insured that China could not play a Japan card against us. The second part of the strategy relied on liberal-ism. We eschewed the language of containment, opened markets with China, and supported its accession to the World Trade Organization (for a fuller description, see Nye, Jr. 1995; Funabashi 1999). I have termed the policy "integrate, but hedge." If China becomes aggressive as its strength increases, Japan will be a key partner in organizing a policy of containment, but if China mellows as it prospers and its ties of interdependence deepen, the world may see a more benign outcome. There are still uncertainties about the future, but the policy is robust against failure, and has had bipartisan support (for an opposite view based on an academic theory of offensive realism, see Mearsheimer 2001).

The point of these two examples is to illustrate how intellectual capital and theoretical ideas produced and stored up in a university setting were useful in making policy changes in Washington. Political science theory was crucial to the way in which I framed and crafted solutions to practical policy issues. It came less from outside articles and consultants (though they played some role) than in the form of embedded intellectual capital. In terms of the earlier discussion, some critics may say this mechanism is too costly, and that I would have been better off staying in the university and developing more academic ideas. Perhaps. Choice involves trade-offs, and there are always opportunity costs. Nonetheless, I am glad I paid them. Not only was I able to contribute to policy on important issues I cared about, but I believe that my writing and teaching were enriched rather than diminished when I returned to the university.

Government practice is a deepening but narrowing experience. There is little time or license for the freewheeling exploration that is possible in a university. For example, when dealing with nuclear nonproliferation, I had no time to explore the broad ethical issues when foreign officials would ask why it was all right for the United States to have nuclear weapons while trying to prevent them from obtaining the bomb. When I returned to the university, I used the lack of pressure on time and politics to teach a course and then write a book on *Nuclear Ethics* (Nye, Jr. 1986). And after I returned from the Pentagon and my work on East Asia, I turned my attention to a book about the future distribution of power in *The Paradox of American Power* (Nye, Jr. 2002). For better or worse, both works were heavily influenced by my experience in government.

My experience of a fruitful interaction between theory and practice may be subjective, but it is not unique. As Vogel (2006, 34) has written:

when I went to Washington and first had to write one-page briefs, I despaired of substituting sound bites for real thinking. I came to appreciate, however, that one pagers can force intellectual discipline. Such space limits impel us to think about what is the absolutely most important idea or two that we want to communicate, and to decide how to communicate those ideas in the most effective way. As a result, I returned to the university and began to encourage students to spend more time compressing their thinking and to work harder to express ideas in a precise and concise way.

Wilson III (2000), Jentleson (2002), and others report similar experiences.

4 CONCLUSION: WHAT IS TO BE DONE?

If such experiences serve as an existence theorem that academic theory and policy practice can interact fruitfully in both directions, what could be done to increase it and bridge the widening gap? On the official side, former ambassador David Newsom (1995–6) advised his colleagues to broaden State Department research grants, to increase scholar–diplomat programs, and to encourage senior officials to participate in scholarly association meetings. The intelligence community, particularly the National Intelligence Council, holds regular unclassified seminars and conferences with academics. Internships and exchanges such as the Foreign Affairs fellowships sponsored by the Council on Foreign Relations in the United States have also helped to introduce young American academics to a policy environment, though, of the dozen or so annual fellowships, the percentage from universities has declined over time. Increased lateral entry at middle levels would be good both for the civil service and for the academy, but this is particularly difficult in countries with a strong civil service tradition. The Internet and blogs also provide new opportunities for scholars to become involved in policy debates on a global basis. On the university side, Walt (2005, 41) argues for "a conscious effort to alter the prevailing norms of the . . . discipline." Departments should give greater weight to real-world relevance and impact in hiring and promotion decisions, and journals could place greater weight on relevance in evaluating submissions. Universities could facilitate interest in the real world by giving junior faculty greater incentives for participating in it (Walt 2005). Since many young academics are (understandably) risk averse, that would require greater toleration of unpopular policy positions.

One could multiply such useful suggestions, but young people should not hold their breath waiting for them to be implemented. If anything, the trends in academic life seem to be headed in the opposite direction. When young scholars ask me about how to combine an interest in theory and policy practice, I give them the following advice:

1. Establish your academic credentials first. Play safe until tenure. The connection between academia and practice is a one-way street. Nail down your academic credentials. It is much easier to go from academia to practice than visa versa.

2. Learn to write clear English with as little jargon as possible. It will make you intelligible to policy-makers, attract a larger audience for your scholarly writings, and make you a better teacher as well.

3. Pick research questions that interest you in substance as well as method. Beware of picking topics that are so manageable that you wind up saying more and more about less and less (which is a current academic affliction). "Better an approximate answer to an important question than an exact answer to a trivial question" (Putnam 2003, 251).

4. Enter the public policy debate. Without taking too much time away from your academic articles, write occasional op-eds, blogs, and policy articles.

5. Get involved in policy networks as well as professional political science associations. The contacts are useful and you can learn things that can enhance your academic work.

6. Understand the transmission belts that link theory and policy and the costs involved with each in terms of time and reputation.

7. Decide what gives a sense of meaning to your life.

8. Do it.

References

Boк, D. 2003. Government personnel policy in comparative perspective. Pp. 255–72 in *For the People: Can We Fix Public Service?*, ed. J. D. Donahue and J. S. Nye. Washington, DC: Brookings Institution Press.

FINNEMORE, M., and SIKKINK, K. 2001. Taking stock: the constructivist research program in international relations and comparative politics. *Annual Review of Political Science*, 4: 391–416.

FUNABASHI, Y. 1999. *Alliance Adrift*. New York: Council on Foreign Relations Press.

GEORGE, A. L. 1993. *Bridging the Gap: Theory and Practice in Foreign Policy*. Washington, DC: United States Institute of Peace Press.

HAASS, R. N. 2002. Think tanks and US foreign policy: a policy-maker's perspective. *US Foreign Policy Agenda*, 7: 5–8.

HILL, C. 1994. Academic international relations: the siren song of policy relevance. Pp. 3–28 in *Two Worlds of International Relations: Academics, Practitioners and the Trade in Ideas*, ed. C. Hill and P. Beshoff. London: Routledge.

HOFFMANN, S. 2006. *Chaos and Violence: What Globalization, Failed States, and Terrorism Mean for US Foreign Policy*. Lanham, Md.: Rowman and Littlefield.

JENTLESON, B. 2002. The need for praxis: bringing policy relevance back in. *International Security*, 26: 169–83.

KAHLER, M. 1997. Inventing international relations: international relations theory after 1945. Pp. 20–53 in *New Thinking in International Relations Theory*, ed. M. W. Doyle and G. J. Ikenberry. Boulder, Colo.: Westview.

KEOHANE, R. O. (ed.) 1986. *Neorealism and its Critics*. New York: Columbia University Press.

——and NYE, J. S. 1977. *Power and Interdependence: World Politics in Transition*. Boston: Little, Brown.

KEYNES, J. M. 1936. *The General Theory of Employment, Interest and Money*. London: Macmillan.

KRUZEL, J. 1994. More a chasm than a gap, but do scholars want to bridge it? *Mershon International Studies Review*, 38: 179–81.

LEPGOLD, J. 2000. Policy relevance and theoretical development in international relations: what have we learned? Pp. 363–80 in *Being Useful: Policy Relevance and International Relations Theory*, ed. M. Nincic and J. Lepgold. Ann Arbor: University of Michigan Press.

LEPGOLD, J., and NINCIC, M. 2001. *Beyond the Ivory Tower: International Relations Theory and the Issue of Policy Relevance.* New York: Columbia University Press.

LIEBERTHAL, K. 2006. Initiatives to bridge the gap. *Asia Policy*, 1: 7–15.

MEARSHEIMER, J. 2001. *The Tragedy of Great Power Politics.* New York: Norton.

MORGENTHAU, H. J. 1974. The new diplomacy of movement. *Encounter*, 3: 52–7.

NEUSTADT, R. E. and MAY, E. R. 1986. *Thinking in Time: The Uses of History for Decision-Makers.* New York: Free Press.

NEWSOM, D. 1995–6. Foreign policy and academia. *Foreign Policy*, 101: 52–67.

NITZE, P. H. 1993. *Tension between Opposites: Reflections on the Practice and Theory of Politics.* New York: Scribner.

NYE, J. S., JR. 1981. Maintaining a nonproliferation regime. *International Organization*, 35: 15–38.

——1986. *Nuclear Ethics.* New York: Free Press.

——1988. Neorealism and neoliberalism. *World Politics*, 40: 235–51.

——1989. Studying world politics. Pp. 199–212 in *Journeys through World Politics: Autobiographical Reflections of Thirty-Four Academic Travelers*, ed. J. Kruzel and J. N. Rosenau. Lexington, Mass.: Lexington Books.

——1995. The case for deep engagement. *Foreign Affairs*, 74: 90–102.

——2002. *The Paradox of American Power: Why the World's Only Superpower Can't Go It Alone.* Oxford: Oxford University Press.

——2004. *The Power Game: A Washington Novel.* New York: Public Affairs.

PETERSON, S., TIERNEY, M. J., and MALINIAK, D. 2005. Inside the ivory tower. *Foreign Policy*, 151: 58–64.

PUTNAM, R. D. 2003. APSA presidential address: the public role of political science. *Perspectives on Politics*, 1: 249–55.

SIVERSON, R. M. 2000. A glass half-full? No, but perhaps a glass filling: the contributions of international politics research to policy. *PS: Political Science and Politics*, 33: 59–64.

SMITH, S. and BAYLIS, J. 2005. Introduction. Pp. 1–14 in *The Globalization of World Politics: An Introduction to International Relations*, 3rd edn, ed. J. Baylis and S. Smith. Oxford: Oxford University Press.

VOGEL, E. 2006. Some reflections on policy and academics. *Asia Policy*, 1: 31–4.

WÆVER, O. 1998. The sociology of a not so international discipline: American and European developments in international relations. *International Organization*, 52: 687–727.

WALT, S. M. 2005. The relationship between theory and policy in international relations. *Annual Review of Political Science*, 8: 23–48.

WALTZ, K. 1979. *Theory of International Politics.* Reading, Mass.: Addison-Wesley.

WILSON III, E. J. 2000. How social science can help policymakers: the relevance of theory. Pp. 109–28 in *Being Useful: Policy Relevance and International Relations Theory*, ed. M. Nincic and J. Lepgold. Ann Arbor: University of Michigan Press.

——2007. Is there really a scholar—practitioner gap? An institutional analysis. *PS: Political Science and Politics*, 40: 147–51.

ZELIKOW, P. 1994. Foreign policy engineering: from theory to practice and back again. *International Security*, 18: 143–71.

PART VII

THE QUESTION
OF DIVERSITY

CHAPTER 38

INTERNATIONAL RELATIONS FROM BELOW

DAVID L. BLANEY

NAEEM INAYATULLAH

CRITICAL theorists seek to defeat claims about modernity's exhaustion by revealing the unrealized "emancipatory" potential of the current social order. Critical theory thereby locates itself mostly within modernity. An "international relations from below," by contrast, necessarily locates itself both within and beyond an "international relations from above." The "below" implies a geopolitical space as well as an evaluative threshold: As space it connotes the global South or the Third World; as threshold it points to those below a certain civilizational or material level, and specifically those below the vital ability of shaping the world according to their own vision.[1] Those who envision themselves as living "below" have, by necessity, a multiple and complex critical vision: They live within the theory and practice of a world largely created by those "above," but also in worlds partly defined by alternative visions that critique praxis "from above." Speaking from this critical

We thank Tarak Barkawi, Gurminder Bhambra, Shampa Biswas, Matt Davies, Kevin Dunn, Xavier Guillaume, Sankaran Krishna, Mark Laffey, Siddharth Mallavarapu, Himadeep Muppidi, Chris Reus-Smit, and Arlene Tickner for invaluable comments.

[1] It might also point to the everyday or the feminine, which are treated as below the threshold of the international or the political. Feminist critiques and engagements with the everyday can be considered as homologous with an "international relations from below."

position invites disparagement from above and casts "international relations from below" beyond the disciplinary pale. Interestingly, this displacement of "international relations from below" is constitutive of the international relations discipline. From its position as simultaneously "cast out" of international relations and as the necessary constitutive other of international relations, "international relations from below" challenges the ontological atomism of dominant modern/Western theories by highlighting the historical co-construction of contemporary institutions and processes (including the mutual constitution of "above" and "below") and by proposing alternative futures usually prohibited by modernity's focus on potential or realized progress.

1 LESSONS FORETOLD: THE DISMISSAL OF DEPENDENCY THEORY

The dependency thinkers of the 1960s presage the status of an "international relations from below." Dependency theories offer a "counter-analysis" of the workings of the international system—the origins of which are traced to the experience of peripheries as imperial subjects (Slater 2004, 118–20) or to the nonaligned movement's political language of "neocolonialism" (Young 2001, 44–5, 51). Primarily associated with Latin American authors, the most prominent of which, not least because their work is available in English, include Fernando Cardoso (1972; 1977; Cardoso and Falleto 1979), Osvaldo Sunkel (1969; 1973), and Theotonio Dos Santos (1970), dependency thinkers and other associated theorists of unequal development, such as Samir Amin (1974; 1976), argue that the historical development of the international system—the structures of the state system and the capitalist global division of labor—produce forms of systematic underdevelopment (stagnation in some places and deformed processes of development elsewhere).[2] Mechanisms of dependence, including external military domination, transnational investment, unequal trade relations, and global financial arrangements, condition national development prospects by subjecting the peripheries to domination by the system's centers. Though global, the system's loci of dynamism, its social structures and attendant class relations, are transnational, existing both internally and externally in relation to the peripheral countries and regions. Nevertheless, these structures of dependence and domination marginalize large zones. The experience of the peripheries cannot, then, reproduce that of the advanced regions, since the latter

---

[2] Many useful summaries of the contributions of dependency theory are available. See Chilcote (1984); Valenzuela and Valenzuela (1981); and Slater (2004, 118–27).

have already asymmetrically integrated the former into this wider system of production and goverance. Representations of peripheries as traditional or less developed are ideological deflections, and conventional policy advice guarantees continued marginalization. Alternative approaches might foster distinctive forms of national economic integration or involve selective delinking from the structures of global capitalism, although any effective response requires the realignment of class forces within the periphery and, eventually, a transformation of global structures.

Leading North American scholars justify the brief sway of dependency theory in disciplinary terms, though perhaps better linked to the waning of the oppositional politics of the Third World movement.[3] Theories of dependency, as Gabriel Almond (1990, 229–30, 233) claims, are "inescapably ideological"—"a backward step" measured against the conventions of social science. Robert Pakenham (1992, 29–30, 43, 103–4) likewise stresses that dependency theory is unscientific because its critical status makes it "unfalsifiable." Confirming its origins in "backward" zones, Pakenham (1992, 255–60) associates dependency proponents, not with science or reason, but with "theatre," "drama," or "symbol and ritual." Not surprisingly, then, dependency theorists ignore the dictates of rationality, eschewing the obvious mutual gains from interdependence (Pakenham 1992, 306).

Others are more deliberative but still place dependency theory beyond the disciplinary pale. In a review, James Caporaso (1980, 622–3) recognizes Cardoso and Enzo Faletto's very different stance toward history; they reject a Newtonian notion of time—"homogeneous, infinitely divisible, and purely formal"—that facilitates generalization, favoring instead a "lumpy" or "qualitative" notion that limits our capacity to generalize beyond particular times and places.[4] Rather than evaluating dependency theory on its own terms, Caporaso (1980, 615) defends disciplinary standards of "falsifiability and verification" without which "the scientific enterprise cannot succeed." Even in this more generous reading, dependency theory is displaced beyond international relations—an outside whose prescientific and politically imprudent (irrational) status serve to confirm the epistemic superiority of international relations proper. Cardoso (1977, 15–16) saw the writing on the wall. To gain disciplinary respectability, theories of dependency were boxed into uniform, static, and thereby testable propositions that misrepresented their historical approach based on a dynamic and dialectical analysis of concrete situations. This "straw man" is "easy to destroy." Caporaso (1993, 470) himself, in later reflections, notes that "dependency theory died out more from neglect than frontal criticism."

The construction of dependency theory as beyond the pale of acceptable knowledge production and policy relevance reveals a crucial feature of international

---

[3] Despite this, theories of dependency sustain interest in Latin America. Arlene Tickner (2003, 317–18) argues that "autonomy" continues to find a central place in Latin American international relations, quite by contrast with contemporary North American international relations.

[4] Cardoso and Faletto (1979, x–xiv, xxiii) defend their emphasis on analyzing concrete situations. See also Gabriel Palma (1978).

relations: the suppression of alternative and competing themes opposed to the standard theory of progress. The political and ethical possibilities of modern life rest on a tension between wholes and parts within the theory of progress. On the one hand, political and economic development is seen as isomorphic with extending modern Western civilization to encompass the entire global cultural space. On the other hand, since the early modern failure of the project to universalize a common blueprint within Europe, political and economic development is also linked to sovereignty, a principle putatively allowing each state to find its own version of meaningful development. International relations theory "proper" conventionally navigates this tension by embracing a monadic vision, by positing that the promise of modernity (that is, political and economic development) is possible only within states. International relations' self-limiting understanding acts to suppress the larger social theory within which this monadic vision nests.

Dependency theorists, by contrast, revive the tension between wholes and parts and between international relations and its larger context by exploring the strains between the imperatives of sovereignty and those of global capitalism (Blaney 1996). By emphasizing the relations of domination central to the global logic of capitalism, they reveal the lie: that development is a set of separable, national projects. Rather, development proceeds within the processes of the global system, enriching some and marginalizing others. Dependency theory thereby is a powerful form of immanent criticism, rooted in a description of current global political and economic arrangements. The spotlight on the ambitions of various Third World states and peoples for development and self-determination should not obscure its deeper insight: The conditions of the periphery are expressions of internal tensions within the values and visions of modern international society itself.

Cardoso himself argued that dependency studies were not something new, either methodologically or in terms of their critical purpose. Rather, they "constitute part of this constantly renewed effort to reestablish a tradition of analysis of economic structures and structures of domination" (Cardoso 1977, 10). The difference in this case is that "a current which was already old in Latin American thought managed to make itself heard in the discussions that were taking place in institutions normally closed to it," including various official agencies and "the North American academic community" (Cardoso 1977, 9). Here, Cardoso stresses more than the Latin American phase of critical thinking; he places this work in a long history of radical responses to modernity (Cardoso 1977, 8–9). He implies that theories of dependency revive a recessive current of thought within modern understandings of social and political life. If so, then despite dependency theory's rightful place as internal to traditions from "above," it is shunted aside, constructed as outside the process of knowledge production and rational political practice.

Nonetheless, residues of the dependency analysis keep emerging. We find one example in the claim that the position of the "Third World" necessitates a shift in our understandings of international security. For Mohammed Ayoob (1989; 1995), the violent incorporation of these areas into international society gives Third World states an intruder status, but it also constructs modern state-building as the main task of Third World political elites. The challenge of modernization appears to leaders as a central security issue. Thus, we can read the "economic" demands of the Third World coalition during its heyday in the 1960s and 1970s as also concerned with securing the state and the position of the elites within it (Murphy 1984; Ayoob 1995, 2). The Third World coalition was eventually forced into submission, and international relations in its realist and liberal versions could return, respectively, to the machinations of great powers, pushing the "internal" problems of Third World states to the margins, or to the building of a liberal global order, constructing these areas as objects of progressive modernization. But we then miss much about the nature of the conflict and insecurity intrinsic to the very structures of international society. Following the underlying insight of dependency theory, we might push deeper. Tarak Barkawi and Mark Laffey (2006, 333, 344–52) attribute the failure of security studies to an inability to "study the weak and the strong together, as jointly responsible for making history." An ontological individualism, rooted in a state of nature mythology or an analogy to neoclassical economics, leads security studies to diagnose conflict originating in the non-West as a lack, as due to the absence of modernization. What is missed is the "mutually constitutive character of world politics" and the insight that the sources of contemporary conflict can be found, not in the "separate objects" that international relations imagines, but in the "relations" between West and non-West.

2 CONSTITUTIVE OTHERNESS

If dependency theory focuses our attention on the differential experience of Third World spaces within the international system, this difference is nevertheless expressed within narrow, often modernist limits. As Dipesh Chakrabarty (2000a, 41) puts it: "European imperialism and third-world nationalisms" together achieved "the universalization of the nation-state as the most desirable form of political community." In its embrace of national autonomy, dependency theory obscures the multiplicity of identities and spaces that express and shape varying experiences of domination and alternative representations of social experience (Manzo 1991, 8–9; Slater 2004, ch. 6). A recent search for a "politics in different guises" was also the result of the eclipse of North–South relations from the agenda of world politics and the sense that the political economy issues raised by dependency theorists had now been "resolved" through the engineering of a liberal "consensus" about free trade and good governance (Darby 2004, 2, 5–6). Though a postcolonial movement expressing an interest in identity and difference had grown up within social theory by the late 1970s, Phillip Darby and Albert Paolini (1994) would later note that its impact on international relations was relatively meager. Geeta Chowdhry and Sheila Nair (2002, 1) later confirm that postcolonial work remains largely marginal to international relations.

Proponents of a postcolonial stance often see their work as a frontal assault on the basic conceptions and methods of international relations.[5] Paolini (1999, 5) argues that the discipline's fixation on states and sovereignty leads scholars to overlook questions about "identity, subjectivity, and modernity" as they apply across global space. He intimates that international relations fails to dig into the "elementary human realm of culture and identity" because it is in that realm, not in its status as science, that its privileged vantage point actually lies. In this respect, the concerns of postcolonial scholars dovetail with deconstructionist work emerging in international relations. For example, David Campbell (1996, 164–5) suggests that international relations is constituted by a discourse of the state that "settles" questions of identity; the centrality of the state is treated as "simply reflecting a reality" that can be objectively apprehended, not as an assertion of authority that obscures other possibilities. Perhaps closer to the spirit of postcolonial scholarship, Roxanne Lynn Doty (1996, 3, 8) calls our attention to the "imperial encounters" at the heart of international relations: "asymmetrical encounters in which one entity has been able to construct 'realities' that were taken seriously and acted upon and the other entity has been denied equal degrees or kinds of agency." Here international relations, even in its critical moment, appears as a set of "representational practices" in which the imperial West has constructed the other, fixing the categories of identity in which people and scholars "make sense."

The task of a "post-colonial analytical sensibility," with its focus on "difference, agency, subjectivity, and resistance," follows from this: It fundamentally challenges these "Western discourses of . . . progress, civilization, modernization, development and globalization" (Slater 2004, 163–4). For Tickner (2003, 302–7), disrupting the universalist and unilinear conceptions central to international relations recovers knowledge lodged in different cultural spaces and times, something international relations has failed to do thus far. Put more sharply perhaps, Chakrabarty (2000a, 29) claims that what passes for social science "has been produced in relative, and sometimes absolute, ignorance of the majority of humankind—that is, those living in non-Western countries." International relations lives in, as Himadeep Muppidi (2004, 3) implies, a state of global illiteracy. Thus, postcolonial scholarship represents an oppositional "frame of reference in [its] mapping of identity in, through, and beyond the colonial encounter;" it celebrates "the particular and the marginal" and hopes to see "peoples of the Third World carving out independent identities in

---

[5] Just as postcolonial thought more broadly provides a challenge to Western modes of representation. See Padmini Mongia (1996) and Leela Gandhi (1998).

a de-Europeanized space of recovery and difference" (Paolini 1999, 6). This process has been spoken of as a "decolonization of the imagination" and a "revalorization of cultural plurality" (Pieterse and Parekh 1995, 4, 14).

However, Chowdhry and Nair (2002, 1) claim that a postcolonial stance requires more. Postcoloniality highlights the "workings of power" that elide "the racialized, gendered, and class processes that underwrite global hierarchies," focusing our attention more convincingly on questions of "global inequality and justice."[6] Similarly, Sankaran Krishna (1999, xviii) calls for a "politics of *postcolonial engagement*," moving us beyond the process of denaturalizing "all identities (national, ethnic, linguistic, religious)" to joining the struggle, not so much to transcend identity, but to "fight for justice and fairness in the world we do inhabit." With the move to the postcolonial, we join, says Slater (2004, 199–200), a struggle over the very definition of the global (see also Muppidi 2004), the uneven consequences of globalization (see also Biswas 2002), and contemporary definitions of security imperatives (see also Barkawi and Laffey 2006). A postcolonial international relations perhaps includes but also moves beyond the concerns of dependency-thinkers.

Postcolonial international relations (as well as other critical approaches, like certain feminisms or post-structuralism, that challenge the modern) receives scarcely a mention in accounts of the state of the discipline (Walt 1998; Snyder 2004). This is not surprising, since, as Robert Keohane (1989, 162, 173) argues, a reflexive emphasis on epistemological and ontological questions merely diverts scholars from the *real* task of studying "world politics;" without adopting the model of a proper "research program," critical versions of international relations "will remain on the margins of the field, largely invisible to the preponderance of empirical researchers." This notion of the profession leaves little space for those who decline the orthodoxy.

Recognizing this, Darby and Paolini (1994, 371) call for a "bridging" of the "diplomatic isolation" of international relations from a postcolonial "international relations from below." The bridging metaphor may not be apt, however, since the oppositional stance of the postcolonial is both outside and inside "international relations from above." More precisely, the representational practices and the processes of identity construction central to the postcolonial are constitutive of international relations itself: A proper international relations "research program" is an effect of a prior assertion of colonial power. We suggested above that dependency analysts shift our vision, insisting that we recognize more fully how the parts—namely, states—are determined by the whole of the states system and the capitalist division of labor (and its imperial history) and therefore are always already inside the whole. Postcolonial analysis calls for a similar shift but, crucially, holds on to the excluded status of otherness. That is, postcolonial visions also call for a broader social theoretical scope that brings our attention to how actors and identities "from

---

[6] The role of gender in the constitution of global structures has a somewhat longer legacy in international relations. The role of race has arisen mostly alongside and within postcolonial international relations (see Manzo 1996; Persaud and Walker 2001).

below" are determined by larger systems of Westernization and modernity. Unlike dependency theory, the postcolonial turn, drawing on a post-structuralist rhythm of argument (Young 2001, 418), sees the non-Western and nonmodern not merely as outside, but also as the excluded other against which the West and the modern are defined. Timothy Mitchell (2000, 4–5, 12–13) refers to this status as the "constitutive outside." He argues that a distinct European identity is a product of the colonial management of difference—forged in relation to "distinctions of race, sexuality, culture and class." Modernity, for Mitchell, "depends upon, even as it refuses to recognize, forebears and forces that escape its control."

This refusal to recognize how the non-West and nonmodern are already integrated as constitutive forces within the West and the modern is precisely how the colonial comes to be externalized. Much of the work of postcolonial theorists is, as it was for dependency-thinkers, immanent, revealing the suppression of this other within international relations. In contrast with the dependency theorists' demands that modernity's promises be fulfilled, the positive aspect of postcolonial critiques is the hope that these revelations of suppressed others help us locate alternative resources for imagining our world (Chakrabarty 2002, xx, ch. 3). For example, Arturo Escobar (1995) claims that denaturalizing the discourse of development opens space for suppressed, often localized imaginations of social life. However, it is not clear that a postcolonial stance itself immediately identifies such alternatives. For international relations, it may require turning to sources beyond the usual fare, like consulting the anthropological or historical archives for accounts of ways of life and organizations of complex intercultural relations previously suppressed or now treated as irrelevant (see Manzo 1999; Euben 2002).

We can read international relations, then, through its refusal to recognize the denial involved in its own constitution (Inayatullah and Blaney 2004, esp. pt. I). The binary of "modernity/anarchy" is pivotal in this suppression: Anarchic disorder acts as the urgent "problem" to which the "solution" of modernization, with its civilizing logic, appears as the sole antidote. Systemic anarchy increasingly is seen as that which must be tamed via the modernization of global relations: international economic interdependence, the community of liberal polities, and global civil society. In this way, an "international relations from above," including seemingly critical approaches that rely on claims of the progressive unfolding of modernity, locates itself on an imagined boundary between the modern and the savage/barbarian. In contrast, "international relations from below," because it attempts to represent, cultivate, and retrieve the voice of the savage/barbarian, appears both as something beyond international relations and as something central to its very constitution. To extend Darby and Paolini's metaphor, what we need is not a bridge, but an excavation; a mining of the culture of international relations in order to reveal the representational practices that hide what is central to its constitution and through which we may find the resources for international relations' reimagination.

3 THE RECOVERY AND CRITIQUE OF POLITICAL ECONOMY

Despite its claims to confront global structures of power, the postcolonial turn to cultural analysis has not adequately engaged the domain of political economy. Darby (2004, 16–17) laments this surprising neglect by postcolonial thinkers within international relations, suggesting that it is part of a general culture of complacency that assumes there is no alternative to globalization. Paolini (1999, 204) notes a general tendency of postcolonial thought to float "above the fray of material circumstances." Both sense something significant in this neglect.

"Economy," claims Mitchell (1998, 84), is thought to refer to a "realm with an existence prior to and separate from its representations, and thus to stand in opposition to the more discursive constructs of social theory." The economy is associated with the natural—fixed laws unfolding across homogeneous time. The postcolonial, in contrast, operates in the domain of human culture(s); it is about revealing that which has been dehistoricized and denaturalized. As Thrift (2000, 692, 698–9) warns, this emphasis on culture has led many thinkers to take "remarkably little...note of economics." Or, suggesting that this opposition is constitutive of the cultural turn itself, he notes that "culture was culture because it had been purified of the taint of the economic." Recent histories of the subaltern movement hint that this separation has been constitutive of cultural studies (Chakrabarty 2000b; Chaturvedi 2000). Sumit Sarkar (2000, 304–5) explains that fears of falling into an economic reductionism led postcolonial scholars to the "bifurcation" of a socioeconomic world of "domination" from a spiritual world of "autonomy." Arif Dirlik (1994, 331) has been more pointed: Postcolonial critics have relieved themselves of the necessity of facing their own role in "contemporary capitalism" by "repudiating a foundational role of capitalism in history."

But there is little reason to limit postcolonial studies in this way. Like Mitchell above, Dirlik (1994, 350) argues that Eurocentrism is "built into the very structure of...capitalist culture;" thus, it is difficult to imagine any serious de-centering or provincializing of the West that does not directly confront political economy. What this suggests is less combining the economic insights of dependency theory with the cultural tools of postcolonialism and more doing to economics and political economy what postcolonial thinkers have already done to "international relations from above." If capitalism, economics, and political economy are constituted by otherness in the manner of "international relations from above," then an international relations from below can move toward revealing how its own status as "constitutive other" contains alternative cultures of political economy.

4 CONCLUSION

"International relations from below" reminds us that conventional international relations—whether structural realist, liberal institutionalist, or constructivist—treats states or groups as parts that are logically independent of the larger systems of capitalism or modernity, and that this methodological device serves political purposes. In the guise of "science," ontological individualism works to deflect our attention from the co-constitution of times and places. While one hand severs holistic threads in order to present states as monadic entities, the other hand pedagogically asserts that the present of the advanced states is the model for those that lag behind. In revealing this sleight of hand, "international relations from below" suggests that contemporary international relations is an expression of the Western theory of progress. It brings our attention to the relation between wholes and parts—to whether development occurs within the boundaries of states or for the system as a whole, and to the unproductive separation between economics and the analysis of capitalism, on the one side, and representational strategies and cultural analysis, on the other. In so doing, it takes advantage of its status as "constitutive other" to foreground international relations' potential as that aspect of social theory that dedicates itself to studying relations of self and other. And it offers us resources for imagining the future beyond those offered by both conventional and critical "international relations from above."

REFERENCES

ALMOND, G. 1990. *A Discipline Divided: Schools and Sects in Political Science.* Newbury Park, Calif.: Sage.

AMIN S. 1974. Accumulation and development: a theoretical model. *Review of African Political Economy*, 1: 9–26.

——1976. *Unequal Development: An Essay on the Social Formations of Peripheral Capitalism.* New York: Monthly Review Press.

AYOOB, M. 1989. The third world in the system of states: acute schizophrenia or growing pains? *International Studies Quarterly*, 33: 67–79.

——1995. *The Third World Security Predicament: State Making, Regional Conflict, and the International System.* Boulder, Colo.: Lynne Rienner.

BARKAWI, T., and LAFFEY, M. 2006. The postcolonial movement in security studies. *Review of International Studies*, 32: 329–52.

BLANEY, D. L. 1996. Reconceptualizing autonomy: the difference dependency theory makes. *Review of International Political Economy*, 3: 459–97.

BISWAS, S. 2002. W(h)ither the nation-state? National and state identity in the face of fragmentation and globalisation. *Global Society*, 16: 175–98.

CAMPBELL, D. 1996. Violent performances: identity, sovereignty, responsibility. Pp. 163–80 in *The Return of Culture and Identity in IR Theory*, ed. Y. Lapid and F. Kratochwil. Boulder, Colo.: Lynne Rienner.

CAPORASO, J. A. 1980. Dependency theory: continuities and discontinuities in development studies. *International Organization*, 34: 605–28.

—— 1993. Global political economy. Pp. 451–81 in *Political Science: The State of the Discipline II*, ed. A. Finifter. Washington, DC: APSA.

CARDOSO, F. H. 1972. Dependent capitalist development in Latin America. *New Left Review*, 74: 83–94.

—— 1977. The consumption of dependency theory in the United States. *Latin American Research Review*, 12: 7–24.

—— and FALETTO, E. 1979. *Dependency and Development in Latin America*, trans. M. M. Urquidi. Berkeley: University of California Press.

CHAKRABARTY, D. 2000a. *Provincializing Europe: Postcolonial Thought and Historical Difference*. Princeton, NJ: Princeton University Press.

—— 2000b. *Subaltern Studies* and postcolonial historiography. *Nepantla: Views from the South*, 1: 9–32.

—— 2002. *Habitations of Modernity: Essays in the Wake of Subaltern Studies*. Chicago: University of Chicago Press.

CHATURVEDI, V. 2000. Introduction. Pp. vii–xix in *Mapping Subaltern Studies and the Postcolonial*, ed. V. Chatuvedi. London: Verso.

CHILCOTE, R. H. 1984. *Theories of Development and Underdevelopment*. New York: Sage.

CHOWDHRY, G., and NAIR, S. 2002. Introduction: power in a postcolonial world. Pp. 1–32 in *Power, Postcolonialism, and International Relations: Reading Race, Gender, and Class*, ed. G. Chowdhry and S. Nair. New York: Routledge.

DARBY, P. 2004. Pursuing the political: a postcolonial rethinking of relations international. *Millennium: Journal of International Studies*, 33: 1–32.

—— and PAOLINI, A. J. 1994. Bridging international relations and postcolonialism. *Alternatives*, 19: 371–97.

DIRLIK, A. 1994. The postcolonial aura: third world criticism in an age of global capitalism. *Critical Inquiry*, 20: 328–56.

DOS SANTOS, T. 1970. The structure of dependence. *American Economic Review*, 60: 231–6.

DOTY, R. L. 1996. *Imperial Encounters: The Politics of Representation in North–South Relations*. Minneapolis: University of Minnesota.

ESCOBAR, A. 1995. *Encountering Development: The Making and Unmaking of the Third World*. Princeton, NJ: Princeton University Press.

EUBEN, R. L. 2002. Contingent borders, syncretic perspectives: globalization, political theory, and Islamizing knowledge. *International Studies Review*, 4: 23–48.

GANDHI, L. 1998. *Postcolonial Theory: A Critical Introduction*. New York: Columbia University Press.

INAYATULLAH, N., and BLANEY, D. L. 2004. *International Relations and the Problem of Difference*. London: Routledge.

KEOHANE, R. O. 1989. *International Institutions and State Power: Essays in International Relations Theory*. Boulder, Colo.: Westview.

KRISHNA, S. 1999. *Postcolonial Insecurities: India, Sri Lanka, and the Question of Nationhood*. Minneapolis: University of Minnesota Press.

MANZO, K. 1991. Modernist discourse and the crisis of development theory. *Studies in Comparative International Development*, 26: 3–36.

——1996. *Creating Boundaries: The Politics of Race and Nation*. Boulder, Colo.: Lynne Rienner.

——1999. The international imagination: themes and arguments in international studies. *Review of International Studies*, 25: 493–506.

MITCHELL, T. 1998. Fixing the economy. *Cultural Studies*, 12: 82–101.

——2000. The stage of modernity. Pp. 1–34 in *Questions of Modernity*, ed. T. Mitchell. Minneapolis: University of Minnesota.

MONGIA, P. 1996. *Contemporary Postcolonial Theory: A Reader*. Oxford: Oxford University Press.

MUPPIDI, H. 2004. *The Politics of the Global*. Minneapolis: University of Minnesota Press.

MURPHY, C. 1984. *The Emergence of the NIEO Ideology*. Boulder, Colo.: Westview.

PAKENHAM, R. A. 1992. *The Dependency Movement: Scholarship and Politics in Development Studies*. Cambridge, Mass.: Harvard University Press.

PALMA, G. 1978. Dependency: a formal theory of underdevelopment or a methodology for the analysis of concrete situations of underdevelopment? *World Development*, 6: 881–924.

PAOLINI, A. J. 1999. *Navigating Modernity: Postcolonialism, Identity, and International Relations*. Boulder, Colo.: Lynne Rienner.

PERSAUD, R. B., and WALKER, R. B. J. (eds.) 2001. Race in international relations, special issue. *Alternatives*, 26: 373–543.

PIETERSE, J. N., and PAREKH, B. 1995. Shifting imaginaries: decolonization, internal decolonization, postcoloniality. Pp. 1–9 in *The Decolonization of Imagination: Culture, Knowledge and Power*, ed. J. N. Pieterse and B. Parekh. London: Zed.

SARKAR, S. 2000. The decline of the subaltern in *Subaltern Studies*. Pp. 300–23 in *Mapping Subaltern Studies and the Postcolonial*, ed. V. Chaturvedi. London: Verso.

SLATER, D. 2004. *Geopolitics and the Post-Colonial: Rethinking North–South Relations*. Oxford: Blackwell.

SNYDER, J. 2004. One world, rival theories. *Foreign Policy*, 145: 52–62.

SUNKEL, O. 1969. National development policy and external dependence in Latin America. *Journal of Development Studies*, 6: 23–48.

——1973. Transnational capitalism and national disintegration in Latin America. *Social and Economic Studies*, 22: 132–76.

THRIFT, N. 2000. Pandora's box? Cultural geographies or economies. Pp. 689–704 in *The Oxford Handbook of Economic Geography*, ed. G. L. Clark, M. P. Feldman, and M. S. Gertler. New York: Oxford.

TICKNER, A. 2003. Seeing IR differently: notes from the third world. *Millennium: Journal of International Studies*, 32: 295–324.

VALENZUELA, J. S., and VALENZUELA, A. 1981. Modernization and dependency: alternative perspectives in the study of Latin American underdevelopment. Pp. 15–42 in *From Dependency to Development: Strategies to Overcome Underdevelopment and Inequality*. Boulder, Colo.: Westview.

WALT, S. M. 1998. International relations: one world, many theories. *Foreign Policy*, 110: 29–46.

YOUNG, R. J. C. 2001. *Postcolonialism: An Historical Introduction*. Oxford: Blackwell.

CHAPTER 39

....

INTERNATIONAL RELATIONS THEORY FROM A FORMER HEGEMON

....

RICHARD LITTLE

THIS chapter assesses whether the status—past and present—of the former European great powers, and more specifically Britain, has had any impact on how theorists in these countries approach the study of international relations. Relatively little thought has been given to this topic. In part, this is because of the widespread acceptance of the positivist assumption that the aim of the social sciences is to develop a view of reality, independent of time and space—a "view from nowhere," as Thomas Nagel (1986) puts it. But it is also because of the widespread belief that the American academy occupies a hegemonic position in the discipline, thereby undermining the potential for international relations theory to develop autonomously outside the United States.

This chapter challenges both of these assumptions. First, it accepts the postpositivist argument that we have no alternative but to adopt a "view from somewhere," and as a result our analysis necessarily embraces a subjective dimension. While positivists insist that the search for knowledge must transcend national boundaries, postpositivists recognize the need for a sociology of knowledge that

I am very grateful to Chris Reus-Smit for his extremely constructive comments on earlier versions of this chapter.

highlights the way that theorists are drawn to problems and solutions that reflect their own historical experience as well as their own distinctive intellectual and institutional foundations. Most disciplines certainly generate national trajectories of thought. But postpositivists insist that there is no reason why these "views from somewhere" should not be objective. Secondly, the chapter questions the hegemonic thesis and argues that, even if we only focus on Britain, it immediately becomes apparent that there have been autonomous developments in British international relations theory that relate specifically to the rise and fall of Britain as a great power.

The first part of this chapter explores the hegemonic thesis and then identifies anomalies that arise when the former European great powers are brought into the picture. In the second part, these anomalies are then reassessed and I argue that, not only is it essential to acknowledge the importance of theory development outside the United States, but also that once these developments are highlighted, then the anomalies can be resolved, but only by reconstituting the conventional account of how international relations theory has developed.

1 AMERICAN HEGEMONY CONFRONTS EUROPEAN ANOMALIES

1.1 The United States as a Disciplinary Hegemon

According to Stanley Hoffmann (1977), international relations emerged as an independent discipline after 1945 when the United States became a global power and its leaders recognized the need for an "intellectual compass" to guide their future actions. But Hoffmann also insists that the United States required and possessed unique institutional advantages for establishing a new academic discipline. First, close relations between American scholars and policy-makers were needed. Secondly, American foundations had to fund research that responded to the needs and interests of government. Finally, the American university system required sufficient flexibility to open up new areas of research and teaching. By contrast, Hoffmann asserts that these institutional features were not present in Europe and, as a consequence, the evolution of international relations has persisted as an essentially American enterprise.

Although Americans do not own the intellectual property rights on international relations, it is widely accepted, nevertheless, that the United States operates as a worldwide disciplinary hegemon, dictating the research agenda for the field. While Britain and other former European great powers can play a role in international relations, at best they are seen to operate as foot soldiers, following a strategy established by the hegemon. So international relations does not supply a "view from nowhere" but one from the United States.

While acknowledging Hoffmann's "brilliant insights," Ole Wæver (1998) insists that there has never been any serious attempt to investigate the sociological development of international relations as a global discipline and he endeavors to rectify the situation, using a sophisticated model to generate national profiles that permit cross-national comparisons. The model not only reveals discernible and explicable national differences in international relations, but also a growing theoretical and methodological divide that is opening up between the United States and Europe.

Wæver (1998) applies his model to Germany, France, Britain, and the United States and demonstrates that key features of the model were in place long before international relations emerged as an independent discipline. But a discipline, he insists, is more than simply the categories used in the organization of knowledge; it is also crucially about the organization of scholars and universities. Knowledge, he accepts, can often be extraordinarily fluid, whereas institutions tend to be highly resistant to change. So, while it may be true that we can trace international relations back to earlier times, Wæver agrees with Hoffmann that it was only in the United States after 1945 that international relations emerged as an independent discipline, although the organizational structures slowly began to be reproduced elsewhere. As the discipline extended, so the United States effectively established itself as a hegemon within the discipline's global arena. But whereas the Europeans were initially very receptive to theoretical developments in the United States, thereby reproducing American hegemony, Wæver forecasts that, with the growing influence of rational choice theory in the United States, they are becoming increasingly hostile to US theory and are starting to plough their own distinctive furrows. Wæver concludes that this development will eventually precipitate the demise of American hegemony in international relations.

Wæver's sociological approach unquestionably creates the space needed to identify the existence of national trajectories and he effectively demonstrates that three of the former European great powers now follow distinctive research trajectories. So he is able to show, for example, that in Germany, during the nineteenth century, international relations, and realist ideas in particular, were embedded in the discipline of history, thereby inhibiting the emergence of international relations as a separate discipline. Nevertheless, in the following century, those European émigrés to the United States interested in international relations found their disciplinary home within political science, in part because of the impact of Germanic ideas on American political science from the nineteenth century onwards.

Wæver's overall argument (1998, 689) highlights the existing hegemonic status of the United States identified by the "huge balance-of-trade deficits" that other countries are currently running with the United States as measured by "patterns of publication, citation, and, especially, theory borrowing." Of course, the importance of the United States is incontestable, but ascribing hegemomic status to the

American academy generates a series of anomalies because the ascription underestimates the degree of autonomy that can be observed in the way that international relations has developed in the former European great powers as well as the impact that theory developed in these countries has had in the United States.

1.2 The European Émigré Anomaly

Despite initiating the idea of international relations as an American social science, Hoffmann—an Austrian trained in France before moving to the United States—admits that one of the important factors that encouraged the development of American international relations was the flow of émigrés from Europe. William and Annette Fox (1961, 339) attribute much of the "ferment, vigor, and variety" in American international relations to scholars "whose origins and, in many cases, entire scholarly training were European." It follows that the emergence of the field in the United States has more cosmopolitan foundations than the unalloyed image of an American social science initially suggests.

But these émigrés have also been viewed as a Trojan horse infiltrating an approach to international relations long associated with the former European great powers. Indeed, Stefano Guzzini (1998) argues that realism was effectively imported into the United States by the émigrés with the express intention of acquainting US leaders with the maxims of nineteenth-century European diplomatic practice. These self-identified realists assumed that the US diplomatic tradition was innocent of the frequently brutal ways of power politics. From Guzzini's perspective, however, international events quickly dislodged realism from the monopoly position that it initially occupied within the newly emerging field of study. But at the same time, he also observes that, from the start, in order to gain influence in the United States, realists had no alternative but to try to give their diplomatic maxims a social scientific sheen, and when classical realism began to lose its scientific lustre, as a more positivist approach found favor in the United States, so classical realism gave way to the more scientific language of neorealism in what Guzzini sees as a vain attempt to ensure that realism retained its prime position.

1.3 The British Anomaly

Wæver's model makes clear that the political and social circumstances that define any state have a significant impact on the trajectory followed by social scientists working within that state. This is not a new line of argument; indeed, it played a central role in E. H. Carr's survey (2001) of thinking about international relations in Britain. From Carr's perspective, between the two World Wars, the British were drawn to what he calls a utopian approach, although he traces this orientation much further back in time. John Mearsheimer (2005, 143) insists, moreover, that this orientation has persisted with British academics and intellectuals continuing to operate as idealists who consistently neglect the crucial role of power when thinking about international politics. So, although Carr dealt idealism "a devastating blow," it nevertheless made an "amazing comeback." From Mearsheimer's perspective (2005, 143), in the contemporary era "almost every British international relations theorist is an idealist." John Haslam (2002, 210) also argues that, since Carr, Britain has "struggled to produce a thinker of any originality in the realist tradition." From Haslam's perspective, moreover, it is Britain's decline in great power status that has discouraged theorists from building on Carr's insights. Although Haslam (2002, 210) acknowledges that intellectuals rarely respond consciously to the kind of fundamental shift in power that Britain experienced after 1945, "the subconscious sensitivity to their working environment is hard to ignore" and so "with the decline in Britain's status in the world ran the decline in original thought about power and international relations."

Chris Brown (2006, 677) offers a more wide-ranging assessment. His starting point is that, as Britain has declined, so theorists now "almost" provide the "dominant voice" in British international relations discourse, although this development has come at the price of theorists shedding their contacts with more substantive areas of discourse. As he sees it, thirty years ago British academics approached theory from the perspective of a range of practical issues within the field. According to Brown (2006, 677), Hedley Bull, for example, set about "theorising a familiar practice" and his theory related to topics that "anyone concerned with IR would have to think about." By contrast, Brown (2006, 680) argues that contemporary English School theorists now feel obliged to "locate their work within traditions of political philosophy and social theory that Bull was hardly aware of." As a consequence, a gap has opened up between theorists and the rest of the community in international relations. But Brown also argues that a crucial part of this story is the way that British theorists have abandoned the search for explanatory theory in favor of interpretative theory, and it is this feature that distinguishes theorizing in Britain from theorizing in the United States. Brown (2006, 683) attributes this development, in part, to the "decline in status of Britain as a world power" with theorists now presupposing that there is no point in trying to change the direction of a state that no longer has influence in the world.

1.4 The Anglo-American Anomaly

The contemporary and ever-widening Anglo-American theory divide appears doubly anomalous if it is accepted that there was a very long-standing tradition of thought that reflected a shared body of ideas about international relations. Indeed, Arnold Wolfers (1956, x), one of the European émigrés, observed a gulf between

Anglo-American and continental theorists that was not, he argued, accidental but "had deep roots in the political experience of England and the United States and in the way this experience has been intellectually absorbed." He focused on the "strategic insularity" of Britain and the United States and argued that the danger of external invasion was low most of the time for these two "island" countries. As a consequence, Wolfers argued that Anglo-American theorists developed an approach to international relations that was quite different from the one adopted by continental theorists. Because the continental countries were constantly confronted by externally generated existential threats, they believed that there was "little leeway if any to rescue moral values from a sea of tragic necessity" (Wolfers 1956, xx). By contrast, the idea of necessity or reason of states "remained foreign to the political philosophers of the English speaking world," and on the contrary, they assumed that statesmen enjoyed the same level of freedom "to choose the right path in their external conduct as they did in their internal policies." Wolfers insists that, although some Anglo-American theorists, for example Thomas Hobbes and Alexander Hamilton, have been depicted as realists, they too emphasized "the moral aspects of political choice" and emphasized the need for moderation and self-restraint, whereas continental theorists invariably stressed the conflict between morality and *raison d'état* (Wolfers 1956, xx).

Wolfers (1956, xxvi) acknowledged, however, that by the middle of the twentieth century, both Britain and the United States had lost their "island" status and "had become 'Continental' in terms of the dangers and compulsions pressing upon them from the outside." As a consequence, their long-established tradition of thinking had become susceptible to two dangerous extremes. One was a cynical acceptance of the continental "philosophy of necessity" and the other was the adoption of purely power-based policies justified not by the philosophy of necessity but by a hypocritical theory that would provide "suitable moral labels, catering thereby to the sense of self-righteousness." By contrast, Wolfers (1956, xxvi) advocated an approach that did not involve a break with tradition and that rested on the assumption that all states possess "freedom of choice between more or less moderation."

Carr (2001, 74–5) also acknowledged the existence of an "English-speaking" tradition of thought, although he saw it as distinctively double-edged and argued that "the view that the English-speaking peoples are monopolists of international morality and the view that they are consummate international hypocrites may be reduced to the plain fact that the current canons of international virtue have, by a natural and inevitable process, been mainly created by them." From Carr's perspective, therefore, the Anglo-American tradition built on a much broader base than simply shared geopolitical circumstances, reflecting a system that had been constructed to promote the interests of both countries. As a consequence, Carr (2001, 65) was not surprised that the Anglo-American tradition embodied utopianism after 1919 because he insisted that "the intellectual theories and ethical standards of utopianism, far from being the expression of absolute and *a priori* principles, are historically conditioned, being both products of circumstances and interests and weapons framed for the furtherance of interests." By the same token, Carr (2001, 97) noted that, especially when these interests are not challenged, utopians themselves fail to recognize the "continuous but silent workings of political power."

2 DECLINING BRITISH POWER AND THE RISE OF THE ENGLISH SCHOOL

Carr was writing at the onset of the Second World War, after resigning in 1936 from a twenty-year career in the Foreign Office to become the Wilson Professor of International Politics in Aberystwyth at the University of Wales. His career epitomizes, therefore, key features that Hoffmann associates with the establishment of a discipline. Yet ironically, Carr almost immediately moved out of the field and, indeed, in the 1970s wrote to Hoffmann, saying that he was not "particularly proud" of the role that he had played in precipitating the formation of international relations. What is this "thing called international relations in the 'English speaking countries' " Carr asked, rhetorically, other than an analysis of how "to run the world from positions of strength." As he saw it, international relations is "little more than a rationalization for the exercise of power by the dominant nations over the weak" (Cox 2001, xiii). And, following the Soviet invasion of Czechoslovakia in 1968, he noted that now Britain was no longer a great power, he discovered that "I don't like Great Powers" (Haslam 1999, 250).

From this perspective, then, international relations is promoted from within the great powers and so it becomes almost axiomatic that in a unipolar world the discipline should take a hegemonic form. But, as noted, this line of argument generates some intriguing anomalies. I now deal with the anomalies in two ways. First I suggest that, on the face of it, the anomalies cancel each other out and provide a coherent but cross-national account of how the discipline has developed. Secondly, I argue that this resolution of the anomalies is problematic because it fails to accommodate the multifaceted nature of the theory propagated by both the European émigrés and the English School. By then focusing on the English School, it becomes possible to assess whether Britain's declining international status factors into the development of English School theory.

2.1 Accommodating the Anomalies

The anomalies discussed above challenge the prevailing hegemonic image of international relations and promote a more nuanced account of how the discipline has developed. According to this account, international relations theory extends back to the eighteenth century in both the United States and Europe, although the major division is not across the Atlantic but between the realpolitik perspective of continental Europe and a more normative position advanced from within Britain and the United States. This normative position significantly influenced how international relations was studied in both countries after the First World War. But after 1945, as the United States acknowledged both its hegemonic position within the West and the emerging existential threat from Eurasia, so the field in the United States was receptive to the influence of an influential group of scholars who had been raised and trained in continental Europe. They helped to propagate a realist approach that for a while dominated the field in the United States, and as a consequence, international relations began to travel along very different tracks in Britain and the United States.

2.2 Reassessing the Anomalies

Taking the anomalies seriously, therefore, pushes the origins of the discipline back in time and accommodates developments in Europe as well as the United States. But this transformed account also becomes a source of new anomalies. For example, although the European émigrés have habitually been associated with the realpolitik or continental view of international politics, they almost invariably subscribed to a much more complex and subtle view of international relations. A sympathetic reading of Hans Morgenthau, for example, demonstrates that he worked on the basis of a multifaceted view of international relations, with his theory distinguishing between the international system, the international society, and world society, thereby blazing a pluralistic trail that was soon to be followed by English School theorists (Little 2003).

The idea of an international society lay at the heart of Morgenthau's approach to international relations. As a consequence, he was strongly opposed to the emergence of methodologies that attempted to establish a "view from nowhere" and that failed to capture the holistic perspective of the actors under investigation. At the start of the cold war, his concern was that the United States and the Soviet Union lacked any common ideas, and yet it was shared ideas that had in the past created and maintained the international society. For Morgenthau, the real danger of the cold war was that international society would give way to an international system governed solely by unconstrained power politics. Although, in the short run, he stressed the importance of sustaining an international society, he pinned his long-term hopes for survival on the evolution of world society.

Morgenthau and his colleagues from continental Europe, however, were quickly misidentified in the United States as hard-nosed realists, and they then lost the methodological battle when positivism prevailed and a holistic understanding of international relations was overtaken by a fragmented approach to knowledge creation. Realism is now reduced to the image of rational actors competing in an an-archic arena, and the approach is contrasted with rival theories that explain, for ex-ample, cooperation and transnationalism—phenomena that realists either are seen to ignore or cannot account for. But, while the hermeneutic and holistic approaches favored by the European émigrés were marginalized in the United States, by contrast the English School pursued a very similar agenda, and according to Dunne (2007, 127), its theorists have now come to occupy center stage in Britain. A substantial trans-Atlantic divide has opened up as a consequence, but to account for the divide we have to discount the influence of the European émigrés in the United States.

2.3 The Rise of the English School

Hidemi Suganami (2003) is undoubtedly correct when he suggests that the well-defined image that now exists of the English School is a relatively recent phenom-enon. The School started as a cluster of theorists trying to make sense of a world where the influence of Britain was clearly on the wane. There was a very strong sense, however, that the contemporary international arena operated on foundations that Britain, as one of the key great powers in the past, had helped to establish. Rather than examining the struggle between the United States and the Soviet Union, therefore, these theorists struggled to understand these foundations, and focused on how the European states system had evolved. They shared a common interest in the idea of an international society that had developed across several centuries. Although Bull (2002) did most to clarify the English School approach to the international society, it was C. A. W. Manning (1957; 1976) who paved the way, stressing the importance of the very distinctive social "structure" of inter-national society and how, in contrast to the world society made up of flesh-and-blood individuals, it was a "quasi-society" constituted by fictional entities (Wilson 2004). But as Brown (2006, 683–4) makes clear, these theorists also recognized that, to understand this society, they needed an "ethno-methodological study of diplomatic culture" and they had to enter the hermeneutic circle to comprehend how practitioners understand the world. At that time, this was still relatively easy to achieve, because there existed a "clubbable relationship" between theorists and practitioners. Indeed, the British Committee on the Theory of International Politics embraced both diplomats and academics when it was established at the end of the 1950s (Dunne 1998).

Wolfers tied British thinking to an Anglo-American tradition that pulled against a continental tradition, but the English School cut these links and identified instead a complementary set of European theoretical traditions: one linked to the interna-tional system (Wolfers's continental tradition), a second to the international society (Wolfers's Anglo-American tradition, although for the English School the main the-orists are unquestionably continental Europeans), and the third to a world society constituted by individuals rather than states. The English School acknowledges the importance of all three traditions (Little 2003), although it is only very recently that world society has been actively interrogated (Buzan 2004; Clark 2007). But, initially, the focus on international society was considered paramount because of the potential apocalyptic ramifications of the cold war. As Carr (2001, 87) acknowledged before the Second World War, pure realism "can offer us nothing but a naked struggle for power which makes any kind of international society impossible." In line with Morgenthau's thesis, therefore, the nascent English School focused on how the fractious Europeans had promoted an international society that ensured a modicum of social order.

2.4 Studying International Society in the Future: Darker and Wider

Although American neorealists such as Mearsheimer (2005) take it for granted that the reference to an international society has idealist overtones, from the start members of the English School recognized that there was a dark side to international society. As Martin Wight (1966, 93) observed, the "quasi" nature of the international society "conceals, obstructs, and oppresses the *real* society of individual men and women." But despite recognizing the repressive potential of international society, this dimension was not highlighted by the first generation of English School theorists. Bull (2002) began by examining order rather than justice because of the dire consequences that can follow if international order breaks down. He emphasized, for example, the dystopian elements that could accompany the erosion of state power and the emergence of a neomedieval world.

The dark side of international society was hidden from view in part because the orientation of the first generation of theorists was so myopically Eurocentric. Of course, they acknowledged that there was a world beyond Europe, but they focused on Europe because they believed that the great power institutions underpinning the European international society continued to provide the best hope for surviving the cold war. In the post-cold war era, however, it becomes more difficult to ignore the evasions of the first generation of theorists. One critic focuses, in particular, on the link between imperialism and the international society and finds it "fascinating how the celebrated historical method of the English School skirts over this historical fact" (Callahan 2004, 310). Barry Buzan (2004) agrees and argues that colonialism must be identified as one of the primary institutions that defined the European international society. But William Callahan (2004, 307) also insists that the emergence of the English School and its emphasis on international society "was part of a moral shift in the valence of imperialism from a positive goal to a negative embarrassment." This assessment is anachronistic. The academics and diplomats who established the English School were part of a generation who still possessed a largely positive image of the Empire.

In the post-cold war era, however, a new generation of English School theorists have emerged who acknowledge that it is necessary to reassess the actions of the European great powers. Edward Keene (2002, xii) argues, for example, that Bull was locked into a conception of international order that had been propagated by the great powers for 200 years. Now that Britain has lost its great power status, it is much easier to step out of the hermeneutic circle and to acknowledge that during the colonial era the great powers established a very different order beyond the boundaries of Europe from the one that operated within those boundaries. This dual order rested, moreover, on racist assumptions, and John Hobson and Jason Sharman (2005) argue that international lawyers played a crucial role in propagating the idea of a racial hierarchy. Shogo Suzuki (2005) notes, moreover, how successfully Japan took advantage of the European dual order, using European international law to promote its own sovereignty while using the standard of civilization to justify the acquisition of territory from "uncivilized" Asian states. But to understand the complex impact of race on international relations, it is necessary to adopt a more holistic approach and embrace world society as well as international society. As Ian Clark (2007) demonstrates, for example, it is not possible to understand how slavery was outlawed from the international arena at the start of the nineteenth century without exploring the interaction between world society and international society. By the same token, to increase their understanding of the dark side of international relations, English School theorists need to widen their frame of reference and draw more effectively on their holistic framework.

3 CONCLUSION

The English School is not the only theory in play in Britain. Nevertheless, it draws on a theoretical orientation that taps into divergent but long-standing traditions of thought within Europe. The first generation of English School theorists focused primarily on the role of international society and, in doing so, drew heavily on the predispositions of British decision-makers when the state operated as a great power. Indeed, they were often so comfortable with these predispositions that they failed to step outside the hermeneutic circle and provide the critical voice that Carr believed was essential for any objective understanding of international relations. A new generation of theorists is now providing this voice and, as a consequence, is beginning to give English School theory a more critical edge. This evolution of English School thinking is unrelated to intellectual developments in the United States, and, on the contrary, it can be seen as a delayed response to Britain's loss of empire and world status. Nevertheless, the central message of this chapter is that we can all too easily overplay the idea of US hegemony inside the discipline of international relations as well as within the real world of international relations.

References

Brown, C. 2006. IR theory in Britain—the new black? *Review of International Studies*, 32: 677–87.

Bull, H. 2002. *The Anarchical Society: A Study of Order in World Politics*, 3rd edn. London: Palgrave.

Buzan, B. 2004. *From International to World Society? English School Theory and the Social Structure of Globalisation*. Cambridge: Cambridge University Press.

Callahan, W. A. 2004. Nationalising international theory: race, class and the English School. *Global Society*, 18: 305–23.

Carr, E. H. 2001. *The Twenty Years' Crisis 1919–1939: An Introduction to the Study of International Relations*, 3rd edn. Basingstoke: Palgrave.

Clark, I. 2007. *International Legitimacy and World Society*. Oxford: Oxford University Press.

Cox, M. 2001. Introduction. Pp. i–cviii in *The Twenty Years' Crisis 1919–1939: An Introduction to the Study of International Relations*, 3rd edn., E. H. Carr. Basingstoke: Palgrave.

Dunne, T. 1998. *Inventing International Society: A History of the English School*. Basingstoke: Macmillan.

—— 2007. The English School. Pp. 127–47 in *International Relations Theories: Discipline and Diversity*, ed. T. Dunne, M. Kurki, and S. Smith. Oxford: Oxford University Press.

Fox, W. T. R., and Fox, A. B. 1961. The teaching of international relations in the United States. *World Politics*, 13: 339–59.

Guzzini, S. 1998. *Realism in International Relations and International Political Economy: The Continuing Story of a Death Foretold*. London: Routledge.

Haslam, J. 1999. *The Vices of Integrity: E. H. Carr, 1892–1982*. London: Verso.

—— 2002. *No Virtue like Necessity: Realist Thought in International Relations since Machiavelli*. New Haven, Conn.: Yale University Press.

Hobson, J. M., and Sharman, J. C. 2005. The enduring place of hierarchy in world politics: tracing the social logics of hierarchy and political change. *European Journal of International Relations*, 11: 63–98.

Hoffmann, S. 1977. An American social science: international relations. *Daedalus*, 106: 41–60.

Keene, E. 2002. *Beyond the Anarchical Society: Grotius, Colonialism and Order in World Politics*. Cambridge: Cambridge University Press.

Little, R. 2003. The English School vs. American realism: a meeting of minds or divided by a common language? *Review of International Studies*, 29: 443–60.

Manning, C. A. W. 1957. Varieties of worldly wisdom. *World Politics*, 9: 149–65.

—— 1976. *The Nature of International Society*. London: London School of Economics/ Macmillan.

Mearsheimer, J. 2005. E. H. Carr vs. idealism: the battle rages on. *International Relations*, 19: 139–52.

NAGEL, T. 1986. *The View from Nowhere*. Oxford: Clarendon Press.

SUGANAMI, H. 2003. British institutionalists, or the English School, 20 years on. *International Relations*, 17: 253–71.

SUZUKI, S. 2005. Japan's socialization into Janus-faced European international society. *European Journal of International Relations*, 11: 137–64.

WÆVER, O. 1998. The sociology of a not so international discipline: American and European developments in international relations. *International Organization*, 52: 687–727.

WIGHT, M. 1966. Western values in international relations. Pp. 89–131 in *Diplomatic Investigations: Essays in the Theory of International Politics*, ed. H. Butterfield and M. Wight. London: Allen and Unwin.

WILSON, P. 2004. Mannings's quasi-masterpiece: *The Nature of International Society* revisited. *Round Table*, 93: 755–69.

WOLFERS, A. 1956. Introduction: political theory and international relations. Pp. i–xxvii in *The Anglo-American Tradition in Foreign Affairs: Readings from Thomas More to Woodrow Wilson*, ed. A. Wolfers and L. W. Martin. New Haven, Conn.: Yale University Press.

PART VIII

··

OLD AND NEW

··

CHAPTER 40

....

THE CONCEPT OF POWER AND THE (UN)DISCIPLINE OF INTERNATIONAL RELATIONS

....

JANICE BIALLY MATTERN

WHERE there are politics there is power. It is no surprise, hence, that the concept of power is fundamental to the study of world politics. What might be surprising is just *how* fundamental it is. Power, or, more exactly, the particular way in which it is conceived at any given time, has been a significant constitutive force defining the discipline of international relations. As an "essentially contested concept" whose meaning has broadened substantially over the years, the developments in conceptual thinking about power have progressively demanded acceptance of new empirical focuses, research methods, and normative logics into the lexicon of what counts as international relations (Connolly 1974). Contestation over the concept of power, thus, has helped broaden the discipline.

And yet, if a broad discipline is desirable for the "engaged pluralism" it facilitates, such benefits seem to have escaped international relations (Lapid 2003). In fact, international relations scholars have responded to the breadth of the discipline by narrowing both their views on power and their empirical, methodological, and normative schemas. The unfortunate result is that international relations is less a discipline than a collection of insular research communities; it is an (un)discipline. If international relations is to amount to more than a cacophony of disconnected views on world politics, these niches need to communicate. A framework that illuminates the relationships among the various aspects of power could help. Such a framework need not force individual scholars to adopt a broader conception of power, nor to engage a broader range of empirical, methodological, and normative angles in their research. To promote productive conversation across the (un)discipline the framework simply needs to allow for those possibilities.

1 POWER IN THE DISCIPLINE

If the way power is used shapes world politics, the way it is conceived shapes international relations. The earliest conception of power among scholars of international politics emerged as the discipline itself emerged. Advanced by early realists like Hans Morgenthau (1948) and embraced by later realists like Kenneth Waltz (1979) and John Mearsheimer (1990), this conception envisioned power as an entity; as intrinsic to tangible things such as the military, wealth, and geography. From this conception, international relations developed into a discipline focused on material resources and the states that controlled them; methodologically preoccupied with tangible measures (Claude 1962); and normatively complicit with militarization and violence (Brown 1992, 77). In turn, international relations designated small states (no less nonstate actors) largely irrelevant (Wight 1946); proclaimed suspect those theories and methods that dealt with "intangibles" (Frey 1971); and pronounced the very idea of morality between states dangerous (Morgenthau 1948).

During the second half of the twentieth century, however, some of these strictures began to widen. Following a trend in the social sciences (Dahl 1961), international relations scholars came to appreciate a distinction between *potential* and *actual* power in which actual power was "a type of causation" rooted in the capacity of actor A to get actor B to do what it would otherwise not do (Baldwin 2000, 178). While material resources were one potential source of that influential capacity, "fuzzier" variables, such as the scope and norms of states' relationships, were also recognized. This helped lessen the discipline's preoccupation with tangible measures. Considering power as a relationship of influence also mitigated the normative complicity of international relations with militarization. Since "no single [power] base . . . is decisive" in crafting influence, states were counseled to marshal all kinds of power resources—not just arms (Guzzini 1993, 454).

Nonetheless, much remained unchanged. For instance, the conception of power as a relationship of influence reinforced the discipline's commitment to materiality because it conceived of influence in terms of an actor's capacity to alter the material costs and benefits of compliance (Guzzini 1993). This fortified the discipline's focus on states (their abundance of material resources makes them effective at manipulating material incentives); and its methodological behavioralism (as a material phenomenon, influence could be observed through overt conflicts between A and B). Finally, this conception did nothing to challenge the realist presumption that world politics is no place for morality.

While this behavioral, material conception of power as a relationship of influence mostly colluded with the realist outline of international relations, other conceptions posed more formidable challenges. The "faces of power" debate in political theory offered international relations scholars three alternative ways of conceiving of power as a relationship of influence, each of which went beyond that "first face." The "second face of power" decoupled power from overt conflict by highlighting how actors can exploit their institutional position to silence dissent (Bachrach and Baratz 1962). Entering international relations through liberal institutionalist work on agenda-setting, decision-making, and compliance in international institutions, this view of power demonstrated the importance of nonevents (Chayes and Chayes 1993). Accordingly, it helped reveal the limits of methodological behavioralism, supporting the turn to scientific realism (Bueno de Mesquita 1985); it helped demonstrate the political relevance (and thus legitimacy) of scholarship on international cooperation (Kratochwil and Ruggie 1986); and it helped justify explicit reflection on the normative dimensions of, at least, formal cooperative relations among states (Meunier 2005).

The third face of power went further. It proposed that one could not sufficiently understand the power relations between actors by focusing on their relative positions in material and institutional arrangements. One must also consider their position in social structures. Arguing that socially privileged actors can use their stature to deceive those less privileged into complicity with their own domination, this view indicated that nonevents could reflect the psychological indoctrination of the weak (Lukes 2005). This Gramscian conception of power pushed international relations scholars to look beyond great powers to materially weak states, since the allegiances of their ruling classes in a global economy also shaped the dynamics of world politics (Chase-Dunn 1989). Moreover, by locating power in the relationship between markets and class (rather than in the relationship between states), this conception challenged the state-centrism of the discipline (Strange 1996). Finally, this conception demanded an explicitly normative systemic international relations theory to cope with questions of oppression and emancipation from structural power (Linklater 1998).

The fourth face of power had the most profound effect on international relations. Rooted in a nonessentialist epistemology, this view offered that power is expressed diffusely through the discourses that create social meaning and make society possible. Power thus is not an exercise carried out by interested agents, but a discursive process through which agents and their interests are produced in the first place (Digeser 1992). Accordingly, world politics happen, not where specific types of actors behave in specific ways, but where social processes produce particular actors and behaviors as meaningful. To study world politics, then, means to study those processes of signification—wherever they occur, among whatever types of actors; through interpretative research methods capable of accessing processes of signification; and with conscious concern for the normative questions provoked by relativism (Campbell 1998). In this way, this constructivist conception of power directly disputed the empirical, methodological, and normative boundaries associated with the realist conception upon which the discipline was founded.

Ultimately, the debate over power was abandoned, unresolved. The problem was that the first and second faces rested upon metatheoretical conceptions of social reality that were incommensurable with those entailed by the, also incommensurable, third and fourth faces (Paolini 1993). This stalemate, however, lent support for the "third debate"—a critical examination of the "ontological, epistemological, and axiological foundations" of international relations' "scientific endeavors" (Lapid 1989, 236). By confronting the discipline with the impossibility of proving its unacknowledged assumptions, this metatheoretical focus forced international relations (however grudgingly) to become more theoretically pluralist, and thus to accommodate a more diverse range of empirical focuses, methodological requirements, and normative dispositions. In this way, contestation over power helped transform international relations into a pluralistic and broad field of study.

2 POWER IN THE (UN)DISCIPLINE

Inasmuch as the theoretic pluralism and substantive breadth of international relations encourages scholars to wrestle with the biases inherent in their own modes of research, it should be celebrated. However, this hardly seems to be the case. As the array of acceptable theories, empirical focuses, methodological approaches, and normative stances within international relations has broadened, the intellectual scope of most international relations scholars has actually narrowed (Kratochwil 2003). Rather than "checking" their research against that of others working on similar issues through different lenses, most scholars have instead ensconced themselves in exclusive research communities organized around specific theories or methods (Smith 2000). So narrow have these niches become that it is hardly possible to arrive at a discipline-wide consensus on the very purpose of the discipline, no less to learn constructively from each other (Tickner 1997). International relations is an (un)discipline.

The fragmentation and silence across international relations' research niches have, in turn, shaped the way that international relations scholars approach power in their research. Rather than confront the thorny metatheoretical issues that dogged earlier efforts to conceptualize power, scholars now tend to substitute grand theories about the phenomenon for studies of its manifestations in various world events. Thus when the end of the cold war and 11 September 2001 raised hegemony as a matter of concern, international relations scholars drew attention, for instance, to the workings of soft power, military and economic power, and caring power in hegemonic systems (Robinson 1999; Brooks and Wohlforth 2002; Nye Jr. 2004). Similarly, as transnational actors, international institutional design, and the United Nations became increasingly important, studies on the powers of "talk" became common (Crawford 2002).

This trend of studying power's modalities is notable in the current context because it is encouraged by, and serves as reinforcement for, international relations' (un)discipline. Specifically, most of these studies have been produced by and for particular, largely insular intellectual niches without much concern to connect them to other such studies in different intellectual niches. Accordingly, it remains unclear how, say, economic standing and care, which are so very different, can both be part and parcel of power. While there have been a few attempts to situate some of these modalities in relation to each other, these have been buried within projects whose primary focus lies elsewhere (Reus-Smit 2004; Bially Mattern 2005). The result is that international relations not only lacks a common conception of power; it also lacks a common framework in which to situate the various conceptions and their expressions. In a peculiar twist, then, as international relations has broadened, power has gone from an essentially contested concept to a concept about which, for lack of a shared vocabulary, international relations scholars cannot even have a discussion. This is ironic indeed for a field to which power is so central.

To remedy this problem, the field, such as it is, could seek common ground upon which the diverse research niches might build collective understandings of the relationships between the various conceptions of power. In this respect, Michael Barnett and Raymond Duvall have taken brave steps. They argue that the different conceptions of power are more accurately different forms of power, understood as "the production, *in and through social relations*, of effects that shape the capacities of actors to determine their own circumstances and fate" (Barnett and Duvall 2005, 3, emphasis added). In light of this, the challenge is to systematize the forms of power according to the social relations from which they issue. Focusing on behavioral versus constitutive social relations and direct versus diffuse ones, the authors construct a typology that recasts the four faces of power as compulsory, institutional, structural, and productive forms of power. This yields analytic clarity on the social relational conditions of possibility for each form of power, and, so, insight into how multiple forms can operate in complementary ways (e.g. Johnstone 2005).

Indeed, as Barnett and Duvall (2005, 4) argue, their framework can promote "cross-fertilization" across the (un)discipline.

Such optimism, however, discounts the complications associated with the social relationalism undergirding the framework. The problem is that as a metatheory, *social* relationalism (as opposed to material relationalism) presumes a non-essentialist view of social reality (White 2006, 47–8). It thus assumes away the possibility of pre-social agents or interests, which in turn assumes away any meaningful distinction between behavior and constitution and direct and diffuse relations. The result is that, in spite of the authors' claims, their framework cannot coherently accommodate behavioral and/or direct forms of power and so, awkwardly, cannot offer analytic purchase on three of the four forms of power—compulsory, institutional, and structural. Rather than identifying common ground upon which scholars across the (un)discipline can situate their varied conceptions of power, this framework is distinctively constructivist and congenial only to productive power.

So what way forward to conversation about power across the (un)discipline? In spite of the limitations of Barnett and Duvall's framework, the quest for common ground remains appealing. The hope is that it is still possible to craft a conception of power sufficiently broad and neutral among metatheoretic logics to accommodate the diversity of views. But concepts, no matter how broad, entail metatheoretical premises. A common-ground definition thus cannot be neutral; it defines away views of power that rest on different premises (Guzzini 2005). Rather than the pluralist inclusion for which it aims, common-ground approaches are necessarily, if unwittingly, exclusive. This dynamic is likely further to entrench the "disciplinary identity politics" behind the dismissive silence across "isms" (White 2006, 1).

Realizing this provokes a suggestion: Rather than pursuing conversation across the (un)discipline by seeking to "split" irresolvable metatheoretical differences, perhaps international relations would do better to face those differences head-on. To propose that conversation about power across the (un)discipline of international relations would be well served by a return to metatheory is not to advocate a return to the third debate. Whereas that discussion responded to the ineluctable yet unknowable character of ontology and epistemology by recognizing *all* metatheoretic logics and the various theories, methods, and normative stances to which they give rise, the discussion I propose would respond to the puzzle of metatheory *pragmatically.* It would ask not "what is the nature of social reality" and "how can we theorize, study, and judge world politics on that basis?" but "what conception of social reality can generate the various processes theorized, methods utilized, and normative issues raised by international relations scholars?" Rather than a metaphysical quest for the "right" foundations, then, this discussion would be a quest for *pragmatic metatheoretic singularism*; an effort to identify one *specific* set of foundational assumptions that can consistently on its own terms give rise to the pluralism that characterizes international relations. Such foundations will offer an inclusive *and* coherent framework upon which to base the "big picture" conversations about power that are currently impossible.

The obvious challenge is how to identify a single metatheory permissive of pluralist theories, methods, and values. As a start, the discussion should focus not on what power *really is*, as did the faces of power debate and Barnett and Duvall's reinterpretation, but on whether there is a conception of social reality that can coherently model the dynamics depicted in each of the four faces. Since antiessentialist "foundations" can accommodate both discursive and behavioral dynamics in a way that essentialist ones cannot, such a conversation will probably end up favoring the very social relationalism that underwrites Barnett and Duvall's framework. However, whereas the latter implicitly privileges that metalogic while presenting itself as neutral, the former makes neither a pretence at neutrality nor a "truth" claim about the social relationalism it adopts. In this way, pragmatic metatheoretic singularism privileges no disciplinary identity in international relations. Rather than fueling exclusion and silence, thus, it encourages productive conversation across the (un)discipline.

REFERENCES

BACHRACH, P., and BARATZ, M. S. 1962. Two faces of power. *American Political Science Review*, 56: 947–52.

BALDWIN, D. 2000. Power and international relations. Pp. 177–91 in *Handbook of International Relations*, ed. W. Carlsnaes, T. Risse, and B. Simmons. Thousand Oaks, Calif.: Sage.

BARNETT, M., and DUVALL, R. 2005. Power in global governance. Pp. 1–32 in *Power in Global Governance*, ed. M. Barnett and R. Duvall. Cambridge: Cambridge University Press.

BIALLY MATTERN, J. 2005. *Ordering International Politics: Identity, Crisis, and Representational Force*. New York: Routledge.

BROOKS, S. G., and WOHLFORTH, W. C. 2002. American primacy in perspective. *Foreign Affairs*, 81: 20–33.

BROWN, C. 1992. *International Relations Theory: New Normative Approaches*. New York: Columbia University Press.

BUENO DE MESQUITA, B. 1985. Toward a scientific understanding of international conflict: a personal view. *International Studies Quarterly*, 29: 121–36.

CAMPBELL, D. 1998. Why fight: humanitarianism, principles, and post-structuralism. *Millennium: Journal of International Studies*, 27: 497–521.

CHASE-DUNN, C. 1989. *Global Formation: Structures of the World-Economy*. Oxford: Blackwell.

CHAYES, A., and CHAYES, A. H. 1993. On compliance. *International Organization*, 47: 175–205.

CLAUDE, I. L. 1962. *Power and International Relations*. New York: Random House.

CONNOLLY, W. 1974. *The Terms of Political Discourse*. Princeton, NJ: Princeton University Press.

CRAWFORD, N. C. 2002. *Argument and Change in World Politics: Ethics, Decolonization, and Humanitarian Intervention.* Cambridge: Cambridge University Press.

DAHL, R. 1961. *Who Governs? Democracy and Power in an American City.* New Haven, Conn.: Yale University Press.

DIGESER, P. 1992. The fourth face of power. *Journal of Politics,* 54: 977–1007.

FREY, F. W. 1971. Comment: on issues and nonissues in the study of power. *American Political Science Review,* 65: 1081–101.

GUZZINI, S. 1993. Structural power: the limits of neorealist power analysis. *International Organization,* 47: 443–78.

—— 2005. The concept of power: a constructivist analysis. *Millennium: Journal of International Studies,* 33: 495–521.

JOHNSTONE, I. 2005. The power of interpretive communities. Pp. 185–204 in *Power in Global Governance,* ed. M. Barnett and R. Duvall. Cambridge: Cambridge University Press.

KRATOCHWIL, F. 2003. The monologue of "science." *International Studies Review,* 5: 124–8.

—— and RUGGIE, J. G. 1986. International organization: a state of the art on an art of the state. *International Organization,* 40: 753–75.

LAPID, Y. 1989. The third debate: on the prospects of international theory in a post-positivist era. *International Studies Quarterly,* 33: 235–54.

—— 2003. Through dialogue to engaged pluralism: the unfinished business of the third debate. *International Studies Review,* 5: 128–31.

LINKLATER, A. 1998. *The Transformation of Political Community: Ethical Foundations of the Post-Westphalian Era.* Cambridge: Polity.

LUKES, S. 2005. *Power: A Radical View,* 2nd edn. New York: Palgrave Macmillan.

MEARSHEIMER, J. J. 1990. Back to the future: instability in Europe after the cold war. *International Security,* 15: 5–56.

MEUNIER, S. 2005. *Trading Voices: The European Union in International Commercial Negotiations.* Princeton, NJ: Princeton University Press.

MORGENTHAU, H. J. 1948. *Politics among Nations: The Struggle for Power and Peace.* New York: Alfred A. Knopf.

NYE, JR., J. S. 2004. *Soft Power: The Means to Success in World Politics.* New York: Public Affairs.

PAOLINI, A. J. 1993. Foucault, realism, and the power discourse in international relations. *Australian Journal of Political Science,* 28: 98–117.

REUS-SMIT, C. 2004. *American Power and World Order.* Cambridge: Polity.

ROBINSON, F. 1999. *Globalizing Care: Ethics, Feminist Theory, and International Relations.* Boulder, Colo.: Westview.

SMITH, S. 2000. The discipline of international relations: still an American social science? *British Journal of Politics and International Relations,* 2: 374–402.

STRANGE, S. 1996. *The Retreat of the State: The Diffusion of Power in the World Economy.* New York: Cambridge University Press.

TICKNER, J. A. 1997. You just don't understand: troubled engagements between feminists and IR theorists. *International Studies Quarterly,* 41: 611–32.

WALTZ, K. N. 1979. *Theory of International Politics.* Reading, Mass.: Addison-Wesley.

WHITE, C. 2006. *Agents, Structures and International Relations: Politics as Ontology.* Cambridge: Cambridge University Press.

WIGHT, M. 1946. *Power Politics.* London: Royal Institute of International Affairs.

CHAPTER 41

LOCATING RESPONSIBILITY: THE PROBLEM OF MORAL AGENCY IN INTERNATIONAL RELATIONS

TONI ERSKINE

QUESTIONS of moral agency are fundamental to the study of world politics. Who—or what—can bear the related moral burdens of duty and blame for specific acts and outcomes has serious implications for practice and theory. We (as politicians, policy-makers, citizens, and scholars) endeavor to identify and assign, and sometimes to deny or deflect, obligations to respond to crises such as famine, environmental degradation, genocide, and disparities in the global distribution of resources and wealth. We also apportion blame—for acts of commission and omission that contribute to these crises and for failures to address them adequately. Thus, rescuing nations from poverty and debt is "a grave and unconditional moral

I am very grateful to Chris Brown, Ian Clark, Neta Crawford, Susanna Karlsson, Andrew Linklater, Cian O'Driscoll, Christian Reus-Smit, Colin Wight, and Michael C. Williams for valuable written comments on an earlier draft of this chapter.

responsibility,"[1] "the developed world has a moral duty to tackle climate change,"[2] and "the international community is guilty of sins of omission" in the context of the Rwandan genocide.[3]

Problematically, such calls to action, claims to duty, and cries of condemnation often precede consideration of the relevant bodies capable of responding. Moreover, the discipline of International Relations offers only limited guidance in addressing this disjuncture.[4] Even in the face of our intuitive sense that entities such as the United Nations (UN), multinational corporations, and states can be held morally responsible, International Relations steadfastly refuses to address this possibility. This refusal is all the more striking given that the discipline travels a considerable distance toward acknowledging the moral agency of such entities by making valuable, and unorthodox, claims about agency. Many approaches, after all, assume that states are agents. Far from being inherently problematic, this move *does not take us far enough*. Hitherto neglected positions on moral agency and responsibility logically accompany such audacious assumptions of agency. Until this is acknowledged and explored, International Relations will be mired in internal contradictions, beset by unnecessary divisions between "normative" and "empirical" pursuits—and of little use in helping us to engage effectively with some of our most urgent global problems.

1 MORAL AGENCY AND RESPONSIBILITY

Moral agents have capacities for deliberating over possible courses of action and their consequences and acting on the basis of this deliberation. Such capacities render moral agents vulnerable to the assignment of duties and the apportioning of moral praise and blame in relation to specific actions and in the context of enabling conditions. In other words, there is a crucial link between the concepts of moral agency and moral responsibility.

Moral responsibility involves being answerable for a particular act or outcome in accordance with what are understood to be moral imperatives. (By contrast, causal responsibility focuses on how a particular outcome is generated and need not be tied to purposive action.) Moral imperatives—especially at the international level—are, of course, variously grounded and conceived. This reality does not,

---

[1] Letter from Pope Benedict XVI to German Chancellor Angela Merkel, dated 16 December 2006.

[2] Attributed to UK Chancellor Gordon Brown, BBC News, 22 April 2006.

[3] Secretary General Kofi Annan at memorial conference for the 1994 Rwanda genocide, 26 March 2004.

[4] Throughout this chapter I am following the convention of using International Relations to refer to the field of study.

however, impede passionate, and often powerful, statements of moral responsibility being made in world politics. Such statements make use of two different, but intimately related, understandings of responsibility. The first involves *ex ante* judgments regarding acts that ought to be performed, or forbearances that must be observed. The second involves *ex post facto* assessments of a particular event or set of circumstances for which an agent's acts and omissions are such that the agent is the object of praise or blame. The forward-looking assertion of moral responsibility is associated with claims to duty and obligation. The backward-looking assertion is linked with claims to blame and accountability. Importantly, to be meaningful, either type of statement must be directed toward those entities capable of responding to ethical imperatives. In short, they must be directed toward moral agents.

This brings us to the important question of where moral responsibility can reasonably be located in world politics. For "individualists," any answer to such a question must refer to individual human beings (Popper 1966, 98; Brodbeck 1968, 240, 283; Weber 1968, 14). From this perspective, the widespread practice of making collectivities (whether corporations, states, or intergovernmental organizations (IGOs)) the objects of statements of moral responsibility is either careless shorthand for describing issues of obligation and accountability at the level of their individual human constituents—or simply nonsensical. Unfortunately, such a strict delimitation of bodies considered to be moral agents leaves much beyond critical scrutiny. It also fails to support compelling descriptions of our expectations and failures in world politics. Individual human beings on their own lack the power, coordination, and resources necessary to achieve many espoused goals (such as preventing genocide). Likewise, explanations of certain harms (such as global warming) cannot be reduced entirely to the individual human constituents of those organizations involved in relevant practices and policies without overlooking an important part of the story. Duty and blame must also, it seems, lie elsewhere.

Significantly, although individual human beings are generally understood to be paradigmatic moral agents, the defining features of moral agency offered above need not preclude certain collectivities from also qualifying. A collectivity with a corporate identity (or an identity greater than the sum of identities of its constitutive parts), an identity over time, a decision-making structure, and an executive function that allows it to act on decisions might also be a moral agent (Erskine 2001; 2003; 2004).[5] By this account, Shell Oil, the US Army, China, Microsoft, the Roman Catholic Church, the European Union (EU), the UN, Hamas, and Amnesty International can conceivably be assigned duties and apportioned blame in ways not reducible to their individual members. It is in this respect that the bold tendency within International Relations to eschew prevalent individualist convictions by portraying certain collectivities as agents with interests, aims, and

---

[5] In proposing these criteria I draw on the work of Peter French (1984) and Onora O'Neill (1986).

decision-making capacities is most promising—and also most disappointing. The disappointment follows from the discipline's reticence to reflect upon its apparent challenge to individualism, to pose it more consistently by considering a wider range of possible collective agents in world politics, and to take this challenge to its logical conclusion by allying it with questions of specifically *moral* agency. Both this potential and these shortcomings warrant attention.

2 Assumptions of Moral Agency in International Relations: Responsibility Misdirected and Obscured

Implicit, and consequential, assumptions regarding moral agency are held in common by a number of otherwise diverse approaches within International Relations. Three tendencies are particularly revealing of the discipline's limited theoretical resources for addressing complex questions of moral responsibility. Each effectively sidesteps consideration of the possible moral agency of collectivities, despite making encouraging gestures toward such an endeavor.

First, there is a fascinating proclivity in International Relations for accepting states as purposive, yet amoral, actors. International Relations thereby flouts, however unreflectively, "individualism," as conventionally understood, by positing the agency of a certain category of collectivity. Nevertheless, while, *inter alia*, realist, neorealist, neoliberal institutionalist, and some constructivist approaches rely on the agency of the state, the idea that the state might be a bearer of moral burdens is either precluded or (perhaps most notably in the case of classical realist positions) allowed but unexamined. This combination of an uncritical acceptance of the state as an agent and the rejection, or evasion, of its possible role as a *moral* agent is a puzzling feature of much International Relations scholarship. Alexander Wendt provides an important exception to this by defending, rather than simply taking for granted, the state's status as an agent. Yet, even while citing the "practico-ethical" motivation for his work, Wendt (1999, 21–2) maintains that he will not deal with ethical issues in his analysis. States may be "people too" (Wendt 1999, 194), but theirs is an oddly amoral, quasi-personhood.

Secondly, while states are generally granted no more than a severely delimited, amoral conception of agency, International Relations is inclined to treat other types of organization—with arguably similar capacities—as neither agents nor moral agents. Nonstate entities have been widely ignored as purposive actors in their own right. Moreover, IGOs, such as the UN, have been variously conceived as "instruments" of states and "structures" within which states pursue their interests. As Michael Barnett and Martha Finnemore (1999, 704) have observed, neorealists and neoliberal institutionalists share the conviction that IGOs "have no ontological independence." Importantly, some positions have explored agency beyond the state. Examinations of transnational relationships present nonstate bodies such as multinational corporations, nongovernmental organizations (NGOs), advocacy networks, and epistemic communities as agents worthy of attention (Keohane and Nye 1972; Haas 1992; Risse-Kappen 1995; Keck and Sikkink 1998). Furthermore, an eclectic collection of theorists have presented IGOs as independent actors and not simply as instruments set up to serve state interests (Ness and Brechin 1988; Cox 1992; Hurrell and Woods 1995; Finnemore 1996; Snidal 1996; Barnett and Finnemore 1999). Yet, even after making the significant move of acknowledging agency in a wider range of collectivities, these positions stop short of taking the plunge into an exploration of their possible moral agency.

Finally, when ethical questions do take center stage in International Relations, individual human beings tend to exhaust the cast of relevant actors. A focus on moral agents as flesh-and-blood individuals is apparent in the range of positions that fall within what is variously labelled "normative International Relations theory" and "international political theory," and is reinforced by its recent surge of cosmopolitan statements (Jones 1999; Pogge 2002; Caney 2005).[6] Notably, then, this body of work does not take the provocative and potentially valuable attributions of agency at the level of organizations found in many International Relations approaches and explore the degree to which they are compatible with assumptions of specifically moral agency. Rather, it separates itself from the anti-individualist posture prevalent across so much International Relations scholarship, and, in doing so, emphasizes the ostensible divide between theories that are and are not self-consciously "normative." This is a loss for positions on both sides of the apparent partition. So-called normative theorizing, with its critical reflection on the significance of borders and concomitant extension of arguments from domestically framed political theory to the global sphere, retains a blinkered view of moral obligations as held only by individual human beings.[7] Much of the rest of International Relations scholarship, although open to some conception of collectivities possessing agency, is left methodologically predisposed to being wary of ethical analyses.

By neglecting moral agency altogether, or recognizing only individual human beings as moral agents, International Relations adopts a theoretical lens through which issues of responsibility in world politics are either profoundly distorted

---

[6] Simon Caney (2005, 2) offers an aside early in his argument that organizations might also have duties, but does not pursue this possibility.

[7] John Rawls (1999) provides a singular exception to the trend by positing the moral agency of states.

or completely beyond view. The result is that the discipline is of little help in analyzing how widespread assertions of duty and blame are directed and apportioned. "Something must be done" and "never again" are common refrains in world politics. If, however, they are divorced from any indication of the relevant moral agents involved, they are meaningless. Alternatively, if expectations to act and charges of wrongdoing are placed *only* at the feet of individual human beings, then responsibility for some acts and outcomes must remain unattributable. Both causing and responding to humanitarian and environmental crises, for example, require institutional *as well as* individual agency. The tendency to speak of moral responsibility with respect to collectivities in world politics therefore makes eminent sense. However, even if one accepts this proposition, a great deal of work remains in exploring to which types of collectivity moral responsibility can be attributed, under which conditions, and to what effect. International Relations, unfortunately, presently lacks a theoretical framework to deal with such questions. So, where do we go from here?

3 THE ROAD AHEAD

There are at least four steps that can be taken to redress International Relations' shortcomings in dealing with issues of moral responsibility. Each challenges existing theoretical assumptions in a way that promises to enhance how the field is able to understand, explain, and respond to practical problems in world politics.

First, questions of agency in International Relations need to be recognized as explicitly moral questions. Exploring moral agency speaks directly to enduring theoretical assumptions in International Relations—and to those important charges that the discipline undertheorizes agency (Wolfers 1962; Wendt 1999; Wight 2006). If collectivities can be moral agents, then International Relations' willingness to treat entities like states as actors in their own right is taken to a logical conclusion. If, on the other hand, those collectivities commonly portrayed as agents in International Relations *cannot* also be considered moral agents, then some doubt should be cast on treating them as purposive actors at all. In other words, the project of focusing on whether collectivities in world politics are moral agents entails either weaving a thicker, richer, tapestry of agency than is presently on display within the discipline, or tugging at a single thread that could unravel, row by row, a whole pattern of assumptions, resulting in an erstwhile intricate (if imperfect) fabric being left threadbare and in need of replacement. Ignoring such a project, however, risks leaving a plethora of theoretical tensions and contradictions unchallenged.

Secondly, even if the potential for collectivities to be moral agents is obvious, difficult questions regarding the capacities and defining features of particular bodies remain. For example, the deliberative capacity evident in an organization's formal decision-making structure might begin to counter the charge that groups cannot be held morally responsible for acts and omissions because they lack the ability to reason and form intentions. Nevertheless, whether or not certain organizations, such as the US Army, can boast a decision-making function that is unified and sophisticated enough to embody this capacity can still be disputed— and demands detailed empirical study. A multitude of bodies invite examination on these grounds. Particularly hard cases include less formal organizations such as Al Qaeda, "coalitions of the willing" (Brown 2003, 60–6; Erskine 2004, 31, 39), transnational advocacy networks, and even "international society" (Brown 2003). Engaging in the sort of ethical, *and empirical*, inquiry needed to identify who the relevant moral agents are in the context of particular problems in world politics improves the likelihood of coherently describing, and effectively addressing, these problems.

Thirdly, taking questions of moral responsibility seriously not only demands careful and consistent analyses of agency, but also requires close attention to the contexts within which agents are charged with performing certain actions. A moral agent can only reasonably be assigned a duty, or blamed for its evasion, if it enjoys the conditions that would make discharging the duty possible. It is, therefore, important to address the structures within which moral agents are situated in relation to specific actions. Structures that are not also moral agents (such as the global capitalist system, for example) cannot be assigned duties or held morally responsible for the consequences of acts or omissions—even though they might be deemed causally responsible for certain outcomes. Structures can, however, be evaluated for their constraining or liberating impact on the duty-bearers situated within them.

Fourthly, the ethical implications of different actors in world politics having disparate internal capacities and experiencing unequal external circumstances warrant attention. Both sets of factors vary wildly among (even nominally indistinguishable) entities. Prescriptions and evaluations of moral responsibility must be influenced accordingly. But what does this mean in practice? Should the considerable capacities and access to resources of some multinational corporate leviathans result in their being shouldered with greater responsibilities (for protecting human rights, for example) than some states? Does the world's remaining superpower have duties that weak states and faltering IGOs do not? Ancillary problems involve how to attend to organizations that cannot bear some moral burdens. Do we have responsibilities to design and restructure an organization, such as the UN, so that it has the internal capacities necessary to act more robustly and consistently in response to what are deemed to be ethical imperatives? Are we similarly obligated to transform structures that prevent agents from discharging specific duties?

Directly confronting questions of moral agency would go a long way toward redressing our often cavalier treatment of the concept of responsibility in world politics—and our equally cursory approach to the concept of agency in the academic study of International Relations. It would, moreover, further bridge the artificial divide (and division of labor) between "normative" and "empirical" approaches to the discipline. Most significantly, perhaps, it would counter the misguided perception that ethical considerations lie at the periphery of much International Relations scholarship and demonstrate their unavoidable centrality to both practice and theory.

References

BARNETT, M. N., and FINNEMORE, M. 1999. The politics, power, and pathologies of international organizations. *International Organization*, 53: 699–732.

BRODBECK, M. (ed.) 1968. *Readings in the Philosophy of the Social Sciences*. New York: Macmillan.

BROWN, C. 2003. Moral agency and international society: reflections on norms, the UN, the Gulf War, and the Kosovo campaign. Pp. 51–65 in *Can Institutions Have Responsibilities? Collective Moral Agency and International Relations*, ed. T. Erskine. New York: Palgrave Macmillan.

CANEY, S. 2005. *Justice beyond Borders: A Global Political Theory*. Oxford: Oxford University Press.

COX, R. W. 1992. Multilateralism and world order. *Review of International Studies*, 18: 161–80.

ERSKINE, T. 2001. Assigning responsibilities to institutional moral agents: the case of states and quasi-states. *Ethics and International Affairs*, 15: 67–85.

——2003. Making sense of "responsibility" in international relations: key questions and concepts. Pp. 1–16 in *Can Institutions Have Responsibilities? Collective Moral Agency and International Relations*, ed. T. Erskine. New York: Palgrave Macmillan.

——2004. "Blood on the UN's hands?" Assigning duties and apportioning blame to an intergovernmental organisation. *Global Society*, 18: 21–42.

FINNEMORE, M. 1996. *National Interests in International Society*. Ithaca, NY: Cornell University Press.

FRENCH, P. A. 1984. *Collective and Corporate Responsibility*. New York: Columbia University Press.

HAAS, P. M. 1992. Introduction: epistemic communities and international policy coordination. *International Organization*, 46: 1–35.

HURRELL, A., and WOODS, N. 1995. Globalisation and inequality. *Millennium: Journal of International Studies*, 24: 447–70.

JONES, C. 1999. *Global Justice: Defending Cosmopolitanism*. Oxford: Oxford University Press.

KECK, M. E., and SIKKINK, K. 1998. *Activists beyond Borders: Advocacy Networks in International Politics*. Ithaca, NY: Cornell University Press.

KEOHANE, R., and NYE, J. (eds.) 1972. *Transnational Relations and World Politics*. Cambridge, Mass.: Harvard University Press.

NESS, G. D, and BRECHIN, S. R. 1988. Bridging the gap: international organizations as organizations. *International Organizations*, 42: 245–73.

O'NEILL, O. 1986. Who can endeavour peace? *Canadian Journal of Philosophy*, supp. vol., 12: 41–73.

POGGE, T. W. 2002. *World Poverty and Human Rights: Cosmopolitan Responsibilities and Reforms*. Cambridge: Polity.

POPPER, K. 1966. *The Open Society and its Enemies*, vol. ii. London: Routledge and Kegan Paul.

RAWLS, J. 1999. *The Law of Peoples*. Cambridge, Mass.: Harvard University Press.

RISSE-KAPPEN, T. (ed.) 1995. *Bringing Transnational Relations Back In: Non-State Actors, Domestic Structures, and International Institutions*. Cambridge: Cambridge University Press.

SNIDAL, D. 1996. Political economy and international institutions. *International Review of Law and Economics*, 16: 121–37.

WEBER, M. 1968. *Economy and Society: An Outline of Interpretive Sociology*, ed. G. Roth and C. Wittich. New York: Bedminster Press.

WENDT, A. 1999. *Social Theory of International Politics*. Cambridge: Cambridge University Press.

WIGHT, C. 2006. *Agents, Structures and International Relations: Politics as Ontology*. Cambridge: Cambridge University Press.

WOLFERS, A. 1962. The actors in international politics. Pp. 3–24 in *Discord and Collaboration: Essays on International Politics*, A. Wolfers. Baltimore: Johns Hopkins University Press.

BIG QUESTIONS IN THE STUDY OF WORLD POLITICS

ROBERT O. KEOHANE

WE do not study international relations for aesthetic reasons, since world politics is not beautiful. If we sought scientific rigor, we would have pursued careers in experimental disciplines. Instead we are motivated by normative questions, often asked urgently in the wake of disasters, from the Sicilian Expedition (416 BCE) chronicled by Thucydides to the Anglo-American invasion of Iraq (2003 CE). Recurring failures lead us to try to understand the conditions under which states and other actors can achieve their collective purposes rather than engage in destructive, and often self-destructive, behavior.[1] Our normative purposes infuse our positive analysis. Political economy came alive as a field in the wake of the economic crises of the 1970s, which recalled the Great Depression of the 1930s. Security studies became a site of creativity after the Second World War and during the height of the cold war. Work on the sources of internal war expanded in the wake of post-cold war internal conflicts. And it is predictable that there will be a new wave of work on the problem of terrorism, in the wake of the attacks of 11 September 2001.

Students of world politics have an obligation to democratic publics to help them understand the most pressing problems of the current day. Yet this moral obligation

---

[1] I use the phrase "world politics" rather than "international relations," since the language of "international relations" leads us to think only about states, which are not central to all interesting questions of world politics.

does not imply that we should focus on topical issues or be "policy-relevant" in a narrow sense by speaking to governments in terms that are acceptable to them. Our task is to probe the deeper sources of action in world politics, and to speak truth to power—insofar as we can discern what the truth is.

The study of world politics begins with the study of war. *Why is war a perennial institution of international society and what variable factors affect its incidence?* In understanding this problem, as well as other issues in world politics, realist theory, which identifies power and interests as the central forces in the behavior of rational states, has played a central role (Morgenthau 1967), although it remained unclear for years why, if states behaved rationally, they could engage in mutually destructive warfare. Scholars have recently made substantial progress on this problem, notably by following the lead of Thomas Schelling (1960) in focusing on the role played by information and credibility (Fearon 1995), and by linking the study of institutions to that of war (Fortna 2004).

The analysis of warfare relates directly to broader issues of discord and cooperation. Work on these issues over the last quarter-century has emphasized that cooperation arises more from discord than from harmony, and that, when complementary interests exist, multilateral institutions can facilitate cooperation (Keohane 1984). A productive line of work has stressed the role of reciprocity in creating incentives for cooperative behavior (Axelrod 1984). These theoretical contributions are beginning to be linked to the literature on the democratic peace, which I do not have space to discuss here.

An important contemporary as well as historical puzzle is how to think about the role of sovereignty. Under what conditions does it promote cooperation by limiting intervention and clarifying the actors in world politics, and under what conditions does it generate civil conflict by providing a shield behind which states can abuse groups within their societies? Recent work on sovereignty (Krasner 1999) has clarified various meanings of this concept, which has regained analytical significance with the increased attention to issues of civil war and intervention.

Behind all these issues lurks the concept of power. Material resources are significant not just for war and threat, but also for the politics of economic relationships. The study of political economy can be viewed as "the reciprocal and dynamic interaction in international relations of the pursuit of wealth and the pursuit of power" (Gilpin 1975, 43). But we need to question the equation of power resources with material resources. Joseph Nye (2004) has emphasized the role of "soft power"—attractiveness that inspires emulation and facilitates persuasion—in world politics. Soft power depends on the beliefs that human beings have and how they process information; hence its systematic study will require engagement with cognitive and social psychology, where recent progress has been rapid. Efforts to understand the sources of beliefs are likely to become more urgent for students of world politics as social mobilization and the ability of people to communicate directly with one another, unmediated by large institutions, continue to grow.

Questions about war and cooperation, and concepts such as power and interest, remain central to world politics. The field has recently become more aware, however, of the inferential biases to which students of international relations are subject. Wars and crises are rare events. Quite naturally, scholars seeking to understand them focus much more on these events than on the situations of peace, especially situations lacking crises at all. Insofar as our purposes are descriptive, this emphasis is unproblematic. However, when we seek to put forward explanatory propositions, we are in danger of selecting our cases on the dependent variable, which will bias our inferences (Achen and Snidal 1989; King, Keohane, and Verba 1994). We need continually to be aware of the uncertainty of our inferences—since our data are not generated by experiments, and often the class of relevant events is small and not independent of one another—and to try to account for sources of bias.

Students of world politics have made theoretical progress in recent decades on issues of war, cooperation, and the role of multilateral institutions; and conceptual progress on issues of sovereignty. Impressive empirical work, guided by improved technical and methodological sophistication, has been carried out on a variety of problems, including warfare. However, most of this progress has focused on seeking to establish static conditional generalizations. Although we are living in a period of unprecedented change, our understanding of change is very inferior to our understanding of fundamental long-term regularities.

1 SIX BIG QUESTIONS ABOUT CHANGE OVER TIME

Compared to the history of civilization, much less of the human race, the known history of world politics is very short indeed, and the period for which reasonably reliable data exist is less than 200 years. Human nature has not changed during that time, nor has the fact that no world government exists. When students of world politics seek to make generalizations based on state behavior during the last two centuries, they implicitly assume that the actors and processes of the early nineteenth century are essentially the same as those operating now. Much, however, has occurred in those 200 years to change some basic factors at work, including the nature of force and the structure of economic life. Furthermore, change seems to be accelerating, generating several new or newly urgent questions.

1. *How has politics been affected by the expansion of force, through technological change, and its dispersion?*
Scholars have explored in depth the effects of changes in the technology of force on international relations in the West over periods of centuries. Recent changes

in warfare, relying on global positioning systems and electronic technology of all kinds, have created huge gaps between the military power of the United States and that of other countries. Some of those who celebrated American military power, however, may have forgotten that ingenious adversaries can create effective "weapons of the weak," such as terrorism, and that possessing a superior resource may lead states to overuse it, or to attempt to use it for purposes for which it is not well suited.

2. How has world politics been affected by changes in capitalism?

Karl Marx and Joseph Schumpeter are the two most famous theorists who saw world politics as fundamentally affected by the nature of capitalist development. Marx, Vladimir Lenin, and their followers viewed war as the result of capitalism, with its limitless demand for markets and investment opportunities. Schumpeter, by contrast, thought that capitalism had peace-inducing effects, limiting imperialism by emphasizing profit over glory and conquest. But he also viewed capitalism as a relentless process of "creative destruction," implying socially disruptive change. Both Marx and Schumpeter thought that change was the essence of capitalism, which implies that how economic structures affect global conflict and cooperation must change over time. Neither would have accepted the static formulations of how world politics operate implicit in much of the statistical work now appearing in the field.

3. Is there any plausible sense in which progress has taken place in international relations, and if so, is this progress due to intellectual or moral advances in human thinking?

Since the Enlightenment, many thinkers in the West have observed fundamental changes in human practices and have concluded, or at least dared to hope, that moral as well as scientific and technical progress was occurring. These hopes peaked in the years before the First World War, when both publicists and practical men of affairs expected economic interdependence to dampen or even prevent wars and sought arbitration and arms limitation treaties to facilitate and institutionalize benign changes. World wars and the Holocaust generated great disillusionment, but in the 1980s and 1990s hopes for progress, through learning or changes in principled ideas, were revived. The effects of changes in the ideas in which people believe are by no means necessarily benign, as illustrated by nuclear weapons and the recent militancy of Islamic fundamentalism. We should expect no simple answer to questions about progress, but they are nevertheless important questions to ask.

4. What is the impact on world politics of the increasing diversity and complexity of social structures in the most powerful societies of the world?

It is a platitude that contemporary democratic–capitalist societies are increasingly complex, a complexity that is magnified by the increasing blurring of lines between societies as transnational relations become more dense. Governments themselves are becoming diversified, along with civil society, which has experienced a vast increase at the transnational level of nongovernmental organizations and social movements (Keck and Sikkink 1998). Traditional gender roles have been changing in Western societies, with potential impacts on decision-making and leadership behavior. Anne-Marie Slaughter has recently put forward the vision of a "disaggregated world order," in which, as a result largely of social complexity, hierarchies have weakened and networks have become the dominant form of connection among individuals and groups in society (Slaughter 2004). There is considerable evidence for Slaughter's argument—from peaceful activities such as accounting and securities regulation and violent ones such as terrorism—but it is largely anecdotal. We need to understand these changes more systematically.

5. *What are the implications of electronic technologies, especially of the Internet, for world politics?*
To exercise influence, sets of individuals with common values or interests need to be able to communicate with each other, to form groups, and to act collectively. Historically, such communication has been very difficult except through formal organizations, including the state; and all but impossible across state boundaries except with the aid of states. This formerly constant reality has been changing with incredible speed during the last two decades, and we have hardly begun to understand the implications of this momentous fact. One implication may be that collective action on a transnational or even global scale, for good or ill, is easier than it has ever been before.

6. *What modes of action can effectively cope with the unprecedented stress that human beings are imposing on the global environment?*
The reality of human-induced climate change has become undeniable, although many uncertainties surround the pace and severity of change and the prospects for relevant technological innovation. The political uncertainties may be even greater, both with respect to the willingness of publics and governments around the world to pay significant costs to mitigate climate change and adapt to it, and with respect to the capacity of existing or feasible institutions to implement measures involving global taxes or tradeable permit schemes (Aldy and Stavins 2007).

2 ISSUES OF INSTITUTIONAL DESIGN

I began this chapter with the argument that the study of world politics is driven heavily by normative concerns, although in our positive research we have an obligation to follow the canons of scientific inference. If we are serious about these normative concerns, we cannot merely pontificate: We need instead to think deeply about these issues so that we can articulate coherent normative points of view, and then to connect these normative issues with practical problems. For me, as a student of institutions, the most pressing practical problems involve institutional design.

The fundamental normative question can be posed as follows: *What is the extent and depth of human obligations to other human beings, extending across political and cultural boundaries?* Do people in Europe and North America have obligations to people in Africa, simply as a result of our common humanity? To what extent are moral obligations limited by shared bonds of historical experience and community? Moral philosophers have reflected profoundly on these issues. Our answers to this question will condition our answers to a related but derivative question: *How should we think about trade-offs among values, such as democracy, liberty, equality (including gender equality), and economic welfare?* It is not obvious that the trade-offs made in wealthy democracies apply fully to developing countries, or to societies with different cultural practices; yet, for liberal cosmopolitans, there is an irreducible core of human rights that must be respected (Okin 1999). What should these rights be considered to be?

The way we think about practical issues such as institutional design will necessarily be shaped by our answers to these fundamental normative questions. I am a cosmopolitan liberal democrat: a cosmopolitan, since I think that basic human rights are universal and not dependent on membership in a particular community; a liberal, because I give priority to liberty as a crucial value for a good society; a democrat, because I believe that elites should not only serve the public good but should be accountable to deliberative public views through institutions that give publics power over leaders. The two basic issues of institutional design that I raise reflect these values.

My first issue of institutional design involves effectiveness. *How can institutions in world politics be designed, or modified, in ways that would make them more effective in attaining collective purposes, from restoring peace in war-torn societies to facilitating nondiscriminatory trade, protecting human rights, and preventing damage to the global environment?* Theoretical and empirical work on institutional design over the last two decades has pointed to the importance of incentives for reaching and complying with international agreements (Koremenos, Lipson, and Snidal 2001). Since institutions vary in the incentives they help to generate, a worthwhile normative project would be to figure out systematically how to get the incentives right in constructing institutions, and what scope global institutions should have in light of the incentives of potential member states and the capacity of domestic and multilateral institutions in a variety of issue areas.

To be worthwhile for a democrat, institutions have to be accountable as well as effective. So the second question can be posed as follows: *How can multilateral institutions be designed, without global government, so that qualified and dedicated leaders are more likely to be chosen, and those leaders who are selected are held accountable to the people whose actions they affect?* Accountability is a basic principle of democracy. Multilateral institutions cannot be fully democratic, since they remain dependent on states. Many states are not democratic, and the connections between multilateral institutions and publics even in democratic states are weak. Yet mechanisms have been devised to make multilateral institutions accountable, and they could be strengthened.

The questions that I have emphasized are necessarily selective. Some issues have been omitted simply for lack of space. But I have deliberately omitted discussion of the alleged incompatibility of broad approaches to the study of international relations such as realism, institutionalism, and constructivism, since I regard these approaches as complementary rather than alternatives. The relevant question is to figure out how they can be combined to address theoretically or practically relevant problems. Nor have I emphasized analytical or statistical tools that are playing an increasing role in scholarship, even though these tools have been valuable both theoretically and empirically. To my taste, there has been an overemphasis recently on tools at the expense of reflection about which questions are most important for the human race and for the ecosystem. Focusing on major problems can help us to figure out which insights from the broad approaches to the field are valuable, and which analytical tools yield genuine insights or evidence. If we then focus on developing testable theories, we can investigate their implications empirically. But if we fail to ask the right questions, there is no hope of getting the answers we need.

References

ACHEN, C. H., and SNIDAL, D. 1989. Rational deterrence theory and comparative case studies. *World Politics*, 41: 143–69.

ALDY, J., and STAVINS, R. (eds.) 2007. *Architectures for Agreement: Addressing Global Climate Change in the Post-Kyoto World*. Cambridge: Cambridge University Press.

AXELROD, R. 1984. *The Evolution of Cooperation*. New York: Basic Books.

FEARON, J. D. 1995. Rationalist explanations for war. *International Organization*, 49: 379–414.

FORTNA, V. P. 2004. *Peace Time: Cease-Fire Agreements and the Durability of Peace*. Princeton, NJ: Princeton University Press.

GILPIN, R. 1975. *US Power and the Multinational Corporation: The Political Economy of Foreign Direct Investment*. New York: Basic Books.

KECK, M., and SIKKINK, K. 1998. *Activists beyond Borders: Advocacy Networks in International Politics*. Ithaca, NY: Cornell University Press.

KEOHANE, R. O. 1984. *After Hegemony: Cooperation and Discord in the World Political Economy*. Princeton, NJ: Princeton University Press.

KING, G., KEOHANE, R. O., and VERBA, S. 1994. *Designing Social Inquiry: Scientific Inference in Qualitative Research*. Princeton, NJ: Princeton University Press.

KOREMENOS, B., LIPSON, C., and SNIDAL, D. 2001. The rational design of international institutions. *International Organization*, special issue, 55: 761–1102.

KRASNER, S. D. 1999. *Sovereignty: Organized Hypocrisy*. Princeton, NJ: Princeton University Press.

MORGENTHAU, H. J. 1967. *Politics among Nations: The Struggle for Power and Peace*, 4th edn. New York: Knopf.

NYE, J. S., JR. 2004. *Soft Power: The Means to Success in World Politics*. New York: Public Affairs Press.

OKIN, S. M. 1999. *Is Multiculturalism Bad for Women?* Princeton, NJ: Princeton University Press.

SCHELLING, T. C. 1960. *The Strategy of Conflict*. Cambridge, Mass.: Harvard University Press.

SLAUGHTER, A.-M. 2004. *A New World Order*. Princeton, NJ: Princeton University Press.

CHAPTER 43

THE FAILURE OF STATIC AND THE NEED FOR DYNAMIC APPROACHES TO INTERNATIONAL RELATIONS

RICHARD ROSECRANCE

THE perennial difficulty in the study of international relations is that general theories holding statically over time are unsatisfactory. The leading theories—emphasizing a single concept ("realism," "constructivism," "liberalism," and so on)—themselves either are unfalsifiable, or if falsifiable, are false. There are few if any theoretical propositions that are both falsifiable and true. As a result, practitioners have to make do with empirical generalizations that hold only part of the time—that is, apply only probabilistically. Both international and domestic factors have to be taken into account in order to develop a reasonable static approach to how nations behave. A three-variable conspectus that comprises (1) international restraints and availabilities; (2) leadership preconceptions; and (3) domestic restraints and pressures can explain international outcomes more fully than any of these variables taken individually. A regression equation, in short, is necessary. The coefficients of this equation, however, may have changed over time, with international coefficients having less strength than they once did and domestic ones more strength (see, *inter alia*, Reus-Smit 1999). I shall elaborate these claims in the first half of this chapter.

In the second half I will concentrate on some dynamic features of the international system that point to the possibility of different and more cooperative outcomes in the years ahead as the influence and content of these factors undergo change.

1 STATIC THEORIES

1.1 Unfalsifiable Theories or Approaches

Both realist and constructivist theories are unfalsifiable. Realist theories have the difficulty of not specifying precisely the conditions under which they might not hold. Suppose, for example, countries did not balance against an aggressor—they surrendered prematurely—or that they conceded sovereignty to a supranational institution. These would be presumed "exceptions" to realist theory. Yet realists have always constructed explanations of such possible events. By redefining the deviant case, realists could extend the meaning of their key terms and emerge unscathed. For example, in strategic contexts, countries facing a strong aggressive power that is expanding territorially would normally be expected to balance against it (see Snyder 1997, 51). Empirically and theoretically, however, they usually do not do so. "Bandwagoning" or "waiting" are usually preferred options to "balancing" in such contexts (see Powell 1999, ch. 5). The public-goods problem also creates formidable difficulties for the general operation of so-called balance of power theory. Unless one confines the strictures of the balance of power hypothesis to resisting actual or threatened attack, it does not hold, and even then, as the examples of interwar Czechoslovakia, Denmark, Austria, and Holland show, some countries do not resist attack at all. And even when occasionally resisting, states frequently underbalance, a notion convincingly propounded by Randall Schweller (2006).

These examples, however, do not technically refute the realist approach. States— so it is said—have to think of maintaining themselves even if defeated. By conserving their population (through concession), they may secure their long-term social and national identity, even when sacrificing short-term autonomy. In this way even "appeasers" or states that surrender are motivated by long-term power considerations. Thus power and realist theories avoid refutation by definitional change. No concrete case that would entail falsification can be stated, with the possible exception of the abolition of the state system itself. Likely then, as well, realists would claim their doctrines would be fulfilled in the relationship then subsisting among subordinate units of the world system.

The same failure to specify the conditions of falsifiability applies to "constructivism." Perhaps states construct their own reality of "self" and "other." The relationship of self and other, however, can vary enormously, depending on the ideas that each hold. It can represent a relationship of Hobbesian conflict, Lockean rivalry, or Kantian "friendship." There is nothing in the "constructivist" canon that requires it to be one or the other. Since "ideas" are critical to the definitions of interest, and states can hold different "ideas," their relationship is always underspecified (see, *inter alia*, Wendt 1999). Some constructivists believe that the international system is undergoing change in a Kantian direction, with friendship superseding preexisting rivalry. But, if so, there are no systemic measures of this degree of friendship offered and no firm foundation on which to declare that war will be averted. The First World War, after all, emerged at a time of a supposed economic interdependence of the parties that should have mandated cooperation among them.

Thus constructivism, by admitting the possibility of divergent ideas dictating the result, gives up any possibility of either prediction or falsification of "constructivist" notions of international behavior.

1.2 Falsifiable Theories that are also False

Neoliberalism represents a valiant effort to conclude that economic and institutional factors will constrain international outcomes. Countries, so it is said, will restrain their separate interests under conditions of interdependence and growing international institutionalism. But institutions have failed to solve major international problems. The United Nations failed to stop the killing in Rwanda and Darfur. The International Monetary Fund did not expeditiously solve the Far Eastern crisis in 1997–8 and may have exacerbated national difficulties. The World Trade Organization (WTO) faltered in completing the Doha Round. On the other hand, though downplayed by American neorealists (see Kagan 2004), the European Union moved from strength to strength. It admitted new members and also deepened in integrative quality via the establishment of a common currency, the Euro. The Euro emerged as a highly valued currency. In the short term, regional institutions may actually have become stronger than more universal organizations, as the Western hemisphere also begins to create new institutions (see Hufbauer and Schott 2005; Katzenstein 2005).

As to the decisiveness of economic factors, some relatively advanced societies have welcomed and embraced globalization, accepting free trade and capital mobility. Others have not done so, preferring instead to keep tariffs, safeguard agriculture, and restrict capital movements. In WTO negotiations, India, China, Brazil, and Argentina failed to lower their industrial tariffs, and France, Germany, Japan, and the United States declined to give up agricultural subsidies (see Cordero and Rosecrance 2006). Liberal institutionalism by no means prescribed the policies of these groups of nations. Though neoliberalism predicted strong institutions, its conclusions have to be questioned. No general pattern emerges to validate the theses of neoliberalism.

There are also falsifiable power theories, which, when investigated, turn out to be false. Theories of great power politics suggest that nations always act according to the amount of power they possess. States remain on their "rational" power line (Mearsheimer 2001), acting neither recklessly (above the line) nor too modestly (below the line).

The surprising fact of international history, however, is how frequently countries act above or below their rational "power lines." This is because leadership strategies and ideology and also the constraints of domestic politics enter the equation and may determine the result. As examples, both the United States and Great Britain should have reacted earlier to stop Nazi Germany in the 1930s, but they did not do so because of the restraints of domestic politics. In the British case, when domestic support for war increased (in 1939), Britain's economic ability to sustain that war had declined and (without help from the United States) nearly disappeared (see Rosecrance and Steiner 1993). Yet Britain went to war anyway. In an opposite example, in the 1840s Great Britain was not only the first industrial nation, it was well-nigh the only industrial nation. Yet it did not seek to use its power to gain new territory on the Continent. It had essentially adopted a strategy of peaceful economic growth, and did not seek to demonstrate that power by acquiring new European territory. Britain acted more modestly than its power line would have permitted. Later, US power after the First World War was as great in relative terms as after the Second World War, yet America did not use that power, except occasionally, economically. It was a de facto European power but exercised that power in name only.

In a similar outcome, after the Second World War, Japan and Germany transformed their policies in a benign direction. They did not couple their signal economic gains with an equally expansive military policy. Either might have challenged the United States, at least in regional terms, but neither sought to do so. Both formally abjured nuclear weapons when the technical possibility beckoned in the 1960s. The United States, of course, would not have been pleased, but Japan and Germany did not move to nuclear weapons, even though they might have increased regional deterrence in doing so. Japan's and Germany's forbearance is difficult to understand in realist terms. Nor is Kazakhstan's and Ukraine's giving-up of their

		Eight cases							
		1	2	3	4	5	6	7	8
Variables	International relations	+	−	−	−	+	+	−	+
	Leadership	+	+	−	−	−	−	+	+
	Domestic politics	+	+	+	−	+	−	−	−

Fig. 43.1. Foreign policy determinants

nuclear arsenals after 1991 any more comprehensible in power terms. Countries do things that might not be expected in terms of theory, and strict realist theory is thereby falsified.

If stronger states have sometimes held back, weaker ones have pushed forward, sometimes heedlessly. Frederick II of Prussia was a profound challenger of the status quo in central Europe, even as he strove to make Berlin a modern and enlightened state. He won, not by superior firepower or economic strength, but because of better organization. He was very lucky. Meiji Japan was also a challenger. It partly succeeded, not by overall strength, but because domestic politics compelled a vigorous policy (see J. L. Snyder 1991). From a position of relative weakness, Prussia and later Japan deliberately challenged the existing order.

What does this tell us about static approaches? It suggests that at least three variables are needed to predict outcomes: (1) the sanctions or permissions allowed by the international system; (2) the policy/ideology of the leadership; and (3) the constraints and requirements of domestic politics. Eight cases devolve from this conspectus (see Figure 43.1).

Under the power theory, one would have expected military expansion in cases 1, 5, 6, and 8 (where international relations permits expansion). In fact, historically, there are many instances where domestic politics or leadership variables overrode external power factors, and the expected expansion did not take place. Equally, under the power theory, one would have expected quiescence in cases 2, 3, 4, and 7. Yet, for instance, Adolf Hitler and Japan expanded in case 2 (with the support of domestic politics) and Hitler's Germany initially expanded in case 7 (without the support of domestic politics). Does this mean that domestic leadership is the single overriding cause of action? Not necessarily. Neville Chamberlain had to be railroaded into war on 3 September 1939 as he faced a parliamentary revolt. Alternatively, does this suggest that domestic politics always tells the tale? Again the response is negative. Leadership sometimes takes risks without domestic support. Still the most peaceful cases are likely to be found in cases 3, 4, and 6, where one or both internal variables (leadership policy/ideology, and domestic politics) are inclined against expansion. Expansion will probably take place in cases 1, 2, 5, and 8, where both internal variables are aligned in favor of expansion or the international system clearly permits it.

The conclusion from this simple conspectus is that the second and third images have to interact together for either peace or war to occur. One of them alone is unlikely to produce the prescribed theoretical outcome. Despite Kenneth Waltz's remarks to the contrary, only a theory that includes both domestic and international levels of analysis can possibly be adequate (Waltz 1979).

2 DYNAMIC APPROACHES

Dynamic approaches suggest that the system is evolving over time. Domestic factors may be rising in influence. The very constituents of what we mean by the term "power" may be in the process of transformation. With domestic constraints on military action increasing, it may be that time horizons have begun to shift from short to long. Instead of seeking results through short-term invasions (with unsatisfactory cost–benefit results), nations may learn to seek influence through economic growth, long-term emulation, and soft power influences. In this way short-term horizons could become more long term, territorial objectives could evolve into economic ones, and tangible power resources could turn into their less tangible equivalents. Normative transformations may have occurred as well. These have permitted states (as in the case of the European Union) to derive benefits of cooperation within regimes, benefits that would not accrue outside an institutional context. Participants in such regimes have been able to save on defense and security costs, attaining rates of growth and low inflation not attainable by heavily armed and indebted states.

There is the possibility that changes in world politics, economics, and technology have altered the currency of power in a secular fashion. What used to be power— territory or real estate—may have metamorphosed into something else—capital, labor, or technology—perceptions aside. If this is true, nations need to modify their notions of power to conform to the new realities. These entail shifts in leadership perceptions/intentions as well as domestic political conceptions and restraints. If nations do not understand this, they will respond inappropriately. Suppose, for example, that high technology proved to be the single most important element in "power"—permitting, for example, vast changes in energy extraction and use. In that case a country with a large and highly educated population could become the strongest nation in the world, and a measure of its strength would be the quality of its educational system. As a means of increasing their GDP, countries would, other things being equal, strive to improve their school systems and bring new students to their shores. Since students frequently work in the country that educates them, this would add a high technological element to the country, generating economic and potentially military power. In this instance as well, new innovations in artificial intelligence—allowing computers to substitute for brains—could partly compensate for a deficiency in population.

In another possible example of secular change, the European Union has pioneered the notion of "peaceful power" as an objective of the partially integrated states of Western and Central Europe (the term was coined by François Duchêne; see Zielonka 2000). As Europe integrates and enlarges, it seeks to create new norms that will guide not only its own practice but others' as well (Katzenstein 1997). The norms that countries seeking to join the Euro area are constrained to accept are now being applied to East Asia to judge national practice there. There could, at the extreme, be the development of "normative power" in which countries following particular norms would benefit and those neglecting them would suffer. Game theorists have demonstrated in simulations that persistent cooperators over time can surpass the apostles of conflict in cost–benefit outcomes. This is because cooperation leads to Pareto optimality and conflict only to Nash solutions.

The influence of these cooperative regimes and practices can be seen in a wider context. Some argue that "authority structures" have begun to emerge in what has been a formal state of anarchy or conflict (Lake 2007). In realist theory, weaker states should technically be forced to spend more on security and defense than larger, stronger states. But any quantitative analysis shows that they do not do so; in effect they spend smaller proportions of their GDP on arms than large states do. How can this be explained? Such states rely on the international system (see Kuwait or Costa Rica) or allies for their protection. Some states economize (see Switzerland or Sweden) even when they do not have formal alliances to protect them. In economic and financial realms, "the hegemonic stability theory" contends that the weakening of the hegemon will result in a failure to cooperate among major players. It has, however, not done so (Snidal 1985). Rising great-power supporters have taken up the slack, if and as the hegemon weakens economically.

The public-goods problem has not forestalled cooperation. Weaker states, moreover, have found ways to influence the domestic politics of their stronger brethren to gain particular benefits. Israel, India, Australia, and Saudi Arabia have invested heavily in influencing the US Congress and with a great deal of success (see Mearsheimer and Walt 2007). Domestic success in this manner can allow them to stint on their military preparations. Two-level games are being played in these cases, with the result depending upon domestic politics as well as international policy (see Putnam 1988; Tsebelis 1990).

3 CONCLUSION

If one expects a single-factor international theory to be validated (which is both falsifiable and clearly true), none is available. The concepts of "realism" and "constructivism" are too broad to be falsified. "Neoliberalism" is more narrowly drawn, and in particular situations is probably false. This does not mean, however, that mid-range theories including domestic, international, and leadership variables are not appropriate and might not hold probabilistically. Dynamically, the very concept of power and the time horizon of maximization are undergoing change. Power is probably becoming less tangible and maximization becoming more long term. Military force is less effective in these circumstances because short-term victories do not produce long-term gains. The result could be greater possibilities for cooperation.

REFERENCES

CORDERO, L., and ROSECRANCE, R. 2006. The "acceptance" of globalization. Pp. 23–33 in *No More States? Globalization, National Self-Determination, and Terrorism*, ed. R. Rosecrance and A. A. Stein. Lanham, Md.: Rowman and Littlefield.

HUFBAUER, G. C., and SCHOTT, J. J. 2005. *NAFTA Revisited: Achievements and Challenges*. Washington, DC: Institute for International Economics.

KAGAN, R. 2004. *Paradise and Power: America and Europe in the New World Order*. London: Atlantic.

KATZENSTEIN, P. J. 1997. United Germany in an integrating Europe. *Current History*, 96: 116–23.

——2005. *A World of Regions: Asia and Europe in the American Imperium*. Ithaca, NY: Cornell University Press.

LAKE, D. 2007. Escape from the state of nature: authority and hierarchy in world politics. *International Security*, 32: 47–79.

MEARSHEIMER, J. J. 2001. *The Tragedy of Great Power Politics*. New York: Norton.

—— AND WALT, S. M. 2007. *The Israel Lobby and US Foreign Policy*. New York: Farrar, Straus and Giroux.

POWELL, R. 1999. *In the Shadow of Power: States and Strategies in International Politics*. Princeton, NJ: Princeton University Press.

PUTNAM, R. D. 1988. Diplomacy and domestic politics: the logic of two-level games. *International Organization*, 42: 427–60.

REUS-SMIT, C. 1999. *The Moral Purpose of the State: Culture, Social Identity, and Institutional Rationality in International Relations*. Princeton, NJ: Princeton University Press.

ROSECRANCE, R., and STEINER, Z. 1993. British grand strategy and the origins of World War II. Pp. 124–53 in *The Domestic Bases of Grand Strategy*, ed. R. Rosecrance and A. A. Stein. Ithaca, NY: Cornell University Press.

SCHWELLER, R. L. 2006. *Unanswered Threats: Political Constraints on the Balance of Power*. Princeton, NJ: Princeton University Press.

SNIDAL, D. 1985. The limits of hegemonic stability theory. *International Organization*, 39: 579–614.

SNYDER, G. 1997. *Alliance Politics*. Ithaca, NY: Cornell University Press.

SNYDER, J. L. 1991. *Myths of Empire: Domestic Politics and International Ambition*. Ithaca, NY: Cornell University Press.

TSEBELIS, G. 1990. *Nested Games: Rational Choice in Comparative Politics*. Berkeley: University of California Press.

WALTZ, K. 1979. *Theory of International Politics*. Reading, Mass.: Addison-Wesley.

WENDT, A. 1999. *Social Theory of International Politics*. Cambridge: Cambridge University Press.

ZIELONKA, J. 2000. Should Europe become a state? Pp. 101–11 in *The Future Shape of Europe*, ed. M. Leonard. London: BSMG Worldwide.

....

CHAPTER 44

SIX WISHES FOR A MORE RELEVANT DISCIPLINE OF INTERNATIONAL RELATIONS

....

STEVE SMITH

THIS chapter looks at how the discipline of international relations should develop over the next twenty years. I start by saying something about the main features of the discipline in the last twenty years. I have previously written on this topic and do not wish to repeat that analysis (see Smith 2000; 2002; 2004; 2007). I follow Ole Wæver's (2007) view of the development of international relations; like him, and following Stanley Hoffmann (1977), I see international relations as an American discipline that dominates by having the largest and best-funded academic community, having the dominant journals, and being able to ignore the work of scholars outside the United States (Wæver 2007, 296). Within international relations, the key journals are almost all US based, and prefer theory testing to the development of new theory (Wæver 2007, 297). This results in a field that prioritizes publishing in the leading journals, for promotion and status reasons, and leads to a focus on

I would like to thank Jodie Anstee for her research assistance on this chapter.

testing and modifying dominant theories rather than confronting them in debates. Despite this generalization, most of the theoretical developments in international relations have come from academics based in the United States; partly this reflects the relative size of the US academic community, but the US community is a varied and diverse one that leads to most innovation in the discipline. Nonetheless, the vast majority of work in the United States focuses on developing existing research paradigms, and the major innovations tend not to come from academics based in the main departments of international politics.

Despite the discipline's fondness for so-called great debates, there have been few; in the main, the differing positions have simply ignored one another. This does not mean that there have not been strong opposing positions within the discipline. Therefore, in this weak sense of the word "debate," there has indeed been a rivalry between competing theoretical frameworks; what there have not been are debates in the strong sense of the word (whereby contrasting positions indicate their superiority over rival positions through explicit debates).

In the period between the late 1980s and the late 1990s the discipline was marked by two key features: first, a coming-together (not debate) of neorealist and neoliberal approaches into a neo-neo synthesis; second, a more general dispute (again, not a debate) between this rationalist core of the field and a group of approaches (feminist, post-structuralist, critical theory, postcolonial, and green theory), collectively known as reflectivism. But these approaches have not debated with rationalism nor have they together constituted a coherent alternative. The contemporary scene is one in which there is a set of debates within broad theoretical positions, and no great debate defining the field. In this sense, the field has a set of powerful theories that almost never touch or confront one another in the major journals. Either the core conversations in international relations are debates within these theoretical positions (for example between offensive and defensive realism, or between the group of theories that comprise neoliberalism), or they are developments of specific aspects of the main theoretical positions.

Importantly, the often-cited concern about theories being divorced from empirical material (the claim that international relations theory is not interested in "real-world" problems) seems not to be the case. Whether the approach is a mainstream one or a reflectivist one, the most common article is one that examines a discrete empirical field through the lens of a specific theory; this is as true of post-structural and gender work as it is of neorealism, neoliberalism, or constructivism. The field, therefore, is not preoccupied with metatheoretical debates, but instead attempts to link theory and empirical domains. Just as the extent of debate involved in the previous four "great debates" has been exaggerated, so it is difficult to find any notion of a fifth "great debate" in the current literature.

1 How should International Relations Develop over the Next Twenty Years?

1. *All approaches should be seen as having normative commitments.*

Since this is an explicit position taken by this volume's editors, I need say little here. International relations is unavoidably normative for two related reasons: first there can be no simple separation between "fact" and "values;" second, international relations is a practical discipline, concerned with how we should act. From the inception of international relations as a distinct discipline, neither of these reasons has been commonly accepted; indeed, the opposite positions have dominated international relations. These were particularly powerful when positivism was the dominant methodology. But accepting that all theories contain normative commitments does not necessarily create a more level playing field, since some normative commitments can be seen as more "natural" or acceptable than others. This could be because some practical prescriptions will be seen as more "accurately" fitting the commonsense reality of world politics. Or it could be because of the dominance of statements about the need to separate "facts" from "values" in analysis; this, of course, assumes that such a distinction is indeed possible, whereas I believe that, following Foucault, disciplines and theories constitute the criteria through which we access the "facts" of the social world. Just as there can never be a theory-neutral account of "reality," so there cannot be a theoretical account that does not have normative commitments and assumptions. Particularly good examples of this problem are contained in two recent articles: first, Stefan Elbe's analysis (2006) of whether HIV/AIDS should be securitized. This is a disease that every day kills three times the death toll from the events of 11 September 2001. Elbe shows that, although there might be advantages of securitizing the discourse—for example, by raising awareness and thereby increasing the resources devoted to dealing with the pandemic—there are also ethical dangers; those living with HIV/AIDS could be seen as the problem, and civil society's role could be increasingly taken over by the military and intelligence services. Similarly, Piki Ish-Shalom (2006) has shown how international relations theories play a political, normative role by shaping the reality that they study, since theorists have agency and therefore automatically have a moral responsibility. For Ish-Shalom this moral ethic should replace the dominant academic ethic of objectivity. All theories have normative assumptions flowing through them, and these are never more powerful than when they are hidden, denied, or eschewed.

2. *International relations has to become less of an American discipline.*

Any academic discipline will take particular interest in the policy concerns of its major subjects, but in international relations the US policy agenda, and its dominant methodology, has been so influential that other voices have been either ignored or placed in a position whereby they are of interest or relevance only insofar as they relate to the dominant agenda. US academic journals set the agenda for the discipline and the US policy agenda constructs the world that international relations theory "sees." While this does not mean that the discipline has been uncritical of US foreign policy (indeed many of the key journals are major sites for the criticism of US foreign policy), this has meant that international relations has been unable to deal with the policy issues that preoccupy the vast majority of the world's people. Dealing with this will require more academics outside the United States building their own academic communities and places of publication; but this will be pointless unless the US academic community is prepared to read material in other languages and publish in journals other than the handful that dominate the promotion process in leading universities. If international relations remains a narrow American social science, then the dangers are that it will be irrelevant to the concerns of large parts of the world's population, and more problematically it may become increasingly part of the process of US hegemony.

3. *International relations has to reject its current, and historic, privileging of a specific, and culturally entailed, social scientific approach.*

International relations has been overwhelmingly focused on one version of social science for the last fifty years. Positivism has legitimized international relations, and has served as the benchmark for what counts as acceptable work. This can be contrasted with the much more eclectic intellectual environment in most other academic communities around the world; but, because international relations is an American discipline, this has meant that only a very specific set of answers to questions of method and knowledge generation have been seen as scientifically legitimate. On the other hand, there has been precious little in the way of accepting the deficiencies and limitations of positivism. Recent papers by Friedrich Kratochwil (2006), Milja Kurki (2006), and Colin Wight (2007) have each shown just how limited and historically specific are the core assumptions underlying positivism. Yet the bulk of the papers in the key US academic journals continue to work within this paradigm without an awareness either of the existence of alternative social scientific approaches, or of the major limitations of positivism. It is as if the entire post-positivist movement never happened. Unless the discipline accepts that there is a wide set of legitimate approaches to studying world politics, then it will become more and more restricted in its ability to relate to other disciplines and it will become a besieged academic fortress validated and legitimized only internally.

4. *International relations academics need to reflect on their relation to power and on their social location.*

I raised this issue in my 2003 Presidential Address to the International Studies Association (Smith 2004). More recently the issue has been discussed in a special section in *Millennium: Journal of International Studies*, 35 (2006). In their introduction,

Karena Shaw and R. B. J. Walker (2006) ask fundamental questions about the relationship between the academic's research and teaching roles and their political responsibility. Merely teaching the received wisdom of the history of the discipline of international relations is certainly not a neutral act, since it predisposes students to accept the categories of debate as natural or given. Therefore, what we research and teach are choices we make as academics; these choices can be explained as simply studying the "main features" of world politics, but this merely covers up what are at base political and ethical choices. When we research or teach, we either explicitly or implicitly give that topic a status and we also locate it within a view of the world that reflects our cultural/social/economic and political location. Unless we question the assumptions we make when we teach and research, then we will simply be reinforcing the existing distribution of power, and reinforcing the agenda of the powerful.

5. *International relations needs to focus on the relationship between the material and the ideational.*
Because the linkages between ideational and material structures are so complex, international relations needs to develop theories that focus on accounts of the linkages. Whereas rationalism assumes that interests construct identity, reflectivists assume the opposite (yet the idea of them existing as separate realms is problematic). One route would be for the return of more materialist accounts to international relations, albeit with more developed accounts of the *relationship* between the material and the ideational than such accounts have tended to have (since they assumed that the ideational was a function of the material). As Chris Brown (2007) argues, Marxism has been much missed in international relations over the last twenty years; it was a theoretical position that had a clear, if contested, view of how material and ideational worlds interrelated. Critical realism is one such account, although that has tended to be discussed in international relations in relation to questions of epistemology.

6. *International relations should not take the core concerns of the most powerful as the dominant issues for the discipline.*
International relations has historically ignored large sections of humanity. This is most obvious when it focuses on US policy interests, but it also follows from the definition of international relations that the discipline works within. International relations has privileged deaths by politics over deaths by economics (ten times as many children die each day from poverty and easily preventable diseases as died in total in the 11 September attacks). Similarly, women have largely been ignored, and, as Alison Watson (2006) has recently noted, so have children. This is a direct result of the core assumptions of the discipline, which determine what we see and what we think international relations has to explain. In a recent article, Tarak Barkawi and Mark Laffey (2006) claim that security studies is Eurocentric, and is thus unable to develop adequate understandings of the security concerns

of the postcolonial world. It contains, they argue, a "taken-for-granted" politics that effectively sides with the strong over the weak. Thus a security studies that was really relevant to postcolonial states would account for how the strong exploit the weak, and would focus on the politics of resistance. Unless international relations is able to deal with agendas outside those of the dominant powers, then it will be completely unable to account for the motivations of all those who fundamentally reject the Western models of development, human rights, and civil society.

Let me summarize my arguments by directly considering the four questions that the editors asked those writing these concluding sections to consider.

2 WHERE SHOULD THE FIELD BE GOING?

The field should be going in no particular direction, since that would assume that there is one thing called international relations. Rather, international relations needs to be pluralistic, in the strong sense of valuing different intellectual approaches; not pluralistic in a weaker sense of "anything goes." International relations should move toward being a truly international field, rather than being a field for one, dominant, part of humanity. It should reject simple dichotomies such as domestic/international, economics/politics, and public/private, and not accept that humanity is moving toward common identities and politics.

1. *What should international relations be about?*
International relations should be about the patterns of international and domestic power, and not assume that those patterns most relevant to dominant powers are those that matter to the rest of the world. International relations should aid the understanding of politics from any social location, and any identity, and not be a discipline written from an Archimedean point of neutrality. It has to be a discipline located in the real lives of real people.

2. *What are the big questions that should animate our scholarship?*
These relate to: identity and how it relates to material interests; how identities are constructed; how they relate to patterns of political, economic, and social power, both between and within societies. How do we categorize our thinking? How do we construct the inside and the outside, or the public and the private realms, and therefore how do we develop the categories within which we "do" international relations?

3. *What are the implications of these questions for how we do research?*
International relations should focus on understanding rather than on assuming a common human identity that can be explained by interest-based models of choice.

It needs to understand the world of the powerless as well as the powerful, and be self-reflective as to the relationship between our scholarship, our stated ethical standards, and our location as scholars. Put simply, could our scholarship be part of a pattern of dominance of one set of interests over another, all carried out in the name of academia and scholarship?

Taken together, these comments lead to a simple conclusion: International relations runs the danger of becoming a discourse applicable only to one part of the world, organized by powerful theories, legitimized by a specific and flawed epistemology, and "disciplined" by the structures of the discipline itself. In place of this, international relations needs to become more applicable to politics outside the world of the dominant power, more interested in the security concerns of the powerless, and better able to account for why we focus on some politics rather than others. When we study international relations, we make choices: Throughout most of its history, international relations has chosen to study the politics of the great powers. Yet these are not the "natural" or "given" focal points; they are choices. In the next twenty years the discipline should opt for choices that will make it a truly international relations.

REFERENCES

BARKAWI, T., and LAFFEY, M. 2006. The postcolonial moment in security studies. *Review of International Studies*, 32: 329–52.

BROWN, C. 2007. Situating critical realism. *Millennium: Journal of International Studies*, 35: 409–16.

ELBE, S. 2006. Should HIV/AIDS be securitized? The ethical dilemmas of linking HIV/AIDS and security. *International Studies Quarterly*, 50: 119–44.

HOFFMANN, S. 1977. An American social science: international relations. *Daedalus*, 106: 41–60.

ISH-SHALOM, P. 2006. Theory gets real, and the case for a normative ethic: Rostow, modernization theory, and the alliance for progress. *International Studies Quarterly*, 50: 287–311.

KRATOCHWIL, F. 2006. History, action and identity: revisiting the "second" great debate and assessing its importance for social theory. *European Journal of International Relations*, 12: 5–29.

KURKI, M. 2006. Causes of a divided discipline: rethinking the concept of cause in international relations theory. *Review of International Studies*, 32: 189–216.

SHAW, K., and WALKER, R. B. J. 2006. Situating academic practice: pedagogy, critique and responsibility. *Millennium: Journal of International Studies*, 35: 155–65.

SMITH, S. 2000. The discipline of international relations: still an American social science? *British Journal of Politics and International Relations*, 2: 374–402.

—— 2002. The United States and the discipline of international relations: "hegemonic country, hegemonic discipline." *International Studies Review*, 4: 67–86.

SMITH, S. 2004. Singing our world into existence: international relations theory and September 11. *International Studies Quarterly*, 48: 499–515.

—— 2007. Introduction: diversity and disciplinarity in international relations theory. Pp. 1–12 in *International Relations Theories: Discipline and Diversity*, ed. T. Dunne, M. Kurki, and S. Smith. Oxford: Oxford University Press.

WATSON, A. 2006. Children and international relations: a new site of knowledge? *Review of International Studies*, 32: 237–50.

WÆVER, O. 2007. Still a discipline after all these debates? Pp. 288–308 in *International Relations Theories: Discipline and Diversity*, ed. T. Dunne, M. Kurki, and S. Smith. Oxford: Oxford University Press.

WIGHT, C. 2007. A manifesto for scientific realism in IR: assuming the can-opener won't work! *Millennium: Journal of International Studies*, 35: 379–98.

Name Index

Beaufre, André 560
Beck, N. 489
Beck, U. 453
Beitz, C. R. 13, 195, 335, 595
Belkin, A. 467, 500 n2, 505
Bem, D. 468
Benedict XVI, Pope 700 n1
Benhabib, S. 353
Bennett, A. 112, 117, 435, 475, 499, 500 n2, 502 n6, 503, 504, 505, 506, 507, 508, 509, 510, 512
Bentham, Jeremy 347
Bergson, Henri 87
Bergsten, C. F. 545
Berki, R. N. 164, 192
Berlin, Isaiah 471
Bernauer, T. 499
Bernhard, W. 491
Bernstein, R. J. 110, 330, 331, 333
Bernstein, S. 113
Best, J. 551
Betts, R. K. 560, 564, 569, 571
Bially Mattern, J. 695
Biddle, S. 566
Bieler, A. 176
Biersteker, T. J. 49 n11, 66, 300, 309, 449, 551
Bilder, R. 614
Bismarck, Otto von 578
Biswas, S. 669
Blaney, D. I. 99, 336, 666, 670
Blaug, M. 18
Blaug, R. 352
Bleiker, R. 101, 366, 368, 369, 370, 413
Blondel, J. 585
Bloom, A. 462
Boff, C. 195
Boff, L. 195
Bohman, J. 113, 114 n2, 115, 117, 349
Bok, D. 649
Boone, C. 53
Booth, K. 367, 564, 637 n3
Boucher, D. 531
Bowden, B. 365
Bowman, K. 513
Boyle, F. 614
Boyle, J. M. 598
Brady, H. 112, 500 n2, 503 n7
Braudel, F. 89 n1, 169, 170
Braumoeller, B. 482
Braybrooke, D. 582
Brecher, M. 588, 589
Brechin, S. R. 703
Bremer, S. 484, 489
Brenner, R. 170, 172, 178

Brewer, A. 166, 168, 169
Bright, John 242
Brilmayer, L. 596
Brodbeck, M. 701
Brodie, Bernard 560, 561, 564, 572, 579, 650
Bromley, S. 177, 181
Brooks, S. G. 14, 143, 244, 302, 438, 695
Brown, C. 188, 190, 191, 270, 320 n2, 335, 531, 549, 595, 679, 683, 692, 705
Brown, Gordon 700 n2
Broz, J. L. 540, 548
Bruck, H. W. 580–1
Brunnée, J. 620, 623–4
Brzezinski, Zbigniew 644, 649
Buchan, B. 365
Buchanan, A. 20, 114 n2, 115, 116, 231, 320 n3
Bueno de Mesquita, B. 112, 428, 439, 481–2, 693
Bukharin, N. 167
Bukovansky, M. 68
Bull, H. 41, 54 n16, 73, 96, 208, 267, 269, 270, 271–2, 274, 275, 276, 277, 278, 279, 280–1, 290–1, 294, 295, 300 n2, 333, 341, 448, 526, 560, 561–2, 563, 571, 572, 639, 645, 646, 679, 683, 684
Bundy, McGeorge 644, 650
Burchill, S. 6, 268
Burke, A. 364, 365, 366, 367, 368, 369, 370, 371, 373
Burnham, P. 176
Burns, J. M. 584
Busch, M. L. 210, 216
Bush, George W. 256, 365, 400–1, 432, 470, 476, 585
Büthe, T. 26
Butler, Judith 30, 367, 381, 386
Butterfield, Herbert 132 n3, 134 n7, 152, 267, 269, 270, 279, 288, 289, 432, 519
Buzan, B. 26, 63, 65, 67, 267, 268, 270, 271, 276, 278, 280, 367, 448, 526, 568, 570, 571, 684
Byers, M. 621, 626

Calhoun, C. 95
Callahan, W. A. 684
Callinicos, A. 198
Camerer, C. F. 463, 464, 476
Campbell, D. 307, 308, 319, 364, 366, 369, 370, 372, 378, 380, 381–2, 383, 384, 385, 386, 387, 388, 504, 668, 694
Caney, S. 596, 703
Caporaso, J. A. 665
Caprioli, M. 414, 417
Caputo, J. D. 382
Cardoso, F. H. 54 n16, 545, 664, 665, 666
Carlsnaes, W. 5, 6
Carlson, A. 110

Subject Index

Abu Ghraib 402–3
academics:
  and advice to young scholars interested in
    practice 658–9
  and influence of real world 651–3
  and policy-making 10, 76–7, 635, 649
    academic obstacles to interaction 654–5
    appropriateness of separation 650, 651
    benefits of interaction 657
    bridging the gap between 658–9
    competitors for influence on 655–6
    complementary relationship 636–7, 640
    cultural gap between 654–5
    gulf between 649–50, 653–4
    influence of 'embedded capital' 656–7
    influence on 650–1
    relationship with 635–6, 645
    relationship with academic
      knowledge 641–2
    split between 636
  and political commitment 642–3, 645
    government service 644
    political bias 643–4, 645–6
  and truth:
    evolutionary 639–40
    nature of 637
    objective 637–8
    subjective 638–9
accountability, and institutional design 713–14
Afghanistan 55, 400–1, 453
agency:
  and political action 362
  and postmodernism 366
  see also moral agency
agency theories:
  and international relations theory 21
  and optimism 24–5
agent-structure debate 456
agreement, and international ethics 599
aid policy 387–8
alliances:
  and formation of 527–8
  and quantitative research 485
    trade patterns 486

American empire 90
  and legitimacy 92–3
  and Marxism 182–3
  and neoimperialism 183–4
American Political Science Association 84, 110,
    230, 500
analytical eclecticism 110
  and conception of 110–11
  and contribution to intellectual
    progress 124–6
  and costs and risks of 125
    conceptual fuzziness 118
  and international law 623
  and international political economy 122–4
    economic strategies of Soviet successor
      states 122–3
    ratings agencies 123–4
    state financial power 123
  and multiperspectival approach 117
  and national security 120–2
    absence of war amongst developed great
      powers 121–2
    American foreign policy 120
    post-Communist Russia 121
    rise of China 120–1
  and pragmatist foundation 111
  and problem solving 117
  and reflexive process 111
  and regions 124
  not theoretical synthesis 118
  and value added by 118–19
anarchy:
  and constructivism 304–5, 308–9
  and international relations 63, 64–5, 77–8
  and postmodernism 364–5
  and questioning of assumption of 444
  and realism 133, 135, 144, 150
    defensive realism 139
    moral behavior 154
    offensive realism 139
argument, and international relations theory
    13
arms control, and strategic studies 563
arms races, and quantitative research 484